THE DRAMA OF DEMOCRACY   American Government and Politics

ABOUT THE AUTHOR   George McKenna is chairman of the Political Science Department at The City College of New York, where he has taught for 25 years. He is the co-editor of two books in The Dushkin Publishing Group's *Taking Sides* series: *Taking Sides* on social issues and on political issues, entering their 6th and 7th editions respectively. Among his other publications are *American Populism* (Putnam, 1974), *American Politics: Ideals and Realities* (McGraw-Hill, 1976), *Media Voices* (Dushkin, 1982), and *Guide to the Constitution* (Random House, 1984). He has led local civic and environmental groups in New York and New Jersey.

THE DRAMA
OF DEMOCRACY

American Government and Politics

GEORGE McKENNA

City College of New York

DPG

The Dushkin Publishing Group, Inc.

Guilford, Connecticut

TO SYLVIA, AFTER TWENTY-FIVE YEARS

Printed in the United States of America

Library of Congress Catalog Card Number 89-82492

International Standard Book Number (ISBN) 0-87967-563-2

First Edition, Second Printing

Credits appear on pages 774-76, which constitute a continuation of the copyright page.

Preface

Those of us who teach American politics love our field. We enjoy talking and arguing, reading and writing about it. It is great fun. What we sometimes forget is that most Americans do not share our enthusiasm. Aristotle characterized man as a "political animal," but abundant evidence supports Professor Robert Dahl's assertion that most Americans think of politics as "a remote, alien, and unrewarding activity."[1] The writer of an introductory American government textbook cannot assume, then, that there is an audience out there that can hardly wait to read about politics. It is better to assume the opposite: that the students reading a text on American government and politics, who may have taken the introductory course to fulfill some core requirement, are rather wary of the whole business.

The implications of this assumption should be clear. Any American government text worthy of the name must have solid factual substance, but it must also have some means of drawing the student into the material, getting the student to *care* about the subject matter. If the reader keeps asking, "Why is he telling me all this?" or "Why is she going on and on?" then something is wrong. The author has not whetted the student's appetite. In this book I have tried to whet appetites.

One way I have sought to do this is by starting each chapter with a story that introduces some of the chapter themes. For example, chapter 17, on campaigns, elections, and voting, begins with a discussion of Richard Nixon's famous "Checkers" speech in 1952. The introductory story tells what it was that prompted Nixon to go on television with the speech, what he said in the speech, how he felt as he delivered it, and what happened afterwards. It then discusses the significance of that speech: the first successful use of a television spot to influence voter opinion on a mass scale in a presidential campaign. Chapter 17 contains much else, from a discussion of critical elections to questions about campaign finances, and here, too, the "Checkers" story ties in. By this point in the text the reader has already been introduced to the chapter themes and may, by now, be interested in the material.

Other examples of how the opening stories draw the reader into the text can be found in chapter 9, on presidential power, and chapter 16, on political parties. In chapter 9, the introductory story on the assassination of John F. Kennedy and the enormous national mourning that followed his death raises questions that are answered in the text: What kind of office is this that created such an aura around a man? What sort of powers go with that office? Similarly, chapter 16 begins with the riots at the 1968 Democratic convention in Chicago and poses the questions: What produced the collision between police and demonstrators? What sort of changes did the Democrats (and eventually the Republicans) adopt as a result, and how have these changes shaped the party system today? And so on. The reader is persuaded—seduced, if you like—by dramatic stories to study their implications. A story will not neatly fit in every item covered in a chapter, but the themes of the story resonate throughout the chapter.

The stories are true. There are no docudramas in this book. The stories are vignettes from American history, and they may help, however modestly, to fill the gaps in American students' knowledge of history. Moreover, knowledge of these episodes is necessary if the student is to understand major developments in our political system. How can the student understand the party reforms of the 1970s unless he or she has some knowledge of what happened at the 1968 Democratic convention in Chicago? How can the student understand the domestic political reaction to the Vietnam War without knowing about the Tet offensive of 1968? The stories, then, are both true and useful. One might call them case studies in American politics, except that the term *case studies* has an academic feel, which is not what I intended in writing the opening stories. Typically, case studies in politics relate an episode, usually a rather complicated one, and then draw conclusions or lessons from it. They are useful and they can even be interesting, at least to those who are interested. But there we see their limitation. If, as I believe to be the case, most Americans care little about politics, the case study is not the best way to arrest their attention. A case study, which is written with a clear analytic purpose, leaves little room for emotion or descriptive detail, unless these clearly fit into the point of the analysis. A story is quite different. It can describe the heat shimmering above a campus roadway at the University of Alabama, or a nervous president, his hands shaking, delivering a speech in Houston, Texas, before going to Dallas. A story is a drama, and I have written the opening stories in a way that conveys this sense of drama.

A vivid opening may arrest the reader's attention, but how does one hold it? I have tried to do this by writing as clearly as I can, by avoiding academic jargon, and by using concrete examples wherever possible. I have also tried to sustain interest by pointing out the unresolved tensions and the clashing points of view in the field of American politics. Since 1978, Stanley Feingold and I have been editing an American government reader entitled *Taking Sides*, in which we present contrasting points of view on a number of political issues. Borrowing the *Taking Sides* format, I have inserted a one-page *Taking Sides* section into each of the chapters in this text. On opposite sides of the page, I summarize the pro and con views of authors who vigorously disagree with each other on one of the issues covered in the chapter. In chapter 5, on civil rights, for example, the *Taking Sides* section summarizes the contrasting views of Professor Glenn Loury and writer Herman Schwartz on the merits of affirmative action. The point of these exercises is not only to help students to think critically, but also to underscore the fact that there *are* tensions in the field of American government, that the "experts" often disagree. The object is to get the student involved in the argument. I am telling the student: "Don't be intimidated. Don't feel that you have to memorize everything because even the 'experts' often disagree. Listen to their arguments. Which seems more reasonable? Try to take sides in the dispute."

The two features of the text, the opening stories and the *Taking Sides* segments, justify use of the term *drama* in the book's title. I have labored long—through five drafts and six years—to work color, tension, and descriptive detail into this text, and these features, I believe, set it apart from others in the field. But there are other features that are also unique to this text that deserve mention.

One is the *Global Perspectives* section in each chapter. As we saw by the events in Eastern Europe, where democracy movements in 1989 rapidly spread from country to country, no nation today can long remain isolated from the events in other countries. For better or worse, we are linked together by channels of economics, culture, technology, ecology, and, of course, politics. Even as we study American government, we should keep in mind the similarities and differences between our political system and those of other countries. In each chapter I included a brief sketch of how another country handles an aspect of government or politics. For example, the *Global Perspectives* section in Chapter 3, on federalism, discusses the federal system of Nigeria and the *Global Perspectives* section in chapter 13, on public opinion and political socialization, discusses changes in public opinion in Argentina. In all, 19 different countries of the world are covered in these sections. *Global Perspectives* are just that: perspectives, glimpses, not definitive studies. They give the reader a sense of how political issues, processes, and institutions are handled in other countries. Perhaps we can learn from their experiences. We can certainly learn more about our own system by seeing how it differs from and resembles other systems in this world.

On a more prosaic level, another unique feature of this text is its system of internal summaries, its lists of key points. In my 25 years of teaching I have encountered the following many times: In trying to help students prepare for exams I have advised them to mark important passages in the text; what often happens then is that students underline nearly everything. Page after page is filled with markings of various kinds; everything is important, so, of course, nothing is particularly important. In this text I have tried to indicate what is particularly important by providing periodic lists within the chapters of *Points to Remember*. These sections are set off from the text and can be ignored by anyone who wants to get on with the reading. The alternative is to include a summary at the end of each chapter, but these final summaries tend to suffer from one of two problems. Either they are too general and skimpy, or they go on so long that the reader has trouble remembering and may need a summary of the summary. My periodic lists permit students to review the material section by section. These also permit me room at the end of each chapter for *Reflections*, another feature which I have not seen in other texts.

The *Reflections* pull together general themes of the chapter and share my thoughts with the reader. Nothing here is graven in stone; there are no final lessons. What I do instead is suggest a few tentative conclusions, without denying that others can be drawn. I want these sections to be less structured and more personal than the body of the text. Here I reveal more of myself and my views than I do in the rest of the text. I think it is wrong for professors to use their lecterns as soapboxes to try to foist their ideologies on their students—it offends my sense of fairness—and this is also true of writers of textbooks. It seems neither possible nor desirable to write a "value-free" textbook, but surely authors of textbooks should try to keep their views from dominating the material. I have striven for a certain kind of objectivity in these chapters. But I have left some room at the end of each, so that the student may get a closer view of what I think about some of the issues raised.

On that last note, I should say a word about my own point of view. I wish I could locate it on an ideological scale of "Left" and "Right," "liberal" and "conservative," but that is not easy to do: The terms seem to be losing their meaning by the day.[2] The news media, for example, call President Gorbachev a "liberal" and his opponents in the Communist leadership "conservatives," even though Gorbachev wants to move his country closer to a market economy, which is favored by "conservatives" in this country. (And where does that leave Cuba's Fidel Castro, who hates Gorbachev's reforms? Is he really a "conservative?") Instead of resorting to such labels, I would rather locate my views within the American political tradition. My allegiances and affinities are to the reform movements of American history, from the abolitionists and populists of the nineteenth century to the civil rights and peace movements of the 1960s. Such movements have been the source of continuing revitalization because they keep reminding us what this country stands for. At the same time, I heed the warnings of such observers as James Madison and Reinhold Niebuhr that human nature has a dark side, so that even good movements and good people can become dangerously arrogant. "In political struggles," said Niebuhr, "there are no saints but only sinners fighting each other."[3] That makes sense to me, and it is why I think that the Madisonian concept of checks and balances also makes sense. Power can only be resisted by power, and tendency by tendency. That does not have to add up to inaction. What it means, as I interpret it, is that we must at once promote reform and force reformers to explain themselves. Democracy, I believe, is well suited to that purpose. As Niebuhr put it: "Man's capacity for justice makes democracy possible, but man's inclination to injustice makes democracy necessary."[4]

ACKNOWLEDGMENTS

During the six years it took me to complete this text I was helped by a number of individuals. I am grateful, first of all, to the academic reviewers who read and offered comments on the manuscript at various stages of development.

Mary L. Carns, Stephen F. Austin State University, TX
Jeffrey E. Cohen, University of Illinois, IL
George F. Cole, University of Connecticut, CT
Anne N. Costain, University of Colorado, CO
W. Douglas Costain, University of Colorado, CO
Robert E. DiClerico, West Virginia University, WV
Joel Diemond, Dutchess Community College, NY
Susan P. Fino, Wayne State University, MI
Charles E. Jones, Old Dominion University, VA
Alan M. Kirshner, Ohlone College, CA
David Magleby, Brigham Young University, UT
Candice J. Nelson, Georgetown University, DC
William H. Rosberg, Kirkwood Community College, IA
Ronald G. Shaiko, Virginia Polytechnic Institute and State University, VA
Lois T. Vietri, University of Maryland, MD

Some of my colleagues from City College and elsewhere have answered a number of questions I put to them at various times while writing this text. My thanks go particularly to Stanley Feingold, David J. Garrow, Thomas Oleszczuk, Edward V. Schneier, and Doru Tagana. John S. L. Holland, managing editor of The Dushkin Publishing Group, has directed this project, an unbelievably complicated task, and I marvel that he did it with such grace. I am grateful as well for the excellent work of editor Jeannine Ciliotta in helping me shape and polish the manuscript. Copy editor Joanne Wlodarczyk, by her careful reading and her good sense, has saved me from many bad slips. Thanks also to Pamela Carley Petersen for her excellent illustrations. Rick Connelly, president of The Dushkin Publishing Group, has given me staunch support and encouragement from the very outset of this project, and I am deeply grateful. My family has also been a source of strength. My daughters, Laura and Maria, and my son, Christopher, have cheered me on and helped in many other ways, and my wife, Sylvia, has done everything from locating hard-to-find data to helping me handle the frustrations that go with writing a book. She sustains me, props me up.

GEORGE McKENNA

1. Robert A. Dahl, *Who Governs? Democracy and Power in an American City* (New Haven, CT: Yale University Press, 1961), p. 279.
2. See further, Christopher Lasch, "The Obsolescence of Left & Right," *New Oxford Review* (April 1989), pp. 6-15.
3. Reinhold Niebuhr, "Leaves from the Notebook of a War Bound American," *Christian Century*, November 15, 1939, p. 1406.
4. Niebuhr, *The Children of Light and the Children of Darkness* (New York: Charles Scribner's Sons, 1972), p. xiii.

Contents in Brief

Contents

5

Civil Rights 102

6

Crime and Punishments 133

11

The Bureaucracy 266

12

The Federal Judiciary 300

13

Public Opinion and Political Socialization   328

14

Mass Media   360

15

Interest Groups   392

16

Political Parties   421

17
Campaigns, Elections, and Voting 457

PART V DOMESTIC AND FOREIGN POLICIES 491

18
Poverty, Welfare, and Taxes 492

19

American Foreign Policy 531

20

National Defense 563

Global Perspectives, Taking Sides, and Other Boxed Material

PART I

The American Republic

Democracy is in the air in the 1990s. Most of the dictatorships of Eastern Europe have suddenly collapsed, and elsewhere in the world—in Asia, Africa, and South America—people are demanding the right to participate in their government. Even in China, where a fledgling pro-democracy movement was crushed, few really believe that the aging Communist leaders can contain for long the people's desire for democracy. Chapter 1 explores the meaning of democratic government, points out its advantages, and provides a brief overview of American democracy. Chapter 2 reviews the work of America's founders, focusing on the Declaration of Independence, the Constitution, and the Bill of Rights. Chapter 3 surveys the theory and practice of federalism in the United States and gives reasons for the great expansion of our national government. Here are some of the basics, essential for starting off the study of American democracy.

Set justice aside, then, and
what are kingdoms but great robberies?

St. Augustine, *City of God*

1

Democratic Government in America

GOVERNMENT: NATURE AND PURPOSE

Why Government? Four Reasons

DEMOCRATIC GOVERNMENT

Direct and Representative Democracy / Four Advantages of Democracy

AMERICAN DEMOCRACY

The Sacredness of the Constitution / Human Rights: Our Birthright
The Attraction of Moderation / Tensions and Contradictions

REFLECTIONS

Show Me a Good Loser

1960—It was a rough campaign. The Republican candidate for president, Richard M. Nixon, was a veteran of 14 years in politics: first as congressman, then senator, then vice president of the United States. To his enemies he was "Tricky Dick," a ruthless politician. Nixon rejected—and deeply resented—that label, but he freely admitted that he hated losing. He had never forgotten the words of his college football coach, Wallace ("Chief") Newman. "Show me a good loser," Newman told his players, "and I'll show you a loser." Nixon made Newman his role model. "There is no way," he later wrote in his memoirs, "I can adequately describe Chief Newman's influence on me."[1]*

* This account is drawn from the following sources: Theodore H. White, *The Making of the President 1960* (New York: Pocket Books, 1961); Richard M. Nixon, *RN: The Memoirs of Richard Nixon* (New York: Grosset & Dunlap, 1978); Richard M. Nixon, *Six Crises* (Garden City, NJ: Doubleday & Co., 1962); Stephen E. Ambrose, *Nixon: The Education of a Politician, 1913-1962* (New York: Simon & Schuster, 1987); Benjamin C. Bradlee, *Conversations With Kennedy* (New York: W. W. Norton & Co., 1984); Julie Nixon Eisenhower, *Pat Nixon: The Untold Story* (New York: Simon & Schuster, 1986).

Both candidates in the 1960 presidential campaign, Richard M. Nixon and John F. Kennedy, were intense, ambitious, effective politicians. Nixon was hard driven and serious of demeanor. Kennedy was equally ambitious, but possessed a sense of humor, a light touch, which he was able to use for political advantage. The Nixon staff dubbed it a "Rock 'em and sock 'em" campaign, and the election itself was extremely close, with the popular vote only 34,221,344 to 34,108,671 in Kennedy's favor. In spite of evidence of fraud in the close race, Nixon refused a recount because he feared it might divide the country and cast doubt on the legitimacy of the presidency.

It was the end of the 1950s, and President Dwight D. ("Ike") Eisenhower was completing his second term. A grandfatherly man with an easy smile, Ike was a very popular president who probably could have been reelected for a third term if his time in office had not been limited by the Twenty-second Amendment. Instead the Republicans had picked his vice president to carry their standard—the intense, hard-driven Richard Nixon. Nixon's opponent in the 1960 presidential race had, in some respects, a very different type of personality. He possessed a sense of humor, which Nixon lacked, and knew how to put on an air of nonchalance when it suited his purpose. "The light touch," it was called. But there was nothing at all nonchalant about John F. Kennedy. Like Nixon, he was wildly ambitious and aggressive, with a sure instinct for an opponent's jugular.

The two went head-to-head in the 1960 campaign, and on both sides it was what Nixon's people liked to call "rock 'em and sock 'em" campaigning. Kennedy charged that the Republicans were allowing Americans to go to bed hungry and letting Communists take over the world. Nixon charged that Kennedy was "running down America" and pushing radical ideas that would ruin us. On the evening of November 8, both candidates—exhausted after months of speechmaking and hand-shaking—sat down to watch the results.

At first, when the votes of the eastern states started coming in,

Kennedy had a comfortable lead. Carried by their big cities, the states of Pennsylvania, New Jersey, New York, Rhode Island, Massachusetts, and Connecticut all went for Kennedy. Most of the South was also holding for the Democrats. By 10:30 P.M., it looked like a Kennedy sweep: "Oh, Bunny," his wife said, "you're president now!"[2]

But then came the votes from the Midwest: Ohio—Nixon; Indiana—Nixon; Wisconsin—Nixon. Predictably, the Dakotas, Kansas, Nebraska, Montana, and Colorado produced solid Republican majorities. Less predictably, all of the West Coast—California, Oregon, and Washington State—went to Nixon.

The election turned out to be a cliff-hanger. The final popular-vote tally was 34,221,344 for Kennedy and 34,108,671 for Nixon. As Nixon biographer Stephen Ambrose has put it: "The American people, finally given the opportunity to make their judgment after one of the longest and bitterest campaigns of the century, split almost fifty-fifty."[3]

Obviously a shift of a few hundred votes in this polling place and a few thousand votes in that one could have tipped the election to Nixon. There was also persuasive evidence of fraud. In Texas, which Kennedy had carried by 46,000 votes, at least 100,000 votes tallied for Kennedy were nonexistent. In one Texas county that had only 4,895 registered voters, 6,138 votes were cast. In Chicago, numerous affidavits testified to widespread cheating. One voting machine recorded 121 votes cast after only 43 people had voted. *Washington Post* editor Benjamin C. Bradlee, a close friend of Kennedy's, wrote in his book *Conversations With Kennedy* that Kennedy called Mayor Richard J. Daley of Chicago on election eve to ask how things were going there. According to Bradlee, Daley replied: "Mr. President, with a little bit of luck and the help of a few close friends, you're going to carry Illinois."

Nixon's daughters, his friends, and many of his supporters urged him to demand a recount. So did the president. Eisenhower called Attorney General William P. Rogers and told him to start an investigation. Rogers replied that he had already spoken to Nixon, and Nixon wanted no investigation or recount.

"Show me a good loser," Nixon's football coach had said, "and I'll show you a loser." Yet Nixon turned out to be a good loser. Why? There may have been two motives. The first, which might be called the public-spirited motive, was that Nixon wanted to spare the nation a long period of turmoil and chaos. It would have taken at least a year and a half to do a recount in Illinois, and Texas had no provision for a recount. There Nixon would have had to go to court and start litigation before a recount could even begin. "I could think of no worse example for nations abroad," Nixon later wrote, "than that of the United States wrangling over the results of our presidential election, and even suggesting that the presidency itself could be stolen by thievery."[4]

Another possible motive was a more self-serving one: Nixon did not want to be tagged a bad loser for fear it would endanger a political comeback. As he interpreted his football coach's recipe for being a winner, it included "the determination to come back after you have been knocked down or after you lose."[5] Nixon had the strong feeling that someday he would be back. Sure enough, within two years he was running again for office, this time for governor of California, and if he had won that race—so he suggests in his memoirs—he would have run for the presidency in 1964.[6] (He lost the governor's race but picked himself up and ran again for president in 1968, this time successfully.) In short, it was good politics for Nixon to be a good sport.

Beyond the question of Nixon's self-interest looms the major point: trust in the political order. Nixon was disappointed about the result of the election and angry about the fraud, but he did not consider our *system* fraudulent. He did not think that the American political order was rigged against Republicans, or conservatives, or any other group lawfully seeking power. He trusted it and wanted it preserved. So Nixon acquiesced in the results and wished Kennedy well.

* * * * *

Thus power passes in America. The day after an election, everything is calm. There are no barricades in the streets, no military takeovers, no revolutions. The victors usually adopt a magnanimous tone, and the losers go on vacation, perhaps consoling themselves—as Nixon did—that they will return to the political arena. In other words, the basics of our government have enjoyed, and continue to enjoy, <u>legitimacy</u>. The term *legitimacy* means the "recognition and acceptance of the exercise of political power"; it is the consensus that those who rule have obtained their power by right, not simply by force.[7] The term derives from *legitimus*, a Latin word that means "lawful" or "according to law." During the Middle Ages, the word was invested with an additional meaning: government by consent of the governed.[8] Gradually, the concept of legitimacy came to be identified with a government that derives its authority through the electoral process, so that today nearly every regime in the world feels obliged to pay lip service to its own origins in "the will of the people." Some even stage phony elections to demonstrate their legitimacy.

Legitimacy, however, can be very precarious. When it breaks down in a nation, some kind of upheaval usually follows. In the 1770s the American Revolution broke out after American opinion leaders reached the conclusion that Great Britain had no right to rule us. The French Revolution in 1789 and the Russian Revolution in 1917 followed similar breakdowns in authority. The People's Republic of China has had a series of revolutions in modern times, all resulting from a breakdown of legitimacy. The most recent of these culminated in the so-called Beijing Spring of April–May 1989. Traditionally, Chinese rulers derived their legitimacy from what was called a "mandate of heaven." After the Chinese revolution of 1949, the new ruler, Mao Zedong relied on his own version of Marxism to justify his rule. Since Mao's death in 1976, however, the legitimacy problem has reappeared. In recent years, writes Nicholas D. Kristof, *New York Times* bureau chief in Beijing, "legitimacy dissipated, not only because ordinary people became embittered by the inflation, corruption and injustice around them, but because fewer and fewer people believed in Marxism."[9] The breakdown culminated in massive demonstrations in Beijing, the Chinese capital. Some 100,000 students and workers occupied Beijing's Tiananmen Square, demanding democracy and civil liberties. The protest was savagely repressed by army units, but the legitimacy of the "People's Republic" was now problematic at best. "Our government is already done with," one student shouted, as tanks moved into the square. "Nothing can show more clearly that it does not represent the people."[10]

In the modern world, then, the mark of legitimacy is the support of the people. Governments today seek to gain that support—or pretend that they already have it.

This chapter will begin with a discussion about government—what it is and what its function is. Then we will move on to the subject of

The intensity of the 1989 confrontation in China's Tiananmen Square, Beijing, is written across this student's face. More than 100,000 students and workers joined together to protest corruption, inflation, and injustice, and to demand democracy and civil liberties for the Chinese people. After two months the demonstration was brutally crushed by the army.

democratic government and some of its advantages. We will end the chapter with some thoughts about American democracy in particular. The chapter, then, is structured around three basic questions: (1) What is the purpose of government, and what makes government legitimate? (2) What is the meaning, and what are the implications today, of the term *democratic government*? and (3) To what extent, in what particular ways, does democracy operate in America? The first of these questions ties in closely with our account of the 1960 presidential election.

Government: Nature and Purpose

At its most general level, government consists of people who exercise power or control over other people.[11] In the United States it consists of legislative bodies, courts, and administrative officials. In other countries it may consist of priests, tribal chiefs, or simply soldiers with machine guns. In primitive societies control usually takes the form of social pressure, which may be combined with more explicit rewards and punishments. A government, together with the people it governs and the territory it occupies, is called a state. Whether a government is primitive or sophisticated, formal or informal, democratic or not, its presence always implies the ability to use force if necessary. Coercion, the use of force, is the ultimate resource available to government. If we do not pay our taxes, we go to jail. If we decide that some laws are worth obeying and others are not, we risk incurring a variety of penalties, from fines to execution. Any government where those who break the law are not punished is no government at all. What then prevails is anarchy, which literally means "no rule." In today's world anarchy seldom lasts long. Typically, it is an immediate prelude to revolution, which means overturning one government and replacing it with another.

Why do we need government? What purposes does it serve? For a neat summary of the reasons for government, we can turn to the Preamble to the United States Constitution. It reads as follows: *(See opposite page)*

The Constitution is one of the most revered symbols of the American nation and schoolchildren are taught to memorize its preamble. As new issues arise in America, such as abortion, the abolition of school prayer, or integration through school busing, each issue must be examined in light of the principles set forth in the Constitution which is the ultimate law. Actions that other countries might condemn as unwise, wrong, or evil are, to Americans, "unconstitutional."

We the People of the United States, in Order to form a more perfect Union, establish Justice, insure domestic Tranquility, provide for the common defence, promote the general Welfare, and secure the Blessings of Liberty to ourselves and our Posterity, do ordain and establish this Constitution for the United States of America.

The idea of forming "a more perfect Union" needs to be studied in connection with the less perfect union we had before the Constitution was written; we will reserve that discussion for the next chapter. For now, let us examine more closely the other purposes set forth in the Preamble.

WHY GOVERNMENT? FOUR REASONS

1. To Establish Justice. Any gun-toting gang can establish a government of sorts. The gang has coercive power; it can command obedience. Such a government would not be a just government, however, because it would rest entirely on force.

The word *justice* is not easy to define. Perhaps it is best understood as Justice, the figure of a blindfolded woman with a set of scales. The scales symbolize balance and fairness; the blindfold stands for impartiality. A just government is a fair and unbiased government.[12] Justice does not necessarily mean treating everyone alike; otherwise all workers would receive the same pay and all students would earn the same grade, regardless of performance or effort. The impartiality of justice is not completely indiscriminate. Aristotle, the ancient Greek philosopher, said that the just is "the proportional," meaning that each person should be given what is due to him or her.[13] Obviously, what is due is not always easy to determine, but the general concept seems clear enough: We should treat people according to *relevant* distinctions.

Justice also has the connotation of humane treatment. A just law, said Martin Luther King, Jr., is one that seeks to "uplift" people; an unjust law "degrades" them.[14] King's formulation reminds us that one of the greatest sins against justice is the humiliation or degradation of people because of race, sex, or religion. Segregation laws in the United States in the past and in South Africa today are examples of unjust laws. A just system of laws, then, must be color-blind. Some argue that our courts and legislatures may *temporarily* have to take race into account in order to correct for the effects of past segregation, but virtually all Americans agree that a legally color-blind society must be our ultimate goal.

These definitions and elaborations are, of course, rather vague. Philosophers have talked about justice for centuries without agreeing on what the word means, and some have even questioned whether or not it has much meaning. But without some concept of justice, it would be hard to criticize any government on moral grounds, much less to intervene in its affairs. How, for example, could we possibly say that Nazi Germany was evil? After all, the Nazi government was a legitimate government: By 1933 it was in firm control of Germany, and it was recognized as a government by most countries of the world. If *justice* is an empty word, what business do we have in passing judgment on the Nazis? Yet we did pass judgment, and we did intervene in the affairs of Nazi Germany; after World War II, the Allied nations not only destroyed the Nazi state, but executed some of its leading officials for "crimes against humanity," including the massacre of millions of people. Today most people agree that we were right to do so. Implicitly or explicitly, then, there seems to be a recognition that justice must be an integral part of the state.

2. To Ensure Domestic Tranquility. This simply means preserving order within the boundaries of the state. "Every community," the philosopher Reinhold Niebuhr has noted, "seeks consciously and unconsciously to make social peace and order the first goal of its life." And, he adds, rightly so, "for the simple reason that chaos means

Above is an engraving from a painting by John Trumbull (1756-1843) of the
signing of the Declaration of Independence. Trumbull served as an aide to
General Washington during the American Revolution and, with the help of
Thomas Jefferson and John Adams, later selected 12 decisive episodes from the
Revolution to record in paintings.

nonexistence."[15] But why does reaching that goal require government? Are people
incapable of living in an orderly, tranquil way without government? To ask this
question is to touch on another profound question: What is human nature, and what
relevance does it have to government?

James Madison, one of the most thoughtful of America's Founders, saw an
intimate connection between human nature and government. "If men were angels,"
Madison wrote, "no government would be necessary." But since we humans are far
from angelic, we require some kind of armed umpire to keep us from harming one
another.[16] That role falls to government. Many years before Madison's time, a British
philosopher named Thomas Hobbes (1588-1679) put the case for government in
even stronger language. He asked his readers to imagine a state of nature in which
there was no government. There would be no police, no jails, no courts, no
legislatures, no government authority of any sort. What would life be like? Hobbes
was sure it would be a nightmare. Everyone would make war upon everyone else,
even the naturally peaceful would participate for their own preservation. In such a
situation, civilization would never take root, for no one could build or save anything.
People would lack the incentive to work because the fruits of their labors would be
stolen before the day was over. Consequently, Hobbes concluded, life in a state of
nature would be "solitary, poor, nasty, brutish, and short." (Hobbes is discussed
further in chapter 6.)

Hobbes may have overstated his case for government. Besides, his preferred
remedy, absolute kingship, sounds worse than the disease. Nevertheless, most
political thinkers would probably agree with him that government is needed to
preserve order. Forty years after Hobbes, John Locke (1632-1704), a British
philosopher much closer to the hearts of Americans, also posited a state of nature.
Locke's version may not have been quite so nightmarish, but it had enough of what
Locke called "inconveniences" to make it decidedly unpleasant. One of its "inconveniences" was the fact that people began robbing and killing one another! (Locke's
influence on our Founders is discussed in chapter 2.) Even Thomas Paine
(1737-1809), the revolutionary pamphleteer of the eighteenth century, said that
government is necessary because of human vice. "Government, like dress, is the
badge of lost innocence." Paine, who loved freedom, called government "a necessary
evil."[17]

3. To Provide for the Common Defense. If James Madison was right that people have a tendency to "vex and oppress" one another, it follows that states (which are composed of people) have the same tendencies. Therefore, we need government to protect us against foreign enemies. Today we hear much argument in America about the size of our defense budget, but no responsible proponent of defense cuts argues that we do not need to defend ourselves. Some years ago, the composer and conductor Leonard Bernstein called for unilateral disarmament and suggested that the Soviets would not take over the United States because they would not know what to do with it. [18] An artist can say that, but any American politician who did so would soon be removed from office.

4. To Promote the General Welfare. Besides establishing justice and controlling the effects of human nature, government can play a positive role. The Constitution speaks of the "general Welfare" and gives the government a number of specific powers, including regulating commerce, establishing post offices and roads, and promoting "the progress of Science and useful Arts." In modern times, promoting the general welfare includes regulating business (making sure, for example, that factories install antipollution devices); helping the needy and the disabled in the form of payments and services; providing free public education; setting aside parkland and wilderness areas for recreation; supervising the economy to make sure that it is sound; and constructing roads, bridges, and other public works.

How far should government go in carrying out these positive functions? The question has been debated since the early years of our republic. Some, like Thomas Jefferson, thought that government should play a minimal role. Jefferson feared that a government that was too energetic would become oppressive. Others, like Alexander Hamilton, wanted government to play an important role, at least in stimulating business. During the New Deal period of the 1930s, the federal government for the first time began to play a major role in helping the poor and providing for old age. The Social Security Act of 1935 was a milestone in this new program of positive government (see chapter 18).

The Social Security Act of 1935, here being signed into law by President Franklin D. Roosevelt, heralded the federal government's first major role as guarantor of the general public's welfare. The act also proved to be one of the most fertile sources of litigation, prompting a legal debate at least as extensive as the current legal controversies over abortion or school prayer.

Most Americans favor some governmental involvement in the economy (Social Security is particularly popular), but people differ on how much involvement is the right amount. Some worry that governmental bureaucracy has gotten too big, that it has taken over too many functions better performed by private individuals and businesses. Others argue that in today's world the state must perform many functions once confined to the private sphere; otherwise, essential needs will not be met (these arguments are reviewed in chapter 20).

Democratic Government

So much, at least for now, on *government*. What about *democratic* government? Let's start with the roots of the term.

Democracy is derived from two ancient Greek words, *demos*, meaning "people," and *kratis*, "rule." The term literally means "people's rule." What people? The majority of people, or at least the majority of those eligible to vote. In some of the ancient Greek city-states, such as Athens in about 450 B.C., rule by the majority of citizens was practiced quite literally. However, citizenship was limited to free adult males who owned property—a small minority of the total population. These few played a direct role in governing. They gathered in the town center to decide matters that affected their city—everything from where statues should be placed to whether or not to go to war. They did not use representatives to govern themselves; they had no members of Congress, no senators. This system is called <u>direct democracy</u>. James Madison called it "pure democracy." Direct, pure democracy also flourished in New England during the seventeenth century. The individual towns held meetings of all citizens and decided questions affecting the town. Again, they used no representatives, though they did appoint people to carry out their decisions. Today no states in the world are governed by direct or pure democracy, although some states have elements of it. For the most part, democratic states rely upon some version of <u>representative democracy</u>; that is, one that relies upon elected representatives to pass laws and do the day-to-day governing.

DIRECT AND REPRESENTATIVE DEMOCRACY

But though no modern state is run by direct democracy, vestiges of it remain here and there. Many New England towns still hold town meetings, though the usual complaint is that few people show up. The townspeople may have better things to do, or they

In ancient Greek city-states such as Athens, the citizens—free adult males who owned property— held open meetings to discuss policy and enact laws. Town meetings were one of the traditions of western civilization that traveled to New England with the colonists. Although many New England towns still hold meetings today, the practice no longer enjoys the prestige it once held.

may think that the real action is no longer at the local level. Another form of direct democracy is the referendum, which is found on both the local and state levels in many places. A referendum is the act of referring legislative or constitutional measures to the voters for approval or disapproval. For example, the voters in Maryland in 1988 were given the opportunity to decide on a measure passed by the Maryland legislature to set up a panel that would have the authority to ban the sale of cheap handguns, the so-called Saturday-night specials. (The voters approved this gun-control measure by a large margin, 58 to 42 percent.) Closely related to the referendum is the initiative, a procedure that permits interested voters to propose a law or constitutional amendment by gathering signatures on petitions. (The number of signatures required varies from state to state, ranging from 5 to 15 percent of registered voters.)

Still, representative, not direct, democracy is the dominant form of popular government in the world today. There are at least two reasons for this. First, modern democracies are too big for direct democracy. Ancient Athens seldom had more than 50,000 people, of which only a small number were citizens. The modern nation-state has millions of voters, and it would be hard to hold a national "town meeting." Second, even if we could hold such a meeting (perhaps through computers or two-way television sets), most voters do not have enough information to debate the many complex questions that modern nation-states have to consider, from interpreting treaties to deciding how to reduce the deficit.

If we cannot have direct democracy in the literal sense, maybe we can at least preserve its spirit, which has to do with participation. Every time you write a letter to a legislator, ring doorbells for a candidate, stand outside a shopping mall soliciting signatures, speak out at a local council meeting, call up a radio talk show on politics, or otherwise become personally involved in the political process, you are getting into the spirit of direct democracy. Everyone who has ever done it knows the feeling of elation it brings. Alexis de Tocqueville, a French observer who watched American democracy back in the 1830s, wrote in *Democracy in America*: "In no country of the world do the citizens make such exertions for the common weal." In the America of *(Continued on page 12)*

GLOBAL PERSPECTIVES:

Democracy in Costa Rica

In Central America, where majority rule is rare, Costa Rica is a remarkable exception. A solidly liberal democracy of 2 million people, Costa Rica has elections every four years, a Supreme Court to protect basic freedoms, a free press, and no army. Two-thirds of its people live above the poverty level, life expectancy is high (about 70 years), and its literacy rates are comparable to ours. Unlike most Latin American countries, Costa Rica does not have sharp divisions between the very rich and the very poor; a large middle class provides the basis for moderation and consensus.

Costa Rica's good fortune is in part a product of its history. When Christopher Columbus discovered it, he called it Costa Rica (Rich Coast) because the Indians wore gold jewelry. But because it was soon discovered that Costa Rica had no mineral wealth, greedy Europeans stayed away from it. Development was largely left to the first Spanish settlers, who drove out most of the Indians and worked the land themselves in small family plots. This pattern was in sharp contrast to that in other Spanish colonies, where the land was worked by huge labor-intensive *haciendas* dominated by rich landlords. Thus, the initial poverty of Costa Rica—its lack of mineral wealth—spared it the legacy of oppression and class division that continues to plague its neighbors. "You see," its information minister quipped in 1984, "there are rewards for being poor and strength in being weak."

But all is not rosy in this model democracy. Two developments cloud its future. First, its economy has become very shaky, in part because of plummeting prices for its chief exports, coffee and bananas. In 1981 Costa Rica defaulted on its foreign debt, and though payments were later resumed, the default triggered a ruinous inflation.

The second big concern of Costa Ricans is geopolitical: They are afraid of being swept into a regional conflict between the United States and Nicaragua, Costa Rica's northern neighbor. Although these tensions have eased somewhat since President Bush took office, they are still present. Costa Rica supported the Sandinistas during their revolution against the right-wing Somoza dictatorship of Nicaragua because the Sandinistas assured them they would bring democracy and independence to Nicaragua. Since then, however, Costa Ricans have become increasingly concerned about what has happened in Nicaragua—the internal repression, the militarization, and the ties to the Soviet bloc. The desperate economic conditions in Nicaragua and the collapse of the U.S.-sponsored Contra resistance there have added a new worry: that Costa Rica will experience a massive influx of Nicaraguan refugees, most of them poor and some of them heavily armed.

(Continued from page 11) those days de Tocqueville felt "the presence of a power which, if it is somewhat wild, is at least robust, and an existence checkered with accidents, but full of animation and effort."[19]

Democracy has always had its critics. Plato, the ancient Greek philosopher, said: "Democracy is a charming form of government, full of variety and disorder, and dispensing a sort of equality to equals and unequals alike." For nineteenth-century Irish author and playwright Oscar Wilde, democracy meant "the bludgeoning of the people by the people and for the people." In 1984 James Reston of the *New York Times*, exasperated that Ronald W. Reagan was about to be reelected, turned his

"Monarchy, while perhaps not necessarily the best form of government in principle, has always seemed the best form of government for me." *Drawing by Ed Arno: © 1982 The New Yorker Magazine, Inc.*

anger on the principle of democracy. Reagan, he said, serves people "baloney" and they swallow it. Why? "Because they like baloney." Unlike the insiders in Washington, Reston wrote, the people at large do not care much about "the vital interests of the nation," or logical consistency, or "complicated facts." They "hate ambiguity and long for simplicity, which Mr. Reagan gives them with a wave and a smile."[20] Reston might have agreed with another journalist and insider from a half-century earlier, H. L. Mencken, who called democracy "boobocracy."

These criticisms, coupled with the fact that democracy is so rarely practiced in the world, should make us think. Why *do* we celebrate democracy? What are its virtues? We can start with a famous quotation from Winston Churchill: "Democracy is the worst form of government—except for all the others." His point, of course, was that we must not judge democracy by some impossible standard of excellence. We may get exasperated by majority rule and we may not like all its decisions, but would we really like to be ruled by philosopher kings or Washington insiders or some other group of know-it-alls? How about a dictator or a tyrant? Most of us would rather take our chances with majority rule. Still, there is a negative quality about the argument so far. It seems to say: "Maybe democracy is not much, but. . . ." We can do better than that. There are some very positive things to say about democracy.

FOUR ADVANTAGES OF DEMOCRACY

1. Peaceful Exercise and Transfer of Power.   By agreeing to be bound by the will of the majority, we ground power on a foundation of nonviolence and fairness: nonviolence because the system settles disputes by ballots instead of bullets, fairness because it offers the hope that today's minority can become tomorrow's majority. This was the hope that sustained Nixon in 1960 and helped to make him a good loser.

Ballots also provide an answer to the age-old problem of succession. Who will be the next leader? In the old days of kings and queens, the question was settled on the basis of heredity: The ruler's son or daughter became the next ruler. This was a high-stakes gamble that often put imbeciles on the throne. In modern nondemocratic systems, a ruler's death or overthrow is often followed by a prolonged power struggle behind the scenes. It may be months or years before the new leader is firmly in control, during which time the country is in turmoil. This was the nightmare Nixon did not want to see in our country after the 1960 election.

2. Safeguard against the Abuse of Power. In the next chapter we will discuss James Madison's theory of checks and balances, the theory of pitting the three branches of government against one another in order to protect us from the abuse of power by politicians. Checks and balances were very important to Madison. What is often forgotten, however, is that he intended them only as "auxiliary precautions." The primary check on the government, Madison contended, is "a dependence on the people."

Representative democracy authorizes certain elites to govern us, but it does so on a temporary and conditional basis. If we do not like the way they wield power, we "throw the rascals out." Of course, a new set of rascals may come in, but the degree of their rascality is limited if they, too, can be thrown out after a few years. This power of democracy, often taken for granted in the United States, is sometimes seen very dramatically in countries where democracy is being born, or reborn, after years of repression. In the Polish parliamentary elections of 1989—Poland's first free elections in more than 40 years—candidates supported by Solidarity, the long-repressed trade union, overwhelmingly defeated candidates nominated by the ruling Communist party. Perhaps more significantly, for the 35 seats set aside for Communist candidates with no opposing candidates allowed, the majority of voters simply voted "No" by crossing off the candidates' names.[21] Their seats were put in jeopardy by an electorate determined to "throw the rascals out."

3. Efficient Communicator of People's Concerns. Ordinary people are usually not experts on farm policy or deficits or the Federal Reserve system, but they know when and where the shoe pinches. They know about inflation and unemployment. They usually know these things better than the experts, not because they have analyzed them carefully but because they have *felt* them, often *experienced* them very directly. Voting is the best way of communicating these grass-roots concerns: Governing elites get the message loud and clear.

4. Educational Process. Democracy means more than counting heads; it also has something to do with what goes on *inside* people's heads. A vigorous political campaign stimulates discussion and debate. It may also, of course, stimulate blather and baloney. This is to be expected, for democracy is not a graduate seminar; it is a real-life struggle to decide who is going to rule. With all its noise and hoopla, democracy affords people the opportunity to hear arguments and to size up candidates. British political theorist Ernest Barker has defined democracy as "government by discussion."[22] The discussion takes place in a number of forums—in legislatures, in administrations, in party caucuses, and in campaigns—but it is always ongoing. There is give and take, talking and listening, and both the majority and the minority learn from it. The result, writes Barker, should be more than just the triumph of numbers.

> If the spirit of discussion—which is the spirit of giving as well as taking, and of learning as well as of teaching—is present from beginning to end, there is genuine reason for thinking that the opinion of the majority, intrinsically and inherently, will possess quality and value.[23]

Barker makes clear that in democracy the discussion process is at least as important as the head count. How we reach the result is as important as the result. That point is bound to be missed by those who think only of results. After the 1979 revolution in Nicaragua, Humberto Ortega, one of the leaders of the Sandinistas, said that elections would be permitted only "to improve the power of the revolution" but that the Sandinistas would not allow "a raffle to see who has power" because the people already had the power "through their vanguard, the Sandinista National Liberation Front and its National Directorate."[24]

To characterize an election between competing parties as a raffle is to misunder-

Once the alternatives to democracy were monarchy and aristocracy. Today these systems are virtually obsolete, though their ceremonial forms remain here and there. The more common alternatives to democracy are authoritarianism and totalitarianism.

An authoritarian regime is one that severely curtails freedom without extinguishing it. It does not hold competitive elections and does not allow free speech and press. But its prohibitions are fairly predictable. People know what they can and cannot do. They cannot openly criticize the rulers, hold protest demonstrations, or organize opposition groups. But if they mind their own business and stay out of politics, they can live their lives without being bothered very much. Authoritarian regimes usually do not intrude into the private sphere; all they want is outward conformity.

Totalitarianism takes away all the freedoms removed by authoritarianism—and goes further. Using indoctrination and terror, it seeks not only outward conformity but total control over its subjects. People are forced to spend evenings at political rallies, children are encouraged to spy on their parents, neighborhood "action" committees are set up to monitor people's behavior, religion is either banned or put into the service of the state. No distinction is made between public and private: everything—art, religion, music, sports—is politicized. Totalitarianism wants its people to march. Its rulers are constantly worried about secret enemies, real and imagined; this paranoia sets off periodic purges, mass arrests, and executions.

Just as there is no perfect democracy, so there is no regime that perfectly fits either the authoritarian or totalitarian model. Some, however, come close. The regimes of General Francisco Franco in Spain (1939-1975) and Iran under the Shahs (1925-1979) would be examples of authoritarian rule. Nazi Germany (1933-1945) and the USSR under Josef Stalin (1929-1953) were classic examples of totalitarianism. The terms do not correlate with any particular ideologies, Communist or non-Communist. The USSR today is Communist but seems to be on the road to democracy, while non-Communist Iran has elements of totalitarianism.

The differences between democracy, authoritarianism, and totalitarianism may be summed up as follows:

	Democracy	Authoritarianism	Totalitarianism
Free elections	Yes	No	No
Free speech, press, assembly	Yes	No	No
Sphere recognized as legitimately "private"?	Yes	Yes	No

stand fundamentally the spirit of modern democracy. In a raffle, the result is dictated by blind chance; debate and deliberation have nothing to do with the outcome. Democracy is something quite different. At its best, it is an educational process because it sets competing points of view before voters and invites them to make judgments. The extent to which it does that successfully varies with time and place, but we should resist the naive and cynical view that people can easily be brainwashed. There is little evidence to support that view, and there is some fairly solid evidence pointing the other way, toward the conclusion that voters learn about issues during political campaigns and make up their minds without being led by Madison Avenue image-makers. We will return to this subject in chapter 11.

Of course, people in democracies do not always behave with perfect rationality. Nor is it necessary to argue that all democracies perfectly represent the views of the majority. We must remember that democracy is an ideal. In no country of the world is there perfect democracy, even perfect representative democracy. We may even question whether or not such a democracy would be desirable. In our own system, we have made the Supreme Court coequal in power with the president and

Points to Remember

1. Democracy literally means "people's rule," that is, rule by the majority. In modern practice, that almost always means majority rule through representatives chosen by the majority.

2. Democracy has always had its critics, those who doubt the wisdom of the people.

3. Democracy has at least four positive virtues: It transfers power peacefully, it serves as a check on power, it communicates people's concerns to governing elites, and it helps to educate people about civic matters.

Congress. The Supreme Court can hardly be called democratic—it consists of nine members appointed for life, yet it has the power to overrule both the president and Congress. We not only tolerate but we revere this elitist institution because we want it to protect minorities and guard the Constitution. In more general terms, we justify the Supreme Court as part of our system of checks and balances.

Our system, then, is a qualified democracy. In some respects, it is also a flawed democracy. There have been a number of cases in which election results have been systematically distorted by accident or fraud. In too many cases and for too long, whole classes of people (women, blacks) have been disenfranchised. While this may be largely behind us, there are still understandable concerns about fairness. There is the issue of money in our electoral process; some fear that the rich have disproportionate power at the polls (see chapter 11). And after the election is over, our day-to-day governing process may not be as democratic as it should be. In this chapter's Taking Sides section, psychologist G. William Domhoff goes so far as to argue that America is ruled by a "power elite." Andrew Greeley—a priest, novelist, and sociologist—opposes that view, although he agrees that our system is not completely majoritarian.

American Democracy

The discussion so far has been about government in general and then democracy and its advantages. In the process, we have touched on some of the features of American democracy, but it deserves a closer look. In a way, of course, this entire book can be seen as a study of the uniqueness of our system. It is important, however, to start with some observations on American-style democracy, which blends majority rule and constitutionalism, natural rights, and moderation.

THE SACREDNESS OF THE CONSTITUTION

To begin with, our democracy operates within the framework of a written constitution, which is not to say that America is the only constitutional democracy. We can argue that every democracy today is in some sense a constitutional democracy—one where the majority rules but there are limits to what the majority can do. It cannot persecute people because of their religion; it cannot imprison people without a trial; it cannot forbid speech because it does not like the content; it cannot torture confessions out of people; it cannot prescribe cruel and unusual punishments. In other words, the majority must respect certain rights that we have come to recognize as fundamental. The majority is thus restrained not only in the United States, but in France, Great Britain, India, Japan, and other countries considered democratic.

It is the almost sacred aura that surrounds our written Constitution that is such a prominent feature of American democracy. Our Constitution is a kind of Torah or

(Continued on page 18)

Is America Ruled by an Elite?

YES G. William Domhoff

Based upon G. William Domhoff, *Who Rules America Now? A View for the '80s* (Englewood Cliffs, NJ: Prentice-Hall, 1983).

Domhoff contends that elite domination of America is obvious during and after the election. In the election process, the rich control the result through donations to candidates. By bankrolling candidates, they "buy" them, Domhoff says, because no politician can afford to be ungrateful to big benefactors. Anyway, because most politicians on the national level are themselves affluent, they see things from the perspective of the rich. When the election is over, they bring into office the same group of advisers and cabinet members who served in previous administrations. Domhoff points to the Carter administration. His close aides swore that they would bring in new faces; instead they brought in people like Wall Street lawyer Cyrus R. Vance and Zbigniew Brzezinski, a member of several corporate-funded foundations. When Reagan took office, he called in people like George P. Schultz, Alexander M. Haig, and Casper W. Weinberger, veterans of the Nixon administration and corporate executives. In short, "the highest levels of the executive branch . . . are interlocked with the corporate community through the movement of executives and lawyers in and out of government."

NO Andrew Greeley

Based upon Andrew M. Greeley, *Building Coalitions* (Chicago: Franklin Watts, 1974).

In Greeley's view, the facts show that there is anything but a power elite running America. In fact, he says, "the most important obstacle to social change in the United States . . . is not the concentration of power but its diffusion." If America were really run by a concentrated power elite, he says, we could appeal to it to decree solutions to problems that plague us all. Take Vietnam, for example. The war was not good for anyone, not even for corporate elites (it caused a terrible inflation). Yet it dragged on for years because no one had the power either to make it a total war or to pull out. Other problems, such as racial segregation, might also yield to a solution by a power elite—but we do not have one. Instead, we have many different "veto" groups that can stop things from happening but have trouble getting together to do things. Greeley believes that pluralism—the interaction of interest groups—is the key to understanding power in America. We may not have straight majority rule, but it takes a broad coalition of minorities to get anything done.

Postscript

The arguments of both Domhoff and Greeley raise questions. Domhoff shows that both Democratic and Republican presidents turn to "old hands" from previous administrations when they come into office. Does that mean that a power elite runs their administrations, or does it simply mean that presidents value experience? As for Greeley, he shows that clear-cut decisions are often blocked by "veto" groups—but isn't that evidence of excessive minority power?

The classic power elite thesis came from a book with that title, *The Power Elite*, by C. Wright Mills (New York: Oxford University Press, 1956). It is still highly readable, though its facts and figures are dated. As for Greeley's side of the issue, the "pluralist" thesis is developed at length in Robert Dahl's *Who Governs?* (New Haven, CT: Yale University Press, 1961).

FIGURE **1-1**

Constitutional Powers and Prohibitions

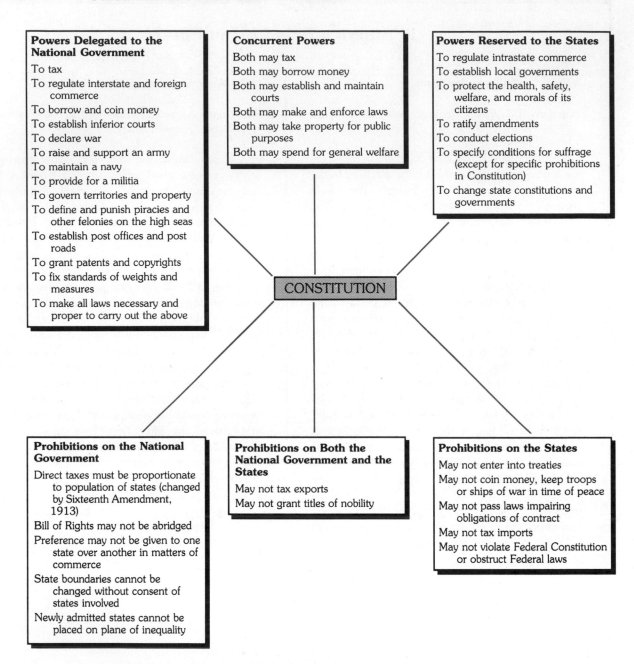

Powers Delegated to the National Government

To tax

To regulate interstate and foreign commerce

To borrow and coin money

To establish inferior courts

To declare war

To raise and support an army

To maintain a navy

To provide for a militia

To govern territories and property

To define and punish piracies and other felonies on the high seas

To establish post offices and post roads

To grant patents and copyrights

To fix standards of weights and measures

To make all laws necessary and proper to carry out the above

Concurrent Powers

Both may tax

Both may borrow money

Both may establish and maintain courts

Both may make and enforce laws

Both may take property for public purposes

Both may spend for general welfare

Powers Reserved to the States

To regulate intrastate commerce

To establish local governments

To protect the health, safety, welfare, and morals of its citizens

To ratify amendments

To conduct elections

To specify conditions for suffrage (except for specific prohibitions in Constitution)

To change state constitutions and governments

CONSTITUTION

Prohibitions on the National Government

Direct taxes must be proportionate to population of states (changed by Sixteenth Amendment, 1913)

Bill of Rights may not be abridged

Preference may not be given to one state over another in matters of commerce

State boundaries cannot be changed without consent of states involved

Newly admitted states cannot be placed on plane of inequality

Prohibitions on Both the National Government and the States

May not tax exports

May not grant titles of nobility

Prohibitions on the States

May not enter into treaties

May not coin money, keep troops or ships of war in time of peace

May not pass laws impairing obligations of contract

May not tax imports

May not violate Federal Constitution or obstruct Federal laws

The U.S. Constitution provides for a federal system of government by delegating separate powers to the national and the state governments. This chart also shows the concurrent, or shared, powers.

(Continued from page 16) Bible, at once a legal code and a set of moral principles. In other countries, people may condemn an act by calling it unwise, wrong, or evil. Americans have a tendency to reject something by saying, "It's unconstitutional." Of course, in the final analysis, we do not leave the question of constitutionality up to citizens. The Supreme Court is the ultimate interpreter of the Constitution, and it has the extraordinary power to strike down laws passed by the other branches if it decides that they violate "the supreme Law of the Land," as the Constitution calls itself.

If the Constitution is one of our holy documents, another is the Declaration of Independence. Unlike the Constitution, it has no legal significance—you cannot sue the government for violating the Declaration of Independence—but it carries enormous moral weight. That is because of the philosophy of <u>natural rights</u>. "We hold these truths to be self-evident," it says, "that all men are created equal, that they are endowed by their Creator with certain unalienable Rights, that among these are Life, Liberty and the pursuit of Happiness." Certain rights are "unalienable": Government cannot take them away because government did not give them to us. John F. Kennedy said in his inaugural address: "The rights of man come not from the generosity of the state but from the hand of God." This is a very old doctrine that has its roots in ancient Greek philosophy. Yet it is also very modern and dynamic. It has been invoked by all sorts of social reformers in American history, from the abolitionists in the nineteenth century to the civil rights activists in the 1960s.

Americans of all persuasions believe in natural rights. It is in this context that we can best understand the observation that Americans are "Lockeans." The single most

These immigrants, viewing the Statue of Liberty, may have mixed emotions: anxiety and hope. The statue (in a poem inscribed at its base) is welcoming them and all others "yearning to breathe free." It symbolizes this nation's commitment to "unalienable rights"—rights that no government may take away.

influential philosopher in America is John Locke. Writing in the seventeenth-century, he taught that humans have left the state of nature—where they had enjoyed natural rights to "life, liberty, and property"—because of its numerous "inconveniences" and have agreed to be ruled by government. But this commitment to being ruled is both cautious and provisional. Rulers hold power "by consent" (through representatives) and must never transgress natural rights. The rights, remember, preceded the government: We had them in the state of nature. Since we already had these precious rights before we had government, government is at best a mixed blessing. We may need it to protect our rights, but there is always the danger that it may get out of hand and trample them instead. This helps to explain the deep-seated American suspicion of big government—and why socialism has made so little headway in this country (see chapter 7 for further development on this topic).

THE ATTRACTION OF MODERATION

Ernest Barker, who defined democracy as "government by discussion," said that discussion and debate may divide people temporarily into opposing parties but should have the effect of bringing people together in the end:

> Discussion is not only like war: it is also like love. . . . If a majority engages in discussion with a minority, and if that discussion is conducted in a spirit of giving and taking, the result will be that the ideas of the majority are widened to include some of the ideas of the minority, which have established their truth in the give and take of debate.[25]

Barker may have been too optimistic about the discussion process—people are not usually so ready to listen to one another—but he was right to imply that democracy requires some amount of agreement, or consensus. If all parties in an election are unyielding extremists, the stakes are so high that no one is willing to accept defeat. Fortunately, this has seldom happened in the United States. (The big exception was the 1860 election, when the nation was so divided over the issue of slavery in the territories that Lincoln's victory brought on the Civil War.)

Americans move toward the center; they seem to do this very self-consciously, as if painfully aware of what can happen if everyone takes extreme positions. *Consensus* and *moderation* are watchwords in this country. In other democracies, political parties do not hesitate to call themselves "radical"; in the United States, they would never do so. "Extremist" is another label American politicians avoid. There are democracies where a politician might say, "Yes, I'm an extremist—I'm extremely correct and my opponent is moderately wrong." But that does not play well here. The only major U.S. candidate to try something like it was Arizona senator Barry M. Goldwater in 1964, who, in accepting the Republican nomination for president, said: "Extremism in defense of liberty is no vice! . . . Moderation in the pursuit of justice is no virtue!" Goldwater was defeated in one of the largest landslides in history.

TENSIONS AND CONTRADICTIONS

Constitutionalism, natural rights, and moderation are central tenets of American democracy. Other attributes of our system, such as checks and balances, federalism, and New Deal capitalism (which we study in subsequent chapters) come from these core commitments. But to discuss each of the three separately does not do their complexity justice, for in reality the three are constantly interacting, and there is often tremendous tension between them.

Constitutionalism Versus Natural Rights.   Constitutionalism implies that we are a government of laws and must live within a legal framework. But natural rights insists that there are laws *beyond* our legal framework: the transcendent moral laws of God's universe. Many of the abolitionists of the nineteenth century were outspoken in their contempt for the Constitution; for them, it was a slave owner's document that put property rights ahead of human rights. America's true charter, they insisted, was the Declaration of Independence, a document that justifies lawbreaking. The civil rights demonstrators of the 1960s were much more reverent toward the Constitution—the Supreme Court had just used it to strike down racial segregation—but their attitude toward government by law was at best equivocal.

Natural Rights Versus Moderation.   The same tension exists between natural rights and moderation. In a way, Barry Goldwater was right to say that extremism in defense of liberty is no vice. The American signers of the Declaration of Independence were surely extremists. They had moved beyond the point of compromising their differences with England. The abolitionists were also extremists; the middle-of-the-road position in the 1800s was that whereas slavery should not be extended into the territories, it could not be eliminated for many years to come. A century later, moderates were saying much the same thing about segregation—their word was *gradualism*. Even the Supreme Court called for caution: Full civil rights were to be awarded not immediately, but "with all deliberate speed." The civil rights demonstrators forced the pace of change by resorting to a variety of tactics then considered extreme—sit-ins, marches, and freedom riding—but today we see as justified.

Still, there is such a thing as bad extremism. There were people in the 1960s who burned down neighborhoods and rioted for "freedom," who threw bags of excrement into the faces of police officers and called them "pigs." There were others who burned crosses on people's lawns and dynamited black churches. Those who did these things probably saw themselves as idealists and crusaders; today we know they were fanatics.

So, in the end, all we can conclude in an abstract sense is that sometimes moderation runs counter to justice and sometimes a passion for rights can lead to fanaticism. The challenge comes in the experience of the concrete words and deeds as Americans play out the drama of politics. Only by getting involved in that drama can we decide where the emphasis should be—on constitutionalism, on rights, or on moderation. There is no precise formula for making such decisions. There is only human judgment based upon an open-minded study of the facts and a measure of common sense.

Points to Remember

1. American democracy mixes majority rule with certain core values: constitutionalism, natural rights, and the spirit of moderation.

2. Virtually all democratic governments in the world are constitutional democracies, but in our case we put great emphasis on a written Constitution. It has become a nearly sacred document, and by reference to it, our Supreme Court some- times strikes down laws passed by the other branches.

3. Our tradition of natural rights has deep historical roots. It developed from the belief, held in ancient Greece, that moral values have greater authority than human laws. It was on the basis of these values that the Declaration of Independence justified the American Revolution.

4. *Moderation* is a watchword in American politics; candidates and programs perceived as radical never succeed.

5. The three core values—constitutionalism, natural rights, and moderation—are often in conflict. Deciding our priorities is no easy task, for we have no formula for doing so.

Reflections

Richard Nixon lost the 1960 presidential election by a whisker—and in at least two key states, the election was apparently tainted by fraud. Yet Nixon accepted the results without a fuss. His motives seem to have proceeded from trust in the long-term justice of our system. You win some and you lose some, but the system is basically fair; there will be another day. After elections, all is calm; there are no barricades in streets, no armed confrontations. The American system enjoys legitimacy. Things are quite different in many other places. For example, political disenchantment in China in the spring of 1989 resulted in huge demonstrations in Beijing's Tiananmen Square. The Chinese government restored order by sending the People's Army into the square—and by so doing, lost its legitimacy.

Government implies coercion, but for a government to enjoy legitimacy, it has to have more than guns. To begin with, it must be perceived as serving the people. What do people want from government? Obviously, that will vary from country to country, but we can present four general goals: (1) to establish justice; (2) to keep order; (3) to defend the people against foreign enemies; and (4) to provide for the "general welfare" in the more positive sense of encouraging industrial productivity, protecting people against harmful products and working conditions, fostering education and culture, keeping the economy sound, keeping the environment clean, and ensuring that the truly needy are helped.

What kind of government does those things best? The question is probably unanswerable because much depends on the people and their traditions. What we can do is recall some of the positive advantages of democracy. First, it provides for peaceful change. Second, it serves as a check on power. Third, in very clear terms, it tells the people in power what we like and do not like. Fourth, at its best, it is an educational process that enriches our minds and hearts. Whether or not all countries can reap these benefits is debatable, but the possibility should not just be dismissed. It may be that our own particular *kind* of democracy is not for export. But different forms of democracy may work very well in countries with very different people.

American opinion leaders once talked about making the world safe for democracy. To our ears, that now sounds presumptuous, and it probably was. But surely there are times when we do have to make value judgments about governments. If we value democracy, then we have to ask how democratic a foreign regime is. The answer to that question then helps determine what our relationship to that country should be.

In the meantime, let us not be reluctant to talk about the merits of democracy. That is not boasting. On the contrary, it helps us to identify the flaws in our own system, the things that need correcting if we are to live up to the spirit of self-government.

Notes

1. Stephen E. Ambrose, *Nixon: The Education of a Politician, 1913-1962* (New York: Simon & Schuster, 1987), p. 66.

2. Theodore H. White, *The Making of the President 1960* (New York: Pocket Books, Inc., 1961), p. 21.

3. Ambrose, p. 607.

4. Richard M. Nixon, *Six Crises* (Garden City, NY: Doubleday & Co., 1962), p. 413.

5. Richard M. Nixon, *RN: The Memoirs of Richard Nixon* (New York: Grosset & Dunlap, 1978), p. 20.

6. Nixon, *Memoirs*, p. 226.

7. Jack C. Plano and Milton Greenberg, *The American Political Dictionary*, 6th ed. (New York: Holt, Rinehart & Winston, 1982), pp. 12-13.

8. Dolf Sternberger, "Legitimacy," in David L. Sills, ed., *International Encyclopedia of the Social Sciences* (New York: Macmillan Co. & Free Press, 1968), vol. 9, p. 245.

9. Nicholas D. Kristof, "China Erupts . . . The Reasons Why," *New York Times Magazine*, June 4, 1989, p. 88.

10. Nicholas D. Kristof, "Troops Attack and Crush Beijing Protest; Thousands Fight Back, Scores Are Killed," *New York Times*, June 4, 1989, p. 20.

11. David P. Apter, "Government," in David Sills, ed., *International Encyclopedia*, p. 214.

12. Stanley I. Benn, "Justice," in *The Encyclopedia of Philosophy* (New York: Macmillan Co. & Free Press, 1967), vol. 4, pp. 298-301.

13. Aristotle, *Ethics* (any edition), Book V.

14. Martin Luther King, Jr., "Letter From Birmingham City Jail," in Hillman M. Bishop and Samuel Hendel, eds., *Basic Issues of American Democracy* (New York: Appleton-Century-Crofts, 1965), p. 291.

15. Reinhold Niebuhr, "Reflections on Democracy as an Alternative to Communism," *Columbia University Forum* (Summer 1961), p. 10.

16. James Madison, *The Federalist* No. 51 (any edition). The background and arguments of the *The Federalist* papers are discussed at greater length in the next chapter.

17. Thomas Paine, *Common Sense* (1776), in Philip S. Foner, ed., *The Life and Major Writings of Thomas Paine* (New York: The Citadel Press, 1961), p. 4.

18. Leonard Bernstein, "Just Suppose We Disarmed," *New York Times*, June 10, 1980, p. 19.

19. Alexis de Tocqueville, *Democracy in America* (New York: Vintage Books, 1945), vol. I, pp. 95-96.

20. "How Reagan Survives," *New York Times*, May 20, 1984: sec. IV, p. 23; "Insiders and Outsiders," *New York Times*, Aug. 19, 1984: sec. IV, p. 19.

21. Henry Kamm, "Communists Concede Victory by Solidarity and Call for Coalition," *New York Times*, June 6, 1989, p. 1.

22. Ernest Barker, *Reflections on Government* (New York: Oxford University Press, 1958), p. 37.

23. Barker, p. 68.

24. "FSLN: Statement on the Electoral Process (August 1980)," in Robert S. Leiken and Barry Rubin, eds., *The Central American Crisis Reader* (New York: Summit Books, 1987), p. 229.

25. Barker, p. 67.

2

Foundations of American Democracy

The Great Compromise

James Madison arrived in Philadelphia eleven days early. It was a typical move for him: He always liked to be prepared. He had come to the convention from New York, where he had been sitting as a member of Congress, representing his home state of Virginia. It was an exhausting two-day journey on a crowded stagecoach, and Madison constantly fretted about his health. Thirty-six at the time, he was small and thin—no bigger, it was said, than half a piece of soap.[1]*

Madison's luggage was crammed with papers and books. A scholarly man, he was not much of an orator and was always ill at ease in crowds, even though he was an experienced politician. Madison thought that the lessons of the past had to be pondered by anyone planning a new constitution—which was just what he was planning. In his view, the

*This account is drawn from the following sources: Christopher Collier and James Lincoln Collier, *Decision in Philadelphia* (New York: Random House, 1986); Catherine Drinker Bowen, *Miracle At Philadelphia* (Boston: Little, Brown, 1966); Charles L. Mee, Jr., *The Genius of the People* (New York: Harper & Row, 1987); William Peters, *A More Perfect Union* (New York: Crown Publishers, 1987).

24

Articles of Confederation was a hopelessly weak basis for government. The central government was a "league of friendship" among 13 independent states. It could not tax; it could only ask the states for money. It could not conscript an army, even if the country were invaded; it could only ask the states for troops. It could not regulate commerce between the states, with the result that the states were engaged in constant trade wars. Perhaps most critical, the Articles could not even be amended unless all 13 states agreed to a change.

Even those who resisted change knew that something had to be done. Commercial rivalries were becoming intolerable. New Jersey, forced to pay tariffs on goods brought from New York on the east and Pennsylvania on the west, was likened to "a keg being tapped at both ends."[2] Maryland and Virginia were feuding about oyster-fishing rights in the Potomac River; Pennsylvania and Delaware, both of which used the river for shipping, soon were dragged into the "oyster war." Adding to the confusion was the use of different currencies. Some states honored Spanish pistoles; others, English sovereigns or Portuguese ducats; still others were printing their own paper money, which quickly lost value. Watching all this, with varying degrees of interest and amusement, were the foreign powers still encamped on American soil: the British in the Northwest, the Spanish in Florida, and the French in the Mississippi delta.

Then there was Shays's Rebellion. In the winter of 1786, angry farmers in western Massachusetts, led by a former Revolutionary War captain named Daniel Shays, took over the court in Northampton in a desperate effort to prevent foreclosures on their farms. The rebellion was soon quelled by the militia, but merchants and creditors feared it might be the start of a whole series of uprisings that would drag the country into anarchy.

Something, then, had to be done: But what? In 1786 representatives of various states met at Annapolis, Maryland, to try to find solutions. The Annapolis Convention was a failure, but under the leadership of Madison and an even younger delegate from New York named Alexander Hamilton, the delegates resolved to call upon the states to send representatives to a new convention to create a government adequate to America's needs. A wary Congress agreed: A new convention was to be held in May 1787 "for the sole and express purpose of revising the Articles of Confederation."

That was all the encouragement Madison needed. Largely unaided, he drew up a series of resolves to be offered at this convention, resolutions that would go much further than revising the Articles. He persuaded another Virginian, Edmund J. Randolph, to introduce them. Randolph rose and was recognized by the president, another Virginian, George Washington. By unanimous agreement, Washington had been made presiding officer. The hero of the Revolution, General Washington was seen as being "above" politics, someone who could be counted on to be fair to all sides.

The Virginia Plan, as it came to be known, provided for a two-house legislature, the second branch (the senators) to be elected by the first. It also proposed a single executive and a national court system. Both the legislature and the executive would have considerable powers, including that of voiding state laws that conflicted with their authority. The Virginia Plan would base all representation on population: the larger the state, the greater the number of voting members in the legislature. That suited Virginia very well, since it had a large population, especially if the slaves were counted.

James Madison has been called, with pardonable exaggeration, "the father of the Constitution." He also worked behind the scenes, getting votes in line, marshaling forces behind the plan, compromising only when necessary. One of his gifts to posterity is the set of notes he kept of the proceedings. No official records of the debates exist; members wanted confidentiality in order to speak frankly. But Madison sat in the front bench each day, writing furiously as each person spoke.

25

Silence followed Randolph's presentation—and then came an uproar. Under the Articles of Confederation, the states were in power. Each was represented equally in Congress, and the central authority could not veto anything a state did. The Virginia Plan submerged the states under a single powerful national government, and the states would be voting units of very unequal power. The small states feared that they would be overshadowed by large states like Virginia. In part, the fight was between the large states like New York and Virginia and smaller states like New Jersey, Connecticut, and Delaware. But it was more than that; it involved different views of how people ought to be represented and how power should be divided between the states and the national government.

The battle began in earnest on Friday, June 15, 1787, when William Paterson of New Jersey presented the plan championed by the small states. Though it proposed some bold departures from the status quo, it was modest in comparison with the Virginia Plan. The New Jersey Plan, as it came to be called, retained the existing one-house legislature, provided for a plural executive, left most authority in the hands of the states, and based representation on the principle of one state, one vote, regardless of population.

It was an angry fight: Madison and his allies were determined to defeat the New Jersey Plan; the Paterson forces were at least as determined not to be stopped. The weather made things worse. A heat wave had hit Philadelphia, and the city was bathed in steamy air. Because the proceedings were supposed to be confidential, the windows had to be kept tightly closed. By midafternoon, the hall was like an oven. When the windows were raised, swarms of hungry black flies entered. A French visitor to Philadelphia expressed his amazement and disgust: "If one writes, the paper is spotted with flyspecks. If a woman is dressed in white her dress is in like manner spoiled. . . . The upholstery and bellpulls are sticky. At table and above all at dessert they light upon and befoul all food, all drinks."[3] They also bit savagely.

The torment continued at night, which meant the delegates scarcely slept. If they opened the windows in their cramped rooming houses, the flies harassed them. If they kept them closed, they suffocated in the heat. They were tired in the morning, and after a day of wrangling, many were ready to go home. Some, including Alexander Hamilton, did pack up and leave (he later came back). George Washington, still grimly presiding over the convention, wrote to Hamilton, his friend and former aide: "I am sorry you went away." Everything, the General said, seemed to be getting worse. "In a word, I almost *despair* of seeing a favorable issue to the proceedings of the Convention, and do therefore repent having any agency in the business."[4]

But somehow a compromise was worked out. The matter was referred to a committee that met over the Fourth of July holidays. The Connecticut Compromise, so called because it was first introduced by Roger Sherman of Connecticut, proposed a two-house legislature in which the lower house would be based on representation by population and the upper house would allow each state two senators, regardless of the state's size. The compromise adopted features from both the Virginia and the New Jersey plans and literally split the difference.

The Great Compromise was probably the result of quiet deals by moderates on both sides, and we know that a few timely departures and absences helped tip critical votes toward it. Maybe the change in the weather played a role. As the delegates adjourned for the weekend on Friday, July 13, a cool breeze swept in from the Northwest. At last they

Visitors to the National Archives can examine four original pages of the Constitution under a mural depicting the Founding Fathers.

could get some sleep. The weather was still cool on Monday when they returned to Independence Hall and voted to accept the committee's recommendation.

Madison was not happy, but he cooperated (and later defended the compromise as a wonderfully well-conceived system). Many tough issues remained, but from now on the delegates would debate without any real threats of dissolution.

Two months and two days later, they were done. The document was written out in the version we know, and on Monday, September 17, the members walked to the front of the hall to sign it. Benjamin Franklin turned to the delegates near him and pointed to the back of the chair Washington had occupied in presiding over the convention, which was decorated with a painting of the sun. During the long convention, he had often looked at that sun and wondered whether it was rising or setting. "But now, at length," he said, "I have the happiness to know that it is a rising and not a setting sun."[5]

*   *   *   *   *

Looking back on the difficulty in reconciling the different attitudes, prejudices, and points of view of the delegates, George Washington later said that the Constitution was "little short of a miracle." The document itself has an almost religious aura about it; like a sacred scroll, the original is kept in a glass case at the National Archives in Washington, D.C.

The Constitution is not the only document in that case. Alongside it are two others: the Declaration of Independence and the Bill of Rights. Here are the great founding charters of the American republic, carefully preserved for following generations of Americans to see. But they are more than relics; they are working documents, full of life and meaning, and still being used to solve controversies. Sometimes vaguely, sometimes quite distinctly, these documents sketch out the American people's sense of legitimacy and political morality. They have not only survived but grown in stature during two centuries of almost bewildering change.

In this chapter we will examine America's basic moral/legal documents: the Declaration of Independence, the Constitution, and the amendments to the Constitution. To do that, we should begin at the beginning, with the American Revolution and the document that explained its purpose to the world.

The Declaration of Independence

This country has always been proud of its revolutionary origins. The events that led up to the American Revolution have been celebrated in poems and plays. The taxes on goods, the futile protests against them, the increasing anger of the colonists, the Boston Tea Party, the vindictive responses of the mother country, the pamphlets and speeches—all served to kindle the fires of what became a successful rebellion against Great Britain. The American Revolution, however, was much more than a successful rebellion. It was also the triumph and culmination of certain ideas about people, government, and human rights. The core of these ideas found their way into the document that summed up the American case for revolution, the Declaration of Independence.

The shooting war between the Americans and British had been going on for over a year before the official break with Britain was announced. Radicals such as Richard Henry Lee, Thomas Jefferson, Benjamin Franklin, and John Adams had long been urging such an announcement. Conservatives and moderates hoped that a final rupture could be avoided. But by the summer of 1776 it was too late; independence was in the air. On June 7 Lee introduced a resolution at the Continental Congress in Philadelphia, which declared that the colonies "are, and of right ought to be, free and independent States."[6] Four days later, the Congress appointed a committee of five to "prepare a declaration." Because the committee included Jefferson, Adams, and Franklin, the delegates knew the result would signal a final break with the mother country. Written under intense emotional pressure and designed to win the support of "a candid World," the Declaration of Independence summed up the American case for independence.

JEFFERSON THE REVOLUTIONARY

Its preamble, which has become its most enduring part, presents its underlying philosophy. Years later, John Adams, perhaps a little annoyed at the fame of the principal author, Thomas Jefferson, remarked that the Declaration of Independence "contained no new ideas, that it is a commonplace compilation, its sentiments

At 6 P.M. on July 9, 1776, some New Yorkers toppled a statue of King George III; they melted it down and used the lead for bullets.

28

Shays's Rebellion (1786-1787) was a series of skirmishes in western Massachusetts that kindled deep fears of anarchy in America. Angry farmers, led by a former Revolutionary War captain named Daniel Shays, forcibly prevented courts from meeting in a desperate effort to prevent foreclosures on their farms. The uprising was soon quelled by the militia and eventually the rebels were pardoned.

hackneyed in Congress for two years before."[7] Jefferson pleaded guilty; its purpose, he said, was "not to find out new principles or new arguments never before thought of, not merely to say things which had never been said before, but to place before mankind the common sense of the subject in terms so plain and firm as to command their assent, and to justify ourselves in the independent stand we are compelled to take."[8] It was intended, Jefferson said, "to be an expression of the American mind, and to give that expression the proper tone and spirit called for by the occasion."[9]

It begins, "When in the Course of human events, it becomes necessary for one people to dissolve the political bands which have connected them with another . . ." To dissolve "political bands" is to stage a revolution. Revolutions should not be undertaken for "light and transient causes," the Declaration says, but when it becomes evident that "a long train of abuses and usurpations" is pushing the people toward "absolute Despotism, it is their right, it is their *duty*, to throw off such Government, and to provide new Guards for their future security" (emphasis added). The idea that people sometimes have the *duty* to revolt was later toned down by some signers of the Declaration, like John Adams, but not by Jefferson.

Take, for example, Jefferson's reaction to Shays's Rebellion, which happened a decade after our break with Britain. Many felt there had been enough revolution, but Jefferson did not agree. "God forbid," he wrote to a friend, "we should ever be twenty years without such a rebellion. . . . What signify a few lives lost in a century or two? The tree of liberty must be refreshed from time to time with the blood of patriots and tyrants. It is its natural manure."[10]

THE IDEAS BEHIND THE DECLARATION

The ideas Jefferson put into the Declaration were widely shared at the time, not only in America but also in England and Europe. The premises behind the ideas are set forth in the preamble: "We hold these Truths to be self-evident, that all Men are created equal, that they are endowed by their Creator with certain unalienable Rights, that among these are Life, Liberty, and the Pursuit of Happiness." The purpose of government, it says, is "to secure these Rights." If a government does so, it is a just and legitimate government. But if it becomes "destructive" of them, then the people have the right and duty to overthrow it.

The Declaration has a logical structure. The pattern is "if . . . then." *If* people are oppressed by their rulers, *then* they have the right and duty to overthrow them. The

29

body of the Declaration fills in the "if" part. It lists several grievances against the English king, including these: "He has erected a Multitude of new Offices, and sent hither Swarms of Officers to harass our People, and eat out their Substance. He has kept among us, in Times of Peace, Standing Armies without the consent of our Legislatures. . . . He has plundered our Seas, ravaged our Coasts, burnt our Towns, and destroyed the Lives of our People." Then came the dramatic conclusion: "We, therefore, the Representatives of the UNITED STATES OF AMERICA . . . solemnly Publish and Declare, That these United Colonies are, and of Right ought to be *FREE AND INDEPENDENT STATES* . . . ." It was a dangerous conclusion. If the Revolution failed, the signers knew they would be hunted down; if caught, they would likely be put to death. Small wonder, then, that they ended their Declaration by invoking "the Protection of Divine Providence."

The Declaration has deep roots. In chapter 1 we discussed the idea that people have certain basic rights that are given to them not by governments but by God. This idea was familiar to Christian theologians in the thirteenth century.[11] The concept of "natural law" had already been developed into a justification for revolution by the end of the seventeenth century by the English philosopher John Locke. Some of the terms and expressions Locke used found their way into the Declaration of Independence.

Many others also influenced the thought of the American Revolution. Some, like the philosophers James Harrington (1611-1677) and Algernon Sidney (1622-1683), are still read today. Most of the hundreds of pamphleteers who wrote in the seventeenth and eighteenth centuries are now unknown. One who is still remembered is Thomas Paine (1737-1809), whose *Common Sense*, written in 1776, helped cut the last ties to the mother country. But long before Paine's famous call to revolution, other pamphleteers were laying the groundwork for it. Historian Bernard Bailyn has traced the development of revolutionary thought in those early pamphlets. At first, the arguments for American freedom were based on what the writers thought were the traditions of the British people. As time went on, pamphleteers started abstracting from those traditions certain basic principles applicable to *all* people, not just the British. The focus had shifted from the rights of Englishmen to the rights of *man*.[12]

SOBER EXPECTATIONS

The American Revolution was finally justified by an appeal to the principle of freedom. In a sense, this is an abstraction, and many revolutions based on abstract principles have ended badly. The French Revolution, begun in the name of "liberty, equality, and fraternity," ended in terror and tyranny. The Russian Revolution, which was supposed to produce a classless society, brought a totalitarian one instead. What distinguishes the American Revolution, according to political scientist Martin Diamond, is that it was based upon a *realizable* principle: Civil liberty—that is, freedom of speech, press, religion, and assembly and protection against arbitrary police actions by the state—can be achieved; it is not a utopian goal.

Diamond characterizes the American Revolution as one of "sober expectations."[13] This does not mean that the Declaration expects little from government or people; on the contrary, it expects a great deal. For over two centuries the Declaration has served as a very severe moral standard. Often it is used to show how short American practices fall from the ideals set forth to justify the Revolution. Long before the Civil War, its statement that "all men are created equal" was quoted by abolitionists to show that slavery should have no place in this country. Jefferson himself was painfully aware of the contradiction between its ideals and the ugly reality of slavery ("Indeed, I tremble for my country when I reflect that God is just. . . .") and, in his original draft of the Declaration, he included a clause mentioning slavery among the abuses of

British rule in this country.[14] The pro-slavery forces knew very well how dangerous the Declaration could be. One called it "a powder-cask."[15] Abraham Lincoln cited it in his debates with Stephen A. Douglas to argue against the extension of slavery; years later, in his Gettysburg Address, Lincoln referred to the Declaration when he spoke of our nation as "conceived in liberty and dedicated to the proposition that all men are created equal."

Down through the years the Declaration has been cited by generations of reformers, especially by those demanding an end to race, sex, and class discrimination. It speaks to us today in as strong a voice as it spoke in 1776, telling us that: (1) Rights are not given to us by government. We are born with basic rights that no government may abridge. (2) Governments are nothing more than agents of the people. If governments continuously fail to protect people's rights, and in fact work against them, then the people have the right, even the duty, to overthrow them. (3) All people are essentially equal. Distinctions based on class or race or sex do not come from nature. They are artificial distinctions. Laws based upon them are therefore arbitrary and unnatural.

These are powerful ideas. The Declaration seems to have lost none of its freshness as a statement of America's revolutionary ideals: It remains what it was in the eighteenth and nineteenth centuries: a cask of gunpowder.

The Constitution

The Declaration of Independence made it clear that government must protect human rights and must be founded on popular consent, but it left open the question of what kind of government the United States should adopt. For the Revolution to be completed, a new government was necessary.

The Articles of Confederation, the first formal charter, provided a "league of friendship" rather than a government. By 1787 a broad consensus had developed that change was needed. The result was the Constitution and a new government.

"A MORE PERFECT UNION"

In its preamble, the Constitution states that one of its purposes is "to form a more perfect Union." In several respects, it did so.

- The Articles of Confederation began, "We the undersigned Delegates of the States," but the Constitution begins, "We the People." The articles of Confederation was a *compact of states*; the Constitution is a *union of people*.

31

"So, then . . . Would that be 'us the people' or 'we the people?' "
Drawing by Gary Larson; © 1982 Chronicle Features.

- Under the Articles of Confederation, the states could print their own money, set up tariffs against each other and against foreign nations, and ignore congressional requests for revenue. Under the Constitution, the power to regulate commerce between states and with foreign nations is exclusively national, as is the printing of currency; Congress can also "lay and collect Taxes."

- Article I, Section 8, of the Constitution contains an impressive list of congressional powers, ending with a clause that gives Congress the right to make "all Laws which shall be necessary and proper for carrying into Execution the foregoing Powers." This so-called implied powers clause resembles a blank check. All Congress has to do to justify new assertions of power is to show that they help carry "into execution" powers explicitly granted to Congress in Article I, Section 8—such powers, for example, as the power to tax and the power to regulate interstate and foreign commerce.

- In the Articles of Confederation it says that "each state retains its sovereignty, freedom and independence," but Article VI of the Constitution says that the Constitution and laws made in pursuance of it are "the supreme Law of the Land," and state judges are bound by them. Article VI, the supremacy clause, has been called the keystone clause because it holds up the arch of our national government.

- The Constitution set up a Supreme Court to have the last word in deciding "cases and controversies" arising under the Constitution. Scholars are still disputing whether or not the Framers meant to give the Court power to strike down federal statutes, but Article VI leaves no doubt that they meant to give it power to strike down *state* laws that violate the Constitution.

- Under the Articles of Confederation there was only a weak, plural executive, a "committee of states," that met for part of the year and was totally the creature of Congress. The Constitution put the executive power in the hands of one person, an independently elected president, and gave that president significant independent powers.

The men who framed our Constitution acted with unusual boldness. Their commission was to revise the Articles of Confederation. Instead, they threw out the old charter and wrote a completely new one. Here were men with great drive and a talent for political action.

THE DELEGATES: AN EXTRAORDINARY GROUP

Seventy-four delegates were named to the convention; 55 showed up, representing 12 of the 13 states. (Rhode Island, heavily in debt and frantically printing paper money, refused to send delegates to a convention it thought would be dominated by creditors and hard-money men.)[16] From the middle of May to the middle of September, delegates drifted in and out of Philadelphia. Some stayed for a few weeks or a month; most stayed till the end. Of those remaining on the last day, all but three signed the document. Most had had considerable experience in politics as lawyers, members of Congress, or as state and local political leaders.

As we noted at the beginning of this chapter, one of the moving spirits behind the convention and the main author of the Virginia Plan was James Madison. Madison has been called, with pardonable exaggeration, "the father of the Constitution." He also worked behind the scenes, getting votes in line, marshaling forces behind the plan, compromising only when necessary. One of his gifts to posterity is the set of notes he kept of the proceedings. No official records of the debates exist; members wanted confidentiality in order to speak frankly. But Madison sat in the front bench each day, writing furiously as each person spoke.

George Washington presiding at the Constitutional Convention.

While Madison was short, his fellow Virginian, George Washington, was a muscular six foot two—practically a giant in those days. In presiding over the convention, Washington said little and avoided any hint of partisanship. A gregarious man who liked to tell jokes, play cards, bet on horses, and dance for hours, Washington also could be very dignified. He had been reluctant to come, but the organizers insisted that his presence was necessary if the convention was to be taken seriously.

At the Annapolis Convention the previous fall, Alexander Hamilton of New York had been part of a small group that persuaded the delegates to call for the new convention the following year. Born in the West Indies, Hamilton had come to America as a teenager and had never developed strong local attachments. He was able to look at America as a whole, seeing it as a nation of continental proportions instead of a patchwork of local interests.

Though Hamilton was influential in getting the convention under way and even more so in getting the Constitution ratified, his role during the convention itself was not a major one. In part, that was because of his extreme views. He expressed his admiration for the British monarchy, his distaste for any government dominated by "the mass of people," and his view that America should have an executive and a Senate elected for life. The other delegates greeted his six-hour speech with profound silence.

From South Carolina came Charles C. Pinckney. Conceited, foppish, wildly ambitious, he was not a beloved figure to his contemporaries—behind his back they called him "blackguard Charlie"—but he played a significant role. For some reason, Madison left out of his notes one of Pinckney's major speeches in which he outlined a plan similar to Madison's. Pinckney's contributions were finally unearthed by twentieth-century scholars.[17]

The Pennsylvania delegation included Benjamin Franklin, James Wilson, and Gouverneur Morris. Franklin had already earned his place in history as a revolutionary publicist, statesman, inventor, and, in the slightly exaggerated words of another delegate, "the greatest philosopher of the present age." At 81, he was slowing down—because of difficulty in walking, he was carried in a sedan chair by Philadelphia jail inmates—and his remarks had little effect on the proceedings, although his humor sometimes helped to break the tension.

Tall, Scottish-born James Wilson wore thick glasses that sat halfway down his nose. He rivaled Madison in learning, and his keen mind could recognize in an instant the weakness of an opponent's argument. These gifts he used relentlessly to make the case for a strong central government headed by a single executive.

Gouverneur Morris was, in the words of one contemporary account, "a very handsome, bold, and—the ladies say—a very impudent man." Among his other

The concept of "natural law" had already been developed into a justification for revolution by the end of the seventeenth century by the English philosopher John Locke (1632-1704). Some of the terms and expressions Locke used found their way into the Declaration of Independence.

distinctions: a peg leg, an aristocratic attitude, a keen desire for a strong central government, and an elegant prose style. It was Morris who put the final polish on the language of the Constitution.

Some other delegates deserve at least honorable mention. Edmund Randolph of Virginia was the first to move the Virginia Plan, which became the basis of the Constitution. At the end, he refused to sign it because it had been changed so much, but he later urged its ratification in Virginia. John Dickinson of Delaware and William Paterson of New Jersey remained out of step with majority sentiments, but they fought a spirited battle for equal representation of small states in the new government. Roger Sherman and Oliver Ellsworth deserve credit for helping to settle the supreme quarrel of the convention, the difference between large states and small over the issue of representation.

On the whole, they were a relatively young group. The average age was 42, artificially raised by Ben Franklin's presence. Madison, at 36, was older than 11 of the other delegates, including Edmund Randolph, 33; Alexander Hamilton, 30; and 26-year-old Jonathan Dayton of New Jersey, the youngest. Few of the delegates were very wealthy, although many held sizable tracts of land. Most were at least comfortable. A minority were men of modest means. About half the delegates were college educated. Most had read Locke and other philosophers popular during the eighteenth century; they also had some acquaintance with the great writers of antiquity. As their debates reveal, they were sophisticated political thinkers and took very seriously the implications of words like *liberty* and *democracy*.

POLITICS AND THE CONSTITUTION

The delegates were also, as political scientist John P. Roche has emphasized, practical politicians.[18] They represented certain constituencies in their home states, and they tried to work out compromises that would balance their principles and their interests. Representatives from small states like New Jersey, for example, knew that they would eventually have to explain to the folks back home why they had backed a plan that diluted the voting power New Jersey had enjoyed under the Articles. Because of the Great Compromise, they could say: "Look, we forced them to modify a plan that would have really put us at the mercy of the big states." Roche shows how some key features of the Constitution were the result of such pragmatic deals.[19]

Constituent interests undoubtedly played a role in the deliberations, but so did other considerations. The three men in the hall on September 17 who refused to sign the Constitution—George Mason and Edmund Randolph of Virginia and Elbridge Gerry of Massachusetts—were all from large states. All three opposed the Constitution because they thought it gave too much power to a central government. Mason and Randolph believed in popular democracy and worried about the elitist tendencies of a central government, but in Gerry's view, from "the evils we experience flow the excess of democracy."[20] What bothered him about a centralized government was that he thought it endangered civil liberties.[21] Obviously, these men were thinking about considerations other than the presumed "interest" of their states. The point is further illustrated by George Mason's passionate denunciation of slavery. Here was a delegate from the slave state of Virginia declaring that slaves "bring the judgment of Heaven on a Country."[22]

The point is this: *It is hard to pull out any single, all-embracing explanation for why these men said what they did and voted as they did.* In part, their decisions were based on their personal views, such as whether or not they thought majorities can be trusted; in part, they were based on what the delegates thought were the interests of their states or the interests of groupings within their states. And there were probably other considerations on their minds as well.

One of these considerations may have been economic self-interest. In 1913 the historian Charles A. Beard published a book entitled *An Economic Interpretation of the Constitution*, in which he argued that, with few exceptions, the Framers were "immediately, directly, and personally interested in, and derived economic advantages from, the establishment of the new system."[23] Specifically, Beard contended, the Framers drew up the Constitution in order to protect mercantile, manufacturing, and investment interests against the threat of majority control. Beard's thesis has been enormously influential but in recent times has come under serious challenge. In 1956 historian Robert E. Brown pointed out that, except for slaves, there was no great propertyless mass in the United States in the eighteenth century and that "practically everyone was interested in the protection of property."[24] Another historian, Forrest McDonald, agreed that Beard's economic hypothesis helps to explain some of the forces at work in the convention but then demonstrated that the hypothesis does not fit very well with the facts concerning the Framers' occupations and interests.[25] In his later writings, Beard himself took a much more positive view of the Framers and their work,[26] and even in 1913 he privately admitted that he had "overemphasized a number of matters in order to get a hearing that might not have been accorded to a milder statement."[27]

Whatever validity Beard's thesis may have, it should not be shocking to think that the Founders' political philosophy was consistent with their economic interests. As John Roche has noted, few people in human history "have espoused a view of the 'common good' or 'public interest' that militated against their private status." Even Plato, when he planned out his ideal republic, "put philosophers on top of the pile."[28]

SLAVERY AND THE CONSTITUTION

One of the property interests protected, or at least tolerated, by the Framers was the institution of slavery. Some members denounced slavery, but Charles Pinckney of South Carolina said that his state would not join if the institution were abolished. In the end, the delegates allowed Congress to prohibit the importation of any more slaves beginning in 1808 and, in the meantime, gave it the right to tax the slave trade. They also called for the extradition of slaves who had escaped from one state to another (Article IV, Section 2), and they let southerners count three-fifths of their slave populations for purposes of representation. (This has given rise to the accusation that the Founders considered a black person three-fifths of a human being.) *(Continued on page 36)*

Doonesbury *Drawing by G. B. Trudeau, © 1987. Reprinted with permission of Universal Press Syndicate.*

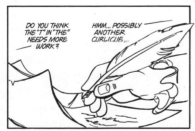

The following is excerpted from a speech delivered by Supreme Court justice Thurgood Marshall on May 6, 1987, at a seminar organized by the San Francisco Patent and Trademark Law Association in Maui, Hawaii:

Nineteen eighty-seven marks the two-hundredth anniversary of the United States Constitution. A commission has been established to coordinate the celebration. The official meetings, essay contests, and various festivities have begun.

Like many anniversary celebrations, this one takes particular events and holds them up as the source of all the very best that has followed. Patriotic feelings will surely swell, prompting proud proclamations of the wisdom, foresight, and sense of justice shared by the Framers and reflected in a written document now yellowed with age. This is unfortunate—not the patriotism itself but the tendency to oversimplify, to overlook the many other events that have been instrumental to our achievements as a nation. The focus of this celebration invites a complacent belief that the vision of those who debated and compromised in Philadelphia yielded the "more perfect Union" it is said we now enjoy.

The men who gathered in Philadelphia in 1787 could not have envisioned these changes. They could not have imagined, nor would they have accepted, that the document they were drafting would one day be subject to interpretation by a Supreme Court to which had been appointed a woman and the descendent of an African slave. "We the people" no longer enslaves, but the credit does not belong to the Framers. It belongs to those who refused to acquiesce to outdated notions of liberty, justice, and equality, and who strived to better them.

And so we must be careful, when focusing on the events that took place in Philadelphia two centuries ago, that we not overlook the momentous events that followed, and thereby lose our proper sense of perspective. Otherwise, the odds are that for many Americans the bicentennial celebration will be little more than a blind pilgrimage to the shrine of the original document now stored in a vault in the National Archives. If we seek instead a sensitive understanding of the Constitution's inherent defects—and its promising evolution through two hundred years of history—the celebration of the "miracle at Philadelphia" will be a far more meaningful and humbling experience.

(Continued from page 35) In recent years, one of the most bitter criticisms of the Constitution has come from a member of the Supreme Court, the institution that has the ultimate task of interpreting it. In 1987 Justice Thurgood Marshall, the Court's only black member, expressed his "dissent" from the bicentennial celebration (see box). In Marshall's view, the Founders deserve little credit for wisdom or foresight; they drew up a document that was defective from the start. Because the Constitution perpetuated slavery, Marshall said, it does not merit respect. If we are to celebrate, we should celebrate the enormous revisions made in the Constitution during the nineteenth and twentieth centuries. Marshall noted that it took a bloody civil war to give us the Fourteenth Amendment, which finally extended equality to blacks. In contrast, the original work of the Framers is based upon "outdated notions of liberty, justice, and equality."[29]

Marshall's anger is understandable, but his argument is open to criticism. The original Constitution was indeed defective, yet it contained the means of remedying its defects. It gave us a strong central government capable of making reforms. Under the original Articles of Confederation, the southern states could have perpetuated slavery indefinitely with no danger of outside interference. The Constitution also gave us an amendment process that eventually allowed the Fourteenth Amendment to come into being. Marshall praises the Fourteenth Amendment while sharply criticizing the document that made it possible; this is like praising the branch of a tree while condemning the trunk. Still, few would dispute Marshall's suggestion that the Framers were less than perfect. The men who drafted our Constitution were human beings with human prejudices and failings. They did their work with utter seriousness—there was little grandstanding at the convention—and in the end demonstrated that it was possible for people to get together, talk about the problems that divided them, and work out peaceful solutions. The product of their labor, says former Supreme Court Chief justice Warren E. Burger, "has permitted us to enjoy a degree of power, stability, and prosperity that eluded mankind during most of the world's history."[30]

THE RATIFICATION STRUGGLE

By mid-September of 1787, the work of drafting the Constitution was complete. The time had come for the delegates to sign, or not to sign, the new charter. Mason, Randolph, and Gerry refused. The rest moved toward the table at the front of the hall; recorded their signatures; and, according to George Washington's journal, "adjourned to the City Tavern, dined together and took a cordial leave of one another."

Yet the struggle to give America a new charter was far from over. The Constitution was as yet only a proposal. It had to be ratified, or approved. According to its own terms (Article VII), that required the approval of the people in at least 9 of the 13 states. The states were to hold ratifying conventions, and a majority vote at the convention was necessary for approval.

The Federalists, as the pro-Constitution people called themselves, faced a determined opposition. Patrick Henry, the fiery Virginia orator, and other Anti-Federalists argued that the Constitution was really an attempt by rich aristocrats to usurp the liberties of the people and crush states' rights. The Constitution obviously needed to be "sold" to the people, and many writers took up the task of promoting it in pamphlets, newspaper articles, letters, and other means.

The Federalist Papers. The most enduring of these political advertisements was a series of articles that appeared in various New York newspapers. The articles were all signed *Publius*, Latin for "public man." *Publius* was really three authors: Alexander Hamilton, James Madison, and John Jay. Jay wrote only a few of the articles; most were the work of Hamilton and Madison. They were later published in a volume entitled *The Federalist. The Federalist* papers, as they are commonly known today, were more than a sales pitch. Though written under great pressure, their tone is remarkably serene: They develop arguments thoughtfully, methodically, and without bombast. They were, and are, brilliant pieces, full of insight into human nature, society, and government. Among the basic themes developed in *The Federalist* papers are these:

- *The dark side of human nature. Federalist* No. 10 addresses the problem of factions, groups of people pursuing benefits for themselves at the expense of others. James Madison, its author, raises the question of whether or not people can be talked out of joining factions. No, he answers, for factions are "sown in the nature of man." Humans have a natural lust for domination, an urge to "vex and oppress" each other. *(Continued on page 39)*

GLOBAL PERSPECTIVES:

The Soviet Constitution

There have been four constitutions in the Soviet Union since the revolution in 1917. The present one was ratified in 1977, when Leonid I. Brezhnev headed the nation.

At first glance the constitution appears to be an extremely liberal and democratic document. It defines the USSR as a federated union of republics controlled by workers and peasants. At the union level, a bicameral Supreme Soviet is the source of all laws and executive appointments. Representatives to it, and to all local legislatures, are chosen by direct democratic elections. All Soviet citizens 18 years old and older are eligible to vote. The Constitution provides for freedom of speech, press, assembly, and religion; freedom from arbitrary arrest; privacy of personal correspondence; the inviolability of the home; and asylum for foreigners. It also provides the right to remunerative employment, rest, leisure, and social security benefits.

On closer examination, one can find an ominous theme running through the constitution. First stated in its preamble, the theme is "the combining of citizens' real rights and freedoms with their obligations and responsibility to society." In almost every place where rights are guaranteed, there is some mention of corresponding duties. In Article 39, which guarantees "personal rights and freedoms," there is an additional paragraph stating that such rights "must not be to the detriment of the interests of society or the state." Article 59 is more explicit, stating that the citizens' exercise of rights "is inseparable from their performance of their duties and obligations," and adding that citizens must "comply with the standards of socialist conduct and uphold the honor and dignity of Soviet citizenship." These are some of the loopholes relied upon by Soviet officials in arresting dissidents for "slander-ing" the Soviet state and jailing demonstrators for "hooliganism."

But even to state the matter in this way is a bit misleading. In fact, it is seldom necessary for Soviet officials to point out loopholes to judges, for they are in no way subordinate to judges. In almost every serious case, the judges take their orders from Communist party officials. Article 6 of the constitution states that the Communist party is "the leading and guiding force of Soviet society and the nucleus of its political system, of all state organizations and public organizations." Unofficially this is referred to as "telephone law": The local party secretary gets on the telephone and tells the judge how to rule.

Winds of change have been gusting through the Soviet Union since the arrival of Mikhail S. Gorbachev and his policy of *glasnost*, or openness. At the moment citizens of the USSR have more freedom than at any time since the 1920s. But this liberalization could be reversed almost overnight with a change of leadership or a change of heart. One purpose of a constitution is to institutionalize freedom, to put it into stone as it were, so that it will survive such changes. It is a purpose that is not well served by a constitution that leaves so much unchecked power in the hands of party officials.

(Continued from page 37)

- *The advantages of a large republic.* We cannot eliminate the cause of factions (at least not without destroying liberty), but we can control their effects. Here the solution is to have a republic large enough to contain a wide variety of factions; the competition among factions will prevent any single one from taking control. That, concluded Madison, is why a federation is better than a single state. A faction might take over one state, but it could never hope to dominate an entire federation.
- *Checks and balances.* In *Federalist* No. 51 Madison discusses another means of controlling factions: checks and balances. Derived from the writings of the French philosopher Baron de Montesquieu (1689-1755), checks and balances were designed to protect liberty by keeping the branches of government in competition with one another. Government, Madison said, must be divided into three separate branches: an executive, a legislature, and a judiciary. Each branch should be given *partial* control over the others. For example, the executive should have a qualified veto over legislation, and the legislature should have the power to turn down executive appointments. By giving these powers to each branch, we also give each the means of warding off a takeover by one of the others. "Ambition must be made to counteract ambition." No single power can take over the entire government and threaten civil liberties. Madison admitted that the need for checks and balances does not speak very well for human nature—"But what is government itself but the greatest of all reflections on human nature? If men were angels, no government would be necessary."

" 'Tis Done." Thanks in part to the work of Hamilton, Madison, and Jay, the Constitution was ratified within two years. Even so, approval did not come easily. In Pennsylvania, for example, the legislature was preparing to call for a ratifying convention when three Anti-Federalists walked out of the chamber, depriving the legislature of the necessary quorum. The next morning the truants were roused from their lodgings, carried triumphantly into the chambers, sat upon, and counted as "present." The majority then voted to call the ratifying conventions, which subsequently ratified for Pennsylvania. Table 2.1 lists the states in the order in which they ratified the Constitution and gives the final vote in each state.

TABLE 2-1

Order of Ratification and Votes Upon Ratification

State	Ratification date	Vote Yes	Vote No
1. Delaware	December 7, 1787	Unanimous	
2. Pennsylvania	December 12, 1787	46	23
3. New Jersey	December 18, 1787	Unanimous	
4. Georgia	January 2, 1788	Unanimous	
5. Connecticut	January 9, 1788	128	40
6. Massachusetts	February 6, 1788	187	168
7. Maryland	April 28, 1788	63	11
8. South Carolina	May 23, 1788	149	73
9. New Hampshire	June 21, 1788	57	46
10. Virginia	June 25, 1788	89	79
11. New York	July 26, 1788	30	27
12. North Carolina	November 21, 1789	195	77
13. Rhode Island	May 29, 1790	34	32

As soon as the nine-state majority was won (when New Hampshire ratified in June 1788), celebrations broke out in state after state. In Philadelphia, the celebration was particularly joyful. Among the horse-drawn floats pulled along Third Street, up Callowhill to Fourth, then west on Market Street, was a perfect replica of a full-rigged warship complete with 20 cannon and a crew of 25. It was named the *Union*, and as it neared Union Green, which was named for the occasion, a sailor on board threw a lead line and cast anchor. Benjamin Rush, the Philadelphian physician who had signed the Declaration of Independence 12 years earlier, was among the spectators. He was to note later in his journal that the crowd was moved to a profound silence by the allegory of the ship coming into port. " 'Tis done," he wrote. "We have become a nation."[31]

The Bill of Rights and Other Amendments

Before we discuss the Bill of Rights and the other amendments to the Constitution, we should examine the amending procedure.

AMENDING THE CONSTITUTION

The amending procedure, as set forth in Article V, sounds a bit confusing. Amendments must first be formally proposed and then ratified. Amendments can be proposed *either* by a two-thirds majority of both houses of Congress *or* by a special national convention called by Congress at the request of two-thirds of the state legislatures. Ratification can be *either* by three-quarters of the state legislatures *or* by special ratifying conventions held in three-quarters of the states. Figure 2.1 illustrates this process.

In practice, this mix-and-match system is not that complicated. Amendments have never been proposed by a national convention called into being by Congress upon petition by two-thirds of the states. It is doubtful that this method ever will be used, since many in Congress fear that a convention might get carried away and propose radical changes. After all, it happened once before; the convention of 1787, which was supposed to "revise" the Articles of Confederation, threw them out and

FIGURE **2-1**

41

The Bill of Rights
and Other
Amendments

Amending The Constitution

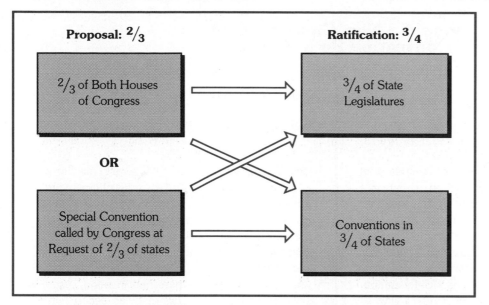

Constitutional amendments are most commonly proposed by a two-thirds vote
of both houses of Congress. The proposed amendment must then be ratified by
at least three-quarters of the 50 state legislatures.

started over. We can have some degree of confidence that the proposal method is
going to remain what it has been—two-thirds of both houses of Congress—but we
cannot be completely certain.

In the 1980s a proposed amendment to require a balanced federal budget picked
up support from state legislatures and at one point came within two states of
achieving the necessary two-thirds endorsement. In June 1989 there was talk of
proposing a constitutional amendment to make flag-burning illegal in response to a
5-4 Supreme Court ruling that found this political act to be protected by the First
Amendment's guarantee of free speech. In a *Newsweek* poll taken in late June,
respondents favored such an amendment by a margin of 71 percent to 24 percent.[32]
What would happen if a proposed amendment did gain the backing of two-thirds of
the state legislatures? No one is quite sure. Article V says that in such a case Congress
"shall" call a convention. Does "shall" mean "must"? The likelihood is that Congress
will, by one means or another, head off that convention. In our Taking Sides section
we explore the issue of whether or not a new convention would be damaging to the
nation.

As for ratification, in every instance except one (the repeal of Prohibition), the
method chosen by Congress has been to submit the amendment not to conventions
but to the state legislatures. To make sure that Prohibition got repealed, Congress
wanted to bypass the state legislatures because the legislatures of the time were
dominated by rural, largely "dry," interests.

In terms of probability, then, we can say that amending the Constitution requires
two-thirds of Congress and three-quarters of the state legislatures. Of course, those
majorities are not that easily mustered. Our history is littered with the bones of
amendment proposals that did not quite make it. In the 1970s, for example, the
proposed Equal Rights Amendment sailed through Congress but could not pick up
the necessary three-quarters of the state legislatures for ratification. We can see the
reason, then, why our Constitution has only 26 amendments—or 16, if we set aside
the first 10. *(Continued on page 43)*

Would a New Constitutional Convention Be a Mistake?

YES   Melvin Laird

Based upon Melvin R. Laird, "James Madison Wouldn't Approve," *Washington Post*, February 13, 1984.

Laird, a former congressman and secretary of defense in the Nixon administration, supports a balanced budget amendment to the Constitution but says that convening a new constitutional convention to draft the amendment "would be an act fraught with danger and recklessness." He recalls that the 1787 convention, which was only supposed to revise the Articles of Confederation, "broke every legal restraint designed to limit its power and agenda" and drafted a whole new charter of government. It could happen again, this time with disastrous results. Civil liberties could be endangered by hasty, ill-considered "reforms," and our whole system of orderly government could be thrown into chaos, says Laird. The effects would be incalculable but certainly devastating. In addition to the perils for the internal workings of our nation, "the potential disruptions to our vital foreign policy—NATO is an example—are disturbing to contemplate." To friends and enemies alike, the convention would appear "as a profound weakness in our national fabric."

NO   Griffin Bell

Based upon Griffin B. Bell, "Constitutional Convention: Oh, Stop the Hand-Wringing," *Washington Post*, April 14, 1984.

Bell, who served as attorney general in the Carter administration, scoffs at "predictions of gloom and doom." He thinks a balanced budget amendment is essential to our economic well-being and notes the failure of Congress to propose it. The only alternative is a convention. Far from being alien to our system, the convention method is "precisely what the Founding Fathers had in mind," especially in cases when Congress has become the problem instead of the solution. Those who think a convention would cause consternation among our allies, says Bell, forget that it is our interest rates, our national debt, and our exchange rates that are really causing the concern, and they are the result of wildly unbalanced budgets. Fears of an irresponsible, runaway convention are also groundless. Since 1787 we have had over 200 state constitutional conventions, and they "have brought out the best, not the worst, in people's governments." In any case, the proposals emerging from a national convention would have to be ratified by the states, and 38 states are not likely to ratify harmful amendments.

Postscript

The Convention of 1787, says Laird, "broke every legal restraint" on its agenda. One "law" apparently broken by the Framers was the clause in the Articles of Confederation that required the approval of all 13 states before any revision could be made. After thoroughly rewriting the Articles, the Framers decreed that the new charter needed the approval of only 9 of the 13 states! No one can say for certain what a new convention would do, but there is no want of speculation. See, for example, John J. Pitney, Jr., "Budget Balancing Act," *Reason* (January 1989); Austin Ranney, "What Constitutional Changes Do Americans Want?" *This Constitution* (Winter 1984); John T. Noonan, "Calling for a Constitutional Convention," *National Review*, July 26, 1985. Donald Robinson, in *To the Best of My Ability* (New York: W. W. Norton & Co., 1987), argues the need for revisions in Article II of the Constitution (on the presidency).

We combine the first 10 amendments because they were proposed and ratified together and because they addressed vital issues of human rights. Together, those first 10 constitute our <u>Bill of Rights</u>, which is revered today even by those who have reservations about the original Constitution. To appreciate the significance of the Bill of Rights, we must know something about how it came to be.

During the ratification struggle, one of the arguments most often heard against the new Constitution was that it contained no explicit guarantees of freedom against possible oppression by a new and powerful national government; it had no bill of rights. To this argument the Federalists replied that a bill of rights was not necessary. The new national government would have only the powers delegated or reasonably implied by the Constitution and thus could not abridge such liberties as the right to speak and the right to a fair trial. Moreover, the Federalists said, to guarantee *some* rights might actually be dangerous because people might start thinking that those not mentioned could be abridged.

But demands for a bill of rights persisted. Thomas Jefferson, who had not attended the convention, approved of its work—but agreed with its opponents that it needed a bill of rights. So did another famous revolutionary, Samuel Adams of Massachusetts, who gave his vote for ratification on the promise that a bill of rights would be added by the First Congress. So in 1789, the First Congress added the first 10 amendments to the Constitution, amendments that by 1791 had been ratified by the required three-quarters of the state legislatures. Each of the amendments was meant to protect specific groups of rights.

The First Amendment guarantees freedom of speech, press, assembly, and religion and prohibits the "establishment of religion." This amendment spells out some of our most vital freedoms. The right to worship—or not to worship—according to one's conscience is a right that lies at the foundation of our democratic system. So too does the right of communication. If free speech, press, and association are curtailed, how can people stop the curtailment of other rights? (Every dictator knows this: First shut people up, then you can do what you want.) In chapter 4 we will take a closer look at First Amendment freedoms.

It may be that all amendments are not created equal. Consider the Second and Third Amendments. The Second Amendment protects our right "to keep and bear arms." Some opponents of gun control cite this clause without quoting its preamble, which reads: "A well regulated militia, being necessary to the security of a free State." In 1789 state militias were manned by volunteers, who kept and maintained their own muskets. Today's "state militias" are National Guard troops, who store their weapons in armories. The Third Amendment also has a slightly antique quality. It forbids the quartering of troops in people's homes without their permission. In the 1990s we seem to have more than enough military bases for quartering troops.

The Fourth Amendment, which prohibits the police from conducting "searches and seizures" without proper warrants, has been greatly expanded by Supreme Court decisions. In 1962 the Court ruled that the Fourth Amendment prevented the use of illegally seized evidence against defendants in state cases. Critics claim that the so-called exclusionary rule has permitted known criminals to go free. (We examine this controversy in chapter 6.) The Fourth Amendment has also become one of the bases for the claim of a general right to privacy, a right nowhere mentioned in the Constitution. That much-debated claim underlies the Court's decisions on birth control and abortion (see chapter 5).

The Fifth Amendment's protection against self-incrimination has figured in plays, novels, and real-life dramas when courtroom interrogators ask questions and are met with the ritual "I refuse to answer on the grounds that my answer may tend to incriminate me." The Fifth Amendment contains other vital rights: protection against being tried (or otherwise held in jeopardy) twice for the same offense, the right to be

(Continued on page 44)

The Bill of Rights, encompassing some of the most important and best known provisions of the Constitution, was drafted by the First Congress in 1789. These first 10 amendments can be grouped into three main categories:

FREEDOM TO PARTICIPATE IN POLITICS

First Amendment: Ensured freedom of religion; freedom from religious "establishment"; freedom of speech, press, assembly, and of the right to petition the government.

PROTECTIONS AGAINST ARBITRARY STATE ACTION

Second Amendment: Established the right of citizens to bear arms.

Third Amendment: Prohibited the quartering of troops in private homes in peacetime.

Fourth Amendment: Prohibited unreasonable searches and seizures.

Fifth Amendment: Required a grand jury indictment before prosecution for a serious crime; Prohibited "double jeopardy": The accused cannot be tried twice for the same offense; Protected witnesses from being forced to testify against themselves; Ensured that no person can be deprived of life, liberty, or property without due process.

Sixth Amendment: Established the accused's right to a speedy, public, impartial trial with defense counsel and the right to cross-examine witnesses.

Seventh Amendment: Preserved the right to jury trials in civil suits where "the value in controversy" exceeds $20.

Eighth Amendment: Outlawed excessive bails or fines and cruel or unusual punishment.

PROTECTIONS OF STATES' RIGHTS AND UNNAMED RIGHTS OF PEOPLE

Ninth Amendment: Proclaimed that unlisted rights are not necessarily denied.

Tenth Amendment: Reserved those powers to the states or to the people that are not already delegated to the United States or denied to the states.

(Continued from page 43) indicted by a grand jury, the right of "due process of law," and protection against government seizure of property "without just compensation."

The Sixth and Seventh Amendments relate to trial rights. The Sixth Amendment gives us the right to counsel in criminal trials. Like the Fourth Amendment, this right has been expanded by the Supreme Court, which has held that a criminal suspect must be supplied with a court-appointed attorney if the suspect cannot afford a lawyer and that the attorney must be present during preliminary questioning. The Seventh Amendment says that people are entitled to jury trials in civil (noncriminal) suits "where the value in controversy shall exceed twenty dollars."

The Eighth Amendment, which bans "cruel and unusual punishments," was meant to ensure that the United States did not torture people or conduct the bizarre executions that were allowed under English law. In recent times, attempts have been made to use the Eighth Amendment to ban all forms of capital punishment and to force prisons to relieve overcrowding, by releasing inmates if necessary. (These issues are discussed in chapter 6.)

The Ninth Amendment says: "The enumeration in the Constitution, of certain rights, shall not be construed to deny or disparage others retained by the people." It was designed to answer the argument that listing some rights might be construed as permitting the abridgment of those not listed. In recent years the Supreme Court has used this amendment to back up its assertion that the right to privacy is a genuine constitutional right, despite the fact that it is not "enumerated" in the Constitution (see chapter 5).

The Tenth Amendment says that the powers not delegated to the federal government or prohibited to the states "are reserved to the States respectively, or to the people." In the nineteenth century and the early years of this century, the Supreme Court struck down federal legislation on Tenth Amendment grounds, but in 1941 a Court with several new appointees asserted that the amendment does not really have much meaning: It "states but a truism that all is retained which has not been surrendered."[33] Others, however, continue to see it as a necessary bulwark against excessive centralization. These issues are explored in the next chapter.

THE BILL OF RIGHTS AND THE STATES

The Bill of Rights was originally intended to apply only to the federal government. The First Amendment begins, "*Congress* shall make no law. . . ." (emphasis added.) While that reference limiting the application to the national legislature is not found in any of the other amendments, there seems to be little doubt that the Framers of the Bill of Rights ended up agreeing with Representative Thomas Tucker of South Carolina, who said: "It will be much better, I apprehend, to leave the State Governments to themselves, and not interfere with them more than we do, and that is thought by many to be too much."[34] Tucker made the remark during House debate of a Madison-inspired amendment that would have protected free speech, a free press, and jury trials against infringement "by any State." Although the House passed Madison's amendment, the Senate defeated it, and the House later concurred.

Forty-four years later, the Supreme Court placed the stamp of judicial approval on the limited, federal-level-only interpretation of the Bill of Rights. The case was *Barron v. Baltimore* (1833). Barron, a Baltimore wharf owner, complained that the city's drainage ditches had deposited silt around his wharf, rendering it useless. He brought suit for monetary damages against Baltimore, citing a clause in the Fifth Amendment that prohibits the taking of private property "for public use without just compensation." But the Supreme Court refused to hear his case, saying that all the amendments in the Bill of Rights apply only to the federal government, not to states and localities.

Today the *Barron v. Baltimore* decision has practically been wiped out by the Supreme Court. Since the Civil War, and particularly since the beginning of this century, the Court has been chipping away at it until now not much is left. Clause by clause, in case after case, the Bill of Rights has been extended to the states. Today most—although not all—of the provisions in the Bill of Rights apply in the same way to states and localities as they do to the federal government. (The reasons for this selective incorporation will be explored in chapter 6.)

THE OTHER AMENDMENTS

The other 16 amendments to the Constitution have been inserted at various times, between 1798 and 1971, in response to perceived needs and pressures. Somewhat roughly, they may be grouped into four categories. *(Continued on page 47)*

THE OTHER AMENDMENTS

Since the First Congress in 1789, another 16 amendments have been added to the Constitution. They can be grouped into four categories:

STATE POWER AND CIVIL RIGHTS

Eleventh Amendment (1798):
Guaranteed that when a state is sued by a citizen in another state, the case must be tried in a state, not a federal, court.

Thirteenth Amendment (1865):
Abolished slavery.

Fourteenth Amendment (1868):
Made former slaves citizens and prohibited the states from denying them due process of law and equal protection under the law.

Fifteenth Amendment (1870):
Prohibited any unit of government from denying people the right to vote because of color "or previous condition of servitude."

Twenty-fourth Amendment (1963):
Outlawed poll taxes in federal elections.

AMENDMENTS EXTENDING DEMOCRACY

Seventeenth Amendment (1913):
Provided for popular election of U.S. senators. (Until that time, senators had been appointed by state legislatures as mandated in Article I.)

Nineteenth Amendment (1920):
Guaranteed women the right to vote.

Twenty-third Amendment (1961):
Permitted residents of the District of Columbia to vote in presidential elections and gave the district three electoral votes.

Twenty-sixth Amendment (1971):
Extended the right to vote to citizens who are at least 18 years old.

AMENDMENTS AFFECTING THE PRESIDENCY

Twelfth Amendment (1803):
Provided separate balloting for the president and vice president. (It was meant to prevent a repetition of the 1800 election, when Thomas Jefferson and Aaron Burr, running on the same ticket, tied in electoral college votes.)

Twentieth Amendment (1933):
Also called "Lame Duck" Amendment. It started the term of the new Congress on January 3 and that of the new president on January 20, rather than in March as previously.

Twenty-second Amendment (1951):
Limited the president to two terms in office.

Twenty-fifth Amendment (1967):
Outlined succession to the presidency and vice presidency and included a solution to the problem of a disabled president who refused to leave office.

MISCELLANEOUS

Sixteenth Amendment (1913):
Put into effect the federal income tax.

Eighteenth Amendment (1919):
Instituted Prohibition.

Twenty-first Amendment (1933):
Repealed Prohibition.

(Continued from page 45)

1. *State power and civil rights.* According to the Eleventh Amendment (1798), if a state is sued by a citizen in another state, the case must be tried in a state, not a federal, court. Also in the category of "state power" are all the amendments designed to protect the rights of minorities. All have had the effect of qualifying the power of the states. The most prominent of these amendments are usually called the Civil War Amendments because they were adopted in the immediate aftermath of the war and sought to resolve problems associated with slavery. The Thirteenth Amendment (1865) abolished slavery. The Fourteenth Amendment (1868) made citizens of the former slaves and prohibited the states from denying them due process of law and the equal protection of the laws. Indeed, those two clauses—due process and equal protection—have played an enormous role in limiting the power of states in such widely diverse areas as civil rights, business regulation, criminal justice, birth control, and abortion. The Fifteenth Amendment (1870) prohibited any unit of government from denying people the right to vote because of color "or previous condition of servitude." A more recently adopted civil rights amendment, the Twenty-fourth (1963), outlaws poll taxes in federal elections.

2. *Amendments extending democracy.* This category somewhat overlaps the previous one; both categories touch on the issues of voting and civil rights. But whereas the previous category is concerned mainly with racial minorities, this one extends to whites and deals exclusively with the question of suffrage. The Seventeenth Amendment (1913) provides for popular election of U.S. senators. Until that time senators had been appointed by state legislatures, as mandated in Article I. The Twenty-third Amendment (1961) extends suffrage in a different way. It permits residents of the District of Columbia to vote in presidential elections and gives the district three electoral votes. The Nineteenth Amendment (1920) guarantees women the right to vote. What the Nineteenth Amendment did for women, the Twenty-sixth Amendment (1971) did for young people. It states that no otherwise-eligible citizen shall be denied the right to vote if he or she is at least 18 years old.

3. *Amendments affecting the presidency.* In this category is the Twelfth Amendment (1803), which provides separate balloting for president and vice president. It was meant to prevent a repetition of what happened in the 1800 election, when Thomas Jefferson and Aaron Burr, running on the same ticket, tied in electoral college votes.

   Another amendment affecting the presidency also affects Congress. It is the Twentieth, or "Lame Duck," Amendment. Before its adoption, members of Congress and the president, elected in November, did not take office until the following March. Meanwhile, a defeated administration and defeated members of Congress ("lame ducks") could continue in power despite their rejection by the voters months earlier. The Twentieth Amendment started the term of the new Congress on January 3 and that of the new president on January 20. Also dealing with the presidency is the Twenty-second Amendment (1951), which limits the president to two terms of office.

   A final presidential amendment is the Twenty-fifth (1967), on presidential disability. Prompted in part by the assassination of John F. Kennedy and still-fresh memories of President Eisenhower's health crises while in office, this amendment sought to tie up a number of loose ends concerning the succession to the presidency and vice presidency. Included was a solution to the problem of what to do if the president were disabled but refused to admit it. (The vice president, the cabinet, and Congress must decide whether or not the president is indeed disabled.)

4. *Miscellaneous.* Two of the three amendments here are mirror images. These are the Eighteenth (1919), instituting Prohibition, and the Twenty-first (1933), *(Continued on page 49)*

TABLE **2-2**

Proposed Amendments Since 1965

No constitutional right to abortion	Rejected by Senate in 1983 by 18 votes.
Balanced budget requirement	Passed by Senate in 1982, rejected in House by 46 votes.
Prohibit busing for school desegregation	House rejected in 1979 by 75 votes.
D.C. voting representation in Congress	Cleared Congress Aug. 22, 1978; ratification deadline expired Aug. 22, 1985, after 16 states (of 38 needed) had approved it.
Equal Rights Amendment	Cleared Congress March 22, 1972; ratification deadline extended by Congress Oct. 6, 1978; deadline expired June 30, 1982, after 35 states (of 38 needed) had approved it.
Voting age of 18	Cleared Congress March 23, 1971; ratified by states June 30, 1971. 26th Amendment.
Direct election of president	Passed by House 1969; died in Senate filibuster 1970; rejected by Senate in 1979 by 15 votes.
School prayer authorization	Rejected by Senate in 1966 by nine votes; rejected by House in 1971 by 28 votes; rejected by Senate in 1984 by 11 votes.
Vice presidential succession, presidential disability	Cleared Congress July 6, 1965; ratified by states Feb. 10, 1967. 25th Amendment.

Source: Congressional Quarterly. Reprinted by permission.

Proposed constitutional amendments that have come to a vote in one or both chambers of Congress since 1965.

Points to Remember

1. Amending the Constitution requires the approval of two-thirds of both houses of Congress and three-quarters of the states. Few amendment proposals are able to clear both hurdles.

2. The first 10 amendments were all passed by the First Congress and ratified together by the states. They are called the Bill of Rights because they were aimed at the protection of rights that were deemed basic at the time.

3. Vital portions of the Bill of Rights are the protections given to speech, press, association, and religion in the First Amendment and those relating to the rights of suspects in the Fourth, Fifth, and Sixth Amendments.

4. The Bill of Rights was intended to protect citizens against possible abuses by the national government; it was not intended to apply to the states. In this century, however, the Supreme Court has gradually applied almost all 10 amendments to the states as well.

5. One of the themes running through subsequent amendments has been the extension of civil rights and suffrage to those formerly left out: blacks (Thirteenth, Fourteenth, Fifteenth, Twenty-fourth); women (Nineteenth); and 18-year-olds (Twenty-sixth). A related theme has been the gradual extension of the power of the voter, represented by the direct election of senators (Seventeenth) and the granting of presidential electors to the District of Columbia (Twenty-third).

(Continued from page 47)
repealing Prohibition. President Herbert C. Hoover called Prohibition "an experiment noble in purpose." After 14 years of this noble experiment, the American people decided to call it quits.

The final amendment in the "miscellaneous" category is the Sixteenth (1916), the income tax amendment. The movement to pass it began after the Supreme Court in 1895 declared an income tax statute unconstitutional. The amendment gives Congress the authority to lay and collect taxes "from whatever source derived."

Reflections

The original copies of the Declaration of Independence and the Constitution are preserved in a helium-filled case at the National Archives in Washington, D.C. In contrast, the spirit of those documents can only be preserved through their use. In this sense, the cheapest printings are as precious as the parchment originals.

Turn to any copy of the Declaration of Independence and read the work of Thomas Jefferson, who expressed the ideas behind our revolution: All men are created equal and endowed by God with unalienable rights; governments are instituted to protect rights; when, instead, governments repress those rights and turn a deaf ear to complaints, people have the right to overthrow them and set up new governments. Here was, and is, the great powder keg we have inherited from our revolutionary forebears. Tyrants and slave masters have always hated it, have called it "abstract," and have tried to belittle it. It is a startlingly sober document that justifies violent revolution for the sake of an ideal—an ideal that is not some lofty utopia, but a republic that protects freedom and equality under the law.

Yet even sober ideals need the means of realization. The vehicle for turning them into the laws of our land is the Constitution. In May 1787, 55 men from 12 states sat down in Philadelphia with a mandate to revise the Articles of Confederation. When they rose in September they had completely rewritten the national charter, setting up a new government composed of three branches with separate but overlapping powers—a solid, strong government that limited state autonomy and made it clear that the new Constitution and laws made according to it were "the supreme law of the land." All this from a convention that almost broke down in angry confrontation—no wonder George Washington called it "little short of a miracle."

Ratification, in some of the states at least, would have been jeopardized had not the Federalists promised to insert a bill of rights into the Constitution once the new Congress met. The promise was kept by the First Congress. Here, in more specific language, were some of the "unalienable" rights referred to in general terms in the Declaration of Independence. Now they were codified into law and protected against interference by the federal government. It took a civil war, new constitutional amendments, and a change of direction in the federal judiciary before these rights were guaranteed against abuse by state governments.

Despite the difficulty of the process, we can be certain that our Constitution will continue to be amended. It belongs, after all, to the living. At various times Americans may need to adapt their charter to meet new needs and expectations. The challenge is to do so with careful consideration, to add only those amendments that advance the purposes set forth at the beginning of the Constitution: to "form a more perfect Union, establish Justice, insure domestic Tranquility, provide for the common defence, promote the general Welfare, and secure the Blessings of Liberty to ourselves and our Posterity. . . ." To do that is to protect and preserve the Constitution even as we change it.

The Constitution is more than the work of a summer, more than the work of the last two centuries. It remains unfinished. The work of democracy will always be unfinished. The solemn commitment of a people to monitor themselves and amend their system when necessary seems to be essential to the survival of popular government. Benjamin Franklin summed it all up in the fewest possible words when he returned to his Philadelphia lodging at the close of the convention in September 1787. His landlady, unable to contain her curiosity about what had been going on behind closed doors, asked: "Well, Dr. Franklin, what have you given us, a republic or a monarchy?" "A republic," Franklin answered, "—if you can keep it."[35]

Notes

1. Charles L. Mee, Jr., *The Genius of the People* (New York: Harper & Row, 1987), p. 7.
2. Christopher Collier and James Lincoln Collier, *Decision in Philadelphia* (New York: Random House, 1986), p. 106.
3. Mee, p. 188.
4. Catherine Drinker Bowen, *Miracle at Philadelphia* (Boston: Little, Brown, 1966), p. 140.
5. Collier and Collier, p. 256.
6. Quoted in Harry J. Carman and Harold C. Syrett, *A History of the American People* (New York: Alfred A. Knopf, 1957), I, p. 150.
7. See discussion in George McKenna, ed., *American Populism* (New York: G. P. Putnam's Sons, 1974), p. xxiv.
8. Edward Dumbould, ed., *The Political Writings of Thomas Jefferson: Representative Selections* (Indianapolis, IN: Bobbs-Merrill, 1955), p. 8.
9. Thomas Jefferson, Letter to Henry Lee, May 8, 1825, quoted in Edward Dumbauld, ed., *The Political Writings of Thomas Jefferson: Representative Selections* (Indianapolis, IN: Bobbs-Merrill, Inc., 1955), p. 8.
10. Jefferson, Letter to William S. Smith, Nov. 13, 1787, in Dumbauld, ed., pp. 68-69.
11. Carl Becker, *The Declaration of Independence: A Study in the History of Political Ideas* (New York: Knopf, 1960), pp. 37-40.
12. Bernard Bailyn, *The Ideological Origins of the American Revolution* (Cambridge, MA: The Belknap Press, 1967), chap. III.
13. Martin Diamond, "The Revolution of Sober Expectations," lecture delivered at Independence Square, Philadelphia, PA, 1975.
14. *Notes on Virginia*, in Dumbauld, ed., p. 61.
15. George Fitzhugh, "Cannibals All!" in Harvey Wish, ed., *Ante-Bellum: Writings of George Fitzhugh and Hinton Rowan Helper on Slavery* (New York: Capricorn Books, 1960), p. 149.
16. Mee, pp. 53-54.
17. Andrew C. McLaughlin, "Sketch of Charles Pinckney's Plan for a Constitution, 1787," *American Historical Review* (July 1904): p. 741. See further, S. Sidney Ulmer, "Charles Pinckney: Father of the Constitution?" *South Carolina Law Quarterly* (Winter 1958), p. 245; Christopher Collier and James Lincoln Collier, *Decision in Philadelphia: The Constitutional Convention of 1787* (New York: Random House, 1986), pp. 64-73.
18. John P. Roche, "The Founding Fathers: A Reform Caucus in Action," *American Political Science Review* (December 1961), pp. 799-816.
19. See especially Roche's explanation of the decision-making process behind the creation of the electoral college, in "The Founding Fathers," pp. 810-12.
20. Max Farrand, ed., *The Records of the Federal Convention of 1787* (New Haven, CT: Yale University Press, 1911), vol. I, p. 48.
21. Gerry did allude to the interests of Massachusetts when he complained that the number of representatives allotted to his state was not sufficient. But after citing this and other objections, he added that they were minor and he could ignore them "if the rights of citizens were not rendered insecure" (in Farrand, vol. II, pp. 632-33).
22. *Farrand*, vol. I, p. 370.
23. Charles A. Beard, *An Economic Interpretation of the Constitution of the United States* (New York: Macmillan, 1913), pp. 324-35.
24. Robert E. Brown, *Charles Beard and the Constitution* (Princeton, NJ: Princeton University Press, 1956), p. 198.
25. Forrest McDonald, *We the People: The Economic Origins of the Constitution* (Chicago: University of Chicago Press, 1958), pp. vii, 415.
26. Michael Kammen, *A Machine That Would Go of Itself: The Constitution in American Culture* (New York: Knopf, 1986), pp. 6, 228.
27. Beard, letter to Max Farrand, May 5, 1913. Quoted in Farrand, p. 459, n. 78.
28. Roche, p. 801.
29. Thurgood Marshall, "Celebrating the Constitution: A Dissent," *Harper's Magazine*, July 1987, p. 19.
30. Warren E. Burger, "The Constitution: A Modern Miracle," *Retirement Life*, July 1987, p. 5.
31. Bowen, pp. 306-10.
32. *Newsweek*, July 3, 1989, p. 18.
33. *United States v. Darby*, 312 U.S. 100 (1941).
34. Quoted in Bernard Schwartz, *The Bill of Rights: A Documentary History* (New York: Chelsea House, 1971), vol. II, p. 1113.
35. Quoted in Emmet John Hughes, *The Living Presidency* (New York: Coward, McCann & Geoghegan, Inc., 1973), p. 40.

The Constitution, in all its provisions,
looks to an indestructible Union,
composed of indestructible States.

Chief Justice Salmon P. Chase,
in *Texas v. White* (1869)

3

Federalism

THE NATURE AND PURPOSES OF FEDERALISM

Three Purposes of Federalism / The Other Side of Local Autonomy

WHY THE NATIONAL GOVERNMENT HAS EXPANDED

Implied Powers: The "Elastic Clause" / *McCulloch v. Maryland* (1819): "Necessary"
Means "Convenient" / The Commerce Clause: A "Hook" for Federal Power
The Civil War Amendments: Nationalizing Rights / Responses to Social and
Economic Change / Grants-in-Aid: Calling the Tune / Reagan's New Federalism:
A Swap

THE STATES TODAY: HOTBEDS OF INNOVATION

REFLECTIONS

1963—Everyone who was there on that June eleventh   **The Schoolhouse Door**
seems to remember the heat. It was 10:30 A.M. in
Tuscaloosa, Alabama, and the temperature was already 95 degrees.
Waves of heat quivered up from the asphalt roadways at the University of
Alabama. Not even a hot breeze stirred. *

A few months earlier, a federal judge had ordered the university to
admit as students two blacks who had been barred because of their race.
Admitting them meant putting an end to Alabama's policy of segregated
higher education. The previous fall, however, Alabama had elected a new
governor, George C. Wallace. Standing on the exact spot where Jefferson Davis stood when he was inaugurated as president of the Confederacy in 1861, Wallace ended his inaugural address with these words: "I
draw the line in the dust and toss the gauntlet before the feet of tyranny.

*This narrative is drawn from the following sources: Marshall Frady, *Wallace* (New
York, Cleveland: World, 1968); George C. Wallace, *Stand Up for America* (Garden City,
NY: Doubleday, 1976); George Wallace, Jr., and James Gregory, *The Wallaces of
Alabama* (Chicago: Follett, 1975); *New York Times*, September 29, 1982, p. 17;
November 3, 1982, p. 22.

51

And I say, 'Segregation now! Segregation tomorrow! Segregation forever!' "[1]

George Wallace had not always been such an outspoken segregationist. When he had first run for governor, in 1958, he had played down the race issue and had been soundly beaten by his opponent, John Patterson, who made racial segregation the center of his campaign. Wallace had learned his lesson. Now, five months after his inauguration, Wallace stood outside the door to the university's auditorium where registration for the fall term was being held. Short, wiry, with his black hair slicked back and precisely parted, the former Golden Gloves bantamweight boxer was ready for action.

At 10:48 A.M. a car rolled up. Out stepped the two black students, accompanied by the assistant attorney general of the United States, Nicholas Katzenbach. Lanky and bald, Katzenbach looked ill at ease as he walked toward the door between the banked lines of reporters. Wallace thrust out his hand to stop him. Katzenbach halted, identified himself, and said that he had an order from the president of the United States that prohibited the governor from interfering with the registration of the students. Katzenbach said: "I have come here to ask you now for unequivocal assurance that you will permit these students, who, after all, merely want an education in the great university . . ."[2] Wallace harshly interrupted him: "Now you make your statement, but we don't need for you to make a speech. You make your statement."[3] Mopping his brow, Katzenbach restated the presidential order. In reply, Wallace read a five-minute prepared statement on his theory of the Constitution. The statement ended with a refusal "to willingly submit to illegal usurpation of power by the central government."[4]

Katzenbach, who towered over Wallace, had to bend to hear him. He folded his arms tightly over his chest and leaned forward in an odd, awkward stance. The two exchanged more words. (In Wallace's later account, Katzenbach asked him three times to step aside, and each time he refused.) Katzenbach then turned and went back to his car. Simultaneously, Wallace pivoted and disappeared into the auditorium.

Four hours later Wallace reemerged, this time to greet a company of the Alabama National Guard that had been "federalized." This meant that the federal government had taken away the governor's command of these troops—they were now under the control of the president. The officer in charge, a brigadier general, saluted the governor and said: "Sir, it is my sad duty to ask you to step aside under orders of the president of the United States."[5] Wallace was prepared for this. He pulled another statement from his pocket. "But for the unwarranted federalization of the Alabama National Guard, I would at this moment be your commander-in-chief. In fact, I am your commander-in-chief. As governor of this state, this is a bitter pill to swallow."[6] Wallace stepped back and let the troops escort Vivian Malone and James Hood, the first blacks ever to enter the University of Alabama, into the auditorium.

*   *   *   *   *

By standing in the schoolhouse doorway, Wallace was violating the Constitution. In 1954 the Supreme Court had ruled that the Fourteenth Amendment prohibited official discrimination on the basis of race. Blacks had as much right as whites to enter the University of Alabama, and by blocking their entrance, Wallace was trying to perpetuate state practices that had been held unconstitutional almost a decade earlier. From our

June 11, 1963: Governor George C. Wallace attempts to block enforcement of a federal court order to admit two black students to the University of Alabama. At right is Assistant Attorney General Nicholas deB. Katzenbach.

perspective today, Wallace's action seems almost incomprehensible. How could a governor pretend to be protecting states' rights by preventing people from going to college? But however absurd the uses to which states' rights have been put, the doctrine itself cannot be dismissed out of hand. The Constitution sets limits on what states are allowed to do, and it also recognizes the independence and autonomy of state power. Wallace, however, was pushing state autonomy past the point allowed by the Constitution.

By standing in the schoolhouse doorway, Governor Wallace was physically enacting an old and by then thoroughly discredited doctrine, interposition. This doctrine states that if the federal government attempts to enforce some law that violates the rights of an individual state, the authorities in that state may "interpose" themselves between (stand between) the federal authorities and the people of the state to prevent local enforcement of the federal law. George Wallace was literally "standing between" the federal government and the people of Alabama.

The Civil War (1861–1865) settled the question of whether states could secede (withdraw) from the union. By implication, it also settled the question of whether or not a state could interpose itself between its people and the federal government. Nevertheless, interposition was long used in the South to stand in the way of civil rights, although that was not the way it was explained by those who used it. Wallace and others defended interposition as an essential part of states' rights. In the speeches and actions of southern segregationists, however, the topic was always intertwined with the race question. In other areas, southern officials had not been reluctant to accept federal aid and even direction. They had been among the warmest supporters of Franklin D. Roosevelt's New Deal, which, as we will see, greatly expanded the role of the central government.

Despite the uses and misuses of interposition and states' rights, these ideas cannot be dismissed as pure hypocrisy. Ours is a federal government. That means that it divides power between one central authority and many regional authorities. Our regional authorities—the states—are more than subdivisions of the central, or federal, government. They have powers and a role to play of their own.

In recent times many people, including some firm supporters of civil rights, have worried that the federal government may have taken away too much state independence. In 1965 Senator Everett McKinley Dirksen of Illinois, who played a major role in steering civil rights legislation through the Senate, said that the way things were going, pretty soon "the only people interested in state boundaries will be Rand McNally," the mapmakers.[7] Since then, the federal government has become even more involved in what were once local decisions, as we will discuss later in this chapter.

How did this federal presence in local affairs come about? Is it a good or bad development? Can it be reversed or somehow stopped? Should it be? When people discuss federalism today, these are some of the issues they raise. To get at the roots of these issues, we must take a closer look at the nature and purposes of federalism and its origin in this country.

The Nature and Purposes of Federalism

The name of our nation, the United *States* of America, is plural. There are good historical reasons for this. Before the American Revolution, there were 13 British colonies along the Atlantic seaboard from Georgia to Maine. The Revolution turned them into separate and independent states that were soon loosely associated in a "league of friendship" under the Articles of Confederation.

The phrase *league of friendship* pretty well summed up the Articles of Confederation, except that the relationship between the states was not always friendly. As we saw in chapter 2, page 25, the states often put tariffs, or taxes, on goods coming in from other states. Some refused to honor court decisions made in other states. There were even threats of military action. A league of friendship also does not permit a central government to use coercion when friendship fails. Here, then, was a true confederation: a compact between independent states. The United Nations (UN) is a close modern example. None of the member states has given up any power or modified its independence in any way in order to belong to the UN. No United Nations army or peacekeeping force can enter a state without its permission. Nor can the UN really tax its member states; it can only assess them and hope they will pay.

The direct opposite of a confederacy is a unitary government, such as those in Great Britain, France, and most other countries of the world. This form of government permits no independent regional powers; the central government is the sole authority. In Britain, for example, the majority party in Parliament, headed by the prime minister, decides what will happen even in local areas.

A federal system lies somewhere between a confederation and a unitary government. A certain degree of independent power is given to local units of government. The exact degree depends upon each country's constitution and traditions. Besides the United States, 18 other countries have federal systems, including Switzerland, Canada, Australia, the USSR, and Mexico (see Table 3.1). Some, such as Canada, leave considerable autonomy in the hands of regional units. Others, notably the USSR, maintain tight central control (although there has been some relaxation of central control under Soviet leader Mikhail Gorbachev). Whatever their differences, federal systems have important features in common, according to political scientist Daniel J. Elazar:

> Federal polities are characteristically noncentralized, that is, the powers of government within them are diffused among many centers, whose existence and authority are guaranteed by the general constitution, rather than being concentrated in a single center.[8]

TABLE 3-1

55

The Nature and
Purposes of
Federalism

Federal Systems

Name	Population (thousands)[a]	Area (sq. mi.)
Argentine Republic	27,863	1,068,302
Commonwealth of Australia	14,616	2,966,150
Federal Republic of Austria	7,507	32,376
Brazil	123,032	3,286,488
Canada	23,941	3,851,809
The Federal and Islamic Republic of the Comoros	298[b]	863
Czechoslovak Socialist Republic	15,312	49,378
Federal Republic of Germany	61,561	96,011
Republic of India	683,810	1,269,420
Malaysia	13,436	127,581
United Mexican States	67,396	756,066
Federal Republic of Nigeria	77,082	356,669
Islamic Republic of Pakistan	76,770[c]	310,403
Swiss Confederation	6,329	15,943
Union of Soviet Socialist Republics	265,542	8,649,540
United Arab Emirates	1,040	30,000
United States of America	227,640	3,618,467
Republic of Venezuela	13,913	352,144
Socialist Federal Republic of Yugoslavia	22,344	98,766

a 1980 or 1981 figures.
b 1976 estimate.
c 1978 figure.

Source: Adapted from Daniel J. Elazar, *Exploring Federalism* (Tuscaloosa, AL: University of Alabama Press, 1987), pp. 43-44.

The above table lists countries that have federal systems of government. A federal system falls somewhere between a confederation and a unitary government. The constitution and tradition of each country determines the exact degree of independent power that the federal system will give to local units of government. Some, like the Swiss Confederation, have historically left much discretion in the hands of local units, while others (India and the U.S.S.R. are examples) have been almost entirely centralized.

In Article I, Section 8, the Constitution delegates certain powers to the federal government. Most of these delegated powers are in the area of foreign and military policy or in an area that cuts across state lines, like regulating "Commerce . . . among the several States," printing a national currency, and delivering the mail. The rest, presumably, is left up to states. The Tenth Amendment puts it in writing: Those powers "not delegated to the United States by the Constitution, nor prohibited by it to the States, are reserved to the States respectively, or to the people." If the powers are not delegated to the federal government, we can assume that they belong to the states. This law leaves to the states a very large, undefined range of reserved powers embracing such areas as health, welfare, morals, education, recreation, and commerce (at least commerce within a state). Still other areas, such as taxation, punishment of crime, and road building are in the hands of both the federal and state governments. These are usually called concurrent powers. The three categories are summed up in Table 3.2.

This table presents a very simplified description. In fact, the boundaries between the federal and state governments are not so neat. For example, normally, education is an area reserved to the states. Yet, as we saw at the beginning of this chapter, the federal government has the authority to step in when a state is practicing racial discrimination or otherwise violating the Constitution. Another example is traffic laws. *(Continued on page 56)*

GLOBAL PERSPECTIVES:

Federalism in Nigeria

Nigeria is black Africa's most populous nation, with a population estimated at close to 100 million. Unfortunately, estimates are all that are available because no reliable official census has been taken since Nigeria achieved independence from Great Britain in 1960. This lack of reliable census data reflects political sensitivities that are bound up with the issue of federalism in this nation.

Nigeria was a creation of British colonialists who carved out a roughly rectangular patch of territory, about 350,000 square miles in extent, that fronts on the West African coast. The territory includes 300 tribal groups professing various religions, including several Christian and Islamic sects. During colonial times the British favored the predominantly Muslim northern part of the country because its native leaders could be counted on to keep order. In return, the British rigorously excluded Christian missionaries from the region. The South, in contrast, was quickly converted, so the basis for religious tension—which was later to add another dimension to ethnic and regional rivalries—was laid.

After independence, Nigeria began as a democratic federation of four regions. Conflict developed almost immediately, and each of the regions at one time or another threatened to secede. In 1966 Nigerian democracy gave way to military rule, and within a year the eastern region broke away and proclaimed itself the Republic of Biafra. Then came civil war, during which an estimated 1 million civilians died of starvation. After three years, the secessionist army disappeared into the bush, as did the name *Biafra*. The victorious military leaders established a magnanimous peace, with no massacres or other reprisals. As insurance

against further revolts, however, the government sought to break up the regions into still smaller units. The result was an increase in the number of states from 4 to 12. (Later the number was increased to 19, where it stands today.)

A census of the Nigerian population has been such a volatile issue because it would become the basis for the representation of each state in the parliament, and the more populous states would get the larger number. At present the issue is moot because there is no parliament. A brief period of civil government in the early 1980s was interrupted by a military coup in 1983. The present ruler of Nigeria, Major-General Ibrahim Babangida, promised a return to democracy in 1990 and later changed the date to 1992. Meanwhile, Nigeria's 19 constituent states remain under the control of military governors appointed by Babangida.

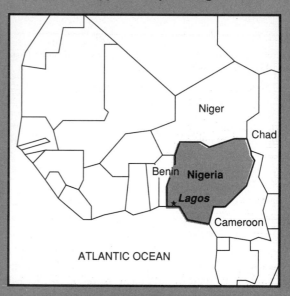

(Continued from page 55) Traditionally, speed limits have been left up to the individual states. But in 1974, in response to the Arab boycott of oil, Congress set a national 55-mile-per-hour speed limit. It was able to do so by threatening to cut off federal highway assistance to any state that did not comply. (In 1987, after many complaints, Congress relaxed the limits, and almost immediately, 38 states raised their speed limits on rural highways to 65 miles per hour.)[9]

But why is it necessary for the states to have *any* autonomous power? Federalism was the only arrangement, besides confederation, that was politically possible in 1787; the states would never have ratified a unitary system. But that is hardly a reason for having a federal system today. Why has federalism persisted?

Reserved powers leave to the states jurisdiction over education, as well as health, welfare, morals, recreation, and commerce within their borders.

THREE PURPOSES OF FEDERALISM

Even those critical of federalism agree that a case can be made for its present-day usefulness. The argument is usually that it serves at least three purposes: (1) it allows for experimentation; (2) it offers diversity; and (3) it gives the average person access to government.

The States as Laboratories.   Policymaking often involves risk. New legislation that looks great on the drawing boards may not work at all when put into practice. Yet we have to take risks if we are to remain innovative. Somehow, we must steer between the danger of a failed experiment and the trap of stagnation. Federalism helps resolve the dilemma by letting one or two states try out a policy. If the new law works, it will spread to other states, possibly even becoming a national policy. If it does

TABLE 3-2

Delegated, Reserved, and Concurrent Powers

Delegated Powers (Exclusively Federal)	Reserved Powers (State Powers)	Concurrent Powers (Shared by Both)
War powers	Education	Taxing
Treaties	Marriage & divorce	Road building
Mail delivery	Drinking age	Punishing lawbreakers
Coining, printing money	Traffic laws	Social welfare programs
Interstate commerce	Local business	
Tariffs	regulations	

This table greatly simplifies what happens in reality: The lines drawn between federal and state governments are often crossed. For example, Congress has influenced state laws concerning legal drinking age by voting in 1984 to withhold part of federal highway funds from those states that allow anyone under 21 years of age to drink. Although challenged by the states, the law was upheld by the Supreme Court in *South Dakota v. Dole* (1987).

not work, at least the whole nation has not been turned upside down. Several years ago, the state of Oregon passed a law requiring a deposit on beer and soda bottles. Its purpose was to eliminate litter and encourage recycling. The experiment worked, and now other states have imitated Oregon. Thus, our state system gives us the flexibility to innovate.

Diversity.   A related advantage of federalism is simply the variety. Anyone who does not like the laws and practices in one state can move to another. For example, during the 1950s and 1960s, millions of black Americans moved out of the South in search of freedom from racism and a better standard of living. Another example is a 1973 obscenity case, *Miller v. California*, in which the Supreme Court said that "the people of Maine or Mississippi" should not have to "accept public depiction of conduct found tolerable in Las Vegas or New York City."[10] And vice versa. Federalism permits a degree of regional diversity.

Grass-roots Government.   The virtues of local government have probably been exaggerated in American folklore, but the fact remains that government at the state and local levels gives citizens a degree of access that they do not have at the federal level. In local government people can go to the town hall or the city council and confront those who make the laws. In Washington, government is largely in the hands of professionals. Even so-called citizen lobbies at the national level are soon dominated by full-time staff members, while local activist groups are run by amateurs. If democracy means "people's rule," then it is surely important for people to have access to those who control their lives. Local governments help facilitate this access.

THE OTHER SIDE OF LOCAL AUTONOMY

Experimentation, diversity, and grass-roots participation are virtues, but they often conceal vices. Experimentation may sometimes lead to hasty, ill-considered projects. Diversity can add up to confusion, especially for those who must do business in more

TABLE 3-3

1988 Per-Pupil Expenditures, Selected States

State	Rank	Per-Pupil Expenditure, 1988
Alaska	1	$7,038
New Jersey	2	6,910
Wyoming	3	6,885
New York	4	6,864
Massachusetts	7	5,396
Minnesota	14	4,513
Michigan	21	4,122
Nebraska	33	3,641
Oklahoma	44	3,051
Georgia	45	2,939
Mississippi	47	2,760
Alabama	48	2,752
Utah	49	2,658
Arkansas	50	2,410

Source: U.S. Bureau of the Census, *Statistical Abstract of the United States 1989* (Washington: U.S. Government Printing Office, 1988), p. xvii.

than one state. Different states have different taxes, different environmental regulations, even different standards of decency. In 1977, for example, Larry Flynt, publisher of *Hustler* magazine, was convicted of "pandering" pornography in Ohio, though his publication was regularly sold in other states without incident. In Great Britain or in any country with a unitary government, Flynt would have been banned everywhere or allowed to operate everywhere because of uniform standards. Diversity also means unequal provision of vital public services, such as education and public health. Per-pupil expenditures for public education in Arkansas, for example, were less than $2,500 in 1988, compared to about $7,000 in Alaska and New Jersey in that same year (see Table 3.3).

As for the virtues of grass-roots government, sometimes local democracy plays into the hands of extremists. George Wallace adopted a segregationist stance in order to win popular support in the governor's race. In *Federalist* No. 10, James Madison warned us against just this kind of fanatical democracy, democracy driven by local majority factions. (Madison's definition of *faction* was discussed in chapter 2, page 37; we will return to the topic in chapter 9.) The beauty of a large and diverse republic, Madison said, is that a faction can be contained in one state or locality; it cannot take over the whole nation.

The merits of our federal system are debated by Michael Kinsley and Daniel Elazar in this chapter's Taking Sides section. In considering the topic, however, we must keep in mind that federalism is constantly changing. Over the past two centuries, the federal government has moved into areas that were once almost exclusively the province of states: health, welfare, morality, and education. In the next section we will take a closer look to see what sorts of changes have occurred, how they have come about, and whether or not they have been justified.

Why the National Government Has Expanded

There are a number of avenues through which the federal government can enter areas once the province of the states—and it constantly does so. A local factory may be forced by the federal Environmental Protection Agency (EPA) to stop polluting the air or water. Or perhaps the federal Occupational Safety and Health Administration (OSHA) may force the factory to make changes to protect workers. The Civil Rights division of the Justice Department may seek court-ordered busing to desegregate local public schools, or it may go to court to compel a city council or state legislature to redraw election districts, charging that those districts discriminate racially. The federal government is involved in numerous functions, from education to the relief of poverty, that were once almost exclusively the province of states and localities. How has this expansion been justified? *(Continued on page 61)*

Points to Remember

1. Federalism is a system that divides power between a central government and regional units such as states or provinces.

2. The Constitution expressly delegates certain powers to the federal government: declaring war and making peace treaties, setting tariffs, ensuring mail delivery, and regulating interstate commerce. Other powers are mainly reserved to the states. Still others, such as the taxing power, are shared by several levels of government.

3. The advantages of federalism include the use of individual states to try out new programs, the preservation of diversity, and the ability to bring government down to the grass-roots level.

4. The disadvantages of federalism appear when it leads to confusion and inconsistency in lawmaking and when it plays into the hands of local extremists.

Should Federalism Be Abolished?

YES Michael Kinsley

Based upon Michael Kinsley, "The Withering Away of the States," *The New Republic*, (March 28, 1981), pp. 17–21.

"Perhaps," says Kinsley, an editor of *The New Republic*, "we should drop it. Federalism, I mean. It was great fun, but it was just one of those things." Kinsley argues that our federal system produces an irrational inequality of treatment. He cites examples of disparate criminal justice systems, noting that "an American will spend more time in prison for robbery in South Carolina than for willful homicide in half a dozen other states." Federalism, he says, also makes sensible regulation impossible. He gives two reasons for this. First, "air and water currents remain unimpressed by the doctrine of states' rights," which means that problems like pollution cannot be addressed at the state level. Second, we cannot regulate business effectively if every state ends up competing to attract businesses. It is time, he concludes, for the United States to strip the important powers—the power to punish crime, to tax, and to make social policy—from the states and hand them over to the federal government. This will save billions of dollars every year, according to Kinsley, and "assure that society as a whole makes rational, democratic decisions about issues that affect society as a whole."

NO Daniel J. Elazar

Based upon Daniel J. Elazar, *American Federalism: A View From the States*, 3rd ed., (New York: Harper & Row, 1984).

Elazar contends that our states are needed today more than ever: "As the population of the nation increases, the states become increasingly able to manage major governmental activities with the competence and expertise demanded by the technological frontier." Meanwhile, Elazar adds, the federal government is becoming more and more remote from the grass roots simply because it has to serve such a large mass. The virtue of the federal system "lies in its ability to develop and maintain mechanisms vital to the perpetuation of the unique combination of governmental strength, political flexibility, and individual liberty, which has been the central concern of American politics." In other words, federalism preserves the best features of American government: strength, flexibility, and liberty.

Postscript

It often happens that the advantages attributed to a governmental system can be viewed from a different perspective as disadvantages. This is certainly the case with federalism, for some of the virtues of federalism cited by Elazar— diversity and flexibility—seem like confusion and irrationality to Kinsley.

The March 1988 issue of the *Annals of the American Academy of Political and Social Science* is devoted entirely to the topic, "State Constitutions in a Federal System." Included are articles on religion under state constitutions, legislative and executive power in various states, and localism in state constitutional law. In *Federalism: the Founders' Design* (Norman, OK: University of Oklahoma Press, 1987), legal scholar Raoul Berger analyzes the Founders' intentions concerning federalism and concludes that they wanted the states to be left alone by the federal government. Ursula K. Hicks, *Federalism: Failure and Success* (New York: Oxford, 1979), is a comparative study of federalist systems, from relatively successful ones like Australia's to dismal failures like the British Central African Federation.

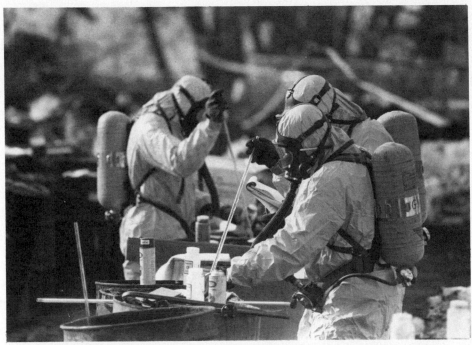

Environmental Protection Agency workers test samples from storage drums at a
paint manufacturer in Phoenixville, PA. The first load of hazardous waste from
this abandoned paint factory was pumped into tank trucks for later incineration
in New Jersey.

IMPLIED POWERS: THE "ELASTIC CLAUSE"

We can start to answer these questions by noting the *omission* of a word from the
Tenth Amendment:

> The powers not delegated to the United States by the Constitution, nor prohibited by it
> to the States, are reserved to the States respectively, or to the people.

The omitted word is *expressly*. When the Framers of the amendment were debating
its language, some wanted it to say that all powers not "expressly" delegated to the
federal government must be reserved to the states or the people. This key word—
which was contained in a similar clause in the Articles of Confederation—would have
limited the federal government's powers to exactly those delegated powers listed in
Article I, Section 8: printing currency, ratifying treaties, declaring war, delivering mail,
regulating interstate commerce, and so on. It would have left no room for expansion.
For that reason, James Madison objected to the insertion of the word. It is impossible,
he said, "to confine a government to the exercise of express powers." Government
should also have powers that can be *implied* by these express grants, powers that do
not have to be explicitly set down in the Constitution. Otherwise, Madison argued,
the Constitution would have to "recount every minutia," and that would turn it into an
unwieldy document.[11]

Madison's argument for implied powers was persuasive in part because the body
of the Constitution had already left room for such powers. Article I, Section 8, lists all
the express powers of Congress; it then goes on to say that Congress has the power
"To make all Laws which shall be necessary and proper for carrying into Execution
the foregoing Powers, and all other Powers vested by this Constitution in the
Government of the United States." This "necessary and proper" clause is sometimes
called the <u>elastic clause</u> because it stretches federal power far beyond the explicit

grants of power in Article I, Section 8. It is more commonly called the implied powers clause because it grants power to the federal government by implication.

In the early years of our nation, the question of implied powers was still largely theoretical. The powers of the federal government were confined almost entirely to the areas explicitly delegated to it. The first real test did not come until 1819, when the Supreme Court upheld the federal government's right to charter a bank.

MCCULLOCH v. MARYLAND (1819): "NECESSARY" MEANS "CONVENIENT"

In the latter part of the eighteenth century, Congress set up the Bank of the United States. Soon the Bank had many enemies—especially state bankers, western farmers, and merchants—who accused it of draining off precious local revenues. "All the flourishing cities of the West," one legislator said, "are mortgaged to this money power. . . . They are in the jaws of the monster!"[12] In an effort to cripple the operation of the Bank, the state of Maryland placed a tax on all banks or bank branches not chartered by the state. James McCulloch, the cashier of the Baltimore branch of the federal bank, refused to pay the tax and was sued by the state. The state won, and McCulloch appealed to the Supreme Court.

The issue was whether or not the federal government has certain powers—in this case the power to charter a bank—not explicitly set down in the Constitution.[13] Writing for a unanimous Court, Chief Justice John Marshall ruled in *McCulloch v. Maryland* that the federal government does have such powers. To justify his ruling, he relied upon a broad reading of the already broad language of the implied powers clause. It says at the end of Article I, Section 8, that Congress may do all things "necessary and proper" for "carrying into Execution the foregoing Powers" and all other constitutional powers. Among the "foregoing powers," those expressly delegated to the federal government are the powers to "lay and collect Taxes," to "borrow Money on the Credit of the United States," and "To coin Money." Marshall argued that a federally chartered bank might be useful to the federal government for seeing that these powers are executed.

Useful, yes. You might even say "convenient," "appropriate," or whatever word

Bank of the United States in Philadelphia as depicted in an engraving of 1800.

you prefer that conveys a similar meaning. But "necessary"? Is a bank really "necessary" within the meaning of the "necessary and proper" clause? Chief Justice Marshall, who wrote the Court's opinion, answered that question by launching into a discussion of the meaning of *necessary*. The word, he said, admits of degrees. "A thing may be necessary, very necessary, absolutely or indispensably necessary." The Bank may not be "indispensably necessary," but it is necessary in the less urgent sense of "convenient" or "appropriate." Once Marshall gave the word that construction, the rest was easy. Maryland would be hard-pressed to show that the Bank was not a convenient or appropriate means for carrying out the federal government's powers to tax and spend, borrow money, or do many of the other things it was given the power to do in Article I, Section 8. If these powers are legitimate, Marshall said, then any means appropriate for carrying them out are also legitimate. Marshall summed it up in this formula:

> Let the end be legitimate, let it be within the scope of the Constitution, and all means which are appropriate, which are plainly adapted to that end, which are not prohibited, but consist[ent] with the letter and spirit of the Constitution, are constitutional.[14]

Marshall's formula opened the way for an enormous expansion of federal power, most of which was postponed until the second half of the twentieth century. Nevertheless, the legal groundwork had been laid. Marshall was saying that the federal government can do *anything*, as long as what it does is appropriate to the government's purposes and not banned by the Constitution.

McCulloch is the arch that supports much of what Congress does today. Congress sets up agencies that do everything from regulating factories to controlling farm acreage; it outlaws drug dealing, gambling, prostitution, securities fraud, and deceptive advertising; it tells auto manufacturers what safety features they must install in cars; it regulates professional football, sets minimum wages and maximum working hours, bans child labor, protects small business from injurious price cutting, and so on, even though none of these functions is explicitly spelled out in the Constitution. All, however, have been deemed "convenient" or "appropriate" for "carrying into execution" the powers delegated to Congress.

Prior to the Fair Labor Standards Act of 1938, young children often worked 72-hour weeks. The Supreme Court had declared earlier child labor laws unconstitutional, in part because they removed power from the states.

THE COMMERCE CLAUSE: A "HOOK" FOR FEDERAL POWER

One delegated power that has been especially useful to the federal government as a "hook" for hanging new powers is the commerce clause in Article I, Section 8. It gives Congress the power "To regulate Commerce with foreign Nations, and among the several States, and with the Indian Tribes." Again, the foundations were laid by Chief Justice Marshall. In 1824 he defined the clause broadly enough to include any kind of travel or "intercourse" that "concerns more states than one."[15] The federal government has used this reading to justify intervention into areas once reserved to the states. Even when a business is purely local (intrastate), if its operation can be shown to have any substantial "effect" on commerce in other states, it can be regulated by the federal government.[16] Congress may even step into areas that seem to have little to do directly with commerce. In 1964, for example, it outlawed racial discrimination in hotels, motels, and restaurants on the grounds that such discrimination was a "burden" on commerce. Even some supporters of the legislation thought that this rationale was a bit strained.[17] After all, racial discrimination is primarily an issue of justice and morality, not of commerce. But when the Civil Rights Act of 1964 was challenged, the Supreme Court said that Congress is not barred from relying on the commerce clause merely because racial discrimination is "deemed a moral and social wrong." It is enough to show that it disrupts commerce, the Court said, and there is "overwhelming evidence" of that.[18] Marshall's formula in *McCulloch*, then, was still at work. "Let the end be legitimate," he had said, and all means plainly adapted to the end are also legitimate. If banning racial discrimination helps ensure the smooth flow of commerce, then banning racial discrimination is a legitimate extension of Congress's power to regulate interstate commerce.

There may be limits on how much the federal government may get involved in matters traditionally reserved to the states, but it is not clear where those limits are. The Supreme Court has never formally overruled some of the decisions of the 1930s that barred the federal government from regulating purely *intra*state businesses,[19] but since the end of the 1930s the Court has blurred the distinction between interstate and intrastate commerce. (As we have seen, John Marshall's earlier decisions also avoided the distinction.) In 1976 the Court struck down federal legislation that sought to extend federal wage-and-hours protections to state government employees.[20] Nine years later, in *Garcia v. San Antonio Metropolitan Transit Authority* (1985), the Court overruled its earlier decision; the position now was that the judiciary should try to stay out of wrangles between state legislatures and Congress. Since both decisions were close (5–4) and since new Supreme Court appointments have been made since 1985, it is hard to say whether or not Congress will continue to be allowed such close control over state employment policies.

THE CIVIL WAR AMENDMENTS: NATIONALIZING RIGHTS

Despite the Marshall Court's broad interpretation of federal power, the federal government played a minimal role in domestic affairs before the Civil War. It confined itself to fighting a few wars, enacting tariffs, building roads, printing money, and delivering the mail. Alexis de Tocqueville, the famous French visitor to America during the 1830s, was much impressed by the vigor and energy of local government in America—and correspondingly unimpressed by the federal government. While acknowledging the potential for centralization, he saw the federal government's powers as confined to specific and limited areas.[21] If anything, Tocqueville wrote, the federal government seemed to have gradually lost power since the writing of the Constitution.[22]

The Civil War changed everything: It not only buried the notion that states could secede from the Union, it left in its wake three important constitutional amendments:

the Thirteenth, which freed the slaves; the Fourteenth, which made former slaves citizens while guaranteeing them "equal protection" and "due process"; and the Fifteenth, which gave former slaves the right to vote. The most far-reaching was the Fourteenth. "Before the Civil War and the Fourteenth Amendment," wrote Carl Sandburg, "the United States were. After the Fourteenth Amendment the United States is."[23] The Fourteenth Amendment helped unify America by standardizing individual rights. Before the amendment's passage, one's rights depended almost entirely on the state in which one lived. Even John Marshall, the great nationalist chief justice, resisted the suggestion that the basic liberties laid down in the Bill of Rights were binding on state authorities. In an 1833 case, he ruled that they applied only to the federal government.[24] But through the due process clause of the Fourteenth Amendment, almost all of the rights in the first 10 amendments have now been made applicable to the states. The application has been slow and piecemeal and did not really begin until the 1920s, but the legal foundations were laid with the ratification of the Fourteenth Amendment in 1868. (The process of "nationalizing" the Bill of Rights is discussed at greater length in chapter 6.)

RESPONSES TO SOCIAL AND ECONOMIC CHANGE

Federal expansion, however, was not just a matter of laws; it was in part a response to social and economic forces. For most of the nineteenth century, America was a rural and technologically primitive nation. People traveled on foot or horseback, worked on farms or in small shops, and had little connection with others beyond their neighborhoods. In this situation, state and local governments served them well enough. But enormous social and technological changes came after the Civil War: Huge industries were born, with giant work forces; people moved from farms to cities; railroads linked the whole nation; millions of immigrants arrived from Europe.

All these changes brought new demands on the federal government, which was now called upon to regulate industry, settle labor disputes, prohibit child labor, help people in distress, punish fraud, stamp out disease, inspect meat, and protect forests and wildlife. It was not only that states lacked the resources and were sometimes controlled by the very corporations they were supposed to oversee; it was also that the new industrial forces were truly national in scope. Industries obtained their raw materials from one state, their work force from another, and sent their products to all. Prices and wage structures in one state would affect all the others. Transport and communications regularly crossed state lines. So did pollution and soil erosion.

The Great Depression made a dramatic case for federal action. When the New York stock market crashed in 1929, it plunged the entire nation into poverty—cities, towns, and farms. With a quarter of the nation's work force unemployed, the states could not handle the problems. Almost by default, the federal government inherited functions that were once almost exclusively the province of states, particularly social welfare and business regulation. This was the period of President Franklin Roosevelt's New Deal (treated more extensively in chapter 20), which produced a staggering increase in the size and power of the federal government. It also brought to Washington a new set of officials—men and women who wanted to transform America. Federal power grew even more rapidly during World War II, from 1940 to 1945, when "Dr. New Deal," as Franklin Roosevelt sometimes called himself, was transformed into "Dr. Win-the-War." Even in the 1950s, when the White House was returned to Republican control under Dwight Eisenhower, the federal government held on to its new power. The fifties have sometimes been called "the Eisenhower doldrums" because nothing much seemed to be going on in government, especially at the federal level. Actually, a great deal was going on. A gigantic complex of interstate highways was being built with federal money, and these highways shifted the American population from the cities to the suburbs; new concerns about health and

Although the Fifteenth Amendment gave blacks the right to vote, it did not guarantee a secret ballot.

education gave rise to a new cabinet department, several new bureaus, and higher spending levels; the civil rights revolution had broken out, and furious southern resistance soon brought federal troops into the South to ensure that schools were desegregated. The federal government was hardly passive, even during this period.

Then came the 1960s. A new generation of reformers came to Washington with John F. Kennedy and stayed on during the years of Lyndon B. Johnson. These reformers were determined to end poverty and racism, clean up the environment, protect consumers, and transform America into a Great Society. The federal government, in a new growth spurt, expanded into local areas that even New Dealers had apparently not considered.

The expansion took several forms. In some cases, federal administrators simply bypassed state and local government. The new federal poverty programs, for example, were supposed to be based upon "maximum feasible participation" from local communities; in practice, this often led to a seizure of power by "community activists" that had power bases outside the structures of local government. Voting rights projects brought federal registrars to local areas to sign up minority voters.

But the most subtle and durable means by which the federal government got involved in matters once considered "reserved" to the states took the form of grants-in-aid. In one sense, these federal grants strengthened the states, since they helped fund state programs. But in another sense, they made the states more subject to federal control because of the strings attached to the money.

GRANTS-IN-AID: CALLING THE TUNE

Grants-in-aid are sums of money awarded to a state or locality to help it carry out its local responsibilities. Grants-in-aid might be used to help a locality finance the construction of day-care centers, sewage treatment plants, or new schools. Often, they take the form of "matching grants," meaning that the state or locality has to put up a certain amount of its own funds in order to qualify for federal assistance.

Grants-in-aid in one form or another can be traced back to 1802. But the truly spectacular growth of this form of federal assistance did not begin until the 1960s. In 1960 the federal government gave $7 billion in such aid; by 1987, the amount had risen to more than $108 billion a year. Figure 3.1 shows the rate of climb between 1950 and 1987.

Thus far, there have been three different types of grants-in-aid given to states: categorical grants, block grants, and revenue sharing. Categorical grants are earmarked for specific purposes: to build an airport, an irrigation project, or to make welfare payments to low-income mothers. Block grants leave more discretion in the hands of the states. Their purposes are defined more broadly: crime control or public health research. Revenue sharing, begun in 1972, provided funds to states with virtually no strings attached. The program, which was always a very small part of grants-in-aid, was discontinued in 1986. (It is discussed further in the next section.)

By far the largest portion of the grants-in-aid—more than 80 percent—takes the form of categorical grants. What this means is that the federal government retains a great deal of control over how the money it gives is to be spent. Federal aid, in short, has become a wedge, permitting the federal government to enter spheres of activity that have traditionally belonged to states and localities. In theory, of course, the states do not have to accept federal direction; they can turn down the money. But since the average state today depends on federal grants for a quarter or more of its budget, the states find it hard to say no.

One reason categorical grants predominate over block grants is that members of Congress can win support from constituent groups by getting them specific projects, such as day-care centers for women's groups or wheelchair ramps for the disabled.

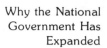

Enormous grants in aid are made by the federal government to states for highway construction.

Block grants do not win politicians the same thanks, since the states have more discretion in deciding how to spend the money. But entirely apart from political self-interest, members of Congress sometimes express concern that if the states are given too much discretion, they may not spend the money properly.

Over the past 30 years, federal controls have mushroomed. One study of federal grant programs in five states found that between 1951 and 1978, over a thousand conditions were added to the programs, nearly 90 percent of them after 1971.[25] The results have not always been greeted with praise; former Arizona governor Bruce Babbitt expressed it succinctly:

Political philosophy aside, it is hard to see why a national Congress, responsible for governing a continental nation, should be involved in formulating programs for rat control, humanities grants for town hall debates on capital punishment, sculpture commissions for local art museums, educating displaced homemakers, training for use of the metric system, jellyfish control, bike paths, and police disability grants.[26]

Points to Remember

1. Article I, Section 8, of the Constitution gives implied powers to Congress.

2. The "necessary and proper" clause was interpreted very broadly by Chief Justice John Marshall in the case of *McCulloch v. Maryland* (1819).

3. The commerce clause has also been a convenient "hook" for new federal power.

4. The Civil War put to rest the claim that states could secede from the Union. It also led to the pas-sage of the Thirteenth, Fourteenth, and Fifteenth Amendments, which further limited state autonomy.

5. The Fourteenth Amendment permitted courts to "nationalize" the Bill of Rights.

6. From the end of the Civil War to the 1960s, industrialization and technology gave us an enormous array of new problems—such as labor disputes, economic depressions, environmental pollution, and uncontrolled urban growth—that demanded federal solutions.

7. Grants-in-aid provide federal assistance to states, but they also attach conditions that give the federal government control over areas traditionally left to states and localities.

8. The three original components of the grants-in-aid program were block grants, categorical grants, and revenue sharing (now defunct).

FIGURE **3-1**

Federal Grants-in-Aid Outlays, 1950-1988

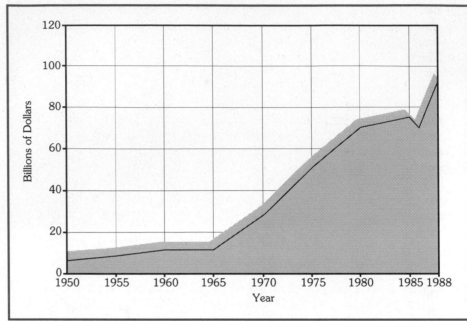

Source: Office of Management and Budget, Special Analyses: Budget of the United States Government, FY 1987, p. H-20; U.S. Dept. of Commerce, *Statistical Abstract of the United States*, 1989, p. 270, no. 450.

> In 1950 federal grants-in-aid to the states totalled approximately $5 billion; by 1988 the grants had increased to almost 23 times the 1950 total ($114.6 billion). Critics complain that these grants represent excessive federal interference in state government since the federal government retains a great deal of control over the use of the money. Proponents say the increases are necessary if the states are to cope with an increasingly complex society.

Perhaps, then, by the 1980s the pendulum had swung too far and Washington planners needed to become more selective about the areas of American life that required federal regulation. The idea of returning federal power to the states was no longer the exclusive province of conservatives. Many, like Babbitt, who considered themselves liberal were now giving it serious consideration.

Still, the most outspoken opponents of federal power are usually conservatives, and this is for two reasons. First, conservatives tend to associate state and local government with their homes and neighborhoods, the places where they think solutions to social problems can best be worked out. George Wallace played on these feelings when he complained about the "intellectual snobs" in Washington and the "hundreds of thousands of bureaucrats . . .looking after matters that ought to be looked after, and could be looked after, by those elected back in the local states and the local political subdivisions."[27] Second, American conservatives tend to believe that government at *any* level—national, state, or local—should play a minimal role.

Both of these premises underlay the domestic agenda of the Reagan administration. President Reagan came into office promising to get government "off our backs." Did he mean just the federal government or all government? Probably all, but there was a built-in ambiguity in his promise. On the one hand, Reagan claimed to be a supporter of state autonomy; from this, it would logically follow that if a state wanted to have an ambitious program of regulation and welfare, so be it. On the other hand,

Reagan made clear his view that government at all levels had become too big; he was a firm believer in *laissez-faire*, or "leave (it) alone," the philosophy that government should play a minimal role in our lives. The ambiguity fueled suspicions about a Reagan administration proposal called the "New Federalism." The proposal was defeated—in fact, it never got off the ground—but it is worth outlining because it was one of the most ambitious initiatives of that administration in the area of federal-state relations.

The term New Federalism actually goes back to the early 1970s and the Nixon administration. President Nixon used it as a label for a program whose keystone was revenue sharing. Its purpose was to turn a share of federal revenues back to the states "without federal strings." In a message to Congress, President Nixon said that this program "marks a turning point in federal-state relations," for it was aimed toward restoring "a rightful balance between the state capitals and the national capital." The program passed Congress in 1972 despite opposition from organized labor and civil rights groups, who feared it would put too much power in the hands of segregationist local officials. It was supported by a broad coalition of Democrats and Republicans, liberals and conservatives—including House Speaker Thomas P. ("Tip") O'Neill of Massachusetts; then-representative Edward I. Koch of New York; and Gerald R. Ford of Michigan, who at that time was House minority leader. Under the law, federal money was distributed according to a complex formula based upon population and each state's effort to raise its own tax revenues. The law required that one-third of the federal money go to the states and two-thirds "pass through" to local governments.

The program was renewed in 1976 and again in 1980, but it never amounted to more than 8 percent of total grants-in-aid. It lacked special interest constituencies to protect it in Congress and at the White House. Under pressure of the Gramm-Rudman-Hollings Act—a law requiring a balanced budget by 1992—President Reagan and Congress killed it in 1986.[28]

REAGAN'S NEW FEDERALISM: A SWAP

Reagan's proposed New Federalism, which he introduced in his 1982 State of the Union address, was different from Nixon's, though it was promoted in much the same way: as a means of returning more authority to the states. What it amounted to was a kind of swap or trade-off. Reagan proposed that the states finance and run some 40 federal programs. The two largest are Aid to Families with Dependent Children (AFDC), which then cost about $13 billion per year, and Food Stamps, costing $11 billion per year. In return, the federal government would assume the full cost of Medicaid, the health program for the poor, which would save the states more than $19 billion annually. However, Reagan's proposal still would have left the states with a large financial burden because the total cost of all the programs handed over to them would have been more than $46 billion. To make up the difference, Reagan proposed to share revenues collected by the federal government on a variety of taxes, notably a windfall profits tax on oil companies. These taxes would be put into a trust fund, and every year about $28 billion would be made available to states and localities for aid programs. Beginning in 1987 the trust fund would begin shrinking, and by 1991 it would disappear. During that time states and localities could decide whether or not they wanted to continue these programs. Those that did would have to fund them with state and local taxes. The result was to be a federal government returned to its traditional sphere of national security, fiscal and monetary control, the regulation of interstate commerce, and aid to the elderly. The rest was back in the hands of state governments.

This, then, was the stated rationale behind the New Federalism: returning federal and state governments to their proper spheres of action. Critics of the proposal,

"Step right up—everybody gets one star and part of a stripe."

Drawing by Herblock in The Washington Post; © 1981.

however, suspected that Reagan's real agenda was to cut back or even kill major welfare programs. A coalition of civil rights groups drafted a strongly worded protest against Reagan's proposal, claiming that it would leave vital national concerns in the uncertain hands of state officials. The proposal also met with a chilly reception on Capitol Hill. Members of Congress did not like the idea of surrendering control of programs that were popular with important constituent groups. Even state officials, the supposed beneficiaries of a plan that would return power and influence to them, were distinctly cool to the idea. Their attitude was "thanks, but no thanks." The National Governors Association objected to having to take over such costly programs as Food Stamps and Aid to Families with Dependent Children; even the prospect of receiving federal aid from windfall oil profits was no sweetener, since the fund would run out by 1991. In 1982 state and local lawmakers were still suffering what the National Council of State Legislatures called the "worst fiscal crisis since [the] Depression," and they feared that the Reagan proposals would simply dump more fiscal burdens on them. This three-cornered opposition—from key members of Congress, from pressure groups, and from many state officials—was too much for the New Federalism: Reagan's proposals never even reached the floor of Congress and were never brought up again.

FIGURE 3-2

Grants-in-Aid, 1981–1987, in Constant 1982 Dollars

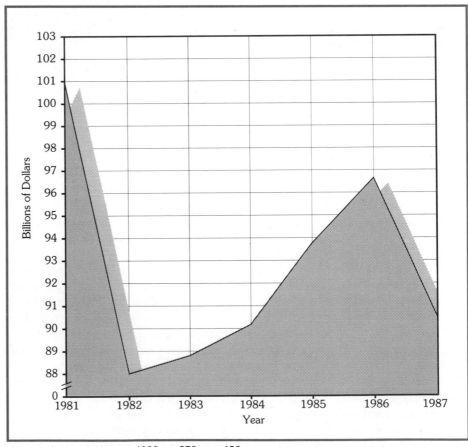

Source: Statistical Abstract, 1989, p. 270, no. 450.

To properly assess the grants-in-aid program, the totals need to be converted to constant dollars. Inflation renders total outlay more variable than it would seem from Figure 3.1 alone.

Reagan's New Federalism thus appeared to be a failure, but was it really? One could argue that what actually happened during the 1980s was a quiet acceptance of its basic rationale, namely that the states themselves must take more fiscal responsibility. Two developments lent support to the spirit of the New Federalism.

The first was a large-scale cutback in federal support. Between 1981 and 1982, about $7 billion was lopped off the federal grants-in-aid program. Although federal aid began to increase again the following year, the rate of ascent markedly leveled off during the Reagan years. This is seen most clearly when the figures are controlled for inflation, as in Figure 3.2.

The first federal cutbacks were particularly alarming to the states because they came at a time when the economy was in near-recession. State governments slammed the brakes on spending and tightened their belts to the last notch. The result of this austerity turned out to be a boon for state independence, for when the economy began to improve after 1982, states and localities found themselves enjoying surpluses. As Robert Rafuse, deputy assistant secretary of the Treasury, somewhat wistfully remarked: "The fiscal outlook for the state and local sector, relatively speaking, is a lot better than it is for the federal government."[29] This new prosperity let state officials replace federal programs with programs of their own, and even add new programs.[30] "The states," said Arkansas governor Bill Clinton, "are pretty much on their own."[31]

The second development that may have nudged states toward greater independence was the partial shift from categorical grants-in-aid to block grants. Although little notice was taken of it at the time, in 1981 Reagan persuaded Congress to consolidate 54 categorical grants into 9 block grants. Governors were jubilant because this move gave them more discretion in deciding how and where to spend the money. Arizona governor Bruce Babbitt saw the consolidation as "an important political and economic resource," and he, along with many other governors, moved quickly to implement the funds.[32]

The States Today: Hotbeds of Innovation

Things have changed dramatically since that hot June morning in 1963 when Wallace blocked the doorway at the University of Alabama. In the South, a new generation of state and local officials, many of them black, have brought new thinking into government. Throughout the nation, state governments have become more modern and efficient than most observers would have imagined then. Fred Graham, law correspondent for CBS News, has remarked on how great the changes have been since he started covering the states in the 1960s:

> When I got into journalism, my first stories were the civil rights revolution in the South and the massive resistance that was occurring across there and the violence. And what was wrong with federalism then was that a lot of our governors were not the quality of people they should have been. . . . And what's happened is that . . . the quality of state leadership is so much better now than it was in those days, that the situation is righting itself.[33]

A similar note has been sounded by former North Carolina governor Terry Sanford. This is all the more remarkable since Sanford was once pessimistic about the future of state government. In 1967, while still governor, Sanford said: "The states are indecisive. The states are antiquated. The states are timid and ineffective. The states are not willing to face their problems." But by 1987 Sanford, now a senator, had brightened his outlook. "Now states are much more innovative and able to get things going than the federal government."[34]

The signs of innovation are everywhere. Massachusetts and 17 other states have created new programs to get people off welfare and into jobs. New York's tax amnesty program has brought millions of dollars into the state treasury. Washington State has led the nation in bringing low-cost health insurance to the poor. Virginia has found new overseas markets for its textiles, hams, and other products. "Enterprise zones" have been set up by 26 states, using special tax breaks to attract new industries into depressed areas. And, without waiting for Washington to act, at least 42 states have passed their own AIDS laws. The states now seem to be on the cutting edge of change in America. The federal cutbacks during the Reagan years forced states and localities to act on their own, and, having gotten the taste of it, they are not ready to surrender their new autonomy. Former Colorado governor Richard D. Lamm probably spoke for many when he said: "Governors and local officials are tired of playing 'Mother, may I?' with federal bureaucrats."[35]

Reflections

This chapter began with an account of George Wallace's confrontation with the federal government "at the schoolhouse door." Wallace was attempting to block enforcement of a federal court order to admit two black students to the University of Alabama. He claimed that the court order violated states' rights and that he was "interposing" himself between the federal government and the people of Alabama.

It was just a publicity stunt. The doctrine of interposition had been discredited a century earlier. At the cost of half a million lives, the Civil War had settled the question of whether or not state officials may block the enforcement of the U.S. Constitution or laws made "in pursuance thereof."

But not all questions of federal–state relations have been settled. If anything, the situation is more difficult today than it was in 1963. The federal government has grown considerably since then. The states, meanwhile, have shown new vitality: They may be able to do things they were unable or unwilling to do in 1963.

For many critics, the question is whether or not the federal government has moved too far into areas that should be left up to states and localities. The beauty of federalism was supposed to be that it left much decision making in the hands of local authorities. This gave us choice (if people did not like the system in one state, they could move to another); permitted selective experimentation with new programs; and gave citizens greater access to government. If the federal government keeps

Points to Remember

1. Aid cuts are a harsh way of encouraging state independence. There may be better ways. One alternative was President Nixon's revenue sharing, which has now been discontinued.

2. President Reagan's New Federalism would have transferred to the states the financing and administration of AFDC and Food Stamps, which are now largely run from Washington; in return, the federal government would have assumed the full cost of the Medicaid program. It would also have made available to the states a temporary trust fund derived from windfall profits on oil.

3. Reagan did succeed in consolidating a number of categorical grants into block grants and generally cutting back on grants-in-aid.

4. One way of giving more responsibility to the states is to cut grants-in-aid. Cuts in federal aid in the 1980s forced some states to start innovative programs.

5. The "new South" has put segregation behind it, and even in the North, state government has been revitalized since the 1960s, so it may now be possible to leave more autonomy to the states.

taking over state and local programs, what will happen to federalism? Will the states soon be of interest only to mapmakers like Rand McNally? Today these questions are being asked not just by conservatives but by many progressive thinkers and leaders. A generation ago, people turned almost instinctively to Washington for solutions. Today, in a time of federal budget cuts and eroding confidence in federal programs, the pendulum may already be swinging in the opposite direction.

As we have seen, the term *New Federalism* can have a variety of meanings. For President Nixon, it meant revenue sharing—giving money to states with no strings attached. For President Reagan, it meant having the federal government take over some programs while handing others over to exclusive state control. Both approaches, of course, are dead at the present: Reagan's proposed swap never reached the floor of Congress, and Nixon's revenue sharing died in 1986. On the other hand, Reagan's consolidation of categorical grants into block grants remains in place. The common theme in all these variants of the New Federalism is discretion: letting state governors and legislatures decide when, where, and how to spend money.

The memory of George Wallace at the schoolhouse door fades slowly—as it should. States' rights has been used as a cover for racism, corruption, incompetence, and do-nothingism. There is always the danger that giving the states more discretion will revive all the abuses of the past. On the other hand, there have been dramatic changes in state and local government since the early 1960s, and at least some of those changes seem to be here to stay. Black voters in the South have made segregation politically unprofitable. White politicians now share power with black officials throughout the South. Elsewhere in the nation, state governments have modernized their procedures, become more representative, and brought men and women of energy and imagination to power. Maybe the time has come to test these new leaders, to see if they can, with sensitivity and competence, take back from the federal government some of the traditional decision-making power "reserved" to the states and the people.

Notes

1. Marshall Frady, *Wallace* (New York, Cleveland: World, 1968), p. 142.
2. Frady, p. 127.
3. George C. Wallace, *Stand Up for America* (Garden City, NY: Doubleday, 1976), p. 81.
4. Wallace, p. 81.
5. Wallace, p. 81.
6. Wallace, p. 81.
7. *New York Times*, Aug. 8, 1965, sec. IV, p. 2.
8. Daniel J. Elazar, *Exploring Federalism* (Tuscaloosa, AL: University of Alabama Press, 1987), p. 34.
9. Some of the states that retained the 55-mile-per-hour limit have complained that the enforcement mechanisms (electronic monitoring of car speeds) may result in penalties for them, while the states that have raised their limits are not subject to monitoring. Thus, they say, the very states that have tried to preserve the lower limits are being penalized. See Clifford D. May, "States With 55 M.P.H. Limit Face Millions in U.S. Penalties," *New York Times*, Jan. 13, 1988, pp. A1, B4.
10. *Miller v. California*, 413 U.S. 15 (1973).
11. Bernard Schwartz, ed., *The Bill of Rights: A Documentary History* (New York: Chelsea House, 1971), vol. II, p. 1118.
12. Thomas Hart Benton, quoted in Harry J. Carman and Harold C. Syrett, *A History of the American People* (New York: Alfred A. Knopf, 1957), vol. I, p. 324.
13. The other issue in the case, of less importance here, was whether or not a state can tax a federal instrument such as the Bank of the United States. Once the Court decided that the federal government could charter the bank, it settled the other issue by logical inference. Since "the power," as the Court wrote, "to tax involves the power to destroy," it follows that to give the states taxing power over a federal instrument would be to make them potential destroyers of legitimate federal power, in violation of Article VI of the Constitution.
14. *McCulloch v. Maryland*, 4 Wheat. 316 (1819).
15. *Gibbons v. Ogden*, 9 Wheat. 1 (1824).
16. *United States v. Darby* (1941).

17. See, for example, the 1963 letter of Stanford Law School professor Gerald Gunther, quoted in Gunther, ed., *Constitutional Law: Cases and Materials*, 10th ed. (Mineola, NY: The Foundation Press, 1980), p. 203.

18. *Heart of Atlanta Motel, Inc. v. United States* (1964).

19. *Schechter Poultry Corporation v. United States* (1935); *Carter v. Carter Coal Company* (1936).

20. *National League of Cities v. Usury* (1976).

21. Alexis de Tocqueville, *Democracy in America* (New York: Vintage Books, 1945), pp. 121, 281-82.

22. Tocqueville, p. 424.

23. Quoted in Fred W. Friendly and Martha J. H. Elliott, *The Constitution: That Delicate Balance* (New York: Random House, 1984), p. 17.

24. *Barron v. Baltimore* (1833).

25. Catherine H. Lovell et al., *Federal and State Mandating on Local Governments* (Riverside, CA: University of California, Riverside, Graduate School of Public Administration, 1979), p. 71.

26. Bruce Babbitt, "States' Rights for Liberals," *The New Republic*, (January 24, 1981), p. 23.

27. Quoted in George McKenna, ed., *American Populism* (New York: G. P. Putnam's Sons, 1974), pp. 223, 227.

28. See James M. Cannon, "Federal Revenue Sharing: Born 1972. Died 1986. R.I.P.," *New York Times*, Oct. 10, 1986, sec. I, p. 39. The Gramm-Rudman-Hollings Act is discussed in more detail in chapter 20.

29. *New York Times*, Nov. 25, 1984, pp. 1, 33.

30. Richard P. Nathan and Fred C. Doolittle, "The Untold Story of Reagan's 'New Federalism'," *The Public Interest* (Fall 1984), p. 99.

31. "Why States Can Do What Uncle Can't," *U.S. News and World Report*, Dec. 28, 1987/ Jan. 4, 1988, p. 35.

32. "Why States Can Do What Uncle Can't," p. 35.

33. "Federalism: The National Government Versus the States," in PBS Television series, *The Constitution: That Delicate Balance*, Dec. 11, 1984: Transcript, p. 15.

34. "Why States Can Do What Uncle Can't," p. 35.

35. Quoted in John W. Mashek and Thomas J. Foley, "Governors Balk: 'We Want a Better Deal,' " *U.S. News and World Report* (March 8, 1982), p. 50.

PART II
Rights and Liberties

Democracy is fraudulent unless it protects human rights and liberties. Yet there are often many who claim these rights and liberties, and sometimes their claims conflict. Political fanatics and those who are offended by them, patriots and flagburners, the religious and non-religious all claim rights, and all interpret the First Amendment differently. In Chapter 4 we examine some of the competing claims involved in our freedoms of speech, press, association, and religion.

Chapter 5 examines conflicts in the area of civil rights, as those on opposing sides of many issues, from abortion to affirmative action, claim constitutional protection. We review the experiences of blacks and women to study the background, nature, and limits of civil rights. Chapter 6 explores crime and punishments and the sometimes competing claims of criminal suspects and society.

Freedom of speech is the right to say
things that people do not want to hear.

George Orwell

4

First Amendment Freedoms

FREE SPEECH

The Defense of Free Speech / *Schenck*: "Clear and Present Danger" / "Symbolic
Speech" / Academic Freedom

PRESS FREEDOM

Prior Restraint: Almost Always Unconstitutional / Obscenity: Changing Standards
Miller v. California (1973): Three Tests of Obscenity / Libel and Slander

THE RIGHT TO ASSEMBLE

CHURCH AND STATE

"Wall of Separation"—Yet "Benign Religion" / "A Religious People" / *Engel v.
Vitale* (1962): Banning Public School Prayer / Religion and State: Total Separation?

REFLECTIONS

In 1977 Sol Goldstein, aged 64, was a resident of Skokie, **The Skokie March**
Illinois, a northern suburb of Chicago. The population mix
in Skokie was unusual. Of its 69,000 inhabitants in 1977, 40,000 were
Jewish, and of the Jewish residents, some 10 percent were refugees from
Nazi concentration camps set up during World War II.*

Mr. Goldstein was one of those refugees. He recalled the Gestapo
tossing his mother, emaciated but still alive, into a mass grave. "When
men went back the next day they saw the earth move."[1] Mr. Goldstein
could not think of Nazis without getting enraged. "I don't know what
would happen to me if I saw a swastika in front of my house."[2] Yet in that
same year, 1977, a group of young men announced its plans to carry a
swastika—many swastikas—in a demonstration in Skokie.

The group called itself the National Socialist Party of America and

*This account is drawn largely from David Hamlin, *The Nazi/Skokie Conflict* (Boston:
Beacon Press, 1980). Other sources include J. Anthony Lucas, "The ACLU Against
Itself," *New York Times Magazine*, July 9, 1978, pp. 9-11; and Hadley Arkes, "Marching
Through Skokie," *National Review*, May 12, 1978, pp. 588-593.

76

1980: Members of the National Socialist Party of America march in Cincinnati, Ohio.

was modeled after its counterpart in Germany a generation earlier. Its members wore brown shirts, jackboots, and armbands decorated with the infamous swastika. Apart from the uniforms, however, there was nothing very terrifying about the National Socialist Party of America. Its total membership was about two dozen. It had been formed and was headed by a young man named Frank Collin, who had been expelled from the larger American Nazi party after the party found out that his real name was Frank Cohn, that he was Jewish, and that he was the son of a concentration camp survivor.

Frank Collin's bizarre form of self-hatred did not much interest Sol Goldstein and the other survivors who were residents of Skokie. The only important thing to them, and to most of the other citizens of the town, was that there be no Nazi march in Skokie. They persuaded the town council to seek a court order preventing the demonstration. At 3 P.M. on April 27, 1977, a process server delivered to Frank Collin notice of the Village of Skokie's suit against him. Collin read the document and then picked up the telephone and called the American Civil Liberties Union.

The American Civil Liberties Union (ACLU) is an organization that goes to court to protect what it considers to be individual rights under the Constitution. At issue in this case was whether or not Frank Collin and his friends had a right to demonstrate in public wearing their Nazi regalia and advocating their doctrine of hate. The First Amendment sounds unambiguous: "Congress shall make no law . . . abridging the freedom of speech, or of the press, or of the right of the people peaceably to assemble." How then could Skokie ban Frank Collin and his friends from engaging in a peaceful demonstration? This was the argument pressed by attorneys for the ACLU as they went to court to challenge the Village of Skokie. As they saw it, their ultimate client was not Frank Collin; it was the First Amendment.

But the First Amendment is more complex than it appears on the surface. Despite its absolute-sounding language ("no law"), the Supreme Court has ruled on a number of occasions that some speech—such as libel, slander, obscenity, "fighting words," and incitement to riot—are not protected by it. This became the case made by attorneys for Skokie, who argued that the demonstration would almost certainly provoke a riot. Individuals have rights, but the community also has a right to protect itself against violence. Another argument was advanced by an attorney for Sol Goldstein, who had launched his own suit against Frank Collin. In society, the argument went, one person's right has to be balanced against that of another person. Holocaust survivors, haunted by memories of what the Nazis had done to them and their families 30 years earlier, should not have to endure that torment again. What about *their* rights?

These issues were argued in state and federal courts, and in the public media, for nearly a year and a half. In practically every public forum, from town meetings to synagogues in the Chicago area, there were debates, shouting matches, even threats of violence. Soon the controversy had become national, even international. The Nazi Skokie march attracted reporters and camera crews from around the nation and the world. Massive counterdemonstrations were planned, and every day brought new threats. The Jewish Defense League vowed to show up and "bust heads." Another group calling itself the International Committee Against Racism (INCAR) was calling on "the people" to come to Skokie and attack Collin.

A major target was the Illinois chapter of the ACLU, based in Chicago, which had initiated the suit on Collin's behalf. Its director, David Hamlin, spent hours each day on the telephone trying to explain to callers why his organization was defending Nazis. Hamlin was not Jewish, but the ACLU's chief counsel in the case was. David Goldberger, 36 years old at the time, was an ardent libertarian. As he saw it, he had a duty to defend free speech—even if it was speech that he hated. Many Jews saw Goldberger as a traitor to his own people. Some 30,000 ACLU members, the vast majority of whom were Jewish, resigned in protest.

The case dragged through state and federal courts for nearly a year and a half and ended in a kind of stalemate. From a strictly legal standpoint, Collin was the winner. Skokie's attempts to keep him out were declared unconstitutional, and an appeal to the Supreme Court failed. But when Collin finally had to decide whether or not to exercise his right to march in Skokie, he opted out. After talking with Hamlin, Goldberger, and members of a special Justice Department mediation team, Collin selected a safer site: Chicago's Federal Plaza, where he would be guarded by a large contingent of city police. In his book *The Nazi/Skokie Conflict*, David Hamlin described the anticlimactic ending to the uproar:

Frank Collin and his followers marched onto the plaza through a corridor of uniformed Chicago police, emerging on the plaza itself to face a crowd of several thousand seething, furious, scream-distorted faces. Although he had a portable amplifier, Collin could not be heard at all; the ceaseless angry roar made whatever Collin said impossible to hear. . . . Frank Collin and his followers left the plaza and returned to their headquarters under heavy police guard all the way.[3]

The story has a brief epilogue. In 1980, two years after the close of the case, Frank Collin was arrested, tried, and convicted for sexually molesting two young boys. He was sentenced to seven years in prison and was expelled from the National Socialist Party of America.

*   *   *   *   *

It is easy to be for rights. But what happens when one person's claim to a right collides with someone else's? Or seems to endanger the peace of the community? Giving Frank Collin and his friends the right to march meant denying Sol Goldstein and other Holocaust survivors the right not to be forced to relive the past. It also meant risking a full-scale riot in the streets of Skokie. Was the case properly decided? Whatever the legal merits of the arguments on both sides, the moral choices are not easy.

The same difficulties appear in other cases involving First Amendment freedoms. Take the case of pornography. The freedom for one person to display sexually oriented material may mean that someone else who is offended by it has to put up with it. Sometimes, of course, we can have it both ways: protect the freedom to display certain material while respecting people's rights not to see it. But the solutions often get caught on one horn or another of the dilemma. They either restrict freedom of expression or else they practically force people to tolerate—and in some cases to fund—material they consider offensive.

There are many other similar dilemmas. The First Amendment protects freedom of press, but that freedom in some cases can collide with other freedoms, such as freedom from libel and slander. The First Amendment also protects freedom of religion. But in concrete cases, such as school prayer, that freedom could run counter to the right of Americans to be free *from* religion if they so choose.

The list of possible dilemmas is practically endless. We cannot examine them all, nor does it seem possible to offer any final answers. In this chapter we will explore some of the tough questions that come up when we contemplate the freedoms protected by the First Amendment: freedom of speech, press, and assembly; freedom of religion; and freedom from any religious "establishment."

Free Speech

"Sticks and stones may break my bones, but names will never hurt me." This familiar children's rhyme is quoted by David Hamlin in his book on the Nazi/Skokie conflict. His point is that words and acts are entirely distinct from one another. Acts, he says, can be harmful, but not words, "for no word ever committed a crime, no name ever violated a law, no speech ever broke a bone."[4] And yet, words do have consequences. They helped bring about the Reformation, the French and American revolutions, the Communist revolution in Russia, and the Third Reich in Germany. Words can inspire people to do great deeds. They can also lead to infamous crimes. In a sense, then, speeches *can* break bones.

THE DEFENSE OF FREE SPEECH

If speech can produce such consequences, should we ban harmful speech? This was once the conventional wisdom in the West (and still is in authoritarian and totalitarian countries). By the eighteenth century, however, it had become clear that such a position suffered from at least three weaknesses.

In the first place, it assumes that we always know what is harmful. History is full of examples of ideas that later generations accepted as sublime truths. Jesus of Nazareth was crucified as an insurrectionist. Four centuries earlier, a jury in Athens found Socrates guilty of "corrupting youth" and sentenced him to death. In seventeenth century Italy, the Jesuits forced Galileo to recant his view that the earth moved around the sun because it seemed to contradict the Bible.

Oliver Wendell Holmes, Jr., wrote, "The best test of truth is the power of the thought to get itself accepted in the competition of the market. . . . That, at any rate, is the theory of our Constitution."

Second, even if a doctrine is wrong, it does not follow that it should be silenced. In fact, as nineteenth-century English philosopher John Stuart Mill argued, it may be good for us to be confronted by wrong and offensive ideas, for by hearing them, we are forced to work out answers to them. "Both teachers and learners go to sleep at their post as soon as there is no enemy in the field."[5]

Third, those who advocate censorship seem to have a low opinion of truth, or at least of people's ability to grasp truth. In 1644 the English poet John Milton observed that if we believe in truth, we must believe in its power to overcome error in a fair debate.[6] Supreme Court justice Oliver Wendell Holmes, Jr., summed up the case for free speech in a dissenting opinion he wrote in 1919. It may be tempting, Holmes said, to persecute people for the expression of ideas.

> But when men have realized that time has upset many fighting faiths, they may come to believe even more than they believe the very foundations of their own conduct that the ultimate good desired is better reached by free trade in ideas—that the best test of truth is the power of the thought to get itself accepted in the competition of the market. . . . That, at any rate, is the theory of our Constitution.[7]

Holmes's "free trade in ideas" has a number of implications, some of which will be explored in chapter 14. For now, we will examine his assertion that it is "the theory of our Constitution." It is—but with some qualifications made by the U.S. Supreme Court, including one written by Holmes himself.

SCHENCK: "CLEAR AND PRESENT DANGER"

The First Amendment says that "Congress shall make no law" abridging freedom of speech. Some have interpreted this language literally. One of them, the late Supreme Court justice Hugo Black, used to get annoyed with colleagues who made exceptions. "I understand," he once remarked sarcastically, "that it is rather old-fashioned and shows a slight naiveté to say that 'no law' means 'no law.' " But Black's position on free speech has never been accepted by the Court; the Court has always been prepared to admit exceptions.

One major exception was spelled out in a landmark case in 1919. It began two years earlier, as America began drafting young men to fight in World War I. Charles Schenck, general secretary of the American Socialist party, mailed to potential draftees 15,000 leaflets that compared military conscription to slavery and urged readers to "assert your rights." Schenck did nothing physically to obstruct the draft; his actions were only verbal. Yet he was arrested under the Espionage Act of 1917 and sentenced to prison for draft obstruction. Schenck claimed that his activities were protected by the First Amendment; the Supreme Court disagreed.

The Court's opinion in *Schenck v. United States* (1919) was written by Justice Holmes, who agreed that during normal times Schenck's leaflets would be protected by the First Amendment. But during a wartime emergency, they constituted a <u>clear and present danger</u> of an evil that government had a right to prevent.

Holmes illustrated "clear and present danger" with a now-classic allegory. "The most stringent protection of free speech would not protect a man in falsely shouting fire in a theatre and causing a panic." The First Amendment protects political advocacy, but certain forms of speech are not merely advocacy; they are incitement. If someone advocates a doctrine, no matter how radical the doctrine is, people have a chance to think it over. But if someone shouts "Fire!" in a theater, it causes a knee-jerk reaction. Such expressions therefore "have all the effect of force."

We can question this view of Charles Schenck's activities. All he did was mail leaflets to potential draftees, which presumably left them time to think. The more enduring part of the *Schenck* case is its general formula, the concept of "clear and

(Continued on page 82)

TABLE **4-1**

81

Public Opinion on Civil Liberties

Issue/year	Allow [a]	Don't forbid [b]
Public speeches against democracy		
1940	25%	46%
1974	56	72
1976[a]	55	79
1976[b]	52	79

Issue/year	Allow to speak	Allow to teach college	Keep book in library
Atheist[c]			
1954	37%	12%	35%
1964[d]	—	—	61
1974	62	42	60
1977	62	39	59
1985	65	45	61
Admitted communist[c]			
1954	27	6	27
1974	58	42	59
1985	57	44	57
Racist[c]			
1943[e]	17	—	—
1976	61	41	60
1980	62	43	64
1985	55	42	60

These were the questions asked:
a. Do you think the United States should allow public speeches against democracy?
b. Do you think the United States should forbid public speeches against democracy?
c. There are always some people whose ideas are considered bad or dangerous by other people. For instance, somebody who (is against all churches and religion/admits he is a communist/believes that blacks are genetically inferior). If such a person wanted to make a speech in your (city/town/ community), should he be allowed to speak? Should such a person be allowed to teach in a college or university, or not? If some people in your community suggested that a book he wrote (against churches and religion/promoting communism/which said blacks are inferior) should be taken out of your public library, would you favor removing this book?
d. In 1964 the question was as follows: Suppose a man admitted in public that he did not believe in God. Do you think a book he wrote should be removed from a public library?
e. In 1943 the question was as follows: In peacetime, do you think anyone in the United States should be allowed to make speeches against certain races in this country?
Dash indicates that figures are unavailable.

Data source: Public speeches against democracy: Howard Schuman and Stanley Presser, *Questions and Answers in Attitude Surveys* (New York: Academic Press, 1981); 1943, 1964: National Opinion Research Center surveys; 1954: Samuel A. Stouffer, *Communism, Conformity, and Civil Liberties* (Garden City, NY: Doubleday, 1955), 32-34, 40-43; data for all other years from General Social Surveys. Adapted from Harold W. Stanley and Richard G. Niemi, *Vital Statistics in American Politics* (Washington DC: Congressional Quarterly Press, 1988, pp. 26-27) with permission.

Oliver Wendell Holmes, Jr., also said, "We should grant freedom to the thought we hate." As this table indicates, Americans seem to be following his advice for it suggests that Americans are coming to terms with views with which they formerly disagreed.

In 1989 the Supreme Court ruled that the City of New York has the right to regulate the sound levels of rock concerts in its parks. At issue was a city regulation, aimed at limiting loud noise, that required musical performers to use a city-supplied sound system and sound technician. The regulation was challenged on First Amendment grounds by Rock Against Racism, promoters of an annual Central Park rock concert. The group won in a lower federal court, but in a 6–3 decision, the Supreme Court upheld New York City's regulation. Speaking for the Court, Justice Anthony M. Kennedy said that the city was not trying to ban free expression but merely regulate it as to "time, place and manner."[a] Justice Thurgood Marshall, dissenting, accused the Court majority of disemboweling the First Amendment. "Unfortunately, the majority plays to our shared impatience with loud noise to obscure the damage that it does to the First Amendment." But city parks commissioner Henry Stern saw it differently. To him, the decision was "a victory for the Eighth Amendment, which protects people from cruel and unusual punishments."[b]

[a] *Ward v. Rock Against Racism*, 1989.
[b] *New York Times*, June 23, 1989, pp. B1, B4.

(Continued from page 80) present danger." If someone writes words in a book or speaks at a meeting, that is one thing; if someone, *using the exact same words*, shouts them to an angry mob, that is obviously something else. "The character of every act depends upon the circumstances in which it is done," said Holmes.[8]

In other cases the Court has qualified its protection of free speech in much the same way as it did in *Schenck*. In *Chaplinsky v. New Hampshire* (1942), for example, the Court said that fighting words do not enjoy First Amendment protection. In that case a member of the Jehovah's Witnesses had gotten into a fight on a sidewalk after calling a city official "a God damned racketeer" and "a damned Fascist." He was arrested and convicted for using that language, and the Supreme Court unanimously upheld his conviction.[9]

"SYMBOLIC SPEECH"

As the Nazi Skokie march and the *Schenck* case illustrate, it is not always easy to draw a line between speech and action. Wearing a swastika is an act, but it is also a way of making a statement; conversely there are speeches that constitute a "clear and present danger" of action. Nowhere, perhaps, is the line between action and speech more blurred than in the case of "symbolic speech." A symbolic speech is an action taken for the purpose of making a public statement. The Court has long recognized this concept and has given it at least some First Amendment protection. It has protected the right of a man to display a Communist flag, the right of a high school student to wear a black armband to school as part of an antiwar protest, and the right of another man to display an American flag partially covered by a peace symbol.[10]

In 1968 the Court rejected the argument of a Vietnam protester who said that burning his draft card was an act of symbolic speech.[11] But in 1989 it agreed that burning the American flag was symbolic speech. In doing so, it struck down a Texas law—and thus similar laws in 47 other states as well as a federal statute—prohibiting desecration of the American flag.[12] The decision resulted from the 1984 arrest of a demonstrator who stood in front of City Hall in Dallas, Texas, and set an American flag on fire as several dozen others chanted, "America, the red, white, and blue, we spit on you." A closely divided (5–4) Court ruled that the act of flag-burning was protected by the First Amendment. The decision set off a stormy controversy. President Bush publicly denounced it, as did 47 members of the Senate. In the House a constitutional amendment was introduced to overturn the decision. ("The Congress

(Continued on page 84)

Do People Have a Right To Burn The American Flag?

YES Justice William J. Brennan, Jr.

From the Majority Opinion, *Texas v. Johnson* (1989).

"If there is a bedrock principle underlying the First Amendment, it is that the Government may not prohibit the expression of an idea simply because society finds the idea itself offensive or disagreeable." That is Justice Brennan's major premise in the flag-burning decision. His minor premise is that flag-burning, disagreeable as it is, is a form of expression. Yes, the flag is an important symbol, but so is the Constitution, the presidential seal, and the flags of our 50 states. Justice Brennan thinks that the Court should not try to decide which symbol deserves "unique" protection because it would then be making a value judgment. Brennan is convinced that this decision will strengthen, rather than harm, the symbolism of the flag because it "is a reaffirmation of the principles of freedom and inclusiveness" that the flag represents. "The way to preserve the flag's special role is not to punish those who feel differently about these matters. It is to persuade them that they are wrong."

NO Chief Justice William H. Rehnquist

From Rehnquist's Dissenting Opinion in *Texas v. Johnson* (1989).

Chief Justice Rehnquist invokes the memory of those thousands who have "died on foreign soil fighting for the American cause." In World War II at Iwo Jima, an island belonging to Japan, 6,000 U.S. Marines lost their lives fighting their way to the top of Mount Suribachi to plant the American flag. Rehnquist feels there must be strong grounds for striking down laws aimed at protecting our flag against desecration, and he does not think that the "symbolic speech" argument is very convincing. "Far from being a case of 'one picture being worth a thousand words,' flag-burning is the equivalent of an inarticulate grunt or roar that, it seems fair to say, is most likely to be indulged in not to express any particular idea but to antagonize others." The flag-burner in this case "had a full panoply of other symbols and every conceivable form of verbal expression" to say what he wanted to say; he did not have to resort to this inarticulate, vicious act against a symbol uniquely sacred to Americans.

Postscript

Rehnquist and Brennan apparently agree that if the individual in this case had only verbally insulted the flag, his action would have been protected speech. Their disagreement turns on whether or not what he did do, physically burning the flag, falls under the category of protected speech. Would Rehnquist deny First Amendment protection to someone who wanted to burn a photo of the flag? Would Brennan extend to the Ku Klux Klan the right to burn a cross in front of the Lincoln Memorial? The logic of both justices can be pushed to awkward lengths.

Nat Henthoff's *The First Freedom: The Tumultuous History of Free Speech in America* (New York: Delacorte, 1980) is a lively study of major free-speech battles. Franklyn C. Haiman's *Speech and Law in a Free Society* (Chicago: University of Chicago Press, 1981) surveys various meanings given to the clauses in the First Amendment. Richard Polenberg's *Fighting Faiths* (New York: Knopf, 1987) is a study of political dissent and American reactions to it.

Drawing by Rob Rogers; © 1989 United Features Syndicate.

(Continued from page 82) and the States shall have power to prohibit the physical desecration of the flag of the United States.") This chapter's Taking Sides section summarizes the majority decision, written by Justice William Brennan, and one of the dissenting opinions, written by Chief Justice William Rehnquist.

What sort of generalizations, then, can we make about the boundaries and limits of political speech in America? It is difficult to generalize—some of the Supreme Court's decisions may simply contradict one another—but perhaps we can safely present these conclusions:

- You can *say* whatever you want about the United States or its government or its officials, provided you do not do so in circumstances likely to incite a riot, a revolution, or other *acts* that government has a right to prohibit.
- There is such a thing as "symbolic speech"—an act whose purpose is to make a statement—but there are limits to what you can do in making such a statement.
- You cannot carry speech to the point of fighting words. Standing face-to-face with someone and calling that person vile names is probably not protected by the First Amendment.

If there is any thread of consistency in these Court opinions, it is the determination to protect unorthodox ideas while also protecting society against imminent danger. "Government," said Justice William Brennan in the flag-burning case *Texas v. Johnson* (1989), "may not prohibit the expression of an idea simply because society finds the idea itself offensive or disagreeable." At the same time, the government may punish someone who falsely shouts "Fire!" in a crowded theater or incites a riot or, indeed, incites any act that the government has a right to prevent. Dissent is protected; incitement to riot is not.

Most people would probably agree that one place where unorthodox opinions ought to flourish is the university. Here, after all, is where ideas can be subjected to disciplined and informed debate. Yet down through the years there have been countless attempts to muzzle free thought in academia. Traditionally, these attempts

On December 2, 1964, students at the University of California at Berkeley stage
a sit-in to protest rules of the institution about political activity on campus.

have come from outside the university, from state and church authorities. In more
recent times, however, there have been pressures from within to silence ideas
deemed offensive. Let us examine for a moment the condition of academic freedom
in America.

ACADEMIC FREEDOM

In 1964 some 800 students staged a sit-in at the administration building of the
University of California at Berkeley. They called themselves the "Free Speech
movement," and they demanded the right to recruit people for civil rights causes and
to bring controversial speakers to the campus. The administration soon gave in to
their demands, and by the end of the decade the spirit of their movement had spread
throughout American campuses. Professors could speak their minds, and students
could bring radical outsiders to the campus. It looked like a giant leap forward in the
history of academic freedom.

Some observers worry that academic freedom is being threatened today. They
contend that students, teachers, and administrators have become wary of offending
activist elites on campus. In theory, academics can still say whatever they wish—but
they may have to answer for it later. They can invite anyone to speak on campus—
but they may have to watch their invitees be humiliated and shouted down by
members of the audience. The threats to academic freedom seem to come from the
Right and from the Left.

Threats from the Right.   In 1985 a new organization called Accuracy in Academia (AIA) began recruiting conservative college students to monitor the classes of
certain professors to see if they showed a liberal bias in their teaching. The students
took down quotations and then reported them in newsletters. In some cases, the
professors were notified of the violations and given a chance to mend their ways
before being exposed. The first major target of AIA, a 52-year-old associate professor

(Continued on page 87)

FIGURE **4-1**

The Status of Freedom in the World

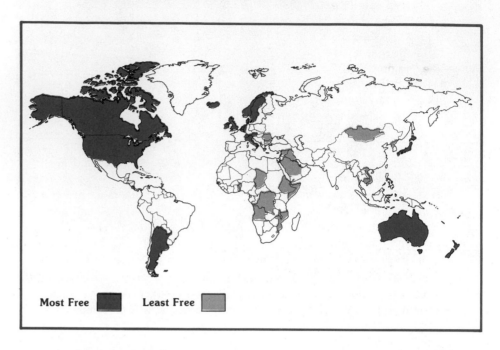

Most Free [ ]   Least Free [ ]

The Most Free Countries
(rated a 1 on both political
rights and civil liberties)

Argentina
Australia
Austria
Barbados
Belgium
Canada
Costa Rica
Denmark
European Community
Great Britain
Grenada
Iceland
Ireland
Italy
Japan
Luxembourg
Netherlands
New Zealand
Norway
Sweden
Switzerland
Trinidad & Tobago
Tuvalu
United States

The Least Free Countries
(rated a 7 on both political
rights and civil liberties)

Albania
Angola
Benin
Bulgaria
Cambodia
Chad
Equatorial Guinea
Ethiopia
Guinea-Bissau
Iraq
Korea (N)
Malawi
Mongolia
Mozambique
Romania
Sao Tome & Principe
Saudi Arabia
Somalia
Syria
Vietnam
Yemen (S)
Zaire

Source: Freedom at Issue (January/February 1989).
Reprinted with permission of Freedom House.

Freedom is a rare commodity in today's world! In a ranking of 168 nations, only
23 countries (and the European Community) achieved high marks for freedom.

(Continued from page 85)

at Arizona State University, claimed that his exposure resulted in telephone threats and verbal harassment.

AIA is an offshoot of Accuracy in Media, a Washington-based watchdog group headed by Reed Irvine (see chapter 14). Irvine has defended AIA by saying that it really amounts to a kind of truth-in-packaging. The Arizona State professor who was its first target was teaching a course entitled "Political Ideologies," which the course catalog described as a study of "leading political ideas and belief systems." Instead, said Irvine, the professor used the course "as a soapbox to indoctrinate students with his obsessive fear of all things nuclear." There was nothing about that in the catalogue's course description. "If you ordered steak in a restaurant and were served liver, you would have a justifiable complaint."[13]

Threats from the Left.   Bullying from the Left often takes a more theatrical form. In February 1983, former UN ambassador Jeane Kirkpatrick came to the Berkeley campus, birthplace of the Free Speech movement, to deliver the annual Jefferson Lecture. But as soon as she appeared on the podium, she was met by the shouts of demonstrators dressed as skeletons. She went home without finishing the lecture when the Berkeley administration warned her that things might get worse. A few months later she attempted to speak at the University of Minnesota, only to be greeted with Nazi banners and heckling. Still later she had to cancel her scheduled commencement address at Smith College after the administration admitted it could not guarantee order if she appeared.

Kirkpatrick was one of many speakers silenced by demonstrators. Eldridge Cleaver, the former black radical who now extols the virtues of capitalism, was shouted down when he tried to speak at Berkeley in 1982. So was Duane Gish, a proponent of the creationist theory of the earth's origins. In another incident, a group of Berkeley students who tried to show an anti-abortion film, *The Silent Scream*, had their equipment broken and stolen by demonstrators.

More recently, many civil libertarians worry about a new movement by college authorities to combat bigotry on their campuses by limiting free expression. At Stanford University, the University of Michigan, the University of Wisconsin, Smith College, and other schools, codes are being drafted which would punish or even expel students who say or write anything considered offensive to various groups in American society. The University of Michigan has already promulgated broadly-worded rules punishing any conduct that "stigmatizes or victimizes" people not only on the basis of race, ethnicity, religion, sexual orientation, and national origin but also marital status, handicap, and "Vietnam-era veteran status."   (Continued on page 88)

Points to Remember

1. The First Amendment guarantees free speech, but key Supreme Court decisions have made it clear that First Amendment rights are not absolute. The landmark decision was *Schenck v. United States* (1919), in which the Court held that government may limit free speech in circumstances that involve a "clear and present danger" of an evil that government has a right to prevent.

2. The First Amendment protects certain forms of symbolic speech, such as the wearing of armbands or flags. It also protects the right to burn an American flag.

3. The Supreme Court's approach to free speech is to protect even the most offensive speech as long as it does not incite unlawful acts.

4. The Free Speech movement at Berkeley in 1964 sought to broaden the right of academic freedom by allowing people to recruit for causes and to bring controversial speakers to campus. In recent years, such freedoms have been challenged by activists on the Right and the Left.

Zaire, formerly the Belgian Congo, has been called the "hub of Africa." It is located at almost the exact center of sub-Saharan Africa, and its territory, which is about one quarter the size of the United States, makes it one of the largest states on the continent. It is also one of the most politically stable regimes in Africa, but its stability has been purchased at the expense of civil liberties.

Since 1965 Zaire has been ruled by Mobutu Sese Seko, who took over in a military coup. Mobutu's ideology, a mixture of socialism and tradition called "authenticity" (*authenticité*), is the ruling doctrine, and Mobutu has used it to justify the takeover of major industries and farms. Bureaucratic corruption is rampant, which is one reason why the Zairean economy is in a state of near-collapse. Zaire has a foreign debt greater than that of any other African country; its bridges, highways, and railroads are in disrepair; and real wages of urban workers are one-tenth of the 1960 level. Yet all attempts to criticize Mobutu's rule have been silenced. Only one political party—Mobutu's—is permitted, and those attempting to organize an opposition have been ruthlessly put down. On two occasions, most recently in 1986, Zaire has been cited as a human rights violator by Amnesty International, which has charged the regime with the illegal arrest, torture, and murder of its critics. Under pressure from the United States, with which

Zaire is allied, Mobutu has admitted the truth of some of the allegations; dissolved the military security agency, which he has blamed for the violations; and appointed a state commissioner for human rights. Still, the campaign of intimidation has had its effect. The chief founder of the stillborn opposition party, released in 1988 after months of internal exile, promised Mobutu to desist from further political activity. He explained the reason: "Always arrested, exiled, banished—it's not fun."

Press Freedom

The First Amendment links freedom of speech and freedom of press. This was quite natural at the time the amendment was written. In the eighteenth century, the word *press* meant a clumsy, long-handled device for printing ink on paper. It enabled one person to reach a few hundred others, at least those who could read. Today the word *press* stands for an institution that employs millions of people and earns billions of dollars every year. It still uses printing presses, but it also uses film and electronic devices that reproduce sound and pictures with the immediacy of live events.

There are two main differences between speech and the modern press. The first is ownership. All of us own a set of vocal chords, but very few of us today are able to own a press or a television station or even get access to either. That difference will be explored in chapter 14. The second difference has to do with resonance. Your average soapbox orator can be heard only by the people gathered around. But newspapers reach far beyond the cities in which they are published, and the electronic media reach national and even worldwide audiences. They can disseminate knowledge, culture, and opinion to millions. They can also stir up mass hatreds, destroy the reputations of innocent people, tell the world a nation's security secrets, and bring violence into our homes. It would be nice if all the press's acts were positive, but that is not the case. The temptation, then, is to say "there ought to be a law" against press misbehavior. In fact, there have been a number of such laws, and many of them have been struck down by the Supreme Court. In this section we will examine how the Court has made its judgments. Beyond that, we will explore ways of distinguishing between proper limitations on press freedom and violations of that freedom.

Like freedom of speech, freedom of the press is not absolute. Even ardent libertarians are reluctant to say that all our libel laws should be repealed. Nor are there many who would say that advertising heroin or selling child pornography ought to be allowed. Still, the question is how to draw the line between what deserves protection and what does not.

PRIOR RESTRAINT: ALMOST ALWAYS UNCONSTITUTIONAL

If there is anything the First Amendment was meant to outlaw, it is prior restraint—stopping the press from printing something.

Prior restraint, also called "previous restraint," sets off alarm bells among American jurists. Historically, the expression is associated with seventeenth-century England, where the royal authorities tried to silence dissenters before they could even get started. A license had to be obtained from the government before anyone could issue any printed matter. The poet John Milton was protesting against this in 1644 when he insisted that truth and error should be allowed to fight it out. As long as truth is in the field, Milton said, "we do injuriously by licensing and prohibiting to misdoubt her strength." Before the end of the seventeenth century, Milton's eloquent appeal had borne fruit: Press licensing was abolished.

This was the English tradition that America inherited: a strong aversion to press censorship. This has to be distinguished from *subsequent punishment* for press activity. It would be hard to find any eighteenth-century thinker, even the most libertarian, advocating the abolition of all laws punishing slander, libel, sedition, and so on. Sir William Blackstone, the great eighteenth-century English jurist, summed up the common understanding when he said that liberty of the press consists of the freedom every man has "to lay what sentiments he pleases before the public." But, Blackstone cautioned, if someone publishes "what is improper, mischievous, or illegal, he must take the consequences of his temerity."[14]

The Supreme Court has adhered to this tradition. As a rule it will not permit the government to stop the presses in advance of publication, although it leaves room for subsequent punishment. In 1931 the Court prevented the state of Minnesota from padlocking the presses of one Jay M. Near, publisher of an anti-Semitic newspaper in Minneapolis.[15] In 1971 the Court relied in part on that precedent in refusing to restrain the *New York Times* and other newspapers from printing parts of the so-called Pentagon Papers.

The Pentagon Papers case, *New York Times et al. v. United States* (1971), involved the issue of whether or not a newspaper should be allowed to print stolen classified documents. Daniel Ellsberg, a former employee of the RAND Corporation (a "think tank" that does a lot of work for the Defense Department), removed from Defense Department files some 7,000 pages of documents stamped "top secret." He photocopied them and turned the copies over to the *New York Times*. The documents, part of a special study of U.S. involvement in Vietnam, suggested that U.S. policymakers had systematically lied and disregarded the law in drawing our country into the war. Ellsberg, who had turned against the war, thought that making this study public would force an end to the war.

Times staffers spent three months poring over the documents and then started printing excerpts. The Nixon administration went to court to stop the *Times* and was successful in doing so for two weeks. Meanwhile, the case went to the Supreme Court, and the Court rendered its decision in record time. A 6-3 majority backed the *Times*. It is hard to draw general conclusions with any great certainty, since each justice in the case wrote his own separate opinion. But perhaps this much can be ventured: The Court regards prior restraint as almost always a violation of the First Amendment (though some of the justices would allow an exception if they were convinced that "grave and irreparable" damage would result from publication). Subsequent punishment, however, is another matter. One justice in the majority went so far as to suggest some of the laws that the government might use in prosecuting the *Times*.[16]

Thus far the discussion has centered on political expression: the right to advocate political views, the right to publish classified documents, the right to engage in symbolic protests. But there is another, extremely controversial kind of expression that has nothing directly to do with politics. Even to bring up its name is to enter into the controversy. The name is "obscenity." Some deny that there is such a thing as obscenity; they consider the term a kind of empty hate-word used by people who are offended by or afraid of certain material. Yet the term remains; Americans will continue to use it, even though they may not be clear about its meaning. Many, probably, would identify with the late Supreme Court justice Potter Stewart, who, referring to "hard core" pornography, said he could not define it, "but I know it when I see it."[17]

OBSCENITY: CHANGING STANDARDS

The problem, of course, is that different people see things differently, especially over the course of time. Less than 70 years ago, women were arrested at public beaches for wearing bathing suits that showed their thighs. At that time, books that are now considered works of art, such as D. H. Lawrence's *Lady Chatterly's Lover* and James Joyce's *Ulysses*, were banned. As late as the 1950s, movie producer Otto Preminger defied Hollywood censors by producing a movie whose dialogue included the word *virgin*, and movie actress Faye Emerson was fired from her job as the hostess of a television show after wearing a gown that displayed a bit of cleavage.

Today situations involving premarital and extramarital sex are the common coin of television entertainment. Movies with nudity and simulated intercourse are showing down at the corner, and there are hardcore pornographic movies for rent at the local video outlet. Newsstands feature magazines like *Penthouse* and *Hustler*, with explicit nude photographs. Major cities have districts, such as New York City's 42nd Street, where the most bizarre kinds of sexual acts can be viewed in theaters and "peep shows." For better or worse, the times have changed.

Our legal standards have changed as well. The Supreme Court first dealt with the obscenity issue in a 1957 case, *Roth v. United States*. Speaking for the Court majority, Justice William Brennan defined obscenity as material "which deals with sex in a prurient manner" and specifically exempted it from First Amendment protection. In this respect, the Court has never changed its view. To repeat, obscenity is *not* protected by the First Amendment.

But what is "obscenity"? By calling it material dealing with sex "in a prurient manner," Justice Brennan invited an obvious question: What does *prurient* mean? In a footnote to his opinion, he quoted a definition from Webster's dictionary: "Itching; longing; uneasy with desire or longing." By itself, this is not very helpful, but Brennan

In July 1922 police arrest women at a Chicago beach for defying an edict banning abbreviated swimsuits.

proposed what he considered a more comprehensive "test" of obscenity: "whether to the average person, applying contemporary community standards, the dominant theme of the material as a whole appeals to prurient interest." His attempt was to get beyond the subjectivity of different people's views of what is offensive. It was to be "the average person." And this person was to apply "contemporary" standards, not those of the 1890s, so that we do not go back to arresting bathers for showing their thighs. Finally, the "dominant theme" had to be prurient, so we do not confiscate books that have occasional erotic passages. It was a good try at balancing liberty and public decency, but it did not hold up very well.

The *Roth* decision was a product of the 1950s. Then came the 1960s. New movies, plays, magazines, and above all, the changing mores of the decade put unbearable strains on the *Roth* formula, and the Court began modifying it. By the end of the 1960s it had become almost impossible to sustain obscenity convictions because the Court now insisted that the material not only had to be prurient but "*utterly* without redeeming social value."[18] Since nearly everything has some tiny trace of social value, a good lawyer and a few "expert" witnesses could get nearly anyone off the hook.

MILLER v. CALIFORNIA (1973): THREE TESTS OF OBSCENITY

In the 1970s a somewhat differently constituted Supreme Court (with four new justices appointed by President Nixon) grappled again with the obscenity issue. In a landmark case, *Miller v. California* (1973), the Court set out new guidelines for defining obscenity: (1) whether or not "the average person, applying contemporary community standards," would find that the work taken as a whole appeals to prurient interests; (2) whether or not the work depicts "in a patently offensive way" sexual material defined by applicable state law; and (3) whether or not the work, taken as a whole, lacks "serious literary, artistic, political, or scientific value" (this guideline has been called the "SLAPS" test).

The *Miller* decision rejected the idea of a national standard for obscenity, instead leaving the matter to the judgment of a local jury using local "community standards." The Court's reasoning was that what is obscene in Mississippi may not be so in New York. People in different geographical areas "vary in their tastes and attitudes, and this diversity is not to be strangled by the absolutism of imposed uniformity." Yet—so it seems today—American tastes and mores are becoming increasingly standardized. The Holiday Inns in Mississippi carry the same cable movies as the ones in New York, television networks bring the same entertainment to rural hamlets and big cities, and *Playboy* sells all over the country. *Miller v. California* (1973) has never been overturned, but the country as a whole has come to accept material that it would not have accepted a generation ago. In 1986 voters in the politically conservative state of Maine overwhelmingly rejected a referendum proposition calling for the prohibition of obscenity. In 1987 a public opinion poll showed that a majority of Americans were opposed to banning pornography for adults, and in 1989 a supposedly conservative Supreme Court unanimously upheld the right of businesses to offer "indecent" sexually oriented telephone messages to callers.[19] It is hard to imagine the Court giving First Amendment protection to a "dial-a-porn" business back in 1957, when *Roth* was decided. In fact, it is hard to imagine such a business even existing then. Today it is a $2-billion-a-year industry. Clearly, the bounds of the acceptable have stretched dramatically over the past generation, and so has the reach of the First Amendment.

The new cutting edge of the obscenity controversy is not what is tolerable but what is fundable. Presently, Congress spends about $225 million each year to fund cultural projects through the National Endowment for the Arts (NEA) and the National Endowment for the Humanities (NEH). In 1989 one of the projects scheduled to be funded was a retrospective exhibit of photographs by the late Robert Mapplethorpe at the Corcoran Gallery of Art in Washington, D.C. The Corcoran canceled the showing after it received complaints from several members of Congress that the exhibit was obscene (it contained photographs of naked children in provocative poses and of naked men in homoerotic acts). Many, particularly in the art world, saw the cancellation as an act of censorship, and at a protest demonstration held outside the gallery, one speaker charged that the Corcoran had "capitulated to the most narrow and mean-spirited redneck prejudices."[20] Others argued that the government has no obligation to fund projects that violate public standards of decency.[21] Another controversial project funded by NEA is a photograph of a crucifix immersed in a glass of urine and entitled "Piss Christ," by Andres Serrano.

Reacting to these publicly-funded projects, Senator Jesse Helms (R-North Carolina) persuaded the Senate in 1989 to pass an amendment cutting off federal grants to any art deemed "obscene or indecent" or that "denigrates, debases, or reviles a person, group, or class of citizens on the basis of race, creed, sex, handicap, age, or national origin." The Helms amendment was later dropped by a Senate-House conference committee and replaced with a formulation that left the status quo virtually untouched. Engineered by Representative Sidney R. Yates (D-Illinois), a long defender of the National Endowment for the Arts, the new wording would use the standards of *Miller v. California* in deciding whether a fund cut-off is justified. Those standards, as we saw above, provide guidelines for defining obscenity, but they put the *application* of the standards into the hands of local juries using local community standards. Under the Yates formulation, the juries to be used in deciding whether an art work is obscene would be the same groups of artists that now award the NEA grants! Still, the whole episode made many people uneasy. Some feared more government intrusions into the arts; others wondered whether artists can reasonably expect to be left alone once they take public money.

"Sticks and stones may break my bones, but names will never hurt me." There has been a lot of argument about whether or not obscenity hurts people (for example, does it provoke sex crimes?). It is very difficult to draw firm conclusions on the subject.[22] It is not difficult, however, to see that some forms of expression can indeed hurt. We talked earlier about shouting "Fire!" in a crowded theater; there can be no question about the harm that can cause. There is another, less physical way to hurt people with words; that is, literally, to use "names" against them. To label falsely someone in writing as a Communist, a Fascist, a crook, or a drunk can cause real harm: The person might lose his or her job, miss the chance for one, lose friends, or be shunned by neighbors. The person's reputation could be destroyed by such words. This is the reason we have laws against <u>libel</u>, which is called <u>slander</u> when it is an oral statement.

In the United States, the legal sanctions against libel are civil, not criminal. Our laws leave the punishment for libel in the hands of the injured party, who can bring a suit for monetary damages. The American press has enormous freedom from libel actions, far more than the press in any other country of the world. This is particularly true of reports on government officials. Since 1964 it has become nearly impossible for these officials to win libel judgments; the crucial case was *New York Times v. Sullivan* (1964).

"Uninhibited, Robust, and Wide-Open" Debate.   The events leading up to the case began with an advertisement in the *New York Times* in 1960 paid for by the Southern Christian Leadership Conference (SCLC), Martin Luther King, Jr.'s organization. Headed "Heed Their Rising Voices," the advertisement alleged that city officials in Montgomery, Alabama, had abused and maltreated civil rights demonstrators. Many of the facts in the advertisement turned out to be nonfacts, and Montgomery's commissioner of public affairs sued the SCLC for libel; he won a $500,000 judgment against the *New York Times* and the SCLC. They appealed, and the case ended up in the Supreme Court.

Written by Justice William Brennan, the Court's opinion turned upon a critical distinction—that between private and public officials. For a private individual to win a libel suit, he or she needs to prove only two things about what was written: (1) it was false, and (2) it was defamatory (damaging to the person's reputation). But a public official who is trying to sue for libel must take on a third burden: He or she must prove that the statement was made with <u>actual malice</u>—that is, "with knowledge that it was false or with reckless disregard" of its truth or falsity. Sullivan proved that the statements in the *New York Times* advertisement were false and defamatory, but because he could not meet this third burden, the judgment against the newspaper was reversed.

The added burden for public officials is based upon the premise that they are different from private individuals in at least three respects. First, they wield power; to make it too easy for them to sue their critics might inhibit criticism of government. In a memorable passage, Justice Brennan said that public debate must be "uninhibited, robust, and wide-open." Second, because their words can command the attention of the media, public officials are better prepared than the rest of us to set the record straight if they have been falsely accused of something. Third, public officials have chosen voluntarily to enter the limelight: "If you can't stand the heat, get out of the kitchen," former president Harry S. Truman used to say.

Since 1967 the Court has extended the *Sullivan* doctrine to cover not just public officials but all those "who by reason of the notoriety of their achievements or the vigor and success with which they seek the public's attention, are properly classified as public figures."[23] Even if they do not occupy public office, said the Court, "public figures" have powers the rest of us do not.

But it is hard enough to prove that a statement is false and defamatory; to prove actual malice is so difficult that most public figures do not even try. Those who do had better be prepared for a tough, and probably frustrating, battle. Take the cases of two generals, one American and one Israeli, who sued the media. In 1984 Israeli general Ariel Sharon sued Time, Inc., for $50 million, charging *Time* magazine with libel for implying that he had encouraged the massacre of Palestinians at the Sabra and Shatila refugee camps in Lebanon. In the same year retired U.S. general William C. Westmoreland sued CBS (and several individuals involved with CBS) for more than $100 million for accusing him of being part of a "conspiracy" to underestimate deliberately enemy troop strength during the Vietnam War.

Westmoreland's suit was dropped before it went to the jury (the case is reviewed in chapter 14). Sharon was more successful; he proved that what *Time* said was false and defamatory, but because he could not meet the burden of proving actual malice, the jury declared *Time* not guilty.

The Right to Assemble

Among the other First Amendment freedoms is "the right of the people peaceably to assemble, and to petition the Government for a redress of grievances." The Nazi Skokie march case was never decided by the Supreme Court, but on the basis of many precedents, we can get a clear idea of how the Court would have decided it. In 1937 it said that "peaceable assembly for lawful discussion cannot be made a crime."[24] During the 1960s, civil rights demonstrations put those words to the test, and in nearly every case, they prevailed. The Court upheld the right of demonstrators to sit in at a "whites only" lunch counter in Louisiana and of "freedom riders" who refused to leave the white waiting room of a bus depot.[25] It also upheld the right of protesters to demonstrate on statehouse grounds and in front of the city halls in South Carolina.[26] In all these cases, the peacefulness of the demonstrations weighed heavily

Points to Remember

1. Press freedom is guaranteed in the First Amendment. It enjoys the same protection, and is subject to the same qualifications, as freedom of speech. Press freedom also implies freedom from prior restraint. Although newspapers and other media may be punished afterward for what they have written, the rule is that they may almost never be restrained in advance.

2. In the Pentagon Papers case, *New York Times et al. v. United States* (1971), the Court upheld the right of the *New York Times* and other newspapers to publish photocopies of 7,000 pages of "top secret" documents stolen from the Pentagon.

3. The Supreme Court has ruled that obscenity is not protected by the First Amendment. The Court has had a difficult time, however, in spelling out the meaning of *obscenity*. Its present position is that material is obscene if its "dominant theme" is designed to appeal to "prurient interests." The Court prefers that particular applications of this rule rest in the hands of local communities, on the grounds that what is prurient in Mississippi may not be so in Manhattan.

4. In 1964 the Supreme Court said that if public officials are to win libel suits, they must prove not only

that what has been said about them is false and defamatory but that it was done with "actual malice" (with knowledge that the statement was false or with "reckless disregard" of whether it was true or false). Since then, the Court has extended its ruling to cover all public figures.

5. The Court has upheld the right of peaceable assembly, even when sponsored by organizations reputed to be violent or revolutionary. Any organization can assemble and demonstrate peacefully as long as it does not interfere with others' rights.

MAJOR SUPREME COURT RULINGS ON FREEDOM OF EXPRESSION

Schenck v. United States (1917)
Government may punish a speech activity if it presents a "clear and present danger" of an action that government has the authority to prevent.

Near v. Minnesota (1931)
Government may not restrain the press in advance of publication, except possibly in cases in which grave and irremedial damage would result from publication.

Chaplinsky v. New Hampshire (1942)
"Fighting words" are not protected by the First Amendment.

Roth v. United States (1957)
Obscenity is not protected by the First Amendment.

New York Times v. Sullivan (1964)
A successful libel or slander suit by a public official requires proof of "actual malice"—proof that the words in question were uttered or written with knowledge that they were false or with "reckless disregard" of their accuracy.

New York Times v. United States (1971)
A newspaper may print material taken from copies of documents stolen from the government and classified "top secret."

Miller v. California (1973)
In order to be considered obscene, material must appeal to "prurient interests," contain "patently offensive" depictions of sex, and lack any "serious literary, artistic, political, or scientific value." Such judgments are to be made by local juries applying local community standards.

Texas v. Johnson (1989)
Burning the American flag is a form of "symbolic speech" protected by the First Amendment.

with the Court. Yet peacefulness is not always enough. When Martin Luther King, Jr., and his followers refused to comply with a state court's injunction forbidding them to parade in Birmingham, Alabama, without a permit, the Court sustained their conviction (though by a narrow 5-4 majority) because "no man can be a judge in his own case, however exalted his station, however righteous his motive, and irrespective of race, color, politics, or religion."[27] For the same reason, any assembly, however peaceful, that blocks an entrance to a building or otherwise prevents people from doing what they have a lawful right to do is not protected by the First Amendment. Gay rights demonstrators, for example, may not disrupt Roman Catholic church services; pro-life demonstrators may not block the entrances to abortion clinics. Civil disobedience may be a moral right, but it is not a legal right.

The one constant in all these decisions is that "the right . . . to assemble, and to petition the government for a redress of grievances" must never turn upon whether or not we agree with the petitioners. Our First Amendment is saying this to all of us: "Whether or not you like civil rights marchers, Communists, homosexual activists, anti-abortion demonstrators—and, yes, even Nazis—they have a right to assemble in public places as long as they do it peacefully, do not incite violence, and do not interfere with the rights of others." Like rain, the right to assemble falls on the just and the unjust alike.

We have examined the issues of freedom of speech, freedom of press, and freedom of assembly in America. But so far we have neglected the topic the First Amendment mentions before anything else: religion.

Church and State

As we have seen, the First Amendment begins: "Congress shall make no law respecting an establishment of religion, or prohibiting the free exercise thereof." Note that there are two clauses: the establishment clause and the free exercise clause. In the minds of the Framers, the two clauses were related. As they understood it, an "established" church is one singled out as *the* church of the nation; it is given official recognition and support by the state, to the exclusion of all other churches. The Church of England was (and is) such a church, as was the Presbyterian church in much of New England. The lesson of history, as the Framers read it, was this: Once a particular church is encouraged to think of itself as the official religion, it gets tempted to persecute other religions or sects.

"WALL OF SEPARATION"—YET "BENIGN RELIGION"

Does this mean that the Founders believed in separation of church and state? Probably the best answer is "Yes, but . . ." They believed that the state should never try to act like a church: deciding what is orthodox, condemning heresy, prescribing particular creeds. Conversely, they believed, a church should never try to act like a state: using physical coercion to enforce conformity. It was apparently the latter danger that President Thomas Jefferson had in mind in 1802 when, replying to a letter from a group of Baptists in Danbury, Connecticut, he spoke of the need to maintain a wall of separation between church and state in America. The complaint of the Danbury Baptists was that they were being forced to observe religious fasts proclaimed by the established Presbyterian church in Connecticut. Such coercion had always troubled Jefferson. In 1785, two years before the Constitution was written, Jefferson wrote the Statute of Virginia for Religious Freedom, which states that since "Almighty God has created the mind free," any attempts to influence it "by temporal punishments, or burdens, or by civil incapacitations, tend only to beget hypocrisy and meanness." Jefferson's bill, introduced by his friend James Madison, became a Virginia law in 1786.

But Jefferson's wall of separation is a metaphor that has to be understood in context. Most of America's early statesmen were enemies of religious persecution, but they were not hostile to religion. In contrast to their European counterparts, American friends of self-government considered religion an essential pillar of republican government. Their belief was that religion teaches self-restraint ("republican virtue"), which is necessary if the restraints of the state are to be relaxed. Jefferson himself shared this view. He was a deist, as were James Madison and some of the other Founders.[28] Deists cared little about religious differences, for theirs was a God of Nature rather than the Bible. "It does me no injury for my neighbor to say there are twenty Gods or no God," Jefferson once wrote. "It neither picks my pocket nor breaks my leg." But he thought that religion *in general* exerts a wholesome influence on society. In his First Inaugural he celebrated the fact that American citizens were "enlightened by a benign religion, professed indeed, and practiced in various forms, yet all of them inculcating honesty, truth, temperance, gratitude, and the love of man." George Washington put it more emphatically in his Farewell Address: "Let us be very cautious," he said, about indulging "the proposition that morality can be maintained without religion."

"A RELIGIOUS PEOPLE"

Washington's belief was widely shared by Americans in the early years of the republic. Alexis de Tocqueville, the famous French observer who visited America in the 1830s, wrote: "I do not know whether all Americans have a sincere faith in their religion—for who can search the human heart?—but I am certain that they hold it to be indispensable to the maintenance of republican institutions." The view was embodied in much early legislation. The Northwest Ordinance of 1787, which was passed again by the First Congress in 1789, stated: "Religion, morality, and knowledge being necessary to good government and the happiness of mankind, schools and the means of learning shall forever be encouraged." Beginning in 1796 and culminating in 1804, Congress passed laws that paid (with enormous land grants) an evangelical Christian sect to spread the gospel among the Indians in the Ohio Territory. In 1803 the U.S. Senate ratified an Indian treaty submitted to it by President Jefferson that included a clause pledging the United States to build a Catholic church and provide a yearly stipend for its priest. And the same Congress that passed the First Amendment also established the congressional chaplain system. An annual salary of $500 was appropriated for public prayer in Congress. In short, though America's early leaders believed in separation of church and state, they welcomed and even promoted religious influence in public life. Their wall of separation was quite porous.

Religion has always been an influence in American public life. Official proclamations have been laced with references to the Deity; "In God We Trust" has been stamped on our coins; chaplains in Congress and the armed services have been paid out of taxpayers' funds; churches have been tax-exempt; and the Supreme Court itself begins every day with its bailiff's cry: "God save the United States and this honorable Court." Looking back over our history in 1952, Supreme Court justice William O. Douglas declared: "We are a religious people whose institutions presuppose a Supreme Being."[29] But in 1962 the Supreme Court seemed to chart a new course when it issued its first and most famous school prayer decision, *Engel v. Vitale*.

ENGEL v. VITALE (1962): BANNING PUBLIC SCHOOL PRAYER

The case grew out of these 22 words: "Almighty God, we acknowledge our dependence upon Thee, and we beg thy blessings upon us, our parents, our teacher, and our country." The prayer, recited in many public school classrooms in New York State, was composed by the New York State Board of Regents. Note that it refers to God but not to Jesus, the Blessed Virgin, or any other figure associated with a particular religious denomination. It was composed after consultation with Catholic, Protestant, and Jewish religious leaders and was intended to be completely non-denominational. The Regents also stipulated that it was to be voluntary. Any child who did not wish to say it could remain silent or leave the room while it was being said.

Nevertheless, it was challenged by a group of five parents (two Jews, one Unitarian, one member of the Ethical Culture Union, and one atheist), whose lawyer argued that the establishment clause was meant "to keep religion out of our public life."[30] The interpretation was essentially that of Justice Black in *Everson v. Board of Education*: The establishment clause forbids aid to religion even if it is aid to *all* religions. As it turned out, Black gave the majority opinion in *Engel*, and he agreed with the parents. Public school prayer, he said, is an establishment of religion— perhaps not a particular religion, but religion—and such a union of government and religion "tends to destroy government and to degrade religion."

The prayer in the *Engel* case was officially composed. What if it had been a traditional prayer said by religious people for centuries? Any hopes for such an exemption to the prayer ban were dashed a year after the *Engel* decision when the Court struck down the recitation of the Lord's Prayer and biblical passages in public schools.[31]

The *Lemon* Law: Three Tests. Building on these and other cases, the Court in 1971 tried to work out a set of principles that would allow the state to benefit citizens who happened to be religious without directly aiding religion. In *Lemon v. Kurtzman*

(1971), the Court ruled that state payment of salaries to teachers of secular subjects at religious schools was an unconstitutional "aid to religion." The Court said that a statute might *incidentally* benefit religion without violating the establishment clause, but for such a statute to pass constitutional muster, it must meet these three criteria:

- It must have a clearly secular purpose.
- It must neither advance nor inhibit religion.
- It must not result in "excessive" government "entanglement" with religion.

The *Lemon* tests raise some obvious questions. What is an "entanglement," and when does it become "excessive"? Why cannot government "advance" religion? And how can religion be aided, even incidentally, without in some way being "advanced"? Still, the *Lemon* tests provided a framework for deciding future cases, although some have put considerable strain on it.

RELIGION AND STATE: TOTAL SEPARATION?

What did the Founders mean by the establishment clause? There are grounds for different interpretations. On the one hand, as pointed out earlier in the chapter, we know that the Framers tended to think of religion in general as a benign force and they encouraged it by various means. On the other hand, we have the language of the clause. Written by James Madison, it forbids Congress to make any law "respecting an establishment of religion." That sounds broader than merely a ban on an "established church." In a major study of the establishment clause, historian Leonard Levy points out that on three occasions the Senate of the First Congress considered narrower wordings of the clause (which would have merely banned preferential treatment) and rejected them; the fourth time they did adopt a narrower wording but then abandoned it in the face of opposition from the House.[32]

In October 1988 presidential candidates George Bush and Michael Dukakis appear pleased to be photographed with a representative of the Roman Catholic church, Cardinal John O'Conner, Archbishop of New York.

Apart from the legal question of what the establishment clause means is this critical policy issue: *Should* religion and the state be kept entirely separate in America? Again, opinions differ. Many Americans would agree with *Time* magazine essayist Roger Rosenblatt's view that religion and state are "natural enemies" because they make "competing claims on the mind." Faith, says Rosenblatt, "implies the refusal to accept any laws but God's." This leads him to ask: "How can a government that relies on the perpetuation of its authority be compatible with an institution that takes dictates from invisible powers?"[33] Other Americans would agree with the Reverend Richard Neuhaus, a Lutheran pastor, who contends that the very authority of our government depends upon its ties to our Judeo-Christian heritage. There will be nothing, says Neuhaus, "but a continuing and deepening crisis of legitimacy if courts persist in systematically ruling out of order the moral traditions" underlying Western law.[34]

Reflections

The theme of this chapter is balance. The Bill of Rights was put into the Constitution to protect individual human rights. But there are limits to those rights. One person's rights must at times be balanced against another person's. And society also has rights. No one has the right to falsely shout "Fire!" in a crowded theater. For the same reason, said the Supreme Court in the famous *Schenck* case of 1919, no one has a right to use speech to incite a criminal act.

The written word may be less likely to incite than oral speech, but it too is subject to restraints. A newspaper does not have the right to print defamatory falsehoods about an individual. Otherwise, its "right" would really amount to a tyrannical power—the power to use lies with impunity to destroy reputations. But to speak ill of government officials is not quite the same as to defame a private individual. Officials, even public figures, have ample means of fighting back, since they have easy access to the media. Also, because they have chosen to be in the limelight, they cannot complain too much when they are criticized. These were two reasons why the Supreme Court, in *New York Times v. Sullivan* (1964), made it more difficult for public figures to sue for libel. But there was a larger reason behind the Court's ruling. The Court wanted to make sure that the threat of libel suits would not make people afraid to criticize their leaders. Public debate, said Justice William Brennan, must be "uninhibited, robust, and wide-open."

The theme of balance is illustrated again by the controversy over church-state relations. It is an emotional controversy. Even so, all sides seem to agree that (1) The First Amendment forbids the establishment of a national Church of America. No particular sect may be singled out for official patronage and financial support. (2) The First Amendment protects not merely belief but the *exercise* of belief. We do not have to keep our religious beliefs "private," confined to our hearts or our homes. The question, then, is not whether religion should be allowed in public or not. The question is to what extent the *state* should be allowed to intermingle with religion.

Concerning all the issues raised in this chapter—speech, press, assembly, and religion—debate has been intense and sometimes emotional. This is understandable. Americans care deeply about these issues and are seriously divided on how to resolve them. Perhaps the only underlying consensus is that it is good to debate. We Americans believe that truth will win out in a fair fight with error. We have staked everything on that faith. For if people cannot, after hearing all the arguments, be trusted to separate truth from error, they should not be allowed to govern themselves. Put the other way, if we are not allowed to hear all points of view, then no matter how much voting we do, we are not really self-governing. That is why Justice Brennan was surely right to insist that public debate in this country must be "uninhibited, robust, and wide-open." It follows that anyone who would shout down a speaker for advocating what may sound like "communism," "fascism," "racism," "imperialism," or any other "ism" that people do not like to hear is fundamentally at odds with American democracy.

Notes

1. J. Anthony Lucas, "The ACLU Against Itself," *New York Times Magazine*, July 9, 1978, p. 10.
2. Lucas, p. 10.
3. David Hamlin, *The Nazi/Skokie Conflict* (Boston: Beacon Press, 1980), p. 174.
4. Hamlin, p. 123.
5. John Stuart Mill, *On Liberty* (1859; reprint, Indianapolis, IN: Hacket Publishing Co., 1978), p. 41.
6. John Milton, *Areopagitica* (1644).
7. *Abrams v. United States*, 250 U.S. 616 (1919).
8. *Schenck v. United States*, 249 U.S. 47 (1919). In *Dennis v. United States*, 341 U.S. 494 (1951), the Court gave the government even more leeway in punishing political advocacy. The Court upheld the constitutionality of the Smith Act of 1940, a law that punishes even the "conspiracy" to advocate violent overthrow of the U.S. government. In subsequent cases the Court whittled down the force of *Dennis* by requiring proof that the advocacy be in the form of "incitement," but the decision has never been overturned.
9. See further, *Feiner v. New York*, 340 U.S. 315 (1951), which raised the related issue of "heckler's veto." Feiner, standing on a street corner in Syracuse, New York, delivered an inflammatory political speech that stirred up the crowd—against *him*. One member of his audience said to a policeman who was present, "If you don't get that son of a bitch off of there, I will go over and get him off myself." The officer then arrested Feiner and charged him with disorderly conduct. Feiner appealed on First Amendment grounds, but the Court, in a 6-3 decision, upheld the conviction. It is questionable whether *Feiner* is still a live precedent, though it has never been overruled. In *Edwards v. South Carolina*, 372 U.S. 229 (1963), the Court reversed breach of peace convictions against 187 civil rights demonstrators who, like Feiner, had angered a large crowd. Justice Potter Stewart, speaking for the majority, insisted that the circumstances in this case were a "far cry" from those in *Feiner*. But were they? In both cases there was no violence nor were there even "fighting words," and the only "clear and present danger" was to the speakers themselves, not to anyone else.
10. *Stromberg v. California*, 283 U.S. 359 (1931); *Tinker v. Des Moines School District*, 393 U.S. 503 (1969); *Spence v. Washington*, 418 U.S. 405 (1974).
11. *United States v. O'Brien*, 391 U.S. 367 (1968).
12. *Texas v. Johnson* (1989).
13. Letter to *New York Times*, Nov. 13, 1985, p. A26.
14. Quoted in Leonard W. Levy, *Emergence of a Free Press* (New York: Oxford University Press, 1985), pp. 12-13.
15. *Near v. Minnesota*, 283 U.S. 697 (1931).
16. See Justice Byron White's opinion in *New York Times et al. v. United States*, 403 U.S. 713 (1971).

17. Justice Potter Stewart, concurring opinion, *Jacobellis v. Ohio* (1964).

18. *Jacobellis v. Ohio*, 378 U.S. 184 (1964); *Memoirs v. Massachusetts*, 383 U.S. 413 (1966).

19. *Sable Communications v. Federal Communications Commission* (1989).

20. Barbara Gamerekian, "Crowd at Corcoran Protests Mapplethorpe Cancellation," *New York Times*, July 1, 1989, p. 14.

21. See, for example, Hilton Kramer, "Is Art Above the Laws of Decency?" *New York Times*, July 2, 1989, part II, pp. 1, 7.

22. Two major government-sponsored studies of the question, one in 1970 and the other in 1986, have reached opposite conclusions. The 1970 study said that it did not cause harm and recommended decriminalization. See *The Report of the Commission on Obscenity and Pornography* (Washington, D.C.: U.S. Government Printing Office, 1970). The later study concluded that at least some forms of it (violent pornography) did have harmful effects, and it recommended tougher enforcement of obscenity laws. See *Final Report, Attorney General's Commission on Pornography* (Washington, D.C.: U.S. Government Printing Office, 1986). Both studies have been accused of faulty methodology and ideological bias.

23. The above formulation is from *Gertz v. Robert Welch, Inc.* (1974), but the extension was first made in *Curtis Publishing Co. v. Butts* (1967).

24. *Dejonge v. Oregon*, 299 U.S. 353 (1937).

25. *Garner v. Louisiana*, 368 U.S. 157 (1961).

26. *Edwards v. South Carolina*, 372 U.S. 229 (1963); *Fields v. South Carolina*, 375 U.S. 44 (1963); *Henry v. Rock Hill*, 376 U.S. 776 (1964).

27. *Walker v. Birmingham* (1967).

28. Contrary to myth, most of the Founders were traditional Christians. See M. E. Bradford, *Worthy Company: Brief Lives of the Framers of the Constitution* (Marlborough, MA: Plymouth Rock Foundation, 1982).

29. *Zorach v. Clausen*, 343 U.S. 306 (1952).

30. See Fred W. Friendly and Martha J. H. Elliott, *The Constitution: That Delicate Balance* (New York: Random House, 1984), p. 122.

31. *School District of Abington Township v. Schempp* (1963); *Murray v. Curlett* (1963).

32. See Leonard W. Levy, *The Establishment Clause: Religion and the First Amendment* (New York: Macmillan, 1986), pp. 81-84. Since the proceedings were conducted behind closed doors and no record was kept, it is hard to say why the narrower constructions were rejected. What we do have of the public debate on the establishment clause is intriguing. In the *Annals of Congress*, we see a number of members of Congress expressing their concern about Madison's broad language. Congressman Benjamin Huntington, in particular, told James Madison he feared that his language "might be taken in such latitude as to be extremely hurtful to the cause of religion." Huntington hoped that the amendment might be written in such a way as to protect freedom of conscience "but not *to patronize those who professed no religion at all.*" Madison hastened to reassure Huntington and the others that this was not his intention. The official stenographer wrote: "Mr. Madison thought, if the word national was inserted before religion, it would satisfy the minds of the honorable gentlemen. He believed that the people fear one sect might obtain a pre-eminence, or two combine together, and establish *a* religion to which they would compel others to conform" (emphasis added). Madison retreated from the word *national* after Congressman Elbridge Gerry of Massachusetts warned that it would alarm people who were already worried that the new government threatened states' rights. But Madison still thought that "no national religion shall be established by law" was a good way to phrase it (*Annals of Congress*, August 15, 1789, in Bernard Schwartz, ed., *The Bill of Rights: A Documentary History* [New York: Chelsea House, 1971], vol. II, pp. 1088-89).

33. Roger Rosenblatt, "Defenders of the Faith," *Time*, Nov. 12, 1984, p. 112.

34. Richard John Neuhaus, *The Naked Public Square: Religion and Democracy in America* (Grand Rapids, MI: Eerdmans, 1984).

5

Civil Rights

The *Bakke* Case

Professor John Tupper had achieved a minor miracle— maybe a major one. A medical professor at the University of Michigan in 1965, Dr. Tupper was recruited by the University of California to build a medical school at its Davis campus. He was given four years to do it. "The standard lead time to build a medical school is 6 to 10 years," he recalled later. "We did it in 32 months."[*]

But Dr. Tupper had little time for self-congratulation. He confronted a host of problems once the school opened. Perhaps the most troublesome was the fact that so few members of minority groups were attending Davis. Only about 3 percent of the medical school's first two classes were minority students, and most of those were Asians. The school had admitted just two blacks and one Chicano.

The members of the admissions committee were bothered by these figures. In the spring of 1971 Dr. Tupper and some of his colleagues met

---

[*]This narrative is adapted from chapter 13, "*Bakke* and the Equal Protection Clause," in Fred W. Friendly and Martha J. H. Elliott, *The Constitution: That Delicate Balance* (New York: Random House, 1984).

with black and Hispanic leaders at a restaurant in nearby Sacramento, where Dr. Tupper made a bold commitment: "I make all of you this promise—next fall we'll have 100 [new] students in the medical school, and I guarantee you that we'll have 16 places for the disadvantaged." A year and a half later, in the fall of 1972, an ex-marine by the name of Allan Bakke filled out applications for 11 medical schools, including the University of California at Davis.

Allan Paul Bakke was born in Minnesota of German descent. A few years after he applied to Davis, all the newspapers would have his picture: a full, wholesome face, with blond hair combed across a high forehead; balding but still boyish-looking at age 32. He wanted to go to medical school. In fact, he was determined to go to medical school. Bakke had put himself through college by serving in the Naval Reserve Officers Training Corps. He did a stint in Vietnam, then went to work at NASA's Ames Research Center in Moffet Field, California. While doing so, he completed work on a master's degree in engineering at Stanford University.

But by then Bakke's dream was to be a doctor. He began taking the biology and chemistry courses required for medical school, and he spent his evenings working as a volunteer in a nearby hospital. To Bakke, medicine had become a calling. An admissions officer at Davis later described him as "a man who felt as strongly as anyone I've ever known about his potential as a healer of the sick and as a benefactor of the community. . . . He struck me as a character out of a Bergman film— somewhat humorless, perfectly straightforward, zealous in his approach. . . . He was an extremely impressive man."[1]

By this time the Davis medical school had made good on Dr. Tupper's promise; it had a two-channel admissions system, one channel for whites and another for nonwhites. Out of the 100 available seats in the entering class, 84 were filled through the regular channel. The other 16 were guaranteed to nonwhites.

Bakke's application was processed through the regular route, in which any applicant with a college grade point average of 2.5 (C+/B−) or below was automatically rejected. Since Bakke's was better than 2.5, he advanced to the next stage, the interview. After the interview, each candidate was given a benchmark score based upon three factors: the impression the candidate made during the interview, the candidate's grade point average, and the candidate's score on the Medical College Admissions Test (MCAT). For the year Bakke applied, a benchmark score of 470 was the minimum for automatic admission. Bakke, given a score of 468, was rejected.

Candidates for special admissions were not automatically rejected if their grade point averages were below 2.5. Instead, those who, in the opinion of the administrators, showed promise were interviewed by members of a committee set up to review nonwhite candidates. During the 1972-73 school year, administrators drew up a list of 16 candidates and recommended them to the interviewing committee. The committee admitted all 16. Not surprisingly, these new Davis students had grade point averages and MCAT scores on the whole significantly lower than those of students who came through the regular admissions route.

Davis had instituted a policy that has come to be called affirmative action. The concept of affirmative action is based upon the assumption that to reach the goal of racial equality, we must do more than simply stop discriminating against racial minorities; we must take positive steps to repair the damage. The common denominator in these steps involves

In 1973 Allan Bakke was rejected by the University of California–Davis Medical School without being allowed to compete for vacancies reserved by quota to minority applicants. He filed suit against the university for racial discrimination, arguing that he had been rejected because he was white. In 1978 the Supreme Court ruled that Bakke's rights had indeed been violated through the use of segregated admission standards, although it left room for "race-conscious" programs benefiting minorities.

giving special consideration to racial minorities (and, in more recent years, women). Affirmative action thus entails a certain degree of race consciousness or gender consciousness. Race and gender must be taken into account in weighing the merits of an applicant.

Bakke, deeply disappointed at being turned down by Davis, wrote to the director of admissions asking if there was any way he could be put on standby or admitted provisionally. After a month went by with no answer, Bakke wrote again, this time in a different tone. "I am convinced," he said, that a "significant fraction" of those admitted to Davis have been "judged by a separate criterion."[2] He hinted that he might begin legal action against the school. Bakke reapplied for the next year's class and was rejected again. This time, he took the school to court.

He said he was a victim of reverse discrimination. A state trial court agreed but refused to order his admittance; the court said that Bakke had not shown that he would have gotten into Davis if it had not been for the special admissions program. Bakke fared much better when the case was appealed to the California Supreme Court. In a 6-1 decision the court not only agreed that Bakke's constitutional rights had been violated but put the burden on the medical school to show why he should not be admitted. When the school was unable to meet that burden, the court ordered it to admit Bakke. The court stayed its order, however, pending a final appeal to the U.S. Supreme Court.

The line of spectators waiting to hear the arguments in the case of *University of California Regents v. Bakke* (1978) snaked down the marble steps of the Supreme Court building and around the block.[3] Five years had elapsed since Bakke, now 37, first applied to Davis and feelings ran high. Some, like Bakke, saw it as a case of reverse discrimination. Others saw it as a ludicrous and shameful attempt by some whites to use civil rights laws as a means of reversing the progress of blacks in America.

There was great bitterness on both sides. How could the Supreme Court decide this controversy without setting off an explosion? Yet the Court did decide the case, and the explosion never occurred. Maybe that was because both sides had trouble figuring out what the Court had said.

The Court split three ways. Four members voted against the Davis admissions system because it used "race-conscious" standards. Another four voted to uphold Davis; for them, its two-track admissions system was a legitimate means of remedying the effects of racism. If there were only eight justices on the Court, it would have been a tie. But there are nine, and the ninth member, Justice Lewis F. Powell, Jr., was of two minds. On the one hand, he agreed that there might be a legitimate purpose in increasing the number of minorities in medical school and that this might justify the use of race as *one* criterion—to be weighed along with others—in deciding on a candidate's merits. Yet he opposed the use of strict quotas: the setting aside of a number of seats exclusively for nonwhites and the use of a separate set of standards for those candidates. That, of course, was Davis's policy. Powell joined the four justices who voted against the Davis admissions policy, making the decision a 5-4 victory for Allan Bakke. *And yet* Powell joined the other four justices in arguing that an applicant's race may be a relevant factor to consider in making admissions decisions.

There was something for everybody in Powell's opinion. It sided with Bakke, but it also sided with the philosophy of remedial race consciousness. Every other justice on the Court agreed with part of it, but, by the same token, disagreed with part of it. Taken as a whole, Powell's opinion was the most minority of minority opinions—an opinion of one. Yet it has been called the controlling opinion of the Bakke case, and in a way it was. It tipped the Court's balance both ways—toward Bakke and toward race consciousness.

The University of California at Davis made a place for Allan Bakke in the entering class of September 1978. He completed his four years without further incident and at graduation received a standing ovation from his classmates. As for Davis, it continued its efforts to recruit minorities, but it was not easy; blacks shied away from the school. Ironically, the *Bakke* case was so widely misunderstood that many thought the school had been taken to court for *excluding* blacks.[4]

*   *   *   *   *

The Declaration of Independence asserts that "all men are created equal." Americans are justifiably proud of their nation's commitment to the ideal of equality. Yet there is a darker side to the American tradition. Blacks, other minorities, and women have all suffered some form of oppression during the course of American history. Even after slavery was abolished by the Thirteenth Amendment in 1865, many Americans were still deprived of some of the most elementary rights: the right to vote, the right to mingle freely with other Americans, the right of access to the job market, the right to an education on an equal basis with others. Not until the 1950s did the Supreme Court begin to challenge official segregation, and not until the 1960s did Congress and the president act vigorously to break its grip.

The scars remain. Women lag behind men in income and are often ghettoized in low-paying "women's" jobs. Blacks lag behind whites in nearly every category, from employment to health. Other minorities also can claim to have suffered from the long-term effects of discrimination. To the extent that we believe in the proposition that "all men are created equal," we know that we must redress these inequities.

In doing so, however, we may end up by taking something away from another group. Allan Bakke's chances of getting into medical school may have been adversely affected by Davis's policy of reserving 16 seats for minorities. In any event, he and other whites were not being treated the same as the minority applicants. In some cases, such unequal treatment may be justified. There were persuasive arguments presented for it in the *Bakke* case. Even so, it always involves difficult questions of ethics and public policy.

The problem of who is entitled to preferential treatment is particularly difficult in America because we are a nation of minorities and few are the minorities that have not suffered discrimination in this country. In the nineteenth century Jews worked in sweatshops under horrible conditions and were excluded from many public accommodations. "No Irish Need Apply" advisories were once common in newspaper want ads. Italian laborers were sometimes paid at a "special" rate, below that of blacks.[5] American Indians were cheated out of their lands, massacred, and reduced to poverty and dependency. Many Puerto Ricans and Mexicans continue to live in poverty in this country, struggling with language barriers and stereotypes. Slavic Americans can recount the brutal treatment their ancestors received when they worked the coal mines of Pennsylvania.[6] More than 100,000 Japanese, including those of American birth, were put into "relocation" camps during World War II; they and other Asians still suffer discrimination despite their tradition of hard work, or perhaps because of it.[7] Homosexual political activists cite examples of what they call American "homophobia," including the Supreme Court's 1986 decision upholding a Georgia law against homosexual activity.[8]

By present-day experience or by inheritance, then, just about every group in America can claim "victim" status.[9] This chapter would be unwieldy if it sought to follow the trials of them all. Fortunately, that is not its purpose. Instead, what it attempts to do is study the background, nature, and limits of civil rights in this country. Civil rights have been defined as "positive acts of government designed to protect persons against arbitrary or discriminatory treatment by government or individuals."[10] The focus of this chapter is not so much on suffering—though it will not avoid the topic—as it is on the positive acts of government designed to remedy discrimination, on the merits of those acts, and on the political struggles behind them. It will single out two groups, blacks and women, not because they are the only groups to have suffered discrimination but because of the wide-ranging nature of the issues raised. The issues concern virtually every other group and probe the most deeply held values of Americans.

Blacks: The Heritage of Discrimination

"We didn't land on Plymouth Rock, my brothers and sisters—Plymouth Rock landed on *us*."[11] Malcolm X's observation is borne out by the facts of American history. Snatched from their native land, transported thousands of miles, and sold into slavery, blacks in America were reduced to the legal status of farm animals. A Supreme Court opinion, *Dred Scott v. Sandford* (1857), made this status official by classifying slaves as a kind of private property.

This is the heritage, "the stain on our history," as the late Supreme Court justice Potter Stewart once called it, whose traces we are still trying to remove. The Thirteenth Amendment, passed in 1865, formally reversed *Dred Scott* by outlawing slavery or "involuntary servitude." The South reacted by passing the Black Codes, which severely limited the rights of the newly freed slaves, preventing them in most states from testifying in court against whites, limiting their opportunities to find work, and relegating them to the status of second- or third-class citizens.

Then came Reconstruction, which seemed like the dawn of a new era to American blacks. Reconstruction was a far-reaching reorganization plan imposed by Congress on the South at the end of the Civil War. Before the defeated Southern states could be admitted to the Union, they had to guarantee suffrage and equal treatment to blacks. The Fourteenth Amendment, passed in 1868, made blacks citizens and promised them—promised all—"the equal protection of the laws." In 1870 the Fifteenth Amendment was passed, which guaranteed the right to vote regardless of "race, color, or previous condition of servitude." Congress also passed a number of civil rights laws barring discrimination against blacks in hotels, theaters, and other public places. Blacks ran for office, and, in some cases, they and their white supporters assumed control of southern legislatures.

But Reconstruction was short-lived. Soon, white vigilante groups like the Ku Klux Klan began to reappear; they terrorized and murdered blacks who tried to exercise their new rights. "Legal" ways were also found for circumventing the new civil rights laws and amendments. Grandfather clauses, which limited the right of suffrage to those who had voted before 1867 or were the children or grandchildren of those who had, were attached to state constitutions. Poll taxes, to be paid before voting, kept poor blacks from casting their votes. White-only primary elections were established. Social discrimination and intimidation were constant: Blacks were expected to move off the sidewalk to make room for whites; they were to address whites with great respect (yet blacks were called by their first names); and a black man who even looked at a white woman ran the risk of hanging or castration. Blacks were excluded from education and from any except the most menial jobs. The condition of blacks took a new turn for the worse after the 1876 presidential election. The Democratic candidate, Samuel J. Tilden, and the Republican, Rutherford B. Hayes, were nearly tied in electoral votes; the outcome depended on those of a few "unreconstructed" states. Democrats and Republicans feuded over whether or not and how to count those votes. The matter was referred to a bipartisan electoral commission and finally to the United States Senate. In the final stages, a deal was cut: The Democrats, who represented the white South, would agree to let Republican Hayes win the election if Hayes would then withdraw federal troops from the South (the troops whose presence was necessary to enforce the Reconstruction laws). The Republicans agreed to the deal, and Hayes honored it in April 1877 by pulling out the troops. The Hayes-Tilden compromise thus permitted the white South to turn back the clock with impunity. By the time the last Union troops left the South in 1877, most of the gains of Reconstruction were badly eroded. Over the next 20 years, they virtually disappeared.

The Supreme Court made it all official. In 1883 it declared unconstitutional a key civil rights statute passed during Reconstruction, the one that barred discrimination in hotels, restaurants, and other places of public accommodation.[12] Not until 1964 would another such federal statute be passed.

PLESSY V. FERGUSON (1896): SEPARATE BUT EQUAL

Then, in 1896, came *Plessy v. Ferguson*. To understand this and later cases, we must keep in mind the distinction between *de facto* and *de jure* segregation. *De facto* segregation (segregation "in fact") results from the movement of people; it is not required by law. For example, college cafeterias and dormitories may show some patterns of *de facto* segregation of races and groups. The wisdom of this separation may be debated, but it does not usually raise questions of justice or legality. *De jure*

Under the *Plessy v. Ferguson* (1896) doctrine of separate but equal, the South adopted a set of laws to deal with their black population. These laws were commonly known as "Jim Crow laws." The Jim Crow laws denied black people the same rights and privileges as other citizens. This situation lasted until the Supreme Court ruled that separate but equal was unconstitutional in the landmark case *Brown v. Board of Education of Topeka, Kansas* (1954), in which segregation was made illegal in public schools and institutions.

When Mrs. Rosa Parks refused to give up her seat to a white man and move to the back of a city bus in Montgomery, Alabama, on December 1, 1955, she provided the catalyst by which the civil rights movement was born. That event also gave rise to a hitherto unknown black preacher named Martin Luther King, Jr., who led the boycott against the city bus company.

segregation is something quite different: It is segregation that is required by law. The coercive arm of the state enforces racial segregation. It was *de jure* segregation that was involved in the *Plessy* case. The state of Louisiana had passed a statute requiring the segregation of railroad cars; blacks were forbidden to enter "white" cars. The U.S. Supreme Court upheld the law as a valid exercise of the state's "police power." The logical extension of this decision was that all states had the right to segregate the races in every public facility, from washrooms to schools. Thus began the heyday of Jim Crow legislation, which in South Africa is called apartheid and in America, "separate but equal." The assumption that people can be separated by race yet treated equally ran through the *Plessy* decision, and only one person on the Court, Justice John Marshall Harlan, knew how wrong that assumption was. In a lone, bitter dissent, Harlan wrote: "The thin disguise of 'equal' accommodations for passengers in railroad coaches will not mislead anyone, not atone for the wrong this day done."[13]

During the early years of this century, the doctrine of separate but equal reigned supreme. *De jure* separation of the races was rigidly enforced in the South and even in some northern areas. Whether it was schools or washrooms, drinking fountains or restaurants, blacks were denied the use of "whites-only" facilities. This state of things went on for nearly 60 years until the Supreme Court's *Brown* decision of 1954.

THE *BROWN* DECISION (1954) AND ITS AFTERMATH

Brown v. Board of Education of Topeka, Kansas (1954) actually consisted of four separate cases involving public school segregation, from the states of Delaware, South Carolina, Virginia, and Kansas. The Court considered them together because they all involved the same issue: whether or not *de jure* racial segregation violates the "equal protection" clause of the Fourteenth Amendment. A unanimous Supreme Court said that it did.

Why? Because, said the Court, it "generates a feeling of inferiority" in the black children, which in turn "may affect their hearts and minds in a way unlikely ever to be undone."[14] For this reason, the Court added, "separate educational facilities are inherently unequal." It was a sweeping decision, and it effectively overruled *Plessy*. Though *Brown* dealt specifically with education, the Court soon extended its scope so as to overrule *de jure* segregation in all areas.

It is one thing to announce a doctrine, another to see it come to life. In fact, separate and unequal conditions remained a way of life in the South and elsewhere. In 1957 President Eisenhower had to call federal troops into Little Rock, Arkansas, after the state's governor forcibly barred black children from entering white schools. In the South of the 1950s, social customs, "private" discrimination, and laws were woven together in a web of humiliation for black Americans.

But by now a grass-roots movement had developed. One day in 1955, a middle-aged seamstress named Rosa Parks refused to move to the back of a bus in Montgomery, Alabama. She was arrested and fined, but her act sparked a citywide black boycott of the bus company that lasted more than a year. The boycott worked, and it set a pattern followed by blacks in other cities. One of the leaders of this historic boycott was a young Baptist minister named Martin Luther King, Jr.

CIVIL RIGHTS IN THE 1960s

Restaurants and lunch counters remained segregated throughout the South. But at the end of the 1950s a group of very serious, very earnest divinity students from black colleges began sitting down at "white-only" lunch counters in Greensboro, North Carolina. Ordered to leave, they refused and were hauled off to jail. Then other black students took their places.

This photograph was taken during the first sit-in at a lunch counter in Greensboro, North Carolina, in February 1960. Students from North Carolina A & T College asked for coffee at Woolworth's lunch counter in Greensboro. When they were refused service they began the first sit-in. Non-violent demonstrations such as these helped to turn the tide in the struggle for civil rights in America.

The sit-ins were still going on when John F. Kennedy began his campaign for the presidency. During the next 10 years, everything happened quickly. Kennedy promised a "New Frontier." Expectations rose dramatically, and there was heightened frustration over the slow pace of change. Riots broke out in northern cities. In the South the civil rights leaders were still in control, however, and they kept demonstrations peaceful. The dignity of their marches was impressive, especially when compared to the ugly reaction they elicited from the southern authorities. And it all appeared, for the first time, on national television. Viewers were shocked at what they saw: police dogs, cattle prods, and fire hoses used against unarmed and nonviolent demonstrators. A new bipartisan consensus began to form around the need for legislation to end compulsory inequality. During the presidency of Lyndon B. Johnson, Congress passed new and sweeping civil rights measures, and the administration enforced them vigorously.

The Civil Rights Act of 1964 had three major provisions. First was a ban on racial discrimination in hotels, motels, restaurants, and other public accommodations involved in interstate commerce—which meant practically all of them. That decision put back into the law what the Supreme Court had removed with its 1883 decision. (This provision too was challenged in the courts, but the Supreme Court upheld it.)[15] Another provision of the act banned discrimination in employment. A third banned discrimination at any educational institution receiving federal money. (Bakke was to cite that provision, along with the Fourteenth Amendment, in challenging the UC Davis admissions system.) The Voting Rights Act of 1965 finally broke the back of southern resistance to black suffrage. It authorized the U.S. attorney general to appoint federal examiners to register voters in areas from which blacks had been systematically excluded. The Civil Rights Act of 1968 prohibited discrimination in the sale or rental of housing. Other laws and executive orders passed during the 1960s supplemented these three major laws. There were also two constitutional amendments that helped to empower black voters. The Twenty-third Amendment, ratified in

Pictures of police dogs lunging at demonstrators in Birmingham, Alabama, in May 1963 shocked America and created the climate for the passage of major civil rights laws in the 1960s.

(Continued on page 110)

Dec. 1, 1955: Montgomery, AL. Rosa Parks is arrested by Montgomery police for refusing to give up her seat on a municipal bus to a white man. Blacks retaliate with a yearlong boycott of the bus company, led by the young Martin Luther King, Jr.

Sept. 25, 1957: Little Rock, AR. When the governor of Arkansas calls out the Arkansas National Guard to block court-ordered integration of the city's all-white Central High School, President Dwight Eisenhower sends federal troops to escort nine black teenagers into the school and keep order.

Feb. 1, 1960: Greensboro, NC. Four black students from North Carolina A & T College stage the first sit-in at a "whites-only" lunch counter in Woolworth's.

May 4, 1961: Alabama. Black and white students, called "Freedom Riders," are beaten and stoned by whites for attempting to sit in the "whites-only" sections of interstate buses and terminals.

Sept. 30, 1962: Oxford, MS. James H. Meredith, a black student, attempts to enroll in the University of Mississippi. Two men are killed in the ensuing riots, and President Kennedy sends in federal troops to protect Meredith as he attends classes.

April 12, 1963: Birmingham, AL. The Rev. King, arrested for continuing a protest march in violation of a court order, is incarcerated in the Birmingham city jail. There he writes his famous "Letter from Birmingham Jail."

May 3-4, 1963: Birmingham, AL. Police in Birmingham use dogs and high-pressure fire hoses against black demonstrators led by the Rev. King. Media coverage of these scenes creates great sympathy for the civil rights movement.

June 11, 1963: Tuscaloosa, AL. Governor George Wallace refuses to permit two black students, Vivian Malone and James Hood, to register at the University of Alabama. When President Kennedy federalizes the Alabama National Guard, Wallace stands aside.

Aug. 28, 1963: Washington, DC. More than 200,000 blacks and whites participate in the peaceful "March on Washington." Jammed between the Lincoln Memorial and the Washington Monument, the crowd listens to the Rev. King's powerful "I Have a Dream" speech.

July 18, 1964: New York, NY. Harlem is the site of the first riot in a black northern ghetto. Others follow that summer.

Jan. 2, 1965: Selma, AL. The Rev. King calls for a 50-mile march from Selma to Montgomery, the state capital. Governor Wallace authorizes state troopers to use tear gas, whips, and night sticks against the marchers. President Johnson federalizes the Alabama National Guard and orders them to escort the marchers to Montgomery in safety.

Aug. 11, 1965: Los Angeles, CA. Two days after the arrest (and rumored beating) of a young black driver by a state highway patrolman, Watts, the city's black ghetto, explodes in riots. They cause millions of dollars of damage and cost the lives of more than 30 people.

Summer 1966: Chicago, IL; Cleveland, OH; New York, NY. Black ghettos in these northern cities erupt in race riots.

Summer 1967: Newark, NJ; Detroit, MI. Huge race riots break out in these two cities, as well as in many others.

April 4, 1968: Memphis, TN. The Rev. Martin Luther King, Jr., is assassinated.

(Continued from page 109) 1961, gave the heavily black District of Columbia a modest say in the selection of U.S. presidents: three votes in the electoral college. The Twenty-fourth Amendment, ratified in 1964, outlawed poll taxes in all federal elections, including primaries.

This flurry of laws, executive orders, court decisions, and constitutional amendments produced dramatic results. By the end of the decade, the days of Jim Crow were over. Blacks and whites could mingle freely in public accommodations. Blacks could vote anywhere, and they flocked to the polls. White politicians everywhere got the message. Yet the goal of full equality remained elusive. It still does. Black unemployment is double that of whites, black life expectancy is a decade less than that of whites, black median income is 55 percent of white income, black infant mortality is twice that of whites, and black participation in the higher professions hovers in the 2- to 3-percent range. If it is difficult to trace all this to present-day racism, it is more difficult to pretend that it has no relationship to racism in the past. But the most difficult problem is how to remedy the situation. The policy of affirmative action—a variation of which was tried at the Davis medical school—may be one solution. The merits of affirmative action are debated in this chapter's Taking Sides section.

1. *The Civil Rights Act of 1957* prohibited any attempt to prevent persons from voting in federal elections and authorized the attorney general to bring suit when a person was deprived of his or her voting rights. It also set up a Civil Rights Commission and a Civil Rights Division in the Justice Department. Except for these last two provisions, the act accomplished little, since resistance to black suffrage in the Deep South was massive and determined, more than a match for the case-by-case approach provided for by this act.

2. *The Civil Rights Act of 1960* strengthened provisions of the 1957 act for court enforcement of voting rights, and it required voting records to be preserved by state officials. It also contained limited criminal penalties relating to bombing and the obstruction of federal court orders: for example, orders to desegregate schools.

3. *The Civil Rights Act of 1964* was the first serious response by Congress, at least since the time of Reconstruction, to the problem of segregation. By this time, sit inners had been beaten, civil rights workers had been killed, and Martin Luther King, Jr., had been jailed. The nation had watched some of these events with horror, including the infamous dogs and fire hoses of Birmingham, Alabama. These provided much of the impetus for the bill.

The key provision of the bill was its prohibition of discrimination in public accommodations—hotels, motels, restaurants, and the like. This provision was later challenged on the grounds that it was trying to prevent a merely "private" discrimination, but it was sustained by the Supreme Court in *Heart of Atlanta Motel v. U.S.* (1964).

Other provisions of the bill included the prohibition of discrimination by unions and employers and the establishment of an Equal Employment Opportunity Commission. These last provisions have also become important to women's rights because they prohibited employment discrimination by sex as well as race.

4. *The Voting Rights Act of 1965* was proposed by President Johnson in a speech culminating in his prediction that "we shall overcome." The appropriation of this language by a former southern senator may have been the high-water mark of civil rights during the 1960s. The ensuing legislation finally broke the back of southern resistance to black suffrage because it authorized the attorney general to appoint federal examiners to register voters in areas of marked discrimination. The effect was electrifying: For the first time since Reconstruction, blacks began to win contests for local offices. White southerners began a mass exodus from the Democratic party.

5. *The Civil Rights Bill of 1968* prohibited discrimination in the sale or rental of housing. It also protected persons exercising such civil rights as attending schools and persuading others to assert their rights. But the bill also contained a "rider" (explained in chapter 12) that was introduced by conservatives as the price for their support. It made it a crime to cross state lines to "incite a riot."

THE FUTURE OF AFFIRMATIVE ACTION

Whatever its merits, the future of affirmative action is clouded. As we saw earlier, the Supreme Court in the *Bakke* case was almost equally divided on the constitutionality of race-conscious remedies. Since then, the Court majority has tipped this way and that on affirmative action cases, usually by narrow majorities. It decided that a factory and a union could ignore seniority and set aside a fixed percentage of trainee positions for black workers (1979) and that Congress could set aside a fixed percentage of public works projects for black construction firms (1980).[16] Yet in mid-decade it ruled that federal courts may not order the firing of white employees during a layoff simply to save the jobs of newly hired blacks with less seniority (1984); nor would the Court let a school board lay off white teachers before laying off minorities with less seniority (1986).[17] On the other hand, it held that local courts can approve settlements that involve the preferential hiring of blacks (1986), and it approved a

FIGURE **5-1**

**Voter Registration in 11 Southern States
by Race, 1960-1986**

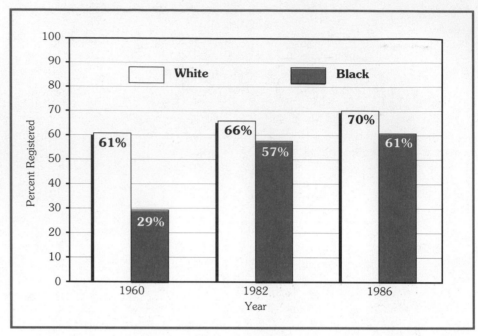

Data source: U.S. Bureau of the Census, *Statistical Abstract of the U.S.*, 1984, p. 261; Voter Education Project, Inc., Atlanta, GA, *Voter Registration in the South.*

Many more blacks registered to vote in the South from 1960 to 1986. In fact, as shown here, voter registration among southern black citizens more than doubled during these years while white voter registration rose by only 9 percent.

lower court ruling requiring a union local to hire a fixed quota of blacks by a certain year (1986).[18]

All of these cases were decided before Justice Anthony M. Kennedy's appointment to the Court. This last of the Reagan-appointed justices may have tipped the Court's balance against affirmative action. In 1989, with Kennedy in the majority, the Court ruled that a city council could *not* set aside a fixed percentage of public construction projects to minority contractors. In another case that year, it ruled that white firefighters could reopen an affirmative action settlement worked out eight years earlier. In still another case, it appeared to reverse an earlier decision by shifting the burden of proof in a discrimination suit onto the plaintiff, forcing the employee/ plaintiff to prove that employer policies having a "discriminatory impact" on minorities are not simply the result of neutral business practices.[19] These cases were decided by narrow majorities, and since some involved the interpretation of statutes, they can be changed by Congress if new laws are passed.

BUSING AND "WHITE FLIGHT"

Another remedy for existing inequality, one implied by the Court's opinion in the *Brown* case of 1954, is to make sure that blacks and whites attend school together. A number of psychological and sociological studies cited by the Court in *Brown* suggested that segregated learning does enormous harm to black children and that

(Continued on page 115)

GLOBAL PERSPECTIVES:

Civil Rights in South Africa

At the southern tip of the vast African continent is the Republic of South Africa, a country that occupies nearly 438,000 square miles and is home to 31 million of Africa's half-billion people. South Africa is one country but two worlds. One, the minority white world, is affluent, healthy, well educated, and in control of political affairs. The other, the nonwhite world, lives in squalor and is largely controlled by the white minority.

More precisely, four racial categories are central to the governing system of South Africa: whites (mainly of British and Dutch descent); Coloureds (people of mixed race); Asians (most of them descendants of Indian workers brought over in the nineteenth century to work on sugar plantations); and Bantus (members of the native black population). The government, social institutions, and the economy are dominated by the whites, who constitute 16 percent of the population. Everyone else is officially consigned to lower status, with the blacks, who constitute 72 percent, situated at the bottom. The Coloureds and the Asians must live in segregated neighborhoods, but since 1983, they have been allowed to elect their own representatives to the three-chambered national Parliament.

Black Africans, however, have no representatives in Parliament and are not permitted to vote in national elections. Indeed, they are not allowed to live within the white regions of South Africa. The government has moved them into black "homelands," territorial regions reserved exclusively for blacks. The government considers these "homelands" embryonic black nations and has already designated one of them, Transkei, an independent republic—though no other nation in the world has recognized it as such. These "homelands" constitute less than 15 percent of the area of South Africa, and they are on the poorest, most unproductive land. To find work, most blacks must travel great distances from their homes to white areas, then return to black townships in the evenings. Until recently, they had to carry passbooks with their photographs and fingerprints and produce them on request. Failure to do so resulted in fines and imprisonment.

The "homelands" constitute one feature of South Africa's system of apartheid (pronounced a-part-hate), or racial separation, that has been the policy of South Africa's ruling National party since it came to power in 1948. While racial discrimination can be found in many parts of the world, it is the systematic and official character of apartheid that makes South Africa unique today.

Since the early 1960s, apartheid has been vigorously, sometimes violently, challenged by many groups within and outside the country. In the past few years the struggle has reached a boiling point as protest demonstrations have been met with government repression of various kinds: censorship, curfews, detainment without trial, and police violence. Under pressure, the government has granted some concessions, such as abolishing the infamous "pass laws," permitting blacks to form labor unions, and moderating its segregation practices. Had these been granted a few years ago, they might have been widely praised, but today most critics consider them too little, too late.

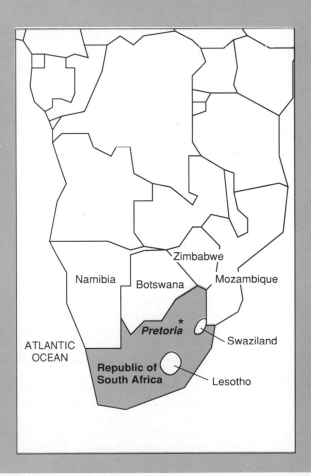

Will Affirmative Action Help Achieve Equality?

YES Herman Schwartz

Based upon *Minority Report: What Has Happened to Blacks, Hispanics, American Indians, and Other Minorities in the Eighties?* (New York: Pantheon Books, 1984).

Schwartz, a law professor, cites statistics on unemployment, poverty, and other factors that show the continued gaps between whites and nonwhites and between the sexes in America. "We must close these gaps so that we do not remain two nations, divided by race and gender." He contends that there is evidence showing that affirmative action programs have made at least modest improvements. "Studies in 1983 show, for example, that from 1974 to 1980 minority employment with employers subject to federal affirmative action requirements rose 20 percent, almost twice the increase elsewhere." Indeed, conservative administrations like Reagan's resorted to their own quiet affirmative action policies—surely Supreme Court justice Sandra Day O'Connor was not appointed solely on merit—even while hypocritically denouncing them. Affirmative action has been with us a long time (immediately after the Civil War, the government instituted programs to help blacks) and will be needed for a long time in the future. In order to get beyond race, Schwartz says, we must first take it into account because "equal treatment of unequals perpetuates and aggravates inequality."

NO Glenn C. Loury

Based upon "Beyond Civil Rights," *The New Republic*, October 7, 1985.

Loury, who worked his way up from a Chicago ghetto to a professorship at Harvard's Kennedy School, is convinced that race-conscious strategies like affirmative action make it impossible for blacks to achieve full equality in American society. He worries about the effect these programs have on black morale and self-esteem. For example, he says, "[In an employment situation,] if it is known that different selection criteria are used for different races . . . it is rational to expect lower performance from persons of the race that was preferentially favored in selection." African-Americans, he says, have a deep need for respect. This, of course, he affirms has been true of other groups excluded from the American mainstream, such as immigrants, but the problem with blacks has been exacerbated by their "continued dependence on special favors from the majority." Using racially preferential treatment to "equalize," Loury concludes, is self-defeating because equality ultimately requires the respect of one's peers, and for that, "there is no substitute for what is to be won through unaided accomplishments of individual persons."

Postscript

Much of the argument between Schwartz and Loury turns on the question of racial color blindness. To what extent should our laws be color-blind? In his "I Have a Dream" speech in 1963, the Reverend Martin Luther King, Jr., said that he dreamed of a day when people "will not be judged by the color of their skin but by the content of their character." Defenders of affirmative action say color consciousness is necessary to bring about color blindness. The logic of this argument suggests that the proponents of affirmative action regard it as a temporary expedient and look forward to the day when it can be abolished.

Richard Kluger's *Simple Justice* (New York: Knopf, 1976) is a classic study of the events and cases leading up to the *Brown* decision of 1954. The focus of Allan B. Sindler's *Bakke, Defunis, and Minority Admissions* (Longman, 1978) is on affirmative action in higher education. Nathan Glazer's *Affirmative Discrimination: Ethnic Inequality and Public Policy* (Basic Books, 1975) is an extended critique of affirmative action.

School busing was and continues to be a very controversial subject. In Boston it has sometimes required a police escort to guarantee the safe arrival of pupils. One of the repercussions of busing is referred to as "white flight"; this occurs when white families flee the city for the suburbs rather than accept the integration of city public schools. Incidents of racial violence following court-mandated busing are an indication of the strong feelings generated by the busing issue.

(Continued from page 112)

this harm will later affect their ability to earn a decent living. The solution, then, is desegregation, and there are cases in which desegregation may require busing children from one place to another in order to prevent segregation or, in some cases, resegregation.

The first busing case decided by the Supreme Court, *Swann v. Charlotte-Mecklenburg Board of Education* (1971), emerged from events in Mecklenburg County, North Carolina, where the city of Charlotte is located. For years, city and county school officials had been running away from the *Brown* mandate. Using a variety of tricks and subterfuges, they had done their utmost to keep the races apart. In the meantime, whites had been moving out of the city into the outlying suburbs, making Charlotte's school population mostly black. After years of litigation, an exasperated federal judge finally told school authorities to set up a busing plan; it would transport some white children into city schools and some black children out into suburban schools. The school board objected, claiming that the black-white imbalance between city and suburban school children was *de facto*, not *de jure*; that is, it resulted simply from the movement of white people out of the city. The school board thus contended that the courts had no authority to order the busing of children away from their neighborhood schools. Not so, said the Supreme Court. The racial imbalance in Charlotte's schools was a result of years of deliberate policies by school officials. The imbalance remained *de jure*, the Court said, even though the original *de jure* segregation that produced it had now ceased. It must be corrected, and if busing is the way to do it, so be it.

Busing soon became an issue in the North as well as the South. In 1974 a federal judge, W. Arthur Garrity, Jr., ruled that the Boston school authorities had deliberately segregated their system. He ordered the state to take control of the city's schools; he

FIGURE **5-2**

White Flight from Boston Schools
Fall enrollment in public schools. Busing began in 1974.

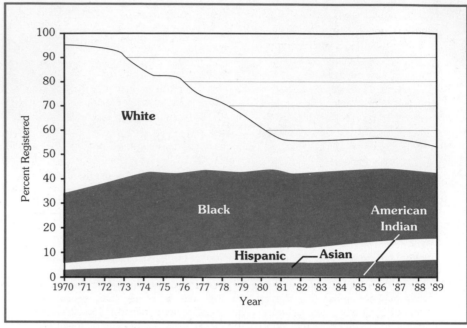

Data source: Department of Health, Education, and Welfare (1970–74); Massachusetts State Department of Education. Reprinted with permission of the *New York Times*.

White enrollment in Boston's public schools has declined rapidly since 1970. Dubbed "white flight" by the media, many white parents have transferred their children to private schools or moved their families to the suburbs. Recently the city has considered revamping the busing policy due to parent dissatisfaction with the public school policy.

then personally administered the state's plan. It called for intensive busing between the predominantly black neighborhood of Roxbury and the white area of South Boston. As the buses of black children arrived in South Boston, white mobs shouted "Niggers, go home!" and pelted the children with bottles and rocks. Later, mobs of black teenagers stoned cars driven by whites that passed through Roxbury and pulled several motorists from their cars and beat them. The brawl continued for years. White resistance was eventually broken, but at a heavy price. In 1972, when Judge Garrity first began hearing the case, the white population of the city's schools stood at 60 percent. Fourteen years later, when Garrity finally returned control of the schools to the city, the white population had declined to 27 percent. The Boston public school system was desegregated—only to become predominantly black.[20]

Where were the white children? Many whites sent their children to private schools. Others simply moved out of the city. There were more than half a million whites in Boston in 1970; a decade later, the number was 393,937. This phenomenon has happened all over the North, and it is known as <u>white flight</u>. As a result, today's inner-city schools tend to be mostly black, while many suburban schools are nearly all white. There would seem to be an obvious remedy for this imbalance: Why not bus white students in from the suburbs and bus black students out into the suburbs? That was what was ordered in the *Swann* case in North Carolina, and for a time it appeared that busing was going to happen in the North as well. But the Supreme Court stopped it.

In a 1974 case involving the city of Detroit and 53 school districts in the outlying

Points to Remember

1. Though blacks were freed from slavery by the Thirteenth Amendment, their rights were at first severely restricted by the southern governments. Congress reacted by setting up a program called Reconstruction, which was supervised by the military.

2. During Reconstruction, blacks made significant gains. They were made citizens, given the right to vote, and guaranteed the equal protection of the laws. Blacks ran for office, and in some cases, they and their white supporters assumed control of southern legislatures.

3. When Reconstruction ended, blacks lost most of their rights again. *Plessy v Ferguson* (1896) gave the Supreme Court's blessing to state-imposed racial segregation.

4. Almost 60 years later, in the case of *Brown v. Board of Education* (1954), the Supreme Court reversed *Plessy* and declared school segregation unconstitutional. Yet segregation persisted, and a grass-roots civil rights movement began a new struggle against discrimination.

5. Not until the 1960s did the president and Congress take vigorous steps to wipe out racial discrimination. Three major civil rights bills guaranteed black voting rights, gave blacks access to public accommodations and the job market, and outlawed discrimination in housing.

6. Inequality of condition remains a stubborn fact of life, and affirmative action is one strategy aimed at remedying it. Its future is precarious because of recent Supreme Court decisions.

7. In the 1971 *Swann* case, the Court said that city-suburb busing is an appropriate remedy where both the city and the outlying areas have deliberately, officially segregated in the past. But in 1974 the Court said that city-suburb busing was not appropriate in the absence of proof that the suburbs too had officially discriminated.

suburb, the Court made this ruling: Unless there is convincing evidence of *de jure* segregation, past or present, in *both* city and suburb, no court may order busing between the two. In the *Swann* case, remember, the city of Charlotte and the outlying suburbs were all tied into the same school district, so city and suburbs were all tainted by the same *de jure* segregation of the past. In the 1974 case, there were two separate school systems, Detroit's and the suburb's. There was clear proof that the city of Detroit had deliberately segregated in the past—but there was no such proof that the outlying suburb had done so. Therefore, city-suburb busing was not required. There was racial imbalance all right, but it was *de facto*, not *de jure*.[21] In part because of this 1974 decision, city-suburb busing never really got underway in the North—the burden of proving *de jure* segregation in both city and suburb is a difficult one—and today it seems to have fallen from favor even among civil rights groups.

Viewed from one perspective, black Americans have made great strides in civil rights. *De jure* racial discrimination has been abolished, voting rights are guaranteed, affirmative action and busing have been used to remedy the effects of discrimination. Yet the goal of full equality somehow eludes us. *De facto* segregation still exists, and in practically every area of material well-being, from income and employment levels to maternal and child health, wide gaps remain. The challenge is to determine the causes and find the cures for these remaining inequities.

Women: Old Attitudes, New Dilemmas

Women are not a minority group. The majority (51 percent) of Americans are female. Yet women share with most minorities in America a history of subjugation and abuse. From the founding of the nation until well into the twentieth century, women were not allowed to vote, hold property, serve on juries, freely use public accommodations, or manage property on the same terms as men in most states. Women today are still subject to discrimination, stereotyping, and harassment of all kinds by men. Their

Those opposed to women's suffrage made up a powerful political force. Until 1920 most states gave the right to vote only to adult white males who owned property. Women could not own property, had limited job possibilities, and had a limited role in the democratic process.

earning power is much less than that of men, and most still remain in jobs traditionally considered "women's work."

To challenge these practices—and the attitudes that underlie them—the women's liberation movement appeared in the 1960s. More accurately, it *reappeared*, since women's liberation movements have surfaced at various times in the United States since the early decades of the nineteenth century. This time the issue caught the public's attention through a book, *The Feminine Mystique*, written by a then-obscure housewife, Betty Friedan.[22] The book criticized the stereotypes of women that were current in the 1950s and early 1960s. Within two years of the book's publication, the National Organization for Women (NOW) had been founded, with Friedan as its first president. Gloria Steinem, another well-known crusader for women's rights, also gained recognition in the 1960s as a feminist writer. In 1972 she founded *Ms.* magazine, which today is the most widely circulated feminist publication.

Friedan, Steinem, and other activists presided over the rebirth of a movement that had died a quiet death 40 years earlier. Its roots, however, went back much earlier.

The first phase of American feminism began in the nineteenth century. Like the feminist revival of the 1960s, its founders were upper-middle-class women sympathetic to the civil rights movement. When the World Antislavery Convention met in London in 1840, American abolitionists of both sexes sailed there to rally against oppression. Ironically, when they arrived, they were told that the female abolitionists were not allowed in the hall. Only after the American men threatened a boycott did the convention's organizers allow the women to sit in the balcony—behind a curtain!

This and other kinds of sexual discrimination were challenged at the first major convention of American feminists at Seneca Falls, New York, in 1848. The convention issued a Women's Declaration of Independence. Drafted by feminist leader Elizabeth Cady Stanton, it read in part: "We hold these truths to be self-evident: that

In the eighteenth century American women were not allowed to vote, manage property, sign contracts, serve on juries, or act as legal guardians for their children. In a half-serious, half-playful exchange of letters, the American revolutionary leader John Adams and his wife, Abigail, traded jibes on the question of whether the liberty for which America was fighting would be extended to the victims of male tyranny.

Abigail Adams to John Adams, March 31, 1776:

I long to hear that you have declared an independency—and, by the way, in the new code of laws, which I suppose it will be necessary for you to make, I desire you would remember the ladies, and be more generous and favorable to them than [were] your ancestors. Do not put such unlimited power into the hands of the husbands. Remember all men would be tyrants if they could. If particular care and attention is not paid to the ladies, we are determined to [instigate] a rebellion, and will not hold ourselves bound by any laws in which we have no voice or representation.

John Adams to Abigail Adams, April 14, 1776:

As to your extraordinary code of laws, I cannot but laugh. We have been told that our struggle has loosened the bands of government everywhere. That children and apprentices were disobedient—that schools and colleges were grown turbulent— that Indians slighted their guardians and Negroes grew insolent to their masters. But your letter was the first intimation that another tribe more numerous and powerful than all the rest [had] grown discontented. This is rather too coarse a compliment, but you are so saucy, I won't blot it out.

Abigail Adams to John Adams, May 7, 1776:

I cannot say that I think you very generous to the ladies. For, whilst you are proclaiming peace and good will to men, emancipating all nations, you insist upon retaining an absolute power over wives. But you must remember that arbitrary power is like most other things which are very hard—very liable to be broken; and, notwithstanding all your wise laws and maxims, we have it in our power not only to free ourselves but to subdue our masters, and without violence throw both your natural and legal authority at our feet.

all men and women are created equal. . . . The history of mankind is a history of repeated injuries and usurpation on the part of man toward woman, having in direct object the establishment of absolute tyranny over her." Although the convention agreed on what women's main grievances were, it split on the question of women's suffrage. Some delegates considered that goal too radical for the times.

Suffrage again emerged as an issue after the close of the Civil War and the passage of the Fifteenth Amendment, which gave blacks the right to vote. Black males, for whose cause feminists had been fighting a few years earlier, now enjoyed rights denied to women. The suffrage struggle continued. The Populist party in the 1880s and 1890s had many female members; not surprisingly, the party championed women's suffrage and other causes popular with women at the time, including the prohibition of alcohol.

In the early 1900s the Progressive movement supported women's suffrage, as did the progressive wing of the Republican party. By 1914 women could vote in 11 states, but this piecemeal progress seemed agonizingly slow to feminist leaders, who decided to direct their energies toward the adoption of a constitutional amendment. Through petitions, demonstrations, parades, pamphleting, and picketing, they focused publicity on their cause and virtually compelled President Woodrow Wilson to support a women's suffrage amendment. In June 1919, Congress approved an amendment that stated: "The right of citizens of the United States to vote shall not be

119

Early feminists campaigning for suffrage were in for a hard fight, but in 1920 they won the right to vote with the passage of the Nineteenth Amendment. At this time the size of the eligible voting population nearly doubled. But it was not until the latter half of the century that the turnout of women at the polls reached the level of male turnout.

denied or abridged by the United States or by any states on account of sex." By August 1920, it had been ratified by the required number of states and became the Nineteenth Amendment to the Constitution.

The passage of the amendment capped a long history of feminist struggle. It also coincided with a cultural revolution in America. Now all women could do what only "loose" women once did: smoke, wear lipstick, go out without a chaperone. Upper-middle-class women began going to college in record numbers. Women had "arrived," and there was no further need for the feminist movement—or so it seemed.

THE RISE AND FALL OF THE ERA

The revival of the 1960s was in part a rebellion against the cultural styles of the previous decade, which contained an uneasy mixture of modernism and tradition. The cars were sleek and streamlined, and youth culture was celebrated. Yet in the relationship between the sexes, traditional roles were stressed. It was the baby boom era and a woman's role as mother and homemaker was glorified; men were seen as breadwinners and protectors. "Sexiness" was fine—the Victorian woman was long gone—but the eroticism of the 1950s always seemed to be bound up with female dependence and passivity.

The new feminism challenged these cultural stereotypes. *Sisterhood Is Powerful*, the title of Robin Morgan's anthology of feminist writings, summed up the spirit of the movement.[23] Women were not content to be homemakers and Playboy bunnies;

they were not going to be denied the pleasures or the freedom men possessed, nor were they going to be crowded out of the workplace or confined to "women's work." Dissatisfied with their situation, feminists tried to change the status of women by proposing a constitutional amendment.

The Equal Rights Amendment (ERA), which Betty Friedan called the "symbol and substance" of the feminist movement, did not look at all controversial. It stated that "equality of rights under the law shall not be denied or abridged by the United States or by any State on account of sex," and it gave Congress the power to enforce it by legislation. The amendment sailed through Congress in 1972 by overwhelming margins and was ratified by 30 state legislatures within a year. Supporters needed 8 more ratifications and had 7 years to get them. It seemed like a sure thing.

Then something happened. An anti-ERA movement sprang up, a movement composed largely of women! Phyllis Schlafly, who had been active in various conservative causes since the early 1960s, formed a group called Eagle Forum, which spearheaded the opposition. By the late 1970s it was clear that the amendment was in trouble. When the deadline came in 1979, only five more states had ratified it. Congress extended the deadline until June 30, 1982, but even with the extended deadline, the amendment failed to garner the necessary ratifications (and some states now voted to "de-ratify"). ERA was defeated. It was reintroduced in the House of Representatives at the beginning of 1983 but failed to get the necessary two-thirds vote to get started again.

What went wrong? Why should such an innocuously worded amendment seem so threatening? The "Stop ERA" movement feared that crusading judges and bureaucrats would use the rather broad language of the amendment to promote abortion on demand, strike down female-only alimony laws, and make women subject to the draft.[24] Supporters insisted that the legislative intent behind ERA was simply to protect women's constitutional rights, but nothing feminists said reassured their opponents. Indeed, the opposition seemed to be directed as much to the feminists as to their amendment. ERA opponents tended to be women from traditional backgrounds who regarded the new feminism as a threat. They resented what they saw as the feminists' contemptuous attitude toward housewives; worried aloud about the lesbian and "man-hating" factions in the movement; and deplored the very style of modern feminism, which they considered coarse and unfeminine.

(Continued on page 122)

FEIFFER®

Drawing by Jules Feiffer. © 1986. Reprinted with permission of Universal Press Syndicate.

TABLE 5-1

Assessing the Women's Movement

Percentage of adults who agreed with these statements:

Women's organizations have done something that "made your life better."			The United States continues to need a strong women's movement to push for changes that benefit women.	
Women	Men		Women	Men
25%	**15%**	**TOTAL**	**67%**	**51%**
		Race		
22	13	White	64	49
39	18	Black	85	63
29	23	Hispanic	76	47
		Age		
29	13	18-29 years	71	56
29	19	30-44 years	72	54
19	13	45-64 years	62	35
19	16	65 years or older	57	63
		Family income		
19	2	Under $12,500	67	44
22	16	$12,500-$24,999	66	55
25	17	$25,000-$34,999	71	47
26	9	$35,000-$50,000	67	53
38	19	Over $50,000	67	50
		Marital status		
22	17	Married now	64	47
26	18	Married previously	73	48
32	10	Never married	70	62
		Employment		
28	14	Employed full time	72	48
21	22	Employed part time	68	54
22	15	Not employed	60	57
33	19	Employed with child under 18	73	50

Based upon interviews with 1,025 women and 472 men, conducted by telephone June 20-25, 1989.

Source: New York Times, August 22, 1989, A18. Reprinted with permission.

(Continued from page 121) Most American women today seem to have ambivalent feelings toward the feminist movement. When respondents to a June 1989 *New York Times* poll were asked if the United States "continues to need a strong women's movement to push for changes that benefit women," 67 percent said "yes." But when asked if women's organizations have done something that "made your life better," only 25 percent agreed (see Table 5.1).

WOMEN IN THE WORKPLACE

In recent years, feminism has turned much of its attention toward issues of the workplace. Feminists have pressed for affordable, quality day care, for tough laws against sexual harassment on the job, and for strict enforcement of laws against job discrimination. Some key laws were in place even before the feminist movement was

FIGURE **5-3**

123

Women: Old
Attitudes, New
Dilemmas

**The Male-Female Wage Gap: Average Weekly Full-time
Earnings, Wage and Salary Workers, by Sex**

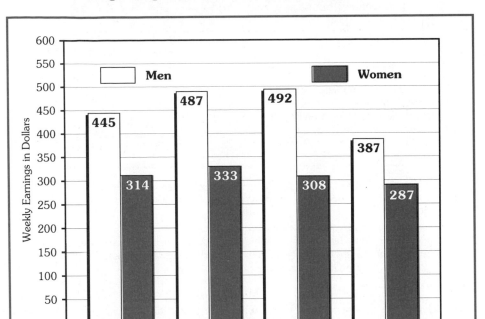

Data source: U.S. Department of Labor, Bureau of Labor Statistics, *News,* August 1988.

In 1988 there is still a significant gap in the earning power of men and women
that continues throughout the average woman's lifespan.

reborn in the mid-1960s. The Equal Pay Act of 1963 forbids employers from paying a
woman less than a man for work that is equal. Section VII of the 1964 Civil Rights Act
prohibits job discrimination based upon sex. Despite these laws, economic inequality
between the sexes still exists.

As Figure 5.3 shows, there is a significant wage gap between the salaries of men
and women. Some feel this discrepancy can be explained by factors not directly
related to past or present sex discrimination, such as women's self-imposed restrictions on working hours, higher absenteeism among women, and less work experience. But an exhaustive study of these factors by researchers Mary Corcoran and
Greg J. Duncan concluded that they "explain" less than half of the wage gap between
white males and white females and even less than half of the gap between white
males and black females.[25] Corcoran and Duncan's findings are presented in Table
5.2.

Feminist leaders argue that more vigorous action is needed to close the wage
gap. They support a number of measures, including affirmative action programs and
what is called "pay equity" or comparable worth. The strategy of comparable worth is
to analyze jobs in terms of their constituent elements—such as the skill and effort
involved, the years of training required, and the working conditions—and then give
each attribute a numerical value. The sum total of all these values provides a
quantitative measure of the job's "worth." Employers would then be required to pay
employees in accordance with these values. If it were found, for example, that a
secretary and a plumber were performing quantitatively similar work, then they

TABLE **5-2**

**Fractions of the Wage Gap Between White Men and Other
Groups of Workers "Explained" by Various Factors**
(All working household heads and wives, age 18–64)

	Black Men	White Women	Black Women
Formal education	38%	2%	11%
Years of training completed on current job	15	11	8
Other work history	3	28	14
Indicators of labor force attachment	− 3	3	− 1
Unexplained	47	56	68
TOTAL	100%	100%	100%

Source: Mary Corcoran and Greg J. Duncan: "Work History, Labor Force Attachment, and Earnings Differences Between the Races and Sexes," *Journal of Human Resources* (Winter 1979). Reprinted with permission.

Some wage disparities are explained by differences in education, training, and experience. Yet a large part of the wage gap cannot be accounted for by rational explanations. Although these figures were estimated with data from 1976, it is likely that they hold true today.

should receive the same pay. This way, many traditional "women's jobs" would achieve pay equity with jobs usually performed by men. Opinions differ as to whether or not such a scheme would be workable and fair. Congresswoman Patricia Schroeder (D-Colorado) called it "the civil rights issue of the 1980s."[26] The Reverend Jesse Jackson made it one of the central planks in his platform when he ran for the Democratic presidential nomination in 1988. The late Clarence Pendleton, head of President Reagan's Civil Rights Commission, called it "the looniest idea since Looney Tunes."[27]

THE LEGALIZATION OF ABORTION

Abortion on demand had been a major objective of feminist groups since the 1960s. They proceeded cautiously at first, calling for "liberalization" of state abortion laws but soon were demanding the repeal of all laws limiting abortion. In this effort they were joined by a number of other groups, from the American Civil Liberties Union to the National Abortion Rights Action League (NARAL). They lobbied various legislatures, with mixed results. Some, like New York's, began changing their laws, but opposition lobbies quickly sprang up, threatening to undo the gains already made. Then came the windfall. In 1973 the Supreme Court struck down all existing abortion laws in the United States. The case was *Roe v. Wade.*

"Roe" was the pseudonym of Norma McCorvey, a woman who sought an abortion in the state of Texas and was told that it was illegal. She had the baby but in the meantime brought suit against the state, claiming that the abortion regulations of Texas violated her right of privacy.[28] The term *right of privacy* can be found nowhere in the Constitution. Critics call it a "judge-made" right. Defenders insist that it is composed of purely constitutional ingredients. The landmark case establishing a right of privacy was *Griswold v. Connecticut* (1965), which struck down a Connecticut law banning the use of contraceptives. In *Griswold,* the Court said that a "right of privacy" can be derived from the "penumbras" and "emanations" of the Bill of Rights. A *penumbra* is a sort of half-shadow or beginning of a shadow. One dictionary defines *emanation* as "that which issues, flows, or proceeds from any source." Deep within the flows and the half-shadows of the Constitution, the Court discovered the right of privacy. That right, said the Court, emanates from a number of provisions in the Bill of Rights, including the Fourth Amendment's prohibition of "unreasonable searches and seizures," the Fifth Amendment's protection against self-incrimination, and the Ninth Amendment, which states that "the enumeration . . . of certain rights, shall not be construed to deny or disparage others retained by the people." Put them all together and you have a right of privacy.

This reading of the Constitution seemed strained and implausible to Justice Hugo Black. Black was one of the Court's foremost libertarians, but he read his Constitution very strictly. In his dissenting opinion, in which Justice Potter Stewart joined, Black said, "I like my privacy as well as the next one, but I am nevertheless compelled to admit that government has a right to invade it unless prohibited by some specific constitutional provision."[29]

Yet *Griswold* had a solid seven-member majority behind it, and its right of privacy ruling became the basis for later Supreme Court decisions. The most controversial of these was *Roe v. Wade*. Here, for the first time, the Court said that the right of privacy included the right of a woman to get an abortion. It was a sweeping decision. *Roe* overturned the abortion laws of all 50 states and attempted to lay down national standards for abortion. The *Roe* opinion, by Justice Harry A. Blackmun, divided pregnancy into trimesters, or three-month segments. During the first trimester of pregnancy, said Blackmun, the state has no "compelling interest" in a pregnancy. It may enact no regulations concerning a woman's right to abortion. During the second trimester, the state may enact abortion regulations but only to protect the *woman's* health. The state still has no "compelling interest" in the life of the fetus. Only for the last trimester may the state enact regulations to protect the "potential life" of the fetus. Even then, however, the state may not ban abortion if such a ban would endanger the health of the mother. And "health" Blackmun defined broadly enough to include not only physical but emotional health. Summing up, *Roe* permitted abortion on demand for the first six months of pregnancy and abortion in some circumstances for the remaining three months.

Why did the Court draw a line at six months? At the time of *Roe v. Wade* the best medical technology might keep a six-month fetus alive, or *viable*, outside the womb, and the Court reasoned that the state could protect a viable fetus without violating the rights of the mother. Justice Blackmun said that the end of the second trimester marked a "compelling point" in the pregnancy when the fetus became capable of "meaningful life outside the mother's womb."

Roe had two dissenters. Writing for himself and Justice William Rehnquist (who is now Chief Justice), Justice Byron White denounced the decision as an act of "raw judicial power" without constitutional foundation. Nevertheless, in later cases the Court not only stuck by the decision but extended its scope. In 1983 it struck down a variety of municipal abortion regulations, including one that required all abortions after the third month to be performed in hospitals.[30] In 1986 it invalidated a Pennsylvania law requiring physicians performing abortions to provide patients with certain information, including the risks associated with abortion and the alternatives to it.

But even as the Court expanded *Roe*, its majority narrowed. There were two dissenters in *Roe*, three in the 1983 decision, and four in 1986. Supporters of legalized abortion worried that one more Court appointment by President Reagan, who had already appointed one of the dissenters, might tip the balance. By 1989 Reagan had appointed two new members and made William Rehnquist Chief Justice—and the balance did seem to tip, or at any rate, shift. In a 5-4 decision, *Webster v. Reproductive Health Services* (1989), the Court approved a series of restrictions on abortion by the state of Missouri. A Missouri law banned abortions in public hospitals and prohibited public employees from performing or assisting at abortions (except for abortions necessary to save a woman's life); it also required

Norma McCorvey as Jane Roe took on Dallas district attorney Henry Wade in 1971. She claimed that she had been raped (she later admitted that this was untrue) and wished to defy Texas law by having an abortion. Her case went to the Supreme Court, which ruled in *Roe v. Wade* that states could not ban abortions during the first two trimesters (6 months) of pregnancy and could not even regulate abortion procedures until the second trimester, when regulations could be enacted only to protect the well-being of the woman, not the life of the fetus. The court ruled that the state had a sufficient interest in the life of the fetus during the last trimester to prohibit abortions, except when the mother's physical or mental health was threatened.

(Continued on page 127)   125

FIGURE **5-4**

Where Abortion Laws Stand

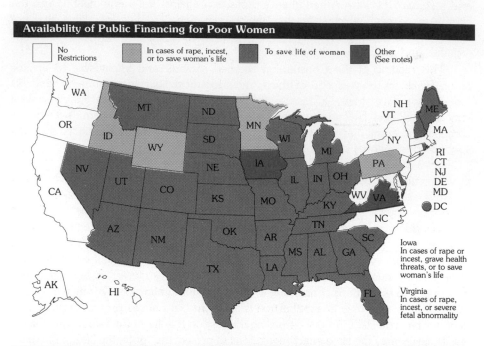

Iowa
In cases of rape or incest, grave health threats, or to save woman's life

Virginia
In cases of rape, incest, or severe fetal abnormality

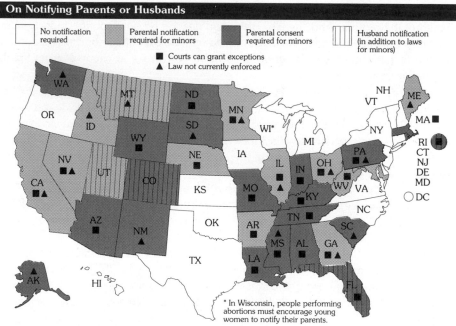

* In Wisconsin, people performing abortions must encourage young women to notify their parents.

Data source: National Right to Life Committee; National Abortion Rights Action League; Americans United for Life; American Civil Liberties Union; Alan Guttmacher Institute; Professor Lynn D. Wardle of Brigham Young University; and individual states. Reprinted with permission of the *New York Times.*

In a majority of states public funding is restricted to cases where abortion is necessary to save the life of the mother. The western coastal states, however, and many of the mideastern and northeastern states still place no restrictions on public funding. Most states, with the exception of the far-western and mid- and northeastern, also have laws that require notification of parents or husbands, but these statutes are often unenforced. Only 14 states have no requirements for notification.

On July 3, 1989 the Supreme Court upheld a Missouri law which outlawed the use of state funding, state personnel, and state facilities for any abortion not necessary to save a woman's life. In addition the Court upheld the Missouri state legislature's right to include a declaration in the Missouri law that "the life of each human being begins at conception." Although this decision does not allow state legislatures to outlaw privately performed and funded abortions, it has intensified the debate over the legality and availability of abortion in the United States and shifted the center of the debate to the various state legislatures.

(Continued from page 125)

medical tests on any fetus more than 20 weeks old to determine whether or not it was "viable," able to live outside the womb. The *Webster* ruling did not directly overturn *Roe v. Wade* but did empower the states to regulate public funding of abortion and to enforce tests of viability. Medical advances since *Roe* had enabled doctors to keep a fetus alive, outside the womb, during the second trimester, and the court acknowledged this change by approving a law requiring viability tests after 20 weeks. Indeed, in dissenting from a 1983 case that struck down limits on abortion, Justice Sandra Day O'Connor suggested that the trimester framework of *Roe*, based as it was on the medical knowledge of 1973, was rapidly becoming obsolete; Justice O'Connor was now part of the *Webster* majority.[31]

The *Webster* decision may have started to shift the major arena for future abortion fights because it left open to state legislatures the possibility of further restricting abortion. Presently, as shown in Figure 5.4, state laws on abortion show considerable variation. There may be even more, as some states move toward sharper restrictions. These moves will be contested by pro-choice lobbies at the state level. The fighting will be bitter, as indeed it has been since 1973. Abortion has been called "the issue that won't go away." Every year, since *Roe v. Wade* legalized abortion in 1973, 1.6 million abortions have been performed in the United States. Those on the "pro-life" side of the controversy say that America has embarked upon a "Holocaust of the unborn," in some ways comparable to the extermination program of Nazi Germany. Those who take the "pro-choice" position say that in 1973 the Court finally recognized a basic right of women, and now this right may be jeopardized by being thrown back into state legislatures. Much of the argument between pro-lifers and pro-choicers turns on the question of whether a human fetus is a human being.[32]

Everything would be much simpler if babies were brought by storks. Instead, they develop over a nine-month period inside women. The process is a continuum. At *some* point the fertilized egg becomes a human being—but when? At conception? At delivery? Sometime in between? A one-day-old fertilized ovum does not resemble a baby. An eight-month fetus does not look like anything except a baby. If a woman

FIGURE **5-5**

Abortion Attitudes: Case by Case

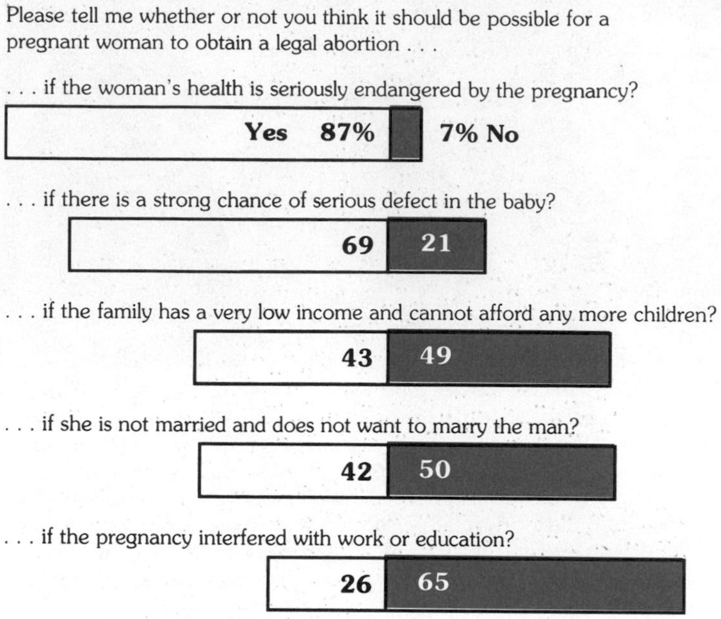

Please tell me whether or not you think it should be possible for a
pregnant woman to obtain a legal abortion . . .

. . . if the woman's health is seriously endangered by the pregnancy?

| Yes 87% | 7% No |

. . . if there is a strong chance of serious defect in the baby?

| 69 | 21 |

. . . if the family has a very low income and cannot afford any more children?

| 43 | 49 |

. . . if she is not married and does not want to marry the man?

| 42 | 50 |

. . . if the pregnancy interfered with work or education?

| 26 | 65 |

. . . and a Spectrum of Acceptance

Those who say abortion should be allowed:

In all five circum-stances	In four of the five circum-stances	In three of the five circum-stances	In two of the five circum-stances	In one of the five circum-stances	None of the five
21%	15%	12%	26%	17%	10%

Data source: Based upon a *New York Times*/CBS News Poll of 1,412 adults nationwide conducted by telephone April 13–16, 1989. Those with no opinion are not shown. Reprinted with permission of the *New York Times*.

Most people would agree that abortion should be legal when the mother's health is in serious danger but not when the pregnancy interferes with her work or education.

may destroy an ovum, may she destroy an eight-month fetus? If a late-term fetus is a baby, is a fertilized ovum also a baby? We continue to grope for guidelines.

It is hard to find much basis for compromise. Abortion probes people's deepest moral convictions. It is not like an argument over taxes or spending, where both sides can eventually "split the difference." In 1989 *New York Times* columnist William Safire predicted that both the pro-life and the pro-choice movements would soon be swamped by a "pro-comp" movement of people who want compromise; the compromise would allow early abortions and place restrictions on late-term ones.[33] There are some grounds for Safire's prediction, since American attitudes toward abortion are quite complicated; most do not neatly fall into the pro-life and pro-choice categories (see Figure 5.5 and Table 5.3). Still, the people whom Safire calls the "absolutists" on both sides of the issue are active and influential; they will not agree to compromise. In *Roe v. Wade* the Court tried its own version of this compromise, but

(Continued on page 130)

TABLE 5-3

How Groups Differ on Abortion

Percent saying abortion should be . . .	Legal as it is now	Legal only in certain cases	Not permitted at all	Know someone who had abortion	Say it was right to do in that case*
Total Adults	49	39	9	51	57
Age					
18-29 years	56	35	8	66	58
30-44 years	49	40	9	64	53
45-64 years	45	39	12	36	63
65 and over	39	45	9	26	52
Sex and Marital Status					
All men	51	38	8	48	60
Unmarried	60	31	7	55	65
Married	46	41	8	45	57
All women	47	40	11	54	54
Unmarried	54	37	7	60	60
Married	42	42	14	50	50
Education					
Less than high school	37	41	16	39	56
High school graduate	47	41	9	47	54
Some college	56	35	7	60	58
College graduate	58	35	5	67	61
Race					
White	49	39	9	51	58
Black	45	42	13	54	51
Religion					
All Protestants	44	44	9	51	53
Religion very important	34	49	13	46	42
Not so important	61	36	1	59	69
All Catholics	48	36	13	45	55
Religion very important	28	49	22	41	32
Not so important	72	22	4	50	76
Political Philosophy					
Liberal	65	28	5	61	66
Moderate	54	38	6	54	61
Conservative	38	46	13	46	46
Exposure					
Women who say they had an abortion	79	12	9	95	81
People who know:					
Someone who had an abortion	58	34	7	100	57
No one who had abortion	39	44	12	0	—

*Percent of those knowing someone who had abortion.

Source: Based upon a *New York Times*/CBS Poll of 1,412 adults nationwide, conducted by telephone April 13-16, 1989. Reprinted with permission of the *New York Times.*

Attitudes about abortion vary according to one's education, age, sex, political leanings, race, religion, and whether or not one knows a woman who has had an abortion. If one is between 18-29 years old, one is more likely to support abortion than if one is 65 or older. If one is very religious, one is also less likely to support abortion than if one has a more secular outlook.

(Continued from page 128) pro-life activists say that the only thing compromised was the life of 1.6 million unborn children every year. Pro-choicers, likewise, are not inclined to compromise. *Village Voice* editor Ellen Willis is a pro-choice activist, but her words could be used by both sides of the struggle:

> But is there a compromise that would satisfy me? No. Is there a compromise that I would consider honorable? No. Is there a compromise that would make me feel I didn't need to keep fighting? No.[34]

Reflections

Everything seemed simpler a generation ago. In the 1950s, civil rights was discussed almost exclusively in terms of blacks and whites. Blacks in the South were denied the most elementary rights: the right to vote, to sit at lunch counters with whites, to attend white schools. "For Whites Only" signs still hung over drinking fountains, waiting rooms, and washrooms.

All that was swept away in the 1960s. The structure of American apartheid came tumbling down, and it seemed for a moment that Martin Luther King, Jr.'s dream was about to be realized: The people of this land would be judged not by "the color of their skin but by the content of their character."

Yet the dream still eludes us. Whatever the legal status of blacks and whites today, stubborn inequalities remain. Examine the statistics on unemployment, on maternal and child health, on longevity, on enrollment in professional schools. Drive through urban America and see the black ghettos and the all-white enclaves. Every segregation law has been struck down, yet the races are still separate and still unequal. Where do we go from here? What approaches do we take? The questions are no longer so easy to answer. The situation is more complicated than it was a generation ago.

Another reason that civil rights has become more complicated is that more and more groups are claiming rights. In the 1960s a revived feminist movement began reminding us of women's rights. It did not take long for the various ethnic groups in America, from American Indians to white ethnics, to demand recognition and rights. Then homosexuals, the elderly, and the disabled began to talk about their rights. At about the same time, the right-to-life movement claimed to represent "the rights of the unborn." Everyone wanted to get into the act, perhaps deservedly.

But what happens when satisfying one group's demands causes another group to claim that *its* rights are being violated? We saw this in the *Bakke* case. Bakke, a white male, claimed that his rights were being sacrificed in order to increase minority enrollment. The situation today is ripe for many such claims. What happens when a black male is passed over for admission or promotion for a white female? Some hard choices lie ahead, not just on affirmative action but on other civil rights issues. Whose rights—the right of one child to attend the school in his or her neighborhood or the right of another child to attend an integrated school—should be paramount in a busing case? Whose rights—the woman's right to control her life or the fetus's right to live—are to be sacrificed?

In some cases, compromise is possible. In its own way, the Supreme Court has been trying to compromise, or at least to make some distinctions and qualifications. It has struck down strict racial quotas but upheld race-conscious programs. It has divided pregnancy into trimesters and permitted the state to ban abortion after the second trimester. More recently, it has permitted a wide range of regulations on abortion. But in the final analysis, some issues can never be compromised. In the last century, slavery was one. In this century, state-imposed racial segregation was another. There was no compromise on these issues; one side won and the other side lost. We look back now and wonder how anybody could have upheld slavery or segregation. Maybe some of the issues now in dispute will look similarly one-sided to people in the future. In the meantime, it would be wise not to think that *we* live in the future. Whether we like it or not, we are caught up in the dilemmas and uncertainties of the present.

Notes

1. "*Bakke* and the Equal Protection Clause," in Fred W. Friendly and Martha J. H. Elliott, *The Constitution: That Delicate Balance* (New York: Random House, 1984), pp. 212-13.
2. Friendly and Elliott, p. 217.
3. *University of California Regents v. Bakke*, 438 U.S. 265 (1978).
4. Friendly and Elliott, pp. 229-30.
5. Richard Gambino, *Blood of My Blood: The Dilemma of the Italian-Americans* (Garden City, NY: Doubleday & Co., 1974), p. 71.
6. Michael Novak, *The Guns of Lattimer* (New York: Basic Books, 1978), p. 216.
7. Fox Butterfield, "Why Asians Are Going to the Head of the Class," *New York Times*, Aug. 3, 1986, special supplement on education (Section 12), pp. 20-22.
8. *Bowers v. Hardwick* (1986).
9. See Joseph Epstein, "The Joys of Victimhood," *New York Times Magazine*, July 2, 1989, pp. 20 + .
10. Jack C. Plano and Milton Greenberg, *The American Political Dictionary, 6th Edition* (New York: Holt, Rinehart and Winston, 1982), p. 53.
11. Malcolm X, *Autobiography* (New York: Grove Press, Inc., 1966), p. 201.
12. *Civil Rights Cases*, 109 U.S. 3 (1883).
13. *Plessy v. Ferguson*, 163 U.S. 537 (1896).
14. *Brown v. Board of Education of Topeka, Kansas*, 347 U.S. 483 (1954).
15. *Heart of Atlanta Motel, Inc. v. United States*, 379 U.S. 241 (1964).
16. *United Steelworkers v. Weber* (1979); *Fullilove v. Klutznick* (1980).
17. *Memphis Firefighters v. Stotts* (1984); *Wygant v. Jackson Board of Education* (1986).
18. *Local 93 v. City of Cleveland* (1986); *Local 28 v. Equal Opportunity Commission* (1986).
19. *Richmond v. Croson* (1989); *Martin v. Wilks* (1989); *Ward's Cove Packing Co. v. Atonio* (1989). The last of these cases was not directly concerned with affirmative action, but it might discourage a business from adopting a "voluntary" affirmative action program, instituted as insurance against costly discrimination suits that it previously would have had difficulty winning. The *Ward's Cove* decision made it easier for the employer to win such suits. Linda Greenhouse, "The Court's Shift to Right," *New York Times*, June 7, 1989, p. A22.
20. For an illuminating account of the Boston busing controversy and its aftermath, see J. Anthony Lukas, *Common Ground* (New York: Alfred A. Knopf, 1985).
21. *Milliken v. Bradley*, 418 U.S. 717 (1974).
22. Betty Friedan, *The Feminine Mystique* (New York: W. W. Norton & Co., 1963).

23. Robin Morgan, *Sisterhood Is Powerful* (New York: Vintage Books, 1970).

24. On abortion, for example, Phyllis Schlafly noted that bureaucrats in the Department of Health, Education, and Welfare had already construed the Education Amendments passed by Congress in 1972—amendments that said nothing about abortion—to require college health services to pay for students' abortions. Phyllis Schlafly, *The Power of the Positive Woman* (New Rochelle, NY: Arlington House, 1977), p. 89.

25. Mary Corcoran and Greg J. Duncan, "Work History, Labor Force Attachment, and Earnings Differences Between The Races and Sexes," *Journal of Human Resources* (Winter 1979), pp. 1-20.

26. Quoted in George McKenna and Stanley Feingold, eds., *Taking Sides: Clashing Views on Controversial Political Issues*, 6th ed. (Guilford, CT: Dushkin Publishing Group, 1989), p. 212.

27. For other opposing views, see Ronnie Steinberg and Lois Haignere, "Now Is the Time for Pay Equity," *Consumer Research*, Oct. 1984, pp. 18-20; Geoffrey Cowley, "Comparable Worth: Another Terrible Idea," *Washington Monthly*, Jan. 1984, pp. 53-57.

28. Friendly and Elliott, chap. 12.

29. *Griswold v. Connecticut*, 381 U.S. 479 (1965).

30. *Akron v. Akron Center for Reproductive Health* (1983).

31. See O'Connor's dissent in *Akron v. Akron Center for Reproductive Health* (1983).

32. History professor Linda Gordon, a pro-choice advocate, thinks that "abstract ethical arguments over when life begins" should be left out of the abortion debate on grounds that they "are not illuminating" and "inevitably become moralistic." *See* her remarks in "Is Abortion the Issue?" a symposium in *Harper's*, July 1986, p. 37. But if all arguments concerning the humanity of the fetus were ruled out, the abortion debate would be stripped of much of its content, and it would be impossible to understand what has generated the controversy. Abortion, then, would not be an *issue*, in the proper meaning of that word, because it would not be debatable.

33. William Safire, "Option 3: 'Pro-Comp'," *New York Times*, July 6, 1989, p. A21.

34. See Ellen Willis's remarks in the *Harper's* symposium, p. 43.

What a country! What a country!
Every day a new frontier.
What a rootin' tootin'
six-gun shootin' country
We've got here.

Lee Adams and Charles Strouse

Crime and Punishments

THE RIGHTS OF CRIMINAL SUSPECTS

State Police Powers / The Bill of Rights and the States / Total Incorporation: Justice Black's Theory / Selective Incorporation: The Process of Absorption Suspects' Rights in the 1960s: Four Cases: *Mapp v. Ohio* (1961): The Exclusionary Rule *Gideon v. Wainwright* (1963): Right to Free Counsel *Escobedo v. Illinois* (1964): Lawyers at the Station House *Miranda v. Arizona* (1966): The Miranda Warnings / Law and Order

PUNISHMENTS

Four Purposes of Punishment: Rehabilitation Deterrence Incapacitation Retribution Some Drawbacks of Punishment / Cruel and Unusual Punishment Overcrowded Jails and Prisons / Capital Punishment: The *Furman* and *Gregg* Cases

REFLECTIONS

It was an early Saturday afternoon in December 1984. He **The Subway Gunman** was sitting in a downtown subway car in New York City. To any would-be mugger he must have looked like a pushover: a skinny guy with wire-rimmed glasses, 37 years old. His name was Bernhard Hugo Goetz. Press accounts would later describe him as "scholarly looking," "frail," and "vulnerable." A wimp. Suddenly, four youths, all under 21 at the time, began to move toward him. Two were carrying long screwdrivers, which they used for breaking into coin-operated video game machines. All of them had police records, mainly for petty crimes, although one of them, Daryl Cabey, was awaiting trial for armed robbery. A total of 10 bench warrants were out for their arrests because of failures to keep court dates.*

*This account is drawn from the following sources: Amy Stromberg, "New Yorkers Rally to 'Vigilante's' Defense," *Washington Times*, January 4, 1985, p. 4A; "Shots in Subway Echo Across Nation as Support Grows," *The Record* (Bergen County, NJ), January 6, 1985, p. A-3; Robert D. McFadden, "Goetz: A Private Man in a Public Debate," *New York Times*, January 6, 1985, pp. 1, 22; (Continued on page 160)

They walked over to Goetz. According to police testimony, two of them later admitted that they were about to mug him.[1] If so, it was no big deal. On the New York City subway, mugging has developed its own routine. You find a guy like Goetz, you ask him for money, and he gives it to you. Then you do what you want with him: hit him in the face, slam your foot into his stomach, scare the hell out of him and make him call you "sir"—have some fun. It happens at all hours and it usually starts with a line like "Gimme a cigarette," or "Gimme five dollars."

Maybe these kids were just panhandling, which is what two of them later insisted. If so, the outcome must have seemed predictable to them. They would ask the skinny guy for money, and more than likely he would give it to them. At any rate, one or more of them did ask Goetz for five dollars. Then everything got very unpredictable.

Goetz reached into his belt, pulled out a nickel-plated .38, and started firing. He shot two of the youths in the stomach and got the others in the back as they tried to run away. Then, after helping two elderly women to their feet and chatting with the train conductor, he jumped off the train at the next station and disappeared into the subway tunnel.

Prior to this incident, Bernhard Goetz had never committed an act of violence. He was an electronics engineer who ran his own business. He was not a "loner." He had friends, was in close touch with his relatives, and was active in community affairs. There was nothing particularly strange about Bernhard Goetz. Yet we have his own words to describe what happened on that Saturday afternoon in December on the IRT subway: "I turned into a monster, and that's the truth."[2]

Why did he?

The human heart is a very dark place. No one can understand all that goes on there. But anyone searching for clues in the case of Bernhard Goetz might take into account something that had happened three years earlier. Again, the scene was the New York subway. Goetz had just gotten off at Canal Street, near his apartment. He was walking out of the station carrying packages of expensive electronic equipment. Three youths jumped him, grabbed his packages, and ran. When Goetz gave chase, they stopped, put down the packages, and began beating him. When a police officer appeared, two of the three ran, but the third, intent on working over Goetz, did not see the officer. The captured assailant was taken to Criminal Court and held for two and a half hours, then released. Goetz and the arresting officer went to the same building to give their accounts of the incident. It took six hours. A doorman in Goetz's apartment later recalled that Goetz "came back all shook up. His coat was a mess. All he could say was, 'Do you believe this? I spent all this time there, and this guy walked out in two and a half hours.' " Three weeks later Goetz was certain that he saw the same youth on the street mugging somebody else.[3]

Goetz bought three guns, two .38 revolvers and a 9-mm automatic. The .38 he was carrying that Saturday in 1984 was loaded with hollow-tipped bullets, the kind that flatten out on impact to inflict maximum damage. Daryl Cabey was hit in the spine and paralyzed from the waist down. He also suffered permanent brain damage and so was never tried on the armed robbery charge. The other three youths made surprisingly fast recoveries, and within months two of them were back on the streets committing crime. In May 1985, James Ramseur, now 20, held a gun on a pregnant woman while another man raped and sodomized her. He was sentenced to a 12- to 25-year term in state prison. In August of that year Barry Allen, also 20, was caught yanking a gold chain from a woman's

The actions of Bernhard Goetz, New York City's "subway vigilante," sparked intense controversy between supporters who believed the government was failing in its duties to protect its citizens and critics who feared such vigilantism would only lead to chaos.

neck and given a 6-month sentence, then paroled; later he violated the terms of probation and was given four years. Troy Canty, 20, committed no new crimes but pleaded guilty to a previous charge of stealing money from video game machines. He was released on condition that he finish a drug rehabilitation program.

Goetz fled to Concord, New Hampshire, after the shooting and turned himself in to the police. He waived extradition hearings and was taken back to New York. After a two-year legal battle with Manhattan's district attorney that was finally resolved by New York State's highest court (the issue was whether or not Goetz's actions were based upon a "reasonable" fear of being harmed), Goetz went on trial in April 1987 on charges of attempted murder, assault, and possession of an illegal weapon. In June a jury found him not guilty of the first two charges but guilty of the weapons charge. In October the judge sentenced Goetz to six months in jail, but in 1988 the sentence was overturned by a New York State appellate court and the case was sent back to the trial judge for resentencing. This time the judge sentenced Goetz to a year. With time off for good behavior, he served eight months and was released in September 1989.

From the outset of his case Goetz enjoyed passionate public support. Even before he turned himself in, police switchboards were jammed with calls running 99 percent to 1 in favor of "the subway gunman," as the press called him. After Goetz turned himself in, his neighbors set up a defense fund; within a few days thousands of dollars poured in. Many donors enclosed notes telling of their own experiences. Even though Goetz was white and the youths were black, support for him cut across racial lines. The Congress of Racial Equality (CORE), a black civil rights group, offered to provide him with legal aid. A *New York Times* poll showed that whites approved of Goetz's action by 56 to 26 percent; blacks supported it by 45 to 33 percent.

Not that there were not dissenting voices. Harlem congressman

Charles Rangel asked what would have happened if the races had been reversed, if Goetz had been black and the youths white. Rangel doubted that there would have been so much support for his actions. William Kunstler, the attorney famous for his defense of radicals and revolutionaries, suddenly turned into a law-and-order advocate who deplored "frontier justice"; Kunstler said that to elevate it to the level of law would "make life in New York infinitely dangerous to all our citizens." (He served as attorney for Daryl Cabey, the paralyzed youth, in a 1-million-dollar damage suit against Goetz.) The *New York Times* took the same view. Any attempt to justify Goetz's conduct, the *Times* said, could only threaten "public safety."[4]

But the most indignant critic of Goetz was Barry Allen, one of the wounded youths. Shortly after the incident—seven months before he was caught chain-snatching and more than a year before he was sentenced for violating probation—Allen pronounced his own judgment in the case of Bernhard Hugo Goetz: "That man took the law into his own hands, man. He got to be punished."[5]

*   *   *   *   *

We cannot be certain why Bernhard Goetz took the law into his own hands, but one apparent reason was that he felt it was not protecting him from violent crime. Many other Americans agree, which explains the deluge of public support for Goetz. The public blames our courts for excessive lenience. In 1972, 66 percent of the public said the courts have not "dealt harshly enough with criminals"; the percentage rose to 79 in 1975 and 85 in 1983.[6] During the 1988 presidential campaign, one of the most potent television commercials for President Bush was one showing criminals going around in a revolving door; it implied that Bush's opponent, Massachusetts governor Michael Dukakis, was letting criminals out of prison as soon as they were put in. The public response to that commercial was so favorable that it helped wipe out a 17-point lead Dukakis had previously enjoyed in the polls.

People are right to worry about violent crime; rates have soared in America since the 1960s. From 1960 to 1987, incidents of assault with intent to kill increased almost 500 percent, from 72.6 per 100,000 people in 1960 to 351 per 100,000 in 1987; during the same period, robbery increased more than 400 percent, from 49.6 per 100,000 people in 1960 to 213 per 100,000 in 1987.[7] Some of the apparent increase in crime may simply be the result of better record keeping. But if we examine crime statistics between 1971 and 1987, when the new methods were already in place, we still see a giant increase (see Figure 6.1).

Today one out of every 31 Americans 12 years of age or older is victimized by a violent crime every year. Blacks are the most frequently victimized. According to a 1985 Justice Department study, Americans as a whole have one chance in 133 of being murdered during their lifetimes: for black males, the chances are one in 21.[8] For some crimes, such as murder and robbery, there has been a decline since the early 1980s, leading criminologists to speculate that the aging of the American population may already be having its effect on the crimes associated with youth. But such statistics are small comfort to people who must live in places like the South Bronx in New York City and the Watts area of Los Angeles, where, as political scientists James Q. Wilson and John J. DiIulio write:

Conditions are not much better than they are in Beirut on a bad day. Drugs, especially crack, are sold openly on street corners; rival gangs shoot at each other from moving automobiles; automatic weapons are carried by teenagers onto school playgrounds; innocent people hide behind double-locked doors and shuttered windows. In Los Angeles there is at least one gang murder every day, Sundays included. A 10-foot-high concrete wall is being built around the junior high school one of us attended, in order, the principal explained, to keep stray bullets from hitting children on the playground.[9]

As for public fears that criminals are not being punished—again, there is some substance to them. Sentencing policies in America are tougher than in a number of other countries, but a large number of violent criminals never get to the sentencing stage. For a variety of reasons, the police in America are not very effective in catching criminals and prosecutors are not very effective in getting them convicted.[10] In 1982, for every 500 crimes reported in the nation, only 100 resulted in arrests. Of those 100 arrests, only 20 adults and 5 juveniles actually went to

FIGURE 6-1

Violent Crimes in the United States

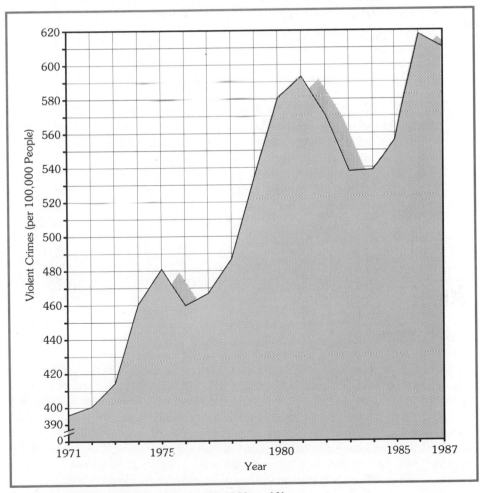

Data source: *Statistical Abstract*, 1981, p. 173; 1989, p. 161.

Violent crimes are homicide, rape, robbery, and assault.

GO AHEAD. MAKE MY DAY...

Drawing by Skelley; © 1985.

prison.[11] In some areas the sentencing rate is even lower. For example, take New York City. In 1980 two *New York Times* reporters sifted through the records and found that 99 percent of felony arrests made in New York City did not lead to a single day in state prison. The overwhelming majority (80 percent) were not even prosecuted as felons.[12]

So Bernhard Goetz bought his own guns and used one of them. People supported his behavior because they felt that the laws were not working. Three centuries ago the British philosopher Thomas Hobbes also worried about this kind of mentality. As you will recall from chapter 1, Hobbes raised the question of what life would be like if we lived in a "state of nature," without laws. In such a state, Hobbes wrote, no one would work because no one could be sure that his earnings would not be stolen. There would be no agriculture, no construction, no navigation, no knowledge, no account of time, no arts, no learning; "and which is worst of all, continual fear, and danger of violent death; and the life of man solitary, poor, nasty, brutish, and short." Hobbes is the patron of people who have to live behind triple-lock doors.[13]

But now consider Hobbes's solution. The only way to get away from lawlessness, he said, is to hand over all power to an absolute government, preferably an absolute monarchy. He thought that any talk of "human rights" or "checks and balances" was dangerous nonsense. Are we ready to go that far to combat crime? Some desperate souls might say yes, but most of us would probably consider the cure worse than the disease. Americans revere their Constitution, and the Constitution contains a Bill of Rights that protects basic human liberties. These liberties include the right to a fair trial, the right to counsel, protection against illegal searches and seizures, the prohibition of "cruel and unusual punishment," and due process of law. Most of us agree that it would be a bad bargain to throw out these essential civil liberties in order to stop crime.

What, then, *is* the solution? Proposals range from getting tougher on criminals to attacking the underlying causes of crime by investing more in social programs. Running like a thread through many of these proposals is the question of whether or not our courts have been too lenient and open in interpreting the liberties guaranteed in the Bill of Rights.

In this chapter we explore some of the facets of the law-and-order controversy. We focus on two broad issues: the rights of criminal subjects and the kinds of punishments handed down to those who are found guilty.

The Rights of Criminal Suspects

Violent crime in America began its dramatic increase in the 1960s, the same decade in which the Supreme Court handed down major new rulings in the field of suspects' rights. In 1961 the Court ruled that evidence obtained without a search warrant may not be used in state trials. In 1964 it ruled that criminal suspects may have their lawyers present during police questioning. And in 1966 it ruled that arrests are not valid unless defendants have been advised of their right to remain silent; warned that anything they say can and may be used against them; told that they have a right to a lawyer and that, if they lack the funds, they are entitled to free legal representation.[14]

Rightly or wrongly, many people suspect that there is a connection between the increase in crime and the new safeguards. Even apart from that suspicion, many people are appalled to think that, in the words of former Supreme Court justice Benjamin N. Cardozo, "the criminal is to go free because the constable has blundered."[15]

Yet there is another side of the argument. Former Supreme Court justice Thomas C. Clark once observed that "nothing can destroy a government more quickly than its failure to observe its own laws, or worse, the charter of its own existence."[16] The "charter" Justice Clark referred to is the United States Constitution. The Constitution may sometimes be inconvenient for law enforcement authorities. But if we condone its violation, our whole system of "government by laws" is imperiled. The remaining question is whether or not the Supreme Court has correctly interpreted the meaning of the Constitution.

STATE POLICE POWERS

What does the Constitution say about the rights that are available to people accused of crimes? To gain some perspective on this question, we need to step back from our immediate concerns about crime and criminals and look for a moment at how the Bill of Rights used to be understood by the Court.

The United States is a federal system. It is composed of a national government and 50 state governments. The national government is in charge of foreign affairs, interstate commerce, currency, and other matters pertaining to the nation as a whole. Those powers are delegated to the federal government in Article I, Section 8, of the Constitution. But all authority not so delegated is "reserved" to the states.

Those reserved powers are extensive: They allow the states jurisdiction over much of everyday life. Getting married, getting divorced, going to school, driving a car, cashing a check, living securely in your home, walking the street—all fall into the area of state jurisdiction. They are usually referred to as state police powers. When it comes to defining crimes and punishing criminals in these areas, the overwhelming majority of cases are handled in state courts. Federal courts get involved only when the case also involves some provision of the U.S. Constitution or a federal statute.

THE BILL OF RIGHTS AND THE STATES

In the past, cases rarely involved the Bill of Rights. In the 1833 case of *Barron v. Baltimore*, the Supreme Court ruled unanimously that the Bill of Rights was meant to apply only to the federal government. Both the language and the history of the Bill of Rights lent support to that interpretation. The Bill of Rights was added to the Constitution by the First Congress to allay fears voiced during the state ratifying conventions two years earlier. The concern was that the Constitution would give the national government excessive power. Thus, the Bill of Rights begins: "*Congress* shall make no law . . ." (emphasis added). It says nothing about limiting state power.

It could be that the *Barron* ruling is now obsolete. It was a pre-Civil War case, and the war brought great changes in nation-state relations. The Thirteenth, Fourteenth, and Fifteenth Amendments, called the Civil War Amendments because they were passed shortly after the war, made it clear that the states were no longer free to do whatever they wanted within their borders. They could not enslave people, or deprive them of the right to vote because of color, or deny them equal protection or due process.

The Fourteenth Amendment is particularly intriguing. Its second sentence begins, "No *State* shall . . ." (emphasis added). Here we have a counterpart to the First Amendment, a specific limitation on *state* power. Another echo of the Bill of

Rights is found in the due process clause of the Fourteenth Amendment. Word for word, it uses language similar to that found in the Fifth Amendment: Authorities cannot deprive people of "life, liberty, or property, without due process of law." Once again, it makes clear that due process applies to the *states*.

TOTAL INCORPORATION: JUSTICE BLACK'S THEORY

Could it be that the Fourteenth Amendment, through its due process clause, has in some way or other taken over the Bill of Rights and made it apply to the states? This was the position adopted at one point by four justices of the Supreme Court, notably by the late justice Hugo Black. It is called the theory of total incorporation. The argument is that the Bill of Rights was "incorporated" by the Fourteenth Amendment, so that it now applies to the states in the same way that it applies to the federal government.

The theory poses serious difficulties. For one thing, there is no evidence that, in the immediate post-Civil War period, the Court itself ever thought that the Fourteenth Amendment "incorporated" the Bill of Rights. In fact, the Court sometimes said just the opposite. In 1884 it refused to hold that the Fourteenth Amendment compelled the states to use grand juries for indicting criminal suspects (the Fifth Amendment requires it in federal cases).[17] In 1896 the Court held that the Second Amendment, which guarantees the "right of the people to keep and to bear Arms," does not apply to the states. In 1900 the Court said that the states were not held to the same standards as the federal government in jury trials,[18] and in 1908 it held that the Fourteenth Amendment did not protect a person against compulsory self-incrimination, although the Fifth Amendment prohibits self-incrimination in federal cases.[19]

The total incorporation theory also has practical problems. It is generally agreed that some provisions of the Bill of Rights are less important than others. We discussed in chapter 2 how the Second Amendment, which guarantees the right to bear arms, is considered by many constitutional scholars to be obsolete. Others disagree, but even they must admit that *some* portions of the Bill of Rights are no longer very important. Take the provision in the Seventh Amendment stating that jury trials in civil suits are necessary "where the value in controversy shall exceed twenty dollars." In 1789, $20.00 was a small fortune; today it is small change. Should the courts force states to hold jury trials in civil suits where the value in controversy is $20.01?

SELECTIVE INCORPORATION: THE PROCESS OF ABSORPTION

In the post-Civil War period the Supreme Court repeatedly denied that provisions in the Bill of Rights applied to the states. But beginning in the 1920s—more than 50 years after the adoption of the Fourteenth Amendment—the Court began the process of selective incorporation, also called absorption. In the 1925 case of *Gitlow v. New York* the Court said:

> For present purposes we may and do assume that freedom of speech and of the press— which are protected by the First Amendment from abridgment by Congress—are among the fundamental personal rights and "liberties" protected by the due process clause of the Fourteenth Amendment from impairment by the States.

The key word is *fundamental*. In various cases, the Court has ruled that certain parts of the Bill of Rights are so "fundamental" that they apply to the states as well as the federal government. *Gitlow* put freedom of speech and press in the "fundamental" category. Less than a decade later the Court ruled that, at least in certain circumstances, the rights relating to a fair trial that are spelled out in the Sixth Amendment are also "fundamental."[20]

Later in the 1930s the Court wrestled with the question of "fundamentals" when it decided *Palko v. Connecticut* (1937), which involved a man who was convicted of second-degree murder and given a life sentence.[21] The state was not satisfied. It wanted him executed, so it appealed the case and this time won a first-degree conviction against him; he was then given the death sentence. The man appealed, saying that the state had violated the clause in the Fifth Amendment that says that no person shall "be twice put in jeopardy of life or limb" for the same offense. The question in the *Palko* case was whether or not the "double jeopardy" clause applied in state cases, or at any rate applied with the same force with which it applied to the federal government. The Court said it did not. The Court's opinion, by Justice Benjamin Cardozo, rested on the distinction between rights that are "of the very essence of a scheme of ordered liberty" and those that are not. Cardozo said that the essential rights are "absorbed" through the Fourteenth Amendment and applied to the states. "Absorption" is a metaphor that brings to mind the digestive process. Food enters the intestines, and its nutrients are absorbed into the bloodstream. The Bill of Rights, then, is a great mix of material, some of it digestible by the Fourteenth Amendment and some—a kind of roughage?—applicable only to the federal government.

The theory of selective incorporation, or absorption, has certain advantages. It avoids the pitfalls of total incorporation yet acknowledges that at least some parts of the Bill of Rights ought to apply to the states. The trouble with this approach is that it seems highly subjective. How is it possible to tell what is and what is not "of the very essence of a scheme of ordered liberty"? We are given no answer, and Cardozo's judgment in the *Palko* case is not very reassuring. As far as he was concerned, the state of Connecticut did not violate any "essential" liberty when it tried Palko twice for the same offense, the second time sending him to the electric chair. How many people would agree? Would you? One constitutional scholar summed up the problem in Cardozo's approach: It "silently assumes that all or most Americans will agree on which rights are and which are not fundamental."[22]

SUSPECTS' RIGHTS IN THE 1960s: FOUR CASES

For better or worse, the Cardozoan standard has become the Court's ruling doctrine in cases involving the Bill of Rights. In the area of criminal justice, it has served as a vehicle for expanding the rights of criminal suspects. Much of the expansion took place in the 1960s, as the following four cases illustrate.

***Mapp v. Ohio* (1961): The Exclusionary Rule.** The Fourth Amendment requires court-issued warrants before the authorities can conduct "searches and seizures." Since 1914 the Supreme Court has held that evidence seized in violation of the "search and seizure" clause cannot be used in *federal* cases.[23] This is called the exclusionary rule. In a 1949 case, *Wolf v. Colorado*, the Court for the first time said that the "search and seizure" clause applied to the states through the Fourteenth Amendment. The Court refused, however, to apply the exclusionary rule to *state* trials.

Not until 1961 did the Court extend the exclusionary rule to the states. Police in Ohio had raided a women's rooming house without a proper warrant and seized obscene materials. In *Mapp v. Ohio* (1961) the Court said that such materials—fruits of an illegal search—could not be used in the trial. The *Mapp* decision remains very

The Fourth Amendment protects citizens from "unreasonable searches and
seizures" by requiring that police first obtain warrants or, in emergency situations, that they at least have "probable cause." The exclusionary rule prevents
illegally seized evidence from being used in criminal cases.

controversial. Many critics agree with the dissenters in the case, who said that the
decision would put a straitjacket on law enforcement officials by denying them the use
of vital evidence against defendants. The critics often quote Cardozo: "The criminal is
to go free because the constable has blundered."[24] To this observation, Justice
Thomas Clark, author of the *Mapp* opinion, offered a tart reply: "The criminal goes
free, if he must, but it is the law that sets him free."[25]

Gideon v. Wainwright (1963): Right to Free Counsel.

In 1964 *New York
Times* columnist Anthony Lewis published a moving account of the facts behind the
case of *Gideon v. Wainwright* (1963). His book, *Gideon's Trumpet*, is the story of a
man with little education and no money who managed to get his case before the
Supreme Court, where it was argued by some of the most brilliant—and expensive—
legal talents in America.

Clarence Gideon, a defendant in a petty larceny case in Florida, was refused a
court-appointed attorney at his trial. He defended himself as best he could, and he
lost. While serving his time he managed to appeal his case to the Supreme Court,
charging that his Sixth Amendment right to "the assistance of counsel" had been
denied. In a 1932 case (*Powell v. Alabama*) the Court had made it clear that
defendants in state cases are entitled to free and adequate counsel in cases where
they could get the death penalty.[26] But in the 1942 case of *Betts v. Brady* the Court
ruled that in noncapital cases the right to free counsel is not one of the "essential"
rights. In *Gideon* the Court reversed *Betts v. Brady*. It explicitly held that in any kind
of felony criminal case defendants are entitled to free legal services if they cannot
afford them, and that this right is "fundamental," binding on the states as well as on
the federal government.

Escobedo v. Illinois (1964): Lawyers at the Station House.

The stage was
now set for a dramatic expansion of suspects' rights. If defendants in state cases are
entitled to counsel, at what point were they entitled to it? At the trial? After being
indicted? Or earlier? In *Escobedo v. Illinois* (1964) the Court extended the right to
counsel to the police station. A young man named Danny Escobedo had been
brought in for questioning by the Chicago police. He asked for but was denied the

right to have his lawyer present during the interrogation. Under persistent questioning, he made a damaging statement that was used against him during his trial, and he was found guilty of murder. In overturning his conviction, the Court ruled that suspects have the right to have a lawyer present during preliminary questioning or at least at the point "when the process shifts from investigatory to accusatory." In an angry dissent, Justice Byron R. White complained that the right to counsel had now become "an impenetrable barrier to any interrogation once the accused has become a suspect."

***Miranda v. Arizona* (1966): The Miranda Warnings.** The 1966 case of *Miranda v. Arizona* marked a kind of culmination in the area of suspects' rights. *Miranda* was a consolidation of four separate cases involving police interrogation. In each of the cases the defendant had not been advised of his right to remain silent and consult counsel and had blurted out a confession that was later used against him. Each defendant's central claim, then, was not that his Sixth Amendment right to counsel had been abridged, but that the failure to tell him about that right had violated his Fifth Amendment protection against compulsory self-incrimination. ("No person . . . shall be compelled in any criminal case to be a witness against himself.") The Supreme Court supported the defendants' claim. "Our holding," the Court said in a 5-4 decision, "is this: the prosecution may not use statements . . . stemming from custodial interrogation of the defendant unless it demonstrates the use of procedural safeguards effective to secure the privilege against self-incrimination."[27]

What "procedural safeguards"? Here we come to the famous Miranda warnings. Before "custodial" questioning (questioning of an arrested suspect) can begin, the police must give these warnings:

- You have the right to remain silent.
- Anything you do say may be used against you in a court of law.
- You have the right to consult an attorney before speaking to the police and to have an attorney present during any questioning.
- If you cannot afford an attorney, one will be provided for you without cost.

Police in most localities now have these warnings written on a card, and they read them aloud to suspects when they arrest them. The police know that any confession or damaging statement obtained from a suspect before the Miranda warnings have been read will probably be thrown out of court.

Many police carry Miranda cards because failure to inform suspects of their rights will result in reversals of convictions; however, when public safety is endangered, police can question suspects without advising them of their Miranda rights.

WARNING

The constitution requires that I inform you of your rights:

You have a right to remain silent. If you talk to any police officer, anything you say can and will be used against you in court.

You have a right to consult with a lawyer before you are questioned, and may have him with you during questioning.

If you cannot afford a lawyer, one will be appointed for you, if you wish, before any questioning.

If you wish to answer questions, you have the right to stop answering at any time.

You may stop answering questions at any time if you wish to talk to a lawyer, and may have him with you during any further questioning.

POLICE DEPARTMENT   NEW HAVEN, CONNECTICUT

AVISO

La Constitución de los Estados Unidos requiere que se le informe de sus derechos:

Tiene derecho de permanecer en silensio. Si le habla a cualquier oficial de al policía, cualquier cosa que le diga puede ser usado en corte en su contra.

Tiene derecho de consultar con un abogado antes de ser interrogado y a que el abogado esté presente durante el interrogatorio.

Si no tiene dinero para pagar un abogado, la corte le proveerá uno, si así lo desea, antes de cualquier interrogatorio.

Si desea contestar preguntas, tiene derecho de dejar de contestar a las preguntas en cualquier momento.

Si desea hablar con un abogado, peude dejar de contestar a las preguntas en cualquier momento, y el abogado puede permanecer con usted durante el resto del interrogatorio.

Si usted es un menor (menor de 16 años) uno de sus padres o un guardián tiene que estar presente durante alguna admisión, confesión, o declaración, escrita o oral, que usted haga.

RENUNCIA DE DERECHOS

¿Entiende estos derechos?

¿Está dispuesto a renunciar estos derechos y contestar a mis preguntas?

The Court had come a long way since 1925. Before then, it had insisted that the Bill of Rights had no application to the states. Then, in case after case, the Court had been "selectively incorporating" much of the Bill of Rights. Now, in 1966, it was telling state and local police what to do when they made an arrest. The *Miranda* ruling set off an angry backlash. One writer called it "the most reviled decision ever issued by the Supreme Court in a criminal case."[28] But *Miranda* itself did not cause this reaction. The anger had been building for years, especially since the 1961 *Mapp* decision, which barred the use of illegally seized evidence in state cases. *Miranda* was the last straw. The public was fed up, and the politicians knew it.

LAW AND ORDER

Richard Nixon made "law and order" one of his campaign themes when he ran for president in 1968. He promised to fill any Supreme Court vacancies that might come up during his term of office with justices who were "tough on crime." To some extent, he kept that promise. Nixon was able to appoint four new justices during his presidency, and these men modified the direction of the Court rulings on criminal justice. Further appointments, notably those of Ronald Reagan, confirmed this shift. In the 1970s and 1980s the Court did not reverse the rulings of the 1960s, but it did qualify them. The following decisions are examples:

- In 1982 the Court ruled that if the police arrest a college student on campus for under-age drinking and accompany the student back to his or her dormitory to check an ID card, they can seize drugs that are in plain view in the dorm room without a warrant.[29]
- In 1984 the Court ruled that if the police obtain a search warrant that is technically invalid (in this case, because the wrong printed form was used) but that they *believe* is valid, the evidence seized may be used in the trial. This is called the good-faith exception to the exclusionary rule.[30]
- Also in 1984 the Court ruled that a police officer need not read the Miranda warnings to a suspect before questioning him or her in order to protect public safety. (A police officer chased a rape suspect into a supermarket, saw his empty shoulder holster, and asked where the gun was. The suspect pointed to some empty cartons and said, "The gun is over there." The Court ruled that the gun and the suspect's statement could be used as evidence.)[31]
- In 1987 the Court ruled that the police may lie to a lawyer to keep him or her from being present during the questioning of a client. Police in Cranston, Rhode Island, assured a murder suspect's lawyer that they were not going to question his client that evening. They did anyway after the man waived his right to have an attorney present. In upholding the man's conviction for murder, the Court ruled that the right to request an attorney belongs only to the suspect, not the lawyer.[32]
- Also in 1987 the Court ruled that police need not tell a suspect in advance of all the crimes about which he or she might be questioned and need not stop asking questions after a suspect requests a lawyer.[33]
- In 1988 the Court ruled that the police may, without obtaining a warrant, search through garbage left outside someone's home for collection, and that any evidence thus obtained may be used against a defendant during a trial.[34]

In spite of these and other modifications, the Court's rulings in *Mapp, Gideon, Escobedo*, and *Miranda* have never been reversed. What the Court said in those decisions remains: The main provisions of the Bill of Rights apply to the states with as much force as they do to the federal government, and any evidence—whether in the

(Continued on page 146)

GLOBAL PERSPECTIVES:

Criminal Justice in China

The system of criminal justice in the People's Republic of China is very different from any in the West. Among the nations of the world, its system is closest to that of its neighbor to the north, the Soviet Union.

Like the Soviet system, the Chinese system of criminal justice is based upon the ideology of Marxism-Leninism. It views "law" as a social tool of the ruling class. Since the ruling class in China is presumed to be workers and peasants, and since in fact the Communist party has been set up as the leader of workers and peasants, all criminal-justice officials—from police and juries to judges and attorneys for the accused—are under the control of party leaders. An independent judiciary, which is central to the Western idea of justice, does not exist in China.

The approach to the defendant is also quite different from that in the West. It is presumed that people brought to trial in criminal suits are guilty. In Communist China the presumption of innocence is held to be incompatible with the principle of "seeking truth from facts." Not surprisingly, 99 percent of all persons brought to trial in China are found guilty.

This does not mean that all criminal suspects in China are railroaded: that is, found guilty of trumped-up charges (although this can happen in political cases). In ordinary criminal cases, a systematic investigation is undertaken long *before* the trial takes place, and no one is brought to trial unless the authorities are reasonably certain of the suspect's guilt. Thus, many accused people do not even come up for trial; their cases are dismissed during the pretrial investigation.

The trial itself is an elaborate ceremony, a ritual in which the accused is expected to confess his or her misdeeds and beg for mercy. The suspect's lawyer does not argue the client's innocence and may even elaborate on the crimes. The lawyer's sole function for the defendant is to plead for a lighter sentence. The main point of a Chinese criminal trial is to remind the Chinese people that criminals are always punished and that the only hope of lenience is to confess one's crimes and vow to amend one's life.

Capital crimes in China include not only murder but rape and major or repeated acts of thievery. Executions are carried out in a circus atmosphere. The condemned are bound standing up in open trucks and slowly paraded through the streets. A sign over each prisoner specifies the crime: "Thief," "Murderer," "Rapist." The crowds run after the trucks and accompany them to the execution site, usually an open field. The condemned walk or are dragged from the trucks and are forced to kneel in front of numbered stakes in the field. Surrounded by the crowd, they are shot in the back of the head at close range.

(Continued from page 144) form of confessions or incriminating material—obtained in violation of these provisions is not admissible in court. The criminal law decisions of the 1960s are thus very much alive—and controversial. As we saw in the Goetz case, many people share Goetz's view that the law has become impotent in dealing with violent crime. They blame the courts for "handcuffing the police," forcing law-abiding people to take the law into their own hands.

Others disagree with what they see as the principle behind this criticism—that the suspect's rights can be sacrificed so that people can feel more secure—and with its assumption that law enforcement has been impaired. They insist that *Miranda* did not have a detrimental effect on the rate of solving crime. One federally financed study in Illinois, Michigan, and Pennsylvania found that convictions were lost as a result of judges throwing out confessions in only 5 out of the 7,035 cases studied, or 0.07 percent.[35] However, these statistics must be read with caution since they do not measure the number of cases never brought to trial because prosecutors knew they would be thrown out in light of the *Mapp* and *Miranda* rulings.

Punishments

Up to this point we have been discussing the rights of criminal *suspects*. We now turn to a different but related topic: What are the rights of those *convicted* of crimes?

Is this pushing things too far? After having been given Miranda warnings, protected by the Fifth Amendment against self-incrimination, given a fair trial—even a free attorney if necessary—should a convicted criminal receive still more rights? A moment's reflection should convince us that the answer has to be yes.

Let us consider an historical example, a form of punishment common in Europe during the seventeenth and eighteenth centuries called "breaking on the wheel." Criminals convicted of capital crimes were bound hand and foot to a large wheel, then beaten to death with a crowbar. It was all done systematically and ceremonially, usually in front of a large, cheering crowd. The executioner began by smashing the wrists and ankles, then gradually worked toward the middle of the body: the legs, the arms, the shoulders, the pelvis. By the time the executioner reached the rib cage, the prisoner was usually dead.

Even though those who were broken on the wheel had been convicted of serious crimes, today we would say that they still have the right to a humane execution. The Eighth Amendment to the Constitution explicitly recognizes that right;

it bans "cruel and unusual punishments." "Breaking on the wheel" is an easy case; we have no trouble recognizing it as "cruel and unusual." Other, larger questions raised by the topic of punishments are much harder to resolve. Does "cruel and unusual punishment" have a fixed meaning or does that meaning change over time? Why do we punish people? What do we hope to accomplish? In this section we will look more closely at these questions.

FOUR PURPOSES OF PUNISHMENT

Throughout history, four purposes of punishment have been identified. Each has enjoyed its season of prominence; some have fallen from grace at various times. The four are rehabilitation, deterrence, incapacitation, and retribution.

Rehabilitation.   The goal of rehabilitation is to restore individuals to the status of law-abiding citizens. In a way, this form is not really punishment; its advocates usually prefer terms like *treatment* or *correction*. This approach to punishment was much in vogue in the 1930s and 1940s, when many prisons in America were renamed "correctional centers." Rehabilitation seeks to employ a variety of resources, from training and education to psychological counseling, to "cure" criminals. One of its foremost advocates and practitioners is Dr. Karl A. Menninger, a psychologist whose famous clinic in Kansas uses these techniques. Menninger is enthusiastic about rehabilitation: "Do I believe there is effective treatment for offenders, and that they *can be changed? Most certainly and definitely I do.*"[36]

Deterrence.   The attempt here is to discourage further crime. If people see that crime does not pay—indeed, causes unpleasant things to happen to the offender—

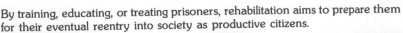

By training, educating, or treating prisoners, rehabilitation aims to prepare them for their eventual reentry into society as productive citizens.

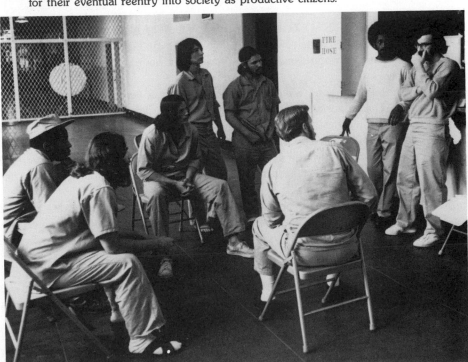

they will think twice before committing it. Perhaps the best-known advocate of deterrence is political scientist James Wilson of UCLA. "Wicked people exist," says Wilson. "They should be punished. And many people neither wicked nor innocent, but watchful, dissembling, and calculating of the opportunities, ponder our reaction to wickedness as a cue to what they might profitably do."[37] Wilson advocates the use of prescribed, fixed sentences for crimes, so that would-be criminals know in advance what will happen to them if they break the law.

Incapacitation.   Despite its rather frightening sound, incapacitation simply means imprisoning people to get them off the streets. Again, the best-known proponent is James Wilson. Citing statistics compiled by researchers on the criminal behavior of 10,000 Philadelphia youths, Wilson noted in 1983 that only 6 percent of them committed five or more offenses before they were 18. Yet these few chronic offenders accounted for *over half* of all recorded delinquencies "and about *two-thirds* of all the violent crimes committed by the entire cohort."[38] In Wilson's view, just locking up these hardened cases would probably make people's lives much easier.

Retribution.   The word *retribution* literally means "paying back." It harks back to the Old Testament law of "an eye for an eye, a tooth for a tooth." On the whole, modern penologists do not recommend this approach to punishment, but in recent years some philosophers have rediscovered a place for it. Consider, for example, this situation. Suppose we were to find that Martin Bormann, or one of the other leading Nazis, were still alive. What would we do with him? Presumably, we would punish him. But why? To rehabilitate him? He would be in his late nineties by now—a little late for rehabilitation! As for deterrence, Bormann's crimes were so unusual that it is difficult to see who would "learn" from seeing him punished. Incapacitation? A 90-year-old Nazi murderer is not a menace on our streets. Unless we just let Bormann go free, the only rationale for punishing him is retribution—"paying him back" for committing genocide.

SOME DRAWBACKS OF PUNISHMENT

All of these reasons for punishment, as we have seen, have certain merits. They also have drawbacks.

The chief drawback of rehabilitation is that there is very little evidence that it works, as even its proponents will admit. Critics, such as James Wilson, cite a number of studies suggesting that in terms of <u>recidivism</u> (repeating crimes after getting out of prison), it seems to make little difference whether or not prisoners have been given therapy, job training, and the like. The tendency toward recidivism apparently depends more on the background and character of the prisoner than on his or her treatment while confined.

Deterrence also has its problems because it assumes that criminals are rational and calculating. In reality a large number of crimes, especially violent crimes, are committed by people who are obviously not rational. This group includes people who are under the influence of drugs or alcohol or are possessed by some uncontrollable rage. Every day the police blotters are full of such crimes: A man finds his wife in the arms of another man and shoots them both; a psychotic woman throws her baby out the window; a friendly card game or drug deal ends in a shootout. Can these crimes be deterred by the threat of punishment? It does not seem likely.

Incapacitation works—for a time—but unless we imprison people for life, we have to let them out eventually. Most prisoners are released after a few years. Then what? Unless we assume that they have been rehabilitated—which most advocates of

(Continued on page 150)

TABLE 6-1

Deterrence and Punishment

	June 8-11, 1989 (telephone)						
	Crime Deterrence Preferences			*Punishment vs. Rehabilitation*			
	Attack social problems	*Improve law enforce- ment*	*No Opinion*	*Punish*	*Rehabil- itate*	*No opinion*	*Number of interviews*
National	61%	32%	7%	38%	48%	14%	1235
Sex							
Men	58	34	8	39	48	13	611
Women	63	30	7	37	49	14	624
Age							
18-29 years	68	27	5	40	48	12	284
30-49 years	63	32	5	42	45	13	508
50 & older	53	36	11	31	53	16	429
Region							
East	63	32	5	40	46	14	294
Midwest	65	27	8	34	53	13	316
South	54	40	6	38	47	15	364
West	62	28	10	39	48	13	261
Race							
White	61	32	7	37	49	14	1097
Non-Whites	61	35	4	42	46	12	127
Education							
College grads.	67	26	7	37	53	10	344
College inc.	69	28	3	37	50	13	267
High School grads.	59	34	7	40	46	14	469
Not H.S. Grads.	51	39	10	35	48	17	145
Politics							
Republicans	58	35	7	41	49	10	427
Democrats	61	32	7	35	51	14	386
Independents	62	30	8	38	45	17	145
Household Income							
$50,000 & over	63	30	7	41	52	7	250
$30,000-$49,999	61	36	3	43	45	12	306
$15,000-$29,999	64	29	7	32	51	17	258
Under $15,000	54	38	8	37	46	17	168
Place							
Large city	61	31	8	34	53	13	244
Suburb	59	35	6	39	52	9	252
Small city/town	63	29	8	38	47	15	518
Rural	60	36	4	40	44	16	210

Source: Gallup poll Report No. 285, June 1989. Reprinted with permission.

Questions asked:
1. To lower the crime rate in the U.S., some people think additional money and effort should go to attacking the social and economic problems that lead to crime, through better education and job training. Others feel more money and effort should go to deterring crime by improving law enforcement with more prisons, police, and judges. Which comes closer to your view?
2. In dealing with those who are in prison, do you think it is more important to punish them for their crimes, or more important to get them started "on the right road"?

Punishment vs. Rehabilitation —Trend		
	1989	*1982*
Punish	38%	30%
Rehabilitate	48	59
No opinion	14	11
	100%	100%

(Continued from page 148) incapacitation would consider unlikely—they will begin committing crimes again, perhaps with some new tricks learned in prison.

Retribution has its own pitfalls. "Paying back" usually means "paying back in kind." If we owe Jack $5, we must pay him back $5; if we owe him $500, we must pay him back $500, maybe with interest. Now, suppose Jack has set fire to his girlfriend. Does it follow that we should pay him back by igniting him? Most of us indignantly reject that suggestion; after all, we are not barbarians. Yet the very idea of "paying back" lifts the lid on some dangerous emotions in the human heart.

This discussion of the weaknesses of the various reasons for punishment does not mean that there is no justification for punishing criminals. It may mean the opposite. Each of the four reasons for punishment has its merits. Rehabilitation may not always work, but apparently it does in some cases, which may be enough to make it worth trying.[39] Deterrence also probably works in some cases; not all criminals are mindless, and there is evidence that the *certainty* of punishment may make people think twice before breaking the law. Incapacitation also works, at least in the short run. And retribution has its own particular rationale, as we saw in the case of punishing Nazi criminals.

Still in punishing criminals, we must punish humanely. We cannot break people on the wheel, tear out their intestines, brand their foreheads, or clip their ears. All these practices were once common, even in "civilized" countries like England, but we consider them savage today.

CRUEL AND UNUSUAL PUNISHMENT

What is "cruel and unusual punishment"? The expression has at least two meanings. First, it means the deliberate, wanton infliction of pain. Pain is not incidental to the punishment; it is the whole point of it. Crucifixion, for example, is a very inefficient way of putting someone to death because it takes a long time. But that is its point—it is supposed to take a long time, in order to maximize the pain. The electric chair or gas chamber may also inflict pain, but that is *not* their primary purpose.

Second, "cruel and unusual punishment" means punishment that is disproportionate to the offense that has been committed. It might not be "cruel and unusual" to imprison a mass murderer for life, but it probably would be to do the same to a first-offense petty thief. The Supreme Court ruled on this issue in the 1910 case of *Weems v. United States*. Weems, a former Coast Guard official in the Philippine Islands (which at that time was under U.S. jurisdiction), was convicted of defrauding the government of 612 pesos (about $120). Using a provision of the old Spanish code, a judge sentenced him to 15 years of imprisonment chained at the ankle and wrist. The Supreme Court ruled that the punishment was cruel because of its disproportionality. The Court conceded that its interpretation of "cruel" may never have occurred to the framers of the Eighth Amendment; the punishment was not breaking on the wheel, or disembowelment, or the other practices that the framers sought to outlaw. Nevertheless, the Court added, the meaning of "cruel" is not limited to those practices.

When considering the Eighth Amendment in light of these previous points, we have to take into account what the Court has referred to as "the evolving standards of decency that mark the progress of a maturing society."[40] Even after the passage of the Eighth Amendment, for example, whippings were administered to prisoners in some states. Such practices today would probably not survive court challenge on Eighth Amendment grounds. The point is that we now consider more varieties of punishment to be "cruel and unusual" than we would have in the eighteenth century. In this respect, our standards of decency have "evolved."

OVERCROWDED JAILS AND PRISONS

Our jails and prisons are becoming increasingly crowded, in part because judges have been imposing stiffer sentences. Since 1970 our prison population has nearly doubled, and it is continuing to grow at an annual rate of 12 percent. Today more than one out of every 600 Americans is in prison. Only the Soviet Union and South Africa have a larger percentage of the population confined. Prison building in America has not kept up with the growth in the numbers of inmates. The overcrowding has put a strain on existing facilities, often resulting in unsanitary conditions, breakdowns in order and discipline, and inadequate medical care. Figure 6.2 on the following page illustrates the rapid rise in the prison population.

Of course, jails and prisons are not supposed to be pleasant places. There have been periodic protests against prison conditions in the past, but the general attitude, even of inmates, is summed up in the prisoners' slogan: "If you can't do the time, don't do the crime." Beginning in the 1970s, however, attitudes began changing. The federal judiciary led the way. Judges began taking a newer and more critical look at prison conditions. In a number of cases they declared those conditions to be in violation of the Eighth Amendment's ban on "cruel and unusual punishments." By the 1980s, prison authorities in at least 30 states were under federal court order to remedy conditions in their institutions.

The orders were coming largely from lower federal courts—district courts and courts of appeal. The Supreme Court was more reluctant to hold that overcrowding violates the Constitution. In *Bell v. Wolfish* (1979) the Court warned the lower courts against getting too involved "with the minutiae of prison administration." The *Bell* case concerned the practice of putting two inmates in cells originally designed for one. The lower federal courts ruled that "double bunking" in jails violates the inmates' right to "due process of law."[41] In a tartly worded opinion, the Supreme Court reversed these rulings. "We disagree with both the district court and the court of appeals that there is some sort of 'one man, one cell' principle lurking in the due process clause of the Fifth Amendment."

But the *Bell* decision did not stop all federal judges from making decisions based on "the minutiae of prison administration." One of the most controversial of these decisions was handed down in 1983 by a district court judge in Manhattan, Morris Lasker. Judge Lasker ruled that overcrowding in the city jail had caused inmates to suffer a number of "privations," including a copying machine that "is frequently out of ink and paper" and "classes that have been offered, and then . . . closed out" at the

Many forms of punishment common in Europe during the Inquisition of the sixteenth century would now be considered "cruel and unusual" and would be banned by the Eighth Amendment.

Today some judges consider overcrowding to be a form of "cruel and unusual punishment" banned by the Eighth Amendment. This has resulted in the early release of criminals and demonstrates the need to balance the rights of prisoners against the rights of society.

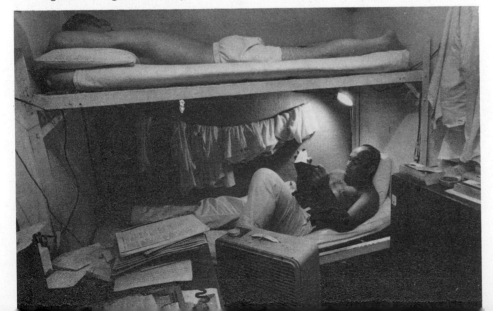

FIGURE 6-2

Our Increasing Prison Population

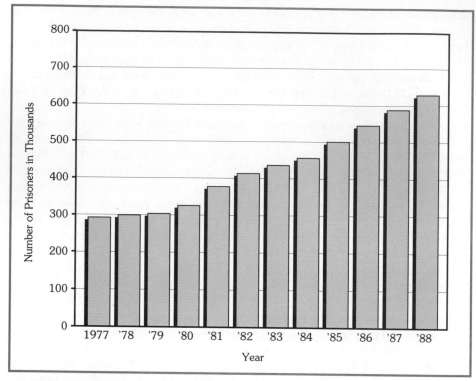

Data Source: U.S. Department of Justice, 1988.

The prison population of the United States, which has more than doubled over the past 10 years, is growing more rapidly than the total population of the country. In 1978 there were 135 prisoners for every 100,000 Americans; by 1988 the number of people in prison had increased to 255 for every 100,000 Americans.

last minute.[42] His ruling forced the city to release 613 jail inmates on nominal bail or no bail. Most of these inmates were career criminals or individuals accused of violent crimes such as rape or armed robbery. Within a month, 55 of them had been rearrested on new charges, and about a third failed to show up for their court dates—double the number that would have been expected under ordinary circumstances.[43]

In citing broken copying machines and closed-out classes as evidence of constitutional violations, Judge Lasker may have gone too far. But the Supreme Court's earlier allusion to "evolving standards of decency" in the treatment of criminals needs to be considered. Our standards have changed; we will no longer tolerate practices that were once acceptable. How far we go—how far our standards have evolved—is a matter for debate and reflection. We need to balance the rights of prisoners against the rights of society. But there can be no simple or static meaning to the phrase *cruel and unusual punishment.*

CAPITAL PUNISHMENT: THE *FURMAN* AND *GREGG* CASES

For a time it seemed that the Supreme Court was prepared to consider the death penalty a form of "cruel and unusual punishment." When the Court struck down all existing death penalty statutes in the case of *Furman v. Georgia* (1972), many thought that it had abolished capital punishment. Actually, only two members of the five-

(Continued on page 154)

FIGURE **6-3**

Who Is Executed, and Where

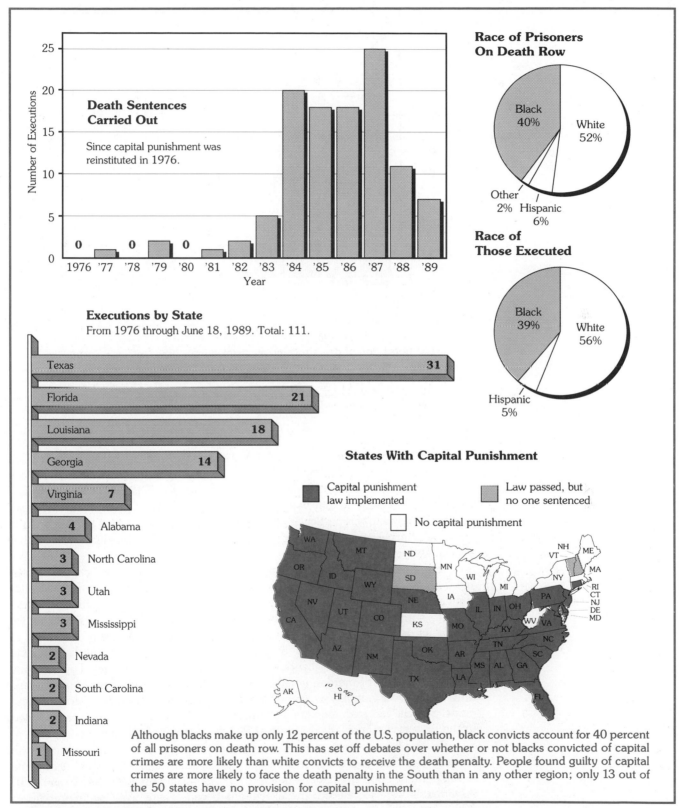

FIGURE **6-4**

Death Row Population, 1980-1989

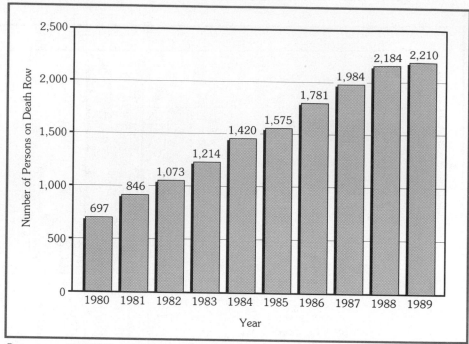

Data source: NAACP Legal Defense Fund; *Statistical Abstract*, 1984, p. 187.

The population of death-row inmates tripled from 1980 (697 convicts) to 1989 (2,210 convicts). In part, this increase may be a reflection of an increasingly get-tough attitude by the public since the reinstitution of the death penalty, but it is more likely a build-up caused by the frequent appeals and stays of execution granted to condemned prisoners.

(Continued from page 152) member *Furman* majority thought that capital punishment violates the Eighth Amendment. The other three members of the majority took the view that capital punishment is unconstitutional only when applied in an arbitrary or a racially discriminatory manner, as they believed it was in this case. There were four dissenters in the *Furman* case, and they were prepared to uphold capital punishment in general and as it applied to this particular case. Not surprisingly, then, with a slight change of court personnel—and a different case before the court—the majority went the other way a few years later.

In the latter case, *Gregg v. Georgia* (1976), the majority upheld capital punishment under certain circumstances. In his majority opinion in the case, Justice Potter Stewart noted that the law in question (a new Georgia capital punishment statute) went to some lengths to avoid arbitrary procedures in capital cases. For example, courts were not given complete discretion in handing out death sentences to murderers but had to consult a series of guidelines spelling out "aggravating circumstances," such as whether or not the murder had been committed by someone already convicted of murder, whether or not it endangered the lives of bystanders, and whether or not it was committed in the course of a major felony. These guidelines, Stewart said, together with other safeguards against arbitrariness included in the new statute, preserved it against Eighth Amendment challenges.

By this time 34 other states had enacted capital punishment statutes with features like Georgia's designed to avoid the "arbitrary and capricious" use of the death penalty. Soon the nation's death rows began filling up again (see Figure 6.4). As appeals were exhausted, the executions began. There were no executions in 1980, but within four years the number had risen to 20. This is a far cry from the

FIGURE **6-5**   **155**

Punishments

Public Support of the Death Penalty, 1936-1988*

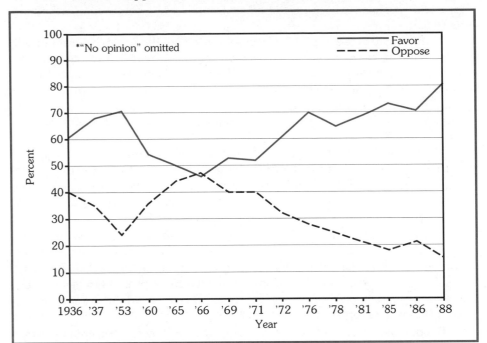

Data source: Gallup Report No. 280, July 1989.

> Public support of the death penalty for murder rose to a high of 79 percent over the past 50 years. Opposition to the penalty was a majority opinion during only one year: 1966. Since that time, public opinion has shifted in response to the rising crime rate and a get-tough attitude by politicians.

1930s, when the average number of executions was just under 200 annually, and today's numbers are unlikely to grow much larger. Judges now go over appeals with extreme care to see if there has been the slightest hint of error. This can mean years of legal maneuvering. Today there are more than 2,000 prisoners on death row (see Figure 6.4), but it will be years before most of them keep their date with the executioner. Some will probably win their appeals.

There are many grounds for appeal, including, of course, evidence of racial prejudice or arbitrariness during the original trial. In 1987 the Court added another. It overturned a capital punishment sentence in Maryland because the prosecutor had discussed the crime's effect on the victim and his family. This was held to be an improper means of influencing the jury.[44] Relying on this precedent, in 1989 the Court threw out the death sentence of a convicted murderer because the prosecutor had talked about the victim's religious and civic commitments. (The prosecutor had read a printed prayer in which the deceased victim had asked God "to help me be a sport in this little game of life.")[45] Other recent decisions, however, may have narrowed the grounds for appeal. In two 1989 cases, the Court rejected the appeals of two death-row inmates who committed their murders when they were 16 and 17 years old. (A year earlier the Court set aside the death penalty in a case involving someone who was 15 when he committed murder; therefore, it now appears that the minimum national standard is 16 years old.)[46] Another 1989 decision considered the issue of executing mentally retarded murderers. The Court set aside the death penalty of a Texas man with an IQ of about 60 because the jury in his case had been limited by Texas law from giving adequate consideration to mental retardation as a mitigating circumstance. However, the Court rejected the contention that the Eighth Amendment "categorically" prohibits the execution of mentally retarded persons, leaving the door open to their execution in some circumstances.[47] Three weeks later, in July 1989, the state of Alabama electrocuted Horace Franklin Dunkins, Jr., a 28-year-old rapist and murderer, whose I.Q. of 69 was considered to be at the borderline of retardation.

The majority of the Supreme Court justices do not think that the death penalty necessarily constitutes "cruel and unusual punishment." Neither, apparently, did the authors of the Eighth Amendment. The same 1789 Congress that passed it also passed death penalty statutes. It also drafted the Fifth Amendment, which prohibits government from depriving people of "life, liberty, or property" without due process of law, implying that government *may* deprive people of their lives if it uses due process.

Yet two justices of the Supreme Court, William Brennan, Jr., and Thurgood Marshall, continue to oppose the death penalty under any circumstances. In their view, the opinions of the Framers should not be controlling. America's "evolving standards" of justice have brought us beyond the rather narrow reading of "cruel and unusual punishments" that prevailed in 1789.

The argument of Brennan and Marshall was more plausible at the time of the *Furman* decision of 1972 than it is today. At that time a majority of Americans opposed the death penalty. Today's polls show, however, that more than 70 percent of Americans favor the death penalty; since *Furman*, capital punishment statutes have been put back on the books of 37 states. The "evolution" of our standards of justice seems to be bringing us back to 1789!

Beyond the question of constitutionality is the question of whether or not capital punishment is morally justifiable. For many, the question turns upon whether or not it deters crimes like murder. If it does, then in taking one life, the state may actually be saving others—those who would have become the victims of a would-be murderer who decided not to murder after considering the penalty for such a crime. This is an extremely difficult argument to prove *or* disprove because murders *not* committed obviously cannot be counted. There have been attempts to compare murder rates in states with and without capital punishment laws and to compare murder rates in states before and after the abolition of capital punishment. These studies, however, have been criticized on a variety of grounds, including their apparent failure to take into account social differences between the states.[48] In any case, proponents and opponents of capital punishment can cite their own favorite empirical studies of its effectiveness as a deterrent. *(Continued at bottom of page 157)*

Points to Remember

1. Four purposes of punishment have been identified: rehabilitation, deterrence, incapacitation, and retribution. *Rehabilitation* seeks to "cure" the criminal; *deterrence* is meant to stop the perpetrator and others from committing crimes; *incapacitation* aims at getting the criminal off the streets; and *retribution* means "paying back" the criminal.

2. Each rationale for punishment has certain weaknesses. Rehabilitation does not seem to work

very well; deterrence assumes that criminals are more rational and calculating than many of them are; incapacitation works only while the criminals are in prison; and retribution can degenerate into a primitive vengeance.

3. The public pressure to get tough on criminals has helped to cause overcrowding in jails and prisons. Federal judges have been forcing states to alleviate these conditions, charging that they vio-

late the due process clause of the Fifth Amendment and the cruel and unusual punishment clause of the Eighth Amendment.

4. Existing capital punishment laws were struck down by the Supreme Court in the 1972 case of *Furman v. Georgia*, but capital punishment—provided it is not administered "arbitrarily and capriciously" or with regard to race— was upheld four years later in the case of *Gregg v. Georgia* (1976).

Is Capital Punishment Justified?

YES Walter Berns

Based upon Walter Berns, *For Capital Punishment: Crime and the Morality of the Death Penalty* (New York: Basic Books, 1979).

For Berns, the essential argument in favor of the death penalty is that justice requires it in certain cases. We should not be ashamed of anger toward those who commit heinous crimes. Anger is our way of recognizing the humanity and moral responsibility of the offender. We live in a moral community, and the criminal calls into question "the very possibility of that community by suggesting that men cannot be trusted freely to respect the property, the person, and the dignity of those with whom they are associated." If, indeed, we are *not* angry with the murderer, that suggests we do not care much for the lives of each other. Our anger makes us recognize that the criminal must repay society for what he or she has taken. Those who take lives must—at least in some cases—pay with their own. It is a terrible punishment, "but there are terrible crimes and terrible criminals."

NO Donal MacNamara

Based upon Donal E. J. MacNamara, "The Case Against Capital Punishment," *Social Action*, April 1961.

MacNamara develops 10 arguments against the death penalty, including: it fails to deter, it is applied prejudicially, it costs the state more than imprisonment, and it is immoral. His moral argument proceeds from the premise that it is wrong for one individual to kill another unless acting in self-defense. What is true for individuals is no less true for the state. The state may take human life only when necessary to protect people against imminent attack by criminals. After the arrest, the rules change. "Once, however, the prisoner has been apprehended and either voluntarily submits to custody or is effectively safeguarded against escape . . . the right of the state to take his life as punishment, retribution, revenge, or retaliation for previously committed offenses . . . does not exist in moral law." Summing up, MacNamara says: "Capital punishment is brutal, sordid, and savage. It violates the law of God and is contrary to the humane and liberal respect for human life characteristic of modern democratic states."

Postscript

MacNamara invokes our Western religious tradition as part of his case against capital punishment. In the past, Christianity and Judaism have justified, and in some cases even prescribed, capital punishment. It may be, however, that "evolving standards" in both religions are moving against capital punishment. Today it is rare to find Christian and Jewish clergy defending it.

In *The Death Penalty: A Debate* (New York: Plenum Press, 1983), Ernest van den Haag and John P. Conrad debate the merits of capital punishment. Hugo Adam Bedau traces the legal and constitutional history of the death penalty in *The Courts, the Constitution, and Capital Punishment* (Lexington, MA: D. C. Heath & Co., 1977).

(Continued from page 156)

Empirically, then, the arguments for and against capital punishment come close to being stalemated, which still leaves the moral question of whether or not it is right for the state to kill killers. In our Taking Sides section above, philosopher Walter Berns argues that it is indeed right, while criminologist Donal E. J. MacNamara emphatically disagrees.

Reflections

At the end of 1984 a skinny, slump-shouldered man with thick glasses became a hero to many Americans after he gunned down four youths in a New York subway car. Bernhard Goetz said that the youths, who had criminal records and were carrying long screwdrivers in their pockets, were about to mug him. When they asked him for five dollars, he pulled out a .38 and administered vigilante justice on the spot.

The trouble with vigilante justice is that any number can play. If everyone packs a gun and nobody trusts the law, many people are going to be shot on real or imagined grounds. As the bullets fly, we find ourselves transported back to the Wild West. Maybe we will even go back to Hobbes's "state of nature," to the war of each against all, where life is "solitary, poor, nasty, brutish, and short."

What is the alternative? If lawbreakers constantly get away with it, should we be surprised if decent people start taking the law into their own hands? Two years earlier Bernhard Goetz had been mugged and badly beaten. So had many other New Yorkers. Yet only a very small percentage of mugging incidents culminate in prison time. Much of the blame for this can be laid on an overcrowded and underfunded justice system. But much of the pressure on the system is the result of a staggering increase in violent crime over the past 30 years, such as the 400 percent increase in aggravated assault that we noted earlier in the chapter. What caused this?

The question of causality in society is hard to pin down. There are so many variables: population shifts, changes in mores, economic conditions, family structures, and so on. The public tends to focus on a single cause, or what it perceives as a cause. People blame the increase in crime on a "climate of permissiveness" fostered by the courts in the 1960s. What angers them are the procedural safeguards extended to criminal suspects in such Supreme Court cases as *Mapp v. Ohio* in 1962 and *Miranda v. Arizona* in 1966.

It may be simplistic to suggest that such decisions could have anything to do with an increase in crime. Very few suspects are released because a confession or incriminating evidence is thrown out of court. But the public's indignation is not based on empirical study. It is based on a gut feeling that our criminal justice system has lost all sense of proportion. Why should a confession obtained without torture be suppressed simply because it was blurted out before the suspect received Miranda warnings? Why should perfectly sound evidence be excluded from the trial just because the police lacked a proper search warrant? If the purpose of a trial is to get at the truth, are we not frustrating that purpose if we keep throwing out the evidence?

These are rhetorical questions, and they can be countered with other rhetorical questions. Shall we violate the Constitution in order to punish lawbreakers? Does the goal of "law and order" permit the authorities to break the highest law of the land? Behind these questions is the implication that the Constitution forbids the use of evidence obtained without a warrant or confessions obtained without Miranda warnings. The Constitution does not—at least not in so many words. It says that no person shall be "compelled in any criminal case to be a witness against himself," and it says that people have a right to be secure against "unreasonable searches and seizures." All the rest has been court interpretation.

Indeed, the whole question of whether or not the Bill of Rights even applies to the states has been a matter of judicial interpretation. By now, the judicial consensus is that most of it does apply—it is "absorbed" through the due process clause of the Fourteenth Amendment.

Procedural safeguards apply to those suspected of crimes. But even those found guilty are entitled to certain protections. The Eighth Amendment forbids "cruel and unusual punishments," which means that people cannot be tortured or made to suffer unduly or disproportionately. Does capital punishment fit any of these categories? The framers of the Eighth Amendment did not think so, but perhaps we are not always bound by their original intent. Those who contend that the death penalty is unconstitutional *today* base their argument upon the premise that our standards have evolved beyond the framers' intentions.

The majority of the Supreme Court rejects the evolutionist view, at least as applied to the case of capital punishment. The Court's position is that the death penalty is unconstitutional only when applied "arbitrarily and capriciously" or in a racially discriminatory manner.

Still, the concept of "evolving standards" is intriguing. Are we Americans ascending, moving onward and upward, in our moral sensibilities? Are we becoming more enlightened and humane, so that punishments that might have once been permissible no longer are? The ramifications of these questions go far beyond the immediate issue of capital punishment.

They apply, for example, to the whole question of punishment. "Cruel and unusual punishment" means the deliberate infliction of pain. But is that not the nature of punishment—the deliberate infliction of pain? When we imprison people, we deliberately deprive them of freedom. Why do we do that? What is the purpose of punishment? In this chapter we have discussed four: rehabilitation, deterrence, incapacitation, and retribution. Some philosophers and criminologists insist that the last three are unworthy motives for incarcerating anyone in modern society. They reject the punitive approach in favor of "treatment"—work training, psychotherapy, and other methods designed to help offenders become law-abiding citizens. So far as the available data show, this rehabilitative approach has had very limited success.

Perhaps that is because rehabilitation has not really been given a chance. Suppose it were, and suppose it worked. "Wicked people exist," says James Wilson. But wicked people would cease to exist once they were rehabilitated. Their wickedness would turn out to be nothing more than a kind of confusion—a confusion that could be dispelled by therapy and training. At that point we would reach the ultimate stage of evolution in our moral standards. Evil would become error, and punishment, treatment. Such a society might be an earthly paradise or it might be a nightmare. It would surely be much different from the unpredictable, chaotic, sometimes violent society of America today.

Notes

1. Esther Pessin, "D.A. Won't Drop Goetz Case," *The Record* (Bergen County, NJ), Dec. 11, 1985, p. A10.

2. Steve Dunleavy, "Tape That Got Goetz Off the Hook," *New York Post*, Jan. 29, 1985, p. 3.

3. Robert D. McFadden, "Goetz: A Private Man in a Public Debate," *New York Times*, Jan. 6, 1985, pp. 1, 22.

4. *New York Times*, Apr. 29, 1986, p. A26.

5. "Youth Shot on Subway Says Goetz Is No Hero," AP Dispatch in the *Record*, (Bergin County, NJ), Jan. 18, 1985, p. A2.

6. Polls taken by National Opinion Research Center, "General Social Surveys," Spring 1983.

7. U.S. Bureau of the Census, *Statistical Abstract of the United States*, 1962, p. 49; 1981, p. 173; 1989, p. 166.

8. John McCaslin, "Odds Are 1-in-133 You Will Be Murdered," *Washington Times*, May 7, 1985, pp. 1, 10A.

9. James Q. Wilson and John J. DiIulio, Jr., "Crackdown," *New Republic*, July 10, 1989, p. 21.

10. See the exchange between James Q. Wilson and Elliot Currie in *Dissent* (Spring 1986), pp. 225, 227.

11. "Crime and Punishment: It Seldom Works That Way," *U.S. News and World Report*, Nov. 1, 1982, p. 41.

12. E. R. Shipp, "99% of Felony Arrests in the City Fail to Bring Terms in State Prison," *New York Times*, Jan. 4, 1981, p. 1.

13. Thomas Hobbes, *Leviathan: On the Matter, Forme and Power of a Commonwealth Ecclesiastical and Civil*, edited by Michael Oakeshott (New York: Collier Books, 1962), pp. 100, 101. (Originally published in 1651.)

14. *Mapp v. Ohio* (1961); *Escobedo v. Illinois* (1964); *Miranda v. Arizona* (1966). These cases will be discussed more thoroughly later in the chapter.

15. *People v. Defore*, 242 N.Y. 13, 21 (1926).

16. *Mapp v. Ohio*, 367 U.S. 643 (1961).

17. *Hurtado v. California* (1884).

18. *Maxwell v. Dow* (1900).
19. *Twining v. New Jersey* (1908).
20. *Powell v. Alabama*, 287 U.S. 45 (1932).
21. *Palko v. Connecticut*, 302 U.S. 319 (1937).
22. Arthur A. North, S.J., *The Supreme Court: Judicial Process and Judicial Politics* (New York: Appleton-Century-Crofts, 1966), p. 118.
23. *Weeks v. United States* (1914).
24. *People v. Defoe*, 242 N.Y. 13, 21 (1926).
25. Majority opinion in *Mapp v. Ohio* (1961).
26. *Powell v. Alabama* (1932).
27. *Miranda v. Arizona*, 384 U.S. 436 (1966).
28. Patrick A. Malone, " 'You Have the Right to Remain Silent': *Miranda* After Twenty Years," *American Scholar* (Summer 1986), p. 367.
29. *Washington v. Chrisman* (1982).
30. *United States v. Leon* (1984).
31. *New York v. Quarles* (1984).
32. *Moran v. Burbine* (1987).
33. *Colorado v. Spring* (1987); *Connecticut v. Barrett* (1987).
34. *California v. Greenwood* (1988).
35. Malone, p. 368.
36. Karl Menninger, *The Crime of Punishment* (New York: The Viking Press, 1968), p. 261.
37. James Q. Wilson, *Thinking About Crime*, rev. ed. (New York: Basic Book, Inc., 1983), p. 260.
38. Wilson, pp. 141-42.
39. See the examples cited by Elliott Currie in *Confronting Crime: An American Challenge* (New York: Pantheon Books, 1985), pp. 239-41.
40. *Trop v. Dulles* (1958).
41. The inmates in this case were not convicted felons; they were suspects awaiting trial. They were thus entitled to the presumption of innocence. They argued that the crowded conditions amounted to a form of punishment for crimes of which they had not yet been convicted. The lower federal courts agreed with them that this violated the due process clause of the Fifth Amendment ("No person shall . . . be deprived of life, liberty, or property, without due process of law").
42. *Benjamin v. Malcolm*, 564 F. Supp. 668 (1983), at 673.
43. Douglas C. McGill, "City's Jail Burden," *New York Times* May 23, 1983, p. B3; Philip Shenon, "Many Inmates Freed on Low Bail Skip Dates in Court in Manhattan," *New York Times*, Dec. 15, 1983, p. A1; "Many Skip Their Day in Court," *New York Times*, Dec. 4, 1983, sec. IV, p. 6.
44. *Booth v. Maryland* (1987).
45. *South Carolina v. Gathers* (1989).
46. *Stanford v. Kentucky* (1989); *Wilkins v. Missouri* (1989).
47. *Penry v. Lynaugh* (1989).
48. See Wilson, pp. 190-93.

(Continued from page 133)

Marcia Chambers, "Goetz Posts Bail and Is Freed; Youths Shot Refuse to Testify," *New York Times*, January 9, 1985, pp. 1, B4; Amy Stromberg, "Subway 'Shane' Brings Cheers in a City Frightened by Muggers," *Washington Times*, January 10, 1985, pp. 1A, 10A; Steve Dunleavy, "Tape That Got Goetz Off the Hook," *New York Post*, January 29, 1985, p. 3; William Tucker, "The Unjust World of Bernhard Goetz," *American Spectator* (April 1985), pp. 18-21; Edwin Diamond and Claire M. Tallarico, "But Where Were the Facts?" *TV Guide*, July 27, 1985, pp. 4-7; Esther Pessin, "D.A. Won't Drop Goetz Case," *The Record* (Bergen County, NJ), December 11, 1985, p. A-10; "The Bernhard Goetz Case," *Gannett Westchester Newspapers* (Westchester County, NY), December 22, 1985, p. B1; Clint Roswell and Thomas Hanrahan, "Ramseur Guilty of Rape," *New York Daily News*, April 8, 1986, p. 5; Todd S. Purdum, "2 of Those Shot by Goetz Face New Jail Terms," *New York Times*, April 9, 1986, p. B5; Kirk Johnson, "Appellate Court Backs Dismissal in Goetz's Case," *New York Times*, April 16, 1986, p. B3; "Man Shot by Goetz Sentenced in Rape," *New York Times*, April 29, 1986, p. B3; Editorial, *New York Times*, April 29, 1986, p. A26; Editorial, *New York Times*, July 6, 1986, p. A26; Kirk Johnson, "State's Top Court Restores Charges in Goetz Shooting," *New York Times*, July 9, 1986, pp. A1, B4; Rick Hampson, Cynthia R. Fagen, and Marsha Kranes, "Goetz Shoots Back," *New York Post*, July 9, 1986, p. 7; Peter Alan Harper, "Goetz: Let the Trial Begin," *The Journal-News* (Rockland County, NY), July 9, 1986, p. A1; Kirk Johnson, "Goetz Is Cleared in Subway Attack; Gun Count Upheld," *New York Times*, June 17, 1987, p. 1; Kirk Johnson, "Goetz Sentenced to Six Months on Gun Charge," *New York Times*, October 20, 1987, p. B1; "Court Overturns Goetz Sentence," *New York Times*, June 29, 1988, p. B4; Ronald Sullivan," Goetz Parole Denied; Must Serve Till September," *New York Times*, March 4, 1989, p. 31.

Lyrics at the top of page 133 are by Lee Adams and Charles Strouse—Strada Music © 1962. All rights of Strada Music are administered by the Songwriter's Guild of America, 276 Fifth Avenue, New York, NY 10001. Reprinted with permission.

PART III

Political Institutions

H ere we examine the chief organs of government in Washington: the Congress, the presidency, the federal bureaucracy, and the federal judiciary. Chapter 7 looks at Congress at work and follows the process by which it passes laws, while Chapter 8 explores the conflicts that often paralyze Congress and suggests some reforms. Chapter 9 describes the enormous powers possessed by the president, but Chapter 10 surveys the equally formidable checks on presiden-tial power by the Congress, the judiciary, the bureaucracy, and the public. In Chapter 11 we see that the federal bureaucracy does not simply carry out the orders of the president but that it has a mind of its own—indeed, many minds—and that it has virtues as well as flaws. Chapter 12 studies the judiciary, another organ that plays a key political role, exercising great discretion as it interprets both the laws and the Constitution of our country.

7

Congress at Work

"Mr. Popham, when he was Speaker, and the Lower House had sat long, and done in effect nothing, coming one day to Queen Elizabeth, she said to him: 'Now, Mr. Speaker, what hath passed in the Lower House?' He answered: 'If it please Your Majesty, seven weeks.' "

Sir Francis Bacon, *Apophthegms* (on the Parliament of 1581)

In 1983 Americans became aware of a major tragedy in **Riders** Africa. Hundreds of thousands of people in Ethiopia, Ghana, Mauritania, Mozambique, and the Sudan were dying of starvation—victims of drought, civil war, and government incompetence. On his return from the area, Senator John Danforth of Missouri said: "I saw what people look like when they're eating leaves off trees."[1] Almost daily, American television carried the pictures: mothers with withered breasts trying to nurse babies with bloated stomachs, desperate families staring at the camera with huge, frightened eyes. Clearly, food had to be sent to these people quickly. President Reagan asked Congress to pass an emergency relief measure, and in March 1984 the House of Representatives passed a bill providing $60 million in aid to the victims. Then the bill headed to the Senate for what appeared to be an easy passage.*

*This account is drawn from the following sources: *Congressional Quarterly Almanac, 1984* (Washington, DC: Congressional Quarterly, Inc., 1985), pp. 90-92, 429-39; *New York Times*, August 19, 1983, I, 4; September 18, 1983, I, 7; March 4, 1984, I, 7;

(Continued on facing page)

That prospect of an easy passage was, in a way, the trouble. A noncontroversial measure like the drought relief bill makes the perfect vehicle for carrying riders. A <u>rider</u> is an amendment to a bill that has nothing directly to do with that bill. In the House of Representatives riders are called "nongermane amendments" and are forbidden. But in the Senate riders are allowed. What happens, then, is that noncontroversial bills function as locomotives, pulling a wide variety of other measures along that might not pass on their own. Moreover, riders can be attached on the Senate floor, whereas separate bills ordinarily must first pass through committees. Riders, then, are very attractive to senators. Once one senator succeeds in attaching a rider to a bill, others are encouraged to offer their pet proposals.

Such was the fate of the emergency relief bill. Senator Alan J. Dixon of Illinois, who had been trying to raise support for a bill to provide a $100-million increase in the summer youth employment program, managed to attach his bill as an amendment to the drought relief bill. What came next was later recounted by Gregg Easterbrook, a writer for *Atlantic Monthly* magazine:

All aboard! The train was about to leave the station. A noncontroversial philanthropic bill—who could be against food for drought victims and summer jobs for youth?—was ideal as a carrier of baggage. Within two days the Senate had attached no fewer than thirty-five more riders to that bill.[2]

Children in the Sheik Sherif settlement in Jijika, Ethiopia, await food distribution. A $60 million U.S. emergency relief measure to aid hundreds of thousands of starving Africans took four months to pass through Congress; the bill had become loaded down with Senate riders, which delayed its passage.

The "baggage" now consisted of an amendment providing $14 million for the Cumberland Gap Bypass Tunnel; $5 billion for the Commodity Credit Corporation; $2.3 billion for the Rural Housing Insurance Fund; $850,000 for recreation in Nassau County, New York; $70 million for the Corporation for Public Broadcasting; $1 million for abandoned-mine reclamation grants for Montana; $25 million for United States Customs Service airplanes; and so on and on. Among the other riders were two especially prized by the Reagan administration: $62 million for military aid to El Salvador and $21 million in aid to the Contras, the insurgent forces fighting the Communist government of Nicaragua.

The House served notice that the Senate had gone too far—"overstepped its prerogatives," in the words of House Appropriations Committee chairman Jamie Whitten. The Senate had attached so many amendments, Whitten said, that the bill looked like "a Sears, Roebuck catalog." He could understand it, he said, if it were later in the year and Congress were about to adjourn: "At the end of a session, if it's the last train going, you jump on."[3] But it was still early in the year; there was plenty of time to board. Because the Senate version was so cluttered with amendments, Whitten decided to start over and write a new House bill. Back to square one.

Then came the news reports that the Contra forces had mined the harbors of Nicaragua, apparently with CIA assistance. A great uproar ensued, and legislators competed with one another to express their outrage. Both houses passed resolutions deploring the harbor mining. Neither of the resolutions was binding—they were merely expressions of concern—but both consumed a lot of time. The House debate lasted 10 hours, not because there was any doubt about passage of the resolution (it carried by a margin of 281 to 11), but because so many members wanted

April 11, 1984, I, 1; April 12, 1984, I, 1; April 13, 1984, I, 4; April 18, 1984, I, 12; Gregg Easterbrook, "What's Wrong With Congress?" *Atlantic Monthly* (December 1984), pp. 62-64.

to make speeches in front of the television camera mounted in the House
of Representatives. By the time the debate was over, it was time to
adjourn for the Easter holiday.

In mid-May the House passed a new version of the emergency aid
bill, one that removed some of the Senate's riders. Since the Senate and
House bills differed, it was necessary to reconcile the two versions and put
together a single bill that could be approved by both houses. This is the
function of a *conference committee*, a special committee composed of
members of the two houses. Shortly before the bill went to conference,
the president of El Salvador, José Napoleon Duarte, met with House
leaders and persuaded them to restore the $62 million for El Salvador
that the House had just deleted. The $21 million for Contra aid, however,
remained in dispute.

Then the White House got back into the act. Its lobbyists let it be
known that President Reagan would not support the bill unless it included
the $21 million in Contra aid. The House continued to insist that it would
not accept any version of the bill that contained such aid. Worried that the
politics of the situation were working against the administration, Senate
majority leader Howard Baker repeatedly warned President Reagan in
June 1984 that the chances of getting the Contra aid were slim. What is
more, the House Democratic leadership was having a field day with the
administration's refusal to compromise. The Democrats were charging
that Reagan was holding up the money for the summer youth employment program that Illinois senator Dixon had first attached to the bill back
in April. Dixon had already demonstrated to his colleagues' satisfaction
that not only Illinois but almost every other state in the Union—44 out of
50—would get some share of the money. The pressure was on Reagan to
give in before school let out for the summer. Finally he did, and so did
administration supporters in the Senate. On June 25, 1984, the Senate
voted to go along with the House and delete the $21 million for the
Contras. The next day the House voted for an identical bill, and the
measure was sent to the president.

When the bill was finally signed by President Reagan in July 1984,
four months had elapsed since its introduction in the Senate. In the
process the bill was transformed from a single-item African relief bill
costing $60 million to an omnibus law containing 22 provisions and
costing $1.1 billion. By now the intended beneficiaries of the summer
employment program were well out of school, and an unknown number
of African drought victims—the original beneficiaries of the bill—had
perished.

*   *   *   *   *

At times the legislative process in America is like a minefield: At any
number of points, a bill faces mortal danger. It can die in committee, or it
can die on the House or the Senate floor. Its different versions, House and
Senate, may turn out to be so different that the two houses remain
deadlocked. The bill can be vetoed by the president. And, as we have
seen, it can become so loaded down with amendments that it is in danger
of collapsing from the sheer weight.

In most other democratic countries, the legislative process is much
more predictable. If this were Great Britain and President Reagan were
prime minister, he could have been certain of getting his African relief bill
passed in short order. The same would be true of aid to the Contras. He
would have gotten these measures passed because his party would

control Parliament, and he would control his party. Or, in President George Bush's case, if Bush were prime minister he would have a secure, obedient Republican majority in Congress that would pass his legislation to implement his "war on drugs" just the way he wants it; instead, Congress threatens to go its own way and shape its own version of the "war." Only by the most delicate negotiations can America's chief executive get what he wants out of Congress. This is especially true when Congress is controlled by the opposition (which can never happen in Great Britain), but even when both branches of Congress come from the same party, a president, unlike a prime minister, can seldom be sure of legislative success. We need to understand why. This chapter, then, will examine the operation of the legislative process in Congress, trace the steps through which a bill becomes a law, and take a look at some of the other things members of Congress do besides making laws.

Congress and Parliament

Most popular governments in the world have a parliament. Parliamentary systems work differently than our congressional system. Both systems have a national legislature with members elected from different geographic areas. But there the similarities end.

THE INDEPENDENCE OF CONGRESS

In parliamentary systems, there is no separation of powers; the executive is elected by the legislature. In theory this makes the executive dependent on the legislature, but in practice it works the opposite way. The chief executive in parliamentary systems— usually called a prime minister or a premier—dominates the parliament. For example, in Great Britain when the prime minister and the cabinet submit a bill to Parliament, Parliament passes the bill. It would be unthinkable for a parliamentary legislature to reject or radically revise a major piece of legislation submitted to it by a cabinet and prime minister. In the American system, that happens all the time.

WEAK PARTY CONTROL

The vehicle that permits an executive to dominate a parliament is the political party. Parties are strong and disciplined in most parliamentary countries. There are no primary elections. Candidates are nominated because they have been loyal to the party organizations; any member of a parliament who failed to support the leadership in a major vote would not be renominated at the next election. His or her career in politics would probably be finished. In Congress the leadership is, by comparison, very weak. Robert Dole, when he was majority leader of the Senate, once remarked that he ought to be called "majority pleader."[4] At that time the Republicans were the majority party in the Senate. Today the Democrats are in control, but the current majority leader, Maine Democrat George J. Mitchell, has to do the same pleading. "I have attempted," he said in 1989, "to accommodate every Senator in every reasonable way."[5]

LOCALISM

Members of parliament represent their party; members of Congress represent their districts or states. Though somewhat oversimplified, that fact sums up an important difference between the two. The parliamentary representative cannot survive politically if he or she falls into disfavor with the party. But if a member of Congress fails to follow the party's line, party leaders can do little about it. At most they can deprive the member of some choice committee assignment, but even then they may overreach themselves. In 1984 former Democrat Phil Gramm of Texas was thus deprived for voting with the Republicans on key issues; he then bolted the Democratic party, ran for the Senate as a Republican, and won. Congressional party leaders are better advised to use carrots than sticks to keep wavering representatives in line.

The real stick-wielders are the constituents. If the legislator falls into disfavor with them, the game is over. This is not true in Great Britain, France, or other parliamentary democracies. There, if a loyal party member loses in his or her district, party leaders may run the member in a more congenial district. Rarely does that happen in America. By law a congressional candidate must establish residency in the state to be represented, and the law is reinforced by custom. A member of Congress who left one district for another would be called a carpetbagger. Since the representative's daily salt comes from the state or district table, he or she is constantly on the lookout for ways of pleasing the folks back home. This helps to explain the popularity of what is called pork-barrel legislation—dams, irrigation projects, day-care centers, and the like—that provide jobs and other benefits for local interests. Many of the Senate riders attached to the African relief bill were of this nature.

BICAMERALISM

Bicameralism, meaning "two chambers," is another feature that sets Congress apart from parliamentary systems. The American legislature was modeled, at least indirectly, after the British Parliament, which has two chambers, the House of Lords and

FINDING OUT ABOUT CONGRESS

If you are not sure who your congressional representative is, call your city or county board of elections. (It may be called "Election Department," "Elections Board," or similar names, and you can find it in the Blue Pages section of the telephone book.) Tell them where you live and they will tell you the names of your representatives and your congressional district number. If you want to get in touch with your representative or senator, call the Capitol Hill switchboard at (202) 224-3121.

The reference room of your local public library may carry *Congressional Quarterly Weekly Report*, a fascinating and informative periodical that tells about the current goings-on in Congress and other branches as they relate to Congress. Congressional Quarterly also publishes an annual *Almanac* summarizing the year's events.

To find out who sits on what committee in Congress and to get other useful information about members of the House and Senate, see the *Con-*

gressional Directory, published every year by the U.S. Government Printing Office.

The *Congressional Directory* includes brief biographical sketches of members of Congress, but for a much better account, see *The Almanac of American Politics*, published every year by Michael Barone and Grant Ujifusa (Washington, DC: National Journal). It includes frank, informal sketches of your legislators and information about their campaign expenditures and ratings by liberal and conservative pressure groups.

If you have cable television service, you can watch live, unedited debates in the House of Representatives and (in some areas) the Senate. You can read somewhat edited versions of the debates in the *Congressional Record*, published daily by the U.S. Government Printing Office. Some local libraries keep current issues of the *Record*; big-city and university libraries keep both current and back issues.

the House of Commons. Today the British House of Lords is powerless; membership in it is an honor but little more. In reality Great Britain has a <u>unicameral</u> (single-chamber) system in its House of Commons, and that is true of almost every other parliament.

In contrast, the American national legislature consists of a Senate, with 100 senators representing the 50 states (2 per state), and a House of Representatives, composed of 435 members elected from congressional districts in the states. (In addition, U.S. insular territories have representatives in Congress. These delegates from Puerto Rico, the Virgin Islands, Guam, and American Samoa have floor privileges and vote in committee but may not vote on the floor. The District of Columbia also has one nonvoting member in the House of Representatives.) To make things more complicated, senators and representatives are elected for different terms. Representatives are elected every two years; senators, every six. (The Senate terms are staggered, meaning that every two years one-third of the senators are up for reelection.) The Framers of the Constitution added yet another distinction between the two houses: Senators were to be appointed by state legislatures, not popularly elected. The Seventeenth Amendment to the Constitution, ratified in 1913, changed that by providing for popular election of senators.

The way we become senator nowadays.

This 1890 cartoon illustrates the public view of the Senate as a "Millionaires' Club."

THE SENATE: SEPARATE AND DIFFERENT

Unlike the House, the Senate was meant to be an elite body and a brake on the more volatile House. At its inception it consisted of only 26 men (2 from each of the original 13 states), who were to serve as special counselors to—and, if necessary, checks upon—the president. The Senate has unique powers: It gives its advice and consent to treaties and ratifies presidential appointments to cabinet and judicial posts. It is relatively immune to short-range shifts of public sentiment, since its members face the voters only every six years. The Senate is a kind of "gentlemen's club" (although there are female members; see Table 7.1 on page 168), and its pace is more leisurely than that of the House. There are no limitations on debate in the Senate, which permits its members to marshal their arguments like philosophers on the Senate floor. Or, if they are interested in obstruction, they can use their unlimited debating time to mount a filibuster, literally to "talk a bill to death." We will discuss this device later in the chapter. For now it is enough to mention that it is typical of the kind of power the Senate has— the power to say no.

President Reagan felt that power when he tried to put Robert H. Bork on the Supreme Court in 1987 and the Senate said no. President Bush felt it when the Senate said no to the nomination of John Tower as Defense secretary in 1989. It is a formidable power. A senator who had been a House member describes the difference between the types of power in the House and the Senate: "In the House, you learn to get something done by putting together a coalition. . . . But in the Senate, people's power arises from their ability to say no, their power to block anything."[6]

The Senate and the House remain separate and rather aloof from one another. Members of the two houses seldom refer to one another's house by name. They say "the other body." Rarely do members of the two houses mingle, except when delegations from the two bodies meet in a joint conference committee to iron out differences between Senate and House versions of a bill.

The gulf between the two houses of Congress is what the Founders intended, for they were believers in a system of checks and balances. An ambassador to the United States from revolutionary France during the 1790s asked President Washington why the United States needed two houses. France had only one house, the National Assembly. Why did the United States need a Senate? As it happened, the two were drinking tea at the time. It was the custom then to pour one's tea from the cup into a saucer (which was conveniently bowl-shaped) before drinking it. Washington asked

(Continued on page 169)   167

TABLE **7-1**

Minorities in Congress

Women in Congress

House (27)

California	Nancy Pelosi, D; Barbara Boxer, D.
Colorado	Patricia Schroeder, D.
Connecticut	Barbara B. Kennelly, D; Nancy L. Johnson, R.
Florida	Ileana Ros-Lehtinen, R (elected Aug. 29).
Hawaii	Patricia F. Saiki, R.
Illinois	Cardiss Collins, D; Lynn Martin, R.
Indiana	Jill Long, D (elected March 28).
Kansas	Jan Meyers, R.
Louisiana	Lindy (Mrs. Hale) Boggs, D.
Maine	Olympia J. Snowe, R.
Maryland	Helen Delich Bentley, R; Beverly B. Byron, D; Constance A. Morella, R.
Nebraska	Virginia Smith, R.
Nevada	Barbara F. Vucanovich, R.
New Jersey	Marge Roukema, R.
New York	Louise M. Slaughter, D; Nita M. Lowey, D.
Ohio	Marcy Kaptur, D; Mary Rose Oakar, D.
Rhode Island	Claudine Schneider, R.
South Carolina	Liz J. Patterson, D.
Tennessee	Marilyn Lloyd, D.
Washington	Jolene Unsoeld, D.

Senate (2)

Kansas	Nancy Landon Kassebaum, R.
Maryland	Barbara A. Mikulski, D.

Blacks in Congress

House (24)

California	Ronald V. Dellums, D; Julian C. Dixon, D; Mervyn M. Dymally, D; Augustus F. Hawkins, D.
District of Columbia	Walter E. Fauntroy, D.*
Georgia	John Lewis, D.
Illinois	Charles A. Hayes, D; Gus Savage, D; Cardiss Collins, D.
Maryland	Kweisi Mfume, D.
Michigan	John Conyers, Jr., D; George W. Crockett, Jr., D.
Mississippi	Mike Espy, D.
Missouri	William L. Clay, D; Alan Wheat, D.
New Jersey	Donald M. Payne, D.
New York	Floyd H. Flake, D; Edolphus Towns, D; Major R. Owens, D; Charles B. Rangel, D.
Ohio	Louis Stokes, D.
Pennsylvania	William H. Gray III, D.
Tennessee	Harold E. Ford, D.
Texas	Craig Washington, D.

Hispanics in Congress

House (12)

California	Edward R. Roybal, D; Matthew G. Martinez, D; Esteban Edward Torres, D.
Florida	Ileana Ros-Lehtinen, R.
New Mexico	Bill Richardson, D.
New York	Robert Garcia, D.
Puerto Rico	Jaime B. Fuster, Popular Dem.
Texas	E. "Kika" de la Garza, D; Henry B. Gonzalez, D; Albert G. Bustamante, D; Solomon P. Ortiz, D.
Virgin Islands	Ron de Lugo, D.*

Asians and Pacific Islanders in Congress

House (5)

California	Norman Y. Mineta, D; Robert T. Matsui, D.
Guam	Ben Blaz, R.*
Hawaii	Patricia F. Saiki, R; Daniel K. Akaka, D.

Senate (2)

Hawaii	Spark M. Matsunaga, D; Daniel K. Inouye, D.

*Non-voting delegate

Source: Congressional Quarterly (Spring 1989). Adapted with permission.

FIGURE **7-1**

Key Differences Between House and Senate

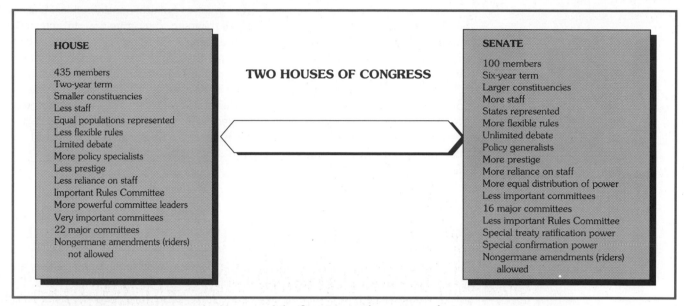

HOUSE	TWO HOUSES OF CONGRESS	SENATE
435 members		100 members
Two-year term		Six-year term
Smaller constituencies		Larger constituencies
Less staff		More staff
Equal populations represented		States represented
Less flexible rules		More flexible rules
Limited debate		Unlimited debate
More policy specialists		Policy generalists
Less prestige		More prestige
Less reliance on staff		More reliance on staff
Important Rules Committee		More equal distribution of power
More powerful committee leaders		Less important committees
Very important committees		16 major committees
22 major committees		Less important Rules Committee
Nongermane amendments (riders) not allowed		Special treaty ratification power
		Special confirmation power
		Nongermane amendments (riders) allowed

The many differences between the House and the Senate provide a system of checks and balances, as the Founders intended. One major difference is that debate in the Senate is almost unlimited; some Senators use this right as an opportunity to filibuster, delaying proceedings of the Senate in order to prevent a vote.

(Continued from page 167)

his visitor why he needed the saucer. Why, to cool my tea, the ambassador is said to have replied. Well, then, said Washington, that is the purpose of the Senate—to cool the steaming legislation of the House.

Some critics complain that the cooling system works too well. In their view, a bill is usually only lukewarm when it emerges from the one house; a journey through the second brings it down to room temperature. Less metaphorically, the complaint is that a bill loses much of its original force as each house qualifies and amends it. To better understand this point, let us follow the passage of a bill on its way to becoming a law.

A Bill Becomes a Law

The first thing to remember is that very few bills *do* become laws, relative to the number that are introduced in every legislative session. Every two years, somewhere around 25,000 bills are introduced, of which approximately 600 make it over the various legislative hurdles to become law. Members of Congress introduce many bills that they know have no chance of passage. But by introducing those bills, the legislators win points with key groups in their constituencies.

INTRODUCING THE BILL

Nearly all bills can be introduced in either house or in both simultaneously. The exception is revenue-raising bills, which, according to the Constitution (Article I, Section 7), must originate in the House of Representatives. Let us suppose that our bill begins in the House. Its introduction is simple: A member drops it in a hopper at the side of the clerk's desk. At the end of the day the clerk opens the box and, in consultation with the Speaker and the Speaker's staff, assigns it to an appropriate committee.

Which committee is "appropriate" often involves political considerations. During the 1960s, for example, a civil rights bill banning discrimination in interstate commerce could have been referred to the Senate Judiciary Committee, which ordinarily considered such bills. But the Senate leadership knew that the bill would have died there, since the committee was controlled by southern conservatives; instead it was divided up and key parts of it were sent to the Senate Commerce Committee, on the grounds they involved interstate commerce. The real reason was that the Commerce Committee was controlled by northern liberals, who would give these sections of the bill more favorable treatment.[7] Today it is not unusual for different parts of bills to be sent to different committees, a practice called multiple referral.

COMMITTEES AND SUBCOMMITTEES: LITTLE LEGISLATURES

The House has 22 standing committees; the Senate, 16. Standing committees are committees that remain from one session of Congress to the next, in contrast to the special committees that Congress creates for some temporary purpose, such as an investigation. In 1973, for example, the Senate created a temporary committee to investigate the Watergate scandal, and 14 years later the Senate and House created a special joint committee to investigate the Iran-Contra scandal.

Standing committees may also conduct investigations, but their main task, at least in the House, is to write legislation. Indeed, it is committees and subcommittees that perform the primary legislative work. To watch the full House or Senate meet, Woodrow Wilson wrote back in 1885, is to watch Congress "on public exhibition," but to watch Congress in its committee rooms is to see "Congress at work." Although slightly exaggerated, the statement was true in 1885 and is still true today. With some justice the standing committees have been called "little legislatures."[8]

The House's 22 standing committees cover a wide range of subjects, from agriculture to ways and means. Some of them, like the Appropriations, Judiciary, and Ways and Means committees, are powerful and influential; others, such as Government Operations and Science, Space, and Technology, are not. New members naturally seek good committee assignments. (What amounts to a good committee assignment may vary with one's district; a legislator from Brooklyn would not be anxious to get on the Agriculture Committee, but many rural members are.) Being assigned to a committee as a first-year member is something like "rushing" at a college fraternity. Incumbent committee members look over each fresh crop of legislators in the quest for new committee members. The final choices are made by a select group within each party's caucus in the House.

The committees have spawned subcommittees, especially since 1946, when Congress passed the Legislative Reorganization Act. This well-intentioned piece of legislation was aimed at cutting back the tangle of committees, then numbering 48 in the House and 33 in the Senate. But by reducing the number of committees, the act opened the way to a multiplication of subcommittees; in 1989 there were almost 300 of them.

Each of these committees and subcommittees has a chair. In the past the member from the majority party with the longest number of consecutive years on the committee automatically became chair. The so-called seniority rule was modified in the early 1970s (see chapter 8). Senior members no longer *automatically* become chairs, although in practice almost all still do. What is important to remember for now

TABLE **7-2**

171

Standing Committees

House		Senate	
Agriculture	8*	Agriculture, Nutrition, and Forestry	6*
Appropriations	13	Appropriations	13
Armed Services	7	Armed Services	6
Banking, Finance, and Urban Affairs	8	Banking, Housing, and Urban Affairs	4
Budget	8	Budget	0
District of Columbia	3	Commerce, Science, and Transportation	8
Education and Labor	8		
Energy and Commerce	6	Energy and Natural Resources	5
Foreign Affairs	8	Environment and Public Works	5
Government Operations	7	Finance	7
House Administration	6	Foreign Relations	7
Interior and Insular Affairs	6	Government Affairs	5
Judiciary	7	Judiciary	6
Merchant Marine and Fisheries	6	Labor and Human Resources	6
Post Office and Civil Service	7	Rules and Administration	0
Public Works and Transportation	6	Small Business	6
Rules	2	Veterans Affairs	0
Science, Space, and Technology	7		
Small Business	6		
Standards of Official Conduct	0		
Veterans Affairs	5		
Ways and Means	6		

*Number of Subcommittees

Source: *Congressional Staff Directory* (Washington, DC: U.S. Government Printing Office, 1987).

Both Senate and House have a variety of committees and subcommittees that prepare bills for floor action. Party leaders in both houses have the final say in deciding which bills are to be sent to which committees. Sometimes bills are divided up into sections and sent to different committees, a practice called multiple referral.

is that the chair is always from the majority party. Thus, from 1981 to 1986, all the committee and subcommittee chairs in the Senate were Republicans, whereas all those in the House were Democrats. The Democrats have since regained the Senate majority, and all Senate committee chairs are now controlled by the Democrats.

Our bill has been assigned to a committee, then a subcommittee. Now what happens? Often nothing. Many bills assigned to committees are *bottled up* and never appear again. At the expiration of the session, they die. If the chair, who initiates action on a bill, refuses to do so, the bill remains his or her captive. By the 1980s many conservative Republicans in the House complained that the House's Democratic committee chairs were bottling up bills that would limit abortions and permit school prayer.

It is very difficult to pry a bill from a committee against the chair's wish. One of the few devices available is a discharge petition. If 218 House members walk up to the Speaker's desk and sign a petition asking that the bill be dislodged from the committee and if the majority later votes to support the petition, the bill is dislodged and reaches the floor of Congress. That very seldom happens. Of the 800 attempts to use discharge petitions in this century, only 24 have succeeded. Democrat Peter W. Rodino, Jr., of New Jersey, whose House Judiciary Committee bottled up school prayer bills in 1984, gloated at the time that few legislators were signing the

"There are days, Hank, when I don't know who's President, what state I'm from, or even if I'm a Democrat or a Republican, but, by God, I still know how to bottle up a piece of legislation in committee." *Drawing by Stan Hunt;* © *1977 The New Yorker Magazine, Inc.*

Republicans' discharge petition. After checking the petition and finding only 40 signatures, Rodino said, "I don't know where all the furor is."[9] Members do not like to put their names on discharge petitions because to do so violates normal procedure and makes those members vulnerable to retribution. Besides, some members who *say* they support a certain bill are privately delighted to see it bottled up.

HEARINGS

Let us assume that our bill is one of the lucky ones. The chair takes it seriously enough to schedule hearings. By this time the bill may have been sent to one of the specialized subcommittees of the committee; the subcommittee chair will preside over the hearings. At this point proponents, opponents, and other witnesses will be invited (subpoenaed, if necessary) to testify before the committee or subcommittee. The witnesses read prepared statements and then answer questions from committee members. Some of the most dramatic dialogues in Congress take place during these question-and-answer sessions. Committee members friendly to the view of the witnesses ask "softball" questions; those opposed try to trip them up.

MARK-UP

Now the work of the committee or subcommittee really begins. Once the hearings are concluded, the members go over the bill line by line, literally "marking it up . . ." amending it as they see fit. They may make only minor changes in language, or they may strike every word after the enacting clause ("Be it enacted by the Senate and the House of Representatives of the United States of America in Congress assembled, That . . .")—in other words, they may write a brand new bill. Rarely does a controversial bill emerge from a committee or subcommittee without changes.

If the bill has been sent to a subcommittee, it must come back to the parent committee before it goes any further in either house. When it does, the committee may make more changes before "reporting it out." Some members may even try to kill it or add crippling amendments. Let us assume, however, that the bill emerges intact and a committee report recommends passage. The House clerk will then put the bill on a calendar (which is simply a list of bills to be debated). Will the full House now vote on it? Not quite yet, at least not if it is a major piece of legislation. First it must go to the House Rules Committee.

HOUSE RULES COMMITTEE

Alone among the standing committees of the House, this committee has nothing to do with the substance of bills. Its function is to serve as a kind of legislative traffic cop. Remember that the House has 435 members, 22 committees, and more than five times that number of subcommittees. The House floor would soon become clogged with bills if it were not for the Rules Committee. It sorts out the bills, decides which should come up for debate and on which dates, sets aside a certain amount of time for debate on each, and decides whether a bill can be amended on the House floor (an open rule) or not (a closed rule).

Although the Rules Committee is supposed to be a traffic cop, it sometimes acts like a roadblock. In the 1950s and early 1960s the committee was controlled by southern conservatives who used it to bottle up civil rights bills. Outraged liberals

GLOBAL PERSPECTIVES:

Standing Committees: Congress and Commons

The standing committees of the American Congress work much differently than their counterparts in the British House of Commons. In Congress, as we have seen, committees serve as "little legislatures." After the bill is submitted, committees make the first revisions, and those revisions are often major ones. Committees hold hearings and take the testimony of witnesses. Then they go into a mark-up session, during which they may completely rewrite the bill. Committee members take pride in the independence of their committees and are respected for the expertise they acquire while working on different types of legislation, especially foreign affairs, armed services, and finance.

In the House of Commons, the committee system is vastly different. This is particularly true of government bills, bills the prime minister wants passed. After being read in the House of Commons, these are brought before one of the standing committees. Unlike ours, British standing committees are not differentiated by subject matter. Any committee can consider any topic. Bills are referred to any committee that is ready to receive them at that point in the timetable. (The single exception to this is the Scottish Standing Committee, to which any measure exclusively concerned with Scotland is referred.) Nor do British committees enjoy the discretion of American committees, at least regarding legislation requested by the executive branch. When it comes to a government bill, the standing committees of Commons are largely committees of detail. Members may tighten and tinker with a bill, but they accept its broad outline. Amendments may be made in committee, but they cannot be attached to the bill without the consent of the government. (If they were to be attached, the government could get them removed on the floor of the Commons.) To be sure, the interaction between committee members and the government is a two-way process in Great Britain, and members of the majority party who sit on the committee can provide valuable advice in the shaping of legislation, advice the Cabinet often accepts. But in Congress, the committee members do more than provide advice; they are writing legislation, and even if the committee majority comes from the president's party, the president can only observe, have friendly chats with committee members, and hope for the best.

With power go prestige and eagerness to serve. In America, service on a powerful committee is an honor, something to brag about to constituents. ("As a member of the House Ways and Means committee, I write tax legislation.") In Great Britain, committee work is a thankless chore to be avoided whenever possible.

demanded reform; majority rule, they said, was being stymied. Eventually reform of a sort came through new liberal appointments and the retirement of the southerners. By the end of the 1970s the Rules Committee was still occasionally blocking bills, but this time the bills were those favored by conservatives, like school prayer and antibusing legislation. Now it was the conservatives' turn to be indignant about the committee's defiance of majority rule.

THE HOUSE FLOOR

Our bill has been reported out of the Rules Committee and scheduled for debate on a certain date. Now, probably, it must pass through one more "committee." All revenue bills, and most others, are first debated by the Committee of the Whole. The Speaker steps down and is replaced by a chair, and the entire House begins *acting* like a

173

Main Display Panels   Chamber Consoles   Voting Station   Summary Display Panel

Electronic voting devices installed in the House in 1973 facilitate the taking of roll call votes. House members are careful not to miss many of these votes because poor attendance records may have to be explained to constituents.

committee. The symbol of this transformation is the removal of the mace, a 3-foot club with an eagle on top, from its pedestal on the Speaker's desk. Once the mace is taken down, the House has become a committee. The advantage of this ritual is that it simplifies and expedites the legislative process. For example, a quorum for debate in the Committee of the Whole is only 100 members, whereas the Constitution requires a majority (218 members) for passage in the House.

The Committee of the Whole debates the bill. If it has been given an open rule, it may amend it. House rules forbid the addition of nongermane amendments—the riders we noted at the beginning of the chapter that the Senate allows.

FINAL HOUSE PASSAGE

Now it is time for final House passage (or defeat) of the bill. For this official act the House must transform itself back into a full legislative body. The mace is put back on its pedestal, and the Speaker returns. The Committee of the Whole now reports to the House, and the official vote of the House is taken. The votes may be by voice only, with the members present shouting "aye" or "nay." At the request of one-fifth of the members present, there must be a roll call vote, in which the name of each person voting is recorded. In the past a roll call vote took a long time because each name had to be called out by a clerk. Since the House installed electronic voting devices in 1973, the process has been greatly accelerated. At the back of every chair is a slot where the member can insert a plastic card; alongside the slot are pushbuttons that allow the member to vote yea, nay, or present. Each member's vote lights up alongside his or her name on a toteboard above the House gallery.

SENATE PASSAGE

Having passed the House, the bill must now pass the Senate, making its way through "the other body" in about the same way that it has maneuvered through the House. There are some differences: The Senate, being a much smaller body, can operate more informally. It has a Rules and Administration Committee, but bills do not have to pass through it on their way to the Senate floor.

In two respects the Senate can be troubling to anyone committed to the orderly

Members of the House and Senate meet in the House chambers to hear President Reagan deliver his State of the Union message to the nation, January 25, 1983.

passage of legislation. One, the rider, we have already discussed at the beginning of the chapter. The other potential roadblock is the filibuster. A filibuster is an attempt to "talk a bill to death." As we mentioned earlier, the Senate, unlike the House, sets no time limits on debate. While the debate goes on, the Senate is prevented from voting or taking any other action. Thus, by monopolizing the floor, a senator can hold up the business of the Senate, which puts pressure on proponents to abandon or modify a bill. A filibuster can be broken by a cloture vote. If 16 senators sign a petition moving to end debate and three-fifths of the entire Senate (not just those present and voting) concur, then each senator has only an hour left to talk about the bill.

Because filibusters are not easy to break, even the threat of one is usually enough to derail legislation. At one time the filibuster was associated almost exclusively with southern conservatives, who used it to block civil rights legislation. But today some northern liberals, like Senator Howard Metzenbaum of Ohio, have become masters of the filibuster and other delaying techniques. "If Metzenbaum's filibuster is overruled," writes Hedrick Smith of the *New York Times*, "he switches to strangling bills by amendment."[10]

CONFERENCE COMMITTEE

Suppose that our bill has passed both the Senate and the House. Is it ready for the president's signature now? Probably not. The chances are that in its current form it is not identical to the original House bill, especially since it can be amended so easily on the Senate floor. In the case of the African relief bill, as you will recall, the Senate tacked 35 extraneous amendments onto the House bill. When the two versions differ greatly, the House and Senate usually appoint a special conference committee to iron out the differences. The conference committee is composed of members from both houses, usually from the committees that wrote the original bills in each.

PRESIDENT'S SIGNATURE OR VETO

If both houses accept the conference committee's version of the bill, it is printed and sent to the president for signature. The president then has three options: to sign the bill (sometimes done reluctantly, sometimes with great gusto and ceremony); to veto the bill; or to do nothing.

I

101st CONGRESS
1st SESSION
H. R. 3199

To amend title 38, United States Code, to establish a program to provide post-secondary educational assistance to students in health professions who are eligible for educational assistance under the Reserve GI Bill program in return for agreement for subsequent service with the Department of Veterans Affairs.

IN THE HOUSE OF REPRESENTATIVES

August 4, 1989

Mr. Smith of New Jersey (for himself, Mr. Montgomery, Mr. Stump, and Mr. Penny) introduced the following bill; which was referred to the Committee on Veterans' Affairs

---

A BILL

To amend title 38, United States Code, to establish a program to provide post-secondary educational assistance to students in health professions who are eligible for educational assistance under the Reserve GI Bill program in return for agreement for subsequent service with the Department of Veterans Affairs.

1   *Be it enacted by the Senate and House of Representa-*

2   *tives of the United States of America in Congress assembled,*

3   **SECTION 1. SHORT TITLE.**

4   This Act may be cited as the "Veterans Health Profes-

5   sionals Educational Amendments of 1989".

Bills are introduced in both houses of Congress, given a number, and put on the calendar for consideration. This bill, H. R. (House Resolution) 3199, which would provide educational grants to veterans, was introduced in the House by Representative Chris Smith (R-New Jersey) in August 1989.

Once signed by the president, the bill becomes a law. If vetoed, it is killed, unless Congress manages to override the veto—a move that requires a two-thirds vote In *both* houses, something seldom achieved. From George Washington's time until the present, there have been thousands of presidential vetoes, but less than 4 percent of them have been overridden.

There remains the third option: A president may decide to take no action. When this option is chosen, the bill will automatically become a law on the tenth day after it was presented (Sundays excepted). Ordinarily, presidents choose to do nothing when they oppose a bill but know they do not have enough support to survive an override. Rather than be humiliated, a president may decide to just let the bill become law. On rare occasions there is another reason why presidents choose not to act. The Constitution (Article I, Section 7) says that if the president does nothing, the bill will become law within 10 days *unless* "the Congress by their Adjournment prevent its

(Continued on page 178)

FIGURE **7-2**

177

How a Bill Becomes Law

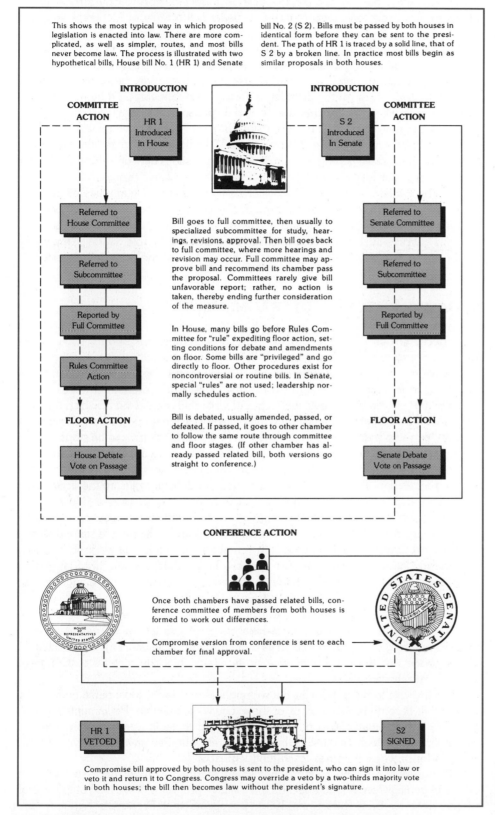

This shows the most typical way in which proposed legislation is enacted into law. There are more complicated, as well as simpler, routes, and most bills never become law. The process is illustrated with two hypothetical bills, House bill No. 1 (HR 1) and Senate bill No. 2 (S 2). Bills must be passed by both houses in identical form before they can be sent to the president. The path of HR 1 is traced by a solid line, that of S 2 by a broken line. In practice most bills begin as similar proposals in both houses.

INTRODUCTION   **INTRODUCTION**

COMMITTEE   **COMMITTEE**
ACTION   **ACTION**

HR 1
Introduced
in House

S 2
Introduced
In Senate

Referred to
House Committee

Referred to
Senate Committee

Bill goes to full committee, then usually to specialized subcommittee for study, hearings, revisions, approval. Then bill goes back to full committee, where more hearings and revision may occur. Full committee may approve bill and recommend its chamber pass the proposal. Committees rarely give bill unfavorable report; rather, no action is taken, thereby ending further consideration of the measure.

Referred to
Subcommittee

Referred to
Subcommittee

Reported by
Full Committee

Reported by
Full Committee

Rules Committee
Action

In House, many bills go before Rules Committee for "rule" expediting floor action, setting conditions for debate and amendments on floor. Some bills are "privileged" and go directly to floor. Other procedures exist for noncontroversial or routine bills. In Senate, special "rules" are not used; leadership normally schedules action.

FLOOR ACTION   **FLOOR ACTION**

Bill is debated, usually amended, passed, or defeated. If passed, it goes to other chamber to follow the same route through committee and floor stages. (If other chamber has already passed related bill, both versions go straight to conference.)

House Debate
Vote on Passage

Senate Debate
Vote on Passage

CONFERENCE ACTION

Once both chambers have passed related bills, conference committee of members from both houses is formed to work out differences.

Compromise version from conference is sent to each chamber for final approval.

HR 1
VETOED

S2
SIGNED

Compromise bill approved by both houses is sent to the president, who can sign it into law or veto it and return it to Congress. Congress may override a veto by a two-thirds majority vote in both houses; the bill then becomes law without the president's signature.

Source: 1987 Congressional Quarterly Almanac, p. 43. Reprinted with permission.

Compromise bill approved by both houses is sent to the president, who can sign it into law or veto it and return it to Congress. Congress may override a veto by a two-thirds majority vote in both houses; the bill then becomes law without the president's signature.

(Continued from page 176) Return, in which Case it shall not be a Law." If Congress adjourns within that 10-day period, the president can kill the bill by refusing to sign it. This is called a pocket veto (the idea being that the president simply puts the legislation in a pocket and walks away). Congress has no chance to override this veto. Fortunately for Congress, adjournments occur only once every two years (each term of Congress lasts two years).

To round out the story, we may assume that our bill has survived the legislative ordeal and become law. But the reality is that most controversial bills do not. They fall through the cracks at one place or another—in committee, on the House or Senate floor, in conference, or on the president's desk—and disappear. Or they may survive, but in such an altered form that their original sponsors vote against them.

We have now completed our excursion through the legislative minefield. In case you have lost the way, Figure 7.2 on page 177 briskly recapitulates the journey.

As we have seen, getting a controversial law passed is difficult at best. Such a bill can fall into jeopardy at any number of places in the legislative process. No doubt this is what the Framers intended. They worried that passionate majorities might force hasty and ill-considered legislation through Congress. For this reason they believed strongly in the need for checks and balances. The system they built for us is full of negative checks—such as the refusal of a committee chair to hold hearings, the use of a filibuster to stop the Senate from voting on a bill, and the presidential veto.

NEGATIVE CHECKS AND FRAGMENTATION

The checks in our legislative process can be overcome, but seldom by a simple majority. For example, a filibuster can be ended, but it takes three-fifths of the entire Senate to impose cloture. A veto can be overridden, but that requires two-thirds of both houses. A discharge petition (which frees a bill from committee) needs only a majority, but the members must walk up and write their names on it, which they are reluctant to do. Negative checks, then, give disproportionate power to minorities. A minority can stop the majority in its tracks, yet minorities in turn can be stopped only by large and determined majorities. One researcher has called this situation "the tyranny of the minorities,"[11] but American democracy was never intended to be purely majoritarian. If it had been, we would find it difficult to justify the activities of the small group of nine non-elected judges who sit on the Supreme Court.

We saw at the beginning of the chapter how the legislative process could tie up a simple emergency relief measure for almost four months while people starved. Many observers of Congress complain about the creakiness of our legislative process, about its tendency toward deadlock. In this chapter's Taking Sides section, historian James Macgregor Burns worries about the "fragmentation of power" in Congress. His critique is disputed by political scientist Gary Orfield.

Whatever people's opinions about how Congress works, most agree that it is hard to predict the fate of a controversial piece of legislation. As we have seen, virtually anything can happen to it on its route through Congress. The unpredictability of the process is, in a way, evidence of its vitality. Nobody dictates to Congress, certainly not the president.

It is impolite to put it this way, but we might as well say it: Most parliaments in the world have become rubber stamps of the executive leadership. Parliaments are very good places for debate. Most parliaments—at least those in democratic countries—are much better at debating issues than is Congress, but they have comparatively little independence when it comes to crafting legislation.

Congress is no rubber stamp, but some presidents enjoy more success than others in getting Congress to enact their legislative programs. If we look at the overall success rate for presidents since 1960, it appears that Presidents Kennedy and Johnson enjoyed the most congressional support and President Nixon the least (see

(Continued on page 180)

Policy Deadlock: Is Congress to Blame?

YES   James MacGregor Burns

Based upon James M. Burns, *The Power to Lead: The Crisis of the American Presidency* (New York: Simon & Schuster, 1984).

"[Congress]," says Burns, "is made up of 535 individualists, most of them of the rugged variety." To be sure, members of Congress do have some ties, but most of those are to their home districts, not to other members of Congress. "So we start with diffusion, not teamwork—with hundreds of men and women fighting separately for their political lives," says Burns.

Leadership is needed, yet, according to Burns, it is sorely lacking in Congress. Power, he says, has been scattered "into a labyrinth of committees, subcommittees, committee staffs, individual legislators, and their assistants." There is party leadership in both houses, but the leaders lack any means of inducing individual members to obey. Burns quotes former House Democratic leader Jim Wright: "You have a hunting license to persuade—that's all." As a result, says Burns, it is hard to get crucial legislation passed and even harder to get cooperation between the executive and legislative branches; the tendency is toward "unholy deadlock."

NO   Gary Orfield

Based upon Gary Orfield, *Congressional Power: Congress and Social Change* (New York: Harcourt Brace Jovanovich, 1975).

Unlike Burns, Orfield sees the obstacles to getting legislation passed as lying not in Congress but in society at large. According to Orfield, "[Liberalism] normally represents a minority position in the United States." We cannot force Congress to pass legislation that only a minority favors. Even at that, Congress has not been inflexible when it comes to reform. It passed important civil rights and anti-poverty legislation, it resisted the efforts of presidents to turn back the clock on social reform, and it forced one of them out of office for misbehavior. These are not the actions of a reactionary or right-wing body. The system works well when there is a clear consensus in the country or when the dominant wing of one party controls both houses. Generally speaking, Orfield says, Americans "have the kind of legislative body they want and deserve."

Postscript

Although it was a Democratic president, Harry S. Truman, who coined the phrase "do-nothing Congress," Republican presidents have assailed Congress for the same reason. This fact underscores the ambiguity in Burns's complaint about congressional inaction. Is inaction always a negative, or does it depend on what Congress is being asked to do?

Arthur Maass's *Congress and the Common Good* (New York: Basic Books, 1983) describes and defends the role of Congress. James Sundquist's *Decline and Resurgence of Congress* (Washington, DC: Brookings Institution, 1981) assesses its weaknesses as well as its strengths. Hedrick Smith's *The Power Game* (New York: Random House, 1988) gives a Washington reporter's "inside view" of a number of our institutions; some of its best chapters center on the maneuvering in Congress.

FIGURE **7-3**

Presidential Success on Votes, 1953-1988*

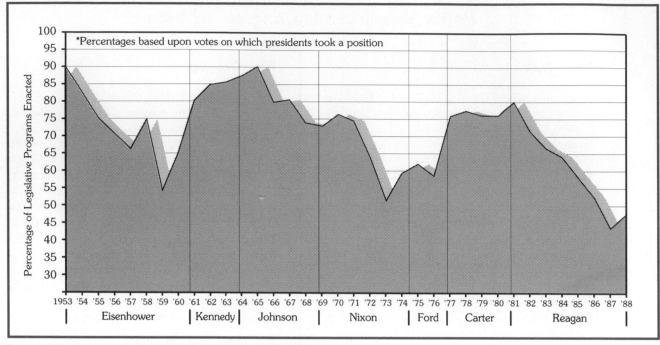

Source: 1988 Congressional Quarterly Almanac, p. 23-B. Reprinted with permission.

It is hard to find clear-cut patterns in the "success rates" of various presidents in congressional votes, although it appears that the rates reached a peak during the time of Kennedy and the early years of Johnson. Some presidents (Reagan, Nixon, Johnson, and Eisenhower) were more successful at the beginning of their administrations, while others (Kennedy, Ford, and Carter) seemed to improve throughout their term in office.

(Continued from page 178) Figure 7.3). More significantly, congressional cooperation with most presidents appears to be higher during the early part of the president's years in office. This shows most dramatically during the Reagan years. In the early 1980s Reagan's success rate in Congress was almost as high as Lyndon Johnson's in the mid-1960s, but by the end of his eight years, it had sunk much lower than Nixon's at its worst.

What Else Do Members Of Congress Do?

We have spent much of this chapter describing the legislative process. But passing laws is only one activity of Congress, and it may not be the most important—at least not to the legislators themselves. What obsesses most legislators most of the time is "how can we please our constituents?" Day and night, members of Congress are devoted to one variety or another of constituency service.

When pollsters ask people to rate the performance of Congress, most say either "fair" or "poor" (see Figure 7.4 on page 182). Yet 99 percent of the members of the House of Representatives and 85 percent of the senators running for election were reelected in 1988. The American people thus seem unhappy with their Congress— but very happy with their members of Congress. There are many reasons for this apparent paradox, not the least of which are all the advantages of incumbency, such as free mailing privileges and support from powerful pressure groups (see chapters 9 and 13). Another important reason is that these legislators work very hard to keep in the good graces of their constituents.

CONSTITUENCY SERVICE

Consider the logic of the American system. In America, parties are weak. Legislators are not dependent on them the way members of Parliament are. There is one master, however, that the representative or senator defies at peril: his or her constituency or the most powerful and active groups within it. Since legislators are not absolutely certain which groups *are* the most powerful, they try to be very nice to everyone back home. House members are particularly concerned about the contentment of their constituents. Senators face election every six years, but House members must run every two, which means that a House member is running for office nearly all the time. Howard E. McCurdy, author of *An Insider's Guide to the Capitol*, says that if by chance you should encounter your representative in Washington, "the appropriate and courteous salutation is 'Hello, sir. . . . How is your campaign coming?' "[12] Charles Peters, editor of *The Washington Monthly*, lays great emphasis on this point. "Nothing," he says, "will help you understand Congress better than the reelection imperative. Do you wonder why the average [congressional] staff member spends four-fifths of his [or her] time on constituent service and one-fifth on legislation?" The reason is that the legislator is working on reelection.[13]

Constituency service is sometimes understood in the narrow sense of doing concrete favors for constituents. Much of this work involves cutting through red tape in the sprawling federal bureaucracy. For example, your father was supposed to begin receiving his Social Security disability check. When he did not, he went to the Social Security office, but without success. Then he went to his representative, who made some telephone calls. One week later your father received a telegram of apology from the Social Security Administration and his first check. This is called casework because your representative functions almost as a social worker. Representatives from inner-city areas do a lot of this kind of work; there are lines of people waiting outside their offices on weekends to talk about such problems.

FIGURE **7-4**

Public's Rating of Congress, 1965-1989*

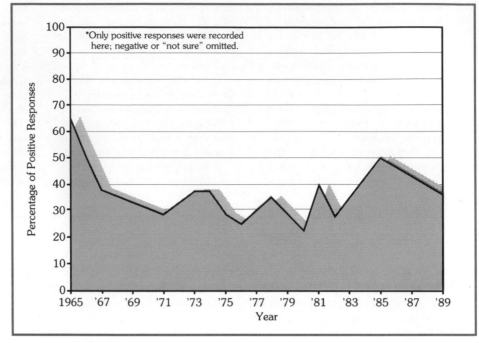

Source: Adapted from a table in *Congressional Quarterly Weekly Report*, July 16, 1989, p. 1812. Adapted with permission.

Responses to Gallup polls taken between 1965 and February 1989 indicate that, overall, the public rated the performance of Congress as fair-to-poor. Based upon the percentage of incumbents reelected, it is likely that individual members would be rated higher. The question asked in this survey was: How do you rate the job done this past year by Congress—excellent, pretty good, only fair, or poor?

But constituency service should be seen in a broader context. Pushing for pork-barrel legislation—legislation that will provide jobs and services in the home district or state—is a kind of constituency service. Then there are private bills. For example, a member of Congress may introduce a bill to waive immigration laws so that a New York City woman can be joined by her Italian husband. Less tangible but no less important are the symbolic favors members of Congress perform. A legislator may introduce a bill knowing full well that it has no chance of passage; the idea is to gain favor back home. Or someone becomes a compulsive "position taker": He or she is often seen on television taking positions on issues. Depending on the tastes of their constituents, the legislators may emphasize patriotism, or peace, or government economy, or compassion. Among congressional colleagues this may be regarded as a joke because nothing so championed ever gets passed. But that does not matter; he or she is a hero to constituents.[14]

We can also put under the category of symbolic favors a multitude of ceremonial tasks, such as dedicating a new wing at a hospital or a library in the district.

Legislators spend much of their time meeting with and writing to individual constituents. For example, anyone wishing to see Congress in session must first stop by his or her representative's office to sign the visitor's book and pick up a pass to the visitor's gallery. (Some representatives actually accompany constituents there.) Nearly every delegation receives an audience. Then there is the mail. As many as 3,000 pieces of mail may arrive each day, most of which are answered by form letters.

As the photo essay on our legislator on the next two pages shows, members of Congress spend much of their days attending committee hearings, voting, performing constituency service, listening to lobbyists, helping their parties, and huddling with staff. It is hard to imagine packing anything else into the day. Yet members of Congress have at least one more role to perform. At this task their performance is uneven: Sometimes they ignore it, and sometimes—especially when television cameras are around—they overdo it. As the day for our congresswoman comes to an end, let us reflect upon the one congressional duty not represented in her typical schedule: overseeing the administration of the laws.

CONGRESSIONAL OVERSIGHT

Congress passes laws. Then what happens? The laws have to be carried out, or administered, which is the job of the executive branch. But are the laws being administered according to the intent of Congress? Are they being carried out—or are they being ignored? Is the administration violating the law or the Constitution? Is it wasting money? Is it harboring Communists or taking payoffs? Is it involved in other dirty tricks? These are the kinds of questions members of Congress might ask as they oversee the administration of our nation's laws.

Congressional oversight is the term used to describe Congress's responsibility for keeping an eye on the bureaucrats in the executive branch—monitoring how well they are carrying out the laws and how effectively they are spending their appropriations. Legislators do not usually have much interest in the issue of bureaucratic performance—the whole question of how the laws are working out in practice. Why should they? Their constituents do not care about such technical and time-consuming things. But like a dozing cat, Congress can suddenly come to life if it smells something interesting. A whiff of scandal, particularly if it seems to be emanating from the other party's closet, may set in motion a full-scale congressional investigation.

Congressional Investigations.   Congress may undertake investigations through its regular standing committees or by means of special, select committees convened for a limited duration. Examples are Senator Joseph McCarthy's investigations of alleged Communist influence during the 1950s, Senator Sam Ervin's Watergate investigation in 1973 and 1974, and the Iran-Contra investigations of 1987.

A congressional investigation is a combination trial, educational forum, and legislative hearing. Witnesses can be subpoenaed to testify, sworn in, and cross-examined. Although the hearings are supposed to be concerned only with fact-finding, the atmosphere usually becomes accusatory, especially when the television cameras are around. A congressional investigation lacks the procedural rigor of a trial: Witnesses may be accompanied by lawyers, but counsel has no right to cross-examine those who accuse their clients; hearsay evidence is admitted; and the whole event can be covered by television and radio.

Congressional investigations can be important learning experiences for the public. Even before the electronic age, Woodrow Wilson contended that the "informing function" of Congress was more important than its legislative one.[15] But here is where the danger lies: Such investigations can degenerate into circuses with members of Congress posturing at the expense of a witness's rights. In the early 1950s, Senator Joseph McCarthy of Wisconsin gave congressional investigations a bad name. Charging that the federal government was infiltrated by Communist spies, he conducted lengthy, well-publicized investigations. His methods, which gave rise to the term McCarthyism, consisted of bullying witnesses, defaming innocent people, using innuendo and smear tactics, and prying into people's personal lives. (For example, McCarthy would insinuate that people were Communists because they had joined a

(Continued on page 186)

1

2

A Representative at Work

After an early morning flight from her home in New Britain, Connecticut, Representative Nancy Johnson arrives at her office in Washington, D.C., at 8:00 A.M. Tuesday morning. Why Tuesday? Because the House of Representatives is usually in session Tuesday through Thursday to allow members of Congress to spend time in their home districts.

Representative Johnson begins her day in Washington with a strategy meeting with leaders in the House to discuss upcoming votes. On her return to her office at 9:00 A.M., Johnson meets with her staff to discuss the day's agenda (1). A series of appointments with constituents and meetings with various organizations interested in legislation begins almost at once. Sometimes Representative Johnson is able to bring in high-level government officials to listen to her constituents' experiences with certain laws. Recently, she brought together officials from the Health Care Financing Administration and members of the Connecticut medical profession to discuss problems with government regulations. This morning she talks with Connecticut students who are visiting Washington (2); she then sees members of the Connecticut Pharmaceutical Association to discuss legislation that will affect their industry (3).

Since members of Congress must, of course, be on hand to debate and vote on bills, Johnson's office is only one block from the House of Representatives. Above right, Johnson is seen leaving the House after voting on the government's budget for fiscal year 1990 (4).

5

6

7

3

4

As a freshman member on the powerful Ways and Means Committee, Representative Johnson voices her opinion on a controversial section of the 1986 Tax Reform Act during a hearing (5). Much of the substantive work on legislation is done in similar committee hearings so that people from the private and public sector may have an opportunity to give their views.

While waiting for the elevator, Johnson reads her mail (6); she takes lunch on the run or during a luncheon meeting with constituents; on trips to and from appointments she often has opportunities to discuss legislative matters with her colleagues. En route to her office, Johnson encounters Representative Cass Bellinger (R-North Carolina) (7).

Later in the day Johnson attends a meeting with U.S. Department of Housing and Urban Development secretary Jack Kemp, who unveils a proposal for eliminating drugs in public housing (8). Members of Congress present their own proposals for addressing the public housing crisis.

At 6:00 P.M. Johnson returns to her office to catch up on correspondence and return telephone calls (9). She often attends dinner meetings where guest speakers lecture on such issues as U.S.-Soviet relations. Her hectic day winds down at 9:00 or 10:00 P.M. when she has a chance to review the day's events and call her husband in Connecticut.

8

9

"Perhaps the witness would care to reconsider his answer to the last question?"
Drawing by Stevenson; © 1979 The New Yorker Magazine, Inc.

(Continued from page 183) left-wing organization while in college or signed a petition circulated by a leftist group.) To the extent that McCarthyism had any content to it, the central ingredient was political paranoia—an obsession with plots and conspiracies.[16] McCarthyites, then and now, find a "small secret team" behind the events of history. Nearly everything that went wrong in our foreign policy, from the loss of China to American reverses in Korea, McCarthy attributed to a domestic "Communist conspiracy."

The Watergate Investigation.   A generation after the McCarthy investigations of the 1950s, another dramatic probe of an administration took place. We will say more about Watergate in chapter 10, but for now a few facts about it can be stated succinctly. In June 1972, Washington, D.C., police apprehended a group of burglars late at night inside Democratic headquarters in the Watergate Hotel Complex; the burglars had been installing a "bug," a small listening device, in one of the office telephones. It turned out that the burglars were acting on orders from people in President Richard Nixon's reelection committee, who in turn were reporting to the highest officials in the White House: Nixon's chief of staff (H. R. Haldeman), his domestic adviser (John D. Ehrlichman), and the attorney general of the United States (Richard Kleindienst).

During most of the summer of 1974, the Senate Watergate investigation preempted television's afternoon soap operas to become something of a soap opera itself. The Watergate hearings helped uncover a very real conspiracy against the democratic process in America and set the stage for major campaign reforms; yet they also had a dark side. From the outset the investigation was conducted like a trial of defendants, and some of the charges made by committee members were without foundation.

The Iran-Contra Investigation.   Since Watergate, there have been other congressional investigations of administrations. During the early years of the Reagan administration, for example, there were probes of the administration's policy in a number of areas, from the environment to the Middle East. For a time it appeared that Reagan himself would not be seriously hurt by any of them. But then, starting at the end of 1986, came the Iran-Contra affair. "Irangate," as the press dubbed it, caused Reagan's reputation to plummet for a time.

We will say more about the Iran-Contra affair in chapter 10. For now it is enough to recall that it had two parts. The first: On November 3, 1986, a newspaper in

Beirut, Lebanon, revealed that Reagan officials had made a secret deal with Iranian officials to ship arms to Iran in exchange for Iranian help in getting American hostages released from a terrorist group in Lebanon. Soon the story was all over the American press. The second part: Three weeks after the Iran disclosures, Attorney General Edwin Meese told reporters that profits from the Iran arms sale had been diverted to the Contras, the antigovernment rebels in Nicaragua. Apparently this had been done at the behest of Lt. Colonel Oliver L. North, an official on the National Security Council (NSC), and Admiral John M. Poindexter, then head of the NSC. In January 1987 both the Senate and the House set up committees to investigate the affair, and between May 5 and August 3 of that year, they held joint public hearings. The testimony and questioning of several key witnesses were carried live on television.

The first part, the arms deal with Iran, was politically embarrassing but not illegal. The second part, the fund diversion, did involve possible criminal violations, since Congress had forbidden government intelligence agencies from using any funds available to them to subsidize the Contras. The purpose of the congressional investigation was to find out what had happened and make recommendations for reform. In the end, the House and Senate committees failed to produce a unanimous report. The Democrats, joined by two Republicans, wrote a majority report, and the others, all Republicans, wrote a bitter dissent.

Opinions differed on the fairness of the Iran-Contra hearings. Defenders said the rules were stacked in favor of witnesses. Witnesses were allowed to consult with attorneys before responding to questions, and their responses could not be interrupted; this permitted the witnesses to deliver long speeches by way of answers. Critics of the hearings claimed that they seemed to prejudge the guilt of some witnesses. Judge Gerhard Gesell, who presided over the trials of North and Poindexter, worried that the hearings endangered their rights. "It's very difficult," he said, "to read portions of the Iran-Contra record to feel that the witnesses were treated decently." Gesell was disturbed by the "political speeches some of the congressmen made before addressing a single question." He said some lawmakers prefaced their questions by saying, in effect, "I know you are guilty; I know you're a traitor."[17]

NO "EXPOSURE FOR THE SAKE OF EXPOSURE"

At various times the Supreme Court has tried to protect the rights of congressional witnesses. One of the more notable attempts was in *Watkins v. United States* (1957), in which the Court ruled that no committee has the power to "expose for the sake of

---

Points to Remember

1. Because legislators owe their presence in Congress more to their constituents than to their parties, they devote much of their time to constituency service.

2. Constituency service includes passing porkbarrel legislation and private bills, doing casework for constituents, and performing a variety of symbolic favors.

3. Members of Congress put in long and hectic days that typically combine committee work, constituency service, voting, reading and answering mail, listening to lobbyists, and meeting with staff.

4. Besides passing laws and serving constituents, legislators are also expected to oversee the federal bureaucracy. This task receives a low priority until a major scandal begins to brew.

5. Concern has often been expressed about the rights of witnesses before congressional committees. Senator Joseph McCarthy's style of investigating, which included bullying and defamation, has given us the term *McCarthyism*.

6. In *Watkins v. United States* (1957), the Supreme Court prohibited congressional committees from engaging in "exposure for the sake of exposure." Any investigation must be related to "a legitimate task of Congress."

exposure." No inquiry, the Court said, "is an end in itself; it must be related to, and in furtherance of, a legitimate task of Congress." In other words, Congress must show that the investigation in some way ties in with the making of laws or the overseeing of the administration. These restraints are extremely flexible, however. The Watergate Committee said its investigations were relevant to the issue of whether or not "new congressional legislation to safeguard the electoral process" was needed. Senator Sam J. Ervin, Jr., of North Carolina, who headed the committee, was more candid when he said that "it was more important that the American people get the truth than that a few people go to jail."[18] Exposure also played a prominent part in the Iran-Contra hearings, which was why they were televised and why some of the legislative members and lawyers for the committees were in close touch with reporters throughout the hearings.

Reflections

When George Washington told his French visitor that the purpose of the Senate was to "cool" the legislation of the House, he was conveying an idea widely accepted in America at the time. The Framers felt that we needed mechanisms to encourage prudent lawmaking so that a bare transient majority could not force legislation upon the nation. That imperative was expressed in their philosophy of checks and balances.

Congress is full of such checks. One of them, which Washington referred to in his conversation, is bicameralism. More fundamentally, checks and balances are built into the relationship between the executive and legislative branches; they are independent of one another to the extent that conflict between the two is almost inevitable. The presidential veto and the possibility of overriding it are aspects of that independence, but its roots go deeper than vetoes and overrides.

Our system is very different from those in other democratic countries. Our legislative and executive branches are separate compartments, elected at different times and by different constituencies. In most other countries the legislature and the executive both come to power at the same time. This occurs because the executive branch, or cabinet, is made up from the leaders of the victorious party. The leaders of the majority, therefore, can send a major bill to the parliament and know that it will pass in substantially unaltered form. Such assurances can never be given in the United States. The passage of bills is by no means a predictable process because they often die in committee, on the floor, in conference, or on the president's desk. At other times they suffocate from the weight of attached amendments, as in the case of the African relief bill.

Bills must pass through so much plumbing in order to become laws that it may seem incredible that any of them make it. The system is frustrating. We should not be surprised if the one official elected by a national majority sometimes gets impatient with that system. It builds in tension between Congress and the president, especially when the president is from one political party and one or both houses of Congress are from the other. President Reagan's inability to raise congressional support for aid to the Nicaraguan Contras caused great frustration within his administration. Some of his officials were thus tempted to embark upon their own aid program, using the receipts from the Iran arms sales. The discovery of their actions triggered the Irangate investigation.

The one task that, as a rule, members of Congress approach with less than enthusiasm is legislative oversight. On some occasions, however, legislators decide that a full-scale investigation of the bureaucracy is in order. These instances usually involve some newsworthy events or scandals, and the investigations can be valuable both to Congress and to the public. The trouble is that they also can degenerate into brutal circuses.

Notes

1. *Congressional Quarterly Almanac, 1984*, p. 430.

2. Gregg Easterbrook, "What's Wrong with Congress?" *Atlantic Monthly* (December 1984), p. 62.

3. *Congressional Quarterly Almanac, 1984*, pp. 437–38.

4. *New York Times*, Nov. 28, 1984, A24.

5. Michael Oreskes, "So Far, Congress Comes Up Short on Ideas," *New York Times*, Aug. 6, 1989, Sec. IV, p. 4.

6. Senator Timothy Wirth (D-Colorado), quoted in Hedrick Smith, *The Power Game: How Washington Works* (New York: Random House, 1988), p. 63.

7. Daniel M. Berman, *A Bill Becomes A Law*, 2nd ed. (London: Collier-Macmillan Limited, 1966), pp. 39–42.

8. George Goodwin, Jr., *The Little Legislatures: Committees of Congress* (University of Massachusetts Press, 1970).

9. *Congressional Quarterly Weekly Report*, Feb. 11, 1984, p. 284.

10. Hedrick Smith, *The Power Game: How Washington Works* (New York: Random House, 1988), p. 63.

11. See Joseph S. Clark, *Congress: The Sapless Branch* (Harper & Row, 1964).

12. Howard E. McCurdy, *An Insider's Guide to the Capitol: The Complete Walking Tour* (Washington: American University, 1977), p. 26.

13. Charles Peters, *How Washington Really Works*, rev. ed. (Reading, MA: Addison-Wesley Publishing Company, 1983), p. 104.

14. David Mayhew, *Congress: the Electoral Connection* (New Haven and London: Yale University Press, 1974), pp. 61–73.

15. Woodrow Wilson, *Congressional Government* (Boston: Houghton Mifflin Company, 1925), p. 303.

16. Richard Hofstadter, *The Paranoid Style in American Politics* (Chicago: University of Chicago Press, 1979). Of course, there have been some real conspiracies in history, and to point them out is not at all paranoid. But that is very different from explaining all major events of history as the work of a vast conspiracy, which is what McCarthyites do. See C. Wright Mills, *The Power Elite* (New York: Oxford University Press, 1959), p. 27.

17. "Judge Has Doubt About Charge in Iran-Contra Trial," *New York Times*, May 27, 1988, p. A12.

18. Quoted in *The Watergate Hearings: Break in and Cover up*, *New York Times* edition (New York: Bantam Books, 1973), p. 7.

8

Congressional Conflict

Don't spit in the soup,
we all gotta eat out of it.

Lyndon B. Johnson

A House Divided

"Mr. Speaker, you know how to win votes the old-fashioned way: you steal them."[1] Those embittered words came from Bob McEwen, a Republican congressman from Ohio. Standing in the "well," the rostrum at the front of the House of Representatives, McEwen was publicly charging that the Democratic leadership of the House of Representatives, headed by House Speaker Thomas ("Tip") O'Neill, had rigged the recount of a congressional election to ensure a Democratic victory. The dispute, which came to a head in the spring of 1985, was the nastiest fight many representatives could remember after years of service in the House. Some Republicans resorted to words like *thugs* and *slime* to describe Democratic colleagues, and Democrats countered with charges of character assassination; one Democrat likened the Republican uproar to a "panty raid," a college prank of the 1950s. Speaker O'Neill called the dispute "one of the silliest things I have heard"—which further inflamed the Republicans. Republican congress-

190

This engraving titled "Congressional Pugilists" depicts an altercation on the floor of the Philadelphia Congress Hall in 1798. Representative Matthew Lyon of Vermont wields fireplace tongs and Representative Roger Griswold of Connecticut fights back with a club. Today, partisan tension and lack of cooperation have replaced physical confrontations such as these as the major threats to the legislative process.

man William Thomas of California said, "He doesn't understand the depth of the feelings on our side."[2]*

All this outrage centered around the hitherto obscure Eighth Congressional District in Indiana, a district drawn, one writer noted, in the shape of "a pregnant praying mantis."[3] The district contains 15 counties and a variety of population centers, from the cities of Evansville and Bloomington to rural hamlets with names like Loogootee, Zipp, Popcorn, Pumpkin Center, and Poseyville. The fight began on election night, November 6, 1984. The Eighth District's incumbent congressman, Democrat Frank McCloskey, was running in a close race against Republican Richard McIntyre. The first count showed McCloskey winning by 72 votes out of a total of 233,000 votes cast. A recount moved McIntyre into the lead by 39 votes, and a second recount, this one by the state, seemed to confirm the Republican victory. It showed McIntyre to be the winner by 418 votes.

Nevertheless, on January 3, 1985, when McIntyre normally would have taken his seat in the House of Representatives, the House voted to keep the seat open until it had performed its *own* recount. More precisely, the Democratic majority in the House voted for a new, House-conducted recount. Democrats controlled the House of Representatives in 1985, as they do today, and as they have done in every Congress since 1956. They set up a special three-member panel to supervise the recount and gave the panel a 2-1 Democratic majority. Their refusal to accept the

*This account is drawn from the following sources: Kent Owen, "Indiana's Bloody Eighth," *The American Spectator* (May 1985), pp. 17-19; Kent Owen, "Stealing it Fair and Square," *The American Spectator* (July 1985), pp. 24-25; *New York Times*, April 28, 1985, p. E5; May 1, 1985, p. A22; May 2, 1985, p. A1; May 3, 1985, p. A16; May 5, 1985, IV, p. 1; Bergen County (NJ) *Record*, May 2, 1985, p. A5; *Washington Times*, May 2, 1985, p. 1A; May 3, 1985, p. 3A; *Time*, May 6, 1985, p. 20; *Congressional Quarterly Weekly Report*, February 11, 1984, pp. 246-49; March 9, 1985, p. 471; May 4, 1985, p. 821-25; *Congressional Record*, April 30, 1985, pp. H2705-H2737; May 1, 1985, pp. H2751-H2786. I am also grateful to Professor Norman J. Ornstein of the American Enterprise Institute for his guidance. Any errors in fact or judgment remain mine.

results of a congressional election was within the legal prerogatives of the House majority. The Constitution (Article I, Section 5) states: "Each House shall be the Judge of the Elections, Returns and Qualifications of its own Members, and a majority of each shall constitute a Quorum to do Business." But it was highly unusual. Only once before, in 1890, had the House done this, and then it was a case of blatant fraud. Here, there were no charges of fraud.

For four months, from early January until the end of April, the three-member panel labored, deciding which votes should be counted. Tension mounted as the committee reached the end of its recount. At issue were two batches of absentee ballots that the state auditors had refused to count. Both batches were considered illegal under Indiana law either because the ballots were unnotarized (unwitnessed) or because they had arrived after election day. One batch had been mistakenly sent on to the district's central voting office by local county clerks; the other batch contained ballots that had been caught by the clerks and retained in county offices. The Democratic majority on the panel decided to count the ballots that had been sent on to the central office. When those were counted, Republican McIntyre's lead disappeared; he was now losing to Democrat McCloskey by four votes.

Now came the question of whether or not the panel should count the second batch of ballots, 32 in all, that had been retained by the county clerks. The lone Republican on the panel, William Thomas, who had opposed counting either batch, said that if the panel counted the first batch then it must count the second because both were in the same category—that of ballots invalidated by state officials. The two Democratic members ruled that the second batch should not be counted, saying there was no way to ensure that the locally retained ballots were still "secure," or untampered with. Some ballots had been kept in unlocked filing cabinets or piled up on desks in county offices. Republican Thomas countered that the panel's staff had already prepared affidavits for the county clerks to sign attesting under oath that the ballots were indeed secure. Nevertheless, the panel Democrats decided not to count any ballots from the second batch. Whether or not McIntyre would have won if the additional ballots had been counted, no one will ever know. By a 2–0 vote, Republican Thomas abstaining, the panel declared McCloskey the winner by four votes. It was the closest election in House history.

The Republican version of what happened was that the Democrats counted both valid and invalid ballots until their man was ahead and only then decided to quit counting. The Republicans called for a new election. Democrat Leon Panetta of California, who chaired the panel, summed up the Democrats' response: There is no rule that says that "when you win by 4 you have a playoff or a runoff." We Democrats, he said, "operate on the basis of majority vote, and this is what we ought to abide by here."[4]

The Republican motion to hold a new election was defeated, and the next day the House formally voted to seat Frank McCloskey. Prior to the vote, every Republican in the House of Representatives rose, marched out of the chamber, and headed for the steps of the Capitol. There they met with a crowd largely composed of reporters and camera crews. Each Republican House member was wearing a lapel button that read, "Thou Shalt Not Steal." As they had filed out of the chamber earlier, the Democrats had applauded, booed, and hissed at them. Distinguished Democratic and Republican lawmakers were seen making obscene gestures at each other.

*   *   *   *   *

Republicans walk out of the House of Representatives to protest the Democratic leadership's handling of the 1985 Indiana election. Republicans charged that Democratic leaders rigged the recount of the congressional election to ensure a Democratic victory.

The Indiana election would not have been so important if it had been just an isolated case. In fact, it was anything *but* isolated. "In some ways," wrote an analyst in the *Congressional Quarterly*, "the anger of the last few weeks is the logical end to a decade of partisan tension that has seemed to increase with every election and every new Congress."[5] Trent Lott of Mississippi, Republican leader in the House, summed up the feelings of many Republicans in this way: "It goes to the fundamental problem about the way the House is run, to the Democrats' arrogance of power."[6] Others, particularly the Democratic leaders, blamed the troubles on the machinations of a small group of conservative Republicans.

Whatever the cause, obviously some very bad feelings exist, feelings that did not exist a few decades ago. The late Clem Miller (D-California), a thoughtful young congressman whose life was cut short in a plane accident in 1962, said that congressmen live "in a cocoon of good feeling."[7] At about the same time that Miller was writing about the House, others were making similar comments about the Senate—at that time members put a premium on courtesy, geniality, and cooperation. Now, it seems the cocoon has shattered. Relations in both chambers are marked by invective and personal abuse. How did that come to be, and what does it mean for the future?

Beyond these questions are some others. Much of the Republican anger in Congress over the disputed Indiana election was directed not at rank-and-file Democrats, some of whom had actually voted with the Republicans, but at the Democratic leadership. Again, Trent Lott's words come to mind: "It goes to the fundamental problem about the way the House is run." How *is* Congress run? Who are its leaders? How do they go about their work? How have things changed in Congress, and have the changes been for better or worse? Should there be new reforms of Congress? These are the questions to be considered in this chapter.

We can gain some perspectives on Congress today by taking a look back at the way Congress used to be.

Decline of the Folkways

In using the expression "cocoon of good feeling," Congressman Clement Miller was referring to an atmosphere that once pervaded both the House and the Senate. In a book published in 1960 political scientist Donald Matthews singled out what he called the folkways of the Senate for analysis: courtesy and geniality, bipartisanship, apprenticeship, and the work ethic.

The Senate, Matthews wrote, was governed at that time by a set of unwritten rules. These rules included a rather elaborate system of verbal courtesy. One senator did not refer to another senator as "Senator Smith" or "Senator Jones." The proper form of address was "The distinguished Senator from _____" or "The able Senator from _____ ," or simply "My wise and venerable colleague." Senators tried at all costs to avoid insulting one another. One senior senator's advice to a newly elected lawmaker was: If you think a colleague is stupid, refer to him as "the able, learned and distinguished senator." If you *know* he is stupid, refer to him as "the *very* able, learned and distinguished senator." A similar atmosphere prevailed in the House. Often cited was the famous Eleventh Commandment of the House: Thou shalt not speak ill of a fellow member.

Hand in hand with the courtesy came geniality, which included all kinds of back-slapping and praise. On some occasions, Matthews wrote, the sentiment could get "as thick as Senate bean soup." Here is Lyndon Johnson, Senate majority leader from 1953 to 1960, talking about Republican minority leader William Knowland of California:

> *Mr. Johnson:* Mr. President, if the Senate will indulge me, I should like the attention of members of both sides of the aisle for a bipartisan announcement of considerable importance. It involves the minority leader, the distinguished Senator from California [Mr. Knowland].
>
> For many years, I have been closely associated with the Senator from California. Like every member of this chamber—on either side of the aisle—I have found him to be able, patriotic, courteous, and thoughtful.
>
> But I wonder how many of my colleagues know that he is also a five-time winner in the contest for the proudest granddaddy in the Senate?
>
> His fifth victory was chalked up last Monday when Harold Jewett II discovered America. Anybody who has found buttons lying on the floor in front of the minority leader's desk in the past few days can know now that they popped right off Bill Knowland's shirt.[8]

Johnson was a tough, hard-driving politician, not given to idle banter. He engaged in this kind of talk because he knew that it helped foster good feelings, which in turn helped to get his bills passed.

An essential aspect of the good feelings was the spirit of bipartisanship. Although Matthews does not use the term in his book on the Senate, it was evident in Lyndon Johnson's speech. Johnson, a Democrat, went out of his way to honor the minority leader, a Republican. Party cooperation was the norm in Congress. Majority and minority leaders often worked closely to get legislation passed. In the late 1950s and early 1960s, party leaders on both sides pressed hard for civil rights bills, pushing aside obstructionists within their own parties. In foreign policy, too, party leaders praised each other's patriotism and insisted that "politics stops at the water's edge"; both parties were to be as one in facing foreign adversaries.

Besides courtesy and bipartisanship, other unwritten rules governed both the Senate and the House. One was *apprenticeship*. Apprenticeship means learning on the job, and learning involves listening. Newly elected members were permitted to ask senior members for advice but otherwise were expected to keep their mouths shut. Professor Matthews noted that the freshman senator who did not "accept his lot as a temporary but very second-class Senator" would meet with considerable hostility.

Senior members of Congress could compel junior members to obey the rules in a variety of ways. They controlled access to committee staffs, decided whether members could be allowed to question witnesses before their committees, and gave or withheld critical support when it came time to vote on a bill. These were powerful inducements to conformity. Sam Rayburn, House Speaker in the 1940s and 1950s, summed up the prevailing wisdom: "To get along, go along."[9]

"There are two kinds of Congressmen—show horses and work horses." Senator Carl Hayden (D-Arizona), who was 91 when he retired in 1969, remembered being told this when he first came to Congress in 1912.[10] "Show horses" always got their names in the newspaper, but they were seldom respected by their colleagues, and their bills went nowhere in Congress. In contrast, "work horses" were rarely in the news. They were content to work quietly behind the scenes, crafting good legislation and getting it passed. These members of Congress were respected within the chamber for their legislative effectiveness. Representatives placed great value on effectiveness, and they saw an inverse relationship between it and celebrity.

THE PURPOSE OF THE FOLKWAYS

The folkways dampened internal rivalry and set limits on political competition and one-upmanship. Courtesy and geniality meant that members of Congress had to learn to restrain their emotions. Bipartisanship meant that, in a House and Senate that were usually closely divided, it was possible to work out deals acceptable to both sides. Apprenticeship taught new representatives the virtues of patience and silence. The ideal of work discouraged members from running to the media to inflame controversies. In sum, the folkways taught compromise, restraint, and legislative pragmatism.

These norms have not completely disappeared; to some degree they surfaced even during the fight over the Indiana seat. There were many on both sides of the issue who sought compromise and who showed moderation in their language. But in the end, if the fight showed anything, it was how much erosion the folkways have suffered. There was no bipartisan compromise: The Democrats won, the Republicans lost, and McCloskey was seated. As for the etiquette of congressional debate, that, too, evaporated in the heat of the fight. The Eleventh Commandment was repeatedly violated as members referred to each other as "thugs" and "slime."

POST-WATERGATE DEMOCRATS AND REPUBLICAN "YOUNG TURKS"

The roots of the 1990s conflicts in Congress go back to 1974, when the Watergate scandal resulted in a major defeat for Republicans in Congress. In the fall elections, voters gave the Democrats their largest House majority in a decade, gaining 43 seats to give them a 291-to-144 majority. Most of the newcomers knew little and cared less about congressional folkways. We have the votes, they reasoned, so why do we have to make deals with the Republicans? Soon the Democratic members of the standing committees were getting together privately and deciding how they would vote when the committee met. The Republicans would discover, usually by reading the *Washington Post*, that everything had already been worked out before the committee even met. That was the "post-Watergate" Democrats' first fateful decision—to abandon bipartisan consensus. The second decision came in 1976, when they decided to keep the 2-1 Democratic ratio on committees, even though the Democrats no longer had a 2-1 majority in the House.

Then came the new breed of Republicans. In the 1978 elections, the number of Republicans in the House increased from 143 to 155, and most of the new members—like their Democratic counterparts in 1974—neither knew nor cared about folkways. The new Republicans were, and are, political conservatives— advocates of school prayer, balanced budget amendments, and abortion restrictions. Much of their case against the Democratic leadership was that it was using parliamentary tactics to prevent the House from even considering these issues.

The new "young Turk" Republicans, as they were soon called, were ready for hardball politics. They harassed the Democratic leadership at every turn, sometimes using parliamentary tactics to delay the House from acting, at other times seeking to force action from a reluctant leadership. They kept up a steady drumbeat of criticism. The Democrats responded by barring the new Republicans from important committee assignments. Since getting on a powerful and prestigious committee is the ambition of every new member of Congress, barring these ambitious young Turks from positions of power only served to make them more restive.

In 1988 the young Turk Republicans, led by Newt Gingrich (R-Georgia), demanded a House Ethics Committee investigation of Speaker Jim Wright (D-Texas). Wright's uncompromising partisanship had infuriated them, and they were looking for vengeance. They charged Wright with a variety of unethical offenses, from taking disguised payoffs to seeking special legislation for favored interests. "This will be a teeth-rattling, eye-gouging, nasty fight to the finish," said Representative Charles Wilson (D-Texas), a Wright ally charged with whipping up Democratic support for Wright.[11] But when the Ethics Committee issued its report, accusing Wright of evading limits on outside income by disguising speech fees as book royalties

"Young Turk" Republicans, angered by House Speaker Jim Wright's partisanship, demanded a House Ethics Committee investigation of his activities. In its report the Ethics Committee accused Wright of evading limits on outside income by disguising speech fees as book royalties. Amid charges of other ethics violations, Wright resigned, giving up his position and his seat.

and accepting $145,000 in unreported gifts from a wealthy Texas friend, two of the six Democrats on the 12-member committee joined the six Republicans to endorse the full report. That took some of the partisan edge off the dispute and made it more difficult for Wright to cast himself as the innocent victim of a Republican vendetta. After a month and a half of behind-the-scenes maneuvering, Wright publicly resigned his position—and his seat. In an anguished speech from the House floor he said, "Let that be a total payment" for all the "bad will" that had accumulated during his tenure.[12] The Democrats selected a new majority leader, Thomas S. Foley (D-Washington), known for his low-key and accommodating style. The hope of many in Congress was that the climate of "bad will" would finally dissipate. It had become oppressive. "Life on Capitol Hill is now about as miserable as anyone can remember," wrote New York Times reporter Michael Oreskes in May 1989. One congressman, he said, dreaded his job so much that he did not want to get out of bed in the morning; another sat up late at night telling his wife how rotten everything was at work. "The institution has begun to devour itself."[13] Many feared that the backbiting would get even worse as a result of the vote of House Republicans to make Newt Gingrich their new minority whip. We will say more about whips, and how un-whiplike they are, later in the chapter; for now it is enough to say that the position is one of party leadership, and giving it to Gingrich—the man who helped start the investigation that ruined Wright's career—seemed to many Democrats a signal that the partisan wrangling would continue. Others hoped that Gingrich's new leadership role would make him more accommodating and statesmanlike. In any case, Gingrich himself was soon being investigated by the House Ethics Committee for possible violations of the ethics code; among the charges against him was that he had accepted financial help from supporters to promote a book he had written.

CAN MEMBERS OF CONGRESS WORK TOGETHER?

In the Senate, as in the House, the art of working together seems to have been forgotten. The new senators know little about the old folkways. One junior Democrat summed up the situation this way: "The Senate has changed; we're all equals."[14] Political scientist Nelson Polsby says, "Today, each Senator is his own mountain peak, with his own staff, his own source of financing, his own pet issues, and his own agenda."[15]

Not all observers agree with this analysis. Political scientist Edward V. Schneier suspects that much of the concern about the breakdown of cohesion is based upon nostalgia for an imagined past. "Just as Grandpa walked further to school through deeper snow," says Schneier, so, it seems, everything was better under Lyndon Johnson's leadership.[16] Schneier presents statistics on legislative behavior suggesting that, in fact, old norms are still working. His analysis is challenged by another congressional scholar, David W. Rohde, who argues that, despite some similarities in legislative behavior, the underlying expectations in Congress have changed radically. Rohde supports the view of other observers that the folkways—apprenticeship, seniority, and working within the system—have just about disappeared.[17]

Sometimes a kind of cohesion is obtained by party leaders, but it is a cohesion based upon partisan anger and retribution. The Senate counterparts to the battles in the House over the Indiana seat and Jim Wright were the fights in the late 1980s over Robert Bork and John Tower. The Bork fight is discussed at greater length in chapter 12. It concerned President Reagan's attempt in 1987 to obtain Senate confirmation of his nomination of appellate judge Robert H. Bork to fill the seat on the U.S. Supreme Court vacated by the retirement of Justice Lewis W. Powell. After weeks of stormy confirmation hearings, the Senate judiciary committee rejected the Bork nomination by an almost straight party vote. All eight Democrats on the committee voted against

When, early in 1989, President Bush nominated former senator John Tower (R-Texas) to be secretary of defense, it set off a bitter partisan fight, with most Democrats opposing him and almost all Republicans supporting the nomination. Oddly, charges of womanizing and drinking, matters about which Senators usually say little, played a role in his defeat.

Bork, plus one Republican. The other Republicans not only voted for Bork, but depicted him as a victim of distortion and misrepresentation. The full Senate vote against Bork (58 to 42) also split along party lines, with only two Democrats joining the Bork supporters and six Republicans opposing his nomination.

In 1989 President Bush's nomination of former senator John Tower as defense secretary set off another partisan battle in the Senate. Although Washington insiders had heard gossip about Tower's alleged drunkenness and womanizing, at the time of his confirmation hearings before the Senate Armed Services Committee, his confirmation seemed assured. (Tower was also accused of conflict of interest—after he left the Senate, he did consulting work for a defense contractor—but few senators paid much attention to this charge.) At some point, however, committee chairman Sam Nunn (D-Georgia) turned against Tower and was supported by the other Democrats on his committee; all the committee Republicans backed Tower. The partisan lines held when the fight went to the full Senate; only two Democrats and two Republicans departed from what was otherwise a straight party vote that defeated Tower.

In chapter 7 we discussed an earlier partisan fight involving both the Senate and the House at the same time: the Iran-Contra affair. The partisanship showed most clearly in the contrasting attitudes toward the chief witness, Lt. Colonel Oliver North. With few exceptions, Republicans in the Senate and House saw North as a persecuted hero (although perhaps a misguided one), whereas almost all the Democrats regarded him as a charlatan and a liar.

These partisan fights may bring a small measure of cohesion to Congress; at least Democrats and Republicans remain loyal to their respective parties. But it is a divisive cohesion, one that ruins the kind of cooperation necessary to produce legislation. It is also negative—it seems to produce only "no" votes. Finally, it is temporary, for after the fight is over, party leaders on both sides lack the means of translating that cohesion into the kind of steady, settled consensus that allows leaders to lead. Fragmentation takes over again.

In short, whether we are speaking of the House or the Senate, Congress has changed greatly since the beginning of the 1960s. In 1981 political scientist Roger Davidson summed it up this way: "Today's Congress is open, egalitarian, and fragmented. It lacks leadership or consensus. . . . The chief impression is buzzing confusion."[18] Senator Alan J. Dixon of Illinois put it more bluntly in 1984: "The system is a mess, and what's amazing is how many members of Congress are fully aware that the system is a mess."[19]

Things could be worse. There was an instance in the nineteenth century when one senator beat another with a cane until blood ran out of his ears during an argument on the Senate floor; in another confrontation, a senator shoved his revolver into an opponent's face and cocked it. In 1798 a fight broke out between two congressmen after one spat tobacco at the other.[20] There have been some more recent physical events in Congress. In 1983 a conservative Republican congressman from California grabbed a liberal Democrat from Long Island by his necktie and yanked it. In 1988 Senate majority leader Robert Byrd (D-West Virginia) ordered late-night sessions to pass a campaign finance bill. When some Republicans refused to show up to make a quorum, he ordered the sergeant-at-arms to bring them in by force if necessary. One senator, Republican Bob Packwood of Oregon, had to be carried into the chamber.

Still, there is no sign that members of Congress are ready to pack pistols and knives, as they did in the nineteenth century. The real violence that threatens Congress today is not to members' persons but to the cocoon of good feeling that once enveloped and shielded the legislative process. Of course, the Founders designed the system to encourage friction; that is what checks and balances are all about. But constant friction can ruin a machine. The situation may not have reached that point yet, but at least one critic was moved to ask in 1984: "Is anyone in charge on Capitol Hill?"[21]

Congressional Party Leadership

The question of who is in charge in Congress today brings us to a discussion of Senate and House party leadership: what the leadership positions are, who fills them today and once filled them in the past, what powers the leaders possess, and what they are doing with those powers.

In the House of Representatives, the highest party leader is the Speaker. As George Galloway notes, the Speaker has "a triple personality."[22] He or she is a member of the House, its presiding officer, and the highest leader of the majority party in the chamber. As a House member, the Speaker has the right to cast a vote on all questions as well as the right to leave the chair and participate in debate. Finally, as presiding officer, the Speaker interprets the rules of the House and calls on members.

Unlike the British Speaker, our Speaker is a party leader—in fact the highest party leader. Although technically elected by the House (the Constitution provides

GLOBAL PERSPECTIVES:

Function of the Speaker: Great Britain/U.S.A

Like the Speaker of the U.S. House of Representatives, the Speaker of the British House of Commons also recognizes members and rules on motions. There the similarity ends. British scholar Kenneth Mackenzie wrote, "The outstanding qualities of the Speakership are its independence and impartiality." Mackenzie noted that this was the result of a long evolutionary process. In the sixteenth century, the Speaker "was first and last a royal servant, paid for his services and afterwards rewarded with great office." But by the end of the next century the Speaker had broken free of royal control and was a servant of the House. By the middle of the nineteenth century Speakers had severed all connection with party activity, whether in or out of the chair. For all practical purposes the British Speaker is not a party official but a neutral moderator; he or she is expected to be well versed in parliamentary rules but scrupulously impartial in applying them.

If the British Speaker comes close to resembling any American legislative leader, it would be the presiding officer of the U.S. Senate—officially, the vice president, although in practice one of the senators with the least seniority. The role is that of a neutral parliamentarian, recognizing members according to formal rules of procedure.

The British Speaker is one of the few vestiges of separation of powers left in Great Britain. The prime minister may control the agenda and majority vote in the House, but he or she may not control the parliamentary rulings of the Speaker, and any prime minister attempting to do so would be subject to severe criticism. In recent years the charge has been leveled against Prime Minister Margaret Thatcher, which she has indignantly denied.

that the House "shall chuse their Speaker and other Officers"), in practice he or she is selected at the start of every Congress by a caucus, or meeting, of the majority party. The Speaker, who is expected to marshal the forces of the majority party to get party-backed bills passed, enjoys much discretionary power in deciding whom to recognize, when to recognize them, and what the rules of debate will be.

The Speaker walks a fine line. Although not expected to be a neutral parliamentarian, he or she must be fair to the minority. Exactly how *fairness* is defined will vary with the Speaker, but today even the blandest of Speakers cannot forget that he or she is a leader of the majority party. Few would disagree with the formulation of Thomas Reed, House Speaker during the last years of the nineteenth century, who said, "The rules of this House are not for the purpose of protecting the rights of the minority, but to promote the orderly conduct of the business of the House." Reed meant, of course, the House *majority*.

Directly below the Speaker in the House party leadership is the House majority leader, who is assisted by the House majority whip and various deputy whips. The name "whip" derives from the phrase "whippers in," used to describe the attendants who ride along on English foxhunts and "whip in" straying beagles. We borrowed the term from the British Parliament, but for Congress—populated largely by lone wolves—it seems singularly inappropriate. Our whip serves as a communications link between the leadership and the rank and file.

The minority party in the House has its own counterpart to the majority's leadership structure. It has a House minority leader, who would become Speaker if that party ever won a majority of seats; a House minority whip; and deputy whips.

In the Senate the arrangement is roughly similar, except that the Senate has no Speaker. The presiding officer of the Senate is the vice president of the United States,

FIGURE **8-1**

Organization of the Majority and Minority Parties of the Senate and House

SENATE	HOUSE
President of the Senate (the vice president of the United States, largely ceremonial) President pro tempore Senior senator of majority party serves as official chair during expected absences of vice president	Speaker of the House (leader of the majority party)
Majority leader Majority whip	Majority leader Majority whip
Minority leader Minority whip	Minority leader Minority whip
Standing committee chairs	Standing committee chairs
Senior committee members	Senior committee members

Data source: Statistical Abstract, 1987, p. 244.

The Senate and House each have a rather formal organization. While real power in the House tends to be shared by the Speaker and the committee chairs and in the Senate by the majority leader and the committee chairs, individual members have in recent years become more powerful.

but the position lacks the discretionary powers of a Speaker. The vice president only votes when there is a tie. Indeed, the vice president is not often seen in the Senate; the chore of presiding is usually handed over to new senators. The true Senate counterpart to the House Speaker is the <u>Senate majority leader</u>, also called the <u>floor leader</u>. He or she is the one responsible for marshaling the majority party's forces. As in the House, there are also majority and minority whips.

The power of congressional leaders is constructed out of bits and pieces—discretion and prerogative, favors and honors. The Speaker has some important formal powers: He or she decides, subject to the rules, who shall be recognized to speak on the floor of the House; rules whether or not a motion is germane (relevant to the business at hand); decides, within certain guidelines, to which committees bills shall be assigned; influences which bills are brought up for a vote; and appoints members to special (but not standing) committees. Since 1975 the Speaker has been able to nominate the majority party members of the Rules Committee. In addition to these formal powers are certain informal ones: The Speaker can decide who goes along on official House visits to other countries, can pick up the telephone and be treated respectfully by high-level bureaucrats, and can rub shoulders with the powerful in his or her party. Except for the power to recognize and rule on what is germane, the Senate majority leader possesses similar powers.

CONSENSUS-BUILDERS: JOHNSON AND RAYBURN

What these fragments add up to depends in part on how skillfully they are assembled. Some observers of Congress long for the 1950s, when Congress was led by Sam Rayburn (D-Texas) and Lyndon Johnson. At the art of assembling the pieces of power, these two were master builders. Johnson's presidency in the 1960s had its problems, but as Senate majority leader a decade earlier he had been highly successful. Senator Johnson would stop at nothing to bring a wavering colleague into line. He was not above calling the senator's wife to ask her husband's neck size so that he could buy him a fancy shirt. Meanwhile, Johnson would be assuring the woman that her husband was one of the most brilliant men ever to grace the Senate, all in a nonstop patter that left little room for reply. It was called "the Johnson treatment." Rayburn, who served as House Speaker from the 1940s until his death in 1961, was more subtle and indirect, but perhaps even more effective. He would say to individual members, "Vote your district first," that is, vote the way you think your constituents want you to vote. However, on certain critical votes, Rayburn would expect members to go along with the party. They usually would; it was a way of buying favors from the Speaker.[23]

Johnson and Rayburn were brilliant tacticians, but as political scientist Norman Ornstein has noted, their power was comparatively modest. What they did for the most part was to negotiate delicate agreements with the chairs of the standing committees—who at that time were the *real* powers in the House—and thus produce votes whose outcomes the leaders could predict in advance. In those days predictability was the hallmark of Congress; today it is "fluidity."[24] Johnson's and Rayburn's great skill was in consensus-building, in bringing Democrats and Republicans, liberals and conservatives, together behind key bills.

THE NEW STYLE

Recent leaders have been less adept, or perhaps less interested, in working out the kind of subtle and complicated deals that Johnson and Rayburn used to make. Senator Robert Byrd (D-West Virginia), who served as majority leader in the Senate from 1977 to 1981 and from 1987 to 1989, had a soft drawl and played a sweet

As Senate majority leader in the 1950s, Lyndon Johnson often used gifts and flattery to sway colleagues to his point of view. Viewed as a consummate negotiator and leader, Johnson arranged complicated deals and his forceful persuasive technique came to be known as "the Johnson treatment."

Representative Sam Rayburn (D-Texas) is usually hailed as the most successful House Speaker of modern times. He occupied the post from the 1940s until his death in the early 1960s and was known for his skill and subtlety in building majority coalitions.

Representative Thomas ("Tip") O'Neill (D-Massachusetts) served as House Speaker from 1977 until his retirement in 1987. A familiar figure to television viewers, he is a giant, red-faced man with a booming voice. His leadership, however, was less impressive. In the early 1980s his leadership was defied by majority coalitions of Republicans and conservative Democrats, and later some of his tactics united the Republicans in angry opposition.

country fiddle, but in the face of opposition he could become stern and cold. It was Byrd, as we mentioned earlier, who in 1988 ordered the sergeant-at-arms to bring Republicans into the Senate chamber by force when they refused to show up for a quorum count. The current majority leader, Senator George J. Mitchell (D-Maine), is more sophisticated in style, although it remains to be seen whether or not he can build a majority stable enough to make public policy. On the House side, Thomas P. ("Tip") O'Neill, Jr., (D-Massachusetts), Speaker from 1977 to 1987, was a familiar figure to television viewers. A giant, red-faced man with a huge head and a booming voice, his presence was overwhelming. His stature as a leader was less impressive. On a number of key issues, from the MX missile to President Reagan's tax cuts, he lost control of his own party, and on some occasions—the Indiana vote count was one of them—he helped unify the Republicans in opposition.

O'Neill's successor was even less popular with Republicans. "I try to be fair. I try to be bipartisan," said Jim Wright (D-Texas), who took over as Speaker in 1987.[25] But virtually all Republicans disagreed, and even some of Wright's admirers worried about his image as a "snake-oil salesman."[26] Formerly a conservative southern Democrat, Wright changed his position on a number of issues, from Contra aid to abortion, to bring himself in line with the liberal wing of his party. He then pushed the liberal agenda with bare-knuckled partisanship. As we discussed earlier in the chapter, Wright's methods provoked the young Turk Republicans, who fought back bitterly, hitting Wright wherever he looked vulnerable.

Yet in fairness to the newer leaders, it must be said that even a Sam Rayburn could not have done much with the power arrangements that now exist in Congress. Wright practiced hardball politics because he needed a reliable power base, and the liberal wing of his party is at least unified on some key issues. If Democratic liberals are not disposed to compromise with Republicans—and they are not, at least not with conservative Republicans—then it is hard for the Speaker to be so disposed. That is the way it has to be: A good leader must be a good follower. In the 1950s, congressional leadership (or "followership") took a different form; it was based not upon ideology but on seniority. Members of Congress got to be committee chairs on the basis of seniority, and these chairs became stable centers of power. But seniority today is no longer a guaranteed basis for advancement in either house of Congress. Congressional reformers have weakened its authority.

Reforms and Their Side Effects

This final section of the chapter focuses on the possibilities and the hazards of "reform." We have used quotation marks around the word because some may question whether or not certain reforms truly *are* reforms. The point is this: Sometimes reforms, even genuine reforms, bring about what sociologists call unintended effects—effects nobody wanted or foresaw. Like the bad side effect of a good medicine, the unintended effect becomes a new problem. This does not necessarily mean that the reform is futile or counterproductive. The unintended negative consequence may be relatively minor. When the side effect is far-reaching and not easily remedied, however, we may conclude that the remedy is worse than the disease.

Who can say at this point whether or not the bad effects of the 1970s congressional reforms have outweighed the good? All we can do with any assurance is describe some of the major reforms and some of their intended and unintended consequences.

DISMANTLING SENIORITY

The seniority system was an unwritten understanding within Congress that the member from the majority party with the longest number of years of continuous service on a committee was to be its chair. The system was derided as "the senility system" because it made longevity rather than merit the criterion for leadership. In 1973 reformers convinced the House Democratic caucus to rule that, in the future, all chairs would be elected by secret ballot of the majority caucus. Then, in 1975, the Democratic caucus actually voted out three aging chairmen. It also passed a subcommittee bill of rights. In the past, committee chairs had ruled subcommittees with an iron hand—deciding whether or not bills could be referred to them, dictating the hearings schedule, controlling the staff available to the subcommittee, and appointing all subcommittee chairs. Now subcommittees had won the right to hold hearings on any subject at any time; committee members could compete for subcommittee chairs; those who chaired committees could hold only one subcommittee chair; independent staff support would be available for each subcommittee; and the number of subcommittees increased.

The tyranny of the "barons" was broken, but there were unintended side effects. The reform decreased cohesion and increased confusion. In-fighting occurred because the chairs were no longer awarded automatically by seniority. And the number of chairs increased dramatically. In the early 1960s there were 47 positions of power available in the House and Senate. By the end of the 1980s there were more than 300. Thanks to the subcommittee bill of rights, each subcommittee chair had separate staff, priorities, and alliances with interest groups. The bill of rights also provided for multiple referrals: Bills and even sections of bills could be referred to several different subcommittees for consideration. This produced redundancy and "turf-fighting," quarreling over who had jurisdiction over what. In short, what one scholar calls the "fluidity" of Congress and what one senator calls "the mess" is in part the result of a reform.

RECORDED VOTES AND OPEN MEETINGS

In the past, much of the voting in Congress went unrecorded. It was not possible to know who had voted for what. On many key amendments to bills there were either voice votes or nonrecorded teller votes. Members would walk down separate aisles for "yea" and "nay" and be counted; however, their names would not be recorded with their votes. In the 1960s reformers criticized that system, saying that it allowed members of Congress to secretly defy their constituents and side with special interests. They demanded accountability. So, in 1970, Congress passed the Legislative Reorganization Act, which required the recording of teller votes. This change has increased the pressure on members to show up for the votes (members do not want to be recorded as "not present"). Everything is now more public, more "official," as it were. Overall, there is less quiet bargaining and compromise and more posturing and haranguing than there was a generation ago. Senator Daniel Evans (R-Washington) quit the Senate in 1988 because he could not continue to tolerate what he saw as unproductive speech-making:

> In the United States Senate, debate has come to consist of set speeches read before a largely empty chamber; and in committees, quorums are rarely achieved. I have lived through five years of bickering and protracted paralysis. Five years is enough. I just can't face another six years of frustrating gridlock.[27]

"Open meetings" were also demanded by reformers. Chapter 7 described the process by which a bill becomes a law. After hearings are held on a bill, the committee or subcommittee goes into mark-up session, where the bill is revised. In the past, almost all mark-up sessions were closed to the public. Reformers wanted them opened. After 1973 most of them were, thanks to sunshine laws passed by both houses. These laws, so-called because they "let in the light of day," made it easier for the average citizen to watch the legislative process, but they had the unintended effect of making that process more difficult. Representatives play to an audience nearly all the time. There is little room for candor and compromise. Also, the pressure of special interests has intensified now that lobbyists can attend mark-up sessions.

STAFF GROWTH

Since the end of World War II, members of Congress have been complaining about the lack of staff. In 1946 staff numbers had not increased perceptively since World War I, yet the workload was multiplying.[28] Staff increases were made, but they were never considered adequate. Good lawmaking requires good information, the argument went, and that requires staff support. By the 1970s some reform-minded writers were beginning to hint that the failure to increase the support staff might have been plotted by senior members. *New York Times* reporter Warren Weaver wrote that the older members did not want new members of Congress to acquire information independently. Instead, "a younger member was to absorb wisdom at his [her] elder's knee," enabling the older member to control him or her.[29] In the early 1970s liberal Republican congressman Donald Riegle (who later became a Democrat and a senator) remarked bitterly that "the men in power" did not want more staff.[30]

Now that has all changed. The subcommittee bill of rights permitted subcommittees to hire their own staffs, which increased total committee staff size from slightly over a thousand (in 1965) to more than three thousand at the end of the 1970s.[31] This figure does not include personal staffs, the staff members available to each member of Congress. From 1973 to 1985, the total number of congressional staff shot up from about 11,500 to more than 24,000; if, in addition, we count the congressional printers, administrators, cooks, barbers, security guards, and gym instructors, we find that by the mid-1980s about 32,000 people were working for Congress.[32]

Why is a large staff a concern? Aside from the enormous cost to taxpayers, there is the problem of having a giant, faceless bureaucracy interpose itself between the people and their elected representatives and threaten to usurp the functions of those representatives. Staffers do much more than type letters and answer the telephone. They ghost-write letters and speeches (and books and articles if the member "writes" them); they organize the member's daily schedule; they feed him or her information and prepare questions for the member to ask at committee hearings. They may even suggest how he or she should vote.

In his book *The Power Game*, *New York Times* reporter Hedrick Smith cites the example of Delaware senator Joe Biden attempting to propose an amendment to a prison reform bill that would provide convicts time off for good behavior:

> "In other words, for every day of good behavior in prison—excuse me, I am being corrected here," Biden said, as his staff aides hastily shoved his own proposal in front of him. After some confusion, Biden—who is known for frankness—candidly confessed: "Obviously, I don't know what the hell I'm talking about. I thought I had a two-for-one provision there. The staff, in its wisdom, rewrote it so I guess I did not want that after all."[33]

Lobbyists are perhaps most aware of the changed situation; for now, they complain, they have to lobby the staff. One said: "In the present environment [members of Congress] spend so much time campaigning that they have no choice but to cede much of the legislative authority to their staffs."[34] A reform—giving members more staff so they could do their jobs better—has resulted in the representatives giving away much of their legislative authority to staff members.

Political scientist Everett Carll Ladd has called attention to another unintended effect of staff growth. Noting the virtual disappearance of competitiveness in House elections—in 1988 about 99 percent of the incumbents were reelected—Ladd lays part of the blame on the use of staff to work on the reelection campaigns of House members. In this capacity the staff functions as "a little electoral machine," paid for by American taxpayers, to protect incumbents against challengers.[35]

Other 1970s reforms are also starting to show some unintended side effects. The campaign finance amendments of 1974 (see chapter 17) have limited the power of wealthy contributors, but in the process they have forced legislators to court a variety of special interests, promising everything to everybody. Electronic voting, adopted in 1973, has made House roll call votes less time-consuming, but in the process it has limited the amount of time members spend getting to know one another while waiting for their names to be called.

SUGGESTED REFORMS: PROS AND CONS

The occurrence of these side effects does not mean that the reforms of the 1970s were futile or counterproductive. It does mean, however, that before any more reforms are put into play, there should be a careful accounting of their effects—not only the anticipated good effects but some of the possible bad effects as well. In that spirit, let us consider some recently advocated reforms.

Restrain Lobbyists.   Many reformers believe that lobbyists have too much influence in Congress. *Atlantic Monthly* writer Gregg Easterbrook went so far as to say in 1984 that lobbyists "should be denied access to the Capitol."[36] Easterbrook was appalled at what he had seen: lobbyists standing outside House and Senate chambers "flashing thumb signs to congressmen like coaches issuing orders to Little Leaguers." Many would agree with him that such spectacles are "a national disgrace."

Barring lobbyists from the building would put an end to these scenes. But what else would it do? To begin with, it would seem to violate the First Amendment, which protects the right of citizens to assemble and "petition the Government for a redress of grievances." The lobbies most hurt would be the small citizens' lobbies that converge on the Capitol to meet with their legislators and advocate their causes. Powerful lobbyists would hardly be restrained. They could continue to give members of Congress the thumbs-up signal by telephone, over dinner and drinks, or while flying them around in company jets.

A Balanced-Budget Amendment.   This proposed reform, a favorite of conservatives, would prohibit Congress from spending more than it receives via taxes in any given year. This tactic might be useful for pressuring Congress to act more responsibly. However, the largest chunk of federal spending (45 percent) goes to so-called entitlement programs like Social Security, which are calculated with set formulas. Spending would continue to increase, therefore, unless the formulas themselves were revised, which would be difficult, especially in the case of the popular Social Security program. The result might be to shift the pressure for big cuts onto the second-largest chunk of federal spending, the defense budget. Would conservatives really want that to happen? (In fact, something like that has already happened as a result of the Balanced Budget and Emergency Deficit Control Act of 1985, better known as the Gramm-Rudman-Hollings Act, which requires an incremental, year-by-year approach to the goal of a balanced budget. The Act is discussed further in chapter 18.) Another result might be more of what already occurs in Congress—the hasty passage of supplementary spending measures that evade the limits set by the budget. If that happened, it would add to the confusion and cynicism.

"Sunset" Laws.   Every major law, it has been argued, should have a "sunset" provision in it. Sunset clauses would provide for the expiration of the law in five years unless Congress voted to renew it. Advocates claim that many laws remain on the books long after their mission has been accomplished. Sunset provisions would automatically sweep away the dead wood. The idea sounds good, but in practice it might have some bad side effects. "A government of laws" implies a legal framework that is stable and predictable. What happens to stability and predictability if all major laws have a five-year life span? Of course, Congress could renew them, but that could bring its own problems. Would it heat up the lobbying wars? As each law neared its limit, proponents and opponents would return to Washington. Would it cut short necessary reforms? Would it give even more power to special interests? It is hard to answer these questions, but they need to be asked.

No Outside Incomes for Members of Congress.   In 1989 members made $89,500 a year in salary, and many of them complained that it was not enough. Because they must maintain two households (one in Washington and the other in their home district) and absorb many other incidental expenses, they turn to outside sources of income. Some run law firms and other businesses, others write articles and books (or have them written for them). Many receive fees, called honoraria, from speaking engagements. This was one of the ways that former House Speaker Jim Wright got into the troubles that led to his resignation in 1989. The present ethics rules in the House limit the amount that members of Congress can collect in honoraria to $2,000 per appearance; there are also overall limits, based upon the congressional salary. The Ethics Committee charged that on several occasions Wright exceeded honoraria limits and disguised the excesses as royalties from his book *Reflections of a Public Man*. (Book royalties are excepted from outside limits on income.)

The current question is whether or not it is proper for a member of Congress to take *any* amount of honoraria money. If a representative from, say, the Distilled Spirits Council were to walk into the office of Senate majority leader George Mitchell, hand him $2,000, and tell him to spend it any way he pleased, both of them could go to jail. But if—as happened in 1988—Senator Mitchell made a speech to the Distilled Spirits Council and the Council then sent a check for $2,000 to his office, that was, and is, perfectly legal (see Table 8.1). Senator Mitchell earned his fee by delivering his wisdom and eloquence, not his vote, to the Distilled Spirits Council. But was that the point of the whole exercise? Did the members of the liquor lobby invite the senator to speak and then pay him $2,000 because they wanted to hear an edifying lecture on public affairs? Maybe so; Senator Mitchell is a good speaker. But is it too cynical to

(Continued on page 208)

TABLE 8-1

Honoraria Collected by Senate Leaders in 1988

Senator	Amount	Senator	Amount
Robert C. Byrd (D-W. Va.), pres. pro tem 1989, majority leader 1988	**Total: $41,000**	Labor Policy Assn. Inc., Washington, Sept. 8	2,000
Donated to charity	**2,000**	National Automobile Dealers Assn., McLean, Sept. 9*	3,000
Paine Webber, Jan. 20	2,000	American Pharmaceutical Assn., Washington, Sept. 19	2,000
Assn. of Reserve City Bankers, Feb. 1	2,000	National Assn. of Medical Equipment Suppliers, Alexandria, Sept. 26	2,000
Gold & Liebengood, Feb. 3	2,000	The FAY Improvement Col., San Francisco, Oct. 4	2,000
Comsat, Feb. 17	2,000	American Dental Assn., Chicago, Oct. 9	2,000
American Hospital Assn., Feb. 19	2,000	American Stock Exchange, New York, Nov. 9	2,000
Timmons & Co. Inc., Feb. 23	2,000	Excaliber Financial Group, Middlebury, Conn., Nov. 10	2,000
Outdoor Advertising Assn., March 14	2,000	American Academy of Dermatology, Evanston, Ill., Dec. 4	2,000
Paine Webber, March 11	2,000	Business International Corp., New York, Dec. 14*	3,000
Mitre Corp., March 18	2,000		
Camp Barsh Bates & Tate, March 22	2,000	**George J. Mitchell (D-Maine), majority leader 1989**	**Total: $42,500**
The Washington Campus Inc., March 24	1,000	**Donated to charity**	**8,000**
Chemical Manufacturers Assn., April 5	2,000	Distilled Spirits Council, Washington, Jan. 19	2,000
National Assn. of Retail Druggists, May 25	2,000	General Electric Co., Washington, Jan. 25	2,000
E. Bruce Harrison Co. Inc., May 28	2,000	American Dental Political Action Committee, Boston, Feb. 2	2,000
American Trucking Assn., June 21	2,000	Paine Webber, Washington, Feb. 2	2,000
C&P Telephone, June 24	2,000	American Hospital Assn., Washington, Feb. 24	2,000
Pharmaceutical Manufacturers Assn., July 15	2,000	Gold & Liebengood, Washington, Feb. 24	2,000
American Insurance Assn., Sept. 16	2,000	Pacific Financial Group, Newport Beach, Calif., March 1	2,000
RJR Nabisco, Oct. 6	2,000	National Assn. of Broadcasters, Washington, March 8	2,000
International Management & Development Institute, Nov. 1	2,000	MCA Inc., Universal City, Calif., March 16	2,000
Charles L. Bartlett-Washington Focus Forum, Dec. 15	2,000	University of Southern California, Los Angeles, March 16	2,000
		American Association of Airport Executives, Alexandria, March 22	1,000
Robert J. Dole (R-Kan.), minority leader 1988-89	**Total: $67,750**	Blue Cross/Blue Shield, Washington, March 23	2,000
Donated to charity	**31,750**	Sutherland Asbill & Brennan, Washington, March 23	1,000
Iowa Assn. of Electric Cooperatives, Urbandale, Iowa, Dec. 3, 1987*	750	Securities Industry Assn., Washington, March 24	2,000
The Liberty Corp., Greenville, S.C., Feb. 18*	2,000	Public Securities Assn., Washington, March 24	2,000
Organization Management Inc., Fairfax, March 3	2,000	American Society of Anesthesiologists, Washington, April 26	2,000
Avon Products Inc., New York, April 21	2,000	American Healthcare Institute, Washington, May 3	2,000
National Commercial Finance Assn., New York, May 10	2,000	American Medical Care & Review, Washington, May 3	2,000
American International Automobile Dealers Assn., Washington, May 15*	15,000	Equitable Financial Cos., New York, May 9	2,000
American Supply Assn., Chicago, May 23	2,000	Avis Licensee Assn., Washington, May 12	2,000
American Health Care Assn., Washington, June 7*	2,000	American Bakers Assn., Washington, May 27	2,000
American Society of Plastic & Reconstructive Surgeons Inc., Arlington Heights, Ill., June 14	2,000	Brookings Institution, Washington, May 27	500
Coalition Against Regressive Taxation, Washington, June 15	2,000	National Academy of Sciences, Washington, July 7	2,000
Ackerley Communications Inc., Seattle, June 20	1,000		
Reagan National Advertising Inc., Salt Lake City, June 20	1,000		
Service Corp. International, Houston, June 22*	5,000		
E. Bruce Harrison Co. Inc., Washington, June 23	2,000		
Merrill Lynch Pierce Fenner & Smith, New York, June 23*	5,000		

*Some or all donated directly to charity.

Source: Washington Post, May 20, 1989. Reprinted with permission.

Influential members of Congress are often invited to speak before groups with large financial stakes in the outcome of votes in Congress. For addressing such groups, the senators and representatives are given honoraria. Many reformers are critical of this practice, regarding it as at least potentially corruptive.

(Continued from page 206)
wonder if they could have had another motive as well: to hand over some money to a powerful politician in hopes of getting favorable treatment from him? Whether or not that was the case, say the critics of this practice, even the appearance of impropriety must be avoided. The thrust of many reform proposals in the 1980s was to abolish outside speaking fees and instead—as a kind of "sweetener" for this medicine—to increase congressional salaries.

Yet it was just that attempt—to raise congressional salaries—that caused a public furor when it was attempted early in 1989. In what appeared to be a largely spontaneous public reaction, congressional offices and radio call-in shows were flooded with protests after the news spread that Congress was about to raise congressional salaries to an annual $135,000. "For almost 40 years," said one South Carolina congressman, "I have been active in the public arena, both as a Democrat and as a Republican. I have seen political storms come and I have seen them go, but never, never have I seen the people so incensed over an issue such as this pay raise question."[37]   *(Continued on page 209)*

TABLE **8-2**

Pay Raise History

Effective date	Salary	Percent Change
March 1789	$ 1,500*	
March 1817	2,000*	33
December 1855	3,000	50
December 1865	5,000	67
March 1871	7,500*	50
January 1874	5,000*	−33
March 1907	7,500	50
March 1925	10,000	33
July 1932	9,000	−10
April 1933	8,500	− 6
February 1934	9,000	6
July 1934	9,500	6
April 1935	10,000	5
January 1947	12,500	25
March 1955	22,500	80
January 1965	30,000	33
March 1969	42,500	42
October 1975	44,600	5
March 1977	57,500	29
October 1979	60,662	6
December 1982	69,800	15
January 1984	72,600	4
January 1985	75,100	4
January 1987	77,400	3
February 1987	89,500	16

*Per diem rates converted to annual rates.

Source: Congressional Research Service. Reprinted with permission of the Congressional Quarterly.

Congressional salaries climbed from an annual $1,500 in 1789 to $89,500 in 1987. An attempt was made early in 1989 to increase salaries to $135,000, but it was virtually shouted down by the American public. Indignant letters and phone calls from citizens flooded Washington and the national media. Congress backed down, but at the end of 1989 it succeeded in passing salary increases for both the House and Senate. The House voted for a larger salary increase in exchange for giving up honoraria.

Should Members of Congress Be Barred from Earning Outside Incomes?

YES   Gregg Easterbrook

Based upon Gregg Easterbrook, "What's Wrong With Congress?" *Atlantic Monthly* (December 1984), pp. 57–84.

Easterbrook, a staff writer for *Atlantic Monthly*, says, "Congressmen should receive a substantial raise and in return be required to forsake all forms of outside income." He worries about the influence special interests have over legislators: To Easterbrook, the honoraria paid to members of Congress for speeches bear a suspicious resemblance to payoffs. As an example, Easterbrook suggests that a legislator could speak before a chemical company one day, receive money for the speech, then vote on a bill favored by the company the next day. Members of Congress, he concludes, "are supposed to function as judges of society's needs; they should be as far above reproach (and influence) as judges."

NO   Howard Baker

Based upon Howard H. Baker, Jr., "Congress According to Baker," *New York Times Magazine*, April 1, 1984, pp. 68–69, 74.

Baker, the former majority leader of the Senate, thinks that members of Congress have become too Washington-centered, too isolated from the people. He believes we ought to go back to the days when a legislator's service in Washington occupied only part of the year. "Congress should be in session for only six or so months of the year," Baker says, which is the way it used to be. The rest of the time should be spent staying in touch with constituents, seeing firsthand how the laws actually affect people's lives, and "experiencing real life in America." Because they would be working only half the time for Congress, members would receive only half their present salary but would be allowed to earn as much as they could from outside sources. "The appropriateness of outside income, fully disclosed and regularly reported, is a political question, not an ethical or moral one," says Baker.

Postscript

Easterbrook would consider Baker's proposal a new and dangerous incentive for members of Congress to get involved with special interests. Baker would no doubt criticize Easterbrook's proposal as one that would further isolate representatives from their home constituencies. If there is merit in both criticisms, then perhaps both proposals need to be re-thought.

Arthur Maas's *Congress and the Common Good* (New York: Basic Books, 1984) defends the role of Congress in the legislative process. James A. Miller's *Running in Place: Inside the Senate* (New York: Simon and Schuster, 1986) sketches a more troubling picture of one house of Congress trying to cope with the burden of legislation. To keep up with current reform proposals, see the *Congressional Quarterly Weekly Report* and the annual *Congressional Quarterly Almanac*, which can be found in almost all college libraries.

(Continued from page 208)

The remaining question is whether or not it would be desirable to forbid members of Congress to make any additional money outside of Congress. In this chapter's Taking Sides section, journalist Gregg Easterbrook argues that it would, while former Senate majority leader Howard Baker takes the opposite view: He would reduce congressional salaries and let members make as much money as they want as long as they report it.

Reflections

A generation ago a young congressman reported that he and his colleagues lived in "a cocoon of good feeling." Political scientists used to talk about the folkways of the Senate: courtesy, geniality, apprenticeship, and quiet legislative craftsmanship. Conformity to these norms was valued and rewarded. "To get along, go along," said House Speaker Sam Rayburn.

The flowery forms of address can still be heard, and so can the praise-swapping. But the "cocoon of good feeling" has sustained heavy damage. Over the 1985 Indiana election dispute, Democrats and Republicans shouted at each other and called each other names. In the end the Democrats won the dispute because they had the votes. That was not the way things used to be done; major disputes were resolved by consensus and compromise. This one was resolved by raw power. In the words of one congressman, "It became a big macho thing."

No American politician was more "macho" than Lyndon Johnson, and it may well have been that belligerent attitude that entangled him in Vietnam when he was president. As majority leader of the Senate, however, he kept his machismo under control. He knew he had to deal with an oligarchy of committee "barons" who would not put up with bullying. They were, however, very amenable to bargaining. They were power brokers, not moral crusaders. Some were lazy, some were venal, and most were well advanced in years, having won their positions through seniority. Collectively, however, they provided a kind of institutional glue for the congressional system. They kept competition under control; they served as a stable power center; and they lent some order to chambers constantly threatened by disorder.

Today the "barons" are gone. Committee chairs must now share power with their committee members, not to mention all the subcommittee chairs who have their own power bases. Now new members can be rude to them with impunity and even band together to vote them out of their chairs. On balance, this may be a positive development. Isn't this what democracy is all about? Yet, as we saw in the case of the disputed Indiana election, the level of anger and bitterness has greatly increased. Whoever heard of members in the 1950s *publicly* making obscene gestures at each other, as occurred in the 1980s!

The fights seem to be getting more partisan and ideological—liberal Democrats versus conservative Republicans. In the past, there were enough liberal Republicans and conservative Democrats to dull the ideological edges. There were also many members of Congress in both parties who seemed to have no clear-cut ideology, and some of them occupied key leadership positions. They enabled a Congress closely divided along party lines to get its work done. In those days, there were "show horses" and "work horses" in Congress, but the "work horses" were the ones rewarded by their colleagues. Today there seems to be no incentive to get work done in an orderly fashion. In the words of one senator, "the system is a mess."

Can anything improve the situation? We have reviewed a few reform proposals, but what seems to be needed is a change in attitude. Our senators and representatives need to think more about what they can do to help shore up their institution and restore some of the goodwill that has been lost. To call for a return of "institutional loyalty" in today's environment may seem quaint, but it is hard to see how Congress can work effectively unless its members start asking not just what Congress can do for them, but what *they* can do for Congress.

Notes

1. Quoted in *Congressional Quarterly Weekly Report*, May 4, 1985, p. 824.
2. *Washington Times*, May 2, 1985, p. 10A.
3. Owen, *The American Spectator* (July 1985), p. 24.
4. *Congressional Record*, Apr. 30, 1985, p. H2719.
5. *Congressional Quarterly Weekly Report*, Mar. 9, 1985, p. 471.
6. Quoted in *New York Times*, May 1, 1985, p. A22.
7. Clem Miller, *Member of the House: Letters of a Congressman* (New York: Charles Scribner's Sons, 1962), p. 93.
8. Donald R. Matthews, *U.S. Senators and Their World* (New York: Vintage Books, 1960), p. 98.
9. Mark J. Green, *Who Runs Congress?* (New York: Bantam/Grossman, 1975), p. 202.
10. Matthews, p. 94.
11. Michael Oreskes, "House Set for Bitter Battle on Wright Ethics Issue," *New York Times*, Apr. 15, 1989, p. 9.
12. *Congressional Quarterly Weekly Report*, June 3, 1989, pp. 1284-90.
13. Michael Oreskes, "Congress," *New York Times*, May 6, 1989, p. B7.
14. *New York Times*, Nov. 26, 1984, p. A1.
15. Quoted in Gregg Easterbrook, "What's Wrong With Congress?" *Atlantic Monthly* (December 1984), p. 64.
16. Edward V. Schneier, "Norms and Folkways in Congress: How Much Has Actually Changed?" *Congress and the Presidency* (Autumn 1988), p. 126.
17. David W. Rohde, "Studying Congressional Norms: Concepts and Evidence," *Congress and the Presidency* (Autumn 1988), pp. 139-44.
18. Roger H. Davidson, "Subcommittee Government: New Channels for Policy Making," in Thomas E. Mann and Norman J. Ornstein, eds., *The New Congress* (Washington: American Enterprise Institute, 1981), p. 131.
19. Quoted in Gregg Easterbrook, "What's Wrong With Congress?" *Atlantic Monthly* (December 1984), p. 58.
20. Alvin M. Josephy, Jr., *On the Hill: A History of the American Congress* (New York: Simon & Schuster, 1979), pp. 109-10.
21. Easterbrook, p. 57.
22. George B. Galloway, *History of the House of Representatives*, 2nd ed. (Rev. by Sidney Wise) (New York: Thomas Y. Crowell Company, 1976), p. 132.
23. Warren Weaver, *Both Your Houses: The Truth About Congress* (New York: Praeger Publishers, 1972), p. 153.
24. Norman J. Ornstein, "The Open Congress Meets the President," in Anthony King, ed., *Both Ends of the Avenue* (Washington: American Enterprise Institute, 1983), pp. 185-211. See particularly pp. 191-93.
25. Irvin Molotsky, "Wright Calls Republican Criticism of House Leadership 'Carping'," *New York Times*, May 26, 1988, p. A24.
26. George Hackett and Eleanor Clift, "Bob and Jim Play a Duet," *Newsweek*, Feb. 9, 1987, p. 29.
27. Daniel J. Evans, "Why I'm Quitting the Senate," *New York Times Magazine*, Apr. 17, 1988, p. 48.
28. Harrison W. Fox and Susan Webb Hammond, *Congressional Staffs: The Invisible Force in American Lawmaking* (New York: The Free Press, 1977), p. 20.
29. Weaver, pp. 165-66.
30. Donald Riegle, *O Congress*, (Garden City, NY: Doubleday & Company, Inc., 1972), p. 175.
31. Ornstein, in King, ed., p. 195.
32. Hedrick Smith, *The Power Game: How Washington Works* (New York: Random House, 1988), p. 281.
33. Smith, p. 285.
34. Easterbrook, p. 75.
35. Everett Carll Ladd, "The 1988 Elections: Continuation of the Post-New Deal System," *Political Science Quarterly* (Spring 1989), p. 6.
36. Easterbrook, p. 84.
37. Rep. Arthur Ravenal, Jr., (R-South Carolina), quoted in *Congressional Quarterly Weekly Report*, Feb. 11, 1989, p. 267.

9

Powers of the Presidency

POWERS OF THE OFFICE

The President as Chief of State / The President as Commander in Chief / The President as Chief Diplomat / The President as Chief Executive / The President as Chief Legislator

PRESIDENTIAL PERSONALITY

Presidential Qualities / In Praise of Active-Positive Presidents

CHANGING ATTITUDES TOWARD THE PRESIDENCY

The Cult of Presidential Activism / The Press and the Presidency: Then and Now
The Turning Point: Vietnam / Nixon and Watergate

PRESIDENTIAL DISABILITY

Order of Succession: Vice President, Speaker, President Pro Tempore / Temporary Disability / Removing Sick, Stubborn Presidents / The Vice President

REFLECTIONS

The president of the United States stood in front of the **The Death of a President**
bedroom mirror. It was early morning. He had already
dressed, fastening his tie with a shiny PT-boat tieclip; now he was
combing his hair. Wedged into the frame of the mirror were various items:
a Washington mass schedule, a Polaroid snapshot of his wife, a postcard
from Italy written by his five-year-old daughter ("I like Italy better than
Hyannis but I like Hyannis a little bit more because there's fairs. I miss you
daddy very much. X Caroline"). On the dresser were his wallet, containing $26 in bills, a gold St. Christopher's medal, and—the only identifica-
tion he carried—a Massachusetts driver's license. He pocketed his wallet
and went down to breakfast. *

* This account is drawn from William Manchester, *The Death of a President* (New York:
Harper and Row, 1967). I have also relied upon Theodore H. White, *The Making of the
President 1964* (New York: Atheneum Publishers, 1965); Arthur M. Schlesinger, Jr., *A
Thousand Days* (Boston: Houghton Mifflin Company, 1965); Theodore C. Sorensen,
Kennedy (New York: Harper & Row, 1965); and my own recollections.

It was November 21, 1963, and John F. Kennedy was about to leave Washington. He was flying to Texas to mend some political fences. The Texas Democratic party was bitterly divided into liberal and conservative factions, which did not bode well for next year's presidential election. Kennedy and his vice president, Lyndon Johnson, were going down to Texas—Johnson's home state—to patch things up. Kennedy flew to San Antonio, then to Houston, and then on to Fort Worth. It was an exhausting day, full of speeches and tours and parades. He hated giving formal speeches; they made him nervous. Before a huge crowd at the Houston Coliseum, his hands shook so badly that he almost dropped his notes. He and his wife, Jacqueline, were glad to go to bed that night at Fort Worth's Hotel Texas.

Friday morning, November 22, 1963: It had rained through the night, but by 9 A.M. the rain had slackened to a light drizzle. After speaking to a crowd in the parking lot next to the hotel, Kennedy flew to Dallas, only 30 miles away. The drizzle had stopped, the sun was shining, and the temperature was climbing. It was going to be a hot, muggy day. He and Jacqueline were exhausted as they walked down the ramp and went through the usual greetings. But they were both good at hiding their feelings. It was almost 11 A.M. Dallas time when the motorcade left Love Field for the Dallas Trade Mart, where the president was to speak at a luncheon. The Kennedys were in the back seat of a blue Lincoln convertible; in front of them, in the jump seats, were Governor John B. Connally and his wife.

11:21 A.M.: The motorcade, moving slowly, turned onto Main Street in Dallas. The crowds along the street were enthusiastic. People were leaning out of the windows of buildings and standing on roofs to get a glimpse of the Kennedys.

11:28 A.M.: The motorcade moved into a seedy neighborhood. Bail bond shops, bars, a public gym. In two blocks they would have to make a right onto Houston Street, then, after another block, a hard left that would take them to the freeway. The last building before they would enter the underpass to the freeway was an old book warehouse. The sign on the building read: Texas School Book Depository.

11:29 A.M.: The crowds were thinner but still enthusiastic. The governor's wife twisted around in her seat and said: "You sure can't say Dallas doesn't love you, Mr. President." Kennedy smiled and said, "No, you can't."[1] At 11:30 A.M. they passed the Texas School Book Depository. The underpass was just ahead. Jacqueline Kennedy thought about how pleasant it would feel in the cool tunnel.

Then came a sudden, loud crack. A high-velocity bullet entered the back of the president's neck, ripped through his windpipe, and exited at the throat. Continuing on, it passed through Governor Connally's back, chest, wrist, and thigh. Kennedy reached for his throat. He looked puzzled. His head slumped toward his wife. Another shot found its mark. The upper part of the president's torso was violently flung forward. The top of his head was blown away.

Everyone over forty can tell you exactly where they were when they heard the news that day. Some heard it on the radio; some, on television; some, from friends. Within an hour the telephone lines across the country were jammed. In New York City a woman driving on FDR Drive to the Triborough Bridge heard about the assassination on her car radio; when she got to the bridge, the tollbooths were empty. The collectors had left their booths to lower the flag. She burst into tears, then noticed that the

President John F. Kennedy, accompanied by his wife, Jacqueline, and Governor and Mrs. John B. Connally, waves to the crowd in Dallas, Texas, moments before his assassination. The bullet-proof transparent top had been removed from the car to allow President Kennedy to wave to the people.

people in the other cars were also crying. Everywhere people grieved together openly and without embarrassment.

The American people loved Jack Kennedy. They still do, although today they see more clearly the flaws in his presidency and his personality. He was always moving, always on the go, but it was never quite clear where he was heading. Yet there was something immensely appealing about him. Author William Manchester put it this way: "There was an air of high drama about the man. Something was always happening to him— something always lay just ahead."[2] Kennedy was in quest of something he could not quite define. "A new frontier," he called it. He might as well have called it the Holy Grail. Journalist Theodore H. White compared the Kennedy White House to Camelot, the court of King Arthur.

Even in death the drama continued. White noted that Kennedy's funeral services were carried by the new satellite system to 22 countries, including the USSR and Japan. "Nothing like this had happened in the history of the human race—so large a participation of mankind in the mortal tragedy of a single individual."[3]

*   *   *   *   *

Yet that single individual, dramatic and exciting as he was, operated in the context of an office, an institution. It was the office of the American presidency that helped make Kennedy what he was. For eight years he had been a senator, a very undistinguished senator. It was the presidency, and the quest for that office, that allowed Kennedy to become Kennedy. Nobody knew that better than he. On repeated occasions he said that he had wanted to be president because "that's where the action is."

Then there were the times. If John Kennedy's clone occupied the White House today, would he get the same reception? It seems doubtful. In the 1990s the press, the public, and the scholars of the office are leery of a presidency with too much power. They worry about *the imperial presidency*, a term never used in Kennedy's day. At that time, the opinion leaders were calling for activism in the White House. Kennedy promised to bring back presidential vigor. In his inaugural address he committed the United States to "pay any price, bear any burden, meet any hardship, support any friend, oppose any foe to assure the survival and success of liberty." In 1961 the American people never thought to question that kind of talk. They would today.

The purpose of this chapter is to study presidential power. What kinds of powers does the president have? What personality seems best suited to the political and emotional demands of the presidency? How has the aura that surrounds the presidency changed since Kennedy's day? What happens to presidential power when the president is disabled? Without trying to provide definitive answers to these questions, let us at least probe them. We can start by examining some of the chief powers given to the president by the Constitution and by nearly two hundred years of history.

Powers of the Office

We do not know exactly what kind of figure the Founders intended the president to be. We do know that they wanted more than a servant of Congress. The office is independently elected and has veto powers, the power to pardon offenses against the United States, the power to negotiate treaties with the "advice and consent of the Senate," and the power "to appoint ambassadors and other public ministers" as well as federal judges. Still, we must look beyond the Constitution itself to discover what the American presidency is today, after two centuries of change.

Perhaps the best way to view presidential power is to examine a few of the several hats the president wears. In a now-classic 1956 book on the presidency, Clinton Rossiter considered the president as chief of state, chief executive, commander in chief, chief legislator, chief diplomat, party leader, and manager of prosperity. Five of those hats—chief of state, commander in chief, chief diplomat, chief executive, and chief legislator—are broad enough to encompass the whole of presidential power.

The Seal of the President of the United States. As chief of state, the president is not only a politician and an administrator but the ceremonial head of the United States, the one who symbolically bears the olive branch and the arrows of our nation.

THE PRESIDENT AS CHIEF OF STATE

As chief of state the president is the ceremonial head of the nation. He is the sole representative of the United States at all formal meetings with the representatives of other countries. (The Constitution says, "He shall receive Ambassadors and other public Ministers.") But as chief of state the president is more than official greeter. He has come to symbolize the nation. The president represents all the people. Unlike members of Congress, he is not elected by a state or a congressional district; he has a national constituency.

But this still does not express the full meaning of chief of state. The presidency today, says philosopher Michael Novak, "is surrounded by a nimbus of magic."[4] The modern president walks in the footsteps of semimythical figures like Washington and Lincoln. The legends of these presidents have charged the office itself with emotional current. In the film documentary based upon Theodore H. White's *The Making of the President 1960* there is a scene in which a youth stands at the curb with his hand outstretched as John Kennedy approaches in an open car. Kennedy thrusts out his hand as he goes by, and the two hands, his and the youth's, briefly touch. The young man leaps back, beaming ecstatically; he grasps his wrist and stares at his own hand as if it were some rare and sacred object.

To what extent can this emotional aura that surrounds the presidency be converted into more down-to-earth power? It is hard to say. President Theodore Roosevelt once called the presidency a "bully pulpit." It permits its occupant to be a kind of preacher who reaches out to the masses. Sometimes, though, presidential sermons fall flat. Lyndon Johnson made frequent special addresses to defend his Vietnam policy, but the policy steadily lost support among the American people. Richard Nixon defended his administration during the Watergate scandal, appearing on television with a bust of Lincoln in the background. Yet he was driven from office. Jimmy Carter used his "pulpit" to tell Americans that energy conservation had to become "the moral equivalent of war," but his energy bill was treated irreverently in Congress. President Reagan's success in getting his 1981 tax cut through Congress can be attributed in part to his "bully pulpit." His grace and gallantry after the March 1981 attempt on his life by John W. Hinckley, Jr., probably also helped. Logically there is no connection between the merits of a tax cut and the president's ability to joke with a bullet in his chest. But we are dealing here with emotions, not logic.

Some critics worry about these emotions. Are they a danger to democracy? Do they promote leader-worship? Other democracies have ceremonial chiefs of state, such as the British queen and the Japanese emperor. Such chiefs of state function as emotional lightning rods. They attract the very dangerous human tendency to worship leaders and sluice it off into harmless channels. This observation has led some to propose that we divide the office of president in two, making one person chief of state and the other chief of government: Let the chief of state have the magic and the chief of government the power. It does not seem likely that the proposal would work in the United States. We are awed by the presidency *because* we know that its occupant possesses enormous power. As Lyndon Johnson put it, the president is the one who can "mash that button." This brings us to the next "hat."

THE PRESIDENT AS COMMANDER IN CHIEF

Since the Vietnam War this power has come under close scrutiny by Congress and the press, most recently in the controversy over the question of covert action in Central America. When Ronald Reagan was president, he lent support to the Nicaraguan Contras, those forces attempting to overthrow the Marxist Sandinista government. As we mentioned in chapter 7, at one point the CIA assisted the Contras in mining the harbors of Nicaragua. An uproar ensued, and military aid to the Contras was cut off.

But covert action, as such, is really a false issue. No responsible person would have objected in 1942 if President Roosevelt had lent covert assistance to a group of Germans trying to overthrow Hitler. The difference is that our involvement in World War II had been authorized by Congress and was widely supported by the American people. The real issue behind covert assistance is whether or not the president has the right to engage American forces in wars without a congressional declaration or at least some kind of implicit permission.

Article II, Section 2, of the Constitution says, "the President shall be Commander in Chief of the Army and Navy of the United States, and of the Militia of the several States, when called into the actual Service of the United States. . . ." Who calls them into "actual Service"? As a rule, Congress does. It has the power "to raise and support Armies" and to declare war. Yet the Founders intended at least one exception to the rule. At the Constitutional Convention some delegates wanted to give Congress the exclusive power to make war, not simply to declare it. That would have ruled out any presidential warmaking. James Madison successfully argued the need for "leaving to the Executive the power to repel sudden attacks."[5]

But does the Constitution allow the president to go further? Can he use troops to repel an attack on American personnel in another country? Can he go to war to head off an anticipated attack? Can he fight a war to protect American interests? Here the limits on presidential power are far less clearly drawn. What we do know is that many presidents have made vigorous use of the armed forces without asking Congress for permission. Instances of purely presidential warmaking are numerous; here are just a few examples:

- In 1801 President Jefferson ordered his navy to seize the ships of Barbary pirates in the Mediterranean.
- In 1846 President Polk sent American troops into territory claimed by Mexico, thus provoking the Mexican-American War.
- Between 1861 and 1865 President Lincoln suppressed the South's rebellion by a variety of acts that the Constitution delegated to Congress: He withdrew money from the Treasury, enlarged the size of the army and navy, jailed people without trial, and blockaded Southern ports, all without congressional authorization.
- In the early 1900s President Theodore Roosevelt invaded several South American countries and set up provisional governments.
- In 1941, several months before World War II was declared, President Franklin Roosevelt ordered his navy to fire at German submarines on sight.
- In 1950 President Truman committed America to fight in Korea without a congressional declaration.
- In 1962 President Kennedy ordered a naval blockade of Cuba—an act of war—without even consulting Congress.
- Between 1961 and 1963 Kennedy sent 16,000 armed "advisors" to Vietnam, and between 1964 and 1968 President Johnson escalated American involvement to 500,000 troops—all without a declaration of war.

For the most part these acts went unchallenged by Congress or public opinion. Not until the early 1970s did Congress react to presidential warmaking by cutting off funds and passing the War Powers Resolution. It was an attempt to draw up statutory regulations and time limits on such warmaking; we will study its effectiveness in the next chapter.

THE PRESIDENT AS CHIEF DIPLOMAT

The Constitution awards the president the power to make treaties "with the Advice and Consent of the Senate." Such advice may or may not be solicited, but no treaty made by a president can become law without ratification by two-thirds of the Senate. The Constitution bestows other powers on the president, however, that do not require Senate approval. It stipulates that the president "shall receive Ambassadors and other public Ministers," which gives the president power to decide whether or not to recognize other governments. A president's decision to receive or not to receive the ambassador of another country can define our relationship to it. When President Nixon, for example, decided to visit China in 1972, he reconnected ties between the two countries that had been severed for more than 20 years. He did this without getting congressional approval or even giving Congress advance knowledge of his intentions. *(Continued on page 218)*

GLOBAL PERSPECTIVES:

Presidential Power: France/U.S.A.

America has one executive, but France has two. The president of the French Republic is elected by popular vote that takes place in periodic elections that are set up so that they do not coincide with the years when the legislature is elected. The president is not politically responsible to the legislature.

The second executive, the premier, is selected by the president and is, along with the government, responsible to the lower house of the French legislature, the National Assembly. In this sense, the premier acts somewhat like the parliamentary leaders in countries (such as Great Britain) with a cabinet system of government.

After suffering years of weak executive leadership, the French adopted a new constitution in 1958 that added the office of president to government. Under the old system the legislature had dominated, but it had been split by factional disputes. General Charles de Gaulle changed all that. Appointed premier in 1958, he obtained power to govern absolutely for six months, during which time he had a new constitution drafted. Submitted to a referendum and overwhelmingly endorsed by French voters, the new constitution retained the premier but made him subservient to a new office, the presidency.

As we said, like the American president, the French president is elected by the people, and, unlike the American president, he is fully independent of the legislature. Also, the American president can be impeached by Congress; the French president may be impeached only by the High Council of Justice, which is appointed by the Senate. But this only begins to describe the differences between the two presidents. The French president's legal powers are much greater than those of his American counterpart. The French president has the legal right to dissolve the national assembly at will, the only limit being that it can be done only once a year. The French president nominates the premier; this enables the president to control the cabinet, and through it, the majority party in Parliament. In addition, the president may call a referendum, issue decrees having the force of law, or, in the words of the French Constitution, declare a state of emergency and "take the measures commanded by . . . circumstances." The American president has none of these powers in writing, though some presidents have assumed extralegal powers during emergency situations.

The French Constitution describes the president as the "arbiter," charged with making the ultimate decision among competing interests and policies. Backed by a large and growing staff, the French president has become the center of decision making in both foreign and domestic matters. In America this could have been said of our presidency prior to the last days of the Vietnam War and the explosion of the Watergate scandal. Since then, however, Congress has taken a much stronger role in challenging the president's initiatives in domestic and even foreign policy.

(Continued from page 217) Another way for presidents to make foreign policy without having to get treaties through the Senate is to make executive agreements, which are bilateral understandings with foreign governments and are not submitted for Senate approval. The executive agreement, which historian Arthur M. Schlesinger, Jr., has called "one of the mysteries of the constitutional order,"[6] began creeping into use early in the nineteenth century, and Congress accepted it without any qualm since it was used almost exclusively for minor and uncontroversial matters. Not until the time of President Theodore Roosevelt in the early years of this century did it become a major, and potentially provocative, instrument. Roosevelt, for example, concluded a secret agreement with Japan giving American approval to Japan's military occupation of Korea. Thirty-five years later, the second Roosevelt, Franklin, concluded an even

President Richard Nixon and Chinese premier Chou En-lai toast each other
during President Nixon's 1972 trip to China. The Chinese government's massacre of pro-democracy demonstrators in Tiananmen Square in 1989 cooled
Sino-American relationships.

more important agreement—the famous "destroyer deal." In one of a long series of
unilateral actions in 1940 that brought the nation to the brink of war with Germany,
President Roosevelt announced that the United States had entered into an agreement
with Great Britain to exchange 50 reconditioned destroyers for American use of
naval bases in the Caribbean islands, then under the control of Great Britain. The
agreement put the United States squarely on the side of Great Britain in its war with
Germany, despite congressional statutes requiring the United States to remain
neutral.[7] Today executive agreements have become major instruments of foreign
policy, far outnumbering treaties (see Table 9.1 on page 220) and, in some cases,
outranking them in geopolitical importance. We have treaties with Mexico, for
example, concerning visits by American archaeologists and executive agreements
with some Middle East countries that have established American naval bases in the
area.

The Supreme Court has interpreted the president's foreign policy powers in very
broad language. In a major case, *United States v. Curtiss-Wright Corporation* (1936),
the Court described the president as the "sole organ" of foreign policy. The president
makes treaties with the advice and consent of the Senate, "but he alone negotiates."
For this important role, said the Court, Congress should give the president plenty of
leeway:

> It is quite apparent that if, in the maintenance of our international relations, embarrass-
> ment—perhaps serious embarrassment—is to be avoided and success for our aims
> achieved, congressional legislation . . . must often accord to the president a degree of
> discretion and freedom from statutory restriction which would not be admissible were
> domestic affairs alone involved.[8]

Congress has not always been ready to grant this leeway. Struggles between
presidents and Congress over foreign policy stretch back to the administration of
George Washington, whose 1793 Proclamation of Neutrality was denounced as a
usurpation of congressional authority. Presidents James Polk, Abraham Lincoln,

TABLE 9-1

Treaties and Executive Agreements Approved by the United States, 1789-1986

Year	Number of treaties	Number of executive agreements
1789-1839	60	27
1839-1889	215	238
1889-1929	382	763
1930-1932	49	41
1933-1944 (F. Roosevelt)	131	369
1945-1952 (Truman)	132	1,324
1953-1960 (Eisenhower)	89	1,834
1961-1963 (Kennedy)	36	813
1964-1968 (L. Johnson)	67	1,083
1969-1974 (Nixon)	93	1,317
1975-1976 (Ford)	26	666
1977-1980 (Carter)	79	1,476
1981-1986 (Reagan)	92	2,019

Note: Varying definitions of what comprises an executive agreement and their entry-into-force date make the above numbers approximate.

Source: 1789-1980: *Congressional Quarterly's Guide to Congress*, 291; 1981-1986: Office of the Assistant Legal Advisor for Treaty Affairs; Harold W. Stanley and Richard G. Niemi, *Vital Statistics on American Politics* (Washington: Congressional Quarterly Press, 1988), p. 226. Reprinted with permission.

Early in our history, the number of treaties and executive agreements were roughly equal. This changed during the twentieth century, particularly after World War II. Executive agreements now far outnumber treaties as instruments of foreign policy. Unlike treaties, executive agreements do not require Senate ratification; supposedly, they merely implement existing laws and treaties, but, in fact, they often deal with important matters and break new ground.

Theodore Roosevelt, and Woodrow Wilson also had confrontations with Congress. In the post-World War II period, however, Congress was largely passive in the face of presidential activism. In 1962 Congressman Carl Vinson (D-Georgia) described Congress as an aging uncle "who complains while furiously puffing on his pipe but finally, as everyone expects, gives in and hands over the allowance. . . ."[9]

Then came the Vietnam War. By the end of that war, Congress was determined to play a more active role in foreign policy. The struggle took on a partisan cast in the 1980s as a Republican president battled a Democratic House of Representatives (and, after 1986, a Democratic Senate as well) over foreign policy issues, particularly Central America. The various Boland Amendments that Congress attached to appropriation bills in the 1980s limited President Reagan's ability to aid the anti-government Contras in Nicaragua. Reagan's attempt to get around these amendments triggered the Iran-Contra affair (see chapters 7 and 10). The resulting scandal further damaged his control of foreign affairs. At one point even the president's authority as "sole organ" of foreign policy was challenged. In November 1987 House Speaker Jim Wright, a Democrat, held a meeting with Nicaraguan president Daniel Ortega Saavedra and Cardinal Obando y Bravo, the Roman Catholic primate of Nicaragua, to seek a solution to the unrest in the area. In justifying his role, Wright said that since the Reagan administration refused to seek peace in Nicaragua, he, Wright, would do so.

It is not clear yet whether or not the Bush administration has won back any of the foreign policy powers lost during Reagan's last years in office. George Bush takes a much different approach to Congress than Ronald Reagan, preferring quiet negotiation with congressional leaders to going public. Bush's conservative critics worry that he may have compromised vital presidential power in foreign affairs, while his supporters commend him for prudent statesmanship.[10]

THE PRESIDENT AS CHIEF EXECUTIVE

Article II, Section 3, of the Constitution says that the president "shall take Care that the Laws be faithfully executed." As chief executive, the president commands a bureaucracy of almost 3 million people, from the local post office personnel to the highest reaches of Washington power. We shall see in chapter 11 that the president's control over the bureaucracy is often more nominal than real. Nevertheless, his attitudes and philosophy shape the way the laws are enforced. Statutes and constitutional provisions often leave room for interpretation in how they are implemented. Does the goal of ending racial discrimination prohibit or demand the use of affirmative action programs? Should church-related colleges be taxed? Does the concept of equal treatment of aliens under the law imply that they are entitled to bilingual education? Laws and court decisions have left these questions open, and presidents have filled in the blanks—each in his own way.

There is also the question of emphasis. How energetically should each law be enforced? Ideally, they should all be enforced vigorously, but this is impossible. As Edward Corwin has noted, there are so many statutes on the books, some of them actually in conflict with one another, that they can not "all be enforced with equal vigor." Consequently, "the President's very *obligation to* the law becomes at times an authorization to *dispense with* the law."[11] Each administration has to decide where it will place its emphasis. Should it concentrate on punishing welfare cheaters or corporate price-fixers? Communist spies or capitalist monopolies? Drug dealers or industrial polluters? Pornographers or strip-miners? All have violated federal laws, but there are not enough federal agents or hours to pursue them all to the same degree. That is where the president's discretion and philosophy become important.

A president sets his bureaucratic machinery in motion by means of <u>executive orders</u>, directives signed by the president that require executive agencies or individuals to take specific actions. Hundreds of these orders are issued every year and published in a giant volume called the *Federal Register*. They do not need congressional approval because technically they are not laws; they are implementations of laws or of constitutional provisions that are often full of presidential discretion. In 1949 President Truman desegregated the armed forces by executive order; he did so not in response to a congressional law (which never would have been passed in those days), but because he wanted the armed forces desegregated. Such orders have been used for a wide variety of purposes. Kennedy's very first executive order expanded surplus food distribution to the poor; he took the money from Customs reserves. Nixon used executive orders to authorize wiretaps on reporters.

Although Congress has sometimes worried about the amount of discretion in the president's hands, it has not shied away from giving more. At various times Congress has allowed presidents to use their judgment in setting prices, adjusting tariffs, impounding appropriated funds, and setting codes of fair competition. What if a president abuses this power? What if the president makes decisions contrary to the will of Congress? Legislators finally came up with a solution to these problems: the <u>legislative veto</u>.

Congress would pass a law delegating broad decision-making power to the

"The question is, do we want to emphasize foreign policy to take the people's minds off domestic policy, or emphasize domestic policy to take the people's minds off foreign policy?
Drawing by Dana Fradon; © 1979 The New Yorker Magazine, Inc.

TABLE 9-2

Number of Pages in the *Federal Register*, 1936-1988

Year	Pages	Year	Pages
1936	2,355	1976	57,072
1946	14,736	1977	63,629
1956	10,528	1978	61,261
1966	16,850	1979	77,497
1967	21,087	1980	87,012
1968	20,068	1981	63,554
1969	20,464	1982	58,493
1970	20,032	1983	57,703
1971	25,442	1984	50,997
1972	28,920	1985	53,479
1973	35,586	1986	47,418
1974	45,422	1987	49,654
1975	60,221	1988	53,376

Source: Norman J. Ornstein et al., eds., *Vital Statistics on Congress, 1987-1988* (Washington, DC: Congressional Quarterly, 1987), 170.

The growing number of pages in the *Federal Register*, which lists executive orders, gives some indication of the growth of executive authority. In 1936 there were 2,355 pages, by 1988 there were 53,376. Executive orders, which do not require congressional approval, implement laws passed by Congress. Unlike executive agreements, which are the joint decisions of the president and the heads of other countries, executive orders are at the sole discretion of the president.

executive branch but retaining the right to strike down any decision it did not like. It would do so by simply passing a resolution reversing the presidential decision. Congress inserted these provisions into at least 126 statutes. Many legislative experts considered this a great way to combine efficiency and responsibility. But in the case of *Immigration and Nationalization Service v. Chadha* (1983), the Supreme Court said that the legislative veto violated the Constitution. In *Chadha* the Court admitted that the legislative veto might be a very efficient device but said that the Founders "ranked other values higher than efficiency." The legislative veto, said the Court, violated the principle of checks and balances because it allowed Congress to legislate—to pass a resolution reversing a decision of the executive branch—without giving the chief executive a chance to veto.

In carrying out the constitutional duty to "take Care that the Laws be faithfully executed," the president must rely upon millions of others, from generals to letter-carriers. The federal bureaucracy as a whole is treated in chapter 11. For now we will discuss those elements most closely connected to the president: the cabinet, the Executive Office of the President, and the White House Office.

The Cabinet. The oldest of these elements is the cabinet. Although the word *cabinet* is not found in the Constitution (which refers to "the principal Officer in each of the executive Departments"), one has existed as a part of the bureaucracy since George Washington's presidency. At that time there were only four cabinet officers: the secretaries of state, treasury, and war, and the attorney general. Today there are 14 executive departments in the cabinet (see Figure 9.1).

The cabinet officials are the president's subordinates. He or she selects them (with the approval of the Senate) and can dismiss them. The president holds cabinet meetings and listens to the advice cabinet members offer as he or she sees fit.

FIGURE 9-1

The President's Cabinet — Executive Departments

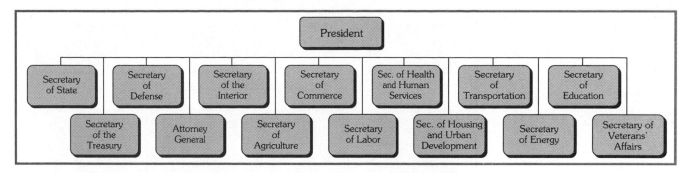

Fourteen cabinet departments are directly answerable to the president. They carry out much of the nation's business, from national defense and foreign policy to matters once left almost entirely to state and local authorities, such as education, housing, and health.

According to one story, President Lincoln, who favored a particular policy, took a vote of his cabinet members and found them all opposed. "One aye, five nays," he said. "The ayes have it." This is not to say that cabinet members have no influence with the president. Some, like Secretary of State Henry Kissinger under Nixon and Defense Secretary Caspar Weinberger under Reagan, have been very influential. But the cabinet itself, the cabinet as a collective institution, is not a decision-making body, and full-dress cabinet meetings are not usually very productive. The cabinet does, however, provide a way for important interests in America to be represented before the president. The Department of Labor, for example, is usually friendly to labor interests, and the Department of Commerce tends to side with the interests of business. Various ethnic and racial groups also find at least symbolic representation in various cabinet departments. President Bush fought hard to fill the position of secretary of Health and Human Services with a black, Dr. Louis Sullivan, despite objections from groups within the Republican party who opposed Dr. Sullivan's apparent pro-choice position on abortion. Bush appointed a Hispanic educator, Lauro Cavazos, to the head the Department of Education. These interests take cabinet representation very seriously, so that once a cabinet department is created it is not soon likely to be abolished. The Department of Education was created under President Jimmy Carter, who promised it to the National Education Association (NEA), a liberal teachers' lobby, when he campaigned for the presidency in 1976. Ronald Reagan, who adopted the conservative view that education should be primarily a state and local function, campaigned in 1980 on the promise of abolishing the Education Department. But once elected, Reagan's proposed abolition met such fierce resistance from the NEA and lawmakers friendly to it that he gave up the idea, contenting himself with the appointment of an education secretary (William Bennett) whose educational policies and preachings delighted conservatives. Now hardly anyone talks about abolishing the Department of Education.

President Bush began assembling his new cabinet even before his inauguration. After his election, while still vice president, he swore in his new secretary of education, Lauro F. Cavazos. Peggy Cavazos, the secretary's wife, holds the family Bible.

The Executive Office of the President. As late as the 1920s only a few dozen people worked for the president in addition to the cabinet. Things changed in the 1930s when President Franklin Roosevelt began hiring special advisers and assistants who answered only to him. Then, in 1939, a special task force appointed by President Roosevelt (the Committee on Administrative Management) recommended the creation of a new office designed to assist the president with a variety of tasks, from preparing the budget to managing personnel. Congress responded by setting up the

FIGURE **9-2**

Executive Office of the President

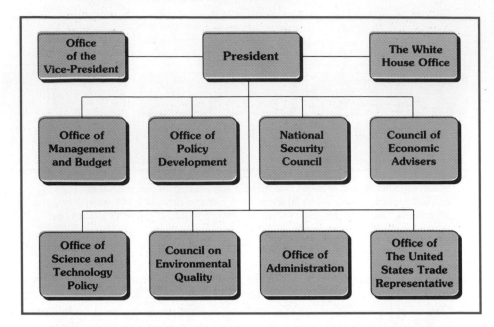

The Executive Office of the President was set up at the end of the 1930s in response to a study of a special commission whose conclusion was that "the President needs help." The bureaus within the Executive Office have very high priority within the executive branch.

Executive Office of the President. Today the Executive Office consists of several agencies with a total of about 1,600 employees. Among the most important agencies housed within the Executive Office are the Office of Management and Budget (OMB), which prepares the executive budget; the National Security Council (NSC), which oversees the operation of the CIA and deals with other sensitive foreign policy operations; and the White House Office.

The White House Office. The White House Office, with about 400 employees, lies close to the heart of presidential power. Closest of all are the handful of senior White House staff members, who include the president's press secretary and various advisers. The positions, which are not formalized, go by various names: domestic adviser, chief of staff, counsel, and so on. The names of the posts tell us little about the power of the occupants. Theodore Sorensen, who played a major role in the Kennedy administration, was called special counsel, but so was Charles Colson in the Nixon administration, and Colson's part was insignificant. The power of these individuals depends largely upon the relationship they have with the chief executive, and that, in turn, depends upon their personalities—and the president's. Franklin Roosevelt liked to give two staff members the same job then compare their work to test their competence and faithfulness. Jimmy Carter often got involved in detailed decision making (such as who should use the White House tennis court on particular days), while Ronald Reagan went to the other extreme by delegating broad areas of decision making to others and making little effort to oversee them.

TABLE **9-3**

225

The Burgeoning White House Staff

Theodore Roosevelt White House (1901–1909)

Secretary (chief of staff)	1
Assistant secretary	2
Executive clerk (handled correspondence)	2
Clerk (stenographers and typists)	11
Telegrapher	1
Messenger	7
Usher	1
Doorkeeper	5
Steward	1
Watchman	1
Fireman	1
Laborer	1
Bookbinder	1
Total	**35**

Ronald Reagan White House (1981–1989)

White House Office (including the Office of Policy Development)	568
National Security Council staff	190
Office of the Vice President	98
Office of Administration	91
Executive residence (including National Park Service staff regularly on the grounds)	129
Military Office	1,300
Engineering and maintenance (including G.S.A. and phone company employees)	190
U.S. Secret Service:	
Uniformed division (White House police)	500
Presidential protective detail	100
Vice presidential protective detail	100
White House technical security	100
Total	**3,366**

Note: There are approximately 2,500 military personnel and 500 volunteers who support the White House on a less than full-time basis.

Source: Edmund Morris, author of *The Rise of Theodore Roosevelt* (New York: Ballantine, 1980); Bradley H. Patterson, Jr., *The Ring of Power: The White House Staff and its Expanding Role in Government* (New York: Basic Books, 1988). Reprinted with permission of the *Wall Street Journal.*

The twentieth century has seen a dramatic increase in the number of presidential assistants—from 35 at the time of Theodore Roosevelt to more than 3,000 by the time Ronald Reagan left office in 1989. "The president needs help" was the conclusion of a commission studying the presidency in the 1930s. The president now has a very large number of "helpers."

THE PRESIDENT AS CHIEF LEGISLATOR

In the Constitution most of the president's legislative powers are either negative or peripheral. He has a qualified veto over legislation passed by Congress (you will recall that the veto can be overridden by a two-thirds vote in both houses). He may, "on extraordinary Occasions" says the Constitution, "convene both Houses, or either of them." If the two houses cannot agree on when to adjourn, "he may adjourn them to such Time as he shall think proper." That is about it, except for one other clause: "He shall from time to time give to the Congress Information of the State of the Union, and recommend to their Consideration such Measures as he shall judge necessary and expedient." This power may not look very impressive on its face, but it has become the springboard for the president's legislative leadership.

Each January the president delivers a State of the Union address to both houses of Congress—jointly assembled in the House chamber—during which he does indeed "recommend to their Consideration" the bills he thinks they should pass. But this address is more than a report to Congress. It has become a grand exercise of the president's "bully pulpit," a chance to pressure Congress by speaking over its head to the American people. Formerly given at noon, the speech was moved to an evening prime-time television slot by Lyndon Johnson. There it has stayed, an all-network media event that pushes everything else off the air.

The State of the Union address is just one of the many ways in which the president exerts legislative leadership. Every year Capitol Hill receives a detailed legislative program and an annual budget setting forth the president's spending priorities. Congress sets to work on these, sometimes with a vengeance. Even though the end product often bears little resemblance to what the president submitted, Congress wants these proposals submitted. In spite of valiant efforts to get its own house in order, Congress is better at responding to total, integrated programs than at crafting them. The president alone is in a position to provide such an initiative and therefore is expected, within the limits of the Constitution, to sponsor programs and lobby for their support.

Presidential Lobbying.   The president possesses some formidable lobbying tools. Some are connected to the magic of the presidency. Take, for example, the telephone. "I do not know what there is about the presidency, when it comes to a call from that lofty and august position," confessed Robert Byrd, minority leader of the Senate. "There is something that likens it to lockjaw. Some individuals, when they receive a call from the president, apparently do not know how to say, 'no.' "[12] There are many other tools of persuasion in the same category. Political correspondent Martin Tolchin gives some examples.

> Presidential blandishments range from the inane, such as a gift of presidential cuff links or an invitation to a White House lunch for a "photo opportunity" with the president, to the presidential appointment of a congressman's supporter, help in a congressman's campaign and support of a congressman's pet legislation.[13]

As Tolchin notes, the presidents have a wide choice of carrots to use on members of Congress. Aside from the photo opportunities and the cuff links, there are pleasing appointments presidents can make, promises of support, and unilateral actions. They can adjust trade barriers to please members' constituents. They can order public works to be built in particular congressional districts. Presidents also have a variety of sticks, most of which are the opposite of the carrots: They can make a member of Congress a *persona non grata* at the White House or turn a cold shoulder to a legislator's proposed appointee, pet bill, or public works project. A president may even visit the member's state or district to campaign for his or her opponent. These instruments are used with varying degrees of skill. In the next section of this chapter, we will talk about those who have used presidential power; for now, we are concerned only with the powers available for use.

Presidential Vetoes.   One power clearly given to the chief legislator by the Constitution is the veto. It can wipe out months of hard work by Congress, and it is not easily overridden. Presidents are aware of its power and know that even the threat of a veto can force changes from Congress. At one point President Reagan borrowed a line from Clint Eastwood's movie *Dirty Harry* in threatening to veto a big spending bill: "Go ahead," he said. "Make my day."   *(Continued on page 228)*

Should the President Have a Line-Item Veto?

YES Senator Mack Mattingly

Based upon Mack Mattingly, "Yes: A Useful Tool to Reduce Government Overspending," *Washington Times*, July 22, 1985, p. B1.

Mattingly, a Republican senator from Georgia, worries about congressional overspending and thinks that the line-item veto would force Congress to spend more prudently. He notes that 43 of the 50 governors have this power, and he denies that it would violate the Constitution if placed in the president's hands. In fact, he says, it would restore the real spirit of the president's constitutional veto power because it would permit him to veto the type of legislation that in recent years has been tucked safely into huge appropriation bills. These items usually call for the kind of spending that, he believes, has created our massive federal deficit. Anyone who has had to balance the family checkbook knows that the government "cannot go on forever spending more than it earns," says Mattingly. The line-item veto would enable the president to cut useless spending without jeopardizing necessary spending. "From this point, the bills would be treated as any other legislation," says Mattingly. "Those spending items vetoed would come back to Congress, and the sponsors would have to stand up in the light of day and defend them."

NO Representative Mickey Edwards

Based upon Mickey Edwards, "No: The President Already Has All the Power He Needs," *Washington Times*, July 22, 1985, p. B1.

To Edwards, a Republican congressman from Oklahoma, a line-item veto would give the president "unprecedented power to determine spending priorities." At least indirectly, it would violate Article I, Section 1, of the Constitution, which says that "All legislative Powers herein granted" belong to Congress. The fact that 43 governors have this power is irrelevant, he insists, since states do not deal with foreign policy or defense questions. Even in domestic affairs, states have much more limited impact. Presidents, Edwards says, have all the veto power they need; what they lack very often is the will to use it. To add to that power with the line-item veto would be to give presidents control over the purse, something the Founders deliberately left in the hands of Congress. "It would be a serious mistake to turn our backs on the separation of powers, and the relative balance of powers between the branches of government, to 'restore' a presidential power that has never been lost."

Postscript

Note that both writers claim that the Constitution is on their side. Edwards relies on the language of Article I, Section 1, stating that "All legislative Powers herein granted" belong to Congress, while Mattingly insists that the Framers of the Constitution never meant to give Congress the power to present the president with a gigantic omnibus bill on a take-it-or-leave-it basis. We can only speculate about which of the two positions would actually be supported by the men who wrote the Constitution.

Presidential power is a much-discussed topic. The classic work on the subject is Edward S. Corwin's *The President: Office and Powers* (New York: New York University, 1957). Some writers, like historian Arthur Schlesinger, Jr., who were strong promoters of presidential power in the 1950s, turned against the activist presidency in the 1970s. See Schlesinger's *The Imperial Presidency* (Boston: Houghton Mifflin, 1973). A more balanced and less polemical view of presidential power is presented in Emmet John Hughes, *The Living Presidency* (New York: Coward, McCann, 1972).

(Continued from page 226)   The veto is a powerful weapon but a clumsy one, more like a shotgun than a rifle. Because it destroys an entire statute, even though there might be some clauses in the statute that the president very much likes, it affords members of Congress, particularly senators, a chance to shield *their* favorite clauses. This is particularly true in the case of so-called omnibus appropriations bills, which may contain money for everything from the Contras in Nicaragua to urban mass transit. A conservative president like Reagan might be forced into accepting money for urban mass transit as the price of aid to the Contras, or a liberal president might be maneuvered into taking the Contra aid to get the urban transit funds. The only alternative is to kill both proposals with a veto.

The president could avoid this dilemma with a line-item veto—that is, the power to veto a single item in a bill. That way, the president could kill some items in an omnibus bill while saving others. Forty-three of our 50 governors have such a veto, but whether it is suited for the president is a matter in dispute. A 1985 bill giving it to the president was co-sponsored by 47 senators and endorsed by politicians of varying persuasions from Ronald Reagan to Edward Kennedy, but it was filibustered to death in the Senate. Its opponents worried that it would give the president too much power. Some contrasting views of the merits of the line-item veto are presented in the Taking Sides section on the previous page.

Chief of state, commander in chief, chief diplomat, chief executive, chief legislator—these are among the important hats worn by the modern president. Yet all these hats sit on the same head, and they all overlap. A clever president can use some of the aura of the office of chief of state to build up power as chief legislator. Doing so may also provide more leeway to do what the president wants as chief executive or commander in chief. An inept president may, by using power badly in one area, lose support in other areas. Much, then, depends on who is sitting in the White House.

Presidential Personality

We have been discussing the powers contained in the office of the presidency today. The powers are there. How skillfully they are used is another question. In part that depends on who is in the White House: Some people know how to use these powers, and some do not.

Take the power of legislative leadership. As noted previously, the president has a variety of carrots and sticks to use on Congress. Some presidents have wielded these with enormous skill. Franklin Roosevelt and Lyndon Johnson were the great virtuosos. Roosevelt visited the districts of friendly members of Congress, posing with them for the photographers, making sure he loaded their state or district with public works projects. Lyndon Johnson used similar carrots but also enjoyed wielding the stick. Former Senate minority leader Robert Byrd said this about Johnson's approach: "I have never known anyone who could twist an arm as well and as painfully as could Lyndon Johnson when he was president of the United States."[14] Byrd, a West Virginia Democrat, once dared to oppose a bill Johnson was determined to get passed. Byrd received a telephone call from the White House. Johnson began the conversation by reminding Byrd that he, Byrd, had sent to the White House the name of a man he wanted appointed federal judge in his state. Byrd recalled the ensuing exchange:

> He said: "Bob, how much do you want that judgeship? How badly do you want that judgeship?
> I said: "I want it pretty badly. I sent a good man's name down to you." The President said, "Bob, send us another name down."[15]

As a legislative leader Johnson was almost unrivaled. But when it came to the use of his power as commander in chief, Johnson marched himself and his nation into a quagmire in Southeast Asia that ended up weakening the presidency. We will look at the darker side of the Johnson presidency in a moment. But for now let us appreciate his true talent, built up through years of experience as Senate majority leader.

President Reagan's legislative leadership was far less impressive than that of giants like Roosevelt and Johnson. Reagan relied more on carrots than on sticks. When critical votes were about to be taken, wavering representatives received telephone calls from the Reagan White House that usually began, "Is there anything you're really interested in that you'd like to talk about?" Those friendly chats brought dividends, at least in the early years of Reagan's presidency. In his first term Reagan won support on such key measures as his 1981 tax cut and the MX missile. Reagan's second term was far less successful. Even before losing control of the Senate to the Democrats and getting hit by the Irangate scandal in 1987, Reagan's legislative influence had waned. His major achievements—securing passage of the tax reform package in 1986 and getting the Senate to ratify the arms control treaty with the Soviets—were possible only because they coincided with the Democratic agenda. On issues opposed by Democratic leaders, he generally lost. Congress limited deployment of MX missiles to a maximum of 50—half of what Reagan wanted. Congress cut funds for Reagan's "Star Wars" program and the overall military budget, and the Senate refused to confirm the nomination of Robert Bork to the Supreme Court.

Still, Reagan—or at least his advisers—had a much better grasp of how to get things out of Congress than did other recent presidents. Nixon, despite his reputation for ruthlessness, hated to put Congress on the spot. As his congressional lobbyist recalled later: "Many times we'd have a key congressman come into the Oval Office and President Nixon would make the argument and then say, 'I know there are two sides to every issue, and whatever you do will be O.K. with me.' " Jimmy Carter was even less effective than Nixon. Nixon knew what he had to do, though he was fainthearted about doing it. Carter seemed confused about what he really wanted from Congress. More accurately, he wanted to do so many things—reform welfare, give tax rebates to all Americans, clean up the environment, solve the energy crisis, make peace with the Soviets—that he could not focus his energies on just one or two issues. *New York Times* reporter Hedrick Smith recalls: "Whenever I would ask White

TABLE **9-4**

Previous Public Positions Held by Presidents

	Number of presidents holding position prior to presidency	
Position	Pre-1900 (24)	Post-1900 (16)
Vice president	7	8
Cabinet secretary	7	2
Subcabinet official	1	5
U.S. representative	13	5
U.S. senator	8	5
U.S. Supreme Court justice	0	0
Federal judge	0	1
Governor	11	6
State legislator	17	5
State executive	10	2
State judge	1	3
Mayor	2	1
City government official	1	3
Diplomate, ambassador	7	1
Military general	5	1

Source: Harold W. Stanley and Richard G. Niemi, *Vital Statistics on American Politics* (Washington: Congressional Quarterly Press, 1988), p. 212; Richard M. Pious, *The American Presidency* (New York: Basic Books, 1979), p. 87. Reprinted with permission.

> It is hard to define the kind of work experience that fits a person for the presidency. Prior to 1900, many presidents had formerly served as U.S. and state legislators. In this century, presidents seem to come from a variety of backgrounds, including the vice presidency and state governorships.

House officials for Carter's top priorities, the list would run past a dozen items."[16] Carter demanded practically everything, and as a result got next to nothing.

Some presidential observers have tried to draw up job specifications for the Oval Office. This is hard to do because successful presidents have come from a wide variety of backgrounds. Kennedy was a rather undistinguished senator. Lincoln was an Illinois legislator and a member of Congress. Other competent presidents have come from such varied fields as the military and state government. Experience may not count for much because, as president after president has testified, there is no job that quite prepares one for being president. More decisive, perhaps, is the president's psychological makeup. American politics is not for introverts or for people who like solitude.

PRESIDENTIAL QUALITIES

Political scientist Clinton Rossiter tried to get more particular about job specifications in a now-classic book on the presidency that he wrote in 1956. Here is Rossiter's list of presidential qualities:

> "Bounce": Not only must the president be healthy . . . he must have that extra elasticity, given to few men, which makes it possible for him to thrive on the toughest diet of work and responsibility in the world. . . .

Affability: The president's heart must not only be stout but warm. He must care deeply about people in the flesh. . . .

Cunning: [A] president cannot get the best out of the dozens of able figures around him or keep them under his command unless he is a master in the delicate art of manipulating men.

A sense of history: This cast of mind raises him above all those around him, sobering him yet exalting him with the thought that he sits in Lincoln's seat. . . .

The newspaper habit: The modern president must be on guard lest he be cut off from harsh reality. He needs badly to know what people are thinking about events and about his handling of them. . . .

A sense of humor: If he reads [newspapers] at all faithfully, he will need a thick skin and a light heart. [17]

The model from whom all these traits are taken is Franklin Delano Roosevelt. His "bounce" is reflected in many of his photographs, particularly the famous one of a beaming FDR clenching a cigarette holder in his teeth. His cunning was as much in evidence to Washington insiders as his affability and sense of humor were to the rest of America. He displayed his sense of history at the outset of his 12-year tenure. Inaugurated in 1933 during the Great Depression, he said in his inaugural address: "This great Nation will endure as it has endured, will revive and will prosper." Its revival and subsequent victory in World War II turned FDR, the man who presided over it all, into a national hero.

Franklin Delano Roosevelt possessed the qualities many political scientists believe are necessary to be a successful president. The times in which a president lives and the climate of expectations surrounding the presidency also have a great effect on presidential success.

IN PRAISE OF ACTIVE-POSITIVE PRESIDENTS

Perhaps the most ambitious attempt to study presidential personality is *The Presidential Character*, by James D. Barber. Barber finds four distinct personality types among various presidents: (1) active-positive, (2) active-negative, (3) passive-positive, and (4) passive-negative. [18] The terms *active* and *passive* measure the president's commitment to hard work, whereas *negative* and *positive* measure his attitude *toward* his work. Does the president enjoy the job or regard it as a burden? The active-negative president works very hard but approaches the task grimly. Barber puts Herbert Hoover and Richard Nixon in that category. The passive-negative president dislikes his work and avoids it as much as possible. Barber thinks Eisenhower was a good example of this type. Then there is the passive-positive president, who relishes the job but is not industrious. Barber finds this combination of qualities in William Howard Taft and Ronald Reagan. Finally, there is the ideal personality type, the active-positive president like FDR and John Kennedy. Here were men who not only threw themselves into their work, but enjoyed it as well. Barber strongly hinted that voters should seek out and elect active-positive presidents because, he believed, they would approach the job with zest, flexibility, and imagination.

Barber's assumption that presidential personality is a good predictor of presidential performance is questionable. Would not the president's philosophy—for example, whether the president favors or opposes welfare spending—be at least as important? Is it really possible to pigeonhole presidents into these categories? Barber himself admits to being uncertain about how to classify Jimmy Carter. When Carter first came to office, Barber suggested that the former governor of Georgia would fall into the active-positive category, but in the third edition of his book he says that such a characterization "rings too hopeful in history's light, for the fact is that Carter had a lot of down days." [19]

Nevertheless, there is much to be said for seeking the right kind of person to be president. People who lack what Clinton Rossiter called "bounce" are probably not suited to a job that demands enormous energy. Affability and a sense of humor are

FIGURE **9-3**

James D. Barber's 4 Types of Presidential Character

	Active	Passive
Positive	ACTIVE-POSITIVE Works hard and enjoys the job. (Franklin D. Roosevelt, John F. Kennedy)	PASSIVE-POSITIVE Enjoys the job but is not very involved in it; is easily swayed by friends. (William H. Taft, Warren G. Harding, Ronald W. Reagan)
Negative	ACTIVE-NEGATIVE Works hard but has a negative emotional reaction to the work. (Woodrow Wilson, Herbert Hoover, Lyndon B. Johnson, Richard M. Nixon)	PASSIVE-NEGATIVE Does not enjoy the job and is not very involved in it. (Calvin Coolidge, Dwight D. Eisenhower)

Data source: James David Barber, *The Presidential Character*, 3d ed. (Englewood Cliffs, NJ: Prentice Hall, Inc., 1985). Adapted with permission.

Political scientist James D. Barber has delineated four different personality types among those who have occupied the White House in this century: active-positive, active-negative, passive-positive, and passive-negative.

also useful qualities. Political savvy, cunning, a love of politics—all of these together capture the meaning of Barber's positive category. But what about the active part of active-positive? Is it always good to have an active president? What if the president is actively getting us into a war? If so, should we go to war? Active-positive President Franklin Roosevelt did indeed steer us toward war with Nazi Germany in 1941, and history's verdict is that he was right in doing so. But some future active-positive president may take us into another war unwisely. Presidential activism, then, needs to be questioned.

A generation ago, hardly anyone would have thought to consider this subject. It is only since Vietnam and Watergate that university professors and journalists have been taking a hard look at it. Ironically, they were once activism's most enthusiastic supporters. To see what has happened, we have to go back to the days of John Kennedy.

Changing Attitudes Toward the Presidency

In the early 1960s John F. Kennedy was perhaps the most dramatic and exciting leader on earth. This was partly because he occupied one of the most powerful offices on this planet and partly because he had a flair for communicating the drama of his office. But we must also consider something else: the period in which he lived. In *The American Presidency* Clinton Rossiter wrote: "A man cannot possibly be judged a great president unless he holds office in great times."[20] Kennedy lived in an era of great hope. America was still basking in the triumphs of World War II. Our country was respected throughout the world. At home, industries were booming; foreign competition was almost nonexistent. Unemployment was low, the economy was stable, and social problems like drugs and crime were considered manageable. The eight years of Eisenhower had been relatively serene. Now it was time for new initiatives. (Kennedy's campaign slogan had been "We've got to get this country moving again.") Kennedy obviously spoke from the heart in his inaugural address when he said, "I do not believe that any of us would exchange places with any other people or any other generation."

So much excitement and hope were centered on the American presidency in the early 1960s. People trusted the presidency. It was a noble office, a clean office. It seemed to be free of politics in the negative sense of the word: free from pettiness, meanness, corruption, and factional wrangling. Those sins, it was thought, could be found in Congress but not the presidency. No, the presidency was different. It was a place for prophets, not hacks. A president could lead us out of the wilderness.

THE CULT OF PRESIDENTIAL ACTIVISM

The biggest boosters of the presidency at this time were university professors. Anyone who went to college in those days can tell you that the professors loved the idea of an expansive, activist presidency. They saw it as an instrument of reform. "The textbook presidency," as Thomas Cronin was later to call it, was a presidency in the image of Franklin Roosevelt: a dynamic, reforming institution. Looking back, historian Arthur Schlesinger, Jr., acknowledged his own role in promoting the activist presidency:

> American historians and political scientists, this writer among them, labored to give the expansive theory of the presidency historical sanction. Overgeneralizing from the prewar contrast between a president who was right and a Congress which was wrong, scholars developed an uncritical cult of the activist presidency.[21]

Kennedy was the personification of activism. He was young and dashing; he kept talking about getting the country moving again. And he did, in a sense. The White House hummed with energy; people were always getting in and out of helicopters on the White House lawn or striding off to crisis conferences. A documentary made just after Kennedy's death was entitled *Years of Lightning, Day of Drums*. Novelist Norman Mailer called Kennedy an "existential president," and while perhaps nobody knew exactly what that meant, it sounded like a good way to characterize the drama that Kennedy had brought to the White House.

Nor was it surprising that Kennedy attracted novelists like Mailer. He appealed to the cultural elites: He was a Harvard graduate who had written two books, and he had a beautiful wife who spoke French. "In his time," wrote Theodore H. White, "poetry was in the White House and music, too."[22] He sought out the young, educated journalists; took them into his confidence; compared notes with them; and joked with them. He became their colleague.

THE PRESS AND THE PRESIDENCY: THEN AND NOW

Kennedy's technique with the press paid off handsomely. If you were to read the transcript of a Kennedy press conference and then compare it to more recent presidential press conferences, you would be amazed at the difference. The reporters used an almost reverent tone when questioning the president in those days. The questions were usually simple requests for information, not attempts to trip up a politician. There were no follow-up questions, no cross-examinations, no harassment. Any questioner who stepped out of line risked being humiliated by Kennedy and laughed at by the other reporters in the room, as in this example:

Reporter: Mr. President, the practice of managed news is attributed to your administration. Mr. Salinger [Kennedy's press secretary] says he's never heard it defined. Would you give us your definition and tell us why it is you find it necessary to practice it? (Laughter)

Kennedy: You are charging us with something, Mrs. Craig [Mrs. May Craig, Portland (Maine) *Press Herald*], and then you are asking me to define what it is you are charging me with. (Laughter) Let me just say we've had very limited success in managing the news, if that's what we've been trying to do. . . . Perhaps you'd tell us what it is that you object to in our treatment of the news.

Reporter: Are you asking me, sir? (Laughter)

Kennedy: Yes.

Reporter: Well, I don't believe in managed news at all. I thought we ought to get everything we want. (Laughter)

Kennedy: Well, I think you should, too, Mrs. Craig. I'm for that. (Laughter)[23]

Actually, Kennedy was quite successful at managing and manipulating the news media. In deference to Kennedy the *New York Times* in 1961 watered down a story it had on the forthcoming invasion of Cuba by a U.S.-backed exile force. In 1962 the newspapers and networks supported Kennedy's blockade of Cuba, even though he failed to consult Congress before committing the nation to what could have become war with the Soviet Union. And when Kennedy gave his special addresses to the nation on television, no analyses or replies were broadcast immediately afterward.

Contemporary presidents are not treated so gently. In 1983 a carefully researched article by political scientists Michael Robinson, Maura Clancy, and Lisa Grand finally laid to rest the contention that President Reagan was getting a free ride from the press. Their findings showed that "Ronald Reagan has received disproportionately critical and negative press from the national media."[24] The respect journalists once gave to the president of the United States has eroded. Contrast the previous description of reporters' treatment of Kennedy with their treatment of Reagan, of which the following excerpt (from a 1986 press conference) is an example:

> *Q.* Mr. President . . . how would you assess the credibility of your own administration in the light of the prolonged deception of Congress and the public in terms of your secret dealings with Iran, the disinformation, the trading of Sacharoff for Daniloff? And I'd like to follow up.[25]

Reagan seemed to inspire the most hostility in academic and cultural circles. Anyone who attended faculty gatherings during the 1980s could hardly fail to notice the contempt for this popular president. Among artists and entertainers, the treatment of Reagan was especially harsh. Comedian Jim Morris did a Reagan imitation at a San Francisco club, staging a "swearing in ceremony" in which the audience was invited to swear at him. "It was a full house of several hundred people all shouting obscenities," Morris later recalled. "The emotion coming from the crowd was so intense that I was shaken, and for the first time I realized what a powerful and polarizing figure this man is."[26]

But Ronald Reagan is not the only recent president to be severely criticized by professors, artists, and journalists. Robinson's research indicates that in the 1980 presidential election campaign the media were rougher on Reagan's opponent, Jimmy Carter, than they were on him.[27] Nor was Jimmy Carter exactly a favorite in academic circles. During the 1980 campaign he was seen as the lesser of two evils. Gerald Ford was even less popular than Carter in academia, and in the press he was portrayed as a good-natured bumbler. Then there were Richard Nixon and Lyndon Johnson. They deserve a longer look, for they both helped to bring on this critical treatment of the presidency.

THE TURNING POINT: VIETNAM

The trouble started with Lyndon Johnson's escalation of the Vietnam War. At first, many leading scholars and journalists supported the war. In 1965 historian Arthur Schlesinger, Jr., was still publicly defending it, and two years earlier the *New York Times* actually had scolded President Kennedy for not being tough *enough* in Vietnam.[28] But as the scale of the fighting increased with no end in sight, the journalists and the professors began having second thoughts. The merits of the war were being publicly questioned on college campuses. Media coverage also was turning critical. It was at this point that President Kennedy's declaration, that America would "bear any burden, pay any price" to protect freedom, began to sound a bit extravagant.

President Johnson was enraged by the criticism. He tried to intimidate the critics by calling them nervous Nellies and questioning their patriotism. This tactic, of course, only inflamed the situation. In response, the professors and the journalists began taking a hard look at Johnson, who soon acquired a reputation as a liar and a manipulator. In the still-polite parlance of the time, the talk was of the president's credibility gap. Former promoters of the activist presidency were dismayed. What kind of man was this in the White House? What kind of power did this man possess? What kind of presidency had they been promoting? But even as they were rethinking the whole philosophy of the activist presidency, Richard Nixon was elected.

NIXON AND WATERGATE

No president in this century ever came into office with as bad a reputation in academic and journalistic circles as did Richard Nixon. In the 1950s, as one example, he was accused of using questionable tactics to defeat his opponents. Nixon reacted with anger to what he regarded as unfair treatment by the press. After being defeated for the governorship of California in 1962, he held a press conference and told reporters he was quitting politics: "You won't have Dick Nixon to kick around anymore." Now here he was back again, ready for a fight. Within a year of his inauguration he was sending his vice president around the country to mobilize public opinion against critics in the media and the universities. Vice President Spiro Agnew called them "effete snobs" and "nattering nabobs of negativism."

For a time, the presidential offensive apparently caused critics to pull back.[29] But then came the Watergate scandal, which destroyed Nixon's power and forced his resignation. The critics' victory was all the sweeter because his downfall was accomplished, at least in part, through the press. Two *Washington Post* reporters, Bob Woodward and Carl Bernstein, broke the stories that implicated high administration officials in a variety of lawless schemes.

If Vietnam had caused former supporters of presidential activism to change their minds, Watergate convinced them that the presidency itself was a dangerous institution—a view that still persists. The presidency, according to the press, needs constant monitoring and its occupants can no longer be trusted to function honorably and within the law. In a panel discussion in 1982, a Washington reporter told a nationwide television audience that he would trust the word of a "leaker" over that of the president because "lying increases the closer you get to the top." Other journalists on the panel, including CBS anchor Dan Rather, agreed with him.[30] In 1985 *Washington Post* editor Ben Bradlee compared President Reagan to terrorists who hijack a plane on the grounds that both were manipulators of the news.[31] These observations would have been unthinkable a generation ago.

The theme of this chapter is presidential power. If, as political scientist Richard Neustadt once argued, power implies the freedom to act without interference, then perhaps we can venture a conclusion: *It is much harder today for a president to be powerful than it was in Kennedy's day.* Freedom to act without interference implies freedom from sustained criticism. Kennedy, for example, was able to blockade Cuba in 1962, risking nuclear war with the Soviet Union, without encountering a storm of criticism. It is hard to imagine that happening in the 1990s.

Perhaps it is all for the best that things have changed. Perhaps the cloud of magic that once surrounded the White House did nothing but harm to this country. "America should feel proud, not apologetic," says Schlesinger about the reaction against the presidency. "That reaction is not a failure but a stirring vindication of American democracy."[32] Yet there is always the danger of an overreaction. If everything the president says is to be doubted and everything he attempts is to be subject to checks, do we not risk crippling the administration of government? The vision offered by Clinton Rossiter in 1956 is still compelling: Our president, he said, should not be "a Gulliver immobilized by ten thousand cords, nor even a Prometheus chained to a rock of frustration." The president should rather be "a kind of magnificient lion who can roam widely and do great deeds so long as he does not break loose from his broad reservation."[33]

So far the discussion has been on the nature of presidential power, the kinds of individuals who know how to use it, and the way presidential power is affected by the times. Let us turn now to the question of what happens to that power when the president becomes disabled.

Presidential Disability

What happens if the president becomes ill, dies, resigns, or is impeached? In that case, says Article II, Section 1, of the Constitution, the powers and duties of the office "shall devolve on the Vice President." Does that mean that the vice president shall then *be* the president? Or is he only an *acting* president? The ambiguity was cleared up in Section 1 of the Twenty-fifth Amendment, ratified in 1967. Section 1 says, "the Vice President shall become President."

ORDER OF SUCCESSION: VICE PRESIDENT, SPEAKER, PRESIDENT PRO TEMPORE

What if the president and vice president *both* die or are removed from office at the same time? For example, Vice President Johnson was riding in the same motorcade as Kennedy in Dallas in 1963. What if both had been killed that day? Article II leaves it up to Congress to settle this question by legislation, and Congress has tried different orders of succession. From 1792 to 1886, it provided that the order be from president to vice president to the president pro tempore of the Senate and then to the Speaker of the House. From 1886 to 1947, Congress redirected the line of succession, making it from the vice president to cabinet officers, in order of the establishment of their offices. That made the secretary of state next in line after the vice president. In the Presidential Succession Act of 1947, Congress changed the order again to what we have today: from the vice president to the House speaker and then to the president pro tempore of the Senate. Secretary of State Alexander Haig must have been remembering his pre-1947 schooling when, after President Reagan was wounded by a gunman in 1981, he told a group of reporters: "Constitutionally, gentlemen, you have the president, the vice president, and the secretary of state, in that order." Because the vice president was flying back to Washington from Texas, Haig announced that he himself was temporarily in control of the White House. Haig may have been in control, but he had no particular authority to be in control.

TEMPORARY DISABILITY

Now we come to a more delicate case. What if the president is not dead but disabled? If the disability is temporary, then the vice president takes over until the president is well enough to resume power. The method of transfer, as set forth in the Twenty-fifth Amendment, is for the president to notify Congress in writing that he or she is "unable to discharge the powers and duties" of his or her office. When the president recovers, the president sends Congress another written message saying that he or she is fit enough to resume the office.

Until 1985 this formal notification procedure was ignored. In 1981 President Reagan underwent five hours of surgery after the assassination attempt. During that time he was totally incapacitated, yet no notice was sent to Congress. Because Reagan and his staff were roundly criticized for this failure, he did notify Congress before his eight-hour cancer surgery in 1985—after a fashion. Reagan and his aides did not think formal notification was necessary for such a short-term disability. (What if the president goes to the dentist to get a wisdom tooth pulled?) They were careful to draft the note so as not to bind future presidents. Reagan said that he was temporarily transferring his power in accordance "with my long-standing arrangement with Vice President George Bush and not intending to set a precedent binding anyone privileged to hold this Office in the future." This may not have constituted formal notification under the terms of the Twenty-fifth Amendment, but it was, in the words of a former Reagan aide, "a close country cousin."[34]

REMOVING SICK, STUBBORN PRESIDENTS

Now we come to the most delicate issue of all. What if the president is disabled but refuses to admit to the disability? Such a case has actually happened. In September 1919 President Woodrow Wilson suffered a stroke while on a speaking tour and returned to Washington a crippled, helpless man. Both his speech and his mind were affected. For the rest of his term (until March 1921) all official business was transacted through his wife, who had had exactly two years of formal schooling. Letters and memorandums would be passed through the door and, sometimes many weeks later, would come back with his wife's childish scrawl on them, saying "The President says," or "The President wants." No one was in a position to know whether it was Wilson or his wife who was running the White House.[35]

What if something like that were to happen today? In Wilson's day everything moved at a slower pace. Today the United States can be reached in only a few minutes by enemy missiles. We cannot afford to have a sick president who clings to power. But what *can* we do? Section 4 of the Twenty-fifth Amendment provides a mechanism for removing the president from office. It is a very complicated mechanism, full of checks and balances to protect the president against the plots of those who would falsely accuse him of incompetence in order to be rid of him. In ordinary language, Section 4 would read something like this:

> 1. If the vice president and either a majority of the cabinet or a majority of a special body appointed by Congress notify Congress that the president is disabled, then the vice president takes over.

After suffering a disabling stroke in 1919, President Woodrow Wilson remained in office, and his wife, Edith Galt Wilson, helped him to carry out his duties as president. The Twenty-fifth Amendment seeks to resolve the problem of presidential disability by providing a procedure for transferring power to the vice president in such cases.

2. But if the president then writes to Congress himself and denies that he is disabled, then he takes his power back.

3. *However*, if within four days of the president's denial the same body mentioned in item 1 writes back to Congress and says that the president is *indeed* disabled, then a vote is taken in both houses of Congress.

4. If two-thirds of both houses agree that the president is disabled, the vice president resumes his role as acting president. If that vote cannot be mustered, the president is assumed to be fit and remains in office.

This is a bewildering process. Is it too complex to be workable? Nobody knows. It has never been put to the test and perhaps never will be. In the meantime, it has plenty of critics. One of them, a former counsel to the House of Representatives, says, "[It] sounds like you're trying to put your aged aunt who is incompetent into conservatorship."[36]

THE VICE PRESIDENT

This talk of presidential disability should remind us of the person who takes over when the president becomes ill, steps down, dies, or is removed: the vice president. Formal succession has happened three times in this century: in 1945, when Harry Truman took over after FDR's death; in 1963, when Lyndon Johnson became president after Kennedy's assassination; and in 1974, when Nixon's resignation made Gerald Ford president. There were also two occasions in the presidency of Dwight D. Eisenhower—once in 1955 when Eisenhower had a heart attack and two years later when he suffered a stroke—when Vice President Nixon came close to taking over. The position of vice president is indeed, as the old cliché puts it, a heartbeat away from the presidency.

Yet nobody really knows what the vice president is supposed to do besides wait to be president. The Constitution is almost entirely silent about job specifications. All it says is that the vice president "shall be President of the Senate, but shall have no Vote, unless they be equally divided." In practice, as we noted in chapter 8, the vice president seldom presides over the Senate, except on rare occasions when a tie-breaking vote is possible. What, then, does the vice president do?

Because the vice president has so little constitutional authority, it is hard even for a skillful politician to do much with the office. "Lyndon," John Nance Garner is supposed to have said when Johnson asked him if he should accept the vice-presidential candidacy in 1960, "it ain't worth a pitcher of warm spit." (Garner, however, did not say "spit.") A fellow Texan, Garner had run with Franklin Delano Roosevelt in 1932 and 1936 to balance the ticket, but Roosevelt had had no intention of giving Garner any power or, indeed, having much to do with him at all.[37]

In recent years, however, the vice presidency has become a more important office. This has been especially true since the Carter administration in the late 1970s. Vice President Walter F. Mondale became almost second-in-command to President Carter. He secured an office in the White House that allowed him easy access to the president (instead of being cooped up in the Executive Office Building next door), and he was given top-level secret information used in presidential briefings. This enabled Mondale to take a meaningful part in the policy debates in which the president's advisers often engaged. Mondale thus became a major player in the administration. During the succeeding Reagan administration, Vice President George Bush inherited some of the new privileges won by Mondale, so that he was able to have regular access to the president and receive much of the top-secret information given to Reagan. But Bush's style was different. He put much emphasis on the vice president's role as team player and did not inject himself into policy debates among the president's advisers; he preferred to express his views in private, one-on-one meetings with Reagan. As president, Bush has extended to Vice President Dan

Walter F. Mondale, who served as vice president under President Jimmy Carter between 1977 and 1981, was an active participant in administration policymaking. Before leaving office he passed along to George Bush the following guidelines for a successful vice presidency:

1. Advise the president confidentially. The only reason to state publicly what you have told the president is to take credit for his success and to try to escape blame for failure. Either way there is no quicker way to undermine your relationship with the president and lose your effectiveness in the government.

2. Don't wear a president down. He should be bright enough to catch your meaning the first time. Give your advice once and give it well. You have a right to be heard, not obeyed.

3. As a spokesman for the administration, stay on the facts. A president should not want, and the public does not respect, a vice president who does nothing but deliver pandering praise of a president. The vice presidency is important enough not to be demeaned by its occupants delivering obsequious flattery.

4. Understand your role as a spokesman. This does not mean that you must defend every idea that comes out of an administration. A wise president, who values the role of his vice president, will not make the mistake of forcing the vice president to speak for something with which he fundamentally disagrees.

5. Avoid line authority assignments. If such an assignment is important, it will then cut across the responsibilities of one or two Cabinet officers or others and embroil you in a debilitating bureaucratic fight. If it is meaningless or trivial, it will undermine your reputation and squander your time, as most vice presidents have found out.

6. A vice president should be ready to assume the presidency. . . . President Carter did not want me to need several months of on-the-job training in the presidency, if the need should have arisen. [The vice president] must be able to get along with the president. The relationship is intensely personal. It is founded on professional need, but it must proceed on personal respect.

Quayle the same perquisites he received as Reagan's vice president. While it is not clear whether Quayle has had any influence on presidential policies, Bush has used Quayle as a liaison to various groups in this country and to convey administration views to other countries.

The vice-presidential slot plays a role during campaigns, where it is used as a means of balancing the ticket. If the presidential candidate is from the East, like Roosevelt or Kennedy or Dukakis, a search is made for an appropriate westerner or southerner, like Garner or Lyndon Johnson or Lloyd Bentsen—all of whom were from Texas. If the presidential candidate is near the Republican center, like Bush, then maybe somebody with close ties to the Republican right, like Dan Quayle, will do.

Or maybe not. Quayle apparently hurt Bush more than he helped him in 1988, in part because many saw him as too inexperienced for the job. Whether or not the perception was justified, it pointed up the underlying dilemma of the vice-presidential office: It is a waste of talent to put a first-rate political leader into an office with marginal responsibilities, yet putting a mediocrity into it risks putting him or her into the White House. The dilemma can be resolved, at least in part, by making the vice presidency into a kind of apprenticeship, allowing its occupant as much hands-on experience as possible in running the executive branch.

Reflections

Presidential power is the result of three factors: the power of the office, the personal qualities particular presidents bring to the job, and the historical times in which they live. *(Continued on page 240)*

Points to Remember

1. Although the office of the presidency contains many powers, whether or not those powers are realized depends on the skill of the person in the White House.

2. It is difficult to draw up job specifications for the presidency. No experience quite prepares one for the task. One basic prerequisite is that the person should like politics and be an extrovert.

3. Clinton Rossiter cited a number of other good presidential qualities: "bounce," affability, cunning, a sense of history, the newspaper habit, and a sense of humor. James David Barber thinks we should seek active-positive people for the presidency.

4. Aside from their own personalities, the times in which particular presidents live affect the power they can wield. In Kennedy's day, presidential activism was celebrated by key opinion leaders.

5. Opinion leaders, particularly scholars and journalists, once celebrated presidential activism, but today they worry about the "imperial" presidency. In consequence, presidents today lack the leeway they had in Kennedy's day.

6. The Twenty-fifth Amendment provides a complicated mechanism for removing a disabled president who refuses to step down. It attempts to balance the rights of the president against the need to have a competent person running the White House.

7. Traditionally, vice presidents have had little involvement in executive policymaking. In recent years, however, they have played a more active role.

(Continued from page 239)

The office of president of the United States has much inherent power. The president today wears a number of hats, of which five were discussed in this chapter: chief of state, commander in chief, chief diplomat, chief executive, and chief legislator. Taken together, these powers are considerable. Yet much depends on what the president does with them. Like musical instruments, they require skill and artistry if they are to be played properly. Some presidents, like Franklin Roosevelt, have performed like virtuosos; others have been booed off the stage.

In fairness, however, to so many of those presidents judged to be weak, much depends upon the times in which they live and the climate of expectations surrounding the presidency. In President Kennedy's day the times were full of hope, and public attitudes toward the presidency were deferential. This public mood was augmented by the writings of journalists and scholars, almost all of whom promoted activism in the White House.

Vietnam and Watergate have caused the promoters to reverse themselves. Now they worry about too much power in the White House. Presidents today are assumed to be liars and manipulators by many of those who occupy influential positions in journalism and higher education. The atmosphere has changed greatly.

Whether this changed atmosphere is healthy or not remains in question. For some, it means that the president is at last being treated the way he should have been treated all along: as a fallible human being. If checks and balances mean anything, they mean that we must keep close tabs on those who hold the powers of a modern presidency. In 1788 James Madison warned that "enlightened statesmen will not always be at the helm." We have certainly had our share of the unenlightened. But there are arguments on the other side. Can a ship be steered by many hands? Isn't there a need for some *one* person to make the tough decisions, and make them quickly in a crisis? "Decision, activity, secrecy, and despatch"—those were the qualities necessary for the successful execution of government, according to Alexander Hamilton. "[Those qualities]," he added, "will generally characterize the proceedings of one man in much more eminent degree than the proceedings of any greater number." Harry Truman put it more simply in the sign on his desk: "The Buck Stops Here."

Hamilton called it "energy in the executive." Kennedy called it "vigor." Whatever this quality is called, we need it. We face dangers of all kinds at home and abroad. There is no logical contradiction between a strong presidency and a restrained

240

presidency, and there need not be one in fact. Perhaps Clinton Rossiter said it best when he expressed his hope that the president could be "a kind of magnificent lion" who can do great deeds as long as he is kept on his "broad reservation."

Notes

1. William Manchester, *The Death of a President* (New York: Harper & Row, 1967), p. 4.

2. Manchester, p. 16.

3. Theodore H. White, *The Making of the President 1964* (New York: Atheneum Publishers, 1965), p. 13n.

4. Michael Novack, *Choosing Our King: Powerful Symbols in Presidential Politics* (New York: Macmillan Publishing Co., 1974), p. 10.

5. James Madison, *Notes on the Debates in the Federal Convention of 1787* (Athens, Ohio: Ohio University Press, 1966), p. 599.

6. Arthur M. Schlesinger, Jr., *The Imperial Presidency* (Boston: Houghton Mifflin Co., 1973), p. 85.

7. Edward S. Corwin, *The President: Office and Powers, 1787-1957*, 4th rev. ed. (New York: New York University Press, 1957), p. 238.

8. *United States v. Curtiss-Wright Corporation et al.*, 299 U.S. 304 (1936).

9. Quoted by R. W. Apple, "Iran Inquiry: Power Battle," *New York Times*, July 26, 1987, p. 14.

10. Rowland Evans and Robert Novak, "GOP Concerned About What Democrats Might Demand Next," *New York Post*, Mar. 29, 1989, p. 21.

11. Edward S. Corwin, *The President: Office and Powers, 1787-1957*, 4th rev. ed. (New York: New York University Press, 1957), p. 122.

12. Quoted by Martin Tolchin, "The Presidency: Mastering the Art of Legislative Persuasion," *New York Times*, July 26, 1985, p. A10.

13. Tolchin, p. A10.

14. Tolchin, p. A10.

15. Tolchin, p. A10.

16. Hedrick Smith, *The Power Game: How Washington Works* (New York: Random House, 1988), p. 339.

17. Clinton Rossiter, *The American Presidency*, rev. ed. (New York: Harcourt, Brace & World, 1960), pp. 179-81.

18. James David Barber, *The Presidential Character*, 3rd ed. (Englewood Cliffs, NJ: Prentice-Hall, Inc., 1985).

19. Barber, p. 451.

20. Rossiter, p. 143.

21. Arthur M. Schlesinger, Jr., *The Imperial Presidency* (Boston: Houghton Mifflin Co. 1973), p. 124.

22. White, 1965, p. 30.

23. News conference, Feb. 21, 1963, *Public Powers of John F. Kennedy*, January 1 to November 22, 1963 (Washington: U.S. Government Printing Office, 1964), p. 204.

24. Michael Robinson, Maura Clancy and Lisa Grand, "With Friends Like That . . . ," *Public Opinion* (June/July 1983), pp. 1-3, 52-54.

25. "President's News Conference on Foreign and Domestic Issues," *New York Times*, Nov. 20, 1986, p. A12.

26. Stephen Holden, "Jim Morris Hails the Chief, Blithely," *New York Times*, July 17, 1987, p. C12.

27. Michael Robinson and Margaret Sheehan, *Over the Wire and On TV: CBS and UPI in Campaign '80* (Washington: Russell Sage Foundation, 1983).

28. *New York Times*, Sept. 6, 1963. This *Times* editorial is discussed in chapter 19.

29. See Daniel Schorr, *Clearing the Air* (New York: Berkeley Publishing Corporation, 1978), chap. 3.

30. The reporter was Lyle Denniston of the *Baltimore Sun*. The remark was made at a videotaped forum first aired in 1982 on PBS in a series entitled "The Constitution: That Delicate Balance." See George McKenna, *A Guide to the Constitution: That Delicate Balance* (New York: Random House, 1984), p. 239.

31. The remark was made on Ted Koppel's "Nightline" program on the ABC television network, July 31, 1985.

32. Arthur Schlesinger, Jr., "Why Not Question the Presidency?" *New York Times*, Jan. 2, 1987.

33. Rossiter, pp. 72-73.

34. *Time*, July 22, 1985, p. 24.

35. Gene Smith, *When the Cheering Stopped* (New York: William Morrow and Company, 1964).

36. *Newsweek*, July 22, 1985, p. 17.

37. By early 1940, according to historian James MacGregor Burns, "Roosevelt was hoping that the vice president would not show up for cabinet meetings." See Burns, *Roosevelt: The Lion and the Fox, 1882-1940* (New York: Harcourt, Brace & World, Inc., 1956), p. 414.

Sits he on never so high a throne,
a man still sits on his bottom.

Montaigne

10

Limits on the Presidency

CONGRESS AS A CHECK

Impeachment: The "Blunderbuss" / Congressional Investigations / The Iran-Contra
Investigation / Executive Privilege: The President's Countercheck / *United States
v. Nixon* (1974): "Presumptive Privilege" / Checking the President by Legislation
The Power to Say No

THE JUDICIARY AS A CHECK

The *Youngstown* Case: No "Inherent" Presidential Power

THE BUREAUCRACY AS A CHECK

THE PRESS AS A CHECK

Muckraking: Watergate and Other "Gates"

PUBLIC OPINION AS A CHECK

THE BALLOT BOX AS A CHECK

REFLECTIONS

Shortly after 1:00 A.M. on Saturday, June 17, 1972, Frank **Watergate**
Wills, a security guard at the Watergate Office Building in
Washington, D.C., was making his rounds. As he passed the garage-level
doors, something caught his eye: A piece of tape had been placed across
the door latch to keep the door from locking when it was pulled shut.*

Thinking the tape had been left by one of the maintenance crew,
Wills removed it and continued his rounds. Soon afterward, he strolled
across the street to the Howard Johnson's for a snack. When he returned
he checked the door again and noticed that the tape had reappeared.
This time Wills called the police.

*This account is drawn from the following sources: Sam J. Ervin, Jr., *The Whole Truth:
The Watergate Conspiracy* (New York: Random House, 1980); J. Anthony Lukas,
Nightmare: The Underside of the Nixon Years (New York: The Viking Press, 1976); John
J. Sirica, *To Set the Record Straight* (New York: W. W. Norton & Company, 1979); Carl
Bernstein and Bob Woodward, *All the President's Men* (New York: Warner Books,
1974); Congressional Quarterly, *Guide to Current American Government*, (Fall 1974).

Eight hours later, at 9:00 A.M., Bob Woodward, a reporter with the *Washington Post* newspaper, was awakened at home by a telephone call. It was the city editor. Five men had been arrested earlier that morning for breaking into the headquarters of the Democratic National Committee in the Watergate Hotel Complex. The Watergate was where the Democrats had chosen to make their national headquarters for the 1972 presidential election. They had been carrying photographic and electronic gear. Could Woodward come in and check out the story?

Woodward went to court to cover the arraignment of the suspects. The judge asked one of them, James W. McCord, Jr., what his occupation was. "Security consultant," McCord replied. The judge asked where. McCord replied that he had recently returned from government service. "Where in government?" the judge asked. "The CIA," McCord answered. "Holy shit," Woodward murmured, "the CIA."[1]

Assigned to cover the story with Woodward was reporter Carl Bernstein—at 28 years old, a year younger than Woodward—who had been with the *Post* for six years. After checking with the police and other sources, Woodward and Bernstein discovered that McCord was now security coordinator for the Committee for the Reelection of the President (the legendary CREEP), President Nixon's campaign committee. On the day the *Post* printed their story, they received a telephone call from another *Post* reporter who had close contacts with the Washington police department. It turned out that one of the burglars was carrying an address book containing the name and telephone number of one E. Howard Hunt. Following Hunt's name in the book was a notation: "W. House." Soon Woodward and Bernstein had another story: "WHITE HOUSE CONSULTANT TIED TO BUGGING FIGURE."

Almost seven months elapsed before the Watergate burglars were brought to trial. The original trial date was scheduled for late October, but the judge assigned to it, John J. Sirica, hurt his back and the trial had to be postponed. When the trial finally got under way in January 1973, Judge Sirica was dismayed at the way the government was prosecuting the case. Throughout the fall of 1972, there had been a series of stories in the *Washington Post* about the burglary: stories about a secret White House fund that had been used to finance the burglary, stories about other break-ins by people connected to the White House, stories about payoffs to the defendants to keep them quiet. Government prosecutors seemed utterly uninterested in these reports. They prosecuted the case as if it were nothing more than a routine burglary attempt by a handful of men acting entirely on their own. Exasperated, the judge began questioning the defendants himself. Were they aware of any larger White House connection? Were they part of a conspiracy? Were any high White House officials involved? Had someone paid them to keep silent?

All of the Watergate burglars either pleaded guilty to the charge of attempted burglary or were found guilty by the jury. All had remained silent about any White House connections, and the case was about to be closed. But Judge Sirica had one last tool for opening it up. He had not yet sentenced the burglars, and the penalty for their crimes could be very stiff—35 years in prison. Around Washington, Sirica was known as "Maximum John." He delayed sentencing and hinted that if the burglars started telling all they knew, they might get off with lighter sentences. The strategy worked. One of the two men who had pleaded not guilty, James McCord, wrote to Judge Sirica that there "was political pressure applied to the defendants to plead guilty and remain silent" and others involved in

The Watergate apartment and business complex in Washington, D.C., lent its name to the scandal that led to the resignation of President Richard M. Nixon.

the break-in "were not identified during the trial."[2] Watergate was about to blow wide open.

The dynamite for blowing it was a series of televised hearings conducted by a special Senate investigating committee: the Senate Select Committee on Presidential Activities. Better known as the Watergate Committee, it was chaired by a 77-year-old senator from North Carolina, Sam J. Ervin, Jr. With 32 years of experience as a trial lawyer and judge before coming to the Senate in 1954, Ervin turned out to be an aggressive questioner. Some witnesses, however, needed no prodding. One in particular proved to be extremely talkative—John Wesley Dean III.

John Dean was a slim, 34-year-old attorney who worked in the White House. His title was Counsel to the President, but, in fact, he was little more than a go-fer. He ran errands for the president's chief domestic adviser, John Ehrlichman; for Chief of Staff H. R. ("Bob") Haldeman; and for the president's friend and former law partner John Mitchell, who also happened to be the attorney general of the United States. Dean listened to the president, praised his ideas, and sometimes, very respectfully, ventured some advice. A colleague of Dean characterized him as "a pilot fish. You know, the little fish who follow beside the sharks."[3]

But by April 1973 Dean was beginning to suspect that the sharks were turning on *him*—in plainer language, that Nixon, Haldeman, and Ehrlichman were setting him up as the scapegoat for the Watergate cover-up. One of the errands Dean had performed was passing the word to the Watergate burglars that their silence during the trial would be rewarded with "hush" money and, eventually, a presidential pardon. Nixon now tried to blame everything on Dean. He ordered Dean to write a false report on the Watergate break-in so that he could say, "Good heavens, I relied on this man's report—how could I know he was deceiving me?" Nixon also wrote a resignation letter for Dean that began, "As a result of my involvement in the Watergate matter . . ." Dean refused to sign the letter or write the report. Instead, he notified Sam Ervin that he was ready to talk.

On June 25, 1973, one year and eight days after the break-in, Dean spent the entire day reading a 246-page statement to the Watergate Committee. The next four days he spent answering questions from committee members. For the first time, a comprehensive story of Watergate was told by one who only months before had been trying to cover it up. It included accounts of various misdeeds:

- Illegal entry and espionage: breaking into Democratic headquarters, installing a "bug" in the telephone, and photographing records; breaking into the office of Daniel Ellsberg's psychiatrist and rifling his files. (The Ellsberg case was discussed in chapter 4.)
- Political sabotage: hiring a man named Donald Segretti to disrupt Democratic rallies, to forge letters from prominent Democrats accusing other prominent Democrats of homosexual acts, and to engage in a variety of other "dirty tricks."
- Perjury, deception, and obstruction of justice: lying under oath and encouraging others to do the same, promising money and pardons to the burglars to keep silent, destroying evidence, coaching witnesses and rehearsing testimony, forging a cable involving the Kennedy administration in misdeeds.
- The planned misuse of government agencies, such as the Internal Revenue Service, to "get" political enemies of the president.

Before the Watergate investigation was over, it was to yield many more "horror stories," as John Mitchell called them, including the systematic shakedown of big corporations for campaign contributions, other practices that looked very much like extortion, and invasions of civil liberties.

"What did the president know, and when did he know it?" That was the question put by then-senator Howard Baker (R-Tennessee). Right after the attempted break-in at Democratic headquarters, Dean alleged, Nixon was told about White House involvement and immediately huddled with his advisers to plot the cover-up. Nixon, of course, denied the allegations, and for a time it was the president's word against Dean's. But then came a new and dramatic development.

At one point in his testimony, Dean recounted a conversation with Nixon in which Nixon kept trying to get him to agree to a point that would make the president look totally innocent. Dean said he had had the impression that Nixon wanted this statement for the record, that their voices were being taped. Later, committee investigators were questioning Alexander Butterfield, Nixon's former appointment secretary. One of the investigators, remembering Dean's comment, asked Butterfield if there was a taping device in the Oval Office. Butterfield, clearly troubled, replied: "I was hoping you fellows wouldn't ask me about that."[4]

There was indeed a taping device, and eventually the Supreme Court forced Nixon to hand over his tapes to federal investigators. The tapes, which turned out to be devastating, did not show Nixon to be involved in the break-in itself. However, they did show the president and his aides actively conspiring to cover up the crime. Covering up a crime is obstruction of justice, a felony.

But you cannot put a president on trial unless you first impeach him and remove him from office. This is what Congress proceeded to do. Late in July 1974 the House Judiciary committee voted to impeach Richard Nixon for obstructing justice, abusing his office, and resisting the committee's subpoenas. Within a few days it became clear that a majority of the House and two-thirds of the Senate would support impeachment. Nixon knew now what he had to do. On August 9, 1974, he resigned from the office of president of the United States. With a last wave and a pained smile, he boarded a helicopter on the White House lawn to begin his trip back home to California. Exactly one month later he would be pardoned by his successor, Gerald R. Ford, for any crimes he might have committed as president.

*   *   *   *   *

What began with a piece of tape over a door latch culminated two years later in the forced resignation of a president. Anyone predicting such an ending in the summer of 1972 would have been considered crazy. This was the presidency of the United States. "We take a few shots and it will be over," Nixon had assured John Dean.[5] There was reason for such optimism. Nixon was head of an executive establishment numbering almost 3 million civilian employees, and that figure included the whole investigative apparatus of the Justice Department and the FBI. In many respects he was independent of Congress. Members of Congress seemed only dimly aware of what was going on in the White House and uninterested in knowing more. Congress had the formal power of impeachment, but impeachment seemed out of the question. Professor Clinton Rossiter, quoting an earlier scholar, scorned it as "a rusted blunderbuss."[6]

After two years of intensive Watergate investigations, Richard M. Nixon resigned from the presidency in 1974. He is seen waving farewell from a helicopter on the White House lawn as he begins his trip home to California and his new life as a private citizen.

As for the news media, they had good reason to worry about the "few shots" that Nixon might give them. Radio and television were licensed by the Federal Communications Commission, and the president appointed the FCC's members. This president had sent his vice president around the country denouncing media "elitists" to cheering audiences. Yet in the end Nixon was driven from office. His presidency turned out to be more vulnerable than he or anyone else had thought. He was undone by forces and institutions beyond his control.

In the last chapter we discussed the powers of the presidency. In this chapter we are going to discuss some of the limitations on the president's power. They come from at least six sources: Congress, the judiciary, the bureaucracy, the press, public opinion, and the ballot box.

Congress as a Check

Potentially, at least, Congress is the strongest check on a runaway presidency. If, at various times in our history, presidents have aggrandized their office at the expense of Congress, this has not happened because Congress has been powerless to act but because it has declined to do so. When it wishes to act, Congress has a formidable array of weapons to use against a high-flying president: impeachment, investigation, legislation, and the simple power to say no. It is appropriate, then, that we devote much of this chapter to a consideration of Congress's checks on the president. We will begin with the most extreme and dramatic one, impeachment.

IMPEACHMENT: THE "BLUNDERBUSS"

As mentioned earlier, in pre-Watergate days Congress's power of impeachment was dismissed as "a rusted blunderbuss." But by the beginning of August 1974 it looked like the old musket was about to go off. The House Judiciary committee had voted to impeach Richard Nixon, and the full House and Senate were about to follow suit. Rusted or not, impeachment is a still-lethal weapon. It merits closer study.

Article II, Section 4, of the Constitution says that the president, vice president, and all officers of the United States may be impeached for "Treason, Bribery, or other high Crimes and Misdemeanors." These terms need explanation.

"To impeach," one dictionary says, is "to charge with a crime or misdemeanor." To impeach a president means only to accuse him or her. In order to be removed from office, a president must not only be impeached but *convicted* of the impeachment. The Constitution (Article I, Section 2) gives the House of Representatives "the sole Power of Impeachment," meaning that it alone can, by majority vote, charge the president with "high crimes and misdemeanors." Proving the charges is the responsibility of the Senate. By a two-thirds vote of the members present, it can *convict* the president of the impeachment, thus removing him or her from office (Article I, Section 3).

Even though the Constitution speaks of "high crimes and misdemeanors," a president does not have to commit a crime in order to be subject to impeachment. In 1868 President Andrew Johnson was impeached for defaming Congress in a series of speeches and for dismissing a member of his cabinet in violation of the Tenure of Office Act, a statute Congress later repealed. (Johnson was impeached but not convicted; the Senate failed by one vote to muster the necessary two-thirds.) In 1974 the House Judiciary Committee voted to impeach Richard Nixon on three grounds: obstruction of justice (covering up Watergate crimes); abuse of authority (using the IRS and other agencies to punish Nixon's enemies); and failure to comply with the

February 25, 1868: Crowds rush to the galleries of the Senate to hear Thaddeus Stevens of Pennsylvania, a leader in the House of Representatives, deliver the House's message impeaching President Andrew Johnson before the bar of the Senate. By one vote, the Senate failed to convict Johnson of the impeachment, so he was able to serve out the remainder of his term. One of the much sought-after tickets to the impeachment is reproduced opposite.

committee's request for tapes and documents. Only the first of these charges describes a criminal offense, and even here the president's defenders were probably right to say that the impeachment was too loosely drawn up for a court of law. But Congress is not a court, and an impeachable offense does not have to be an indictable offense. The Founders used the expression "high crimes and misdemeanors," but they meant it broadly enough to include "the misconduct of public men," as Alexander Hamilton phrased it in *Federalist* No. 65.[7] Even though impeachment is an extreme measure, it does not have to be confined to outright criminal behavior. Gross misconduct in office is enough.

CONGRESSIONAL INVESTIGATIONS

The impeachment proceedings against Richard Nixon did not materialize out of thin air. They were the result of nearly two years of congressional investigations. The best-known of these investigations was Sam Ervin's special Senate committee, but there were others conducted during the same period by regular standing committees of the House and Senate. For example, the House Judiciary Committee, which drew up the articles of impeachment, conducted its own lengthy investigation. Together, these congressional committees and their staffs uncovered the series of abuses that moved Congress to take action.

As we noted in chapter 7, a vigorous, well-publicized congressional investigation can shake up an administration. The Watergate probes of 1973 and 1974 forced Nixon out of office. In 1982 and 1983 a series of congressional investigations into the practices of the Environmental Protection Agency (EPA) caused major quakes within the Reagan administration. Top officials of Reagan's EPA, including its head, Anne Burford, were investigated concerning charges that they had let chemical industries foul the environment and had mismanaged a $1.6 billion "superfund" that was supposed to be used for cleaning up toxic wastes. At one point no less than six House committees were collecting testimony and documents on what came to be called "Sewergate." The investigations culminated in the resignation of Burford and 20 other EPA officials.

FIGURE **10-1**

Roll Call Vote

COMMITTEE ON THE JUDICIARY					
HOUSE OF REPRESENTATIVES					
930 CONGRESS					
ROLL CALL					
ARTICLE 1					
REPUBLICANS	Ayes	Nays	**DEMOCRATS**	Ayes	Nays
Mr. Hutchinson		✗	Mr. Donohue	✓	
Mr. McClory		✗	Mr. Brooks	✓	
Mr. Smith		✗	Mr. Kastenmeier	✓	
Mr. Sandman		✗	Mr. Edwards	✓	
Mr. Railsback	✓		Mr. Hungate	✓	
Mr. Wiggins		✗	Mr. Conyers	✓	
Mr. Dennis		✗	Mr. Eilberg	✓	
Mr. Fish	✓		Mr. Waldie	✓	
Mr. Mayne		✗	Mr. Flowers	✓	
Mr. Hogan	✓		Mr. Mann	✓	
Mr. Butler	✓		Mr. Sarbanes	✓	
Mr. Cohen	✓		Mr. Seiberling	✓	
Mr. Lott		✗	Mr. Danielson	✓	
Mr. Froehlich	✓		Mr. Drinan	✓	
Mr. Moorhead		✗	Mr. Rangel	✓	
Mr. Maraziti		✗	Ms. Jordan	✓	
Mr. Latta		✗	Mr. Thornton	✓	
			Ms. Holtzman	✓	
	6	11	Mr. Owens	✓	
			Mr. Mezvinsky	✓	
			Mr. Rodino, Chairman	✓	
				21	0
Total				27	11

The Judiciary Committee of the House of Representatives voted to impeach President Nixon in 1974. The 21 Democrats on the committee voted for impeachment, and so did six of the 17 Republicans. The measure almost certainly would have passed in the full House, but Nixon headed off the vote by resigning.

Sewergate was nothing compared to Irangate. Congress's 1987 investigation of the Iran-Contra affair cracked the foundations of the Reagan White House, and it may have also done some damage to Congress. We need to take a closer look at this affair and the congressional response to it.

THE IRAN-CONTRA INVESTIGATION

Arms-for-Hostages. The hyphen in "Iran-Contra" reminds us that the affair had two parts. The first part, "Iran," emerged early in November 1986 when an Arab newspaper in Beirut, Lebanon, revealed that high-ranking Reagan officials had made a secret deal with Iranian officials to ship arms to Iran in exchange for Iranian help in

In 1974, the same year that Richard Nixon was forced from office because of the Watergate scandal, the chief executive of the Federal Republic of Germany (West Germany) also resigned in the midst of a major scandal. In April 1974 it was disclosed that a close aide to Chancellor Willy Brandt was a Communist spy. The aide, Gunter Guillaume, had left the communist German Democratic Republic (East Germany) 18 years earlier, pretending to flee the Communist regime. In reality he had been sent by it to do just what he had done—get a job with the West German government and spy on it.

Chancellor Brandt was profoundly shocked. Guillaume was even closer to him than Haldeman and Ehrlichman were to Richard Nixon; Brandt and Guillaume were not only professional colleagues but intimate friends who had vacationed together. To Brandt's supporters, his resignation was a high-minded act. In their view he did not really have to resign. Unlike Nixon's situation, Brandt's involved no official charges of wrongdoing against the chief executive. And, legally, he was in a better position than Nixon to cling to power if he had wanted to do so. A German chancellor cannot easily be removed between elections. Unlike an American president, he cannot be impeached by the legislature. He can only be removed by what is called a "constructive vote of nonconfidence" in the *Bundestag*, or popular assembly. That means that the *Bundestag* must not only depose the chancellor but at the same time decide whom it wants as his successor. Since that could lead to months of painful political infighting, West German legislators are not eager to depose chancellors.

Brandt's resignation may not have been quite as generous an act, however, as his supporters claimed. Some years earlier, Brandt had had an affair with a woman from East Germany who turned out to be yet another East German agent. There were unconfirmed rumors that the woman had then blackmailed Brandt for large sums of money and that Brandt had obtained the blackmail money from official funds budgeted for his intelligence agency. If the rumors were true, Brandt was guilty of a very serious crime: embezzling public money. Some of Brandt's critics charged that the whole blackmail story would have come out if Brandt had not resigned. We will probably never know if the story is true; Brandt's resignation apparently closed the book on it.

getting American hostages released from a terrorist group in Lebanon. When the American media got wind of the deal, Reagan and his people tried to explain: The administration did not deal directly with terrorist groups, it had traded arms not for hostages but for goodwill in Iran (which would help get hostages released), and the arms sale was a small part of a larger effort to open channels of communication with Iranian moderates. These distinctions seemed unconvincing to most Americans; it all came out in the press as "arms for hostages," a devil's bargain that sent all the worst signals about American resolve and toughness to our allies.

The Fund Diversion. The second part, the "Contra" of "Iran-Contra," suddenly surfaced at a hastily convened news conference on November 25, 1986. President

Reagan summoned the press to the White House and announced a new development in the affair. He brought out Attorney General Edwin Meese, who told reporters that the profits from the arms sale had been diverted to the Contras, the antigovernment rebels in Nicaragua. Since Congress had barred giving funds to the Contras, this discovery raised legal questions: Had crimes been committed by Reagan officials? If so, had Reagan himself been involved, or was he at least aware of what was done?

A central figure in the Iran-Contra affair was Marine Lt. Col. Oliver L. North, a 41-year-old staff member of the National Security Council (NSC). North, who coordinated the dealings with Iran and the diversion of funds to the Contras, claimed to be acting under the orders of Admiral John M. Poindexter, head of the NSC from the end of 1985 until November 1986. Special prosecutor Lawrence M. Walsh, who was appointed to investigate the case, brought criminal charges against North, Poindexter, and others for a variety of offenses, including conspiracy to defraud the government by illegally providing the Contras with funds from the sale of American weapons to Iran. The fraud charge was connected with an alleged violation of the so-called Boland Amendment, named after its sponsor, Congressman Edward Boland (D-Massachusetts). In fact, there was not one but a series of Boland Amendments, passed in successive years by Congress, that restricted Contra aid in varying degrees.[8] North and Poindexter were accused of violating the 1984 version of the amendment, which barred the use of any funds available to the CIA or any other federal agency "involved in intelligence activities" for aiding any military or paramilitary operations in Nicaragua. When the case against North reached the court, the special prosecutor dropped the fraud charges against North when it became clear that the defense would try to force disclosure of top secret documents that might compromise national security. In all, 12 charges were brought against North. In May 1989 a jury found North guilty of three: obstructing Congress by giving it misleading chronologies of what had happened, destroying documents, and receiving an illegal gratuity (a $13,800 security system for his home). North was fined $150,000, given a 3-year suspended sentence, and was required to perform 1,200 hours of community service.

Congress's role in uncovering the facts behind Irangate began early in 1987, when it created committees of investigation. Hearings began on May 5, 1987. For the next three months a 26-member panel composed of House and Senate committees heard more than 250 hours of testimony from 28 public witnesses; much of the testimony was carried live on the television networks. The Senate committee, which played the more prominent role, was chaired by Senator Daniel Inouye (D-Hawaii), who had been on the Watergate panel 14 years earlier. The hearings were even conducted in the same rooms in which the Watergate hearings were held.

Many observers were convinced that this was going to be a full-blown Watergate. Within a few weeks of the news conference, the old question kept surfacing: What did the president know, and when did he know it? But despite the parallels to Watergate, there were some key differences. For one thing, the American people were already a little weary of the scandal by the time the hearings began. Most of the important facts had been exposed months earlier in the press or by the Tower Commission. The latter, appointed by Reagan and headed by former Texas senator John G. Tower, issued a report in February 1987 that sharply criticized Reagan for poor judgment and inadequate staff supervision but found no criminal wrongdoing on his part (see chapter 19). The congressional hearings added few important new facts, at least few that lingered long in the public's memory. A second difference, which probably affected the way television viewers looked at the hearings, was the size of the panel. Whereas the Watergate panel had consisted of only 7 members, the Iran-Contra panel had 11 senators and 15 House members. Such numbers prevented the media from showcasing any particular questioner and also contributed to a kind of inquisitional atmosphere, which may have increased public sympathy for some witnesses. In the case of Lt. Col. Oliver North this certainly happened. ABC News correspondent Brit Hume later wrote:

Here were twenty-six members of Congress, attended by countless staff, seated on a two-tier, red-draped dais to watch their hired inquisitors take on a youthful Marine Lieutenant Colonel seated below, with only his bespectacled lawyer at his side.[9]

The bespectacled lawyer, Brendan Sullivan, turned out to be a ferocious fighter who intimidated the panel into allowing North to respond to questions by delivering passionate speeches. While not everyone agreed with North, his testimony tended to turn the tables on his accusers. A poll taken later by the *Los Angeles Times* revealed that 43 percent of respondents thought Congress was to blame for the Iran-Contra affair, as against 30 percent who blamed Reagan (12 percent blamed both equally, and 15 percent were undecided). Unlike Watergate, Irangate hurt Congress at least as much as it hurt the president.

Still another difference between the two is that the Iran-Contra investigation never produced a "smoking gun," definite proof of presidential involvement. What did the president know, and when did he know it? Two days before the hearings began, Senate committee chairman Inouye flatly declared that Reagan knew of the fund diversion, but the panel failed to come up with any convincing evidence to sustain his assertion. Admiral Poindexter, in fact, declared emphatically and under oath that "the buck stopped" with him. A final difference between Watergate and Irangate is that Reagan generally cooperated with Congress. Truckloads of executive documents were handed over to congressional investigators, and several executive officials, including the secretaries of State and Defense, were sent to testify. During the North trial two years later, a few government documents turned up that had apparently been withheld by the Reagan administration from Congress during its investigation— perhaps it was an oversight, perhaps a deliberate move. In either case, Reagan's actions were different from what Nixon tried to do in 1973 and 1974. Reagan never attempted to "stonewall" the committees, to shut off all access to executive documents or witnesses. Nixon *did* try to stonewall and had to be forced into complying with requests for information. He claimed executive privilege, a claim that culminated in a major Supreme Court decision on the issue.

EXECUTIVE PRIVILEGE: THE PRESIDENT'S COUNTERCHECK

Executive privilege is a claim of confidentiality that has been occasionally invoked by presidents when investigators have demanded materials or summoned administration officials to testify. The term is not found in the Constitution and was apparently never used until Attorney General William Rogers coined it in 1958. The concept may not have had a name, but it had a long history. In 1796 George Washington invoked executive privilege against the House of Representatives. Over the next century or more, presidential claims of privilege were rare. Only since the late 1940s has executive privilege been invoked as a general principle. In 1947 when the House Un-American Activities Committee demanded the security files of a physicist serving in the Truman administration, the president responded by reserving the right to determine whether or not such disclosures would serve the public interest. An even more sweeping assertion of executive privilege was contained in a letter from President Eisenhower that was read before Senator Joseph McCarthy's investigating committee in 1954. Eisenhower stated, "It is not in the public interest that *any* of their conversations or *any* documents or reproductions [relating to what McCarthy was investigating] be disclosed (emphasis added)."[10]

As a young congressman, Richard Nixon had been an outspoken critic of the Truman administration's claim of privilege. Yet during the Watergate investigation he pushed executive privilege further than had any previous president. At the outset of the Senate investigations he asserted the right to withhold not only documents but

Marine Lt. Col. Oliver North was the key witness during the Iran-Contra hearings. His striking appearance and passionate testimony made him a prime media figure throughout the investigations. In a rhetorical manner, North turned the tables on the congressmen who had been attacking the Reagan administration; he put many of them on the defensive by charging Congress with tying the hands of the president and preventing the president from protecting the security of the United States. Later a jury convicted North of three relatively minor charges, including the receipt of a burglar alarm system as a gift from an arms dealer.

testimony from any "member or *former member* of the president's personal staff" (emphasis added).[11] His attorney general went him one better, announcing to a startled Senate panel that executive privilege covered not only the president's aides, but any one of the 2.9 million employees of the federal government!

UNITED STATES V. NIXON (1974): "PRESUMPTIVE PRIVILEGE"

Nixon was forced to back down from these sweeping claims. Soon his closest aides were testifying before congressional committees. But he clung to the principle of executive privilege, and in the end he won at least a partial vindication. In *United States v. Nixon* (1974) the Supreme Court gave judicial recognition to executive privilege.

The case came to the Supreme Court after a special prosecutor appointed to the Watergate case asked Nixon to provide the tapes he had made of his conversations with aides and Nixon refused to do so. In an 8-0 opinion delivered by Chief Justice Warren E. Burger, the Court held that the president's White House conversations should enjoy presumptive privilege. Courts must start with the assumption that the records of all White House conversations belong to the president alone. Chief Justice Burger said that anyone trying to gain access to such records against the president's wishes must show why an exception should be made. If investigators could pry into confidential White House discussions whenever they wished, said the Court, the president could never get frank advice from his aides.

But if *United States v. Nixon* was a partial victory for the presidency, it was a total defeat for Richard M. Nixon. Chief Justice Burger said that exceptions have to be made to executive privilege in certain cases, and this was one of them. Serious criminal charges had been made against members of Nixon's administration. The requests had been made not by members of Congress but by a special prosecutor empowered to bring criminal charges. His requests were limited and carefully specified. The tapes were first to be heard by a District Court judge in his chambers, who would then decide whether or not they could be heard in open court. The president had not claimed that the tapes contained any military or diplomatic secrets. These qualifications, Burger said, were enough to overcome the president's presumptive privilege. Nixon was forced to hand over the tapes by a unanimous vote of eight justices (Justice William Rehnquist did not participate). Ironically, Chief Justice Burger, the author of the opinion, was one of the Nixon appointees.

Eight years later, Ronald Reagan also invoked executive privilege when he refused to let EPA director Anne Burford testify before a House subcommittee investigating the $1.6 billion "superfund." Congress responded by citing her for contempt of Congress, which could have resulted in a jail term. In the end, a confrontation was avoided when Reagan backed down and let Burford testify. What, then, are we to make of the claim of executive privilege? In the main, what we are left with is *United States v. Nixon*, which holds that presidential communications as a rule should be confidential but which also leaves room for exceptions.

CHECKING THE PRESIDENT BY LEGISLATION

One obvious power that Congress has is the power to pass laws. By this means Congress has at various times sought to limit the powers of the president. Sometimes this has required a congressional override of a presidential veto, not an easy task (a two-thirds vote of both houses is required). One such attempt at curbing presidential power, in this case the power to conduct undeclared wars, was the War Powers Resolution of 1973.

If Watergate made Congress suspicious of presidential power, so did the Vietnam War. Under three presidents there had been a steadily increasing American involvement in Vietnam, but under Lyndon Johnson the American commitment had escalated sharply, from about 16,000 "advisers" to half a million troops. After 1968 Johnson's War became Nixon's War, with still no end in sight. This was a presidential war, a war that had never been declared by Congress, although each year Congress dutifully supplied the funds for it.

By 1973 Congress was tired of Vietnam, angry about being maneuvered into supporting it, and determined to see that there would be "no more Vietnams." In that mood it passed the War Powers Resolution—indeed, produced the necessary two-thirds votes to pass it over President Nixon's veto. It contains the following provisions:

- *Notification*. A president who introduces American troops into any situation where a shooting war is about to break out must notify Congress within 48 hours. The notification must set forth the reasons for the use of troops and an estimate of how long they will be needed.
- *Sixty- to Ninety-Day Limit*. Unless Congress declares war or extends the time period, the president must bring the troops home within 60 days. However, if more time is needed to protect the troops as they are being withdrawn, another 30 days can be added.
- *Consultation*. The president must answer any questions about the war that Congress raises and must submit periodic progress reports.

The resolution was an attempt to strike a balance between giving the president too much leeway and not giving enough. It leaves the president free to handle military emergencies but prohibits the fighting of a long, expensive war without Congress's express permission. Both "hawks" and "doves" have attacked it. Former president

Critics have charged that despite the War Powers Resolution of 1973, presidents still engage in warmaking without proper authorization from Congress. President Carter sent an armed group mission into Iran, in an attempt to rescue the hostages; President Reagan kept marines in Lebanon until they suffered large casualties from a terrorist attack (shown below); and it is feared that future presidents may be tempted to ignore the terms of the act.

Gerald Ford, a self-declared hawk, has called it "gutless." If Congress wants to end a presidential war, Ford says, it should end it, which it can do by cutting off funds. He sees the War Powers Resolution as an attempt to duck that responsibility, to say that the war must end automatically in 60 to 90 days and then "we'll sit back in our cozy way and do nothing."[12] Critics at the other end of the spectrum, so-called doves like *New York Times* columnist Tom Wicker, think the War Powers Resolution errs in the opposite direction. They think it gives the president too much power: a 60- to 90-day license to conduct an all-out undeclared war.[13]

It is easy to find flaws in the War Powers Resolution and also easy to point out that presidents have paid little attention to it. President Ford notified Congress but otherwise ignored the resolution in 1975 when he sent the marine corps in to rescue U.S. citizens held captive by Communists in the waters off Cambodia; President Carter never mentioned the resolution when he made his ill-fated attempt to free the American hostages in Iran in 1980; President Reagan ignored it when he invaded Grenada in 1983, nor did he admit that it had any relevance to his use of troops in Lebanon or of "advisers" in El Salvador. Despite these examples, the resolution is not completely toothless. It was Congress's way of telling the president that it wanted no more protracted wars without congressional authorization. In that respect, it has at least sent a clear message to the executive branch.

THE POWER TO SAY NO

Yet President Ford makes a good point when he says that Congress could end any war simply by refusing to fund it. This is a power to be reckoned with, even if Congress must screw up its courage in order to use it. "The real power of Congress," said Clinton Rossiter, "is essentially negative in character."[14] It is the power to deny presidential requests.

The president may want a law passed, an appropriation made, a treaty endorsed, an appointment approved. Congress can simply refuse to act, frustrating the most determined president. Take the case of Woodrow Wilson. In 1919 Wilson came back from Europe with an almost mystical vision. He had negotiated a treaty to end World War I that included U.S. participation in a new League of Nations. He saw the League as an essential guarantor of peace. The Senate did not share his vision and refused to ratify the portion of the treaty calling for U.S. membership in the League. Infuriated, Wilson went off on a nationwide railroad tour trying to mobilize public opinion. In Pueblo, Colorado, he suffered a paralyzing stroke that ended his active life as president and his dream of a U.S.-led League. He died a bitter man, still cursing the Senate.

Then there was Richard Nixon, another determined man. He came into office promising to transform what he saw as a too-liberal Supreme Court. When a vacancy appeared on the Court, he nominated a conservative South Carolina judge. The Senate, for the first time in 40 years, denied confirmation. Less than a year later a second nominee for the position was also turned down because of his position on civil rights. Nixon's two consecutive defeats were embarrassing but not humiliating in the way that Reagan's would be 14 years later. Reagan first nominated Federal Court of Appeals judge Robert Bork, and after lengthy hearings—during which Bork was branded as a right-wing ideologue—the nomination was defeated in the Senate by a 58-42 vote. Then Reagan nominated another Court of Appeals judge, Douglas Ginsberg, but after the press revealed that Ginsberg had smoked marijuana, the administration pressured him into withdrawing. (The Bork and Ginsberg debacles are discussed at greater length in chapter 12.)

President Bush tried a more bipartisan approach to Congress, using friendly persuasion and quiet meetings with Democratic leaders. But within the first seven months of his administration Bush had already suffered serious rebuffs. In March

1989, as we saw in chapter 8, his nomination of former senator John Tower to head the Department of Defense was defeated by the Senate in an almost straight party vote. In August another major Bush nomination failed, again along party lines. The Senate Judiciary Committee voted not to confirm the nomination of William Lucas to the post of assistant attorney general. Lucas, the first black nominated to the post, was opposed by all but one of the eight Democrats on the committee. They charged that he lacked the required knowledge and experience for the job, and they cited other matters in his background, but their main complaint appeared to be Lucas's refusal to condemn recent Supreme Court decisions limiting affirmative action and requiring a greater burden of proof in racial discrimination cases.[15]

Some presidents have derived political advantage from congressional negativism. In 1948 Harry Truman won an uphill reelection battle against a Republican challenger by blaming the nation's troubles on a "do-nothing" Republican Congress. More often, however, lack of congressional support is a net loss for the president, for it calls into question the ability to lead. Congress's tardy and watered-down support for President Carter's energy program—which he had characterized as "the moral equivalent of war"—did nothing to help Carter's reputation as a weak leader. Ronald Reagan, originally called "The Great Communicator," also suffered after he got rebuffed by Congress. When Reagan was unable to get consistent support for arming the Contras in Nicaragua, administration zealots tried to maneuver around Congress—which, of course, led to the Iran-Contra affair, the biggest blow of all to Reagan's reputation.

The Judiciary as a Check

"It is emphatically the province and duty of the judiciary to say what the law is." With those famous words from *Marbury v. Madison* (1803), Chief Justice John Marshall made it clear that the Supreme Court is the ultimate interpreter both of our laws and our Constitution. The Court has the power to decide whether or not presidential actions are illegal or unconstitutional, and it can order the president to stop such actions. It may even order him to do something, as it did in *United States v. Nixon* (1974). Nixon was ordered to hand over tapes and documents to the special prosecutor investigating the Watergate affair.

What is remarkable is that Nixon complied. Why did he? The Court had no visible means of forcing him: no armies, no police, no control of the treasury. Nixon was a great believer in hardball politics. Why would he give up information that was so damning to his presidency? Almost a century and a half earlier, another president, Andrew Jackson, reportedly had challenged Chief Justice Marshall to enforce a particular decision. Why didn't Nixon respond similarly to Chief Justice Burger's decision in the tapes case? It is hard to say, but Nixon's attorney may have played a key role. When the decision came down, Nixon asked his attorney if there was any way around it. No, the attorney answered, and if Nixon defied the Court he would certainly be impeached; moreover, he, the president's attorney, would be obliged by ethics to withdraw from the case.[16] So Nixon obeyed, knowing full well it meant the end of his presidency.

Like Nixon (although with results that were less personally damaging), President Reagan was also rebuffed by a Supreme Court consisting of some of his own appointees. In 1988 the Court decided by a 7–1 vote to uphold the federal law that provides for independent prosecutors to investigate suspected crimes by high-ranking officials. The facts behind the case go all the way back to Watergate. The attorney general is usually the one who investigates federal lawbreaking, but because Nixon's attorney general, John Mitchell, was himself a suspect in Watergate (he was later convicted and sent to prison), Congress pressured Nixon into appointing a special prosecutor. Nixon chose Archibald Cox, a former solicitor general, but when Cox started demanding the tapes, Nixon dismissed him and his entire staff. The resulting firestorm of public indignation again forced Nixon's hand. He was pressured into appointing a new prosecutor, and it was the new prosecutor's demand for tapes that brought *United States v. Nixon* to the Supreme Court.

Dissatisfied with the rather improvised status of the special prosecutor, Congress sought to put the office on a more secure footing. The 1978 Ethics and Government Act provides that, in cases involving criminal allegations against high-level administration officials, the attorney general must ask a special three-judge Appeals Court to appoint a "special counsel" to prosecute the case and may remove the counsel only for "good cause" and subject to judicial review. During the 1980s several Reagan administration officials were investigated by special counsels appointed under this law, and some (including North and Poindexter) were prosecuted. The administration challenged the constitutionality of the special counsel law, contending that it violated separation of powers by handing over to Congress and the judiciary a power that properly belongs only to the president: the power to enforce the laws of the United States. The administration's position was decisively rejected by the Supreme Court in the case of *Morrison v. Olson* (1988), when, by a 7–1 majority, it declared that the law "does not violate the separation-of-powers principle by impermissibly interfering with the functions of the executive branch." Joining the majority was Justice Sandra Day O'Connor, a Reagan appointee, and writing the opinion was William Rehnquist, a conservative and a Nixon appointee elevated by Reagan to the position of Chief Justice. Whether or not the case was rightly decided—Justice Antonin Scalia, another Reagan appointee, passionately dissented—it does suggest that our Supreme Court justices do not feel obligated to the president who appoints them. They can, and sometimes do, bite the hand that feeds them.

Nixon and Reagan were not the only presidents to feel the bite. A generation earlier another proud president had to bow before a decision of the Supreme Court— a decision that, in his opinion, actually interfered with his ability to fight a war. The war was in Korea. The president was Harry S. Truman.

Supreme Court appointees sometimes vote contrary to the presumed or expressed wishes of the president who appointed them. Sandra Day O'Connor is no exception. In the case of *Morrison v. Olson* (1988), O'Connor, a Reagan appointee, voted to uphold the "special prosecutor" law, in opposition to the Reagan administration.

THE *YOUNGSTOWN* CASE: NO "INHERENT" PRESIDENTIAL POWER

During the Korean War a wage dispute broke out between union and management in the nation's largest steel mills. It led to a strike, which in turn crippled the nation's steel production. After unsuccessfully attempting to settle the dispute, Truman seized the

During World War II, President Roosevelt ordered the relocation of thousands of Japanese-Americans to special camps in California. The Supreme Court upheld his decision despite much controversy. In this picture, the first contingent of "evacuees" prepares to leave Los Angeles under Army escort for Manzanar, California.

mills, put through a wage settlement satisfactory to the union but not to management, and said that the mills would run on that basis until the parties worked out their own settlement, at which time they would revert to private ownership. Truman justified his seizure of private property on the basis of what he called the "inherent powers" of the president. Even though there was no statute authorizing him to seize the steel mills, Truman said he had that power by virtue of his position as commander in chief and chief executive. This was an emergency. There was a war on, and we needed steel to fight the war. According to Truman, as supreme commander of our forces and as the man who must "take care that the laws be faithfully executed," he had to act. The steel companies disagreed. They took Truman to court and won their case. In *Youngstown Sheet and Tube Co. v. Sawyer* (1952) a 6-3 majority ruled that Truman must return the mills to their owners.[17]

Despite the authority of the Supreme Court, it has at times seemingly gone out of its way to avoid confrontations with the president. During the Civil War the Court was asked to declare unconstitutional Lincoln's blockade of the South. It declined to do so.[18] During World War II the Court was asked to declare unconstitutional the Roosevelt administration's forced relocation of Japanese-Americans who lived on the West Coast. Again, it declined to do so.[19] During the Vietnam War the Court was asked to rule on the constitutionality of the administration's war in Vietnam. Once again, it declined to do so.[20] The Court cited quite different reasons in each of these cases, but the bottom line may have been this consideration: It is not prudent to challenge a popular president when the country is at war. During the Korean War the Court made Truman give back the steel mills, but Truman was not a popular president; during the 1930s the Court repeatedly challenged Roosevelt, but there was no war on at the time. The combination of a popular president and a war may be something that the Court considers too dangerous to challenge. However, this is sheer speculation. In theory courts are not supposed to be intimidated by public opinion polls or wars.

The Bureaucracy as a Check

It may seem odd to list the federal bureaucracy among the checks on a president. The president, after all, is the head of the executive branch and is the boss of its 3 million bureaucrats. What kind of power can employees have over the boss? Yet they do have that power. In the next chapter we will examine it more closely. For now let us confine ourselves to a brief overview of the bureaucracy's ability to check presidential power.

1. *Inertia*. One dictionary defines *inertia* as "a tendency to remain in a fixed condition without change." In a famous quotation, Harry Truman once put it very concretely. Commenting on Dwight D. Eisenhower, the man who was about to take over the presidency, Truman said: "He'll sit here and he'll say, 'Do this! Do that!' *And nothing will happen*. Poor Ike—it won't be a bit like the Army."[21] Even now we can see Truman's point: The federal bureaucracy can stymie the president simply by dragging its feet or refusing to act. In theory the bureaucracy takes its orders from the president, but in fact it is subdivided into many bodies that have their own views on how to proceed. Some of them may not want to proceed at all. It is one thing, therefore, to give an order, and quite another to see it carried out. In one of his secret White House tapes we hear Nixon fuming: "Nobody follows up on a God damn thing."[22] By simple inertia, then, the bureaucracy can quietly sabotage the most ambitious presidential plans.

2. *Fighting Back*. Instead of just ignoring the president, bureaucrats can fight back by running to their friends in Congress and the media. Many bureaucrats have spent years carefully cultivating these friendships. Like the kid who brings a big brother to beat up the bully at the playground, a bureaucrat may complain to members of Congress or reporters about a president who has been trying to force him or her to do something that seems unethical or unwise. This is called "blowing the whistle," and whistle-blowers are usually portrayed in the press as martyrs and heroes. Their friends in Congress can threaten the president with an investigation, or a fund cutoff, or other sanctions. Their friends in the media do not bother threatening. They run front-page stories based upon the bureaucrats' "leaks." These stories usually assume a breathless tone: "Reliable sources have disclosed that evil schemes are being hatched at the highest levels of the administration." Much of what Woodward and Bernstein wrote in the *Washington Post* from 1972 to 1974 was in that vein and was based upon such leaks.

3. *Here Today, Here Tomorrow*. One of the reasons that bureaucrats are able to cultivate lasting friendships in the press and Congress is that most of them have been around for years. Civil service reforms that began in the last decades of the nineteenth century have given us the "career civil servant." Most federal bureaucrats now are hired not on the basis of political ties to the president but through more objective means, such as competitive exams. Their jobs are virtually lifetime ones; they can be fired only through special procedures that require evidence of wrongdoing. Consider the implications of these facts. First, most bureaucrats now consider themselves professionals, experts who operate in accordance with well-established procedures. Their primary loyalty is not to the president but to their bureau and their task. The second implication is even more obvious. Bureaucrats usually acquire their positions before the president comes into power, and they remain after the president steps down. As two students of the subject have put it: "Presidents come and go, the bureaucracy stays."[23]

This cartoon from the 1940s depicts Harry Truman as a man grasping after excessive presidential power. *Drawing by Carrey Orr in the* Chicago Tribune. *Courtesy of the Chicago Historical Society.*

"I have seen a senior aide to a president, sitting over an early morning cup of coffee, rise and literally punch the front page of the *New York Times*." Daniel P. Moynihan, now a senator from New York, wrote this shortly after leaving the Nixon administration, where he served as an adviser.[24] To which senior aide was Moynihan referring? Haldeman? Ehrlichman? It hardly matters. All modern presidents have had senior aides who have become angry when they have seen their boss being roughed up in the press. Jody Powell, one of President Carter's chief aides, wrote a blistering book, entitled *The Other Side of The Story*, on the press coverage of the Carter administration. Reagan's aides, too, complained about hostile press coverage. Attorney General Edwin Meese was often the object of barbed stories in the press, as were many others in the administration, including, of course, Reagan himself.

MUCKRAKING: WATERGATE AND OTHER "GATES"

Reagan was wary of the press. He held fewer press conferences than any president in the previous half-century (see Figure 10.2 on the following page), and when reporters tried to ambush him on the White House grounds, there always seemed to be a helicopter parked nearby with its engines roaring. Still, Reagan seemed to take press criticism good-naturedly. Some of his predecessors were more thin-skinned. Nixon was the worst; he battled with the press during his presidency and for a time seemed to intimidate it. Then came Watergate. As the scandal deepened, Nixon blamed his loss of public support on the "leers and sneers of commentators."[25] He complained that "a constant barrage—12 to 15 minutes a night on each of the three major networks for four months—tends to raise questions in the people's minds with regard to the president."[26] In a sense these charges were true. The media were more than happy to take credit for alerting the public to Nixon's misdeeds. In the early years of this century Theodore Roosevelt called this kind of reporting "muckraking." He used the term in disgust, but in recent years the press has worn the label with pride.

Watergate revived the muckraking tradition. Indeed, since then there have been new "gates" for every presidency. During the Carter administration the press aired accusations against his budget director, Bert Lance. Lance was accused of using his position to help his Georgia bank. This controversy was christened Lancegate. Then there was Billygate, named after Carter's brother, who was accused of trying to tilt U.S. foreign policy in favor of Libya, which employed him as a lobbyist. Under Reagan there was Sewergate, which was discussed earlier in this chapter; Debate-gate, a flurry of accusations that Reagan's campaign staff in 1980 had received stolen copies of papers intended to prepare Carter for his debate with Reagan; and Irangate, which damaged Reagan's reputation for toughness in fighting terrorism.

None of these has packed the wallop of Watergate, and it may be that the public is starting to get tired of muckraking. Still, the press today is a potent check on the presidency. No president can rely on it to keep secrets, as John Kennedy could in the early 1960s, nor can any president expect the gentle treatment at its hands that Kennedy received (see chapter 9). Indeed, as we shall see in the chapter on the mass media, reporters today are not merely passive purveyors of news. They are newsmakers, active players in the game of politics, and their chief adversary, as often as not, turns out to be the president. George Bush's efforts to please reporters— holding frequent informal meetings with them, even taking them with him on vacation—may ease some of the strain and bad feelings in the relationship, but it remains inherently adversarial. Howard Simons, of the *Washington Post*, put it neatly when he talked about the conflicting jobs of the president and the press. It's the job of the White House, he said, to keep secrets, and "my job is to find 'em."[27]

FIGURE **10-2**

The Disappearing Presidential News Conference

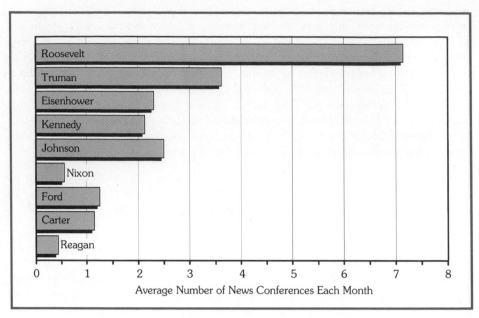

Average Number of News Conferences Each Month

Source: *New York Times*, Oct. 17, 1988, p. A20. Reprinted with permission.

No modern president has even come close to President Roosevelt in the average number of news conferences held each month. Most of Roosevelt's conferences were very informal, with no live coverage or even transcripts of the proceedings. In today's nationally-televised performances, presidents must worry about verbal slips that could damage them politically or even cause harm to United States' interests. President Bush has attempted to bring back a more informal relationship between the president and the press.

Public Opinion as a Check

The public's perception of the president's job performance can also limit presidential power. A generation ago, political scientist Richard E. Neustadt wrote about the effects of the public's esteem for the president—the president's "prestige," as Neustadt called it. According to Neustadt, prestige gives the president leeway to prevail in Washington. Congress and members of the president's bureaucracy, the other major players in Washington politics, are less likely to hassle a president who has strong public support. By the same token, they may conclude that they can defy and criticize him or her with impunity if the president suffers a loss of public confidence.[28] Neustadt had worked in the Truman administration and saw, first-hand, how hard it is for a president with low ratings in the polls—Truman's ratings were among the lowest in modern times—to get what he wanted. More recent presidents have also suffered the consequences of low poll ratings. When President Johnson's prestige declined in the late 1960s, largely because of his Vietnam policies, so did his influence over Congress and even within his own party. Johnson's successor, Richard Nixon, saw the collapse of his own precarious influence in the Washington community after the Watergate scandal caused his poll ratings to fall even below Truman's. Presidents Ford and Carter experienced similar resistance after their poll ratings declined.

President Reagan was more successful than any recent president in obtaining leeway through high public-approval ratings. However, when his ratings dropped as a result of the Iran-Contra affair, so did his ability to get his way in Washington. During

FIGURE **10-3**

Presidential Approval, Gallup Poll, 1938-1987

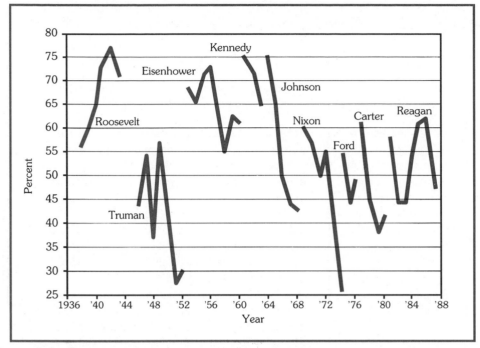

Source: Harold W. Stanley and Richard G. Niemi, *Vital Statistics on American Politics* (Washington: Congressional Quarterly Press, Inc., 1988), p. 227. Reprinted with permission.

In modern times, scientific polling has enabled us to get a clearer picture of the ups and downs of presidential popularity by measuring the president's "approval rating" among representative samples of the public. Presidents Roosevelt, Eisenhower, Kennedy, and, at least at the beginning of his term, Johnson enjoyed the highest ratings, while Truman and Nixon scored the lowest. The question asked in this survey was: Do you approve or disapprove of the way (last name of president) is handling his job as president? Shown are the percentages approving.

Reagan's last two years in office, Congress made deep cuts in his defense budget, sharply scaling back funds for MX missiles and Reagan's cherished "Star Wars" missile defense program (see chapter 20, pg. 586); it was during this period, too, that prominent Democratic congressional members began openly negotiating with the principal actors and nations in Central America, almost taking over the president's role as chief diplomat (see chapter 9).

President Bush, during his first year in office, enjoyed an unusually long honeymoon with the American public. Among recent presidents, public opinion ratings usually sagged after the first few months in office, but Bush's ratings kept going up, and by October 1989 almost 70 percent of Americans polled thought Bush was doing a good job. This is the kind of reservoir of goodwill that gives a president leeway; it does not guarantee that the president will prevail, but it helps.

The Ballot Box as a Check

One check on the president is so obvious that it is sometimes overlooked: the ballot box. Americans can always exercise the option of "throwing the rascal out." In this respect the Constitution provides a double check on the president: He or she must be *(Continued on page 263)*

TAKING SIDES

Do We Need More Checks on the Presidency?

YES Theodore Lowi

Based upon Theodore J. Lowi, "Presidential Power: Restoring the Balance," *Political Science Quarterly* (Summer 1985), pp. 185-213.

In Lowi's view, there are not enough checks on the presidency—the president still has too much power. Little, he says, has been learned from our experiences with Watergate. In a sense, the president is the "victim" of excessive power because people expect him to work wonders with it. When he cannot, they become disappointed and cynical.

Lowi advocates more sharing of power. There should be "a real cabinet around the presidency," a cabinet whose advice the president could not ignore. "A cabinet combines the advantages of a single chief executive with those of a plural executive. A cabinet would cut down, without eliminating, the personification of government in the plebiscitary presidency," says Lowi. Unfortunately, he adds, a strong cabinet system would probably not be feasible under our present party system. Cabinets are instruments of political parties, and our parties are weak. The ultimate solution, then, lies in making our parties tightly disciplined, like those in Europe, and even in encouraging a strong third party to give people more choice. The presidency, he says, "must be turned into a more parliamentary office." Presidents should be encouraged to veto bills that give them too much discretion.

NO Theodore Sorensen

Based upon Theodore Sorensen, *Watchmen in the Night* (Boston: M.I.T. Press, 1975).

Sorensen worries that if the critics of presidential power had their way, the presidency would become an "impotent" institution. He favors a strong executive. Congress cannot do the president's job. Just because Nixon abused his executive powers "does not mean that those powers could be better exercised by Congress," argues Sorensen. When Congress did try to run the executive branch after Ulysses S. Grant left office, "it was not a period of greatness in Washington."

What the critics forget, says Sorensen, is that "the power to do great harm is also the power to do great good." He cites numerous examples of the good use of expanded presidential power, from Kennedy's executive order in 1961 that gave food to hungry Americans in Appalachia to Nixon's opening of relations with China in 1972. By weakening the presidency, we weaken the ability of future presidents to act in the national interest. Instead of doing that, Sorensen concludes, we should renew the powers of the presidency while holding those powers more accountable—"more closely watched, more precisely defined, more carefully kept within constitutional bounds, and more clearly answerable to the electorate, Congress, and our other institutions."

Postscript

The question of whether or not the presidency needs more or fewer checks continues to be debated. It is a debate that may have partisan overtones. Presidential activism used to intrigue Democrats and worry Republicans, but now that Republicans have been controlling the White House for a decade, they seem more favorably disposed toward what President Kennedy used to call "vigor." Today the Democrats see greater need for congressional checks.

The Presidency Reappraised, edited by Thomas E. Cronin and Rexford G. Tugwell (Praeger, 1977), contains some interesting essays on the limits of presidential power, particularly in parts four and five. In 1970 a former press secretary to President Johnson wrote about the "monarchical" White House, and his book is still valuable. See George E. Reedy, *The Twilight of the Presidency* (New American Library, 1970). Wilfred E. Binkley's *President and Congress*, 3rd ed. (Vintage, 1982) is a classic study on the "ebb and flow" of presidential power in American history.

Points to Remember

1. The Supreme Court is a formidable check on presidential power. The Court may command no army, but it does command respect. Even though Richard Nixon appointed four members to the Supreme Court, his appointees joined in a 1974 decision that forced him to give up the secret White House tapes.

2. In the 1952 *Youngstown* case involving President Truman's seizure of the steel mills, the Court told the president he must return the mills to private ownership.

3. Bureaucrats check the president in at least three ways: by bureaucratic inertia, by fighting back (going to their friends in Congress and the press), and by "waiting out" the president. Presidents come and go, but the bureaucracy remains.

4. The press checks the president by muckraking. No president can expect the press to keep secrets or accept his or her word

without question. The press is an active player in American politics, and its opponent is often the White House.

5. Elections serve as a means of removing a president who does not measure up to expectations. Presidential elections cannot easily be manipulated by incumbents, as ex-presidents Ford and Carter can testify.

(Continued from page 261)

elected every four years and, thanks to the Twenty-second Amendment, can serve for no more than two terms.

In some circles it has become fashionable to deride the American political system. It is asserted that presidential elections are not really meaningful because they provide no real choice, and that incumbent presidents can use their office to manipulate public opinion and thus stay in power. Both these assertions are untrue. American presidential elections provide the public with significant choices. Could anyone doubt that in 1984 and 1988 the Republican and Democratic candidates differed on a wide range of issues, from abortion and the death penalty to the MX missile? As for the president's supposed power to manipulate public opinion, that would certainly surprise Gerald Ford and Jimmy Carter, who were voted out of office despite their efforts to use incumbency in their favor. American voters are nobody's puppets. They make up their own minds. They decide, partly on issues and partly on "horseflesh," whom they want to entrust with the powers of the presidency.

Elections by themselves are not enough. Historian Arthur Schlesinger, Jr., and political scientist Theodore J. Lowi have both written about the dangers of a plebiscitary presidency.[29] By that they mean a system in which the president goes to the people every four years but is otherwise free to operate without interference. Carried to its logical conclusion, a plebiscitary presidency would amount to a four-year dictatorship. In view of all the other checks on the presidency that we have discussed in this chapter—checks imposed by Congress, by the Supreme Court, by the bureaucracy, by the press, and by public opinion—America seems very far from having a dictatorship. Nevertheless, Lowi and others continue to worry. They think the president still has too much unilateral power. That view has been vigorously opposed by Theodore Sorensen, a former Kennedy aide. Lowi and Sorensen present the arguments on both sides in the Taking Sides section of this chapter.

Reflections

In the 1950s and the early 1960s American government courses taught in colleges and universities conveyed the idea that the race for the presidency was a kind of purifying event that screened out unprincipled people. After Nixon's presidency it was hard to maintain confidence in that idea. The Watergate investigations raked up plenty of evidence that lack of principle was rampant in the Nixon White House.

There were plots against enemies, telephone taps, burglaries, bribes, dirty tricks, and cover-ups. Watergate ended in prison sentences for most of Nixon's key aides, a forced resignation for their chief, and a rather strange pardon for him—a pardon granted by his successor for deeds for which he would never be tried.

When the Watergate scandal was still fresh in people's memories, there was much talk of the lessons to be learned from it. There were proposals for a plural presidency, for forcing the president to take members of Congress from the opposition party into the cabinet, for making impeachment easier, and so forth. Although many of these suggestions were thought-provoking, few were feasible, and by the end of the 1970s nearly all had disappeared from the agenda of public debate.

This does not mean that we have no lessons to learn from Watergate. Certainly one lesson is that presidential power must be adequately checked, in two senses of that word. It needs to be "checked up on" or "checked out"—that is to say, carefully investigated. And it needs to be "checked," in the sense of restrained; obstacles or barriers must be placed in its way to prevent it from getting out of hand.

It may be that checking presidential power is more a matter of will than of means. We already have the means for checking the president. Congress can check presidential power by legislation, by refusing to approve presidential treaties and appointments, by investigating the president, and, in extreme cases, by impeachment. The Supreme Court can check the president by declaring presidential actions unconstitutional, as the Court did with Truman; or by ordering the president to do something, as the Court did with Nixon; or by upholding congressional checks, as the Court did in 1988 when it upheld the special prosecutor law. The bureaucracy can check the president by dragging its feet, by going for help to its friends in Congress and the press, or simply by "waiting out" the president. The press can check the president by relentless exposure and muckraking. Public opinion can check the president by depriving him or her of "leeway." The voters can check the president by limiting him or her to one term in office.

If the means of checking the president exist, what about the will to use them? There was once a cult of presidential activism, fostered by journalists and college professors, the very people who should have been watching the presidential office with a wary eye. They helped lead public opinion to the belief that the American people should trust the president. Vietnam and Watergate turned everything around. Now many journalists and professors see the presidency as an imperial office that breeds arrogance, dishonesty, and contempt for law. They want Congress to take over much of the decision making once left to the executive branch.

Has the pendulum swung from one extreme to the other—from uncritical celebration of presidential power to jaded distrust of it? This is a question to be answered in the future. All we can do for now is to keep in mind the insights of both James Madison and Alexander Hamilton. They have to be embraced as a unit, each qualifying the other. In *The Federalist* papers, Madison warned against the concentration of power anywhere, including the presidency, and favored a system of checks and balances to keep all units of government in their place. But in that same volume of *The Federalist* papers, Alexander Hamilton also discussed power, or "energy," as he called it, in the executive branch. Such "energy," he said, "is a leading character in the definition of good government." Deprive the president of power and we will have a feeble executive, which means that we will have a feeble government.

Between the insights of Hamilton and Madison there is a tension, not a contradiction. What is wrong with giving a president great power yet watching that power very carefully—making it accountable, limiting its reach, and being sure that its abuse is swiftly punished? We can always argue about where the limits of legitimate power lie, but the formula itself—the necessity of both considerable power *and* limits—may help to keep us from slipping toward one extreme or the other as we confront the presidency today.

Notes

1. Carl Bernstein and Bob Woodward, *All the President's Men* (New York: Warner Books, 1974), p. 19.
2. Quoted in J. Anthony Lucas, *Nightmare: The Underside of the Nixon Years* (New York: The Viking Press, 1976), p. 303.
3. Quoted in J. Anthony Lucas, p. 280.
4. Quoted in J. Anthony Lucas, p. 371.
5. *The Presidential Transcripts*, in conjunction with the staff of *The Washington Post* (New York: Dell Books, 1974), p. 37.
6. Clinton Rossiter, *The American Presidency*, rev. ed. (New York: Harcourt, Brace and World, Inc., 1960), p. 52.
7. See further, Raoul Berger, *The Impeachment: The Constitutional Problems* (Cambridge, MA: Harvard University Press, 1973).
8. Joel Brinkley, "Boland and the Contras: Curbs That Vary," *New York Times*, May 13, 1987, p. A13.
9. Brit Hume, "Ollie North and the Fools on the Hill," *American Spectator* (Sept. 1987), p. 16.
10. *U.S. News and World Report*, May 28, 1954.
11. *New York Times*, Mar. 13, 1973, p. 16.
12. See transcript of "War Powers: The President and Congress," *The Constitution: That Delicate Balance*, 13-part PBS television series, p. 9.
13. Transcript, "War Powers: The President and Congress," *The Constitution*, p. 10.
14. Clinton Rossiter, p. 54.
15. "Lucas Rejection a Blow to Bush, Thornburgh," *Congressional Quarterly Weekly Report*, Aug. 5, 1989, pp. 2036-39.
16. J. Anthony Lukas, p. 519.
17. *Youngstown Sheet & Tube Co. v. Sawyer*, 343 U.S. 579 (1952).
18. *The Prize Cases*, 2 Black 635 (1863).
19. *Korematsu v. United States*, 323 U.S. 214 (1944).
20. *Mora v. McNamara*, 389 U.S. 934 (1967).
21. Quoted in Richard E. Neustadt, *Presidential Power: The Politics of Leadership* (New York: John Wiley & Sons, Inc., 1962), p. 9.
22. Quoted in the *New York Times*, July 19, 1974, p. 14.
23. Peter Woll and Rochelle Jones, "Bureaucratic Defense in Depth," *The Nation*, Sept. 17, 1973, p. 231.
24. Daniel P. Moynihan, "The Presidency and the Press," *Commentary* (Mar. 1971).
25. *New York Times*, Sept. 5, 1973, p. 1.
26. News conference, San Clemente, CA, Aug. 22, 1973. Reprinted in *The Watergate Hearings: Break-in and Cover-up*, *New York Times* edition (New York: Bantam Books, 1973), pp. 726-27.
27. Transcript, "National Security and Freedom of the Press," *The Constitution: That Delicate Balance*, p. 12.
28. Richard E. Neustadt, p. 90.
29. Arthur Schlesinger, Jr., *The Imperial Presidency* (Boston: Houghton Mifflin Co., 1973), pp. 254-55; Theodore H. Lowi, "Presidential Power: Restoring the Balance," *Political Science Quarterly* (Summer 1985), pp. 185-213.

11

The Bureaucracy

Glendower: I can call spirits from the vasty deep.
Hotspur: Why, so can I, or so can any man;
But will they come when you do call for them?

William Shakespeare, *King Henry IV, Part I*

THE NATURE OF THE FEDERAL BUREAUCRACY

Weber's Model Bureaucracy: Hierarchy, Specialization, Rules / The U.S. Bureaucracy: A Distinctive System

DEVELOPMENT OF THE FEDERAL BUREAUCRACY

The Spoils System / The Rise of the Merit System / The Hatch Act / The Growing Power of Federal Bureaucrats / Political Appointees and Career Bureaucrats

PROBLEMS OF THE FEDERAL BUREAUCRACY

Red Tape and Waste / Lack of Accountability / Incompetence and Mediocrity / Suggested Reforms

HUG A BUREAUCRAT

REFLECTIONS

The Bureau and the Attorney General

As far as it is possible for any human being to look like a bulldog, J. Edgar Hoover looked like a bulldog. He was stout and solid in build, and he had a thick neck. But it was his face that stood out. It was a round face, yet there was no softness in it. The jaw was set and thrust forward, the nose was squat, the eyes were alert and fierce. It was not the face of a man anyone would want to trifle with.*

*This account is drawn from the following sources: Richard G. Powers, *Secrecy and Power: The Life of J. Edgar Hoover* (New York: The Free Press, 1987); Arthur M. Schlesinger, Jr., *Robert Kennedy and His Times* (Boston: Houghton Mifflin Co., 1978); Sanford J. Ungar, *FBI: An Uncensored Look Behind the Walls* (Boston: Little, Brown and Co., 1975, 1976); Ralph deToledano, *J. Edgar Hoover: The Man in His Time* (New Rochelle, NY: Arlington House, 1973); Ovid Demaris, *The Director* (New York: Harper's Magazine Press, 1975); William C. Sullivan (with Bill Brown), *The Bureau: My Thirty Years in Hoover's FBI* (New York: W. W. Norton & Company, 1979); Victor S. Navasky, *Kennedy Justice* (New York: Atheneum, 1971); William Safire, "The President's Friend," *New York Times*, December 15, 1975, p. 31. Thanks also to Professor David Garrow of The City College of New York; any errors are entirely my responsibility.

In 1961 Hoover could look back on 37 years as the director of the Federal Bureau of Investigation (FBI) and know it was more than his face that had earned respect. In 1924 when Hoover became director, the FBI was a corrupt, patronage-ridden enclave in the Justice Department. Hoover had turned it around.

Hoover began with a written promise from the attorney general that he could run the bureau without political interference and without being bound by civil service requirements. Then he went to work: He fired all the incorrigibles and frightened the rest into a sudden change of heart. He set up new hiring practices, including the requirement that all future agents have degrees in law or accounting. He laid down strict codes of dress and conduct. Agents were to dress conservatively and comport themselves with dignity. They were to keep their suit jackets on at the office; during Prohibition, any agent caught drinking was dismissed, and so was any FBI man (there were no female agents) discovered to be sleeping with someone other than his wife. Hoover was a Puritan.

His puritanism may have been right for the times. It instilled a sense of discipline and mission in an agency that had been conspicuously lacking in both. It boosted morale. His agents worked long hours and never seemed to mind; the pay was modest, but the prestige that Hoover brought to the bureau was theirs to share. They became known as G-men, a term coined by gangster George ("Machine-Gun") Kelly, who reportedly said, "Don't shoot, G-men. I'm coming out!" By the 1930s kids were wearing G-man pajamas to bed and bringing G-man machine guns out to play.

By the end of the 1950s J. Edgar Hoover had turned himself into a national monument. He had served under five presidents and become a living symbol of morality, patriotism, and honesty. The public adored him, and the politicians treated him gingerly. One reason the politicians were so nice to him was that he kept files on them. The files were kept under lock and key in his office, but he would sometimes share them with the individuals involved. This senator had had a homosexual affair; that congressman had a friend who was a Communist or had signed a petition for a Communist front group. Hoover would invite the individual into his office, close the door, and show him what he had on him. The individual would thank him profusely and walk out of Hoover's office with heightened respect for J. Edgar Hoover. That is the way it went, through five administrations.

But in the 1960s change was in the air. John F. Kennedy, the youngest man ever elected president, came into office proclaiming that "the torch has been passed to a new generation of Americans—born in this century. . . ."[1] J. Edgar Hoover was born in 1895. What did all this mean, this talk of torches being passed? Hoover soon found out. Like his predecessors, Kennedy reappointed J. Edgar Hoover as director. But he also appointed Robert F. Kennedy attorney general. The attorney general is the head of the Justice Department. Robert Kennedy was to be J. Edgar Hoover's new boss.

In 1961 Robert Kennedy was 35 years old, young enough to have been one of the kids wearing the G-man pajamas back in the 1930s. He had worked for eight years as counsel to a Senate investigating subcommittee—Senator Joe McCarthy's old committee. In the early 1950s Robert Kennedy had helped McCarthy investigate communism. Later, when the Democrats took over the Senate, he turned his attention to labor racketeering. That was the sum of his legal experience. Now he was the most powerful legal officer in the United States. (President Kennedy

J. Edgar Hoover served as director of the FBI from 1924 until his death in 1972. The lifelong bureaucrat was appointed and reappointed to his office by seven different administrations. Although he molded the FBI into one of the most efficient law enforcement agencies in the world, he was often criticized for exceeding his jurisdiction.

had said of the appointment: "I see nothing wrong with giving Robert some legal experience before he goes out to practice law.")[2] He wanted to make sure Hoover knew who was boss. Early in 1961 he dropped by Hoover's office to have a talk with him. No one knows what was said at this first meeting, but afterwards Hoover was red-faced and steaming with rage. Apparently, Kennedy had proposed setting up some kind of supplementary group within the Justice Department to take over part of Hoover's work. When Hoover threatened to resign, Kennedy pulled back. Whether Kennedy made the proposal in earnest or simply to put Hoover on notice that things were going to be different under the new administration, Hoover concluded that the Kennedy brothers were out to humiliate him at the very least and possibly to force him out of office.

Hoover was right. The Kennedys saw him as a relic of bygone times. To them, he had done a good job against the gangsters of the thirties, but times were different now. Robert Kennedy considered Hoover's methods ill-suited to fighting well-organized crime networks like the Mafia. He thought Hoover's shop needed closer supervision, which would be difficult because Hoover had spun a cocoon around his bureau, shielding it from any outside interference. Hoover had forgotten that the FBI was subordinate to the Justice Department and its chief, the attorney general of the United States. From Hoover's perspective, the Kennedys were attempting to politicize the FBI, to make it the servant of their ambitions, to weaken its discipline and morale, and, in the long run, to reduce it to what it had been when Hoover took over in 1924—a corrupt patronage organization. To Hoover, everything about the Kennedy brothers seemed to point in that direction, including their way of comporting themselves. Bobby Kennedy strolled around the halls of the Justice Department in his shirtsleeves, dropping in on FBI offices without announcement. He let his dog have the run of one of the halls, in violation of bureau rules. There was beer-drinking in his office, and a dartboard; sometimes darts missed the board and went into the paneling. Hoover considered this a "desecration of government property."[3]

Following that first meeting with Hoover, Robert Kennedy abandoned his plan for setting up a parallel investigatory group. But he remained determined to assert his personal control over the FBI. Hoover fought back. Periodically, flurries of identical letters would arrive at the White House; the gist of them was that Hoover was a fine public servant who deserved the president's full support. There were also speeches in Congress in support of the director. The extent to which Hoover encouraged these campaigns is still not clear, but he never hesitated to tell his friends about the treatment he was getting from the Kennedys. In other, quieter, ways he resisted control. He would drag his feet in carrying out some directives, particularly when Robert Kennedy wanted him to use the FBI to enforce civil rights in the South.

In the spring of 1962 Hoover played his trump card. He discovered that President Kennedy was having an affair with a woman named Judith Campbell. Judith Campbell was the girlfriend of Momo Salvatore (Sam) Giancana, the don of organized crime in Chicago. When Robert Kennedy had served as counsel to the Senate investigating committee on labor racketeering, he had grilled Sam Giancana. He had characterized Giancana as the "chief gunman for the group that succeeded the Capone mob" and had taunted him for taking the Fifth Amendment.[4] Now here was Robert Kennedy's own brother, the president of the United States, sleeping with Giancana's mistress! On March 22, 1962, Hoover had a luncheon meeting with the president. A few hours after that meeting was over, the president made his last telephone call to Judith Campbell. Still, the Kennedy brothers insisted on trying to control Hoover.

Then, on November 22, 1963, everything changed. John Kennedy was assassinated, and the new president, Lyndon Johnson, had an old grudge against Robert Kennedy. Bobby had fought against putting Johnson on the presidential ticket in 1960 and had even tried to get his brother to withdraw the offer after it had been made. Hoover, of course, knew about this and used it. Soon Hoover was able to bypass the attorney general's office completely. He replaced a Kennedy intimate as White House liaison to the bureau with someone who was a personal friend of Johnson's. It was like the old days again: Hoover reported to the president—largely through intermediaries—and ignored the attorney general.

President Johnson and J. Edgar Hoover got along splendidly. They were old friends and former neighbors. Hoover began supplying Johnson with files on various high-level politicians. Then, too, Johnson had a few indiscretions of his own to hide. It was better, he confided to a friend, "to have Edgar inside the tent pissing out than outside the tent pissing in."[5] Hoover stayed on under Johnson and was reappointed by Nixon in 1969. He was still director in May 1972 when he died of a heart attack at the age of 77. By that time he had worked under seven administrations and outlived both brothers who had tried to retire him.

* * * * *

J. Edgar Hoover was a bureaucrat. The term derives from the French word *bureau*, meaning a writing table or desk and was meant to apply to those who sat at desks and wrote the orders that implemented government policies. As a bureaucrat, Hoover was not elected to his post but was appointed to it—in his case, appointed and reappointed by a succession of presidents going back to Calvin Coolidge.

In some important respects Hoover was an atypical bureaucrat. He was a political appointee, not, like most, a "career bureaucrat," who gets his or her job through civil service examinations. Hoover was also quite unique in terms of his rather strange, quirky personality and the historic situation that brought him to power and kept him there for so long.

Yet despite the unique features of the J. Edgar Hoover story, it does reveal much about how bureaucrats operate in Washington. Like other federal bureaucrats who are appointed, Hoover supposedly answered to those who are elected, the president and the Congress. But in fact, he was able to insulate himself and his bureau from direct control of either elected branch. He did not just implement policies, he made them. Finally, he learned how to survive and increase his power by building political ties in the Washington community. In all these respects, Hoover was not unlike many other key players in the federal bureaucracy.

In this chapter we will study our national bureaucracy. We will consider what bureaucracy is and how it has developed in the United States. Next, we will discuss the problems posed by the bureaucracy and some of the attempts that have been made to solve those problems. We will also argue that our extensive bureaucracy is needed in today's world and that ours, despite its flaws, provides indispensable services to the public.

The Nature of the Federal Bureaucracy

If we reflect a moment, we suddenly realize that the bureaucracy is the real point of contact between the federal government and the people. Congress can pass laws, but laws do not mean anything until they are put into effect. That is what bureaucrats do. They take us beyond abstractions and good intentions; they give the orders; they make the regulations; and they deliver the goods and services. We rely on bureaucrats to:

- deliver our mail
- write our Social Security checks
- police our borders
- manage our national forests
- shape our foreign policy
- regulate our businesses
- give money to states and localities
- collect our taxes
- arrest federal lawbreakers

The list goes on and on. It is impossible to live through a single day without encountering the work of federal bureaucrats. The cars we drive have had to meet federal standards written by bureaucrats. Many of the roads on which we drive have been built with federal highway funds disbursed by bureaucrats. The food we eat has been inspected by bureaucrats. Chances are that some of you are partially financing a college degree with student loans facilitated by bureaucrats. There are 2.9 million federal bureaucrats scattered around the country and overseas (only 12 percent of them are in Washington), plus 3 million more in the armed services. Without them, the business of the nation would quickly come to a halt.

The federal bureaucracy contains three main areas: the cabinet; the independent agencies; and government corporations, foundations, and institutes. The best-known is the cabinet. Making up the cabinet are 14 departments, each headed by a secretary (except the Justice Department, which is headed by the attorney general). They are shown in Figure 11.1.

The cabinet heads, who report directly to the president, oversee the work of various deputies and undersecretaries who help manage the department. Within

FIGURE 11-1

The Bush Cabinet

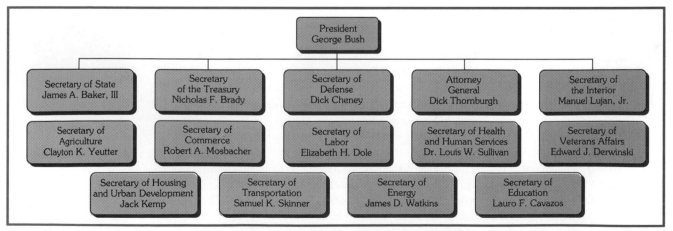

The cabinet of our 41st president as of January 1990.

FIGURE **11-2**

Organization of the Justice Department

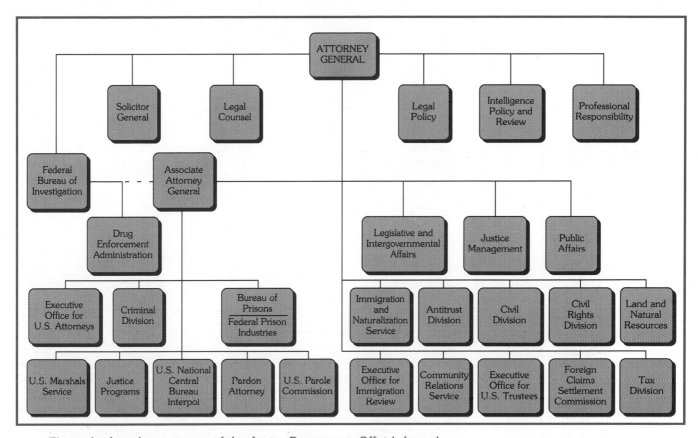

This is the formal organization of the Justice Department. Officials from the Immigration and Naturalization Service are on hand to greet those who land on our shores and to decide whether or not they have a right to stay. The Civil Rights Division looks into allegations of racial and other forms of discrimination. Agents from the Drug Enforcement Administration often work side by side with city police during local drug busts. Another kind of "bust"—breaking up illegal monopolies—is the job of lawyers from the Antitrust Division.

each department are the <u>bureaus</u>, called by various names (bureaus, offices, divisions, services, and so on), which are the working agencies of the cabinet departments. Indeed, the cabinet departments are really sprawling collections of bureaus that do the real work of government; each department is a kind of umbrella held over its bureaus. Under this umbrella the bureaus can be arranged in an organizational tree; such diagrams provide some understanding of the formal relationships and hierarchies within each department. Figure 11.2 shows the formal organization of the Justice Department, which has many functions.

Keep in mind that formal organization charts can be very misleading; they do not tell us anything about the *informal* lines of power and influence within a department. Often we find bureaucrats in the lower regions of the chart who in fact swing a lot of weight. They may have powerful friends in Congress; they may have a lot of seniority; they may have built strong friendships with people on the president's staff or with close associates of the cabinet secretary. As we saw earlier, J. Edgar Hoover was virtually untouchable—by his nominal boss, the attorney general, and even by the president of the United States.

FIGURE **11-3**

Spending by Cabinet Departments, 1988

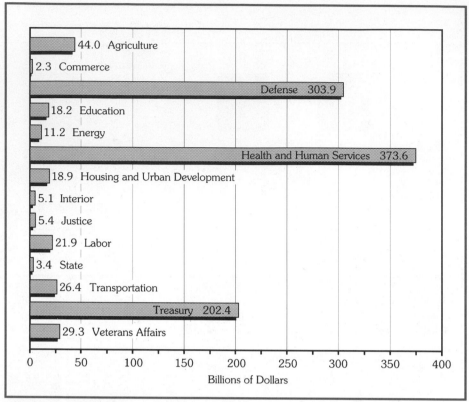

Source: Fiscal 1990 Budget.

Many Americans believe the Defense Department is the biggest spender of all
the cabinet departments. Actually, even during the Reagan years, the largest
federal expenditures have been made by the Department of Health and Human
Services. Defense is second, the Treasury third, and all the other departments
are far behind in the amounts they spend each year.

The second area of the bureaucracy consists of the more than 50 <u>independent</u>
<u>agencies</u>, so called because they are independent of the cabinet. These include the
Central Intelligence Agency (CIA), the Environmental Protection Agency (EPA), and
the National Aeronautics and Space Administration (NASA). Although they have no
ties to any cabinet department, these independent agencies are not necessarily
independent of presidential control. Most of their heads are appointed by and
answerable to the president. There are, however, some exceptions. The head of the
U.S. Postal Service, the postmaster general, is appointed by an 11-person board of
governors and takes direction from that board. (The board itself is appointed by the
president, but its members serve nine-year overlapping terms, so that the influence of
each president is limited.)

Another type of independent agency that is more or less free of direct
presidential control is the <u>independent regulatory commission</u>. There are several of
these commissions, including the Federal Communications Commission (FCC), the
Interstate Commerce Commission (ICC), and the Federal Reserve Board. These
boards have quasi-legislative and quasi-judicial powers: that is, they (1) make rules
and (2) decide if their rules have been violated in particular cases. For example, the
FCC sets certain standards for broadcasting and then hears cases involving accusa-

(Continued on page 274)

TABLE **11-1**

273

The Nature of the
Federal
Bureaucracy

Independent Agencies of the Federal Government

Independent Establishments and Government Corporations

ACTION

Administration
Conference of
the U.S.

African
Development
Foundation

American Battle
Monuments
Commission

Appalachian
Regional
Commission

Board for
International
Broadcasting

Central Intelligence
Agency

Commission on the
Bicentennial of
the United States
Constitution

Commission on
Civil Rights

Commission of Fine
Arts

Commodity Futures
Trading
Commission

Consumer Product
Safety
Commission

Environmental
Protection
Agency

Equal Employment
Opportunity
Commission

Export-Import
Bank of the U.S.

Farm Credit
Administration

Federal
Communications
Commission

Federal Deposit
Insurance
Corporation

Federal Election
Commission

Federal Emergency
Management
Agency

Federal Home Loan
Bank Board

Federal Labor
Relations
Authority

Federal Maritime
Commission

Federal Mediation
and Conciliation
Service

Federal Reserve
System, Board of
Governors of the

Federal Retirement
Thrift Investment
Board

Federal Trade
Commission

General Services
Administration

Inter-American
Foundation

Interstate
Commerce
Commission

Merit Systems
Protection Board

National
Aeronautics and
Space
Administration

National Archives
and Records
Administration

National Capital
Planning
Commission

National Credit
Union
Administration

National
Foundation on
the Arts and the
Humanities

National Labor
Relations Board

National Mediation
Board

National Science
Foundation

National
Transportation
Safety Board

Nuclear Regulatory
Commission

Occupational Safety
and Health
Review
Commission

Office of Personnel
Management

Panama Canal
Commission

Peace Corps

Pennsylvania
Avenue
Development
Corporation

Pension Benefit
Guaranty
Corporation

Postal Rate
Commission

Railroad Retirement
Board

Securities and
Exchange
Commission

Selective Service
System

Small Business
Administration

Tennessee Valley
Authority

U.S. Arms Control
and Disarmament
Agency

U.S. Information
Agency

U.S. International
Development
Cooperation
Agency

U.S. International
Trade
Commission

U.S. Postal Service

Veterans
Administration

Source: Office of Federal Register, *The United States Government Manual,* 1988–89 (Washington: U.S. Government Printing Office, 1988), p. 21.

The Central Intelligence Agency, the Environmental Protection Agency, and the National Aeronautics and Space Administration remain independent of any cabinet department even though their heads answer to the president. The president has less influence over the Federal Communications Commission, the Interstate Commerce Commission, and the Federal Reserve Board; these agencies have overlapping terms, thus limiting control by any one president.

The Sequoyah Nuclear Power Plant located near Chattanooga, TN, is a government-owned project of the Tennessee Valley Authority (TVA), a government corporation, and provides electricity to the local communities at wholesale rates.

(Continued from page 272) tions that a broadcaster has violated one or more of the rules. These commissions are headed by three or more individuals with overlapping terms, and they cannot be removed by the president. For some of the commissions, there is a provision that they must be bipartisan. Table 11.1 on the previous page lists the independent agencies of the federal government.

A third general area of the federal bureaucracy is one that is still more loosely connected to the central spine of the federal government. It includes government corporations and government foundations and institutes. In the former category are the Tennessee Valley Authority (TVA) and the Federal Deposit Insurance Corporation (FDIC). These are money-making agencies. For example, TVA operates dams and hydroelectric plants and sells power to customers. These corporations are run by the government but are freed from many of the regulations most government agencies must follow. They also are free to make their own decisions, such as how to spend their earnings. The idea is to enable them to serve the public's needs without being paralyzed by too much regulation. Government foundations and institutes are also given a fairly long leash. Their purpose is to promote science, the spread of knowledge, and scholarship. The most famous is the Smithsonian Institution. Anyone who has ever gone to Washington, D.C., and visited the National Air and Space Museum, which houses some of America's historic air and space vehicles, has seen one of the Smithsonian's most dramatic exhibits. Other government foundations and institutes include the National Institutes of Health, the National Science Foundation, the National Endowment for the Arts, and the National Endowment for the Humanities. As long as these government institutes follow certain statutory guidelines, they can run themselves as they see fit, and they are shielded against direct political interference. The National Science Foundation, for example, is run by a 24-member National Science Board, appointed for six-year terms by the president with the advice and consent of the Senate.

TABLE **11-2**

275

The Nature of the
Federal
Bureaucracy

Selected Government Regulatory Agencies

Agency	Year Created	Regulates
Agencies that regulate specific industries:		
Interstate Commerce Commission (ICC)	1887	Railroads, trucking, pipelines, barges, express carriers
Federal Reserve Board (FRB)	1913	Banks
Federal Power Commission (FPC)	1930	Public utilities
Food and Drug Administration (FDA)	1931	Food, drugs, cosmetics
Federal Communications Commission (FCC)	1934	Radio, television, telephone, telegraph
Federal Aviation Administration (FAA)	1967	Airline safety
National Highway Traffic Safety Administration (NHTSA)	1970	Motor vehicles
Agencies that regulate specific functions:		
Securities and Exchange Commission (SEC)	1934	Sales of securities
National Labor Relations Board (NLRB)	1935	Labor-management relations
Equal Employment Opportunity Commission (EEOC)	1964	Hiring practices
Environmental Protection Agency (EPA)	1970	Pollution of the environment
Occupational Safety and Health Administration (OSHA)	1971	Conditions in workplaces
Consumer Product Safety Commission (CPSC)	1972	Design and labeling of goods

Federal regulatory agencies first appeared at the close of the nineteenth century in response to public pressures to supervise interstate businesses accused of engaging in practices injurious to the public. The first of these, the Interstate Commerce Commission (ICC), established in 1887, was aimed primarily at the railroad industry. In this century, the number of new regulatory agencies has mushroomed.

WEBER'S MODEL BUREAUCRACY: HIERARCHY, SPECIALIZATION, RULES

Before we take a look at the distinctive qualities of U.S. bureaucracy, it might be useful to examine first one of the best-known theories of bureaucracy. We can then compare the reality of the American bureaucracy to it.

One way to view bureaucracy is to see it as an assemblage of offices. An office is an impersonal place; it functions the way it does regardless of the personal qualities of its occupants. That was the approach taken by the German sociologist Max Weber (1864–1920). In a posthumous work published in 1920, Weber described a bureaucracy in its ideal form as an organization that rests upon *hierarchy*, a layering of offices from high to low; *specialization*, meaning that "only persons who have the . . . qualifications to serve are employed"; and *the rule of law* rather than the personal dictates of any individual.[6]

Even though the term *hierarchy* implies a gradation of offices from high to low, it does not mean that the lower offices are automatically subservient to the higher ones.

On the contrary, the lower offices are protected against unwarranted intrusions from the upper ones. The authority to give commands "is distributed in a stable way," according to Weber, meaning that each level enjoys its own degree of authority. A bureaucratic order is not the same as a despotism, in which the person at the top rules by whim. Each level of the hierarchy is bound by rules and regulations. One level does its task and then passes the work along to the next level. For Weber, a true bureaucracy was an impersonal machine that operated smoothly and logically, in accordance with stable, well-understood rules.

THE U.S. BUREAUCRACY: A DISTINCTIVE SYSTEM

There is much to be said for Weber's model. Our bureaucracy does function by rules and regulations, and these have become increasingly dense and complicated in recent years. Weber's description also helps to account for the spirit of professionalism among career civil servants—their image of themselves as technicians who perform specialized tasks and their corresponding annoyance when political superiors try to meddle in their affairs. We saw this in the case of J. Edgar Hoover. Yet Weber's description obscures at least as much as it illuminates. As we also saw in the Hoover case, the machine metaphor fails to take into account all the moving and maneuvering that go on within the federal bureaucracy.

A machine leaves no room for discretion; its cogs turn in only one direction. But the "cogs" in our federal bureaucracy can move in all sorts of ways, exercising a wide range of options. The bureaucratic process in America is *political*: there is negotiation, deal-making, and compromise; there are alliances and confrontations, vendettas and conspiracies. There are rules, but often there are ways around the rules. None of this is very machinelike.

American bureaucracy has three distinctive qualities: two masters, shared functions, and private agencies.

Two Masters. First, because of our system of separated powers, American bureaucrats serve two masters, the president and Congress. Both the president and Congress share in the lawmaking function, and both oversee the implementation of

The bureaucracy often appears to be an impersonal machine. A portion of the staggering amount of paperwork generated by the federal government can be seen in this one IRS office. These specially designed desks are used to sort the millions of income tax returns that are received each year.

laws. Yet the president and Congress serve different constituencies, are elected at different times, and often come from different parties. The result is frequently a tug-of-war, with bureaucrats being pulled in opposite directions. Bureaucrats cannot always follow the orders of their superiors or even follow up on what they regard as congressional mandates. To do so may put them on a collision course with key members of Congress. In his book *Smoking and Politics*, political scientist A. Lee Fritschler notes that the Federal Trade Commission got into trouble with Congress for proposing warning labels not only on cigarettes but on other products as well. This made a lot of businesses uneasy, and they contacted some key members of Congress. Oversight hearings were held, and new legislation was passed limiting the FTC's authority—all of which, Fritschler says, left the commission "a bit shaken."[7] Of course, Congress cannot control every action of the bureaucrats; that would be impossible. But Congress does function as a check on bureaucrats, according to Fritschler:

> The fact that Congress has the power to rise up in awesome dissent, at least occasionally, serves to remind administrators that the road to success is paved with quietly negotiated accommodation of agency policy to the views of key Congressmen.[8]

The bureaucratic machine does not operate this way in Europe and in most other countries. Parliaments pass laws but play only a small role in the administration of them. Bureaucrats serve one master—the executive cabinet.

Shared Functions.   Second, because of our system of federalism, federal bureaucrats in America share functions with state and local bureaucrats. There are federal tax collectors and state and local tax collectors, federal meat inspectors and state and local ones, federal agricultural agents and their counterparts in states and localities. In some cases—when both federal and local laws are involved—federal and local agents work hand in hand. Local police departments have worked with the FBI for decades, and in more recent years, Federal Drug Enforcement Administration (DEA) agents have often helped local police arrest offenders. The closest most of us come to dealing with agents of the federal government, however, are contacts with U.S. postal employees and those who work at the local office of the Social Security Administration. Federal bureaucrats are usually much less visible to the average citizen than state and local ones. Of course, much of what state and local bureaucrats do is now at least partly underwritten by the federal government. As we saw in chapter 3, federal grants to states and localities have grown enormously since the 1960s. Still, the federal government's *presence* is not as obvious as it is in most European countries, where the central government runs all public institutions—such as schools, health clinics, and housing developments.

Private Agencies.   Third, many of the services for which the federal government pays are performed by private agencies. Despite the huge increase in federal expenditures and regulations over the past generation, there has been hardly any change in the *numbers* of federal employees. There were about 2.9 million executive branch employees in 1970 and the same number in 1985. The federal government has held down the numbers of public employees by turning over the work to private agencies and companies and paying them to do it. This practice, called contracting out, has boomed since the end of World War II.

The Department of Defense spends billions on the development of weapons, but nearly all the research and construction is done by private firms that have been given Pentagon contracts for the work. The Department of Health and Human Services spends money to provide birth-control services to women, but these services are provided through Planned Parenthood, a private organization that receives federal money. These are two of many examples. Hundreds of offices in the Washington, D.C., area house contractors that specialize in services to the government. Some are very small operations that are set up for the purpose of administering a specific program. Others are divisions of some of America's largest corporations, such as Westinghouse and General Electric.[9] In our country the national government gets involved in public services largely by financing them rather than by running them. Publicly operated enterprises account for less than 3 percent of all services in the United States, compared to about 12 percent in France and Great Britain.

Why does our federal government avoid direct involvement? One reason is ideological. If the government actually ran things, that would smack of socialism, and, as we discussed in earlier chapters, *socialism* is a bad word in this country. Second, contracting out is a good way for politicians in both the executive and legislative branches to nourish alliances with key interest groups. Supporters of and contributors to legislative campaigns are often the same people who are running the enterprises that the members of Congress have set up. Many executive branch officials retire and go to work for the same businesses they helped finance and supervise. This is not to suggest that there is anything dishonest or wrong in contracting out public services. It may at times be a more efficient way of getting things done than having the government do them.

Development of the Federal Bureaucracy

Our federal bureaucracy is not even mentioned in the Constitution. In George Washington's administration (1789-1797), there were five executive departments, each consisting of a secretary and a few clerks. The State Department, for example, started with nine employees. These, plus other federal employees (such as postal employees and tax collectors), added up to less than 800 bureaucrats in 1789.

THE SPOILS SYSTEM

Over the next 30 years, however, the federal bureaucracy began a period of steady growth, so that by the time Andrew Jackson was elected in 1828 there were almost 11,000 federal officials. How did one get to be a federal official? By patronage—that

(Continued on page 279)

GLOBAL PERSPECTIVES:

The Bureaucracy in Mexico

Mexico has a strong presidential system, which means that its bureaucracy is highly centralized and cannot be influenced easily through the legislative branch. It can, however, be reached through its top administrators.

In the Mexican bureaucracy, power is largely concentrated at the top. Members of the Mexican bureaucracy charged with implementing policies always raise their eyes upward for cues. Powerful economic interests thus find it to their advantage to cultivate friends among high-level administrators. These then pass the word to their subordinates, who obey without question. There is very little sense of professionalism in the Mexican bureaucracy; its members tend to think of themselves less as technical specialists than as loyal retainers. They are unlikely to implement any policy that would adversely affect their superiors—or any powerful friend of their superiors. They also look out for their own friends and relatives when they implement policies, and in many cases "friendship" is something that can be purchased. Bribery, which is not uncommon in Mexico (it is known familiarly as *la mordida*, or "the bite"), reinforces the Mexican class system. The middle class, like the economic elites, can afford to pay; workers usually have to rely on union leaders to distribute such rewards; landless rural workers or recent migrants to cities have almost no means of influencing decisions.

Another drawback of the Mexican bureaucracy—one that also results from the dominance of its top layers—is the lack of continuity in policymaking. Since everyone's position depends on loyalty to superiors rather than on devotion to task or mission, an upper-level management shift will often mean a shift of an entire bureaucratic team

(*equipo*) as well. The superior who has been shifted will take his or her people along to wherever he or she is going. This disrupts not only the old bureau, by depleting it of experienced workers, but also the new one, by flooding it with bureaucrats new to its ways.

There have been recent attempts to improve the Mexican bureaucracy. One of them has been the establishment of a national school for public administration. At existing colleges, such as El Colegio de México, more courses on public administration are now being taught. The hope is that with improvements in living standards and educational opportunities, the middle levels of the Mexican bureaucracy will gradually develop a greater degree of professionalism.

(Continued from page 278)

is, by having a friend in Congress or the White House who arranged the job for you. When Jackson came into the White House, the existing jobs had been filled during previous administrations. Jackson immediately set to work firing large numbers of these holdovers and filling the positions with his own supporters. His political opponents professed to be shocked at this purge (although Jefferson had done much the same thing in 1801), but the Jacksonians justified it by reference to the old maxim "To the victor belong the spoils." Thus was born the spoils system, or "rotation of offices," as Jackson preferred to call it.

In 1881, President James A. Garfield was shot and killed by a disappointed candidate for a federal appointment. The outrage over Garfield's assassination led to a review of the spoils system and the passing of the Pendleton Act in 1883, which requires competitive written examinations for filling most appointive government positions.

The system continued under subsequent administrations. President Abraham Lincoln appointed many fellow Republicans to positions formerly held by Democrats or Whigs during James Buchanan's administraton. Although the system was criticized from time to time, it did not produce a scandal until the presidency of Ulysses S. Grant (1869–1877). Riddled with corruption, his administration created "no-show" jobs to reward political supporters, appointed incompetents to high positions, and tolerated public officials who solicited bribes. Grant, concerned about the scandals, persuaded Congress to set up a Civil Service Commission to seek better ways of making appointments. But Congress refused to fund the commission adequately, and reform was postponed until 1883 and the administration of Chester A. Arthur.

THE RISE OF THE MERIT SYSTEM

As is often the case with reform, it took a tragedy to bring it about. In 1881 Chester Arthur was vice president in the administration of President James A. Garfield. Garfield had personally interviewed one Charles J. Guiteau for a post in the diplomatic service and had turned him down. Guiteau then purchased a revolver and shot Garfield as he waited for a train in Washington's Union Station. The president died 80 days later, and Guiteau was hanged. Arthur, as the new president, championed the cause of civil service reform for a number of reasons, not least of which was the desire to take politics out of the appointments. Guiteau may have been a madman, but his reaction was sparked by the same hard feelings that most disappointed office-seekers shared. As President William Howard Taft later lamented, every White House appointment produces "nine enemies and one ingrate."[10] The way to avoid making these enemies—and to resolve the other problems associated with patronage appointments—was to fill positions by objective examinations based upon *what* people knew instead of *whom* they knew. This view was embodied in the

TABLE **11-3**

**Number of Civilian Federal Government Employees and
Percentage Under Merit Civil Service, 1816-1985**

Year	Total number of employees[a]	Percentage under merit	Year	Total number of employees[a]	Percentage under merit
1816	4,837	—	1940	1,042,420	69.7
1831	11,491	—	1947	2,111,001	80.2
1861	36,672	—	1950	1,960,708	84.5
1881	100,020	—	1955	2,397,309	83.6
1891	157,442	21.5	1960	2,398,704	85.5
1908	356,754	57.9	1965	2,527,915	85.2
1909	372,379	63.1	1970	2,981,574	82.3
1913	396,494	71.3	1972[b]	2,608,000	65.6
1919	794,271	86.6	1975	2,741,000	62.5
1925	553,045	76.6	1980	2,772,000	61.0
1930	601,319	87.9	1985	2,902,000	58.9
1935	780,582	58.3			

Dash indicates not available.

[a]Excludes employees of the Central Intelligence Agency and the National Security Agency.
[b]Under Postal Reorganization Act of 1970, U.S. Postal Service employees were changed from competitive (merit) service to excepted service.

Data source: 1816-1970: U.S. Bureau of the Census, *Historical Statistics of the U.S.* (Washington, D.C.: U.S. Government Printing Office, 1975), 1102-1103; 1972-1985: U.S. Bureau of the Census, *Statistical Abstract of the U.S., 1977,* 268, *1980,* 279, *1987,* 309. Harold W. Stanley and Richard G. Niemi, *Vital Statistics on American Politics* (Washington: Congressional Quarterly Press, 1988), pp. 218-219. Adapted with permission.

The merit system, which uses written civil service exams or other "objective" means of determining the qualifications of bureaucrats, grew enormously during the early years of this century. Its use remains high today, though "merit" levels dropped after 1970, when the U.S. Postal Service employees were excepted from it. Today, almost 60 percent of federal employees are recruited through merit, compared to 21.5 percent in 1891.

Pendleton Act (the Civil Service Act), passed by Congress in 1883. It set up a system of competitive written examinations for filling offices.

The beginnings of the merit system were modest. Only about 10 percent of all federal offices were filled by competitive examinations in the 1880s. Gradually the system spread throughout the federal government. Today most bureaucratic positions are filled through civil service examinations or agency-designed examinations not under the control of the White House. All that is left of the old spoils system are about 2,000 executive positions, fewer than there were when Jackson came to power in 1828.

THE HATCH ACT

Another measure designed to ensure a politically neutral bureaucracy was the law passed in 1939 entitled an "Act to Prevent Pernicious Political Activities." Commonly called the Hatch Act after its chief sponsor, Senator Carl Hatch of New Mexico, this statute prohibits federal civil service employees from taking an active part in elections. They may vote, but they may not campaign or raise money for any party or candidate. The Hatch Act also makes it illegal to dismiss any civil servant below cabinet or subcabinet level for partisan reasons. This law was prompted by the fear

FIGURE **11-4**

Paid Civilian Employment, Executive Branch

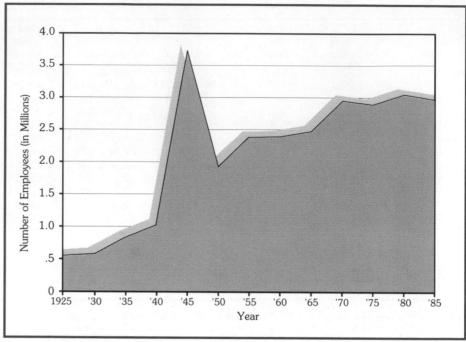

Data source: U.S. Census Bureau, *Historical Statistics of the United States, Colonial Times to 1970, Statistical Abstract of the United States,* 1976, 1980, 1987.

In the 1920s, about half a million people worked for the executive branch of the federal government. Today, the number of paid civilian employees in that branch has jumped to nearly three million. The biggest leap in the number of employees occurred during World War II, when over two million bureaucrats joined the executive branch to plan and direct the war effort.

that the growing federal bureaucracy would soon become a major political force that, because of its size, could make parties beholden to it and force them to champion measures (such as pay raises) that might not be in the public interest. Another reason was the fear that political appointees might put pressure on civil service employees to go out and campaign for the party in power. Many federal workers consider the law to be a violation of their First Amendment rights of free speech, press, and assembly, but in 1973 the Supreme Court upheld its constitutionality.[11]

THE GROWING POWER OF FEDERAL BUREAUCRATS

Although the civil service bureaucracy has been neutralized in terms of active partisanship, it plays an enormous role in American life by operating and funding programs of all kinds. As we noted earlier, the actual numbers of bureaucrats have not grown much over the past generation. Even so, if we compare the bureaucracy today to what it was in the early days of the republic, the growth has been enormous. In Andrew Jackson's day the 11,000 federal bureaucrats were housed mainly in one frame building in Washington. Today the 2.9 million federal bureaucrats occupy 470,000 buildings in the United States and other countries.

In terms of numbers, two of the biggest increases occurred during the Great

Depression of the 1930s and again during World War II. In the former period, several hundred thousand people were recruited to administer the various New Deal programs designed to help the poor and get the economy back on its feet. Then, when World War II came, hundreds of thousands more were needed to run the various defense-related programs. As Figure 11.4 shows, employment in the executive branch of the federal government doubled between 1925 and 1940, then tripled between 1940 and 1946.

The number of federal employees has remained relatively stable since the mid-1950s. But if we look at bureaucratic growth in terms of moneys disbursed and regulations issued, the increase over the past generation has been phenomenal. By 1975 the *Code of Federal Regulations*, which includes all regulations developed by the federal government and currently in force, had grown to 72,200 pages. Today it is a massive set of 50 volumes numbering hundreds of thousands of pages. As for spending, in constant (1982) dollars, federal budget outlays have increased from $395 billion in 1965 to more than $860 billion in 1989. Even leaving out defense expenditures, federal spending almost tripled in constant dollars between 1965 and 1985.[12]

The growth of spending and regulation that took off in the late 1960s became even more pronounced in the 1970s. That growth was fueled by a number of developments. We will discuss four:

1. *Expansion of New Deal Programs.* Old Age Survivors and Disability Insurance (OASDI), usually referred to today as "Social Security," was the heart of the original Social Security Act of 1935. It is by far the most popular of all the New Deal social programs, and it was greatly expanded during the 1970s. In 1970 the Social Security Administration paid out about $32 billion in benefits. By 1986 the payments totaled $194 billion. Other social programs established during the New Deal, such as Aid to Families with Dependent Children (AFDC), also grew dramatically during this period.
2. *"Great Society" programs.* This was a series of antipoverty measures passed by Congress in the 1960s under the leadership of President Lyndon Johnson. Many are still in place. They include projects like Head Start, designed to improve the education of preschoolers, and the Food Stamp program.
3. *Civil rights programs.* These also had their origins in the Johnson years. They began with the passage of the Civil Rights Act in 1964; today they include programs for blacks, Hispanics, Native Americans, and the handicapped. In the

During the 1960s, President Lyndon Johnson expanded government services and the bureaucracy by creating new programs such as Project Head Start. The president's wife, Lady Bird Johnson (third from right), was an active advocate of this program and traveled throughout the country working to improve the education of pre-schoolers.

1970s, for example, laws were passed requiring wheelchair ramps for any buildings financed by federal funds, and monies were appropriated for that purpose.

4. *Safety, consumer, and environmental regulation.* In response to pressure from various public interest groups, such as the ecology movement and the Ralph Nader organizations, Congress passed a series of laws to protect consumers, clean up the environment, and make cars safer. These laws, of course, have to be administered, which requires money and regulations.

In 1980 Ronald Reagan campaigned against this burgeoning growth of bureaucratic spending and regulation; he promised to "get government off our backs," cut back on spending and regulation, and abolish the two new cabinet departments, Energy and Education, established during the Carter administration. By the time Reagan left office in 1989, these two new departments were still intact, and a third, Veterans Affairs, had been added. Reagan succeeded in slowing down the rate of spending and regulation, but his promised "deregulation" never went very far. The reach and importance of the federal bureaucracy keep growing. We live in an age of big business, big social problems, and big demands for public service. The result is bound to be some form of big government.

POLITICAL APPOINTEES AND CAREER BUREAUCRATS

Whether or not the Reagan administration tried hard to resist the growth of bureaucracy, it did try its best to bring the bureaucracy under presidential control. *New York Times* reporter Hedrick Smith describes the process:

> The Reagan White House aggressively centralized the appointment process. It insisted on the litmus of Reaganite conservative ideology, pushed names from Reagan's conservative movement onto cabinet secretaries, and required White House political screening of all appointees. Out of roughly three thousand names for high-level presidential appointments, earlier administrations were content to review about one-tenth, the Reagan team reviewed and approved the full slate. . . . In the process they provided the White House with a political network for monitoring and managing the executive branch.[13]

Despite these efforts, the Reagan team did not succeed in making any permanent changes in the bureaucracy. That was because the vast majority of people in the bureaucracy were career bureaucrats, people who got their jobs through civil service examinations or from some other credentials unrelated to their partisan loyalties. Protected by bureaucratic rules and political alliances, and enjoying job security, these bureaucrats were relatively shielded from the ideological currents at the top of the administration. They were part of the permanent government of bureaucrats entrenched to last through several administrations. In some cases, their spirit even infected the political appointees. The late Malcolm Baldrige, Reagan's secretary of commerce, is an example. When first appointed, Baldrige was eager to implement the administration's plan to trim domestic spending, absorbing big cuts in his own department. But within a few years, according to Edwin Feulner of the conservative Heritage Foundation, "Mac Baldrige would be over there fighting for every 35 cents and trying to get more. Instead of being the President's representative to Commerce, Baldrige had become Commerce's spokesman at the cabinet table. He was there to make sure that 'by God, my guys back at Commerce don't get their ox gored.' "[14] Baldrige had become what is often called a captured appointment. In effect, he had joined the career bureaucrats. By the end of Reagan's eight years in office, most of his political appointees had either been "captured" or had quit. "The real right-wingers

"Think of it! Presidents come and go, but WE go on forever!" *Drawing by Jim Berry;* © *1976 NEA, Inc.*

who used to be around here aren't visible any more," said Andrew Feinstein, chief counsel of the House Subcommittee on Civil Service, an observation echoed by Ray Kline, president of the National Academy of Public Administration, a congressionally chartered research organization: "If you look across the board at all the many different cultures of the Federal government, you just have to say that there has been no deep penetration. If that is what the conservatives intended, it just hasn't happened."[15] In 1989 the Bush administration, more moderate and pragmatic in its leanings, made its own accommodations with the right wing of the party but generally steered closer to the center in making appointments.

Problems of the Federal Bureaucracy

Ultimately, the federal bureaucracy is supposed to serve the people, but sometimes that simple truth gets obscured. Although people criticize many aspects of the federal government's operation, three defects in particular are often mentioned: (1) red tape and waste; (2) lack of accountability; and (3) incompetence and mediocrity.

RED TAPE AND WASTE

Every year our federal bureaucracy uses 66 billion sheets of paper, enough to fill the Washington monument 11 times. This astounding amount of paperwork is generated because bureaucrats have to fill out forms for everything—from hiring new people to keeping track of expenses. Much of this paperwork is needed to satisfy legal requirements imposed by Congress. Governmental agencies must hire on the basis of merit, must observe strict accounting rules, must provide detailed information on what they are doing, and must allow for citizen access. Adding to the confusion is the competition and bureaucratic infighting that go on, often as a result of two executive agencies serving different purposes. Perhaps the most striking example of this is the Department of Agriculture's policy of subsidizing tobacco growers and the surgeon general's warnings on the link between cigarette smoking and cancer.

President Bush's "war on drugs" points to the difficulty of getting competing federal agencies to work together. Bureaucratic tensions were already building in September 1989, as President Bush prepared his address to the nation outlining his antidrug strategies. His "drug czar," William J. Bennett, was supposed to bring together all the major departments and agencies in a coordinated effort. Part of the problem was that key units of the bureaucracy had different priorities. The Justice Department favors punitive approaches, but the State Department tends to be more interested in building alliances with other countries than in punishing them for not doing enough about drugs in their countries. The Pentagon, which was supposed to play a role in the drug war, is uninterested in military efforts that might fail and make it look ineffectual. Infighting also resulted from duplication of effort. The Customs Service and the Drug Enforcement Administration, both charged with intercepting drugs coming into the country, were fighting each other to see who got the most funds.[16] "Too often," said Bush in his address to the nation, federal bureaucrats have acted "as if their part of the problem—whether fighting drug production, or drug smuggling, or drug demand—was the only problem. But turf battles won't win this war. Teamwork will."[17] Achieving this teamwork will be a major challenge in the war on drugs.

Conflict and duplication help generate wasteful government expenditures. In 1982 a presidential commission headed by industrialist J. Peter Grace undertook a major study of government waste. At the end of 1983 the Grace Commission (formally known as the President's Private Sector Survey on Cost Control) issued a series of reports detailing the extent of government waste. Here are some examples:

- Pentagon purchasing procedures resulted in payments of $91 for a 3-cent screw, $100 for a 25-cent breather cap, $114 for a 9-cent battery, and $511 for a 60-cent light bulb.
- The Department of Energy has eight different accounting and payroll systems, each with a different monthly closing day, which results in unnecessary costs estimated at $12 million annually.
- Mismanaged mailing lists result in an unnecessary $32 million being spent every year. The Grace Commission cited the example of one addressee who received 29 copies of the same government publication; since it was a periodical, that meant 29 copies of *each issue*.
- The federal government spends $12 billion each year on computers, but it sometimes takes four years to acquire one because of the involved internal approval process. What is more, many of them cannot interface (communicate with each other); the Department of Health and Human Services has 10 different brands, all incompatible.

The Grace Commission proposed 2,478 measures that could realize savings of $424 billion in the first three years of implementation. What has happened to these proposals? So far, not much. They have met with stiff resistance from key interest groups that benefit from current levels of spending. One writer summed up the situation as follows:

> Those who stand to benefit by the spending are a concentrated, coherent, organized group whose members have a large vested interest in the contest and therefore fight effectively; but those who benefit from cuts are the general public, who are diffuse, unorganized, not a coherent group, and therefore virtually unrepresented on the political battlefield.[18]

It should also be added that the first group has influential friends—in Congress, in the press, in the public, and among the bureaucrats themselves. This brings us to the next problem, which is the lack of any central authority or direction.

LACK OF ACCOUNTABILITY

The ideal bureaucracy is a chain of command: Orders are issued at the top and get transferred downward through the layers of the bureaucracy, at each level becoming more concrete. They emerge at the bottom as specific directives to be implemented.

FIGURE **11-5**

287

Problems of the
Federal
Bureaucracy

An Example of an Iron Triangle

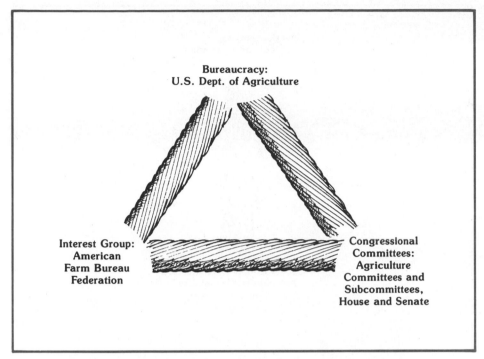

An iron triangle is a three-way, mutually beneficial power relationship between an executive bureau, a committee or subcommittee in Congress, and an interest group. Above is depicted an iron triangle related to agriculture.

Although this may sound authoritarian (armies are usually run like this), it actually fits very well with the theory of democracy. We elect a president, whom we hold responsible for campaign promises. The president then implements those promises by giving orders to the bureaucrats, who carry them out. If something goes wrong, we know who to blame: the president. As Harry Truman used to say, "The buck stops here."

The theory rests on the assumption that the bureaucracy *does* carry out the president's orders. But does it? Truman did not think so. He thought that his successor, Dwight D. Eisenhower, with his strict military background, would become easily frustrated when his orders were not followed. Sure enough, when Eisenhower came into office, he began to feel some of this frustration. "The President still feels," an Eisenhower aide remarked in 1958, "that when he's decided something, that *ought* to be the end of it . . . and when it bounces back undone or done wrong, he tends to react with shocked surprise."[19] Every modern president has encountered this intractability. The reason for it is not simply that bureaucrats are stubborn or perverse. Its roots lie in the fact (already mentioned earlier in the chapter) that *federal bureaucrats serve more than one master.* They serve the president, but they also serve Congress. And they serve other masters as well, including interest groups.

The three-way relationship between bureaucrats, interest groups, and congressional committees has been studied for a number of years.[20] It has been depicted as an <u>iron triangle</u> (see Figure 11.5). The three sides represent, respectively, an executive bureau, an oversight committee in Congress, and a client group.

The iron triangle is a useful metaphor for explaining the way things used to work in J. Edgar Hoover's era, but it may need some updating. Since the end of the 1960s

FIGURE **11-6**

An Example of an Issue Network

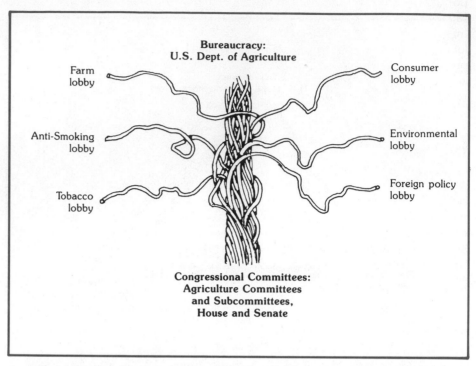

If we imagine an iron triangle as three individuals connected together by telephone in a conference call, then an issue network is very similar, except that the telephone cable connecting the three callers has become frayed. Strands of cable now shoot out in all directions, enabling large numbers of people to tap into the conversation. This is not a conference call any more, but a party line. In fact, it's a kind of free-for-all: Everybody in the neighborhood is listening, talking, kibbitzing, arguing, and shouting. Telephones are constantly being picked up and hung up as new parties get on the line and old ones get off.

a number of new interest groups have become involved in bureaucratic politics, and this fact has modified the iron triangle. Political scientist Hugh Heclo prefers to picture the new relationships as issue networks.[21] Today a wide variety of groups, some of them at odds with one another, may be interested in what a particular government bureau is doing. Look what happened to Hoover's FBI. Instead of a three-way conversation between Hoover, "his" congressman, and their friends, we now have a cacophony of voices. There are police associations, and there is the American Civil Liberties Union, concerned about FBI snooping and break-ins. There are civil rights groups wondering how many blacks are employed by the FBI (few were in Hoover's day) and whether or not the FBI is advancing or impeding civil rights. Then there are feminists and pro-choicers who wonder if the FBI is pursuing those who bomb abortion clinics. Above all there is the press, which serves as an echo chamber for all these interests. Not much is private or confidential anymore, as it used to be in Hoover's day.

Heclo contends that issue networks have produced a new type of bureaucrat. It is no longer enough to cultivate the friendship of a few powerful allies, for authority is now more diffused in Washington. As a rule, then, it is unwise for the bureaucrat to be too closely associated with a single point of view on the issues.[22] The smart bureaucrat knows how to dance around a bit, displaying knowledge of the issues but not tilting too obviously toward one position or another.

But are dancing bureaucrats any better than stolid, Hoover-type bureaucrats? From the president's standpoint, the answer is no. Presidents like to have bureaucrats who do not play politics and who content themselves with carrying out presidential policies. What is the best arrangement from the public's standpoint? It is not easy to say. People who are part of a well-organized interest group with a Washington office may be better off today than ever, for the bureaucracy is extremely sensitive to lobbying pressures. On the other hand, people who think that a popularly elected president deserves a decent chance of getting his policies implemented should be concerned about iron triangles and issue networks. How can we hold the president responsible to the voters if the bureaucracy is not responsible to the president?

INCOMPETENCE AND MEDIOCRITY

Another problem with today's federal bureaucracy is how extremely difficult it is to get rid of bureaucrats who perform poorly. Sometimes performance is spectacularly poor, as with employees who drink or suffer from disabling emotional problems. More often, however, it is simply mediocre—a routine, spiritless performance. Editor and author Charles Peters says that the primary goal of the typical Washington bureaucrat "is not to serve you, the citizen of the United States":

> His primary goal is to survive, get promoted, get those annual increases. If you say, "Find out what excites a Washington bureaucrat," it is any threat to his parking space. Real passion is produced at those times.[23]

That incompetence and mediocrity in the federal bureaucracy are protected—and thus rewarded—is partly due to our civil service system. During the heyday of the spoils system in the nineteenth century, there was no legal block to firing. Indeed, as we mentioned earlier, there were mass firings every time a new administration took office. Then came the Pendleton Act of 1883. Bureaucrats were to be hired by competitive examinations. The corollary was that they could no longer be fired without sufficient cause, which was determined by formal complaints and hearings. Over the years the layers of protection grew thicker and thicker. Everything became more legalized; the employee now had to be given "due process of law." There were cross-examinations, lawyers, and appeals.

Even by the 1920s it was becoming difficult to fire a bureaucrat. Hoover demanded exemption from civil service laws as a condition for taking over the FBI in 1924 so that he could sweep out the dead wood and rebuild the bureau. True, Hoover was often eccentric and arbitrary in his hiring and firing practices, but at least he was in control of his agency. By 1960 civil service employee protections had become even denser. In the late 1950s federal judges began ruling that dismissed federal workers who had exhausted all their executive-branch appeals could go to court. The courts then added still more protections, further strengthening the "due process" rights of employees. Result: We now have a system that makes it almost impossible to fire an incompetent! An agency must first give the employee 30 days' notice of its intention to do so. The employee may then take his or her case to a regional branch of the Merit Systems Protection Board (MSPB); this process takes four months. If the branch board upholds the firing, the employee may then go to the MSPB's national headquarters in Washington. If he or she loses the case there, there is still the court system. All this requires reams of paperwork, countless hours of work, and substantial expenditures of taxpayers' money.

Agency heads find it so difficult to fire unproductive or problem employees that they often look for other ways to get rid of these people. They may hire new people to duplicate their tasks; try to transfer them to another area; send them off for a year to special "training programs" or "study projects" known as "turkey farms"; or try to persuade them to retire early, promising them glowing letters of recommendation. Failing all this, they may make the working conditions miserable in a final attempt to drive them out. Ultimately, many agency heads and cabinet chiefs simply resign themselves to the situation. "You see that happening over and over again," says Charles Peters, "with Cabinet members who come to Washington and who think they're going to do all these wonderful things. And within a matter of six months they become a prisoner of the Washington establishment."[24]

SUGGESTED REFORMS

For the complex of problems discussed here—red tape and waste, lack of accountability, and the protection of incompetence and mediocrity—there is probably no single solution. Various remedies have been proposed, which we will discuss briefly.

Ombudsmen and Whistle-Blowers.   In 1809 Sweden began experimenting with an ombudsman, an officer appointed to investigate citizen complaints about bureaucratic incompetence and corruption. An ombudsman has no power but issues reports to the governing organs on the validity of the charges brought by citizens and may recommend corrective action. The system has worked well in Sweden, and the idea has gained support here. A number of states and cities have ombudsmen, as do a variety of institutions, including some universities. There have been various proposals for installing an ombudsman's office in the federal bureaucracy. So far, nothing has come of them, in part because of several unresolved questions: To whom would the ombudsman report? Who would staff the office? Could it be used to cover up problems? Would it become a giant bureaucracy itself?

At various times unofficial, self-appointed ombudsmen have appeared. Called whistle-blowers by the press, they are federal bureaucrats who "go public" with stories about abuses in their bureaus. The most celebrated of these whistle-blowers was a man named A. Ernest Fitzgerald, a $32,000-a-year management analyst in the Pentagon. In 1968 Fitzgerald alerted Congress and the public to a $2 billion cost overrun in the production of the C-5A transport plane being made by Lockheed Aircraft. After his congressional testimony Fitzgerald was suddenly transferred to Thailand to review the construction of a bowling alley, then discharged from the Air Force in 1970.[25] After a four-year fight, he was reinstated with back pay, but he was never returned to his old position.

While some whistle-blowers are simply troublemakers or people with unjustified grudges against their superiors, others are authentic, like Fitzgerald, and deserve protection. The question is how to do it? In 1978 Congress created an independent Office of Special Counsel to investigate complaints of harassment against whistle-blowers. Its performance has been uneven at best because it forces whistle-blowers into making public charges, which they would prefer not to do.[26] The question of how to protect whistle-blowers against reprisals warrants a fresh examination by Congress.

Pay More, Get Better Bureaucrats.   Whistle-blowers are a rare breed. Not many bureaucrats can be expected to expose publicly wrongdoing in their agencies. But the public has a right to expect bureaucrats at least to perform their own tasks with the requisite knowledge and competence. For this we need to attract qualified personnel. There is some evidence that this is becoming increasingly difficult, both in the upper and middle levels of the bureaucracy. In the summer of 1989, after six months in office, President Bush was still having trouble filling high-level administration positions. The shortage was interfering with important administration goals, such as restructuring the wasteful management procedures in the Pentagon and cleaning up nuclear weapons plants. Some administration officials despaired of ever finding

"Whistle-blower" Ernest Fitzgerald worked as a cost expert in the Pentagon until he exposed the skyrocketing costs of the production of the C-5A plane. As a direct result of his actions, he was removed from his position, transferred abroad, and later discharged from the Air Force. Sometimes it takes a whistle-blower to expose abuses of power in federal bureaus, but given the experiences of past whistle-blowers, few people are likely to assume this role without protection from Congress. In 1989 Congress passed a new law designed to provide a degree of protection.

TABLE 11-4

291

Problems of the
Federal
Bureaucracy

Pay: Public v. Private

Occupation	Federal	Private sector
File clerk GS-1 (entry level)	$ 9,811–$12,275	$ 11,461
Chemist GS-5 (entry level)	15,118– 19,654	25,314
Secretary GS-5 (mid-level)	15,118– 19,654	19,504
Engineer GS-5 (entry level)	15,118– 19,654	29,222
Computer operator GS-6 (mid-level)	16,851– 21,480	22,682
Systems analyst GS-9 (entry level)	22,907– 29,783	31,130
Chief accountant GS-14 (senior level)	46,679– 60,683	88,223
Engineer GS-15 (top level)	54,907– 71,377	85,725
Attorney GS-15 (top level)	54,907– 71,377	110,489

Data source: Bureau of Labor Statistics. Reprinted from the *New York Times* with permission.

> Shown here are the average annual salaries in 1988 for selected federal civil servants and private-sector employees in jobs involving comparable training and responsibility. Federal figures describe a range, starting salary to highest available salary, in job categories from GS-1 to GS-15. Private-sector figures are national averages based on a federal survey. Pensions and other benefits are not included.

enough qualified people. One Pentagon official said, "We're approaching the point where we're going to have to settle for mediocrity."[27] Many reasons were cited for this delay in finding qualified bureaucrats. There were complaints that the FBI background checks were taking too long, to which FBI officials replied that their job was made burdensome by demands for more intensive screening. Some excellent candidates from the private sector turned down administration job offers because of the new government ethics rules, which, among other things, would ban them for a year from lobbying the federal agency that had employed them. But one of the greatest obstacles to finding good men and women may not be the regulations but the salary. As Table 11.4 shows, the salaries for jobs in the federal bureaucracy tend to lag far behind those in the private sector.

In the 1970s political scientist Hugh Heclo suggested the creation of a new elite corps of high-level bureaucrats who would be well paid and expected to play a major leadership role in the bureaucracy. These new leaders would not get their jobs simply by fitting into a particular civil service classification.

> Instead, individuals would be appointed to a new Federal Service on the basis of their nonpartisan qualifications for high-level government work and would carry a rank and salary dependent on their individual record of performance. . . .[28]

The Carter administration liked this idea and persuaded Congress to implement it. The Civil Service Reform of 1978 set up a Senior Executive Service (SES), composed of about 7,000 high-level bureaucrats. They could be hired, fired, and

The Federal Executive Institute, housed in a converted hotel in Charlottesville, Virginia, conducts courses for the most promising of the career bureaucrats in the Senior Executive Service of the federal government. They are given special leaves from their jobs in order to attend four-week sessions taught by university professors and public officials. The institute, which includes dormitory rooms in the former hotel, hosts 68 executives at each of the nine sessions held each year. The $4,700-per-student cost of each session is paid for by the federal government.

The institute teaches 15 different courses on a variety of topics, from studies of the American constitutional system to work-group effectiveness. The courses are designed to learn about the operation of the federal government and to develop leadership skills and potentials. "Our emphasis is less on moving papers than on critical thinking, problem-solving, strategic thinking for the government with a large view," said Pamela Gwin, assistant director for Academic Programs. The curriculum uses a variety of approaches, from lectures to group discussions and role-playing. At the end of the 1980s the institute began a major overhaul of its curriculum, which had been criticized as mired in the "touchy-feelie" styles of the late 1960s, when the institute was inaugurated. The directors of the institute also began improving the physical plant, which had become seedy and unkempt. The changes, at an anticipated cost of $4 million, were designed to make its classrooms and dorms more livable. One of the directors insisted, however, that the changes would be made with the taxpayers in mind. "It will not be a posh hotel," he said, "but it will be very comfortable." *(Adapted from "Molding a Higher Cut of Bureaucrat,"* New York Times, *Aug. 30, 1989, P. A18.)*

transferred more easily than those not in this corps, and they would be eligible for large cash bonuses on the basis of excellent job performance. In practice, however, SES has not been very successful in creating a new spirited leadership cadre. Because of federal budgetary problems, the bonuses have turned out to be very slight, and it has become almost impossible to weed out mediocrities, since members cannot be transferred against their will and hardly any receive unsatisfactory job ratings.

The Reagan administration, which tended to downplay the role of the federal bureaucracy, did not much care about creating incentives within it, but there are signs that the Bush administration is more concerned. To make some of the pay scales more competitive with those of the private sector, in July 1989 President Bush proposed pay increases for senior employees and a new category for highly specialized workers, such as doctors, that would raise their pay to an annual $124,000. Some observers regard these moves as long overdue. In constant dollars the salaries in the higher reaches of the federal bureaucracy are lower today than they were in the 1960s (see Figure 11.7).

But there are reasons to doubt whether or not higher salaries will make for better government. In 1986 congressional researchers were unable to find any systematic empirical evidence linking low federal salaries with the erosion of services.[29]

Sunset Laws. Some critics think the basic problem is that we have too many government organizations and agencies that no longer serve any good purpose. Their solution is to enact sunset laws. These are discussed in chapter 18 in the course of considering how Congress might make its workload easier, but they also have relevance here. A sunset law is a law that creates an agency with a limited life span. Unless Congress renews the law after a certain time period, it automatically ceases to exist. Some reformers think these laws might prevent agencies from hardening into permanent institutions that survive their usefulness and waste taxpayers' money.

FIGURE **11-7**

293

Problems of the
Federal
Bureaucracy

The Pay of Upper-Level Bureaucrats

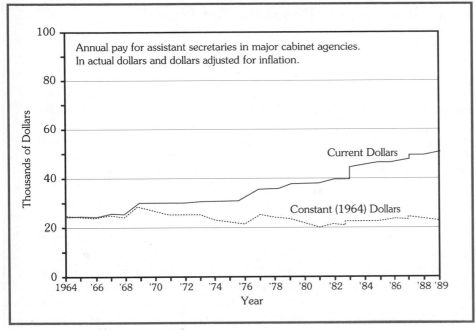

Annual pay for assistant secretaries in major cabinet agencies.
In actual dollars and dollars adjusted for inflation.

Current Dollars

Constant (1964) Dollars

Source: New York Times, July 23, 1989, sec IV, p. 4. Reprinted with permission.

In current dollars, the pay of upper-level federal bureaucrats (assistant secretaries in major cabinet agencies) has been steadily rising since the 1960s. But when adjusted for inflation, their salaries have sagged slightly since 1968.

They might also prevent the barnacle-like growth of interest groups around an agency. About 25 states have experimented with sunset laws, and several federal statutes have sunset provisions. So far, however, they have not been very successful. Once employees realize that the sun might go down on their agency (and their jobs), they mobilize to raise support in Congress for continuing the agency.[30] Still, the idea of sunset legislation seems to make sense, and it may be that adjustments can be made to correct the practical defects.

Deregulation and Decentralization. Some critics think that the problems of bureaucracy really stem from one basic cause: Over the past two decades the federal government has taken on too many responsibilities. Today it does everything, from specifying the type of toilet seats to be used in factories to laying down standards for high-school athletic fields. Perhaps it has gotten too deeply involved in regulation. In this chapter's Taking Sides section (on the following page), Barry Crickmer makes the case for deregulation, while Susan and Martin Tolchin argue against it.

Another means of reducing the federal government's administrative responsibility is to delegate some of it to the state and local levels. This approach has long been a goal of conservatives; part of the motivation behind President Reagan's "new federalism" proposals (see chapter 3) was to turn over parts of the welfare system to states and localities. Liberals have long been suspicious of this idea, fearing that it may result in massive cutbacks. In recent years, however, liberals have been reconsidering their views on state and local government in view of the modernization that has taken place over the past 20 years. *(Continued on page 295)*

Does the Government Regulate Too Much?

YES Barry Crickmer

Based upon Barry Crickmer, "Regulation: How Much is Enough?" *Nation's Business* (March 1980), pp. 26-30+.

Crickmer, a senior editor of *Nation's Business*, thinks that well-meaning regulations have done the nation more harm than good. He cites a number of examples of what he considers either worthless or harmful regulations: drug regulations that have kept life-saving remedies off the market for years, auto safety regulations that have not reduced death or injury but have raised repair costs and wasted gasoline, and silly or destructive regulations imposed by the Consumer Products Safety Commission.

Crickmer contends that the news media, in pursuit of dramatic stories, have exaggerated the danger to our safety and environment; this in turn has played into the hands of zealots who promise government panaceas for imaginary crises. He acknowledges that genuine problems exist but suggests that the forces of the marketplace will correct most of them. According to Crickmer, it is not profitable to operate unsafe factories or sell unsafe products. He agrees that air and water pollution may warrant government intervention but argues that intervention must be cautious and moderate. We must not expect perfection. Zero defects and zero pollution equal zero profits, zero economic growth, and maximum government intervention according to Crickmer. We must balance and trade off one good against another.

NO Susan and Martin Tolchin

Based upon Susan J. Tolchin and Martin Tolchin, *Dismantling America* (Boston: Houghton Mifflin, 1983).

Political scientist Susan Tolchin and her husband, Martin Tolchin, a *New York Times* reporter, contend that government regulation has been turned into "the national whipping boy," blamed for everything from low profits to foreign competition. Egged on by the Reagan administration, industry officials have successfully lobbied for deregulation. What took years to build is being rapidly dismantled, to the detriment of the nation. Industry now has the power to alter genes, invade privacy, wreck the environment, and endanger lives. "Only the government has the power to create and enforce the social regulations that protect citizens from the awesome consequences of technology run amuck," say the Tolchins.

The Tolchins cite examples of successful government regulation. Because the drug thalidomide was banned in this country, Americans were spared the horrible birth defects it caused in Europe between 1957 and 1961. Government regulation also helped revive the Great Lakes in the late 1970s after their near-death from years of industrial dumping. Another success story is the progress made by the government in forcing industry to clean up the air: Sulfur emissions have been reduced 17 percent since 1972. Now all this progress is in danger of being reversed.

The Tolchins admit that government regulators have sometimes overstepped their bounds, but they contend that occasional excesses do not justify the wholesale dismantling of the regulatory structure. In its effect, such a campaign amounts to an attempt to "dismantle America."

(See Taking Sides Postscript on facing page)

Postscript

Note that both the Tolchins and Crickmer concede some ground to their opponents in the argument. Crickmer admits that market forces are not always sufficient to right the wrongs committed by industry. The Tolchins agree that sometimes federal regulators get out of hand. The debate, then, turns on degree. How much regulation is too much? How much deregulation would hurt America? Perhaps a consensus can be shaped on these questions.

Regulation and deregulation have been much studied in recent years. Kenneth J. Meier's *Regulation: Politics, Bureaucracy, and Economics* (St. Martin's Press, 1985) develops a conceptual framework for studying regulatory policy, then uses it to survey the process in several areas, including agriculture, the environment, and the workplace. The obstacles to compliance are the main focus of Herbert Kaufman's *Red Tape: Its Origin, Uses, and Abuses* (Brookings Institution, 1977). Charles T. Goodsell develops *The Case for Bureaucracy* (Chatham House, 1985) in a well-argued book that he frankly calls "a public administration polemic."

(Continued from page 293)

More Presidential Control. The president is elected to run the administration. Yet the bureaucracy often goes its own way and plays politics with Congress and interest groups. The president can do very little about that, since only a small number of bureaucrats are under direct presidential control. The rest are protected by complicated civil service rules. This has prompted one critic of the bureaucracy, Charles Peters (whom we quoted earlier, complaining about spiritless bureaucrats), to make a radical proposal. Peters wants to bring back the spoils system:

> Now let me give you my final, what most people regard as my lunatic, theory. . . . What I want to do is take about half the civil service jobs and, as they become open, instead of replacing them with another civil servant, make them available for political patronage appointments so that people from out in the country can come here. [Appointments] would be limited to 2½ to 5 years.[31]

Peters contends his plan would do three things. First, "you would get a more dedicated group of people affecting the policies"; these political appointees would be in tune with the president's goals. Second, "you would bring a different personality type into the civil service. . . . [Instead of lifetime appointees], you'd have people who were definitely going back home after 2½ to 5 years. They couldn't be concerned with security." Third, "these people would go back home knowing what Washington was like, knowing what kind of actions on their congressman's part it was important for them to support."[32]

Peters's proposal is thought-provoking, but its critics may not be altogether unjust in characterizing it as lunatic. If adopted, it would risk bringing back precisely what the Pendleton Act of 1883 was intended to abolish: rampant corruption. In the old days of patronage appointments, jobs were given to people who lacked qualifications. Some job-holders contented themselves with collecting their salaries without working; others worked, but badly; still others made themselves available for bribes.

Another danger of replacing career bureaucrats with political appointees is that of creating a monster political machine. The Internal Revenue Service (IRS), located in the Treasury Department, is a good example. With 123,000 employees, the IRS is the largest tax-collection system in the world, pulling an annual $1 trillion into the Treasury. It makes crucial decisions on what organizations can be tax-exempt, decides whose tax returns should be audited, can impose stiff civil penalties that are difficult to appeal, and can decide to refer criminal cases to the Justice Department. Enormous discretion is left in the hands of IRS bureaucrats, and some of them undoubtedly abuse that discretion. But would it help if all the tax bureaucrats were put under direct presidential control? The history of presidential use of the IRS is not reassuring. President Franklin D. Roosevelt used his influence to reward friends and punish enemies. In 1944 he persuaded the agency to call off a tax investigation involving a loyal Roosevelt supporter, then-congressman Lyndon B. Johnson; a decade earlier, Roosevelt forced the IRS to press tax fraud charges against former Republican treasury secretary Andrew Mellon, even though IRS auditors knew that Mellon was innocent.[33] President John F. Kennedy also used the IRS for partisan purposes by calling for special tax audits of right-wing fundamentalist organizations that had criticized his administration; several of the groups subsequently lost their tax-exempt status.[34] President Richard M. Nixon followed this tradition by placing his own loyal lieutenants in the IRS bureaucracy, seeking from them tax breaks for his friends, and, for his foes, submitting an "enemies list" to the IRS for special tax auditing.[35] To their credit, it was the career bureaucrats in the IRS who tried to resist these pressures.

Hug a Bureaucrat

Whatever its imperfections, the federal bureaucracy plays a vital role in modern America. Gone are the days of Andrew Jackson, when the bureaucracy could all be housed in a single two-story building. Modern problems and expectations are too great for that. If we want protection from tainted meat, harmful chemicals, quack medicines, filthy air and water, nuclear waste, interstate criminals, racial discrimination, unsafe cars, and all the other threats to our lives and our well-being, then we need bureaucracy.

The bureaucracy has not only been needed, it has performed—it has done its job. Not perfectly, not by any means, but the survey research done so far shows that most Americans who have dealt with it are satisfied (although they imagine that *others* are dissatisfied).[36] There are good reasons for this general satisfaction. As we

Safety experts see the air bag as the best possible way to protect drivers and passengers in an accident. After a twenty-year fight with automakers, the federal government has mandated that by the early 1990s all automobiles sold domestically must be equipped with either automatic front seat belts or air bags.

noted earlier in the chapter, bureaucrats perform a variety of vital functions, from delivering our mail to investigating crime. Political scientist Charles Goodsell elaborates:

> Bureaucracies exist for the enforcement of civil rights, promotion of minority employment, alleviation of urban poverty, protection of migrant workers, education of pre-school blacks, safeguarding of the environment, advancement of solar energy, enhancement of worker safety, promotion of labor unions, and receipt of consumer complaints. Very few causes are completely without an administrative spokesman.[37]

Our much-maligned federal bureaucracy has done much good. The Consumer Products Safety Commission's regulations on childproof caps on medicine bottles have significantly reduced accidents and deaths; Federal Trade Commission rules mandating greater competition among optometrists have lowered prices on eyeglasses. The list could go on and on.[38] As Goodsell remarks, the bureaucracy should not be viewed as some imaginary *they*, but as "collective action in our behalf."[39] In a very real sense, then, the bureaucracy is *ours* and exists *for* us.

Reflections

This chapter began by considering the conflict between J. Edgar Hoover and Attorney General Robert Kennedy. On an organization chart, the attorney general, head of the Justice Department, was Hoover's superior. In point of fact, Hoover ran his shop in his own way from the time he first took over the FBI directorship in 1924. Previous attorneys general and five presidents had left him alone. Robert Kennedy was determined to change these arrangements. He made some inroads—in the process infuriating Hoover—but in the end he failed. Hoover continued in full command of his FBI, and it remained an institution largely outside the control of the attorney general, at least until Hoover died.

It is hard to think of any other bureaucrat who stayed on as long as Hoover did or who had his combination of resources for resisting control—a near-legendary reputation, powerful allies, and, of course, his files on politicians. Although Hoover is an extreme case, to some extent the federal bureaucracy is rife with independence. In theory, bureaucracy is a pyramid. The elite at the top give the orders, which filter down through successive layers until they are translated into particular commands at the bottom level. The German sociologist Max Weber said that a true bureaucracy is marked by hierarchy, specialization, and the rule of law. Weber would agree that when the president says, "Do this"—provided he has the authority to say it—it gets done. In practice, this often does not happen. Why?—because the U.S. bureaucracy is very complicated, because its rules are malleable, because it is divided into federal and state levels, because it contracts out much of its work to private corporations, and because it serves more than one master.

Our bureaucracy resembles less a pyramid than an old Victorian house with many rooms and stories, plus a few strange-looking extensions. It has regular cabinet agencies and agencies within the Executive Office of the President, but it also has a number of independent agencies beyond direct control of the president. Moreover, even cabinet agencies have ties with interest groups and congressional committees, ties that often conflict with their loyalty to the president. These ties have been variously depicted as iron triangles and issue networks. Outside ties make the bureaucracy responsive to pressures, but they also create confusion, irresponsibility, and wasteful expenditures.

How can we reform the bureaucracy? It will not be easy, in part because we do not all agree on what constitutes reform. Charles Peters wants to bring back some elements of patronage, hoping thereby to make the bureaucracy more responsible to the public. Would this be reform—or retrogression? It has its dangers. However, the present system, which protects mediocrities and time-servers, also poses dangers. Then there are proposals for an ombudsman, for sunset laws, for deregulation, and for giving more responsibility to state and local governments. All these proposals need careful weighing, for reforms often bring unintended results.

Perhaps we have stressed too much the dark side of our federal bureaucracy, its problems and its pathologies. There is much to be said on the positive side. The bureaucracy is flawed, but it still delivers a remarkable range of goods and services, from food stamps to airline safety regulations, and it does so with a reasonable degree of honesty. It has adapted itself to the giant increase in government programs that began with Lyndon Johnson's Great Society in the 1960s. These are real accomplishments.

Some of the bureaucracy's exasperating features actually may be needed at times. Intractability, for example. When the president gives an order, there is no certainty that it will be carried out. But perhaps some orders should not be obeyed. When Richard Nixon was in the White House, one of his advisers concocted an elaborate scheme for domestic spying; it included bugging, burglary, and mail-opening. Nixon was all for the plan, but because of J. Edgar Hoover's objections, it was never put into effect. When the bureaucracy serves as a check on such dangerous, ill-conceived schemes, its very intractability becomes a virtue. James Madison, who advocated checks and balances, never thought of the bureaucracy as a check on presidential ambition, but he might approve of it today. If, as Madison warned, "enlightened statesmen will not always be at the helm," then—at times—it may be necessary to have people down in the engine room jamming the machinery.

Notes

1. Quoted by Robert F. Kennedy in Pierre Salinger and Sander Vanocur, eds., *A Tribute to John F. Kennedy* (Chicago: Encyclopaedia Britannica, Inc., 1964), p. 160.

2. Remarks at Alfa Club, Washington, D.C., Jan. 21, 1961, in Bill Adler, ed., *The Kennedy Wit* (New York: Bantam Books, 1965), p. 104, and compare with Theodore C. Sorensen, *Kennedy* (New York: Harper & Row, 1965), p. 268.

3. Richard G. Powers, *Secrecy and Power: The Life of J. Edgar Hoover* (New York: The Free Press, 1987), p. 355.

4. Arthur M. Schlesinger, Jr., *Robert Kennedy and His Times* (Boston: Houghton Mifflin, 1978), p. 172.

5. Ralph de Toledano, *J. Edgar Hoover: The Man in His Time* (New Rochelle, NY: Arlington House, 1973), p. 300.

6. Max Weber, "Bureaucracy," in H. H. Gerth and C. Wright Mills, *From Max Weber: Essays in Sociology* (New York: Oxford University Press, 1946), p. 196.

7. A. Lee Fritschler, *Smoking and Politics: Policymaking and the Federal Bureaucracy*, 3rd ed. (Englewood Cliffs, NJ: Prentice-Hall, 1983), p. 112.

8. Fritschler, p. 112.

9. For a critical treatment of this practice, see Daniel Guttman and Barry Willner, *The Shadow Government* (New York: Pantheon Books, 1976).

10. Quoted in Emmet John Hughes, *The Living Presidency* (New York: Penguin Books, 1973), p. 195.

11. *Civil Service Commission v. National Association of Letter Carriers, AFL-CIO*, 413 U.S. 548 (1973).

12. U.S. Bureau of the Census, *Statistical Abstract of the United States, 1988* (Washington: U.S. Government Printing Office, 1987), No. 472, p. 294.

13. Hedrick Smith, *The Power Game: How Washington Works* (New York: Random House, 1988), p. 102.

14. Quoted in Philip Longman, "Reagan's Disappearing Bureaucrats," *New York Times Magazine*, Feb. 14, 1988, p. 56.

15. Longman, p. 45.

16. Richard L. Berke, "Disunity is Feared As Bush Maps War on Drugs in U.S.," *New York Times*, Sept. 5, 1989, p. 1.

17. Text of President's Speech on National Drug Control Strategy, *New York Times*, Sept. 6, 1989, p. B6.

18. Peter Samuel, "Battling the Budget Bulge—Gracefully," *Reason*, May 1984, p. 36.

19. Quoted in Richard E. Neustadt, *Presidential Power* (New York: John Wiley & Sons, 1962), p. 9.

20. See J. Leiper Freeman, *The Political Process* (New York: Random House, 1965) and Douglas Cater, *Power in Washington* (New York: Vintage Books, 1964).

21. Hugh Heclo, "Issue Networks and the Executive Establishment," in Anthony King, ed., *The New American Political System* (Washington: American Enterprise Institute, 1978), pp. 87-124.

22. Heclo in *The New American Political System*, p. 106.

23. Charles Peters in an interview "Tragedy of the Beltway Syndrome" in *Insight*, Sept. 30, 1985, p. 17.

24. Peters, p. 16.

25. Congressional Quarterly, *The Power of the Pentagon* (Washington: Congressional Quarterly, Inc., 1972), p. 88.

26. Hedrick Smith, *The Power Game: How Washington Works* (New York: Random House, 1988), p. 165.

27. Andrew Rosenthal, "It's Loneliest at the Top of the Bureaucracy," *New York Times*, July 23, 1989, Sec. IV, p. 4.

28. Heclo, *A Government of Strangers: Executive Politics in Washington* (Washington: The Brookings Institution, 1977), p. 249.

29. Robert D. Hershey, Jr., "The Civil Service: Doubts from Within and Without," *New York Times*, July 23, 1989, Sec. IV, p. 4.

30. Kenneth J. Meier, *Regulation: Politics, Bureaucracy, and Economics* (New York: St. Martin's Press, 1985), p. 296.

31. Peters, p. 17.

32. Peters, p. 17.

33. David Burnham, "The Abuse of Power: Misuse of the IRS," *New York Times Magazine*, Sept. 3, 1989, pp. 52, 58.

34. Bob Kuttner, "The Taxing Trials of the IRS," *New York Times Magazine*, Jan. 6, 1974, p. 66.

35. Kuttner, p. 66.

36. Charles T. Goodsell, *The Case for Bureaucracy*, 2nd ed. (Chatham, NJ: Chatham House Publishers, Inc., 1985), pp. 139, 156; Roberta L. Kahn et al., "Americans Love Their Bureaucrats," in Francis E. Rourke, ed., *Bureaucratic Power in National Policy Making*, 4th ed. (Boston: Little, Brown and Company, 1986), pp. 285, 290.

37. Goodsell, p. 138.

38. Meier, p. 4.

39. Goodsell, p. 149.

12

The Federal Judiciary

He was tall, lanky, and not very particular about his **The Midnight Appointments**
clothing. Stories used to circulate about people mistaking
him for a menial worker or a servant. Except for almost frightening jet-
black eyes, there was nothing in his appearance that caught one's
attention. But on February 24, 1803, John Marshall, the 47-year-old
chief justice of the Supreme Court, delivered an opinion that left an
indelible stamp on our system of government. In the words of his
biographer Albert Beveridge, Marshall's opinion "set up a landmark in
American history so high that all the future could take bearings from it."*

*This account is drawn from the following sources: Albert J. Beveridge, *The Life of
John Marshall* (Boston and New York: Houghton Mifflin Company, 1929), II; George L.
Haskins and Herbert A. Johnson, *History of the Supreme Court of the United States*
(New York: Macmillan Publishing Co., 1981), II; Patricia C. Acheson, *The Supreme
Court: America's Judicial Heritage* (New York: Dodd, Mead & Company, 1961; Bill
Severn, *John Marshall: The Man Who Made the Court Supreme* (New York: David
McKay Company, 1969); *(Continued on facing page)*

The opinion grew out of some very bitter partisan struggles. In the election of 1800 the Federalist party, which had controlled the presidency and Congress since the adoption of the Constitution, was challenged by a new party called the Republicans (later the Democratic-Republicans). The Republican presidential choice was Thomas Jefferson, who had founded the party in the late 1790s.

The Federalists, headed by President John Adams, knew they were in trouble. The stout and rather pompous Adams lacked the charisma of his predecessor, George Washington, and during his administration serious splits developed within the party. In the election of 1800 Jefferson won the White House and carried a Republican majority into Congress.

The Federalists were appalled. To them, the Republicans were dangerous radicals—freethinkers in matters of religion, friends of the French Revolution, champions of "mobocracy." Now they were about to take over the government! Something had to be done.

The Federalists hit on an idea: They would use their remaining months in office to appoint themselves and other Federalists to judicial posts. In this way their party would survive its defeat at the polls. Someday they would make a political comeback, but in the meantime they could use the judicial power of the United States to modify the force of Republican legislation.

The Adams administration had plenty of time to carry out the plan. In those days the new administration did not take office until March 4 (this was changed by the Twentieth Amendment in 1933). Between the November election and the swearing-in of Jefferson there was a period of nearly five months, during which the Adams administration—called a lame duck administration because it was mortally wounded but still flying—could make its appointments.

The man who signed and sealed most of these appointments was Secretary of State John Marshall. Early in 1801, Marshall had himself been appointed chief justice of the Supreme Court. Now he was staying on as caretaker secretary of state. He would occupy the two posts until March 4, when James Madison, Jefferson's secretary of state, was to take office. Like Madison and Jefferson, Marshall was a Virginian. He was also a distant cousin of Thomas Jefferson. Yet he had a profound dislike for Jefferson's party. In his view, the Republicans were "divided into speculative theorists & absolute terrorists." He allowed that Jefferson was a theorist rather than a terrorist, but he suspected that most of Jefferson's comrades belonged in the latter category. The lights burned late in Marshall's office on the evening of March 3. The secretary was hard at work signing and sealing the last batch of judicial appointments. But then he mistakenly left some of them on his desk when he left the office, perhaps preoccupied with tomorrow's duties. As chief justice of the Supreme Court, he would be the one to swear in Thomas Jefferson as president of the United States.

"Today," he wrote in his diary the next morning, "the new political year commences—the new order of things begins." After administering the oath of office to his red-haired cousin, Marshall sat back to listen to Jefferson's inaugural address. Later in the day Jefferson surveyed his new quarters. As he strolled into the Department of State, he spotted the undelivered appointments lying on a table. No one knows for sure what

Leonard Baker, *John Marshall: A Life in Law* (New York: Macmillan Publishing Co., 1974); Francis N. Stites, *John Marshall: Defender of the Constitution* (Boston: Little, Brown and Company, 1981); and Robert G. McCloskey, *The American Supreme Court* (Chicago: University of Chicago Press).

happened after that. According to one report, the papers were burned in a State Department fireplace.

One of the "midnight" appointees whose commission was left on the table was a man named William Marbury. Little is known about Marbury except that he was a Federalist and was appointed a justice of the peace. He waited almost 10 months before bringing a lawsuit to force the new secretary of state, James Madison, to deliver his appointment. Marbury took his case directly to the Supreme Court and asked for a writ of mandamus, a judicial order commanding a public official to carry out some specific duty. Marbury brought his suit under Section 13 of the Judiciary Act of 1789, which authorized the Supreme Court to issue writs of mandamus "in cases warranted by the principles and usages of law." Marshall presided over a court composed of six Federalist justices. Marshall himself was the man who had signed Marbury's appointment. Could anyone doubt the outcome?

But consider the situation more carefully. Suppose Marshall had followed what we can assume were his inclinations and granted Marbury the writ. Would Madison have obeyed it? Probably not. More than likely, Jefferson would have instructed Madison to ignore it. Then what? How could the Supreme Court have forced Madison to deliver the appointment? The Court was the least respected branch of the federal government in those days. It did not even have its own building, but was housed in a shabby little committee room underneath the House of Representatives.

Marshall faced a dilemma. If he granted Marbury his writ, the order would be defied. But if Marshall bowed to the realities of the situation and refused the writ, he would be seen as caving in to the Republicans. What could he do? John Marshall delivered a three-part opinion based upon what he said were the three issues in the case. First, did Marbury have a right to his appointment as justice of the peace? Second, if he had the right, should he have a remedy for it? Third, if he had the right and deserved a remedy, should the remedy take the form Marbury wanted—a writ of mandamus? Then he answered his own questions.

First, did Marbury have a right to his commission as justice of the peace? Yes indeed, said Marshall. Sweeping his arm in dramatic circles, he spent the next hour and a half lecturing Thomas Jefferson on his duty to deliver commissions that had been duly signed and sealed. Second, if Marbury had a right, should he have a remedy for that right? Of course, Marshall said. Every right had to have a remedy; otherwise there was no point in having a right. Third, if Marbury had a right and deserved a remedy, should the remedy take the form of a writ of mandamus? No, Marshall replied. The writ must be denied because the section of the Judiciary Act of 1789 (Section 13) that authorized such writs was unconstitutional.

Unconstitutional! The decision was a bolt out of the blue. Nobody saw it coming. And what did it mean—why was Section 13 of the Judiciary Act unconstitutional? Marshall answered that the clause tried to add to the Supreme Court's original jurisdiction in violation of Article III, Section 2, of the Constitution. Original jurisdiction was reserved only for cases involving ambassadors, other foreign ministers, and cases involving states. Marbury fit none of these categories, so in authorizing such litigants to come to the Court under original jurisdiction, Section 13 violated the Constitution. Marshall's reasoning here is certainly open to challenge, but it hardly matters any more. The real historical significance of *Marbury v. Madison* lies in its bold assertion of judicial review, the authority of federal

John Marshall was appointed chief justice of the Supreme Court in 1801. Two years later, his decision in *Marbury v. Madison* gave the federal courts the authority to declare congressional legislation unconstitutional. This act of judicial review enhanced the power of the Supreme Court and established it as an equal third branch of the government. The above portrait was painted by Ferre de Saint Memin the year Marshall joined the Supreme Court.

courts to declare federal statutes unconstitutional. Judicial review is not explicitly mentioned anywhere in the Constitution. Marshall teased it out by his reasoning in *Marbury*. In the process he resolved the political dilemma he had faced: on the one hand, giving in to the Jeffersonians; on the other hand, issuing an order that Jefferson would have contemptuously ignored. As constitutional scholar Robert G. McCloskey put it, the Court was "in the delightful position . . . of rejecting and assuming power in a single breath."

*   *   *   *   *

Article III, Section 1, of the Constitution states that federal judicial power shall be vested in one Supreme Court "and in such inferior Courts as the Congress may from time to time ordain and establish." Beginning with the Judiciary Act of 1789, Congress did indeed "ordain and establish" a federal court system.

Our federal courts decide cases and controversies that arise under the Constitution and federal law. In presiding over these courts federal judges engage in <u>statutory interpretation</u>: They decide what the statute means in application to the facts of the case. There is nothing remarkable about this; judges do it in *every* country with an independent judiciary. What *is* remarkable, and almost unique to America, is that our federal judges also have the power to declare statutes unconstitutional—to undo the work of the legislative branch. This power is unheard of in most countries. Thanks in great part to John Marshall, American courts often resort to it.

It still generates intense controversy. True, nobody really fights anymore about *Marbury v. Madison*. The question today is not whether or not judicial review can be used but whether or not it is being used too much and for insufficient reason. This chapter will take a close look at judicial review, and at judicial power in general. Broadly speaking, the chapter will study three major issues: how the federal judiciary is organized and the role it has played in our history; the grounds on which present-day complaints against the Supreme Court are based; and the types of restraints there are on the future direction of Supreme Court opinions. Let us start by examining the organization and history of our federal court system.

Organization and History of the Federal Judiciary

Because ours is a federal system, we have two systems of courts, one at the state and local level and one at the federal level. Cases such as breaking and entering, disturbing the peace, and speeding will be tried in state or local courts. Only about 2 percent of all cases begin in federal courts. These involve some offense against the U.S. government or its officers; crimes committed on the high seas; or interstate commerce, civil rights, or any other area protected by the federal government.

DISTRICT COURTS

The Constitution says little about the federal courts. The Founders knew they wanted a Supreme Court of the United States but could not make up their minds about lower federal courts and left the decision to Congress. Congress responded in the Judiciary

Act of 1789 by setting up 13 <u>district courts</u>, one for each original state. In *Marbury v. Madison* Marshall struck down one section of the Judiciary Act but left the rest intact, so the district court system remains part of our basic judicial structure. Over the years Congress has increased the number of courts to 94, spread out over the 50 states plus one each for the District of Columbia, Guam, Puerto Rico, the Marianna Islands, and the Virgin Islands. Each state has at least one district court; the most populous states have up to four. These district courts are where most federal trials originate and end. Most of their decisions are not appealed.

U.S. COURTS OF APPEALS

For those district court decisions that are appealed, the next step up the judicial ladder is likely to be the <u>U.S. Courts of Appeals.</u> They too were first set up by the Judiciary Act of 1789. They were called "circuit courts" because, lacking their own judges, they were presided over by individual Supreme Court justices who "rode circuit" from court to court. This proved extremely burdensome to the justices, and over the years Congress made a number of modifications. Today courts of appeals have their own judges. In 1948 the name circuit courts was dropped, although the term *circuit* is still used to denote the geographic area covered by each appeals court. Today there are 13 courts. Each one covers a broad area usually including a number of states, except for the one that encompasses only the District of Columbia.

U.S. Courts of Appeals hear no witnesses and have no juries because their job is to determine if there was *legal* error in the original trial. Suppose, for example, that a lower court judge had allowed the prosecution to introduce as evidence a confession

FIGURE **12-1**

The Thirteen Federal Judicial Circuits and Ninety-four U.S. District Courts

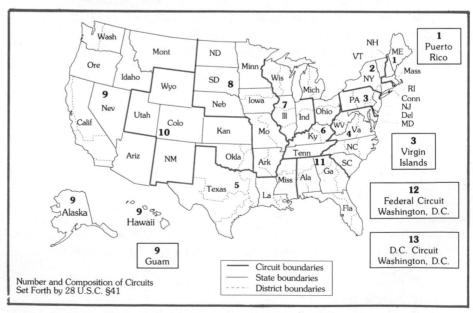

Source: Administrative Office of the United States Courts (January 1983).

Most decisions by our 94 federal district courts are not appealed, but those that are usually go to one of the 13 federal courts of appeals. These courts of appeals may reverse the decision of a lower court if a judicial error has been made.

that had been coerced. That would violate the Fifth Amendment (which says that no defendant in a criminal trial shall be compelled "to be a witness against himself") and a number of Supreme Court rulings barring the use of coerced confessions. It would be a serious legal error on the part of the district court judge, and in all likelihood the court of appeals would reverse the conviction of the defendant.

SPECIAL COURTS

There are, in addition, a number of courts with specialized jurisdiction. The Court of Claims hears suits for damages brought against the federal government by private individuals and companies. The Court of International Trade decides cases involving tariffs (taxes on imports). The Court of Customs and Patent Appeals hears appeals from the Court of International Trade, the U.S. Patent Office, and the U.S. Tariff Commission. Congress has also established a series of legislative courts, of which the most prominent is the Court of Military Appeals, created in 1950 to hear appeals from military tribunals (courts martial). These are called legislative courts because they are not set up under Article III of the Constitution (concerning the judicial branch) but under Article I (concerning the legislative branch). As such they are not courts in the full sense of the word, but administrative arms of Congress. Their judges are appointed for specific periods, instead of for life or "good behavior." There are other special courts as well, but they are not within the scope of this discussion.[1]

FIGURE **12-2**

Major Federal Courts

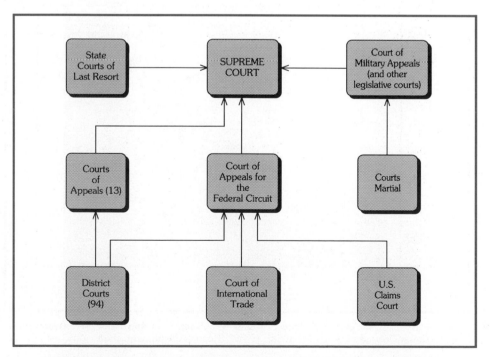

There are several major federal courts, but the ones that handle the most fundamental constitutional questions are the district courts, the federal appeals courts, and the Supreme Court.

THE SUPREME COURT

At the top of the whole structure is the United States Supreme Court. Cases are appealed to it not only from lower federal courts, but also from the highest level of state courts—*if*, in the Court's view, a substantial federal question (a question involving the U.S. Constitution, a federal statute, or the actions of a federal official) is presented. In the *Bakke* case (see chapter 5), Alan Bakke's claim that he was the victim of reverse discrimination came up through the California state courts. After the Supreme Court of California ruled on the case, it was taken up by the U.S. Supreme Court because it involved claims under the federal Civil Rights Act of 1964 and the Fourteenth Amendment of the U.S. Constitution.

In certain limited categories (for example, when a lower federal court declares a state law to be unconstitutional), cases reach the U.S. Supreme Court on appeal. That means that the Court *must* hear the case. However, the vast majority of cases come to the Supreme Court by a <u>writ of certiorari</u>. It requires a vote of four out of the nine justices to "grant cert," and they do it in very few cases. A person may talk about taking a case "all the way to the Supreme Court," but it is rare for a federal case to get beyond the appeals court level. Although the number of cases filed in the Supreme Court has grown dramatically since the 1930s (see Figure 12.3), the Court is only able to hear about 3 percent of them.

Before the Court hears oral arguments by attorneys for both sides of the case, the justices read the written arguments, or <u>briefs</u>—a rather ironic term for documents

FIGURE **12-3**

Cases Filed in the U.S. Supreme Court, 1938-1986

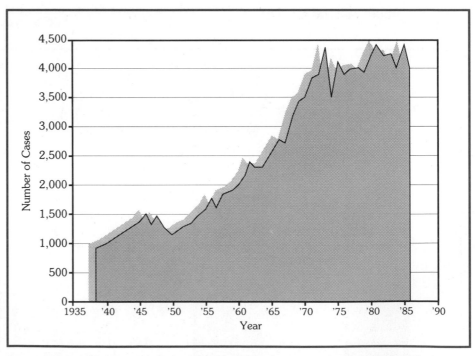

Source: Harold W. Stanley and Richard G. Niemi, *Vital Statistics on American Politics* (Washington: Congressional Quarterly Press, Inc., 1988), p. 252. Reprinted with permission.

The number of cases filed before the Supreme Court has increased steeply since the 1950s. The Supreme Court's schedule has become increasingly crowded and the Court can only hear a tiny fraction of the cases filed.

that may run to hundreds of pages. In addition to the briefs filed by the immediate parties to the suit, there may also be _amici curiae_ (friends of the court) briefs, brought by groups and individuals interested in its outcome. They have no official role, but these briefs are submitted in the hope of influencing the Court's thinking. Major cases usually attract many of these briefs. In _Webster v. Reproductive Health Service_, the 1989 abortion case, 78 _amici_ briefs were submitted, more than had ever been filed in the Court's history.

After studying the briefs, the justices hear the arguments. At precisely noon, Monday through Thursday, the red curtains at the end of the Supreme Court room open and the justices enter. The Court Crier shouts: "Oyez, oyez, oyez! All persons having business before the Honorable, the Supreme Court of the United States, are admonished to draw near and give attention. . . . God save the United States and this Honorable Court." The Court hands down its opinions on Mondays; the arguments are heard Tuesdays through Thursdays. The attorney representing the petitioner (the "moving party") steps forward and says: "Mr. Chief Justice, may it please the Court. . . ." The time of each presentation is severely limited; as a general rule, each side gets half an hour. A white light goes on on the attorney's lectern when five minutes remain; a red light goes on when the time has expired. The attorney must then stop immediately, even if in midsentence. During the arguments, the justices may interrupt the attorneys to ask questions; often these questions turn into dialogues. During the oral argument in the 1989 _Webster_ case, Justice Antonin Scalia got into an exchange with the attorney representing the abortion clinic on whether or not it is permissible to kill a fetus. Six of the other justices also interrupted with questions.[2]

Having read the briefs and heard the arguments, the justices move toward a decision. They confer with their clerks and then meet together. In order of seniority, each justice states his or her views and conclusions. Once it is clear that a majority exists, the chief justice assigns one member to write the opinion. Successive drafts are circulated to get as many members as possible to endorse a single opinion of the Court. This may be impossible; aside from those who dissent, each member of the majority may have a different reason for going along with the ruling. This produces concurring opinions, meaning that a member or members agree with the Court's ruling but disagree with the reasons for it.

In its basic procedure and style, our Supreme Court is not very different from the highest courts in other constitutional republics. There is the same aura of honored ritual, the same assumption that the judicial determinations must be free of political influence. In substance, too, there are obvious similarities. In all countries, courts must resolve disputes between parties and interpret the statutes passed by legislatures.

But our federal courts have another power that sets them apart from courts in almost every other country of the world: They can nullify statutes and decisions by the president of the United States by declaring that they violate the Constitution. This awesome power of the federal courts and the Supreme Court derives from John Marshall's decision in _Marbury v. Madison_.

Ascending the courthouse steps to argue a case before the Supreme Court.

MARBURY RECONSIDERED

Although it had a lasting importance, Marshall's decision caused little stir at the time. There is evidence that the idea of judicial review—even though it was not authorized in the Constitution—was then widely accepted. In _Federalist_ No. 78 Alexander Hamilton argued that judicial review was an essential means of enforcing the limitations of government prescribed in the Constitution:

> Limitation of this kind can be preserved in practice no other way than through the medium of courts of justice, whose duty it must be to declare all acts contrary to the manifest tenor of the Constitution void.[3]

Of course, Hamilton's distrust of popular majorities was well known. But even the radical Patrick Henry voiced similar views. "I take it as the highest encomium of this country," Henry said, "that the acts of the legislature, if unconstitutional, are liable to be opposed by the judiciary."[4] Constitutional scholar Raoul Berger, who studied the remarks of delegates to various state conventions called to ratify the Constitution between 1787 and 1789, concluded that judicial review was regarded "as a necessary instrument of the new system [and] was taken for granted."[5] Yet we know at least one of Marshall's contemporaries did not take judicial review for granted: Thomas Jefferson. In an 1804 letter to Abigail Adams, Jefferson wrote: "The opinion which gives to the judges the right to decide what laws are constitutional, and what not, not only for themselves in their own sphere of action, but for the legislative and executive also, in their spheres, would make the judiciary a despotic branch."[6]

In the *Marbury* case Marshall was almost nonchalant about the justification for judicial review. It was very simple: We have a written constitution that is supposed to be the law of our land; if the legislature can violate it at will, why have a constitution? Jefferson agreed. But the remaining question was this: Why should the Supreme Court have the *exclusive* power of interpreting the Constitution for the other branches? In his answer, Marshall relied heavily on Alexander Hamilton's argument in *The Federalist* No. 78, which was based upon the expertise of courts. "It is emphatically the province and duty of the judicial department to say what the law is." (Hamilton had said, "The interpretation of the laws is the proper and peculiar province of the courts.") That was the major premise. The implied minor premise was that the Constitution is a law. Thus the conclusion: Therefore, it is the unique province of the judiciary to interpret the Constitution.

If there is any weakness in Marshall's argument, it lies in the assertion that the Constitution is a law. In one sense the Constitution is indeed a law, "the supreme Law of the Land," as it says in Article VI. But as Marshall himself observed in a later case, the Constitution is much different from a statute.[7] It does not attempt to spell out everything but leaves room for interpretation and growth. And its language is accessible to anyone; in a sense it is a people's document, for it was meant to be understood by the public at large.[8] The legal training of judges may make them experts at interpreting technical legal codes, but does it make them experts on the Constitution? Should not prudence and common sense play a great role in interpreting it? Do judges have a monopoly on common sense? These critical questions were not raised at the time of the *Marbury* decision.[9] Judicial review has thus remained largely unchallenged. In fact, it was not even used again for another 54 years. But when the Court did begin using it, it set off a gigantic explosion that nearly destroyed the authority of the federal judiciary.

DRED SCOTT: A SELF-INFLICTED WOUND

The second time in the Court's history that it struck down a federal statute was in *Dred Scott v. Sandford* (1857). The case is probably best remembered for the Court's ruling that slaves were not human beings, but articles of property to be bought and sold like cattle.[10] It was on this premise that it ruled unconstitutional the Missouri Compromise of 1821, a statute passed by Congress outlawing slavery in the territories. The facts of the case were these: Dred Scott, a slave, accompanied his master into free territory and there claimed his freedom under the statute. But the Court said this would deprive the master of his property without due process of law. Therefore, the statute was unconstitutional.

The uproar began almost immediately. A Washington newspaperman observed, "If epithets and denunciations could sink a judicial body, the Supreme Court of the United States would never be heard of again."[11] The decision upset a delicate

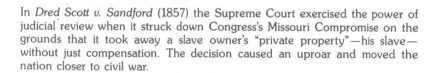

A PUBLIC MEETING
WILL BE HELD ON
THURSDAY EVENING, 2D INSTANT,
at 7 o'clock, in ISRAEL CHURCH, to consider the atrocious decision of the Supreme Court in the
DRED SCOTT CASE,
and other outrages to which the colored people are subject under the Constitution of the United States.
C. L. REMOND,
ROBERT PURVIS,
and others will be speakers on the occasion. Mrs. MOTT. Mr. M'KIM and B. S. JONES of Ohio, have also accepted invitations to be present.
All persons are invited to attend. Admittance free.

In *Dred Scott v. Sandford* (1857) the Supreme Court exercised the power of judicial review when it struck down Congress's Missouri Compromise on the grounds that it took away a slave owner's "private property"—his slave—without just compensation. The decision caused an uproar and moved the nation closer to civil war.

compromise between North and South, inflamed abolitionist sentiment, and helped bring on the Civil War. Even northern supporters of the South were embarrassed by it. For the abolitionists, it signified moral bankruptcy. Writing in his influential *New York Tribune*, Horace Greeley said that the decision was "entitled to just so much moral weight as would be the judgment of a majority of those congregated in any Washington bar-room."[12]

It took years for the Court to recover from this self-inflicted blow to its reputation. As Hamilton pointed out in *Federalist* No. 78, all the Court has is its judgment, and even there it needs the help of the executive branch to carry it out. When its judgment seems to be chronically bad, its reputation suffers, and so does its authority. To see the point more clearly, let us leap ahead 80 years from the time of *Dred Scott* to the late 1930s.

THE COURT IN THE 1930s: NINE OLD MEN

In the 1930s the Court's use of judicial review again embroiled it in controversy. The nation was in the grip of the Great Depression: A quarter of the work force was out of work; poverty and starvation were widespread. President Franklin Delano Roosevelt had promised the country a "New Deal." He quickly persuaded Congress to pass his New Deal legislation, which regulated businesses in various ways: setting up codes of fair competition, establishing wage and hours standards, and compelling businesses to provide retirement and pension plans. The Court, however, ruled that these statutes violated the Constitution and struck them down.[13] The rulings outraged many people who believed, along with Congress and FDR, that one cause of the Depression was irresponsible business practices. "Nine old men," Roosevelt called the justices. In 1936 all nine were over 60 and seven were over 70. This seemed to Roosevelt to be an opportunity. After his landslide reelection in 1936, FDR proposed enlarging the size of the Court by appointing a new justice for every justice over the age of 70, with 15 set as the maximum number. (The Constitution does not specify any particular number of justices to sit on the Court. The amount is set by congressional statute.)

Had his proposal been adopted by Congress, Roosevelt would have been able to pack the Court with justices friendly to his views. The crudeness of the scheme shocked even many of the president's supporters in Congress, and the bill that contained it never got out of committee.

Roosevelt lost a battle, but two subsequent developments allowed him to win the war. First, shortly after Congress rejected Roosevelt's proposal, Justice Owen Roberts, an inconsistent supporter of Roosevelt, began casting his votes solely in favor of New Deal legislation. (Fairly or not, this has been called "the switch in time that saved nine.") Second, the death or retirement of some of the "old men" enabled Roosevelt to replace them with justices of his own choosing.

JUDICIAL SELF-RESTRAINT

With Roosevelt's new men came new ideas, particularly judicial self-restraint. The most vigorous exponent of this new philosophy was a man Roosevelt appointed in 1939, Felix Frankfurter. A Harvard Law School professor at the time of his appointment, Frankfurter believed the Supreme Court should defer to the legislative branch whenever possible. It should assume that whatever the legislature does is constitutional unless there is clear and convincing evidence of unconstitutionality. At first all the Roosevelt appointees agreed with Frankfurter. Was it wise for appointed judges to make a habit of striking down the work of the people's elected representatives? Within a few years, however, a split developed among Roosevelt's appointees that was caused by the emergence of civil liberties as the dominant issue before the Supreme Court.

JUDICIAL ACTIVISM

With some notable exceptions, the cases that concerned the Court of the 1930s involved the regulation of business. But beginning in 1940, the Court was called upon to decide a succession of cases involving compulsory flag salutes, religious proselytizing, aid to parochial schools, the prosecution of Communists for "conspiring to advocate" revolution, and other matters concerning freedoms guaranteed in the Bill of Rights. As Figure 12.4 shows, by the early 1940s the Court was inclined to leave economic statutes standing; in the next decade it turned its attention to statutes regulating civil liberties, striking down many of them on constitutional grounds. Some of the Roosevelt appointees thought that these liberties deserved special protection. They began to call them preferred freedoms. When cases involving these basic freedoms reached the Court, they looked very hard at any statute that limited them. Like Frankfurter, they believed in judicial self-restraint in cases affecting property; unlike Frankfurter, they did not believe in self-restraint when cases involved the Bill of Rights, particularly the First Amendment. In such cases these Roosevelt appointees came to be called judicial activists. The most famous of these were Justices William O. Douglas and Hugo Black. In cases involving civil liberties, Douglas and Black almost always voted together. Black himself, as we saw in chapter 4, believed that the First Amendment's protection of free speech was an absolute.

For Frankfurter, judicial activism was a throwback to the philosophy of the Court in the 1930s. He considered it to be judicial arrogance and was unimpressed by the doctrine of preferred freedoms on which it rested. "I deem it [preferred freedoms] a mischievous phrase," he said, "if it carries the thought, which it may subtly imply, that any law touching communication is infected with presumptive invalidity."[14] Nevertheless, this philosophy has won out. Today if a statute limits property rights the Court

Felix Frankfurter served on the Supreme Court from 1939 to 1962. Although a liberal activist in his private life, he was famous for his advocacy of judicial restraint. He believed the courts should defer to the legislative branch whenever possible.

FIGURE **12-4**

311

Organization and
History of the
Federal Judiciary

Number of Economic and Civil Liberties Laws (Federal, State, and Local) Overturned by Supreme Court

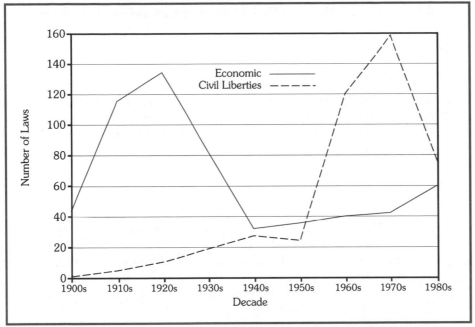

Source: Lawrence Baum, *The Supreme Court*, 3d ed. (Washington: Congressional Quarterly Press, 1989), p. 188. Reprinted with permission.

Between the 1920s and the 1940s, the Supreme Court's "activism" in economic matters (that is, its tendency to strike down laws regulating business) declined dramatically. Its activism in the area of civil liberties (striking down laws on grounds that they violated personal liberties in the Bill of Rights) increased dramatically between the 1950s and the 1970s.

will assume the statute is constitutional unless shown otherwise; but in cases involving personal freedoms, the Court will scrutinize the statute very strictly. In a sense, this involves a double standard; but defenders of judicial activism contend that a double standard is appropriate since freedoms like speech and religion are more basic than the freedom to run a business without state interference. Nevertheless, judicial activism has continued to embroil the Court in controversy.

Points to Remember

1. Judicial review, the power of federal courts to hold statutes unconstitutional, was first asserted by Chief Justice John Marshall in *Marbury v. Madison* (1803).

2. Marshall based his decision on the need to uphold the Constitution and on the "province and duty of the judicial department."

3. The second time the Court struck down a congressional statute was in *Dred Scott*—a disastrous decision that helped to bring on the Civil War.

4. The Court's decisions came under fire again in the 1930s, when the "Nine Old Men" repeatedly struck down New Deal legisla-

tion. After trying unsuccessfully to pack the Court, Roosevelt changed its membership by filling vacancies.

5. Roosevelt's appointees were committed to judicial self-restraint in cases involving the regulation of business; in Bill of Rights cases, however, some advocated judicial activism.

The Court Today

In 1953 President Eisenhower appointed California attorney general Earl Warren to be chief justice of the Supreme Court. At the time Warren seemed a logical choice for someone like Eisenhower to appoint. Warren had long been active in Republican party circles, was well liked, moderate, and yet considered tough on lawbreakers.

THE WARREN COURT

Within a few years, however, Eisenhower came to regret his choice. He later described it as "the biggest damned-fool mistake I ever made."[15] Eisenhower was far from being a radical right-winger, but his temperament was conservative. However one would describe the Supreme Court under the leadership of Earl Warren, it certainly would not be classed as conservative. By the time Warren stepped down in 1969 the Court had done the following:

- Outlawed racial segregation in public schools and other state institutions.
- Abolished prayer and Bible reading in public school classrooms.
- Forced states to redraw their legislative districts to make them all approximately equal in population size.
- Redefined *pornography* to extend First Amendment protections to sexually explicit material.
- Prevented state authorities from using evidence seized without proper warrant against a criminal defendant.
- Thrown out the murder conviction of a man who confessed without his lawyer being present during police questioning.
- Required police to give Miranda warnings to suspects before questioning them: The suspect must be told he or she has a right to a lawyer (and that the authorities will provide one free if necessary), that anything the suspect says may be used against him or her, and that the suspect has the right to remain silent.

In 1953 President Dwight D. Eisenhower appointed Earl Warren chief justice of the Supreme Court. The Warren Court was known for its bold and liberal interpretations of the Constitution, which expanded and affirmed civil rights and civil liberties.

In all these cases Warren was in the majority, and in some he wrote the majority opinion. By the time Frankfurter left the Court in 1965, he was often in dissent. In his view, the Court had forgotten the lesson of the 1930s that in a democracy courts ought to defer to the elected branches of government. There were other thoughtful critics of the Warren court, such as Philip Kurland and the late Alexander Bickel, two distinguished professors of law who faulted the Court for its quirkiness, inconsistency, and disregard of precedent.[16] There were other angrier voices. In the Deep South billboards said "Impeach Earl Warren" because of the desegregation decisions. The Warren Court was also accused of "taking God out of our schools" and "handcuffing the police." It seemed as if the justices had gone on a rampage of activism, rewriting much of our legal and even our moral system by reading their own views into the Constitution. In his 1968 election campaign, Richard Nixon promised that he would fill any Court vacancies with "strict constructionists who saw their duty in interpreting and not making law."[17]

THE BURGER COURT

Shortly after his election, Nixon got a chance to deliver on his promise. When Warren retired in 1969, Nixon appointed Warren Burger as chief justice. A federal court of appeals judge at the time, Burger had often criticized Court opinions in the area of criminal justice. Over the next few years there were three more retirements, enabling

Nixon to place a total of four new justices on the Court. His successor, Gerald Ford, added another in 1975. Another member of the Warren Court retired in 1981, enabling Ronald Reagan to appoint the first female justice, Sandra Day O'Connor.

During Burger's tenure as chief justice, the Court seemed to retreat from the Warren Court's judicial activism in some areas. In matters relating to criminal justice, the Burger Court refused to strike down the death penalty, and it allowed to police and prosecutors certain exceptions to the rules the Warren Court had formerly laid down concerning illegal confessions and searches.[18] In some areas of civil liberties, too, such as pornography, the Burger Court allowed states and localities more latitude in interpreting the law.[19] But in at least one area of the law, abortion, it carried judicial activism further than the Warren Court. In the 1973 case of *Roe v. Wade*, the Court ruled 7-2 (with Burger in the majority) that women have an unrestricted right to abortion during the first six months of pregnancy. The decision, which forced all 50 states to revise their abortion laws, set off a controversy that shows no sign of abating.

In another area of the law, civil rights, it is hard to find the right classification for the Burger Court. Perhaps the best way to put it is to say that the Burger Court leaned toward a liberal version of judicial self-restraint. It generally tended to approve—or at least to refrain from striking down—affirmative action, i.e., the use of quotas or numerical goals based upon race. To be sure, in the famous *Bakke* case of 1978, the Burger Court struck down the practice of using strict quotas guaranteeing a certain percentage of minority seats in medical school.[20] But it did allow the use of "race-conscious" remedies for racial imbalance, and, with some exceptions, it adhered to that approach in later cases. In this case, judicial self-restraint pleased liberals (since they support affirmative action) and displeased conservatives (who regard it as a form of reverse discrimination.) Thus it appears that the champions of "activism" can become "self-restrainers," and vice versa, depending upon what it is that the Court is examining.

THE REHNQUIST COURT

In 1986, during the second term of President Reagan, Chief Justice Burger retired, and Reagan made Nixon appointee William Rehnquist the chief justice; he then filled Rehnquist's old seat with a new justice, Antonin Scalia. In 1987 still another Nixon appointee retired, and after two tries, Reagan finally managed to secure Senate approval for Anthony M. Kennedy. Only two justices sitting on the Court now remain from the Warren days, and both are in their eighties: Thurgood Marshall and Byron White.

What is the Rehnquist Court like? Most observers agree that it has modified many of the precedents set during Warren's tenure. In matters of criminal justice, for example, it seems to have redefined the requirements for valid confessions, searches, and seizures.[21] Nevertheless, it has not repudiated the protections for criminal suspects established during the 1960s, nor has it reversed some of the protections added during the 1970s.[22] In other areas, such as pornography and church-state relations, it has reaffirmed the decisions of the 1960s while modifying them in certain situations. But in the two areas where the Burger Court went even further than the Warren Court in extending or affirming new rights regarding affirmative action and abortion, the Rehnquist Court has made some important modifications. In affirmative action the Rehnquist Court has declared unconstitutional municipal ordinances setting aside certain percentages of public works jobs for minority contractors. It has, in some cases, placed the burden of proof on minority complainants to show that intentional discrimination is the cause of racial imbalance in the workplace, and it has ruled that court-approved affirmative action settlements are open to subsequent legal challenges by white workers.[23] In abortion cases, it has approved of state regulations prohibiting state facilities or personnel to be used for abortion for any reason except to

The Supreme Court, 1989. From left front, Thurgood Marshall, William
Brennan, Chief Justice William Rehnquist, Byron White, and Harry Blackmun.
From left rear, Antonin Scalia, John Paul Stevens, Sandra Day O'Connor, and
Anthony M. Kennedy.

save the life of the mother, and it has opened the door to other state limitations on
abortion.

In the 1930s the Court was called "Nine Old Men." Today the Court would more
accurately be called "Three Old Men, Three Aging Men, One Middle-Aged Woman,
and Two Fairly Young Men." Justices Harry Blackmun, Thurgood Marshall, and
William Brennan are in their eighties; Justices John Paul Stevens, Byron White, and
Chief Justice Rehnquist range from the late sixties to the early seventies; Justice
Sandra Day O'Connor is in her early sixties; and Justices Antonin Scalia and
Anthony Kennedy are in their early fifties. There are also ideological divisions in
today's Court. While such terms as *liberal* and *conservative* have to be used cautiously
in classifying Supreme Court Justices since judicial judgments are not the same as
political preferences, it is generally agreed that the Court's two most conservative
justices are Rehnquist and Scalia, and that the two most liberal are Brennan and
Marshall. The rest seem to be either in the middle (Stevens), leaning toward the
liberal side (Blackmun), or leaning toward the conservative side (O'Connor, White,
and Kennedy).

The present Court is sometimes referred to as a "Reagan Court," but this is
somewhat misleading. President Reagan appointed only three of its nine members
(although he also elevated William Rehnquist, a Nixon appointee, to the chief
justiceship). The other six were appointed by Presidents Ford, Nixon, Johnson,
Kennedy, and Eisenhower. Interestingly, Eisenhower, a rather conservative president,
appointed one of the Court's most liberal members, William Brennan, while the liberal
Kennedy appointed Byron White, who leans toward the conservative side. Again, as
we saw in the case of Eisenhower's appointment of Earl Warren ("biggest damned-
fool mistake I ever made"), we see that the judicial behavior of prospective Supreme
Court justices is sometimes hard to predict.

Unpredictability is not necessarily a virtue. For some critics, another word for
"unpredictable" is "arbitrary." For them, what is worrisome about the justices of the
Supreme Court is that they seem to be making things up as they go along, reading
the law arbitrarily instead of the way it is set forth in the Constitution.

(Continued on page 316)

GLOBAL PERSPECTIVES:

The Judiciary in Japan

The Japanese constitution guarantees the independence of the judiciary, including Japan's highest court, the Supreme Court. It consists of 15 justices appointed by the cabinet. The Supreme Court's chief justice is appointed by the emperor but approved by the cabinet. The appointments are for life, but they must be confirmed by popular vote at the next general election and then once every 10 years. The judges generally receive confirmation, largely because the Japanese public pays little attention to them and has little knowledge of what they do. Article 81 of the Japanese Constitution gives the Supreme Court the power of judicial review, but it is rarely exercised because Japan has no tradition sanctioning such a practice.

Below the Supreme Court, there are eight high courts of appeals throughout Japan. Below these are district courts having original jurisdiction in all civil and criminal cases except for those involving petty offenses, which are handled by special courts. After experimenting with the kind of jury system used in Great Britain and the United States, the Japanese decided it was too erratic and chose a system permitting judges to mete out both verdicts and sentences. This system, which closely resembles that of continental Europe, also permits judges to conduct the inquiry and question witnesses instead of relying on the adversary system used in Great Britain and the United States.

Persons qualify for the judiciary in much the same way as they do for positions in higher civil service. A few hundred university graduates are selected each year through examinations; they are then put through a two-year training program conducted by the Japanese Legal Training and Research Institute. Successful trainees may then choose careers as judges, public prosecutors, or jurors.

In general, the Japanese have tended to downplay the role of law and the courts in settling disputes, preferring more informal methods and stressing conciliation. Local police stations provide special conciliation rooms, and elders are often utilized as go-betweens. However, as the stresses of modern industrialization continue to weaken old customs and traditions, it is likely that Japan will follow the path of the West toward an increasing reliance on lawyers rather than conciliators.

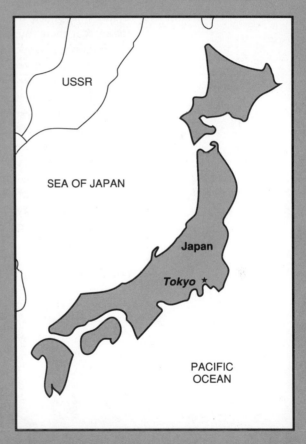

IS THE COURT MAKING UP ITS OWN LAWS?

In defending judicial review in *Marbury*, John Marshall posed a hypothetical case: Suppose a state were to pass an *ex post facto* law (a law punishing people for acts that were not crimes when they did them), which is prohibited by the Constitution. Now, Marshall went on, suppose further that someone is hauled into court and found guilty of violating this unconstitutional statute. Should the judge sentence the person without first asking whether or not the statute violates the Constitution? "Ought the judges to close their eyes to the constitution, and only see the law?"

If the meaning of the Constitution were always as evident as it is in the case of *ex post facto* laws (explicitly forbidden in Article I, Section 10), there would be no controversy. But key phrases in the Constitution are anything but self-evident. What is an "establishment of religion"? What is "commerce among the several states"? What is "due process of law"? The critics of judicial activism charge that the members of the Court have often read their own meanings into these phrases. To put it more bluntly, critics charge that the members of the Court have not been content to interpret the law; they have been *making* law, usurping the role of the legislature.

Take the landmark school prayer case of 1962, *Engel v. Vitale*. In that case the Court interpreted the establishment of religion clause of the First Amendment to mean that there must be a "wall of separation" between church and state. "Wall of separation" is found nowhere in the Constitution; it was a phrase used by Thomas Jefferson in a letter to a group of Baptists in Danbury, Connecticut. Yet it was by reading the establishment clause in light of that phrase that the Court struck down school prayer. Was the Court twisting the meaning of the establishment clause?

The same question may be asked of the abortion decision. The Court ruled that laws against abortion violate a woman's "right of privacy." But, like "wall of separation," the phrase "right of privacy" is found nowhere in the Constitution. The Court took it from an earlier case concerning birth control.[24] In that earlier case the Court said that the right of privacy was formed out of "emanations" from various clauses in the Bill of Rights. Do all these miscellaneous clauses or emanations from them add up to a right of privacy? The majority thought so, but not the dissenters. They saw it as a judge-made right not authorized by the language of the Constitution. The same complaint was made by the dissenters in the *Roe v. Wade* decision of 1973. "The Court," wrote Justice White, "simply fashions and announces a new constitutional right for pregnant mothers and . . . invests that right with sufficient substance

"Do you ever have one of those days when everything seems un-Constitutional?" *Drawing by Joe Mirachi;* © *1974 The New Yorker Magazine, Inc.*

to override most existing state abortion statutes." It was, he said, "an exercise of raw judicial power."[25]

Controversy over the role of federal courts and judges grew increasingly heated during the Reagan years. Attorney General Edwin Meese charged that many of the Supreme Court's opinions were "more policy choices than articulations of constitutional principle."[26] He argued that federal judges should interpret the Constitution according to the "original intent" of its Framers. The critique provoked spirited responses, some of them from members of the Court. Justice John Paul Stevens said it was very difficult to make generalizations about the Framers' intentions, since the Framers had diverse views.[27] Justice William Brennan charged that "it is little more than arrogance cloaked as humility [to] pretend that from our vantage we can gauge accurately the intent of the Framers on application of principle to specific, contemporary questions."[28]

CONFIRMATION POLITICS: BORK, GINSBURG, KENNEDY

The controversy reached a flashpoint when on July 1, 1987, Reagan nominated Court of Appeals judge Robert H. Bork to fill the seat vacated by the retirement of Justice Lewis F. Powell. A former Yale Law School professor, Bork had served as Solicitor General in the Nixon and Ford administrations and been appointed to the Washington, D.C., Court of Appeals by Reagan in 1982. The Senate Judiciary Committee held televised confirmation hearings.

The nomination came at a time when the Court's ideological balance was very delicate. As regards criminal justice, the Court had already modified some of its earlier rulings on defendants' rights, but many of the decisions were closely divided between those who wanted to extend the rights of the accused and those who felt that they had already been extended too far. A similar close division existed on civil liberties, civil rights, and church-state issues. Affirmative action decisions had been 5-4 and 6-3 since the famous *Bakke* case of 1978 (see chapter 5). The Court had been handing down abortion decisions supporting and even extending the *Roe v. Wade* decision of 1973, but the decisions had been increasingly close. Lewis Powell, the retiring justice, had consistently supported *Roe*; his position on other cases was more difficult to pin down, but he was generally regarded as a centrist.

Bork was certainly not seen as a centrist. He was squarely opposed to a number of doctrines laid down by the Court since the middle of the 1960s. One of these was the idea of a right to privacy, which Bork considered fuzzy and subjective. Bork's views on civil rights law were at least as controversial. He originally opposed passage of the Civil Rights Law of 1964, and although he later publicly changed that view, he criticized affirmative action because he said that the law must be color-blind.

A few days after the nomination, Senator Edward Kennedy (D-Massachusetts) fired the first volley: "Robert Bork's America is a land in which women would be forced into back alley abortions, blacks would sit in segregated lunch counters, rogue police could break down citizens' doors in midnight raids, schoolchildren could not be taught about evolution, writers and artists could be censored at the whim of government. . . ."[29] The same theme was pursued in television advertisements, the first ever to be used to influence the outcome of confirmation hearings (see chapter 17).

Then the hearings began, conducted by the Senate Judiciary Committee, of which Senator Kennedy was a member. Millions watched the hearings on television as over 100 witnesses testified for and against confirmation; Bork himself testified for 32 hours and was asked questions ranging from why he grew a beard to how he would treat gender in cases involving the Fourteenth Amendment. On October 23, nearly four months after Reagan nominated Bork, the Senate refused its consent to

Although presidents have the power to appoint judges, the nominees must be approved by a majority of the Senate. In 1987 President Reagan told reporters that he would nominate Judge Robert Bork to serve on the Supreme Court, but after months of hearings and debates, the Senate rejected Bork on a vote of 58–42.

the nomination by a vote of 58 to 42. This capped a battle that reporter Stuart Taylor of the *New York Times* called "the most contentious in the modern history of the Supreme Court."[30]

Six days after Bork's defeat, Reagan introduced a new nominee, Court of Appeals judge Douglas H. Ginsburg. Bork supporters and detractors now wondered about how Ginsburg would vote if he were on the Court; he probably would have been closely questioned had he appeared before the Judiciary Committee. But that never happened because Ginsburg withdrew his name from consideration nine days after being nominated. It was learned that Ginsburg had smoked marijuana while a student at Cornell University and later while teaching law at Harvard Law School. Behind the scenes, Reagan officials pressured Ginsburg into withdrawing. He was the 27th Supreme Court nominee in the nation's history not to receive Senate confirmation (see Table 12.1).

When insiders in the Reagan administration first started debating about a replacement for Bork, one of the runners-up was Court of Appeals judge Anthony M. Kennedy. President Reagan nominated Kennedy three days after Ginsburg withdrew. Like Ginsburg—and distinctly unlike Bork—the new nominee kept a very low ideological profile. Kennedy had written over 400 opinions and had given many speeches in his 12 years as an appeals court judge, but he had avoided definitive pronouncements on controversial topics. "His opinions are more sensitive than strident," said Harvard law professor Lawrence H. Tribe, who had testified against the Bork nomination. Kennedy was unanimously confirmed by the committee and went on to win an easy confirmation by the full Senate early in 1988.

Justice Kennedy had been on the Court less than a year when it became clear that he was not as centrist as he had appeared during the confirmation hearings. In closely divided decisions in 1988 and 1989, Kennedy usually tipped the balance in favor of the Court's conservatives.[31] One of the cases was not without irony. In the

TABLE **12-1**   **319**

Nominees Not Confirmed by the Senate

Nominee	President	Senate Action	Date of Senate Action
John Rutledge (for chief justice)	Washington	Rejected	Dec. 15, 1795
Alexander Wolcott	Madison	Rejected	Feb. 13, 1811
John J. Crittenden	John Quincy Adams	Postponed	Feb. 12, 1829
Roger Brooke Taney	Jackson	Postponed*	March 3, 1835
John C. Spencer	Tyler	Rejected	Jan. 31, 1844
Reuben H. Walworth	Tyler	Withdrawn, 1844	
Edward King	Tyler	Postponed	June 15, 1844
Edward King	Tyler	Withdrawn, 1845	
John M. Read	Tyler	Not Acted Upon, 1845	
George W. Woodward	Polk	Rejected	Jan. 22, 1846
Edward A. Bradford	Fillmore	Not Acted Upon, 1852	
George E. Badger	Fillmore	Postponed	Feb. 11, 1853
William C. Micou	Fillmore	Not Acted Upon, 1853	
Jeremiah S. Black	Buchanan	Rejected	Feb. 21, 1861
Henry Stanbery	Andrew Johnson	Not Acted Upon, 1866	
Ebenezer R. Hoar	Grant	Rejected	Feb. 3, 1870
George H. Williams (for chief justice)	Grant	Withdrawn, 1874	
Caleb Cushing (for chief justice)	Grant	Withdrawn, 1874	
Stanley Matthews	Hayes	Not Acted Upon, 1881†	
William B. Hornblower	Cleveland	Rejected	Jan. 15, 1894
Wheeler H. Peckham	Cleveland	Rejected	Feb. 16, 1894
John J. Parker	Hoover	Rejected	May 7, 1930
Abe Fortas (for chief justice)	Lyndon Johnson	Withdrawn, 1968	
Homer Thornberry	Lyndon Johnson	Not Acted Upon, 1968	
Clement F. Haynsworth, Jr.	Nixon	Rejected	Nov. 21, 1969
G. Harrold Carswell	Nixon	Rejected	April 8, 1970
Robert H. Bork	Reagan	Rejected	Oct. 23, 1987
Douglas H. Ginsburg	Reagan	Withdrawn, 1987	

*Later nominated for chief justice and confirmed.
†Later nominated and confirmed.

Data source: Library of Congress, Congressional Research Service. Reprinted from Congressional Quarterly, Inc. with permission.

From 1789 through mid-1988, 28 Supreme Court nominations failed to receive Senate confirmation. Of these, 12 were rejected outright and the remainder were withdrawn or allowed to lapse when Senate rejection appeared imminent.

spring of 1988 the Court listened to arguments about whether or not a civil rights law passed during the post-Civil War Reconstruction era applied to the case of a woman who claimed she had been racially harassed on the job. The woman's case rested in part on a precedent set by the Court in a 1976 decision, *Runyan v. McCrary*. The Court had interpreted the Reconstruction statute very broadly in the *Runyan* opinion, allowing plaintiffs to sue private schools and businesses on grounds of racial harassment.

In arguing the 1988 case before the Court, lawyers for both sides accepted the *Runyan* interpretation. Surprisingly, the Court ruled that both parties to the suit must come back in the fall to reargue the case in terms of whether or not *Runyan*'s liberal interpretation was correct.[32] The Court's 1988 decision was 5-4, with Kennedy in the conservative majority. Liberals were appalled that the Court should seek to question a settled civil rights precedent. Almost forgotten in the uproar was the name of the man who had originally argued for the expansion of civil rights in the 1976 case. He was the United States solicitor general at the time, Robert H. Bork.

Restraints on the Supreme Court

As Alexander Hamilton noted in *Federalist* No. 78, the Supreme Court lacks the power of the sword and the power of the purse. All it has is judgment. If that judgment no longer enjoys the support of the president, Congress, and the people, the Court is in danger of being ignored, defied, or tampered with. The Court at times seems to be aware of its vulnerability. Sometimes it pulls back, avoiding decisions that may embroil it in political battles. In discussing restraints on the Court, then, we must not leave out self-restraint.

SELF-IMPOSED LIMITS: CASES AND CONTROVERSIES

The Court usually practices the doctrine of self-restraint in cases involving economic freedoms but not in cases involving preferred freedoms. Yet even the most vigorous champions of preferred freedoms readily admit that judges are not supposed to make rulings simply on the basis of their own predilections.[33] Judges are not legislators. They cannot decide what they think is good for the country. As Article III of the Constitution makes clear, they are limited to deciding "Cases and Controversies." This limitation on the Court's power has a number of implications; three are especially important.

No Advisory Opinions.   The Court is not supposed to issue advisory opinions. The Court may decide only on the immediate issues of the case. This rule is sometimes broken when the Court makes an *obiter dictum* (Latin for "remark by the way"), a parenthetical comment indicating how the Court *would* rule in a certain hypothetical case. Nevertheless, the rule is that the Court sticks to the issues raised by the opposing attorneys in the case before it.

Avoiding Political Questions.   Since 1849, in the case of *Luther v. Borden*, the Court has tried to stay away from what it calls political questions. The Court ruled in the *Luther* case that it had no authority to decide which of the two factions claiming to be the legitimate government of Rhode Island was in fact the legitimate one. It said that this struggle should be settled in the political arena; courts had no business meddling in it. Since that time, the Court has refused to rule in cases it considers political.

What precisely is a political controversy? The question is not easy to answer, but the Court has provided three guidelines. First, a political question is a controversy that is better resolved by one of the other two branches of the federal government (legislative or executive); second, it is a controversy for which judicially manageable standards are lacking; and, third, it is a controversy in which a judicial decision would risk embarrassment abroad or grave disturbance at home. Questions of war and peace fit these criteria. During the Vietnam War, several legal challenges were made to the war, all claiming that the war was illegal or unconstitutional. The Court refused even to hear the arguments in these cases.[34]

Standing to Sue.   The Court refuses to hear a challenge against a statute or action unless the challenger can show that he or she is being personally and substantially injured by it. The landmark precedent here was the attempt to bring a taxpayer's suit against the federal government to prevent it from making payments under a 1921 law aimed at reducing infant and maternal mortality. The petitioner claimed that the government had no authority to pass such a law and said she did not want her tax money used for it. The Court dismissed her suit on the grounds that she could not claim any substantial personal injury. The taxpayer's "interest in the moneys of the treasury [is] shared with millions of others; is comparatively minute and indeterminable; and the effect upon future taxation . . . so remote, fluctuating and uncertain, that no basis is afforded for an appeal. . . ."[35]

CONSTITUTIONAL AMENDMENTS

The surest way of checking the Court is also one of the most difficult: amending the Constitution. As we saw in chapter 2, constitutional amendments must be proposed by at least two-thirds of Congress or by a convention called by Congress at the request of at least two-thirds of the states. Then the amendment must be ratified by at least three-quarters of the state legislatures' ratifying conventions. An amendment becomes the final word; the Court may never overrule it on grounds of unconstitutionality, for the amendment *is* the Constitution. In three instances Court decisions have been overruled by amendments: *Chisholm v. Georgia* (1793), which allowed a plaintiff living in one state to sue another state, was overruled five years later by the Eleventh Amendment; *Dred Scott* was overruled by the Thirteenth and Fourteenth Amendments in 1865 and 1868; and the *Income Tax Cases* of 1895, which struck down the income tax, were reversed by the Sixteenth Amendment in 1913. In recent years efforts have been made to add amendments to the Constitution reversing the abortion, busing, school prayer, and flag-burning decisions, but proponents have never been able to muster the necessary two-thirds vote in Congress.

LIMITING THE COURT'S JURISDICTION

As part of the frustration at being unable to pass amendments, some opponents of the Court's decisions have sought another route that requires only a majority vote in Congress. Article III, Section 2, of the Constitution says that the Court shall have appellate jurisdiction, both as to law and fact, "with such Exceptions, and under such Regulations, as the Congress shall make." On the face of it, this excepting clause seems to give Congress the power to withdraw areas of law from the Court's appellate jurisdiction by majority vote.[36] In 1868 Congress passed a law that did just that, and in the case of *Ex parte McCardle* (1869) the Court upheld the constitutionality of the law.

The jurisdiction issue is like a dormant volcano in Congress: Every so often it erupts. In 1957 Senator William Jenner of Indiana managed to get a bill limiting the Court's jurisdiction reported out of the Senate Judiciary Committee. As he complained that recent Supreme Court decisions were "undermining the efforts of the people's representatives . . . to meet and master the Communist plot," Senator Jenner proposed a long list of areas to be removed from the Court's jurisdiction.[37] The Jenner bill was defeated on the Senate floor by only one vote. Bills were introduced again in 1968 after the Court's decisions on suspects' rights and in 1971 after the decision on busing for the sake of racial balance. Between 1979 and 1984 a number of bills introduced in Congress would have limited the Court's jurisdiction in such areas as abortion and school prayer. These bills died in the House's Judiciary Committee; they were killed on the floor by Senate filibusters.

But the issue of whether or not Congress has the right to limit the Court's jurisdiction is far from dead. It is really part of a larger, almost perennial, issue in the United States: Should Congress attempt to curb the powers of the Supreme Court? This question is debated by William Stanmeyer and Judge Irving Kaufman in this chapter's Taking Sides section.

IMPEACHMENT

If worse comes to worst, Congress can impeach members of the Supreme Court. The procedure is the same one used for impeaching the president: The House of Representatives brings the impeachment (an indictment) by majority rule, and the Senate tries the case. It takes a two-thirds majority in the Senate to convict and remove the justice.

Impeachment is an extreme remedy, and it is unlikely to be pursued in any serious way unless a justice's conduct at least borders on the outrageous. Presumably, a justice who makes decisions with total disregard for the meaning of the Constitution would be a suitable candidate. Supreme Court justice Samuel ("Bacon-face") Chase, an intemperate colleague of John Marshall, was impeached by the House in 1805 for reading his own Federalist biases into the law and jailing Republicans under any pretext he could find, but even Chase won an acquittal from the Senate.

(Continued on page 324)

FEDERAL JUDGES CONVICTED OF IMPEACHABLE OFFENSES

1804: John Pickering, federal judge in New Hampshire. Convicted of irregular judicial procedures, immorality, alcoholism.

1862: West Humphreys, federal judge in Tennessee. Convicted of advocating secession, accepting appointment as a Confederate judge.

1913: Robert Archibald, federal commerce court judge. Convicted of using improper influence and accepting favors.

1936: Halsted L. Ritter, federal judge in Florida. Convicted of filing false tax returns.

1986: Harry E. Claiborne, federal judge in Nevada. Convicted of filing false tax returns.

1989: Alcee L. Hastings, federal judge in Florida. Convicted of eight charges, including making false statements, producing false documents, and conspiring to receive a bribe.

Should Congress Curb the Powers of the Supreme Court?

YES William Stanmeyer

Based upon William A. Stanmeyer, "Judicial Supremacy," in Robert Whitaker, ed., *The New Right
Papers* (New York: St. Martin's Press, 1982).
Stanmeyer contends that the Court has commanded radical changes—such as the legalization
of abortion, the expulsion of prayer from public
schools, and the transformation of state criminal
procedures—with very little support either from
public opinion or the Constitution. The Supreme
Court today "reminds us of the kings and their
courts in the Middle Ages: a royal elite wearing
special robes and sometimes speaking a different
language from the ordinary people. . . ." He considers various proposals for curbing the Court's
power, including restricting the appellate jurisdiction of the Court, and believes them all justified if
not equally feasible. One proposal he especially
likes is a constitutional amendment permitting
Congress to override Supreme Court decisions by
a two-thirds vote of both houses.

NO Irving Kaufman

Based upon Irving R. Kaufman, "Congress vs. the
Court," *New York Times Magazine*, September 20,
1981, pp. 44+.
A federal Court of Appeals judge, Kaufman is
horrified at the thought of stripping the Supreme
Court of jurisdiction over such questions as abortion, school prayer, and busing. "One may disagree with these decisions. . . . But one cannot
doubt that they were based upon informed interpretation of the Constitution—and not on the
basis of political or ideological expediency." He
thinks that depriving the Court of jurisdiction by
federal statute would be unconstitutional and that
the Court would be right to strike down such a
law. If it ever did succeed, it would leave vital
constitutional rights in the hands of state judges,
which the Framers of the Constitution never
intended. It should be "self-evident," Kaufman
says, "that the framers saw independent, tenured
Federal judges . . . as more appropriate arbiters
of conflicts between constitutional and state law
than elected state judges, many of whom are
popularly elected and who might be partial to
state law."

Postscript

Kaufman considers it self-evident that appointed federal judges can do a better
job of interpreting the Constitution than elected state officials. A self-evident
proposition is one of which it is impossible to think the opposite. Is it impossible
to think that elected state representatives could have a better grasp of the
Constitution than appointed federal judges?

   One famous legal scholar, the late Alexander Bickel, was not ready to put
the Constitution in the hands of state officials, but he did cast doubt on the
omniscience of federal judges in *The Majority of Consent* (New Haven: Yale
University Press, 1975); on the other side, making a strong case for judicial
activism is former Watergate prosecutor Archibald Cox in his *The Role of the
Supreme Court in American Government* (New York: Oxford University Press,
1978).

(Continued from page 322) Soliciting bribes or favors from litigants would also seem to be sufficient grounds for impeachment. Although no Supreme Court justice has ever been removed on such grounds—no Supreme Court justice has ever been convicted by the Senate—two judges in lower federal courts have been removed for seeking payoffs. In 1913 Robert A. Archibald, a federal commerce court judge, was impeached by the House and convicted by the Senate for using improper influence and accepting favors from litigants. More recently, in October 1989 federal district judge Alcee L. Hastings was removed from the bench after being convicted in the Senate on a number of counts, among them conspiring to obtain a $150,000 bribe.[38] From 1804 to the present, a total of six federal judges have been found guilty of a variety of offenses, from public drunkenness to filing false tax returns, and have been removed from office (see box on page 322).

APPOINTMENT

Perhaps the best way to change Supreme Court opinions is to change the people who deliver them. We saw in the 1930s situation that President Roosevelt was eventually able to shape a Court that was more receptive to New Deal legislation. The same has been true during the last 20 years of Republican appointments to the Court. Richard Nixon was able to appoint four members of the Court between 1968 and 1972. Justice Harry Blackmun has turned out to be more liberal than conservative, but the other three, in combination with the Reagan appointments, helped to shift the direction of opinion into a more conservative path. There will probably be more shifting over the next couple of years as Justices Marshall and Brennan, the Court's two oldest and most liberal members, retire. Chief Justice Rehnquist probably summed it up best when he said that the greatest agent for change in the Supreme Court is Father Time.[39]

Reflections

This chapter has studied the powers of and limitations on the federal judiciary, particularly the Supreme Court. Perhaps *powers* is not the right word because in a certain sense courts have no power. They wield no sword and they control no purse. What they have, instead, is something more delicate. Alexander Hamilton called it "judgment."

Points to Remember

1. The limits on the Supreme Court and other federal courts are self-imposed limits, constitutional amendments limiting a Court's jurisdiction, impeachment, and appointment of new members.

2. Among the most important self-limitations are the prohibition against advisory opinions (sometimes violated by *obiter dictum*) and the doctrine of political questions.

3. Constitutional amendments are hard to pass, but they are a certain means of overruling the Court; for example, constitutional amendments overturned Court decisions protecting slavery and invalidating the federal income tax.

4. Unlike a constitutional amendment, a congressional bill stripping the Court of jurisdiction over particular issues can be passed by a simple majority of Congress. However, such a statute is constitutionally questionable and might be struck down by the Supreme Court itself.

5. Justices of the Supreme Court and of lower federal courts can be impeached in extreme cases. However, there is no clear consensus on what constitutes impeachable behavior.

6. Probably the most successful means of changing the direction of Court opinion is by the appointment process. Some presidents, like F. D. Roosevelt, Nixon, and Reagan, have had a significant impact on Court decisions in this way.

The judgment granted to our federal courts is very broad indeed. Since Chief Justice John Marshall's historic opinion in *Marbury v. Madison*, they have been given the authority to strike down laws as being unconstitutional—an authority almost unique to American courts.

If the judgment of courts is broadly accepted as legitimate and reasonable, then they can exert great leverage over the political process. But if judges seem to be abusing their judgment—by pushing it too far, by making decisions that destroy the public peace, by substituting their own personal biases for the law—they risk a reaction that could end up weakening their influence. The Court did that when it decided the 1857 *Dred Scott* case, and it did it again during the 1930s when it struck down a number of New Deal laws. After *Dred Scott* came the Civil War and a blow to the Court's prestige; in the 1930s the reaction took the form of Roosevelt's "court-packing" proposal.

Today the members of the Supreme Court are generally in agreement that in economic cases—cases affecting property rights—great deference should be paid to the legislative branch. The assumption is that these laws are constitutional unless clear and convincing evidence shows that they are not. On the other hand, most justices lean toward judicial activism when Bill of Rights freedoms are involved: They cast a hard eye on any statute that seeks to limit these preferred freedoms.

Alexander Hamilton called the Supreme Court "the least dangerous branch" of the federal government because he considered it the weakest. But Hamilton died in 1804, well over 150 years before the Court decided that public school prayer violates the establishment clause and abortion restrictions violate "a right of privacy." Has this "least dangerous branch" *become* dangerous by overreaching and straining at the meaning of the Constitution in order to substitute the policy preferences of appointed judges for those of our elected legislators? The issue is much debated today.

A related issue is whether or not anything should be done about our federal judges. Shall we impeach them, override them by constitutional amendment, limit their jurisdiction by statute, or wait for them to die or retire? Another option is to stop worrying and learn to live with them. After all, they sometimes limit *themselves* by staying away from political questions and refusing (with some exceptions) to issue purely advisory opinions.

A third option is to realize what a contribution our Supreme Court has made. It was the first branch of our federal government to end legally imposed racial segregation. The overwhelming majority of Americans now agree that the Court's 1954 decision in *Brown v. Board of Education* was the right decision; there was not such overwhelming agreement at the time. Perhaps some more recent controversial decisions may turn out to be as broadly approved by the nation as *Brown* is today.

Then again, perhaps not. Whether it wants to or not, the Supreme Court finds itself in a prophetic role. Some of its decisions are almost bound to go against contemporary public opinion; that is the way it is with prophets. Yet there are true prophets and false prophets. The "Nine Old Men" of the 1930s were not very good prophets, nor were the judges who handed down the *Dred Scott* decision of 1857. So it comes down to this: When the Court makes decisions that stir the wrath of the majority (or even a sizable minority), it is taking a large and visible gamble that history will be on *its* side. Since the 1950s and particularly since the middle of the 1960s, the Court has been staking a great deal on the verdicts of history. Some of its bets, such as the *Brown* decision of 1954, have paid off. Other decisions, such as those legalizing abortion on demand and setting up a wall of separation between church and state, still lack the broad and untroubled support that constitutes a genuine consensus. Can this unsettled situation continue indefinitely? It is hard to say, but if past experience is any guide, time will finally sort out the arguments. Some will be honored; some will end up in the dustbin of history.

Notes

1. For a more complete picture of the structure and components of the lower federal courts, see Henry J. Abraham, *The Judicial Process*, 5th ed. (New York: Oxford University Press, 1984); Sheldon Goldman and Thomas Jahnige, *The Federal Courts as a Political System*, 3rd ed. (New York: Harper & Row, 1985); Richard A. Posner, *The Federal Courts* (Cambridge, MA: Harvard University Press, 1985).

2. Linda Greenhouse, "High Court Asks Sharp Questions in Abortion Case," *New York Times*, Apr. 27, 1989, pp. 1, B14.

3. *Federalist* No. 78, any edition.

4. J. Elliot, *The Debates in the Several State Conventions on the Adoption of the Federal Constitution* (Philadelphia, 1836), II, p. 325.

5. Raoul Berger, *Congress v. the Supreme Court* (Cambridge, Massachusetts, 1969), p. 49.

6. Quoted in L. Baker, *John Marshall: A Life in Law* (New York: Macmillan, 1974) p. 412.

7. *McCulloch v. Maryland* (1819).

8. In *McCulloch v. Maryland* Marshall said that if the Constitution tried to spell out everything in the manner of legal code, it could scarcely be embraced by the human mind and "would probably never be understood by the public."

9. The first systematic critique of Marshall's reasoning was made by Pennsylvania state judge John B. Gibson in the case of *Eakin v. Raub* (1825).

10. See above, chapter 5.

11. Quoted in Charles S. Hyneman, *The Supreme Court on Trial* (New York: Atherton Press, Inc., 1960), p. 31.

12. Quoted in Harry Carman and Harold Syrett, *A History of the American People* (New York: Alfred A. Knopf, Inc., 1957), II, p. 584.

13. *Schechter Poultry Corp. v. United States* (1935); *Panama Refining Co. v. Ryan* (1935); *Railroad Retirement Board v. Alton Railroad Co.* (1935); *Carter v. Carter Coal Co.* (1936). The Court gave various reasons for ruling these laws unconstitutional; the two most common reasons were that the statutes exceeded the bounds of federal authority and that they delegated too much discretionary power to the president.

14. Frankfurter's opinion in *Kovacs v. Cooper*, 336 U.S. 77, at 90 (1949).

15. Quoted by Alden Whitman, "For Sixteen Years, Warren Saw the Constitution as Protector of Rights and Equality," *New York Times*, July 10, 1974, p. 24.

16. Philip B. Kurland, *Politics, the Constitution, and the Warren Court* (Chicago: University of Chicago Press, 1970), p. 186; Alexander M. Bickel, *The Supreme Court and the Idea of Progress* (New York: Harper & Row), 1970, pp. 50ff.

17. *Nixon on the Issues* (New York: Nixon-Agnew Campaign Committee, 1968), pp. 85-86.

18. See cases discussed in chapter 6.

19. *Miller v. California* (1973), discussed in chapter 4.

20. *Bakke v. Regents of University of California* (1978), discussed at the beginning of chapter 5.

21. See chapter 6, pp. 141-44.

22. *Brewer v. Williams* (1977); *Dunaway v. New York* (1979); *Jenkins v. Anderson* (1980).

23. See chapter 5.

24. *Griswold v. Connecticut*, 381 U.S. 479 (1965). See the discussion of this case in chapter 5.

25. See White's dissent in *Roe v. Wade*, 410 U.S. 113 (1973).

26. U.S. Department of Justice, "Address of The Honorable Edwin Meese III, Attorney General of the United States Before The American Bar Association," July 9, 1985 (Mimeo), pp. 14-15.

27. *New York Times*, Oct. 27, 1985, Part IV, p. 1.

28. "Excerpts of Brennan's Speech on the Constitution," *NYT*, Oct. 13, 1985, p. 36.

29. Quoted in *New York Post*, July 6, 1987, p. 1.

30. Stuart Taylor, "Of Bork and Tactics," *New York Times*, Oct. 31, 1987, p. A23.

31. "Kennedy Cast Key Votes in 7 Conservative Rulings," *NYT*, July 3, 1988, p. 14.

32. *Patterson v. McLean* (1988).

33. "Justices are not platonic guardians appointed to wield authority according to their personal moral predilections." Justice William Brennan, "Excerpts of Brennan's Speech on the Constitution," *New York Times*, Oct. 13, 1985, p. 36.

34. *Mora v. McNamara* (1967); *McArthur v. Clifford* (1968); *Holmes v. United States* (1968); *Velvel v. Nixon* (1970); *Massachusetts v. Laird* (1970); *Dacosta v. Laird* (1972).

35. *Frothingham v. Mellon*, 262 U.S. 447 (1923).

36. But see Raoul Berger, referred to in chapter 9. Berger concedes that "the inference is warranted if we look no further than the terms of the clause itself" (p. 285). However, Berger's study of the background of the excepting clause has convinced him that the clause was intended to qualify the Court's appellate jurisdiction over matters of *fact* but not over matters of *law*.

37. "Hearings Before the Sub-Committee to Investigate the Administration of the Internal Security Act and Other Internal Security Laws of the Committee on the Judiciary," United States Senate, 85th Congress, 1st Sess., Part I, pp. 2-13.

38. David Johnston, "Hastings Ousted as U.S. Judge by Senate Vote," *New York Times*, October 21, 1989, p. 1.

39. Quoted in the *New York Times*, Oct. 27, 1985, Part IV, p. 1.

Political Participation

In this section we look at the dynamic, often confusing, processes by which American citizens make their voices heard and get involved in the political process. In a democracy, public opinion must play a key role in policymaking. What sort of a role does it play in America? What are the beliefs of Americans, how are they formed, and how are they measured? These questions are studied in Chapter 13. In Chapter 14 we see the changing role of the mass media—and the people who run the media—in shaping public opinion.

Chapter 15 studies interest groups and lobbies: the different types, their purposes, and the factors affecting their success. Chapter 16 examines how our political party system has changed and developed over the years and how it fits in with American democracy. Chapter 17 takes a broad look at our national political campaigns and elections and also studies the electoral college system, examines the role of television advertisements in campaigns, and looks at the controversy over the importance of money in American elections.

The good sense of the people
will always be found to
be the best army.

Thomas Jefferson

13

Public Opinion
and Political Socialization

OPINIONS, ATTITUDES, AND VALUES IN AMERICA

    Qualities of Public Opinion: Intensity, Stability, Direction / Elite and Mass Opinion:
    On Tolerance / Ideologies of the Left and the Right / Liberalism and
    Conservatism: The Meanings Change

POLITICAL SOCIALIZATION

    Childhood: Trusting Authority / Adolescence: Questioning Authority / Peer Group
    and Community Influences / The Mass Media

MEASURING PUBLIC OPINION

    Sampling Techniques / The Wording of Questions / The Interview
    Bandwagon Effects / The Role of Public Opinion Polls

REFLECTIONS

The Ups and Downs of Jimmy Carter

On January 20, 1977, President-elect Jimmy Carter refused the traditional limousine ride after his inauguration.
On that bright, chilly morning he and Rosalyn walked hand in hand down
Pennsylvania Avenue from the Capitol to the White House. They waved
to the crowds lining the street, and the crowds waved back. Everyone was
in high spirits.*

    Carter had good reason to be happy. He had won only a narrow
victory over Gerald Ford in the November election, but by January it was
clear that he had tapped a large reservoir of goodwill within the nation.

*This account is drawn from the following sources: Kathleen A. Frankovic, "Public
Opinion Trends," in Gerald Pomper et al., eds., *The Election of 1980: Reports and
Interpretations* (Chatham, NJ: Chatham House, 1981); *Gallup Opinion Index*, Report
Nos. 173 (December 1979), 175 (February 1980); Gallup poll news releases, August 5,
1980; September 10, 1980; *Washington Post*, October 28, 1980, p. A1; November 3,
1980, p. A9; Ted J. Smith III and J. Michael Hogan, "Public Opinion and the Panama
Canal Treaties of 1977," *Public Opinion Quarterly* (Spring 1987), pp. 5-30.

Perhaps in reaction to charges that the presidency had become an "imperial" institution, President Jimmy Carter wanted to show himself to be a humble "man of the people." Shown here walking with his wife Rosalyn and daughter Amy, Carter refused the traditional limousine ride to the White House after his inauguration. Carter also liked to dress informally and carry his own luggage.

People liked Jimmy Carter. They liked his earnestness and his humility. Under presidents Johnson and Nixon, critics had complained of how regal, how imperial, the presidency had become. There was certainly nothing imperial about Jimmy Carter. He said he wanted to be a people's president, a populist, and he went to great lengths to show it. He often dressed casually (blue jeans and cardigan sweaters), he did a national call-in radio program with CBS's Walter Cronkite, and he carried his own suitcase on and off Air Force One.

Carter's down-home style seemed to play well. A Gallup poll in February 1977 showed that 66 percent of Americans approved of his performance; only 8 percent disapproved. Through the spring and most of the summer of 1977, large majorities continued to think Jimmy Carter was doing a good job.

But then his ratings began to slip. Charges were made in the media that Bert Lance, Carter's budget director and close friend, had abused his office for personal gain. ("Lancegate," some called it, suggesting parallels to President Nixon's Watergate scandal. Lance later resigned.) Then there were the two Panama Canal treaties that had been negotiated by the Carter administration in 1977 and ratified by the Senate in 1978; critics charged that the treaties were sellouts because they provided for the eventual transfer of the Canal, owned by the United States since its construction in 1905, to Panama. Whether or not these controversies were the cause, by August 1978 only 39 percent of those polled approved of the way Carter was handling things.

Then, after he successfully mediated peace talks between Egypt and Israel at the presidential retreat in Camp David, Maryland, the ratings began to climb. A few weeks after the signing of the Camp David Accords in the fall of 1978, the polls showed that 48 percent of Americans approved of Carter's performance, and 34 percent disapproved. By January 1979, 50 percent approved, and 36 percent disapproved.

Then the slippage began again. By mid-summer, the polls showed only 28 percent approving of Carter's performance, while 59 percent disapproved. As the president's ratings continued to dip, Democrats became jittery. A presidential election was coming up the following year. Could Carter win it? Would it be better to field a stronger candidate? At informal meetings of prominent Democrats, the name of Edward M. Kennedy kept surfacing. Perhaps the Massachusetts senator would make a better vote-getter than Carter. Many thought so, including Kennedy himself. After mulling it over for a few months, the senator decided to challenge Carter for the nomination by entering the 1980 Democratic presidential primaries and caucuses.

Kennedy's hopes of winning seemed justified. By mid-October, 60 percent of Democratic voters were saying that they preferred him to Carter, and only 10 percent were undecided. These numbers seemed to forecast a landslide for Kennedy. A few weeks later, he announced his candidacy.

Then something happened. On November 4, 1979, just two days before Kennedy announced his candidacy, a mob of Islamic militants in Iran stormed the American embassy in Teheran and took its employees hostage. The increasingly fanatical government in Iran not only made no attempt to rescue the embassy personnel but actually supported the militants who held them prisoners. This strange melodrama, which was to last 444 days, had a double effect: It utterly destroyed Kennedy's challenge to Carter, and it helped elect Ronald Reagan.

Almost immediately, Kennedy's lead began to dissolve. By early December, Carter was slightly ahead. A month later, 51 percent of Democrats wanted Carter, 37 percent wanted Kennedy. By the end of January, 63 percent wanted Carter; only 24 percent, Kennedy. This erosion of Kennedy's popularity set the stage for some critical primary defeats. In the New Hampshire primary, important because it is the first, Carter won by a small margin. Kennedy won, as expected, in his home state of Massachusetts, but in Illinois, the first real test of the candidates' strength in the big states, Carter beat Kennedy by a 2-1 margin. By the time of the Democratic convention in August, Carter had piled up enough primary victories to be certain of renomination.

Unfortunately for Carter, by convention time his popularity had once again plummeted. The delegates pledged to vote for him at the convention had been elected in the early spring, a few months after the hostage takeover. Now, many months later, the public was getting impatient with his inability to resolve the crisis. This impatience was aggravated by an abortive rescue attempt in April, a complicated scheme involving helicopters and commandos that ended in tragedy when two U.S. helicopters collided in an Iranian desert, killing all on board. Figure 13.1 illustrates the public response to Carter's actions in the White House.

Carter won the nomination, but at the end of the convention he was only one point ahead of Ronald Reagan in the Gallup poll. The election, it seemed, was going to be close. Earlier, Carter had challenged Reagan to a debate, and Reagan had accepted. Most people who watched the televised debate held on October 28 thought Reagan had won it. The pollsters stopped polling a week before the election, and Gallup's last poll showed a three-point lead for Reagan. At that stage, it still looked like a horse race, but the election was to show a decisive victory for Reagan — 10 percentage points, a popular vote margin of 8 million. Apparently the pollsters stopped polling too soon, missing the big shift away from Carter in the remaining few days before the election. It was the last plunge of the roller coaster that had taken Carter from the height of his popularity shortly after being sworn in, through several intermediate swoops and

FIGURE **13-1**

President Carter's Approval Rating, 1977-1980

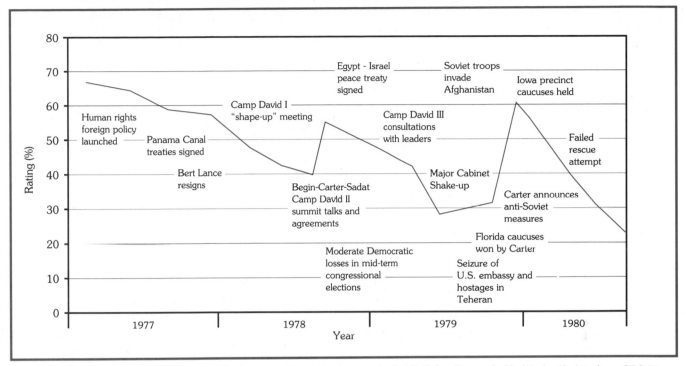

Data source: Reprinted with the permission of the American Enterprise Institute for Public Policy Research. Updated with data from CBS/*New York Times* polls, April, June, and August 1980.

In response to pollsters' questions about Jimmy Carter's performance as president, respondents gave increasingly negative ratings between January 1977 and the summer of 1978. Then came a remarkable series of positive and negative ratings, which culminated in a final ratings nosedive just before the November 1980 presidential election.

*　　　*　　　*　　　*　　　*

climbs, to the final trough of public displeasure on election day. "Never," said pollster George Gallup, "in the 45-year history of presidential surveys has the Gallup poll found such volatility and uncertainty."[1]

*　　　*　　　*　　　*　　　*

It was not to be the last time polls would show such volatility. In July 1988 George H. W. Bush was trailing the Democratic candidate, Massachusetts governor Michael S. Dukakis, by 17 points in the polls, but by early August he was ahead of him by 8 points. In slightly more than two weeks, the percentage of Americans who preferred Bush to Dukakis jumped by 25 percent.

What does all this mean? Alexander Hamilton would have had no trouble interpreting it. At the Constitutional Convention of 1787, he argued against giving direct control of the government to the people because, he said, "the people are turbulent and changing; they seldom judge or determine right." Could the changing fortunes of Jimmy Carter and Michael Dukakis be cited as proof? Do they show that the people are indeed "turbulent and changing"? Hamilton's complaint should not be

331

lightly dismissed. Carter left the White House with a reputation for weakness, softness, and ineffectiveness. Yet he was the same man whose humility the public had first regarded as a virtue.

If Carter had wanted some bittersweet consolation, he would have had no difficulty finding parallels to his experience in that of other presidents. Lyndon Johnson started off with a tremendous burst of public approval, but by the time he left office the public had serious doubts about his leadership. President Nixon experienced an even steeper decline in approval once the Watergate scandal broke. Ronald Reagan also had his ups and downs during his eight years in office. He was once called the "Teflon president" because none of his critics seemed to be able to make anything that they threw at him stick; the mud just slid off. But the Iran-Contra scandal in 1987 finally scratched the Teflon: At that point Reagan's popularity took a sudden plunge, although by the end of the year it had partly recovered.[2]

Over the long haul, American opinion is sometimes very kind to once-scorned leaders. Take the example of Harry Truman. Truman was one of the most unpopular presidents of this century, yet today he is revered as a spunky, courageous man who did a good job under difficult circumstances. Truman did not change, yet today he is looked upon with different eyes. There you have it, Hamilton might say, is this not proof of how "turbulent and changing" public opinion is?

What causes these fluctuations in American public opinion? Are there any constants? Is public opinion rational, or is it, as Hamilton implied, an arbitrary, mindless force? How is it measured? What role should it play in a constitutional democracy? Let us begin by taking a closer look at what public opinion is and what sorts of opinions Americans have.

FIGURE **13-2**

President Reagan's Approval Rating, 1981-1988

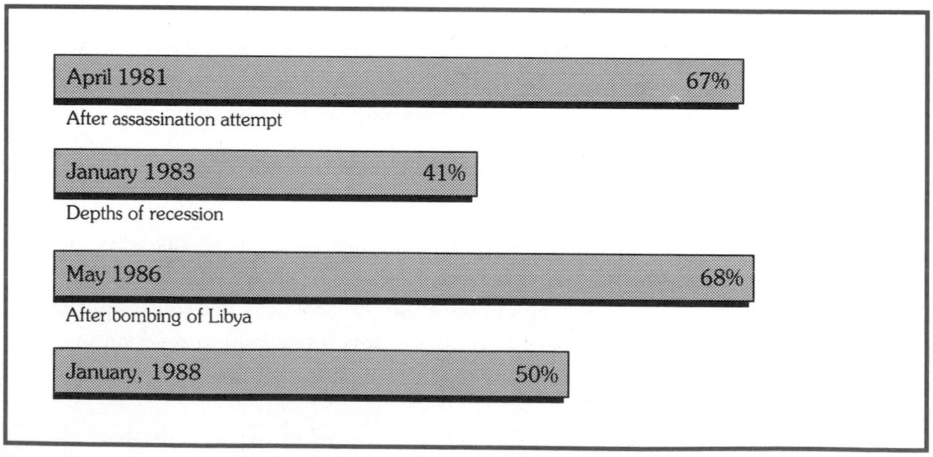

April 1981	67%
After assassination attempt	
January 1983	41%
Depths of recession	
May 1986	68%
After bombing of Libya	
January, 1988	50%

Data source: New York Times/CBS News polls. Reprinted with permission.

Like his predecessor Jimmy Carter, President Ronald Reagan had his ups and downs in public approval ratings. Overall, he was one of the most popular of American presidents since Franklin Roosevelt, but he suffered declines in public approval ratings during the recession of the early 1980s and during the period when the Iran-Contra affair dominated the news.

Opinions, Attitudes, and Values in America

Political scientist V. O. Key defined public opinion as "those opinions held by private persons which governments find it prudent to heed."[3] The definition points up the connection between public opinion and democracy. In totalitarian countries, the term *public opinion* has almost no meaning, for the rulers do not have to pay attention to the people's opinions. There are no meaningful ways—such as elections or public demonstrations—by which people's opinions can be translated into policy. Indeed, it usually works the other way around: The people play it safe and do not voice opinions on public issues. There may be some public reactions, such as isolated food riots, deliberate work slowdowns, or worker morale low enough to ruin the economy. The rulers may decide at some point that it would be prudent to change policies in order to minimize these reactions. But they certainly have no obligation to do so and may decide instead to repress the people by force. In any case, these half-conscious protests hardly add up to a public voice; they are more like muffled sighs and groans.

Key's definition also tells us something about public opinion in a democracy. Even a freely elected government does not have to pay attention to the opinions of everyone. Some people do not vote or even care much about politics. Those who are well-informed and politically active are the ones the politicians "find it prudent to heed." Take the issue of gun control. Even though a majority of Americans polled favor more strict controls over the manufacture and sale of firearms, Congress has voted down all attempts to enact strict gun control legislation. It has done so because members of Congress know that groups of people, such as those who belong to the National Rifle Association (NRA), are adamantly opposed to gun control legislation and quite prepared to mobilize against legislators who vote for it. A majority of representatives therefore find it prudent to heed these voters. Even though the people who are opposed to gun control are a minority, they are a very intense and active minority. So whether we like it or not, it is *their* opinion that is politically relevant. This does not mean, of course, that proponents of gun control must just give up. If enough of them care enough, and for long enough, and get organized enough, their opinions will indeed be relevant. This brings us to a closer examination of the qualities of public opinion.

QUALITIES OF PUBLIC OPINION: INTENSITY, STABILITY, DIRECTION

Intensity is a measure of how deeply people feel about a given issue. You may have an opinion about some controversial issue, such as abortion or school prayer, but the political significance of your opinion depends in large part on how intensely you feel about the issue. If you feel very strongly about it, chances are you will translate your feelings into letters to a legislator or a newspaper, donations to an organization devoted to the issue, willingness to talk to friends and relatives about it, or at least the determination to vote for or against a candidate on the basis of that one issue. This makes your view "worth" more than that of someone who is relatively indifferent. At least that is the way politicians view it, and they may be right, for people who are politically active are usually better informed than those who are not.

Another quality of public opinion is its stability—the extent to which it stays the same over time. As we have seen when it came to evaluating Jimmy Carter's job performance, public opinion was very unstable, or volatile. Carter started off, as every president does, with a honeymoon period—a period of public trust and goodwill—when his ratings were high. Then began a roller coaster ride of peaks and valleys as his approval rating was affected by current events, such as the Camp David Accords and the Iran hostage crisis.

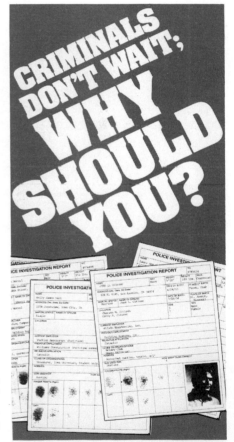

CRIMINALS DON'T WAIT; WHY SHOULD YOU?

The Case Against Waiting Periods

Public opinion has been defined as those opinions that governments "find it prudent to heed." Our legislators find it very prudent to heed the opinions of NRA members, who are adamantly opposed to gun control.

Initially, the hostage crisis, like almost every foreign policy crisis, caused Americans to "rally 'round the flag"—to support their nation against a perceived threat from abroad. This increased nationalism translates into approval of the president, who is the symbolic head of the nation. As the months went by, however, increasing frustration at Carter's failure to resolve the crisis led to his final slump in 1980. Yet even then it was by no means certain that Carter would be defeated by Ronald Reagan. Neither Reagan nor Carter was very much loved, and as one pollster noted, "The polls fluctuated as people tried to decide which of the two unlovable candidates to choose."[4] By 1984, though, the public's opinion of Reagan had gone up and stayed up, at least when it came to choosing between him and his Democratic opponent, Walter Mondale. From the outset of that campaign, a large, almost unchanging majority backed President Reagan.

Political scientists, media pundits, and other observers of American public opinion often try to locate opinions somewhere to the right, middle, and left of a scale. They also use terms like *liberal* and *conservative* to characterize political opinions; these too, they arrange in a scale or spectrum and try to see where people's opinions lie. In this manner, they speak of the direction of an opinion, meaning where it sits on the observer's scale. The scale itself is a bit elusive. It exists in the minds of observers—particularly among those in academia and the media—but most Americans are not clear as to what the scale means or where their views fall. We will look more closely at this problem of placing opinions along a spectrum when we discuss political ideology later in the chapter.

First, however, it is necessary to make some distinctions. In analyzing American public opinion, we must keep in mind the differences among (1) opinions, (2) attitudes, and (3) core beliefs.

Opinions: Ups and Downs.   Opinions are judgments about current events. They can be factual ("Which Democrat do you think will win the New Hampshire primary?") or evaluative ("How do you think the president is doing in foreign affairs?"). Either way, they do not go very deep. The response to a question like "How is the president doing?" does not spell out what kind of evaluative framework the respondent is using. For example, someone who thinks the president should not even meet with Soviet leaders might well say that President Reagan was "doing poorly" when he signed a treaty with Soviet leader Gorbachev. On the other hand, another respondent might give the president an "excellent" rating precisely because of the treaty signing. Opinions, then, tend to be rather superficial. They can also be extremely volatile, and for two reasons. First, opinions are tied to current events, and events can change quickly. Second, opinions can change as Americans learn more about a current event or situation. Americans are often asked questions about which they know next to nothing. In response, they toss off answers that are practically arbitrary. Such answers can thus fluctuate greatly over time.

Perhaps this is the place to point out what you probably already know: that Americans are generally ignorant of political facts. Study after study, year after year, confirms this. A 1973 poll by Louis Harris Associates showed that only 46 percent of respondents could name their representative. A 1978 poll by the National Opinion Research Center showed that only 34 percent of respondents could name the current secretary of state and only 30 percent were aware that the term of a House member is two years.[5] Other polls have shown that 45 percent of the respondents did not know how many U.S. senators are elected from each state and that 60 percent did not know the number of justices on the U.S. Supreme Court.[6] A poll on the Bill of Rights conducted for the Hearst Corporation in 1986 revealed that 59 percent of the respondents could not identify the Bill of Rights as the first 10 amendments to the Constitution; an earlier poll showed that 79 percent could not name a single provision contained in the Bill of Rights. In the Hearst poll, 64 percent thought that the Constitution establishes English as our national language.[7] Therefore, when you see polls saying that such-and-such a percentage of Americans support the Contras or Star Wars or a new arms treaty with the Soviets, remember that a large percentage of these people may be holding opinions on subjects about which they know practically nothing. The percentages can change dramatically as people's knowledge of the topic increases. There is certainly a lot of potential volatility here. Alexander Hamilton would call it turbulence.

Hamilton would not be bothered by the statistics on voter ignorance; he had little use for democracy anyway. We are the ones—those of us who believe in democracy—who should be concerned. "If a nation," said Thomas Jefferson, "expects to be ignorant and free in a state of civilization, it expects what never was and never will be."[8] Jefferson kept hoping that the combination of public education and a free press would gradually dispel political ignorance. Yet, here we are, two centuries later, with 59 percent of the public unable to identify the Bill of Rights. Why this civil illiteracy? It is hard to say. It could be that people do not have the time to learn about politics, or perhaps the distractions and diversions of modern society keep their minds off politics. Possibly our educational system has failed by watering down the civics curriculum too much or trying to spread it too far. It may also be that people simply do not care. Why not? We do not have any definitive answers yet; we are just learning to ask the right questions.

Attitudes: Gradual Changes.   An attitude runs deeper than an opinion; it may be defined as a general outlook or perspective on social policies. A good example would be one's outlook on race relations: Is racial segregation ever justified? Would you be opposed to voting for a well-qualified black candidate for president? Is affirmative action a good strategy for achieving equality? These kinds of questions elicit people's attitudes.

Attitudes can change, although the change is usually gradual. When Americans were asked in 1958 if they would vote for a well-qualified black male for president if their party nominated one, slightly more than 40 percent said yes; by 1965 the percentage was more than 60 percent; by 1988 it was 85 percent (see Figure 13.3, Panel A, on page 336). Another long-term shift can be seen in American opinion concerning support for a female president. Less than 35 percent of those polled in 1937 would have voted for a woman, but the percentages gradually increased: as is shown in Figure 13.3, Panel B, 45 percent of Americans polled in 1945 would have voted for a female candidate, almost 60 percent of those polled in 1965 would have, and by 1989 close to 87 percent of Americans were prepared to elect a female president. In other areas of race relations and sex roles, similar long-term trends can be traced. Greater and greater numbers of white Americans have supported school desegregation since the 1950s; today more than 90 percent favor it (compared to slightly more than 50 percent in 1956). Almost 80 percent of Americans today believe that married women have a right to a career in business, as opposed to less than 30 percent in 1945, and less than 25 percent in 1938 (see Figure 13.3, Panel B).[9]

We often hear that America is a racist country. The long-term polling data suggest that Americans are considerably *less* racist (and sexist) than they used to be. From what we can record and measure, it appears that a gradual but enormous change in attitude has occurred.

Core Values.   Deeper than attitudes—and much deeper than opinions—are core values. These are basic commitments. Attitudes concern the means of achieving certain ends. Core values touch upon the ends themselves. It is at this level that American public opinion seems to be the most stable. Admittedly, it is more difficult to measure long-term stability because scientific polling goes back only to the 1930s; but we can supplement polling data with a good deal of other evidence: evidence from our history and our literature, from the statements of our politicians and judges, from the insights of observers, and from revealing anecdotes. On the basis of all these data,

(Continued on page 337)

FIGURE **13-3**

Changing Attitudes in America

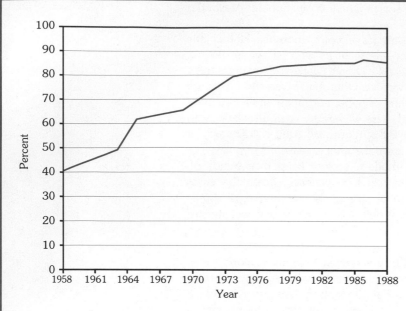

Panel A:
Voting for a Black Presidential Candidate

The question asked in this survey was: If your party nominated a well-qualified black man for president, would you vote for him? The percentage of people who answered "yes" is recorded on the graph at left. The wording of the question in the Gallup and the National Opinion Research Center polls was essentially the same, with only minor variations.

Data source: Surveys by the Gallup Organization, 1958–1969; National Opinion Research Center, University of Chicago, 1974–1988.

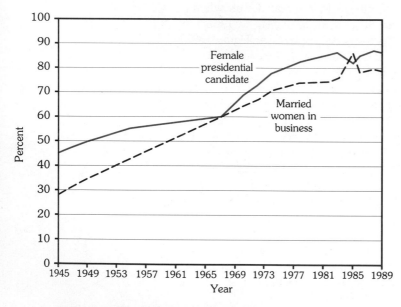

Panel B:
Voting for a Female Presidential Candidate/Approving of Married Women in Business

The questions asked in this survey were: If the party whose candidate you most often supported nominated a woman for president of the United States, would you vote for her if she seemed qualified for the job? (1949, 1955). If your party nominated a woman for president, would you vote for her if she were qualified for the job? (1967–1989). Do you think married women whose husbands make enough to support them should or should not be allowed to hold jobs if they want to? (1945). Do you approve of a married woman earning money in business or industry if she has a husband capable of supporting her? (1970). Do you approve or disapprove of a married woman earning money in business or industry if she has a husband capable of supporting her? (1972–1989). The percentage of people who said they would vote for a female presidential candidate and the percentage of people who said they approved of married women earning money in business or industry is recorded at left.

Data source: Female presidential candidate: Surveys by American Institute of Public Opinion (Gallup), 1937–1971; National Opinion Research Center, General Social Surveys, 1972–1989. Married women in business: Surveys by the Roper Organization for *Fortune*, 1945; American Institute of Public Opinion (Gallup), 1970; National Opinion Research Center, General Social Surveys, 1972–1989.

we can hazard at least four general categories of core beliefs for most Americans: (1) belief in God; (2) belief in individualism and equality of opportunity; (3) pride in America; and (4) belief in moderation.

1. *Americans believe in God.* In a landmark 1952 Supreme Court opinion, Justice William O. Douglas wrote: "We are a religious people, whose institutions presuppose the existence of a Supreme Being."[10] There is abundant evidence of this. In response to the question "Do you believe in God or a universal spirit?," 94 percent of Americans answered yes to Gallup pollsters in 1976.[11] The percentage has stayed at that level, with very small variations, since Americans were first polled on the question in 1948.

Admittedly, the inclusion of "universal spirit" leaves a lot of room for unorthodoxy, but the answers to other questions on religion in polls show how traditional most Americans are in matters of religious belief. In a 1968 survey, 85 percent said that they believed in heaven and 65 percent indicated a belief in hell.[12] A 1982 Gallup poll found that 71 percent of Americans believed in life after death.[13]

Americans also think—or, at least, say—that religion matters in their lives. In the 1976 survey, 86 percent claimed that their religious beliefs were either "very important" or "fairly important," with over half being in the first category. It is in this area that we can really see the contrast between Americans and people from other industrial democracies. Look at Table 13.1. Italians, in second place to Americans, say that religion is "very" important—but notice the dropoff of more than 20 points. Notice also that in Great Britain and France, 20 percent of those polled consider religion "not at all" important, compared to only 5 percent here. Small wonder that American politicians often talk about God! Yet it would be a mistake to think that religion can be put on the political agenda. Most Americans think that churches should keep out of political and social matters and that the main purpose of religion is to "comfort the individual."[14] Fully 78 percent of Americans think that religious convictions should not be the basis for political action.[15] When asked whether it was a good or bad idea for clergy to run for public office, 53 percent thought it was a bad

TABLE 13-1

Importance of Religious Beliefs

Nation or Region	Very	Fairly	Not Too	Not at All	Don't Know
United States	58%	30%	7%	5%	2%
Italy	36	42	16	6	*
Canada	36	36	19	9	*
Benelux†	26	30	22	19	3
Australia	25	33	29	13	*
Great Britain	23	26	26	20	5
France	22	33	23	20	2
West Germany	17	30	37	14	2
Scandinavia	17	28	39	13	3

*Less than .5%
† Belgium, the Netherlands, and Luxembourg

Source: Harry Holloway, with John George, *Public Opinion: Coalition, Elites, and Masses,* 2d ed. (New York: St. Martin's Press, 1986), p. 81. Reprinted with permission.

Religion is very important to most Americans. This is an interesting fact that points out the differences in basic values between citizens of this country and those of other Western countries. Only the citizens of Canada and Italy come close to those of the United States in their attitudes toward the importance of religion.

idea; only 34 percent thought it was a good idea.[16] On the other hand, 80 percent would support a constitutional amendment allowing prayer in public schools and roughly 90 percent have endorsed the idea of "more emphasis" on conservative social values based upon traditional religious concepts.[17] Still, many politicians oppose school prayer, saying things like "My family and I believe in prayer, but we pray at home and in our church."

2. *Americans believe in individualism and equality of opportunity.* American thought has been much influenced by the work of the seventeenth-century English philosopher John Locke. It was Locke who insisted that individual labor is the only rightful basis of ownership. Locke supplied the philosophical grounds for economic individualism, the belief that individual effort is what gives people the right to wealth. "Lockeanism," as historian Louis Hartz called it, runs deep in American history.[18] From the frontier settlers to the Yuppies of today, Americans say: "I worked for it, I took risks for it—it's mine." They oppose limits on the amount of money people can earn. When respondents were asked in a 1981 poll if they thought there should be a $100,000-limit on incomes, 71 percent said no.[19] Even in 1940, when America was barely out of the Depression and many were supposed to resent the rich, a poll showed that 74 percent opposed any law limiting incomes.[20]

Believing as they do in economic individualism, Americans are not keen on socialism, the doctrine that calls for state (or community) ownership of basic industries. The high point of socialism as a national movement in the United States came in 1912, when Eugene V. Debs, the Socialist candidate for president, won 900,000 popular votes, 6 percent of the total. Socialism then declined in popularity, almost expired in the 1920s, rallied briefly in the "radical" 1930s, and finally collapsed. By 1940 it was politically dead.[21] Today socialism remains popular in Europe but not here.

Americans approve of capitalism, but they do so in qualified terms. They are often critical of specific business practices, and a 1985 poll showed that almost 73 percent believed that "there is too much power concentrated in the hands of a few large companies for the good of the nation."[22] Americans do accept a positive role for the state in regulating business and helping the poor. They consistently support the proposition that the United States spends too little on health and education, as Figure 13.4 indicates. In one poll, 73 percent said they would support an amendment to the Constitution guaranteeing the right to adequate health care to all citizens, even those who cannot afford it.[23] This brings us to the discussion of equality, a related American core value.

The Declaration of Independence affirms that "all men are created equal." But note the kind of equality in which Americans believe. It is really another facet of individualism. American-style equality is equality of opportunity—the equal right of each individual person to better his or her lot in life. This is far different from equality of condition, the notion that people are entitled to an equal share, regardless of effort or output. Americans are receptive to the idea of helping those who need it, but their idea of lending assistance usually means helping people to help themselves—"a hand, not a handout." In that sense, then, Americans support what is sometimes called welfare capitalism. The late socialist writer Michael Harrington used to claim that there was a kind of masked, hidden socialism popular here, but "its socialist aims are phrased in capitalistic rhetoric."[24] On the other hand, political scientist Donald J. Devine, a former Reagan official, thinks that when poll questions are properly framed, they show that most Americans prefer to deal with social problems through private and local government agencies, not the federal bureaucracy.[25] George Bush played on this theme when he ran for president in 1988. He used the phrase "a thousand points of light" to emphasize how important the volunteer efforts of individuals are to the nation.

3. *Americans are proud of America.* We saw earlier that President Carter benefited from the Iran crisis in the short run. Americans always "rally 'round the flag"

These Fourth of July marchers display their pride in their country. A 1982 Gallup poll indicated that such feelings of national pride are more common among Americans than they are among citizens of other countries. Recent events seem to support these findings: When the Supreme Court ruled in 1989 that burning the flag, the symbol of America, was a form of self-expression protected by the First Amendment, patriotic Americans protested and many called for an amendment to the Constitution banning desecration of the flag.

FIGURE **13-4**

339

Opinions,
Attitudes, and
Values in America

Too Little Public Spending on Health and Education

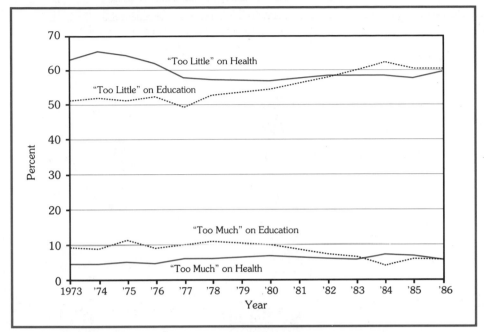

Source: Robert Y. Shapiro and John Young, "Public Opinion and the Welfare State: The United States in Comparative Perspective," *Political Science Quarterly* (Spring 1989), p. 61.

Polls taken from 1973 to 1986 show a high level of public support for spending on health and education. This support remained relatively stable over the years; 60 percent of those polled in 1986 stated that we spend too little on health and education and only 5 percent stated that we spend too much.

at the outset of a foreign policy crisis, and it causes them to support—at least initially—almost any presidential response. Americans do this not because they love their president but because they love their country. This may happen in other countries as well, but there is reason to believe that it is more likely to happen here.

A 1982 poll taken by the Gallup organization for the Center for Applied Research in the Apostolate, a Roman Catholic organization, asked people in different countries about their feelings on various religious and secular topics. When asked how they felt about their country, 80 percent of Americans said they were very proud to be Americans. Only 30 percent of the Japanese, 21 percent of the West Germans, 33 percent of the French, 55 percent of the British, and 41 percent of the Italians felt that way about their own countries. "In many European countries, pride in nationality is regarded as a rather outdated concept," the Center commented.[26]

Of course, love of one's country does not have to mean an uncritical attachment to its leaders. In the late 1970s, some polls were showing a widespread loss of faith in the leaders of government, business, labor, and other private and public institutions in this country. Other polls suggest that Americans have a kind of "well . . . okay" attitude toward key institutions in their country, like the military, the press, and the Supreme Court. The majority of poll respondents in America register "some confidence" in these institutions; a minority say they have "a great deal of confidence." Only small minorities, however, say they have "hardly any" confidence (see Figure 13.5 on the following page). *(Continued on page 341)*

FIGURE **13-5**

Confidence in Key Institutions

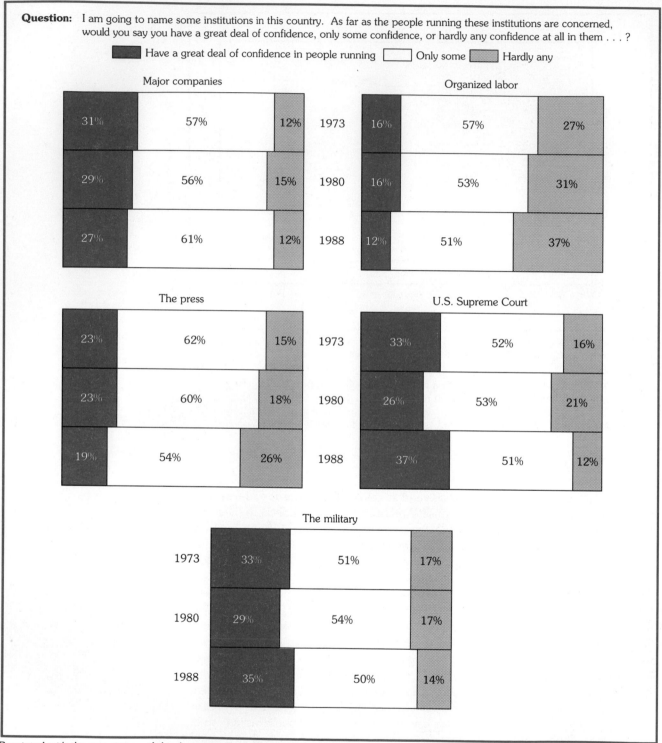

Question: I am going to name some institutions in this country. As far as the people running these institutions are concerned, would you say you have a great deal of confidence, only some confidence, or hardly any confidence at all in them . . . ?

■ Have a great deal of confidence in people running   □ Only some   ▨ Hardly any

Major companies

31%	57%	12%	1973
29%	56%	15%	1980
27%	61%	12%	1988

Organized labor

1973	16%	57%	27%
1980	16%	53%	31%
1988	12%	51%	37%

The press

23%	62%	15%	1973
23%	60%	18%	1980
19%	54%	26%	1988

U.S. Supreme Court

1973	33%	52%	16%
1980	26%	53%	21%
1988	37%	51%	12%

The military

1973	33%	51%	17%
1980	29%	54%	17%
1988	35%	50%	14%

Reprinted with the permission of the American Enterprise Institute for Public Policy Research.

"Well . . . okay," perhaps sums up the attitudes that Americans have toward the major institutions in this country. With remarkable consistency, majorities keep telling pollsters that they have "some" but not a "great deal" of confidence in the institutions. Only minorities say that they have a great deal of confidence, but when their numbers are added to those who have some confidence, these groups far outnumber those having "hardly any" confidence in American institutions.

(Continued from page 339)

In any event, the confidence gap in the 1970s was more a matter of attitudes than of core values; people were still happy with America and happy to live here.[27] The gap disappeared in the early 1980s but by the end of the decade seemed to be returning. A poll taken at the end of 1988 for the American Political Action Committee showed a large majority (64 percent) agreeing that our "traditional leaders" are "less trustworthy now than 10 to 15 years ago." Only 29 percent thought they were "more trustworthy."[28] It is hard to tell whether this marked the beginning of a trend or was simply a temporary dip in confidence. Whatever the case, Americans' changing opinions of their leaders apparently leave undisturbed their basic faith in their nation and its institutions.

4. *Americans believe in moderation.* The meaning of *moderation* is a bit elusive. Moderate in relation to what extremes? Yet it has connotations that are important in understanding American core values. Moderation gives us the sense of "caution" and "consistency." Reform is fine, but not if it seems to bring abrupt change. Americans quickly turn against leaders who say one thing and do the opposite. What really disturbed Americans about the Iran-Contra affair was that the same president who had warned against "negotiating with terrorists" had then negotiated with terrorists. Even Reagan's strongest supporters were shocked at this behavior.

Another aspect of American "moderation" can be seen when we contrast it with "radicalism." In Europe and in other countries, individuals, groups, and parties are proud to be associated with the idea of radical change. Americans are not. American radicals prefer to be called "progressives." Americans associate radicalism with extremism, which they reject completely. This distaste for extremes shows itself in many ways. Experiments have demonstrated that people are likely to select the middle alternative in public opinion polls.[29] Outside the laboratory, American moderation shows up in electoral campaigns. In 1964 Arizona Republican senator Barry Goldwater tried to rehabilitate the word *extremism* and lost to Lyndon Johnson in one of the largest landslides in our history. In 1972 South Dakota Democratic senator George McGovern suffered the same fate. The Republicans called McGovern "the triple-A candidate: abortion, amnesty [for Vietnam draft-dodgers], and acid [LSD]." The label was unfair (just as it was unfair for the Democrats to call Goldwater "the mad bomber"), but McGovern could never shake off the "extremist" tag. Richard Nixon beat him by a margin of 61 percent to 38 percent.[30] Since then, successful presidential nominees in both parties have learned to portray themselves as "mainstream" candidates and their opponents as "extremists." The lesson was driven home during the 1988 presidential campaign when George Bush managed to describe his Democratic opponent, Massachusetts governor Michael Dukakis, as being "outside the mainstream." In a series of stump speeches and television advertisements, Bush and his staff portrayed Dukakis as being permissive on crime, soft on defense, and generally too liberal for the American public. Dukakis tried hard to counteract the "extremist" label—he rode around on a tank, visited bowling alleys and other gathering places in conservative Middle America, and accused Bush of distorting the facts—but he never quite succeeded.

Moderation does not have to mean gradualism. America has changed enormously over the past two decades, and Americans have welcomed many of the changes. Much depends on context. Is the proposed change in "the spirit of America," or is it some departure that mocks our way of life? The genius of a leader like Martin Luther King, Jr., was his ability to show Americans that his agenda did not violate the traditions of this country. "I have a dream," King said. Then he went on to show that *his* dream was also the American Dream.

In sum, the American people share certain values, which remain stable. "The people," Alexander Hamilton said, "are turbulent and changing." At the most superficial level, that is often true. But the deeper we probe, the more we discover the solidity of American beliefs. Religion, free enterprise, equality of opportunity, patriotism, moderation: These are fixed stars in the American sky. The political

(Continued on page 343)

GLOBAL PERSPECTIVES:

Public Opinion in Argentina

To get some sense of public opinion in Argentina, we must start with an outline of the nation's stormy history. After winning its independence from Spain in 1810, the nation careened back and forth between anarchy and dictatorship. In this century, Argentina's longest period of democratic government was during the presidency of Hipolito Irigoyen, leader of the misnamed Radical party. (The Radicals were, and are, a middle-class liberal party.) Although Irigoyen was swept into power in 1916 by an enthusiastic majority, few mourned when he was overthrown in 1930 by a handful of military officers. By the 1940s, the country had grown even more impatient with military rule. Then came Juan D. Perón, elected president in 1946, whose regime combined leftist economics with right-wing nationalism. Perón was at first immensely popular, especially with the working class and the poor, but his free-spending programs ruined the economy. There was little resistance when he was overthrown in 1955.

After 15 years of weak civilian government interrupted by military coups, many Argentinians had begun to miss Perón. He came back triumphantly in 1974, winning the presidency by a record 62 percent of the vote. Sick and half-senile, he died within nine months. His third wife, whom he had made vice president, took over, and chaos followed as left- and right-wing guerrillas embarked on a nationwide campaign of terrorism and assassination. The generals took over again in 1976 and stopped the unrest by suspending all basic freedoms and ruling through terror, torture, and murder. Then in 1983 the generals, disgraced by their defeat in the war with Britain over the Falkland Islands, stepped down. They were replaced by a new civilian government headed by Raul Alfonsin, a Radical. The initial popular enthusiasm for Alfonsin quickly faded in the face of a monthly inflation rate of 115 percent and massive foreign debt. In the next presidential election, he was defeated by a Perónist, Carlos Saul Menem, who took office in July 1989 and promised tough measures to restore the nation's economic health. It was the first peaceful transfer of political power to the opposition through elections in Argentina since 1916.

As can be seen, public opinion in Argentina is subject to extreme mood swings. Wild enthusiasm for new leaders quickly evaporates when those leaders fail to keep their promises. The hope now is that these mood swings can be contained within a constitutional framework so that failed leaders can be removed through elections instead of military coups. The basic problem may have deeper roots in the political culture of Argentina. Argentinians usually applaud the concept of democracy, but—as a number of Argentinian intellectuals have complained—there seems to be little realization that successful democracy requires patience, tolerance, and a willingness to make temporary sacrifices for long-term gains.

implications of these values, although not always clear, must be noticed and taken into account by anyone seeking public approval.

ELITE AND MASS OPINION: ON TOLERANCE

There are at least three kinds of elites in America: *economic elites*, the rich and the very rich; *educational elites*, those with college and graduate or professional degrees; and *sociopolitical elites*, the people who occupy leadership positions in major American institutions. Public opinion researchers often contrast the views of the elites in the last two categories (the educational and leadership elites) with mass opinion. In doing so, they usually find large differences, particularly in matters relating to civil liberties.

The classic study of those differences was conducted by Samuel Stouffer in 1954.[31] Stouffer found community leaders to be more tolerant of Communists, atheists, and nonconformists than the masses of politically uninvolved Americans. Among the public, only 27 percent were ready to allow a Communist to speak in public and only 37 percent would allow an atheist to speak. A 1983 study by political scientists Herbert McCloskey and Alida Brill came to much the same conclusion. While noting that the mass public has become more tolerant since the 1950s, McCloskey and Brill wrote:

> If one judges by the responses of the mass public to survey questions, one has little reason to expect that the population as a whole will display a sensitive understanding of the constitutional norms that govern the free exercise of speech and publication.[32]

Still, we should be cautious about assuming that elites are *always* more tolerant. For example, there are some academic elites whose tolerance for dissent seems to be quite selective. In 1965 Marxist philosopher Herbert Marcuse argued that free speech should not be extended to speakers who "promote aggressive policies, armament, chauvinism" or racism.[33] Since then, as we discussed in chapter 4, some faculty members and students at various colleges and universities have shouted down and even physically threatened speakers who have come to their campuses—and they have done so without incurring the censure of the rest of the academic community. There have also been cases where faculty governing bodies have barred certain outside speakers, such as CIA recruiters, despite the desire of students to hear those speakers.

The data clearly show that educated elites are relatively tolerant of leftist doctrines like communism. It is not yet clear how tolerant they are of speakers who seem to promote racism or, in the words of Herbert Marcuse, "aggressive policies." There is also some evidence suggesting that liberals are more tolerant of opposing opinions than are conservatives.[34] Since academic elites are more likely to be liberals than conservatives, this may indicate a willingness to tolerate views they consider offensive. But it is difficult to draw conclusions from analyses based upon the terms *liberal* and *conservative*, for the meanings of the terms are hard to pin down and apparently vary from generation to generation. The next section will take a closer look at political labels and ideologies.

The term *ideology* has been defined in a variety of ways.[35] The most common definitions in American social science literature stress the idea of a link between particular beliefs. If someone with a clearly defined ideology has a certain view on *this* issue, we can predict what that person's view will probably be on *that* issue. In a very general sense, then, ideology is a set of political beliefs or values that are systematically and predictably linked.

IDEOLOGIES OF THE LEFT AND THE RIGHT

In political writings and in the media there are often attempts to measure political ideologies along a scale or continuum. One end of the scale is marked the "Left"; the other extreme, the "Right." Then there are various places along the continuum, such as "Center," "Center-Left," and "Center-Right."

Practically everybody who writes and talks about politics uses these terms. The terms the *Left* and the *Right* go back to the French Revolution in the eighteenth century. By an accident of seating, the more radical members of the French National Assembly—the ones who wanted the Revolution to wipe out all remnants of the Old Order—happened to sit on the left side of the room and those who were more cautious about change sat on the right side.

Today the terms are still used to designate attitudes toward political change. On the extreme Left are those who want the American system changed from top to bottom. A revolutionary would be considered an extreme leftist. On the extreme Right are those who want no change at all or may even want a restoration of conditions that once existed. (These latter individuals are sometimes called "reactionaries.")

Located much closer to the middle of these two poles are the important political groups and politicians in America. Many observers would locate the Democratic party at a point somewhat left of center and the Republican party somewhere on the Right. How far to the Left or Right depends in part on which politician or group we are discussing. Some commentators would put the Reverend Jesse Jackson at the extreme Left of the Democratic party and "the other Jesse," North Carolina senator Jesse Helms, at the far Right of the Republicans. But not all would agree with these placements. Much depends on where one thinks the center is. Like beauty, it seems to be in the eye of the beholder.

The underlying problem with the terms the *Left* and the *Right* seems to be that they do not have much content. To say that leftists are committed to change without spelling out the *kinds* of changes they want is to gloss over important differences. For example, Pope John Paul II wants social change, and so does the head of the American Communist party. Are they, then, both leftists?

LIBERALISM AND CONSERVATISM: THE MEANINGS CHANGE

The terms *liberalism* and *conservatism* are sometimes used in place of the *Left* and the *Right*. Liberals are supposed to be somewhat left of center (although not as far to the Left as Socialists or Communists), and conservatives are considered to be on the

"The two Jesses"—Jesse Jackson and Jesse Helms—represent Left and Right wings of the Democratic and Republican parties respectively. The Rev. Jesse Jackson (left) supports affirmative action, deep cuts in the Pentagon budget, the establishment of a Palestinian state in the Middle East, and other policies generally favored by the Left. In contrast, North Carolina Republican senator Jesse Helms (right) belongs to the Right. He has sponsored legislation cutting off federal funding for "indecent" art and has tried to defeat legislation making Martin Luther King's birthday a national holiday; in foreign policy, Helm's hard-line anti-Communism has earned him the title of "the Rambo of the Geritol Set." Despite their differences, "the two Jesses" share certain qualities. They are both highly visible politicians who can mobilize minorities within their own parties.

Right (although not as far to the Right as Fascists or the Ku Klux Klan). During the 1988 presidential campaign, George Bush and his campaign committee called Bush's Democratic opponent, Michael Dukakis, a "liberal," a term they associated with extreme positions on such issues as national defense and criminal justice. Dukakis himself seemed to be uncomfortable with the label. In accepting the Democratic nomination, he insisted that the campaign was not about "ideology" but "competence," and at first he avoided answering reporters' questions as to whether or not he was in fact a liberal. Eventually he acknowledged that he was a liberal in the tradition of Franklin Roosevelt and Harry Truman, but he avoided mentioning any contemporary figures. Bush and President Reagan seemed to enjoy needling Dukakis about his discomfort with the term; they referred to it derisively as "the 'L' word."

The meaning of the term *liberal* is hard to pin down because its content keeps changing over time. If we were to go back, say, to 1840, a liberal would be a person who favored as little government as possible. In those days liberals fought state intervention in any sphere—economics, religion, culture, or morality. Today these people are usually called classical liberals.

Now move the clock forward a hundred years, to 1940. By then, liberalism favored state intervention, at least in the economic sphere. It worried about the power of big business, and it concluded that only big government could control big business. It supported the idea of a welfare state to protect our "freedom from want." Move on to 1960. Liberals still favored the welfare state, but they also favored a strong presidency and large military expenditures. They worried about Soviet power in the world and about Soviet advances in rocketry and space technology. Today, on the other hand, those who call themselves liberals worry about "the imperial presidency" and think the government spends too much on the military. Liberals have reversed much of what liberalism stood for in 1960.

Conservatives have done their own flip-flops. They used to oppose American involvement abroad, but today's conservatives often support it—at least when the aim is to defeat communism. Conservatives today also support large military budgets; in the past they opposed them. In domestic affairs today's conservatives sound like the classical liberals of the nineteenth century because they oppose government intervention in the economy. In contrast they favor government intervention in the social sphere, for they believe that the government should ban abortion, pornography, and prostitution.

As you can see, then, it is hard to assign any fixed meanings to *liberalism* and *conservatism*. But it is not so hard to spell out where liberals and conservatives stand *today*.[36] Profiles of their respective beliefs are shown in the box below. To get some idea of who and what might be considered liberal and conservative today, see Table 13.2 on page 348. The table also tries to incorporate degrees of "leftness" and

---

LIBERALS v. CONSERVATIVES

LIBERAL BELIEFS TODAY

Economic Issues

1. Capitalism should not be abolished—it works better than socialism—but it should be regulated. Businesses often exploit workers, waste resources, make unsafe and shoddy products, pollute the environment, and discriminate on grounds of race and sex.

2. We need major new spending programs to deal with the causes and consequences of poverty—more money for housing, education, job training, health care, income supplements, and food programs. Government should ensure jobs, if necessary by hiring people itself.

Social/Moral Issues

1. Since a woman has the right to control her own body, the government should not restrict abortion and should pay for the abortions of poor women. Absent solid proof that women are exploited, it should not ban pornography or prostitution.

2. Those suspected of crime, especially the poor, have been so often abused by the police in the past that they require the protections given them by the Supreme Court during the 1960s.

3. There must be a "wall of separation" between church and state: Religions must not receive state funds, at least not directly; religious activities have no place in public institutions.

4. Racial justice in America requires the use of such strategies as busing and affirmative action.

Military/Foreign Policy Issues

1. Government spends too much on the military. We can have a "lean, mean" military for less money.

2. America should conduct more of its foreign policy through international agencies like the UN and less of it unilaterally.

3. The cold war between the United States and the USSR is nearing an end. As for communism in the rest of the world, the best way to fight it is to rely on economic assistance and set an example of fair and just dealing.

"rightness" by using the terms *Left* and *Right* to designate positions somewhat closer to the extremes of the political spectrum. Keep in mind, particularly in the case of the politicians and celebrities, that the designations are at best approximations.

How do most Americans line up on the liberal-conservative scale? If you look at their preferences among labels submitted to them, you will conclude that Americans are not very liberal—and are getting less so. In 1976, 23 percent of those polled said that they were "liberals." In 1980 the figure was 20 percent. By 1984 it had shrunk to 18 percent. By the end of the 1988 presidential campaign, it was 15 percent. But this does not mean that the ranks of conservatives have grown. In 1976, 32 percent of Americans polled called themselves "conservatives," while in 1984 the percentage was down to 30. The growth has been among self-declared "moderates"—from 38 percent in 1976 to 46 percent in 1984.[37]

These labels can be quite misleading. The majority of Americans may call themselves "conservative" or "moderate," but their views on many specific issues are liberal. Most Americans support welfare spending, business regulation, gun control, and tough environmental laws; they favor negotiation rather than confrontation with the Soviets and think that defense spending should be trimmed. On many other issues, ranging from capital punishment to prayer in schools, they fit the conservative profile.

"I guess I'm a conservative, if you mean do I put up a lot of jams and jellies." *Drawing by Weber;* © *1976 The New Yorker Magazine, Inc.*

LIBERALS v. CONSERVATIVES

CONSERVATIVE BELIEFS TODAY

Economic Issues

1. Much business regulation is unnecessary, wasteful, and harmful. It has lowered our productivity, tied up business in red tape, and cost taxpayers a fortune. We should deregulate.

2. Welfare spending hurts the very people it is supposed to help because it mires them in dependency. The way to cure poverty is to stimulate business so that it can create jobs. In the meantime, poor relief is best left to private agencies or state and local government.

Social/Moral Issues

1. Abortion is not a "victimless crime" because it kills an unborn baby. If it can be justified at all, it is only in cases where the woman's life is at stake. Pornography and prostitution victimize women and debase society's morals and should be outlawed.

2. Criminals have literally been getting away with murder because of excessive leniency in the courts. We need judges who will ease restrictions on the police and hand out tougher sentences. We also need the death penalty as the ultimate deterrent.

3. Americans are a religious people. There should be a place in our public institutions for the nonsectarian exercise of religion.

4. Racial quotas or other programs that give preferential treatment to minorities amount to racism in reverse.

Military/Foreign Policy Issues

1. The cold war is not over. We need adequate military expenditures to prevent the spread of communism in the world and to guarantee our security.

2. Negotiation will not work unless we negotiate from strength. We must demonstrate our willingness to use force if necessary; otherwise, our diplomacy will simply be appeasement.

TABLE **13-2**

Ideological Positions — Some Representative Examples

	Left	Liberal	Conservative	Right
Magazines	*The Nation* *The Progressive* *Mother Jones* *Dissent*	*The New Republic* *The Washington Monthly* *Ms.*	*National Review* *Policy Review* *Insight* *Commentary*	*Human Events* *American Spectator*
Pressure Groups	Institute for Policy Studies National Lawyers' Guild	Americans for Democratic Action People for the American Way National Organization for Women	Americans for Constitutional Action American Taxpayers Union	Young Americans for Freedom Concerned Women of America
Politicians	Rev. Jesse Jackson Rep. Ted Weiss (D-NY) Rep. Ronald Dellums (D-CA)	Sen. Edward Kennedy (D-MA) Gov. Michael Dukakis (D-MA) Sen. Paul Simon (D-IL) Sen. Christopher Dodd (D-CT)	Ronald Reagan Sen. Robert Dole (R-KS) Pres. George Bush Jack Kemp	Sen. Jesse Helms (R-NC) Rev. Pat Robertson Rep. Robert Dornan (R-CA)
Celebrities	Ed Asner Dick Gregory Jane Fonda	Phil Donahue Paul Newman Betty Friedan Bill Moyers	George Will William F. Buckley Charlton Heston	Morton Downey, Jr. Phyllis Schlafly Rev. Jerry Falwell Patrick Buchanan

It is often difficult to identify ideological positions in the United States, but, in a very imprecise way, we can place them on a spectrum from left to right, with "Left" and "Right" being at the outer edges and "Liberal" and "Conservative" closer to the middle. Magazines like *The Nation*, for example, would be considered "Left," while *Human Events* could be called a "right-wing" magazine. This table is highly tentative; the reader may well quarrel with placement of some of the magazines, pressure groups, politicians, and celebrities. Some, perhaps, belong further to the right, others to the left, and possibly some have no place anywhere in the spectrum.

Political Socialization

We have been discussing some of the basic values of Americans. The question to be considered now is where Americans acquire these values. What influences our political beliefs? They do not suddenly spring into our heads at the age of 18 or 20. We develop them gradually, and they undergo a number of changes. Obviously, our social environment has much to do with our beliefs. We form our views after listening to parents and other relatives, to friends, teachers, spiritual leaders, other students, coworkers, bosses, the mass media. Political scientists have devoted much time and effort to studying this process, which they call political socialization. The term may be defined as the process by which, at various stages of their lives, people acquire views and orientations about politics and political life.[38] One could call it the process by which a child is transformed into a citizen.

Socialization starts very early in life, in the home. Gradually, the influence of the home diminishes as the child spends more time outside it, listening to teachers, friends, and, eventually, coworkers. Throughout this process, the person is also exposed to the mass media. We will now take a closer look at the entire process.

CHILDHOOD: TRUSTING AUTHORITY

Political socialization starts very early—as early as five or six years of age. At this point, the major influences come from the home, particularly from parents or guardians. The natural tendency of children is to trust their caretakers, and this attitude apparently gets transferred to other authority figures.[39] Children tend to associate power with benevolence, so they trust police officers and other people in uniform. They also trust our system of laws and identify our president with those laws. Only when they get older, usually in their teenage years, do they learn to separate particular authority figures from the laws themselves.

As children go through school, other influences enter their lives. From their peers they learn that other families think differently about politics. And of course teachers can exert a powerful influence, since they are themselves authority figures. Complexity and perplexity come into the lives of children. Which political views are right, and which are wrong? Which leaders should they listen to? Children recognize that there are serious disagreements. They retain their earlier disposition to trust authority figures, but by about the eighth grade, they have begun to differentiate between the office (such as the presidency) and the person holding it. They also have a better awareness of collective institutions and processes, such as Congress and elections, and do not focus only on individuals.

ADOLESCENCE: QUESTIONING AUTHORITY

In high school, attempts are usually made to give students a more critical perspective on the institutions of their country. They may take field trips to state legislatures or Congress and be encouraged to debate issues and policies. The effect this has on high school students is not altogether clear, but what apparently happens is this: High school students may question authority yet retain their faith in the government. They "acknowledge a greater amount of unfairness, reveal less heroic pictures of government leaders, and show an awareness of the distinction between roles and the people who fill them."[40] At the same time, they believe that whatever is wrong can be made right by their governmental system. Even during the Watergate era of the 1970s, most high school students trusted the system to correct itself.[41]

What happens after high school is even harder to pin down. There seems to be a decline of confidence in the government, but its causes are not well understood. College courses and teachers expose students to much that is critical of American institutions, but political cynicism seems to correlate more with age—the older the person, the more cynical—than with years of schooling.[42]

PEER GROUP AND COMMUNITY INFLUENCES

Peer group influence is often sharply opposed to that of teachers and parents. At the college level, peer group influence can be especially important. There is reason to believe that this will become increasingly important in the future. First, peer group influence has increased as families have grown smaller and more dispersed geographically. Second, the peer group is most important in people's lives in the period after they move away from the family "nest" and before they start their own families.[43] This period is lengthening in the United States, another reason why people's friends will probably play a greater role in the development of their opinions. Among other community influences are those encountered at work. The work environment can be quite challenging and may lead to marked changes in political attitudes. The former liberal arts student who became politically liberal during four years of college may alter those beliefs after getting a job in a large corporation.

THE MASS MEDIA

The next chapter is devoted entirely to the role, the power, and the political outlooks of those who run the news media. But in fact researchers do not know a great deal about the effects of the mass media. We have barely gone beyond the extremely modest conclusion reached by one social scientist more than a generation ago: "Some kinds of communications, on some kinds of issues, brought to the attention of some kinds of people, under some kinds of conditions, have some kinds of effects."[44] But although we are not sure what the effects are, we can assume that there are major effects. Television is a good example. Here is a medium found in virtually every American home. It requires no reading skills or much effort to absorb. It offers large doses of sex, violence, music, loud noises, and quick movement. It is extremely vivid, almost hypnotic. Its sitcoms, dramas, and commercials are skillfully written, and they contain all kinds of messages. The television set is turned on for six hours a day in the average American home, and kids often spend more time in front of it than they do in school.

One study reported that students rate the media as being the most important source of opinion influence—more important than parents, teachers, and friends.[45] But how is it important? What effects does it have? Is it making young people more liberal or more conservative? More patriotic or more critical of their country? We do not know. There is evidence that people who rely on network television for their news get "turned off" to politics and that television news programs help to shape the framework by which we judge politicians.[46] But that tells us little about television's effect on the young because few young people watch network news. Young people prefer entertainment programs and music videos. One study of the change in television programming between the 1950s and the 1970s suggested that modern television entertainment pushes "social liberalism," especially when it comes to issues like premarital sex and abortion.[47] That fits some of the attitudes found among college students today, but there is no proof that the programming caused the attitudes. About the only causal links that have been found—and even those are in dispute—are between prolonged exposure to violent television entertainment and a disposition toward aggressive behavior.[48] It is hard to draw any political conclusions from that. There is no proof that television violence is making young people more warlike or more prone to solve political problems by violence. In short, we can suspect that the role played by television in the political socialization process is very great, but we still are not sure what it is.

We know that the home, the school, peers, and the media all help to shape political attitudes. However, we are still generalizing from studies that were done in the 1960s, when public school curriculums emphasized patriotic themes and respect for authority. By the late 1970s, the Vietnam War and Watergate had caused many academics to rethink their views. A new generation of teachers started coming into the public schools, most of them products of 1960s colleges. Do the attitudes they picked up in college affect the way they teach children in elementary and secondary schools today? What is happening? Again, at this point, we do not really know.

The mass media have also undergone great changes since the 1950s and early 1960s. Some movies and television dramas now identify the villain as the CIA, rather than the KGB. Does that affect children's attitudes toward their country? And what about the changes in the family, the very heart of the socialization process? When one out of two marriages ends in divorce and one out of every four children is being raised by one parent, do small children still have the same trusting attitude toward authority they once had? It could be that much of the knowledge we have accumulated about socialization no longer applies. There is much new ground to break for scholars in this area.

Measuring Public Opinion

Many Americans have seen the photograph on page 352. In 1948 the editors of the *Chicago Tribune*, who had a fierce dislike for Harry Truman, rushed out the morning edition before half the votes were counted on election eve. They wanted to be the first to announce Truman's defeat and Thomas E. Dewey's victory. Since then, Dewey's name has been a byword for failed hopes and overconfidence.

That overconfidence was nourished by the pollsters in 1948. Their tallies kept showing Dewey with a comfortable lead; the last Gallup poll, conducted a week before the election, showed that if the election were to be held then, Dewey would win. The problem was that the pollsters stopped polling too soon. In the last week of the campaign Truman did some furious barnstorming in the Midwest, and that final effort apparently tipped the balance in his favor. The pollsters made a somewhat similar error in 1980 when they predicted a close race between Jimmy Carter and Ronald Reagan. Reagan beat Carter by a 10-point margin. Again, the pollsters had quit polling too soon. A last-minute surge of undecided voters toward Reagan made the difference.

In 1984, determined not to repeat the Dewey mistake, the pollsters kept polling until Election Day. The result, at least for the George Gallup organization, was a direct hit: It predicted that Reagan would get 59 percent of the vote and Mondale 41 percent, which was exactly the way it came out. Other polling organizations were less

President Harry S. Truman grins as he holds up an edition of the *Chicago Tribune*: Its headline erroneously proclaims his defeat by Thomas E. Dewey in the 1948 presidential election.

accurate, but all predicted a substantial Reagan victory. A headline in the *New York Times* summed it up: "A Good Election for Poll Takers."[49]

The mistakes of 1948 and 1980 were slight compared to the one made back in 1936 by the *Literary Digest*, a magazine of conservative sympathies. On the basis of its own public opinion poll, it predicted that Alfred E. Landon, the Republican presidential nominee, would beat President Franklin Roosevelt. The magazine's method of sampling public opinion has become a classic example of how not to do it. It derived its sample from a list of Americans who owned telephones and automobiles. Since many Americans owned neither in 1936, the sample was skewed toward the more affluent, who were more likely to vote Republican. The election was a landslide for Roosevelt.

SAMPLING TECHNIQUES

Today the pollsters have learned how to avoid obvious sampling errors. In fact, sampling has become a highly sophisticated procedure, using probability laws and other mathematical formulas. The most common type of sampling is random sampling.[50] As the name implies, random sampling involves selecting interviewees on an absolutely random basis. Each person within the area to be covered in the poll must have an equal chance of being selected. The probability, then, is that the sample will reflect the approximate divisions of opinion within the entire area. The sampling has to be done very carefully to avoid any systematic bias. For example, if interviewers were to build a sample by selecting people who live in the corner house of every block, their sample could be biased by the fact that certain types of people — perhaps with certain income levels or certain preferences — buy only corner houses. Done properly, however, random sampling can work very well. One of the amazing facts about sampling is how few people need to be interviewed in comparison to the total area being measured. One often hears the complaint, usually by those who do not like the result of a poll, "They didn't interview me." The answer is, they did not need to. For the entire United States, with its more than 240 million people, a properly selected random sample of only 1,500 to 1,600 persons will produce responses accurate within three percentage points 95 percent of the time. The Gallup poll uses a national sample of 1,500 persons, and Louis Harris uses 1,600.

Since sampling is based upon the laws of probability, there is always a chance of error. Statisticians allow for this; they tell us the range of sampling error, the percentage above or below the actual numbers by which the poll's numbers could be off. (The percentage varies with the size of the sample.) If a poll with a sampling error of 4 percent shows candidate A running ahead of candidate B by four percentage points, it could mean anything—from that the two are tied exactly to candidate A is actually running eight points ahead. It is best to dismiss close races in public opinion polls; unlike real elections, where every ballot is counted, they are more subject to distortion.

THE WORDING OF QUESTIONS

But selecting interviewees is only the first step in sampling opinion. Next, the interviewees must be questioned. The wording of the questions can greatly influence the outcome. Ask people if they favor welfare, and most say no; ask them if they favor caring for the poor, and most say yes.[51] Ask people if a woman should have a right to an abortion if she is raped, and most say yes; ask them if they favor abortion on demand, and most say no. Probably no wording is totally free from bias. The pollster must at least be aware of how the wording of a question can shape the response to it, however, so as to take account of possible ambiguities by using several wordings of the question. A 1987 poll conducted for NBC and the *Wall Street Journal* asked this question: "Should imports be limited to save jobs?" Over 60 percent of the respondents said yes. But the question is loaded to the extent that it assumes that import quotas *do* save jobs instead of (in the long run) costing them, as opponents argue. A better wording would have been, "Should imports be limited if the *intention* in doing so is to save jobs?" Better still, a little preface would have been helpful, something like this: "Some people say that import quotas will save American jobs, while others say that they will end up costing us jobs. How do you stand on import quotas?"

THE INTERVIEW

The best interviews are conducted face to face in people's homes, where they are more relaxed and prepared to give the questions some thought. Second best is the telephone interview, where the people being polled are in their homes. The street-corner interview is worse, and worst of all is the mailed questionnaire, which only the unrepresentative few bother to answer. (In the case of the wildly inaccurate *Literary Digest* poll of 1936, 10 million ballots were mailed out, but only about 20 percent were returned.) In face-to-face and telephone interviews, it is important that the interviewer be trained to register neither approval nor disapproval of the answers. Even a raised eyebrow can influence the respondent's answers. Indeed, there is reason to suspect that people sometimes give even poker-faced interviewers the answers they think the interviewers want. Take the issue of gun control. A majority always claims to favor it, yet the popularity of movies like Charles Bronson's *Death Wish*, which glorifies vigilanteeism, or the enormous support we saw in chapter 6 for Bernhard Goetz,

...WHAT 98% OF AMERICANS WOULD LIKE THE SHUTTLE TO PUT IN ORBIT...

Drawing by Wiley; © 1988 San Francisco Examiner.

suggests that Americans are not always opposed to frontier justice. It is hard not to share one congressman's "nagging apprehension" that "the voters . . . are not telling Dr. Gallup everything he ought to know."[52]

This raises a question: Do polls just register public opinion or do they *influence* it? During the 1988 presidential election there were complaints that the pollsters had the race settled weeks before the election. Their polls gave George Bush such a wide lead that it seemed almost a waste of time for Michael Dukakis to go on with the campaign. Other media reporters reminded viewers that a poll is merely a "snapshot" of relative standing with the voters at any given point in time. Still, there was concern that many who would have voted for Dukakis were discouraged because of the repeated announcements of his poor showing in the polls. The concern may be justified: Voter turnout for the 1988 election was lower than it had been in a generation. If the logic behind "low poll ratings discourage supporters" is accepted, however, it is hard to see how Bush managed to recover from his own poor showing in polls taken during the early stages of the campaign.

BANDWAGON EFFECTS

Consider the other side of the coin. Does a good showing in the polls produce more supporters? It has been suggested that Americans love to back winners. If they think someone is far out in front in a race, they consider that good enough reason to vote for him or her. This is called "jumping on the bandwagon."

Understandably, candidates—especially losing candidates—worry about the bandwagon effect. Yet there is very little systematic evidence to prove that polls directly influence grass-roots opinion. Opinions are influenced more by the views people hear from their friends and family than from polls; many do not even know what the polls say. Pollster Elmo Roper has argued that if a bandwagon effect actually existed, polls would always underpredict the margin of victory, "since the whole theory of the bandwagon is that more and more people jump on it." In fact, Roper says, polls have overpredicted the margin of victory as much as they have under-predicted it.[53]

A more basic question than whether or not public opinion polling affects opinion is the question of whether or not the polls should guide the decisions of our leaders. This question is raised indirectly in the Taking Sides section for this chapter, which presents opposing views on the issue of whether or not public opinion polls aid democracy. But let us ask the question very directly: Should our political leaders follow the public opinion polls?

The first impulse is to say yes. After all, our system is a democracy. Therefore, anything that tells politicians what the people want should guide their decision making. Such a position is certainly arguable, but we need to give it more thought.

We should remember that our system is not a pure democracy, but a *representative* system. We elect people to make decisions, and Americans seem to like it that way. They want leadership from public officials. Would public officials be leaders if they simply followed public opinion polls? And do the often vague questions asked by pollsters really provide much guidance in making the concrete decisions that must be made by officials? Finally, there is the question of knowledge. We live in a republic where 60 percent of the people do not know how many justices there are on the Supreme Court and 79 percent cannot name a single provision in the Bill of Rights. Do we want these people making particular decisions in complicated areas of civil justice and civil liberties? Then there is foreign policy. Only 34 percent of Americans know who the secretary of state is. Do we want them directly involved in making foreign policy? Ratifying treaties? Deciding whether or not to recognize a country or wage war with it or to build a certain kind of missile? Surely there is a place for expertise in policymaking. Granted, public officials do not always know what is best, but they frequently possess detailed information on subjects of which the public is ignorant.

Yet the "expertise" argument can be overstated. Experts are very impressive when they give advice on public policy, but that advice is sometimes wrong. In the early 1960s, for example, it was not the American people who advised the Kennedy administration to become involved in Vietnam. It was Kennedy's civilian "experts"— Ivy League intellectuals with all kinds of academic credentials. Policymaking requires more than factual knowledge; it requires judgment and common sense, and "experts" have no monopoly on these. In fact, the premise behind any system of popular government is that the public at large is a better judge of the larger, broader issues of public policy than is any elite. *(Continued on page 357)*

Points to Remember

1. Proper sampling techniques enable pollsters to get a sense of the community's opinions without having to poll a very large number of people. The most common method is random sampling.

2. Poll questions must be carefully worded to avoid influencing the opinions of respondents. Certain words, such as *welfare*, can evoke automatic negative responses.

3. The best interviews are conducted in the home; the worst are on-the-street interviews and mailed questionnaires. Few people respond to mailed questions, and those who do are probably not representative of the sample.

4. There is little evidence to prove that public opinion polls produce bandwagon effects.

5. Public opinion polls raise a broader question: What role should public opinion play in a democracy? Because the people are often ignorant of political facts, democracy needs leaders and experts. Yet the general public may well be more competent than any elite to determine the broad ends of public policy.

Do Public Opinion Polls Aid Democracy?

YES John C. Ranney

Based upon John C. Ranney, "Do the Polls Serve Democracy?" *Public Opinion Quarterly* (Fall 1946), pp. 349-60.

The late John C. Ranney, a Smith College professor, wrote what is now considered a classic defense of polls. "No principle, in democratic theory, has been more fundamental than the belief that political decisions ought to be made by the people as a whole or in accordance with their desires." Yet until recently, we have lacked a sensitive mechanism for measuring the people's will. With the arrival of scientific polling techniques, we have such a device. Polls have made a major contribution to democracy "by reflecting sensitively and flexibly the currents of public feeling, by making this information available to political leaders in such a way that is neither rigid nor mandatory, and by testing the claims of special interests to represent the desires of the people as a whole." As for the argument that public officials invariably "know more" than the people polled, Ranney replied that this argument puts us "on the road to what, since the days of Plato, has been the radically undemocratic position of urging rule by some elite." This is not to deny that democracy requires leadership, but surely our leadership should be given accurate information about the feelings of the people. The polls, then, should be applauded for giving new substance and meaning to democracy.

NO Lindsay Rogers

Based upon Lindsay Rogers, "The Pollsters' False Premises," in Hillman M. Bishop and Samuel Hendel, eds., *Basic Issues of American Democracy*, 5th ed. (New York: Appleton-Century-Crofts, 1965), pp. 23-31.

The late Lindsay Rogers, a Columbia University professor, considered polls an unsuitable tool for guiding a modern democratic state. He said, "There are few questions suitable for mass answers by yes or no." Moreover, Rogers believed, the polls lumped together the answers of the ignorant and the informed, the bright and the stupid, the caring and the indifferent, treating them as if they were all the same. Our system was not built upon this kind of mindless majoritarianism. "Under the American system of government we take many fateful decisions by less than a majority and sometimes prevent the larger part from having its way against the smaller part." Citing the views of Edmund Burke, the eighteenth-century British statesman who told his constituents that he would not be bound by their instructions, Rogers said that government is not a matter of "will" but of "reason and judgment." That reason and judgment can best be exercised by the people elected to do it. Pollsters can tell us which policies a majority of their respondents prefer, but their false premise is that "our political system must accept and act on their answers." What we need, he said, is thoughtful political leadership, not people who take their cues from public opinion polls.

Postscript

Both Ranney and Rogers concede key points made by the other side. Ranney acknowledges that we need political leadership, and Rogers admits that the polls can supply leaders with accurate information about the feelings of voters. Perhaps both would agree that it cannot hurt for politicians to poll voters, or at least to read polls.

In *Polls: Their Use and Misuse in Politics* (New York: Basic Books, 1972), Charles W. Roll, Jr., and Albert H. Cantril argue that polls can provide a good estimate of people's feelings, and it is precisely at "feeling level" that public opinion is so valuable. W. Lance Bennett in *Public Opinion in American Politics* (New York: Harcourt Brace Jovanovich, 1980) suggests the need for well-defined theories of public opinion. Some important theories are discussed in Harry Holloway and John George, *Public Opinion: Coalitions, Elites, and Masses*, 2d ed. (New York: St. Martin's Press, 1986).

Reflections

"The people are turbulent and changing," said Alexander Hamilton. "They seldom judge or determine right." On the surface, the ups and downs of Jimmy Carter's popularity seem to confirm Hamilton's impression. Yet on closer view, it appears that the American people have a yearning for firm leadership; they want consistency and resolution from their officials, and they are harsh on those who seem irresolute or contradictory. They turned against Carter because he seemed unable to deal firmly with foreign crises or domestic ills. They turned against Ronald Reagan when the revelations of the Iran-Contra affair showed a president who was neither consistent nor, apparently, in firm control of his own administration.

Public opinion polling as a science goes back only to the 1930s. Since then, the art of measuring opinion has become increasingly sophisticated. Sampling techniques, interviewing methods, the wording of questions, all play a role in determining the outcomes of polls. But what is the underlying premise behind these polls? The premise is that the American people can be trusted in their overall judgments. They may not be suited to deal with the specifics of lawmaking—there is no evidence that they *want* to handle the specifics—but they are capable of judging outcomes.

What is more, Americans have shown an overall steadiness of purpose as they judge the policy outcomes and the politicians they hold responsible. Far from being "turbulent and changing," the American people have been remarkably consistent, at least when it comes to core values. Religion, patriotism, individualism, equality of opportunity, and moderation are perennial ideals in America, as vital today as they were two centuries ago.

It is hard to say precisely how Americans acquire their political beliefs. The process, known as political socialization, is extremely complicated because we are influenced by so many factors: the environment, school, peer group relationships, work experiences, and the mass media. We know that it begins very early, with the influence of parents and guardians, and we know that children tend to personalize government institutions, identifying figures like the president with persons of authority in their lives. It may well be that somewhere in these very early processes American patriotism gets imprinted into American children, but by high school and college, patriotism is mixed with a critical attitude toward government. The other core values also appear during early socialization. To what extent has American socialization changed over the past generation? What political effects have resulted from the changes? These are intriguing questions for further research. What we know right now is that the basic, perennial American values remain intact and that no armor or Teflon can protect any leader who flouts them.

Notes

1. *Washington Post*, Oct. 28, 1980, p. A1.
2. Everett Carll Ladd, "The 1988 Election: Continuation of the Post-New Deal System," *Political Science Quarterly* (Spring 1989), p. 1.
3. V. O. Key, Jr., *Public Opinion and American Democracy* (New York: Knopf, 1961), p. 10.
4. Michael Kagay, vice president of Louis Harris and Associates, in Pamela Fessler, "Pollsters Right on Reagan But Mixed on Margin," *Washington Times*, Nov. 16, 1984, p. 6A.
5. Robert S. Erikson, Norman R. Luttbeg, and Kent L. Tedin, *American Public Opinion: Its Origins, Content, and Impact*, 2d ed. (New York: Wiley, 1980), p. 19.
6. William J. Crotty, "Introduction: The Nature and Meaning of Public Opinion," in Crotty, ed., *Public Opinion and Politics: A Reader* (New York: Holt, Rinehart and Winston, Inc., 1970), p. 23.
7. "Many Confused on Bill of Rights," *The Record* (Bergen County, NJ), Feb. 15, 1987, p. O-9; Crotty, *Public Opinion and Politics*, p. 23.
8. Edward Dumbauld, ed., *The Political Writings of Thomas Jefferson* (Indianapolis, IN: The Liberal Arts Press, 1955), p. 93.

9. These statistics were derived from the following sources: On a black for president—American Institute of Public Opinion (Gallup Organization) Surveys, 1958-69; National Opinion Research Center (NORC), University of Chicago, 1974-86. On a female president—Gallup Organization Surveys, 1937-71; NORC General Social Surveys, 1972-86. School desegregation—NORC, 1956-70; NORC General Social Survey, 1988. Married women in business—Surveys by Gallup Organization, 1938; Roper Organization for *Fortune*, 1945; NORC General Social Survey, 1988.

10. *Zorach v. Clausen* (1952).

11. *Gallup Opinion Index*, 1976, Report No. 130, p. 5.

12. *Gallup Opinion Index*, 1969, p. 16.

13. *New York Times*, May 19, 1982, p. 23.

14. *New York Times*, Apr. 12, 1968, p. 10.

15. John M. Benson, "The Polls: A Rebirth of Religion?" *Public Opinion Quarterly* (Winter 1981), p. 584.

16. Times-Mirror/Gallup poll, 1987.

17. Peter Kerr, "Rating the Things Americans Value," *New York Times*, Jan. 28, 1982, III, p. 3.

18. Louis Hartz, *The Liberal Tradition in America* (New York: Harcourt, Brace & World, Inc., 1955).

19. Poll by Civic Services, Mar. 1981.

20. Poll by Elmo Roper for *Fortune* magazine, Mar. 1940.

21. Irving Howe, *Socialism and America* (San Diego: Harcourt Brace Jovanovich, 1985).

22. Seymour Martin Lipset and William Schneider, "The Confidence Gap During the Reagan Years, 1981-1987," *Political Science Quarterly* (Spring 1987), p. 12.

23. *The Record* (Bergen County, NJ), Feb. 15, 1987, p. O-9.

24. Michael Harrington, *Socialism* (New York: Bantam Books, 1973), p. 161.

25. Donald J. Devine, *Reagan Electionomics, 1976-1984* (Ottawa, IL: Green Hill Publishers, 1983), chap. 1.

26. *New York Times*, May 19, 1982, p. 23.

27. Harry Holloway, with John George, *Public Opinion: Coalitions, Elites, and Masses*, 2d ed. (New York: St. Martin's Press, 1986), pp. 140-42.

28. *Wall Street Journal*, Feb. 17, 1989, A16.

29. George F. Bishop, "Experiments With the Middle Response Alternative in Survey Questions," *Public Opinion Quarterly* (Summer 1987), pp. 220-32.

30. Goldwater and McGovern were not simply victims; some of their own remarks may have contributed to their reputations. At one point Goldwater said that he would not mind lobbing an H-bomb "into the men's room of the Kremlin." McGovern, for his part, said that he would "crawl to Hanoi on my knees" in order to get peace in Vietnam.

31. Samuel Stouffer, *Communism, Conformism and Civil Liberties* (New York: Doubleday & Co., 1955).

32. Herbert McCloskey and Alida Brill, *Dimensions of Tolerance: What Americans Believe About Civil Liberties* (New York: Russell Sage Foundation, 1983), p. 92.

33. Herbert Marcuse, "Repressive Tolerance," in Robert Paul Wolff, Barrington Moore, Jr., and Herbert Marcuse, *A Critique of Pure Tolerance* (Boston: Beacon Press, 1965), p. 100.

34. Herbert McCloskey and John Zeller, *The American Ethos: Public Attitudes Toward Capitalism and Democracy* (Cambridge, MA: Harvard University Press, 1984), chap. 7 (see particularly, Table 7-7, item 2); John L. Sullivan et al., *Political Tolerance and American Democracy* (Chicago: University of Chicago Press, 1982), pp. 184-85.

35. For a survey of various definitions, see David W. Minar, "Ideology and Political Behavior," *Midwest Journal of Political Science* (Nov. 1961), pp. 317-31.

36. For an attempt, see the Introduction to *Taking Sides: Clashing Views on Controversial Political Issues*, 6th ed., by George McKenna and Stanley Feingold (Guilford, CT: Dushkin Publishing Group, 1989).

37. Speakers for the Left and the Right like to make predictions about which way the opinions of Americans are moving. Liberal historian Arthur M. Schlesinger writes that Americans have shaken off Reaganism and are moving toward the Left. But Ben Wattenberg, a more conservative political analyst, thinks that Reagan moved the political "center" to the Right, so that even liberals are now more conservative than they used to be. Arthur M. Schlesinger, Jr., *The Cycles of American History* (Boston: Houghton Mifflin Company, 1986). Wattenberg's remarks were made on "The MacNeil-Lehrer News Hour" on PBS, Jan. 26, 1988.

38. Adapted from the definition in Jack C. Plano and Milton Greenberg, *The American Political Dictionary*, 6th ed. (New York: Holt, Rinehart and Winston, 1982), p. 138.

39. W. Lance Bennett, *Public Opinion in American Politics* (New York: Harcourt Brace Jovanovich, 1980), pp. 135-37.

40. M. Kent Jennings and Richard G. Niemi, *The Political Character of Adolescence: The Influence of Families and Schools* (Princeton, NJ: Princeton University Press, 1974), p. 274.

41. Bennett, p. 137.

42. Jennings and Niemi, p. 275.

43. Jennings and Niemi, p. 230.

44. Bernard Berelson, quoted in Harold Mendelsohn and Irving Crespi, *Polls, Television and the New Politics* (Scranton, PA: Chandler Publishing Co., 1970).

45. S. H. Chafee, I. S. Ward, and L. P. Tipton, "Mass Communications and Political Socialization," *Journalism Quarterly* (Winter 1970), pp. 647-59.

46. Michael J. Robinson, "Public Affairs Television and the Growth of Political Malaise: The Case of 'The Selling of the Pentagon,' " *American Political Science Review* (June 1976), pp. 409-32; Sahanto Iyengar and Donald R. Kinder, *News That Matters: Television and American Opinion* (Chicago: University of Chicago Press, 1988).

47. Michael J. Robinson, "Television and American Politics: 1956-1976," *The Public Interest* (Summer 1977), pp. 31-39.

48. R. E. Goranson, "Media Violence and Aggressive Behavior: A Review of the Experimental Research," in *Advances in Experimental Social Psychology* (New York: Academic Press, 1970), V, pp. 1-31.

49. *New York Times*, Nov. 8, 1984, p. A19.

50. Another type, less common and less accurate, is called *quota sampling*. The idea behind it is to try to build a microcosm of the entire community. This involves interviewing a certain number of people from the various ethnic, religious, age, gender, and other groups in the community. For example, if the total community includes 10 percent who are black, 3 percent who are Jewish, and 50 percent who are female, the sample should reflect these same percentages. The advantage of quota sampling is that if you do it right, you can get a sense of the community with a very small sample. The disadvantage is subjectivity: A lot of choices have to be made in setting up the sample. Random sampling is a more objective way of selecting the people to be interviewed.

51. Tom W. Smith, "That Which We Call Welfare By Any Other Name Would Smell Sweeter," *Public Opinion Quarterly* (Spring 1987), pp. 75-83.

52. Rep. Michael Harrington, "The Politics of Gun Control," *The Nation*, Jan. 12, 1974, pp. 44.

53. Bernard Hennessy, *Essentials of Public Opinion* (North Scituate, MA: Duxbury Press, 1975), pp. 70-71.

Americans. We know who we are.
And we know who we trust. Dan Rather,
CBS News.

Commercial for CBS News.

14

Mass Media

In the early morning hours of January 31, 1968, a taxi and **Tet**
a small Peugeot truck sped down Thong Nhut Boulevard
in Saigon, South Vietnam. They carried a 19-member team of Communist guerrillas, armed with rockets, machine guns, and high explosives.
Their mission, not quite clear even to them, apparently included blasting
their way into the main building of the American embassy, killing whoever
was inside, and then using the building as a fortress to hold off the
Americans when they tried to retake it.*

The main building of the American embassy was a six-story structure
of concrete and glass with a helicopter pad on the roof. It was set inside a
large, landscaped compound and surrounded by an eight-foot wall. The
main gate was sealed at this hour, but an open side gate was guarded by

*This account is drawn from the following sources: Peter Braestrup, *Big Story* (New
Haven and London: Yale University Press, 1983); Don Oberdorfer, *Tet!* (Garden City,
NY: Doubleday and Co., 1971); David Halberstam, *The Powers That Be* (New York: Dell
Publishing Co., 1979).

only two members of the American military police. As the guerrillas reached this side gate, they opened fire. The two MPs fired back, ducked inside, slammed and locked the gate. The guerrillas then blew a three-foot hole in the wall and began crawling through. Inside, the MPs fired at the invaders as they came out of the hole. One MP shouted into his radio: "They're coming in! They're coming in! Help me! Help me!" His body was found later with bullet holes in the head. Next to it was the body of the other MP, shot through the chest.

Thus began one phase of the Tet offensive in Vietnam. American media coverage of Tet marked a turning point in the way the media portrayed the rest of the Vietnam War. It may even have marked the turning point in the war itself—a war that was to culminate in the most humiliating defeat America has ever suffered.

In the fall of 1967, the Vietnam War was still broadly supported by Congress and the American public, but resistance was growing on American campuses and in the press. The press coined the term *credibility gap* to suggest that President Lyndon Johnson was being less than truthful in telling people about the war. In response, the administration launched a major public relations campaign to convince Americans that we were winning in Vietnam.

The most impressive of these administration boosters was the Supreme Commander of the Allied forces in Vietnam, General William Westmoreland. In a speech to the National Press Club in November 1967, Westmoreland said: "I am absolutely certain that whereas in 1965 the enemy was winning, today he is certainly losing."[1] The president's public relations blitz was still fresh in the memory of news correspondents as the new year got under way. In Vietnam, the New Year holiday is celebrated according to the Asian lunar calendar. In 1968 the lunar New Year, Tet, fell on January 29. Traditionally, Tet was celebrated for several days with parties and fireworks. A temporary cease-fire had been declared by both sides in the war, and the government of South Vietnam had given half its troops holiday leave.

Back at the American embassy, the invaders, after killing the two MPs, laid siege to the chancery building, which was guarded by a handful of marines with light arms. The firefight went on for the rest of the night. At dawn the compound was stormed by U.S. Marines. In the end, the guerrillas never penetrated the chancery building. They were all killed or gravely wounded, their bodies strewn around the carefully tended embassy grounds. Vietcong propaganda depicted the attack as a mighty victory over "the American bandits." Privately, the commander of the Communist forces in South Vietnam sent a critical inquiry to his underling commander of the Vietcong, asking for an explanation.

The embassy attack was a small (and militarily insignificant) part of a synchronized series of surprise attacks throughout South Vietnam that took place that morning. For years, the Vietcong had confined itself to hit-and-run attacks. This time, the leadership decided to go for broke. Timing the offensive for the Tet holidays, they struck more than 100 cities and towns in South Vietnam, committing some 84,000 guerrillas to the assault. Their objectives were to take and hold the cities, to spark popular uprisings against the puppet regime in South Vietnam, and to cause panic within the South Vietnamese army.

They failed to achieve any of these objectives. Though the surge caught the Americans and South Vietnamese by surprise, they recovered quickly. What began so fiercely on January 31 had ebbed by February 4. By February 7, the Vietcong had been forced to withdraw from most

Saigon, South Vietnam, 1968: United States soldiers peer through a damaged window of the U.S. embassy after Vietcong guerrillas attempted to seize the building in a daring attack. The strike on the embassy and simultaneous attacks on scores of important towns began what was known as the Tet offensive. Although the Tet offensive was a military disaster for the Vietcong forces, media coverage made it appear to be a stunning victory for them.

urban areas. The only city they held for more than a week was Hue, in the north. The Allied force could not reclaim Hue until February 25 (during which time the Vietcong executed more than 2,000 civilians and buried them in mass graves). At that point, all urban fighting in South Vietnam was effectively over. Only at Khe Sanh, an isolated U.S. Marine base close to the Laos border, did enemy pressure continue, and even there the Vietcong was forced to withdraw by mid-March. The South Vietnamese army did not flee in panic; it stood and fought. Nor did the civilian population rise in revolt. Most of the population seemed to be either indifferent or hostile to the invaders. Tet took a terrible toll of Communist guerrillas: The Vietcong lost more than 50,000 of its best cadres. For the rest of the war, North Vietnamese regulars had to be sent to the South to replace them. Even some observers sympathetic to the Vietcong conceded that Tet had been a military disaster.

But that is not how Tet was depicted in the American media. Press accounts sent back to the States made it appear a disaster for the Americans. To CBS anchor Walter Cronkite, the enemy's "stunning series of coordinated attacks" showed the hollowness of American talk of "progress." Tet was a "defeat," and "the only rational way out" for America was to negotiate, "not as victors, but as an honorable people who lived up to their pledge to defend democracy, and did the best they could." The same line was taken by other commentators. "The war in Vietnam is unwinnable," said *Washington Post* columnist Joseph Kraft. NBC anchor Frank McGee was more emphatic. The war, he concluded, "is being lost."[2]

Much of this analysis was based upon extremely pessimistic reporting from news correspondents in Saigon. For example, Cronkite, who had formerly supported the war, visited his CBS staff in Saigon after the Tet offensive and came back an opponent of the war. *Washington Post* columnist Don Oberdorfer recalled the reaction of reporters when General Westmoreland, standing in the blood-spattered yard of the American embassy, told them that "the enemy exposed himself . . . and he suffered great casualties." The assembled reporters "could hardly believe their ears. Westmoreland was standing in the ruins and saying everything was great."[3] What Westmoreland said turned out to be correct, and some would later acknowledge that what he had said had been true—from a military standpoint. But, they insisted, Tet was a psychological victory for the Communists. The only trouble was that the Vietcong had never intended Tet to be a psychological offensive; all the evidence suggests they were seeking a military breakthrough.[4]

The attack on the American embassy became the centerpiece of early Tet reporting. Though militarily insignificant, it represented for reporters an enormous symbolic victory for the enemy and proof that American claims were nonsense. In fact, it was not reported accurately. Early wire service reports said the Vietcong had gotten *into* the embassy building. One creative reporter even recounted a six-hour gun battle through "the carpeted offices of the chancery." (The chancery had linoleum floors.) Because the wire service reporting became the basis for television reporting, the mistake was repeated and amplified by all three networks.[5]

Even the best war correspondent can confuse the facts, but this misreporting continued long after the battle was over. Two hours after the recapture of the embassy grounds, the Associated Press (AP) reported that while General Westmoreland had *said* that no one had gotten into the chancery, "dozens of persons on the scene said some of the Vietcong were in the lower floors of the main building." The "dozens of persons" turned out to be some of the Vietnamese staff of the AP, who had gotten their information from Vietnamese police, usually regarded by the press as the most suspect of sources.[6]

The Tet coverage set the reporting style for the remainder of the Vietnam War. Indeed, as David Halberstam later observed, Tet reporting may have started America moving toward withdrawal: "It changed the country, it forced the beginning of the end of the American combat participation, and it changed Walter Cronkite."[7] Yet all this was based upon overheated, often misleading accounts of what actually happened. "At best," concluded Peter Braestrup, former Saigon bureau chief for the *Washington Post*, "this was overwrought instant analysis; at worst, it was vengeful exploitation of a crisis. Historically, it proved unfounded."[8]

*   *   *   *   *

"With public sentiment," said Abraham Lincoln, "nothing can fail; without it, nothing can succeed. Consequently, he who molds public sentiment goes deeper than he who enacts statutes or pronounces decisions." Tet reporting did not directly mold public sentiment. Public opinion polls indicated a high level of support for the war even after Tet. But it did have an immediate and lasting effect on the sentiments of American elites—writers, journalists, editors, and politicians. Tet reporting, notes journalist-historian James Boylan, "had vast historical consequences, finally tipping the balance of the Washington establishment toward those who wanted to cut the losses."[9]

The press has been called the fourth branch of government. On its face, that statement seems an exaggeration. After all, the press cannot make laws, like Congress, or administer them, like the president, or interpret them, like the Supreme Court. But if Lincoln was right, if the press molds opinions, then perhaps its power is even more basic than that of the three official branches of government. Whether or not it is able to shape public sentiment directly, it has an unquestionable effect on the views of our political and cultural leaders.

The press helps to "move the movers." Already true in Abraham Lincoln's day, how much more true that statement is today! In the 1860s, the press consisted of many little newspapers, each with a small number of subscribers. In the 1990s, giant media conglomerates—newspaper chains, mass-circulation magazines, and radio and television networks—spew out news and opinion to millions every day. They create a dazzling world of images, and every day this image world gives us the most vivid pictures and the most authoritative voices. It is a magical world, "where the image has more dignity than the original."[10]

It may be asking too much to expect this image world to reflect the real world all the time, but at least we may ask whether or not it reflects more than one point of view of the real world. Does it allow for diversity, and do the people who control it try to present a balanced view of controversial issues? Finally, does the public at large have a role to play in deciding what will be presented and how it will be presented? These are the questions we consider in this chapter. Perhaps the best way to start is to examine the basic rationale for press freedom.

Agenda Setting: Is There a Media Monopoly?

The American press is perhaps the freest in the world. It prints classified documents, exposes wrongdoing, and aggressively criticizes high government officials. These practices—some of which would immediately land reporters in jail or in front of firing squads in, for example, the People's Republic of China—go on almost routinely here. The press is protected by the First Amendment guarantee that "Congress shall make no law . . . abridging the freedom of speech, or of the press."

But why *should* the press be free? The question is so basic that we usually forget to ask it. Press freedom cannot be taken for granted; we need to understand its roots and its rationale.

FREE TRADE IN IDEAS

The theory behind freedom of the press is this: In a democracy, we need press freedom because it exposes us to the widest variety of ideas. We can then sort through them all in search of the truth.[11]

A famous American jurist, Supreme Court justice Oliver Wendell Holmes, Jr., once compared free speech to free trade, trade that is unhindered by government restrictions. He suggested that the ultimate good for society is best reached by "free trade in ideas." The "best test of truth," Holmes wrote, "is the power of the thought to get itself accepted in the competition of the market."[12] Thus, when government jails dissidents or censors their publications, it does not hurt just the dissidents; it hurts *us*, the audience, as well because it deprives us of the full range of alternative ideas. The marketplace has been rigged by the government.

This is a compelling argument, but notice something. It is an argument not only against government interference, *but also against private monopolies*. Monopoly has always been the enemy of free trade. If we can buy gasoline only from Exxon, or make telephone calls only through AT&T, how can we compare products and services? The whole idea behind antitrust legislation is that we need to break up monopolies if we are to give people an opportunity to decide which product is best.

If that is true of products, it would seem to be no less true of ideas. In arguing against punishing people for expressing controversial viewpoints, Holmes was affirming the importance of "free trade in ideas." Government repression stifles free speech; a press monopoly has the same effect. Governments usually repress debate by crude methods—jails and firing squads. Media monopolies can operate much more smoothly and nonviolently—they can simply refuse to give space to competing points of view. In other words, they can control the agenda.

Is there a media monopoly in America, or do we enjoy a "free trade in ideas"? The question is itself the subject of heated debate. Let us work our way into that debate with some historical perspective.

PEASANTS AND THEIR HOUSEWIVES

In eighteenth-century America, there were hundreds of little print shops throughout the nation turning out countless newspapers, magazines, pamphlets, and broadsides (one-sheet papers). It was not difficult to gain access to one of these presses or even to own one. Benjamin Franklin started his own paper six years after arriving in Philadelphia with nothing in his pockets but "three great puffy rolls."[13] In those days, debates between rival newspapers were often vigorous. A Tory writer in the *Boston*

364

Evening-Post in 1769 complained that the Whig press had made it possible for "the peasants and their housewives in every part of the land . . . to dispute on politics and positively to determine upon our liberties."[14] Small wonder that Thomas Jefferson, who would tolerate any error "so long as reason is left free to combat it," put such emphasis on press freedom. Given the choice between a government without newspapers and newspapers without a government, Jefferson said, "I should not hesitate a moment to prefer the latter."[15] However, after Jefferson had served in the White House for six years, he wrote that "the man who never looks into a newspaper is better informed than he who reads them, inasmuch as he who knows nothing is nearer to truth than he whose mind is filled with falsehoods and errors."[16] After he left the presidency, he went back to his extravagant praise of the press. In 1816, for example, he said: "Where the press is free and every man able to read, all is safe."[17]

CONCENTRATION IN THE NEWS MEDIA

Our system of communication has undergone a radical change since the time of Franklin and Jefferson. Instead of a large number of small newspapers, we have a small number of huge media outlets pouring out a massive flow of words and pictures. We have media conglomerates like Time, Inc. (owner of *Time, Life, Sports Illustrated, People, Money,* and *Discover,* among other holdings) and the Hearst Corporation (which owns 13 magazines, including *Cosmopolitan, Good Housekeeping, Popular Mechanics,* and *Redbook*). We have giant newspaper chains, wire services like the Associated Press and United Press International, and national newspapers like *USA Today,* all of which tend to give us standardized news reporting.

Much of the concentration in the print media has occurred since World War II. In 1945 there were 1,381 independent daily newspapers in America; by 1985 the number had shrunk to 531.[18] In the cities and towns of America today, competition between newspapers is exceedingly rare. In any case, whether competing or not, the papers rely largely on national wire service dispatches for news of the nation and the world. Even opinions in newspaper columns are becoming standardized as local newspapers reprint syndicated columns from papers like the *Washington Post,* the *Los Angeles Times,* and the *Chicago Tribune.*

THE RISE OF NETWORK NEWS

This century also saw the rise of electronics. Almost from the outset, it was clear that the air waves could provide only limited access. Signals from local radio stations in the early 1920s kept running into each other, producing a babble of voices on radio sets. The government had to step in and assign frequencies to particular stations and, of course, there were only so many frequencies to go around.

Diversity was limited still further by the networks. The National Broadcasting Company (NBC) came first, then the Columbia Broadcasting System (CBS) and the American Broadcasting Company (ABC). The networks put together high-priced entertainment programs in New York City studios, carried them by wire to local stations, and allowed the stations to "clear" them for local broadcast. Advertisers paid huge sums to sell their products on these national programs and, as a result, the networks quickly became big businesses.

At first network news was largely an adjunct of entertainment, but by the 1940s, correspondents like CBS's Edward R. Murrow brought polish and professionalism to news broadcasting. The prestige of broadcasting was enhanced further in the 1950s, when television programs like Murrow's "See It Now" explored controversial issues. In

With the advent of cable television and UHF, viewing options have dramatically increased over the years, but the news industry is still dominated by the three major networks: ABC, CBS, and NBC.

the 1960s, the networks' nightly news programs were expanded from 15 minutes to 30, and by the time of President Kennedy's assassination in 1963, television had displaced newspapers as both the most trustworthy and the most common source of news for most Americans. Walter Lippmann, America's great journalist-philosopher, once remarked, "It's as though this nation had three mighty printing presses. *Only three*."[19] Lippmann was exaggerating to make a point. Yet his statement contains elements of truth, for television has become the preeminent news medium, and it is largely dominated by the three networks. In recent years, network news executives have begun to worry about a slippage in their audience size and the aging of their most loyal viewers; networks must also worry about competition from local news programs, which are now more popular than network news.[20] Nevertheless, television is still the major source of national and international news (see Figure 14.1).

The dominance of television news translates into enormous prestige for network stars. In the 1960s, CBS anchor Walter Cronkite was so influential that President Johnson mounted a frantic effort to lobby for his support of the Vietnam War. When, after Tet, Cronkite turned against the war, Johnson told his press secretary that it was a turning point: If he had lost Walter Cronkite, he had lost Mr. Average Citizen.[21] In the 1980s, Cronkite's successor, Dan Rather, was considered by the majority of Americans to be more believable than President Ronald Reagan. So were the two other network anchors. And that was before the Iran-Contra scandal eroded Reagan's enormous popularity. (After the scandal broke, *both* Reagan and the anchors suffered credibility losses, but the anchors' credibility ratings remained well above Reagan's.[22])

These developments raise troubling questions. If newspapers do not compete with one another, and if the most trustworthy source of national news is controlled by three giant networks (see Figure 14.2 on page 368), what happens to the ideal of "free trade in ideas"? Who is going to correct Dan Rather if he gets his facts wrong? Who is going to challenge Mike Wallace if he misleads viewers? And how many people will hear? It may not have been difficult for ordinary people to gain access to the media in Ben Franklin's day, but no peasant or housewife today has much chance of challenging the words of news conglomerates and multibillion-dollar networks. As one critic put it: "Freedom of the press belongs to the man who owns one."[23]

Certainly there are some counter-trends, such as the phenomenal growth in the

"Attention out there! We now bring you an opposing viewpoint to a CBS editorial!" *Drawing by Richter; © 1975 The New Yorker Magazine. Inc.*

FIGURE **14-1**

367

Agenda Setting:
Is There a Media
Monopoly?

Sources of News Information

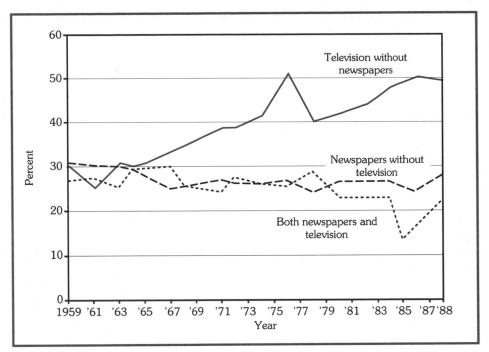

Source: Surveys by the Roper Organization for the Television Information Office from 1959 through 1988

> Since 1965 more Americans have been getting their news from television alone, which gives the networks ABC, CBS, and NBC greater power to influence their audiences. The question asked in this survey was: Where do you usually get most of your news about what's going on in the world today—from the newspapers or radio or television or magazines?

number of local AM and FM radio stations and the increased importance of cable television and UHF channels. The trouble is that when it comes to *news*, there are still very few sources. Local radio broadcasters are largely in the entertainment business. Their brief public affairs segments tend to rely upon the "rip and read" method: Wire service dispatches are yanked off machines and read to listeners. The impact of cable and UHF programming is still unclear, but it has not yet realized its potential of greater diversity of viewpoint.[24] There can be no doubt that cable television has made deep inroads into the viewing audience that once watched the networks. The network share of the prime-time audience has been steadily falling as cable's rises. But at present there is little reason to hope that cable will usher in a new era of programming diversity. First of all, cable is itself controlled by big media conglomerates. The giant of the business is Tele-Communications, Inc., with interests in systems that reach more than 20 percent of the 50 million national subscribers. Time, Inc., is also a key player, with more than 5 million subscribers.[25] (Table 14.1, on page 369, shows the major companies with a stake in cable programmers.) Second, and more to the point, what is cable television? At present, it consists largely of televised sports events, movies, and old network re-runs. Apart from the Cable News Network (CNN), there is little news on it, and CNN's new agenda, format, style, and content do not seem much different from what we see on ABC, CBS, and NBC. In any case, the majority of Americans still depend upon network television for news and opinion.

To be sure, there are many media outlets—radio and television stations,

FIGURE **14-2**

Perceived Trustworthiness of News Sources, 1959-1988

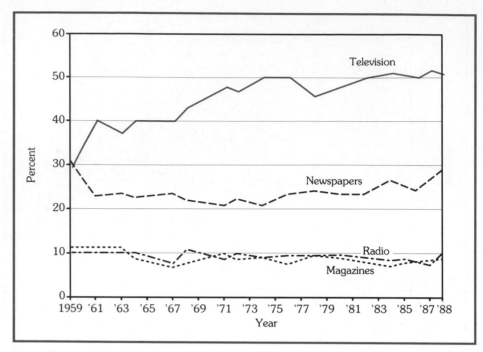

Source: Surveys by the Roper Organization for the Television Information Office from 1959 through 1988.

Americans are more likely to trust a television news account of a story than they are to trust other news media accounts. The survey question asked was: If you got conflicting or different reports of the same news story from radio, television, the magazines, and the newspapers, which of the four versions would you be inclined to believe—the one on radio or television or in magazines or newspapers?

magazines, newspapers, and so on.[26] But in the presentation of news, there is a tendency to follow the leader. "To an ever-growing extent," says press analyst Michael J. Bennett, "correspondents for [major] newspapers no longer are writing not so much for the folks back home as they are for their peers on the *Washington Post* and the *New York Times*, and for their colleagues at ABC, NBC, CBS, and PBS." Looking back on his days as a reporter, sociologist Robert Darnton says: "We really wrote for one another. Our primary reference group was spread around us in the newsroom."[27] In this kind of environment, there is a tendency to engage in what journalist Timothy Crouse has called "pack journalism."[28]

If that is the case, then it is important to know who the leaders are. They are not the hometown newspapers or radio stations. They are the agenda-setting papers like the *New York Times*, the *Washington Post*, and a few others; they are the wire services; they are the three network news shows watched by 50 million people every night; they are the two mass-circulation newsweeklies, *Time* and *Newsweek*. The people who run these media are the press leaders. They are the media elites.

Media elites can be used as a neutral, descriptive term. Usually, though, people who use terms like *elitism* in the media are pushing some political agenda. During the Nixon administration, Richard Nixon's vice president, Spiro T. Agnew, delivered a series of speeches attacking the "small group of men, numbering perhaps no more than a dozen," who operate network news. Today leftist critic Michael Parenti writes

TABLE **14-1**

Media Companies with a Stake in Cable Programmers

Tele-Communications Inc. 11 million subscribers	*Time Warner Inc.* 5.5 million subscribers	*Cable Vision* 1.4 million subscribers	*Viacom* 1 million subscribers
American Movie Classics	Black Entertainment Television	American Movie Classics	Cable News Network
Black Entertainment Television	Cable News Network	Bravo	Cable Value Network
Cable News Network	Cable Value Network	Cable News Network	Fashion Channel
Cable Value Network	Cinemax	Cable Value Network	Lifetime
Discovery Channel	Fashion Channel	CNBC	Headline News
Fashion Channel	Headline News	Fashion Channel	Movie Channel
Headline News	Home Box Office	Headline News	MTV
Home Sports Entertainment	Movietime	Shop Television Network	Nickelodeon
Rocky Mountain Sports Network	Shop Television Network	Sports Channel America	Showtime
Think Entertainment	Travel Channel	Travel Channel	Turner Broadcasting System
Turner Broadcasting System	Turner Broadcasting System	Turner Broadcasting System	Turner Network Television
Turner Network Television	Turner Network Television	Turner Network Television	VH-1
	Viewers' Choice		Viewers' Choice

Source: National Cable Television Association.

> As the table indicates, four major media companies, Tele-Communications, Time Warner, Cable Vision, and Viacom, hold equity interests in more than 50 cable subscribers, networks, and programming services. Cable television was supposed to open up and expand the marketplace of ideas. Some observers worry that it, too, may be headed toward control by the few.

about a small group, "numbering between ten and twenty-five persons," who ultimately control the media.[29] The critics, of course, differ on whether the media elites tilt to the Left or to the Right. But on the importance and power of these "captains of consciousness," as Parenti calls them, there is no disagreement.

The critics do not have to be discounted because of their ideologies. Their ideologies, however, sometimes distort their vision. This is nowhere more evident than in the assertion that the press is simply a tool of big business. Critics on the Left put more emphasis on big money control of the media, but the idea is often implicit in right-wing critiques as well. Conservative activist Phyllis Schlafly says: "Our First Amendment right to speak on radio or television should not be limited only to those who have the money to buy the station."[30] It is true that news *is* a business in America, and bottom line considerations sometimes play a major role. Newspapers like to increase circulation, and the television networks are always anxious about ratings. But the idea that tycoons dictate news content has a slightly quaint quality. It recalls the time when reporters wore straw hats and sat at rolltop desks. In those days, of course, it *was* largely true. In the days before the news correspondent, reporters had had very little power or status.

THE OLD DAYS: OWNER AND SPONSOR CONTROL

In the early years of this century, the working reporter tended to be self-educated. He (there were few women in journalism) earned a meager salary and was not expected to have any profound insights into national or world affairs. The term *working press* in those days could be used almost synonymously with *working class*. Thus came the image of the rummy-playing reporter with the rumpled suit, the chin stubble, the bottle in the drawer—a caricature, but recognizable.

A reporter's beat in those days was usually limited to local stories about crime or corruption. (The Washington press corps was minuscule; in the 1920s, even major

These 1936 newspaper reporters call in election results from a campaign headquarters. In those days, the working reporter tended to be self-taught and poorly paid. Opinions and philosophies were established by the owner of the paper and any reporter who printed material counter to the interests of the owner would probably be dismissed.

newspapers generally sent no more than one reporter to cover the entire government.) The large papers were owned by press barons like William Randolph Hearst and Colonel Robert McCormack. Reporters and editors were kept on a tight leash: Anyone who tried to print material that ran counter to the interests or philosophy of the paper's owner would not be working for the paper the next day.

The same was true in the early days of electronics. When CBS was wholly owned by the heir of the La Palina Cigar Company, one would hardly expect to hear antismoking messages broadcast on the network. Even when news professionals like Fred Friendly and Edward R. Murrow came to CBS at the end of the 1930s, they could not ignore the wishes of the owner, William Paley, nor of their sponsors. The controversial programs presented on "See It Now" in the 1950s (such as the program criticizing Senator Joseph R. McCarthy) were possible only because Friendly persuaded its sponsor, Alcoa Aluminum, to continue to back the series. Even so, there was some bargaining and trading with network officials and sponsors.[31]

THE NEWSROOM REVOLUTION

All this changed dramatically in the 1960s. Even at the beginning of the decade, there were signs of change. Washington was swarming with reporters, many of them quite young. Unlike the seedy ambulance chasers of an earlier generation, these new reporters were well-paid, college-educated, and sophisticated. These members of the press corps thought of themselves as professionals, not as the hired hands of editors and publishers and producers and sponsors. The stage was set for the newsroom revolution.

What set off the revolution was the Vietnam War. David Halberstam's *The Powers That Be* is a brilliant chronicle of the change wrought by the war. According to Halberstam's account, what happened was a kind of revolution: The war radicalized a younger generation of reporters, and by the end of the decade, they had moved into leadership positions in the media. At the *Washington Post* in the mid-sixties, the top level of the paper was committed to the Vietnam War, while its lower echelons were turning against it.[32] At *Time*, the reporting on Vietnam was "schizoid, with Saigon bureaus often essentially pessimistic and Washington bureaus essentially accepting the word of the government."[33] The *Los Angeles Times* was "almost hydra-headed, two papers merged into one."[34] CBS had similar divisions. When Walter Cronkite went to Vietnam in 1965, he was shocked by "the brashness of the younger correspondents who sat at the military briefings, tearing into the military officers."[35]

It was this younger generation that took control of the major media at the end of the 1960s. In doing so, it acquired layers of protection against dictation by owners or sponsors. Today Dan Rather and Mike Wallace at CBS are virtually untouchable news celebrities. Not only do they earn salaries much higher than those of their nominal bosses (in 1986 Dan Rather earned $3 million, compared to the $200,000 annual salary of the CBS News president), they have the power to override and in some cases get rid of those bosses. Such was the fate of two CBS News presidents, Ed Joyce and Van Gordon Sauter, who got into power struggles with Rather.[36]

Top management at the networks can indirectly affect news by cutting the news budget and firing employees. This happened at CBS in 1987, when management fired more than 200 employees in an effort to cut costs—a move that was fiercely resisted. Dan Rather "went public" with his complaints, writing pieces in the *New York Times* that were highly critical of his superiors.[37]

Today whatever indirect effects management policies may have on the news, it would be almost unthinkable for management to try to dictate news content. This is also true in the print media, where Washington correspondents are regarded with considerable awe by home editors.[38] To sum up: The left-wing and right-wing critics of the media indeed have a point when they talk about a news media elite. But the assumption that this elite is identical to or controlled by big business is no longer tenable. Since the 1960s, the people who bring us the news have acquired an unprecedented degree of autonomy and independence. If anything, their political views run counter to those of business elites, and many large corporations have hired public relations experts to try to neutralize unfriendly press coverage.

The Media Bias

If the newsroom revolution has permitted working journalists to break free of owner and sponsor control, it becomes all the more important to find out what journalists are thinking—and whether or not their thoughts affect their reporting. What are the political and social attitudes of our leading journalists? Do those attitudes creep into their news reports? This brings up the issue of bias in the media.

Points to Remember

1. The classic defense of a free press is that such freedom permits people to judge between truth and falsity. The assumption is that freedom will lead to diversity of opinion and debate between competing viewpoints.

2. Today diversity and debate may be threatened by concentration in the news media. In Benjamin Franklin's day, it was relatively easy for people of modest means to own their own newspapers and compete on equal terms with other papers. Today it is impossible.

3. Since the early years of this century, newspaper ownership has become increasingly concentrated. In the electronic media, concentration is even more obvious. The majority of Americans depend upon the three main television networks for information about national and world affairs.

4. Today there are many media outlets, but they often follow the lead of a few major news sources, such as the wire services and prestigious papers like the *New York Times*.

5. Left-wing and right-wing critics of the media seem to agree that the major media are controlled by a small number of individuals. In this they are not wrong, but they mislead themselves and others in suggesting that big business controls the media. The newsroom revolution of the 1960s transferred much power to the working press. In understanding the role of the press, therefore, it is important to recognize the views of the journalists themselves.

Are journalists biased? The question is rather silly. Of course journalists are biased. All other human beings are biased if by *bias* we mean "a mental leaning or inclination" (Webster's Unabridged Dictionary, 2d ed.).

The question of bias starts to get interesting only if evidence is shown that (1) major journalists *share* certain biases that set them apart from other Americans and (2) the journalists *carry their biases into their reporting.* Let us see what evidence there is for these propositions. *(Continued on page 373)*

GLOBAL PERSPECTIVES:

Television Viewing in East Germany

It all happened within a few weeks in November 1989: the demonstrations against the Communist government of East Germany, the flood of East Germans to the West, the disgrace and removal of the old hard-line leaders, the opening of the Berlin Wall, the prospect of real democracy in a country its rulers had called "the German Democratic Republic." No one predicted these remarkable events, yet in retrospect they seem utterly predictable. How long could barriers of brick and concrete separate a people when their pictures and voices could so easily cross the borders?

Under the old regime in East Germany, all of the mass media, including newspapers, magazines, and television, were owned by the government and controlled by the Communist Party. Border guards carefully searched all luggage and confiscated any publications deemed "subversive." What the authorities were unable to control were the electronic radio and television signals from the West.

Most estimates show that 75 to 80 percent of East Germans watch Western television regularly. Particularly popular among East Germans are television programs from West Germany, Denmark, and Sweden, and Western news programs. In contrast, fewer than 10 percent of televisions in East Germany are tuned to the country's state-run channels. For East Germans, Western television has long been a kind of umbilical cord linking them to the West, a substitute for forbidden travel. The Dresden Valley area of East Germany, which cannot pick up Western signals, is popularly known as "Dead Eyes Valley." It is hard for the government to attract workers—even top party functionaries—to the area.

All this had worried the government. It attributed the popularity of Western television to a taste

for "diversion" and "decadence," but there was little it could do to stop it. Day after day, East Germans had their windows open to the West, and they watched a very different world from the one around them. Television may even have contributed to an idealized picture of the West, all the more so since the travel ban prevented East Germans from comparing television images to the realities of life in the West. Now that the barriers are down, East Germans may experience the freedom and abundance of the West but also see some of its less attractive features.

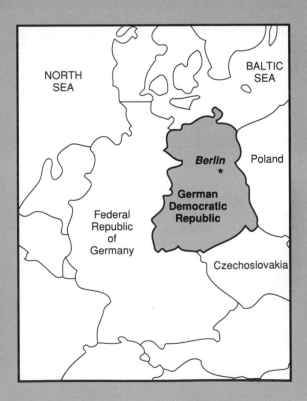

In a 1981 article and a 1986 book, *The Media Elite*, political scientists S. Robert Lichter and Stanley Rothman studied the views of journalists from America's most influential media: the *New York Times*, the *Washington Post*, the *Wall Street Journal*, *Time*, *Newsweek*, *U.S. News and World Report*, and the news departments at CBS, NBC, ABC, and PBS, along with major public broadcasting stations.[39]

The media elites in their sample were 95 percent white and 79 percent male. Most were in their thirties and forties. Ninety-three percent had college degrees, and a majority (55 percent) had attended graduate school. Most were from the northeast sector of the country and were products of upper-middle class homes. Their views on social and political topics sometimes diverged markedly from the views of the American majority. In religion, for example, most Americans consider themselves believers, but, according to Lichter and Rothman, the "predominant characteristic of the media elite is its secular outlook."[40] Half had no religious affiliation. Only one in five identified themselves as Protestant, one in eight as Catholic. Only 8 percent attended religious services weekly, and 86 percent seldom or never attended services.

TABLE 14-2

Media Elite Attitudes on Social Issues

	Strongly Agree	Agree	Disagree	Strongly Disagree
Economics				
Big corporations should be publicly owned	4%	9%	23%	65%
People with more ability should earn more	48	38	10	4
Private enterprise is fair to workers	17	53	20	10
Less regulation of business is good for USA	16	47	24	13
Government should reduce income gap	23	45	20	13
Government should guarantee jobs	13	35	33	19
Political Alienation				
Structure of society causes alienation	12	37	32	20
Institutions need overhaul	10	18	31	42
All political systems are repressive	4	24	26	46
Social-Cultural				
Environmental problems are not serious	1	18	27	54
Strong affirmative action for blacks	33	47	16	4
Government should not regulate sex	84	13	3	1
Woman has right to decide on abortion	79	11	5	5
Homosexuality is wrong	9	16	31	45
Homosexuals shouldn't teach in public schools	3	12	31	54
Adultery is wrong	15	32	34	20
Foreign Policy				
U.S. exploits Third World, causes poverty	16	40	25	20
U.S. use of resources immoral	19	38	27	16
West has helped Third World	6	19	50	25
Goal of foreign policy is to protect U.S. businesses	12	39	28	22
CIA should sometimes undermine hostile governments	26	19	36	19
	None	*Democracies*	*Friends*	*Anyone*
To what countries should we sell arms?	19	29	48	4

Source: S. Robert Lichter and Stanley Rothman, "Media and Business Elites," *Public Opinion* (October/November 1981). Reprinted with the permission of the American Enterprise Institute for Public Policy Research.

The media have been accused of being biased to the Left and to the Right. Although many reporters are more liberal than the American public, this does not, by itself, prove that they are biased in their reporting of the news.

Most called themselves liberals. (Only 15 percent of the public at large consider themselves liberals.) Only 19 percent considered their views right of center. One of the litmus tests for liberalism-conservatism in the 1970s was the presidential election of 1972, when Senator George S. McGovern of South Dakota ran against President Nixon. McGovern, whose positions on defense and social issues were too liberal for many voters, won only 38 percent of the vote. But 81 percent of the journalists in the Lichter-Rothman study voted for McGovern.

On economic issues, the majority of the journalists were moderately liberal, but not radical or socialist. While 68 percent agreed that government should reduce the income gap between rich and poor, only 13 percent thought that big corporations should be publicly owned, and 70 percent agreed that "private enterprise is fair to workers." The media elites were more liberal on foreign policy and national security issues. A bare majority was convinced that American foreign policy was interested mainly in protecting American business, 55 percent were opposed to the use of the CIA to undermine hostile foreign governments, and 57 percent considered U.S. use of resources to be immoral. Where the media elite's liberalism was most evident was in the area of social issues like abortion and homosexuality. Only a quarter of the respondents thought that homosexual behavior was wrong, and 91 percent took the pro-choice position on abortion (see Table 14.2 on the previous page).

Some critics faulted the methodology used by Lichter and Rothman; one charged that the authors were themselves biased in a "conservative-populist" direction.[41] Whatever comfort or discomfort anyone gets from Lichter and Rothman's work, it has one critical—and admitted—limitation. It discusses the political views of journalists but does not tell us whether or not the journalists allow their political views to color their reporting. *Do* journalists bring their political opinions into their reporting? This is a very tough question. We will begin to try to answer it by providing some history on the subject.

FROM PROFESSIONALISM TO THE NEW JOURNALISM

Journalists' "personal beliefs," says Herbert Gans, "are left at home, not only because journalists are trained to be objective and detached, but also because their credibility and their paychecks depend on their remaining detached."[42] Whether or not this is an accurate description, it sums up an ideal once held in high esteem by journalists. That ideal was professionalism.

Professionalism had its origins in the late nineteenth century when the educated classes, disgusted with the sensational "yellow journalism" of the time, sought to make journalism into a respectable profession. Schools of journalism were created that taught aspiring reporters the basics of their craft. These schools also taught their students a kind of ethic: Get the facts straight and keep personal sentiments out of reporting. Eventually, the ideals of detachment and objectivity permeated the profession. They were not always practiced, but they were widely preached. Some newspapers took them seriously—perhaps too seriously. *New York Times* reporters grumbled that their paper's copyreaders deleted everything that sounded remotely lively or colorful.[43]

All this changed in the 1960s. The change coincided with the newsroom revolution, and it was brought about in part by the same catalyst: Vietnam. To the young reporters covering the Vietnam War, the so-called objective journalism seemed a farce. The objective journalist would faithfully report what the various military briefers had said, then perhaps go into the field and report on a skirmish: how long it lasted, where it took place, what the casualties were. At best, these reporters thought, such objective journalism left out what they regarded as this war's particular essence—savagery, absurdity, and hopelessness. To tell the real truth about

Vietnam, they thought it necessary to include personal observations. But at home, editors kept sanitizing their reports.

Tet changed everything. Even Walter Cronkite dropped his cloak of impartiality and thus became, in David Halberstam's words, "a personal journalist."[44] Within a few years, the revolution in the newsrooms had brought a new generation into power, and the new generation brought with it the views that were popular among young journalists in the 1960s. One view much in vogue at the time was the belief that authentic news reports were ones in which the reporter mixed observations with feelings, much in the manner of a novelist. It was called the "New Journalism," and it was made popular by reporter-novelists like Tom Wolfe and Norman Mailer.[45] Today even the *New York Times* carries items written in this style.

NEWS SPIN

If personal journalism has only just crept into the *New York Times*, it has become almost a staple of television reporting. Former NBC correspondent John Chancellor, who still clings to the old ethos of objectivity, has expressed deep misgivings about the New Journalism:

> One of the things that troubles me is the way television reporters end the minute-and-a-half or two-minute pieces they have on the news (you see I'm not a reporter anymore so I can criticize)—they always seem to have some nasty hook right at the end. "Tomorrow the President goes to Cleveland, but no one knows why"—and I keep saying, "Hey guys, why don't you just say he's going to Cleveland?"[46]

NEWS SPIN

Political scientists Maura Clancy and Michael Robinson study news spin, which they define as "the way the correspondent interprets or embellishes the facts in a story." The following, taken from various sources, are some examples of news spin:

"[Eleanor] Smeal [then-president of NOW] denounced Phyllis Schlafly, the vehement high priestess of ERA critics." (Ellen O'Brien and Bob Cunningham, *The Record*, Bergen County, NJ, June 25, 1982, p. A1)

"[President Reagan conducts] a campaign in which he highlights the images and hides from the issues." (Leslie Stahl, "CBS News," October 4, 1984)

"When it suits their purposes, they [President Reagan and his aides] cite North; when it suits their purposes, they say, 'Ah, who's gonna believe him?' " (Chris Wallace, "NBC News," July 1, 1987)

"Col. North spent the morning preaching. His speech contained the now-familiar mix of patriotism, piety, and anger." (Carol Martin, "WCBS-TV News," New York City, July 9, 1987)

"Through the smirks and winks and teary eyes, through the 'Peck's Bad Boy' grins and the earnest altar-boy gazes, Oliver North seemed, as always, to be starring in his own movie." (Maureen Dowd, *New York Times*, July 8, 1987, p. 1)

"With his characteristic keep-the-press-at-bay-and-blame-them-when-necessary strategy, the vice president [George Bush] acted as though the reporters and cameramen, who were there for the candidate's precise aim of getting himself on the evening news, were interlopers." (Maureen Dowd, *New York Times*, October 31, 1988, p. B4)

FIGURE **14-3**

**Good Press-Bad Press TV-News Seconds for Each Candidate
in the 1984 Presidential Election**

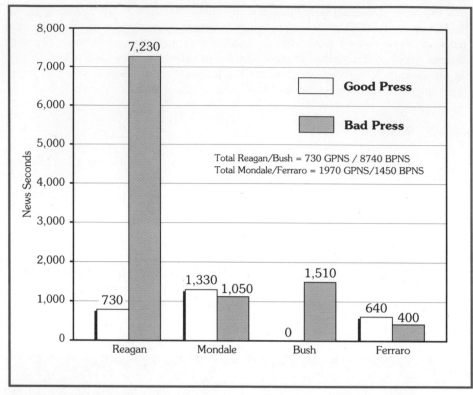

Total Reagan/Bush = 730 GPNS / 8740 BPNS
Total Mondale/Ferraro = 1970 GPNS/1450 BPNS

Source: Maura Clance and Michael Robinson, "General Election Coverage," Part I, *Public Opinion* (December/January 1985), p. 50. Reprinted with the permission of the American Enterprise Institute for Public Policy Research.

Studies by political scientists Maura Clancy and Michael Robinson reveal that in 1984 the TV news media gave much more "bad press" to Republicans Ronald Reagan and George Bush than to Democrats Walter Mondale and Geraldine Ferraro. "Good press" and "bad press" were measured by the number of seconds of positive or negative "spin" (judgmental comments by television correspondents) given to each of the candidates.

Political scientists Maura Clancy and Michael Robinson have looked more closely at the use of devices like the "nasty hook" that Chancellor mentions. (See also the Box on news spin on the previous page.) In studying television news coverage of presidential campaigns, the two researchers focus on what they call news spin. Spin, defined as "the way the correspondent interprets or embellishes the facts in a story," involves the tone of the story—"the part of the reporting that extends beyond hard news." Clancy and Robinson cite the following example: During the 1984 presidential campaign, President Reagan's train trip through western Ohio was hard news, but "when Dan Rather chose to label the ride 'a photo-opportunity train trip, chock full of symbolism and trading on Harry Truman's old turf,' Rather added 'spin.' "[47]

Clancy and Robinson neither praise nor condemn news spin, they simply measure it. Their purpose is to determine whether or not television news correspondents are biased in their election coverage. By quantitatively comparing the number of seconds of favorable and unfavorable news embellishments for each candidate (the spin ratio), they seek to determine whether or not television news tilts in favor of one side or the other.

For the presidential race of 1984, the results were unambiguous. President Reagan received 7,230 seconds of bad press, compared to Walter Mondale's 1,050 seconds; Reagan's good press amounted to 730 seconds, compared to Mondale's 1,330. Reagan's running-mate, George Bush, "had a spin ratio that defied computation: 1,510 seconds of 'bad press' pieces and zero seconds of good press."[48]

Does this prove that television news correspondents are giving us biased election coverage? Clancy and Robinson's answer is yes—and no. Yes, the coverage is biased (at least it was in 1984). No, it is not *politically* biased. If the bias were political, we would expect television to have given Reagan unfavorable treatment in the 1980 election. That did not happen. According to Robinson's earlier research, it was Jimmy Carter who suffered more in 1980 at the hands of television correspondents.[49] The authors think that Reagan's unfavorable 1984 coverage is better explained as the result of "the four I's: impishness, irritation, incumbency, and irrevocability." "Impishness" was the reporters' desire to make the contest more of a horse race; since Reagan was so far ahead, they needed to slow him down. The reporters' "irritation" was over Reagan's seemingly impenetrable Teflon coating. Reagan's "incumbency," they felt, gave him an unfair advantage; hence the desire to even things up. "Irrevocability" was determined by the Twenty-second Amendment's "two-term only" rule; since the president was entering his second term, this was the journalists' last chance to rough him up during a political campaign. None of this, Clancy and Robinson insist, has anything to do with ideology. Their "four I's" hypothesis is interesting but speculative. All we can conclude from the statistical data gathered by Clancy and Robinson is that *for some reason* network television news was slanted against Reagan and Bush in 1984. However, a cautionary note must be added: This was not, apparently, the way the public saw it. A 1989 poll conducted jointly by the Television Information Office and the Roper Organization asked respondents how they thought the media treated each of the major presidential candidates in the 1980, 1984, and 1988 presidential elections. In 1984, 23 percent of the respondents thought Reagan had been given favorable treatment, compared to 9 percent who thought that Mondale had been favored; in 1988, 21 percent thought Bush was favored, and only 9 percent thought Dukakis had been favored (see Table 14.3). In

(Continued on page 379)

TABLE 14-3

Media Coverage of Presidential Candidates: The Public's View

| | The 1989 TIO/Roper Report | | | | | | |
| | 1980 | | | 1984 | | 1988 | |
	Carter	Reagan	Anderson	Mondale	Reagan	Bush	Dukakis
Favored	7%	19%	3%	9%	23%	21%	9%
Treated him about right	69	69	54	70	64	54	55
Were unfair	17	5	30	16	8	13	23
Don't know	7	7	13	5	5	12	13

Source: Survey by the Roper Organization for the Television Information Office, 1989.

When asked if they thought news coverage was biased toward a certain candidate in the 1980, 1984, and 1988 presidential campaigns, the public responded that overall media treatment was generally fair and unbiased. The question asked was: First, (name of candidate), do you think television news people favored him, or treated him about right, or were unfair to him? This was asked about each candidate in turn.

Do the Media Have a Liberal Bias?

YES William Rusher

Based upon *The Coming Battle for the Media* (New York: William Morrow Company, 1988).

Rusher, publisher of *National Review*, a conservative magazine, contends that the news media are biased against conservatives and that news coverage promotes liberal points of view. He cites the Lichter-Rothman study of leading journalists, which, he says, shows that they "are far to the Left of American public opinion in general on the great majority of topics." For example, the overwhelming majority of leading journalists voted for George McGovern in 1972, although the vast majority of Americans voted against him. Rusher acknowledges that detecting bias in coverage "is almost inevitably somewhat subjective" and that "one man's 'bias' is another man's 'robust journalism,' " but he claims that empirical research has taken much of the subjectivity out of the argument. He cites studies of how television covered the 1972 and 1984 presidential elections—studies based upon "favorable" and "unfavorable" word-counts—to show how liberal journalists injected bias into their coverage. George Bush, for example, got zero favorable spin in television news reports of the 1984 election. Such objective, measurable evidence proves, according to Rusher, that the media's conduct is "neatly congruent" with the "demonstrated liberal preferences of the overwhelming majority of the media elite."

NO Mark Crispin Miller

Based upon "TV's Anti-Liberal Bias," *New York Times*, November 16, 1988, p. A31.

Miller, a social commentator who teaches writing at Johns Hopkins University, contends that the media have an anti-liberal bias. He cites examples from media coverage of the 1988 presidential election. Although most Americans thought Michael Dukakis won the first debate with George Bush, most media commentators called it a draw, as they did the debate between the vice-presidential contenders, Dan Quayle and Lloyd Bentsen. "Analysts would admit the obvious only after scanning polls that showed that Quayle had seemed normal to only a minority of believers." The media played up issues that hurt the Democrats—such as the whisperings of a Dukakis nervous breakdown—while ignoring or dropping stories of improprieties by Quayle and Bush. "Far from showing liberal bias, then, television news helped do the liberals in," Miller contends, and he suggests two reasons for this. First, television is a "majoritarian" medium: It aims for high viewer ratings and can thus be very easily manipulated by the Right, which can "flood a switchboard or fire off a million threatening letters." Second, news reporters *are*, by and large, liberal, and this makes them "bend over backwards not to seem at all critical of the Republicans."

Postscript

One of the problems in determining whether or not news reports are colored by political bias is trying to decide what kind of evidence to admit. Rusher accepts studies based upon quantitative data that tabulate the use of "favorable" and "unfavorable" words or expressions; Miller relies upon what he considers key examples. Ultimately, both rest upon judgments about what is important, what is favorable or unfavorable, and where emphasis should be placed.

S. Robert Lichter et al., *The Media Elite* (Bethesda, MD: Adler and Adler, 1986) lends support to Rusher's thesis, while Ben Bagdikian's *The Media Monopoly* (Boston: Beacon Press, 1983) leans more toward Miller. Edward Jay Epstein's *News from Nowhere* (New York: Random House, 1973) remains one of the most balanced studies of the bias issue.

"When you quote a Presidential candidate, Gorman, you do not—
I repeat—do not roll your eyes." *Drawing by Stevenson: © 1988 The
New Yorker Magazine, Inc.*

(Continued from page 377)

both elections, the majority of respondents thought *all* the major-party candidates
were treated "about right." Thus, if the news media are slanted in their election
coverage, the general public apparently does not think so—although, of course, the
public may be mistaken.

But the issue of liberal bias continues to spark vigorous debate. In this chapter's
Taking Sides section, journalist William Rusher and social analyst Mark Crispin Miller
offer us very different points of view on this issue.

THE MEDIA AND THE MILITARY

World War II was an enormously popular war in which our opponents—the German
Nazis and the Japanese warlords—were obvious villains. Most Americans were
united in open hatred of them, particularly after the Japanese launched their surprise
attack on our naval base at Pearl Harbor, Hawaii, in December 1941. It was an
intensely patriotic period, and America's military leaders came out of the war with
their prestige at an all-time high—they were heroes, guardians of democracy.
Reporters shared this view and helped to foster it. The Vietnam War generation of
journalists had a very different opinion of military leaders. The tendency was to
regard these leaders as bumblers and liars, some honorable exceptions aside. The
generals sent young men to kill and be killed in pointless battles, lied about enemy
body counts and about progress, covered up American atrocities, and tried to
manipulate the press.

Do the attitudes of this generation of reporters affect the way the military is
covered in the media? There has been little systematic research, so we do not know if
it happens often. But it does happen. In 1971 CBS broadcast a program entitled "The
Selling of the Pentagon," which won a number of journalism awards at the time. The
documentary's message was that the Pentagon spends huge sums of money to sell
itself to the public and that it does so through public relations programs that glamorize
war and manipulate people's fears of communism. It was an arguable position. The
trouble was that in presenting the story, CBS relied upon editing techniques that were

themselves manipulative. It used *nonsequential editing*, editing that switched portions of film footage recorded earlier with those recorded later. For example, in one place in the film, reporter Roger Mudd was shown interviewing the Pentagon's public relations director. Mudd asked the director some questions, which were answered. However, those answers were clipped out by the program's editors and replaced by answers the director had given to *earlier* questions. The effect was to make the director sound evasive and unresponsive.[50]

Although CBS has never specifically repudiated nonsequential editing, it has done so in effect by stating that it will give viewers prior notice if documentary material is to be shown out of sequence. But there are other deceptive ways of processing documentaries, and CBS later admitted that some of those were used in the making of a 1982 documentary about General William Westmoreland.

GENERAL WESTMORELAND AND CBS

As Supreme Commander of the Allied forces in Vietnam, General William Westmoreland was profoundly distrusted by the American press. He was a zealous promoter of the Johnson administration's thesis that the war was being won. Still, until 1982 no serious journalist had ever accused him of consciously lying about the number of enemy troops in Vietnam. A special 90-minute program aired by CBS on January 23, 1982, was therefore especially dramatic as well as a real departure from usual coverage. The title was "The Uncounted Enemy: A Vietnam Deception," and in advertisements for it, CBS proclaimed that it had found a "conspiracy," a "deliberate plot to fool the American public, the Congress, and perhaps even the White House."

The program grew out of an article written for *Harper's* magazine in 1975 by an ex-CIA agent named Sam Adams. Adams charged that the top military authorities in Vietnam had deliberately underestimated the number of Communist guerrillas operating in South Vietnam in the 1960s. He had calculated that there were 600,000 Vietcong operating in South Vietnam; the figure officially reported, 270,000, was less than half that number. The charge seemed odd at first. American military commanders are usually suspected of *overestimating* enemy troop strength in order to wheedle more soldiers and arms out of their commander-in-chief. Adams's theory was that Westmoreland had underestimated the number in order to convince America that the war was being won—that the enemy was retreating.

Adams had been persuaded to write the article by a young editor at *Harper's* named George Crile. Crile, 30 years old at the time, had heard of Adams through a friend and was impressed by his troop-count thesis. Five years later, in 1980, Crile and Adams decided the subject would make a good television documentary. By now Crile held a position that allowed him to realize such ambitions; he was a CBS producer. Crile hired Adams as the program's chief consultant and went to work. Interviews were arranged, and one of CBS's top correspondents, Mike Wallace, was picked to conduct the on-camera interviews. Among those interviewed was Adams himself, the program's paid consultant, although he was never properly identified as such in the broadcast.

The most dramatic of all the interviews was the one with General Westmoreland, who had agreed to be interviewed because he thought the discussion was going to be an overall review of the Vietnam War. Westmoreland was thunderstruck when the interview turned into a high-pressure inquisition. During a pause, he stalked over to Crile and growled, "You rattlesnaked me!"[51]

Crile was delighted with the result. Before the interview, he had written to Wallace, "Now all you have to do is break General Westmoreland and we have the whole thing aced."[52] Westmoreland may not have been broken by the interview, but he was red-faced and seemed flustered; some of his answers sounded wobbly. Watching it in the screening room, Crile, according to one account, leaped to his feet at one point and shouted, "I got you, I *got* you, I *got* you!"[53] Westmoreland had a tough question of his own that he kept throwing back to Wallace: Why, if the enemy had 600,000 fighting guerrillas in South Vietnam, did it commit only 84,000 to the Tet offensive? Tet was the great all-out Vietcong offensive, yet *every* informed source agrees that there were no more than 84,000 guerrillas committed to it. If Sam Adams was right that there were really 600,000 Vietcong in South Vietnam at the time, what were the other 516,000 doing? Westmoreland never got an answer.

The general was predictably furious when the documentary was broadcast, but he waited eight months to bring his $120-million libel suit against CBS. Westmoreland did not want to sue because he knew that the odds were against any public figure winning a libel judgment against the media. For a public figure to win such a suit, he or she must demonstrate that the allegations carried in the media were (1) false; (2) defamatory, that is, hurtful to one's reputation or career; and (3) made with actual malice, that is, with knowledge that the allegations were false or with reckless disregard to whether they were true or false.

What finally convinced Westmoreland that he could leap all of these impediments and win his case was an article in *TV Guide* in May 1982. Based upon two months of intensive probing and interviews with CBS staffers, the article charged that CBS had done the following:

General William Westmoreland leaves the courthouse with one of his lawyers during a break in the proceedings of the general's $120 million libel suit against CBS. In 1985, almost two and a half years after filing the suit, Westmoreland withdrew his case.

- Rehearsed interviews with witnesses against Westmoreland (one was interviewed twice to improve his testimony).
- Made little attempt to investigate Adams's thesis.
- Misedited some interviews and distorted the content of others.
- Failed to interview knowledgeable witnesses who would have refuted the conspiracy thesis.
- Allowed an anti-Westmoreland witness to watch the testimony of others in the screening room in order to prepare better for his own testimony.

Since many of these charges were violations of CBS's own standards, the network launched an internal investigation. Burton Benjamin, a senior executive producer, was given the task. Three months later, the Benjamin Report was completed. It not only substantiated most of *TV Guide*'s charges, but added some of its own. The report charged that the premise behind the show was flawed, since there had never been any proof of a conspiracy. It also pointed out that Adams had never been properly identified as a paid consultant, that sympathetic witnesses were coddled, that not enough effort was made to contact knowledgeable witnesses who might have exonerated the general, and that the program was unbalanced (General Westmoreland and his one defender received a total of 5 minutes and 59 seconds on the program; his accusers got 19 minutes and 19 seconds). In his later account of the controversy, Benjamin defended the substance of the broadcast but summed up the "three essential elements" of it that, in his opinion, could not be denied: "The use of the word 'conspiracy' was unwarranted; the broadcast was out of balance in reflecting the opposing sides; and the CBS News Standards had been violated repeatedly."[54]

Despite all these revelations, Westmoreland's libel suit went nowhere. In February 1985, almost two and a half years after Westmoreland had filed suit, he withdrew from the case. He and CBS signed a joint statement in which CBS agreed that Westmoreland had been a patriotic general but otherwise conceded nothing. Westmoreland simply gave up. Renata Adler of the *New Yorker*, who made an exhaustive study of the case, concludes that it was because Westmoreland's chief counsel "was seriously, even vastly, overmatched."[55] A 39-year-old lawyer with no previous trial experience, he became increasingly awed by CBS's legal talent and in the end accepted its view that he could not win.[56]

In effect, CBS won its case against Westmoreland. But that did not change the facts confirmed by CBS's own internal investigation—for example, that witnesses hostile to Westmoreland had been coached and witnesses friendly to him had been ignored or given short shrift. The questions raised by the documentary, therefore, are still unresolved. Why were these practices followed? Apparently, Crile was convinced that Westmoreland was guilty and that he, Crile, was going to prove it on the air. But why did he feel compelled to do that? Was he out to get Westmoreland, or was there some deeper message behind the documentary, a message not unlike that in "The Selling of the Pentagon" 11 years earlier?

Both documentaries seemed to say: "This is what the cold war brings—lying, deception, manipulation by the military." Westmoreland became the symbol of the "cold war general." By the 1970s, especially after Richard Nixon and Watergate, the media became increasingly suspicious of appeals to national security or patriotism. In the 1980s this put the press on a virtual collision course with the Reagan administration.

When the United States invaded Grenada in 1983, reporters were excluded from the battle zone until the operation was virtually complete. They were indignant. This was the first time, they complained, that the American military had barred the press from a war. Secretary of State George Shultz replied that in the past journalists were on "our" side. "These days, in the adversary journalism that's developed, it seems as though reporters are always against us."[57]

A generation ago, this would not have been an issue. When, early in 1961, a *New York Times* reporter discovered preparations for a CIA-sponsored invasion of Cuba, the *Times* watered down his copy and shrank the headline as a favor to President Kennedy. As late as 1967 the *New York Times* backed away from printing classified cables supplied by Daniel Ellsberg, the Pentagon employee who eventually supplied the press with 47 volumes of stolen documents. But by 1971, as we saw in chapter 4, the *Times* was no longer awed by "top secret" stamps. It received Ellsberg's stolen documents and printed portions of them. And got away with it: In *United States v. New York Times* (1971), the Supreme Court barred the government from stopping the presses.

By the 1980s, many journalists would probably agree with former CBS News president Richard Salant that the journalist cannot be on the side of *any* nation: "We're on the side, to be pompous about it, of truth."[58] Salant said this in 1985 at a nationally televised symposium on the media and the military. The moderator, law professor (and later Yale president) Benno Schmidt, laid out this hypothetical case: Imagine you are in a country like El Salvador, where American advisers are helping the government resist Communist guerrilla forces. You get a chance to interview some guerrillas, and during the course of the interview, you discover that they are planning to attack a government-controlled village the next day. Would you share that information with the American authorities? CBS correspondent Jane Wallace answered that she "would not feel at all compelled, or even tugged, about sharing that information." Schmidt asked if she considered herself "a stateless person for this purpose. That is, the fact that the Americans are on our side doesn't matter?" Wallace: "Doesn't matter." Charles Lewis of the Associated Press said that journalists should be loyal to their readers and viewers "rather than to the security of any particular group."[59] As Figure 14.4 shows, these views are not uncommon among journalists, but they are uncommon among other Americans.

The question of whose side the press is on had already come up, although more indirectly, in an earlier seminar. In 1983 some of the nation's leading journalists, including Dan Rather of CBS, Jack Nelson of the *Los Angeles Times*, ABC's Brit Hume, and *Washington Post* editor Howard Simons, got together to discuss the press and national security. Again, Benno Schmidt served as moderator. At one point

FIGURE **14-4**

383

The Media Bias

Battle Reporting: Journalists' and Public's Views

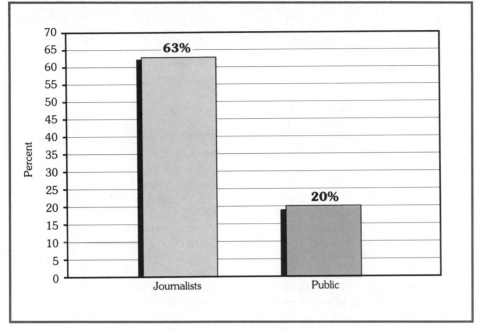

Data source: Minnesota Opinion Research, Inc.

During World War II and the Korean War, the American press was seldom in an adversarial relationship with American military leadership, but Vietnam changed everything. Today, a majority of journalists would publish a battlefield story even if military authorities ruled it "off limits." In contrast, only a small minority of the public at large would approve of publication under such circumstances. The question asked in this survey was: The press should always publish a story from an area where American troops are fighting, even if "off limits"—do you agree or disagree? Shown are the percentages agreeing.

Schmidt asked *Baltimore Sun* reporter Lyle Denniston (who also frequently appears on PBS's "MacNeil-Lehrer News Hour") if he would accept a document stolen from the Pentagon. This produced the following exchange:

Denniston: Professor Schmidt, as a journalist I have only one responsibility and that is to get a story and print it.

Moderator: Would you steal it yourself?

Denniston: I would.

Moderator: Right off [the CIA director's] desk?

Denniston: Exactly. And hopefully without his knowing it.

Moderator: Would you hold a gun to his head?

Denniston: Mayhem might well be ruled out, but I'm not even sure of that.

Moderator: But breaking and entering?

Denniston: Breaking and entering is benign.[60]

Some of the other journalists were put off by these flourishes, but all agreed with Denniston's position. Brit Hume would not take the stolen documents, but "I'd take a

Xerox, frankly." Howard Simon put it in terms of jobs: The government's job is to keep secrets, and "my job is to find 'em." Jack Nelson said he "might be a little concerned" if he knew he was receiving stolen documents. "But in the end it wouldn't make any difference." Dan Rather said, "As a professional, my job is to publish and be damned." Schmidt pressed: Would it bother you that the documents came to you "with this taint of criminality?" Rather replied, "Some, but frankly not a great deal."[61]

These views are not uncommon among today's journalists. Many of the leaders in journalism today are the peers of the young reporters David Halberstam saw in Vietnam. Others are post-Vietnam reporters who inherited views on national security issues that they now take for granted. Whether or not their attitudes—biases if one prefers—affect the way they cover the news remains a matter of dispute.[62] But it should not be difficult to understand why the military was reluctant to take reporters along when it went to Grenada.

What to Do About the Media?

What bothers some critics of the press is the apparent casualness with which reporters today talk about such matters as their willingness to accept stolen documents and give away military secrets. Has the press become an arrogant and irresponsible institution? The question is being raised not just by right-wing critics, but by many who wish the press well—including some journalists. "Rather than adopting a self-righteous ideology," wrote *Washington Post* columnist Joseph Kraft in 1981, " . . . I think we need to acknowledge—to ourselves at least—that we are the shapers and movers; that we are biased; that we are not representative." In 1985 Robert MacNeil, co-host of PBS's distinguished "MacNeil-Lehrer News Hour," criticized the kind of "advocacy" journalism "which regards fairness as *effete* and unmanly, and thinks telling both sides of the story and letting the public decide on the merits is wimpy and even irresponsible."[63] If we agree that these criticisms have merit, the next question is whether or not there is anything that can or should be done to reform the press.

That last sentence may sound a bit ominous. But reform can include a wide range of options, including self-criticism. Let us look at a few of the options.

MEDIA SELF-CRITICISM

The comments quoted by Kraft and MacNeil exemplify the willingness of some journalists to take a critical look at their own profession. Still, some feel that more is necessary: a permanent institution through which the press itself can call attention to press abuses. For a time there was such an institution, the National News Council. Founded in 1973 with a $400,000 grant from the Twentieth Century Fund of New York, the council was given the task of investigating charges of press bias and unfairness, attempting to mediate disputes, and releasing its findings. Membership was voluntary, and its powers went no further than tongue-lashing. Even so, the *New York Daily News* called it "a sneak attempt at press regulation," and the prestigious *New York Times* served notice that it would refuse to cooperate with any of its investigations. Lacking publicity, prestige, and, in the end, operating funds, the National News Council went out of business in 1985.

This does not mean that the media leave no room for criticism. Most newspapers have letters-to-the-editor sections, where scathing criticisms of the paper sometimes appear. Op-ed columns also occasionally carry criticisms of the press. Television programs like "Sixty Minutes" regularly feature reactions from viewers, and on talk shows, we sometimes hear derogatory comments about the media. Still, all these forums are subject to the control of the media that carry them. Media people decide what criticisms—if any—they want to carry and how they want to edit them. Long ago James Madison observed that "No man is allowed to be a judge in his own cause, because his interest would certainly bias his judgment and, not improbably, corrupt his integrity."[64] Madison's point was that we should not trust any group to govern itself without bias; there needs to be some sort of outside check. What are some possible checks on the press?

GOVERNMENT REGULATION

There is always government regulation. On its face, this seems to be unconstitutional. The First Amendment states that "Congress shall make no law . . . abridging the freedom of speech, or of the press." For some interpreters, like the late Supreme Court justice Hugo Black, "*no* law" means exactly that. Nevertheless, as we saw in chapter 4, the Supreme Court has left room for exceptions. Nobody has a right to falsely shout "Fire!" in a crowded theater, and, the Court has said, nobody has a right to incite violent revolution or display hard-core pornography in public or commit libel and slander. Still, as we have seen, it is very difficult for the government or a public figure to win a judgment against the print media. They have been able to publish classified information stolen from the Pentagon, false and defamatory charges against public figures, the most sexually explicit books imaginable, and open calls for revolution. When the print media deal in the public realm, there is very little the government can do to stop or punish them.

For the electronic media, the situation is a little different. From the earliest days of radio, it was clear that not everybody could have access. There are only so many

Tax-Form Checkoff

To the Editor:

Let's end the debate about tax increases to finance the war on drugs. We already have a box to check on our Federal tax return if we want to help fund elections; why not add a new box for a $5 donation to aid the war on drugs?

WILLIAM BROWN

Letters to the editor give readers the opportunity to express opposing viewpoints and to exercise their First Amendment rights. Whether or not those alternate viewpoints ever reach the public depends upon the editor's willingness to publish them.

frequency bands available, so not everyone who wants to can just start broadcasting. Since the 1920s, the federal government has been assigning the various bands of the broadcasting spectrum to individual stations, giving each an exclusive license to broadcast within its band. In return for this license, the government demands that the stations operate in the public interest.

What is "operating in the public interest"? The Communications Act of 1934 says it means, among other things, bringing to the public a diversity of viewpoints. The act requires any station that endorses a political candidate to allow equal time for the endorsement of competing candidates. It set up the Federal Communications Commission (FCC) and gave it the power to make and enforce rules for broadcasting. Acting on that mandate, the FCC in 1949 promulgated its fairness doctrine, which required radio and television stations to air controversies and to allow at least some time—not necessarily equal time—for replies to any controversial viewpoint that it might broadcast.

In *Red Lion Broadcasting Co. v. Federal Communications Commission* (1969), the Supreme Court upheld the fairness doctrine against a challenge to its constitutionality. A radio station claimed that the doctrine violated its First Amendment right to broadcast—in this case, its asserted right *not* to broadcast a listener's reply to a commentator. But the Court insisted that "it is the right of the viewers and listeners, not the right of broadcasters, which is paramount." Alluding to Oliver Wendell Holmes's ideal of "free trade in ideas," the Court said that the purpose of the First Amendment is "to preserve an uninhibited marketplace of ideas in which truth will ultimately prevail."

During the 1980s, the fairness doctrine came under increasingly heavy attack by the broadcast industry and by the FCC itself. Most of its commissioners made no secret of their distaste for government regulation, and they interpreted "fairness" so loosely that it was enough if a broadcaster consigned dissenting views to the small hours of the morning. Finally, in August 1987, the FCC voted unanimously to abolish the doctrine: "We seek to extend to the electronic press the same First Amendment guarantees that the print media have enjoyed since our country's inception," said chairman Dennis R. Patrick.[65] Congress later tried to reinstate the doctrine by legislation, but the bill was vetoed by President Reagan.

For a time it was argued that there ought to be a fairness doctrine for newspapers. In his book *Freedom of the Press for Whom?* law professor Jerome Barron argued that since competing newspapers are practically nonexistent, people should have a "right to reply" to newspaper attacks on them.[66] Barron took his case to the Supreme Court by defending the state of Florida's "right to reply" law. The Court sympathized with his position but struck down the law (*Miami Herald v. Tornillo*, 1974). A "responsible press," the Court said, "is an undoubtedly desirable goal, but press responsibility is not mandated by the Constitution and like many other virtues it cannot be legislated."

That sums up the situation as it applies to both broadcast and print media. Judges and legislators have taken the view that while it might be nice if our media were more responsible and balanced, there is little that the law can do to make them so. There are, however, other ways of trying to affect the content and style of the media. In general, these take the form of economic and social pressures.

ECONOMIC AND SOCIAL PRESSURES

Organized groups have tried to influence media content by using economic and social pressures. In the early 1970s, the leading feminist organization, the National Organization for Women (NOW), complained of sex role stereotyping in the media. It urged the media to hire more women specialists, use *Ms.* instead of *Miss*, use *girl* only to refer to females under the age of sixteen, and avoid terms like *gals* and *ladies*. NOW also lent its support to various women's caucuses that grew up within media organizations.[67]

NOW was only one of many organizations trying to make the media more responsive to its agenda. Most, like NOW, supported liberal causes such as feminism, defense spending cuts, increases in welfare spending, and gay rights. By the 1980s, however, conservative organizations had become more visible among those pressuring the media. Fundamentalist Christian groups objected to the casual sex on entertainment programs and what they saw as the secular humanist bias of news reporters. Some attempted to organize consumer boycotts of the products advertised on the programs. Business organizations, notably Mobil Oil, began buying advertisements in which they complained about media coverage. Groups opposing gun control, supporting the Contras in Nicaragua, and favoring greater defense expenditures and other right-wing goals began demanding access to the media.

The success of these groups is hard to measure. The consumer boycotts of the Christian Right certainly did not work: Today's television shows have so many sponsors that it is hard to focus economic pressure. Other methods—such as NOW's combination of picketing, threatened legal action, and negotiating—may have achieved greater results. More women are now in broadcasting and the print press, and in made-for-television movies and sitcoms; they are now seen in the strong roles once reserved for men. (NOW also persuaded the *New York Times* to call unmarried women *Ms.*) Mobil Oil's media critic, Herbert Schmertz, has become something of a celebrity because of his aggressive stance: Instead of trying to soothe the press, he attacked it by pointing out instances of factual inaccuracy and advocacy journalism. He has won the respect of major media outlets and may have persuaded journalists to qualify their writing on issues relating to "big oil."

The Left and the Right sometimes exchange accusations about their attempts to influence the media; often these accusations reflect unconscious double standards. One side accuses the other of trying to harass the media, while characterizing its own attempts to influence the media as citizen action. They come to the same thing, of course; it is simply that "yea" words are substituted for "boo" words, depending on which side a person favors. Someone addressing his or her adversary might put it this way: *(Continued on page 388)*

Connie Chung of CBS is one of many well-respected female news reporters. More women than ever before are now in broadcasting and many hold positions that were once the exclusive domain of men.

MEDIA GADFLIES—LEFT AND RIGHT

Left: Fairness & Accuracy in Reporting
Jeff Cohen, Director
666 Broadway, Suite 400, New York, NY 10012
(212) 475-4640
Founded in 1986, Fairness & Accuracy seeks to counter what it considers to be the center-right bias of the media in coverage of such issues as minorities, national defense, and the environment. It claims to be a friend of working reporters and seeks to guard them against the pressure of corporate interests and to raise their consciousness. It publishes *Extra*, a monthly newsletter.

Right: Accuracy in Media (AIM)
Reed Irvine, Chairman
1341 G Street, NW, Suite 312, Washington, DC 20005
(202) 783-4406
Founded in 1968, AIM seeks to bring pressure on the news media to provide more balanced programming content. Its chairman, Reed Irvine, claims that news reporting is skewed toward the Left, especially on issues relating to defense and internal security. Irvine edits the *AIM Report*, a newsletter published twice a month.

(Continued from page 387)

- "Your protest is intemperate; mine is robust and vigorous."
- "You want to intimidate; I want to nail a lie."
- "You want to censor; I want to get that garbage off the air."
- "Your people are shrill; mine have a right to be angry."
- "Your picketing will chill free speech; my picketing will raise consciousness."

Whatever peoples' views or motives, they have a right to be heard. The First Amendment applies to everybody—Dan Rather, Leslie Stahl, Mike Wallace, *and* their critics to the Left and Right. Indeed, we should welcome critics of all persuasions. At his trial in ancient Athens, Socrates described himself as a "gadfly" and said that his role was to sting the public out of its stupor. Many reporters and columnists picture themselves in this socratic role. But the press in America is more than a gadfly. It has become a powerful political institution—an actor, a mover, and a shaker, not just a commentator. Today's gadflies, then, are not only the people in the press but those in the public who criticize the press. Their stings, annoying as they are, may force the press to re-examine its own framework of values and assumptions.

Reflections

In 1919 Oliver Wendell Holmes said that truth is best reached through "free trade in ideas." Freedom of the press, as guaranteed in the First Amendment, is meant to foster free idea-trading. If everyone is allowed to publish his or her views, no matter how extreme, people can sort them out and decide which ones are valid.

Holmes was giving his version of what has become the classic defense of press freedom. Most of us probably accept it. The trouble comes not when we think about the theory of press freedom, but when we try to figure out how to apply it. At the time the First Amendment was written, there was a large number of little printshops, all of them more or less equal in power. It was not that expensive to buy your own press or at least get access to one. Trade in ideas was brisk. There was a lot of competition.

Today less than three percent of the metropolitan areas of the United States have competing newspapers; newspaper chains have taken over independent papers. Wire services have helped to standardize reporting, and syndicated columns have begun to standardize opinion. Radio and television have, on the one hand, opened up new channels of communication and, on the other, contributed still more to standardization and nationalization. Television, the news medium of choice for most

Americans, is dominated by three networks, giant media conglomerates that reach audiences of 60 million and more every night.

It is hard to compete with these giants; the average person certainly cannot buy a network! That is why questions about bias and balance have become so important. Bias would not matter if we could all compete on equal terms in the marketplace of ideas. Then everybody who wanted to could deliver his or her own biased news and we could judge between them. Obviously that is not possible, so we expect the news giants to leave room for a variety of viewpoints, while giving us news reports that are objective.

Objectivity was once the highest journalistic virtue. Schools of journalism taught it, and newspapers like the *New York Times* tried to practice it. "The good gray *New York Times*," they used to call it. But objectivity fell into disrepute during the Vietnam era. The younger reporters came to the conclusion that in order to tell the truth about the war, a good reporter had to venture some personal journalism—advocacy journalism. Today even the *New York Times* is no longer gray. Reporters often put their own colorful spins onto their stories. This makes for livelier writing, but it also raises the question of ideological bias.

Ideological bias may simply be in the eye of the beholder. But that, in a way, is the whole point. It is we, the beholders, that the mass media are meant to serve. We have to devise ways of getting access to the giant conglomerates or at least ways of contradicting them when we think they are wrong. The fairness doctrine was meant to serve this purpose, as was the National News Council. But the fairness doctrine and the National News Council are both gone. Perhaps the best course left to us is to bring pressure on the media. We can write letters to newspapers when we think their coverage is unfair or inaccurate. We can call local radio and television stations or call or write the networks themselves. We can picket. We can affiliate ourselves with watchdog groups like Fairness & Accuracy in Reporting and Accuracy in Media. The First Amendment gives the media the right to broadcast and publish what they see fit. It also gives us the right to talk back.

Notes

1. Peter Braestrup, *Big Story* (New Haven and London: Yale University Press, 1983), p. 51.
2. Braestrup, pp. 133-37.
3. Don Oberdorfer, *Tet!* (Garden City, NY: Doubleday and Co., 1971), p. 34.
4. Braestrup, chaps. 4-5; Oberdorfer, pp. 238-57.
5. Braestrup, p. 89.
6. Braestrup, p. 85.
7. David Halberstam, *The Powers That Be* (New York: Dell Publishing Co., 1979), p. 511.
8. Braestrup, p. 142.
9. James Boylan, "Declarations of Independence," *Columbia Journalism Review* (November/December 1986), p. 36.
10. Daniel J. Boorstin, *The Image* (New York: Atheneum, 1977), p. 37.
11. This classic defense of free speech goes back at least to 1644, when the English poet John Milton argued that truth and falsehood should be allowed to "grapple" with one another, for "who ever knew the truth put to the worse, in a free and open encounter" (see *Areopagitica*, any edition). This argument or some variation of it is found in virtually every serious defense of free speech.
12. Holmes's dissenting opinion, *Abrams v. United States* (1919).
13. L. Jesse Lemisch, ed., *Benjamin Franklin: The Autobiography and Other Writings* (New York and Toronto: Signet Books, 1961), pp. 39, 77.
14. Quoted in Clinton Rossiter, *The Political Thought of the American Revolution* (New York: Harcourt, Brace & World, 1963), p. 11.
15. Edward Dumbauld, ed., *The Political Writings of Thomas Jefferson: Representative Selections* (Indianapolis, IN: Bobbs-Merrill Co., 1955), pp. 76, 94.
16. In Dumbauld, ed., p. 95.
17. Jefferson, in Dumbauld, pp. 93, 95.
18. Alvin P. Sanoff, "Behind the Demise of Family Newspapers," *U.S. News and World Report*, Feb. 11, 1985, p. 60. See further, Ben Bagdikian, *The Media Monopoly* (Boston: Beacon

Press, 1983), p. 9. See also Bagdikian's testimony before the Federal Trade Commission in 1978, in George McKenna, ed., *Media Voices* (Guilford, CT: Dushkin Publishing Group, 1982), p. 28.

19. Walter Lippmann, quoted in Fred Friendly, *Due to Circumstances Beyond Our Control* (New York: Vintage Books, 1967), p. 294.

20. Eleanor Randolph, "Is Network News Going Down the Tube?" *National Weekly Edition, Washington Post*, Feb. 23, 1987, pp. 10-11.

21. David Halberstam, *The Powers That Be* (New York: Dell Publishing Co., 1979), p. 716.

22. *The People and the Press*, special *Times-Mirror* investigation of public attitudes, conducted by the Gallup Organization, Jan. 1986, p. 25; "Poll Finds TV News Anchors More Trusted Than Reagan," *New York Times*, Feb. 15, 1987, p. 34.

23. A. J. Liebling, quoted in Michael Parenti (see endnote 17).

24. Malcolm Gladwell, "Ted Turner's Cable Scam," *American Spectator* (March 1987), p. 22.

25. Bill Carter, "With America Well Wired, Cable Industry is Changing," *New York Times*, July 9, 1989, p. 20.

26. See former FCC Commissioner Lee Loevinger's remarks at the FTC hearings 1978, in McKenna, pp. 31-37. See also the views of William Paley, founder and former chairman of CBS, in George McKenna and Stanley Feingold, eds., *Taking Sides: Clashing Views on Controversial Political Issues*, 4th ed. (Guilford, CT: Dushkin Publishing Group, 1985), pp. 166-70.

27. Michael J. Bennett, "The 'Imperial' Press Corps, in Ray Eldon Hiebert and Carol Reuss, *Impact of Mass Media* (White Plains, NY: Longman, Inc., 1985), p. 266; Darnton is quoted in Stephen Hess, "Fear and Fraternity in the Washington Press Corps," in Hiebert and Reuss, p. 275.

28. Timothy Crouse, *The Boys on the Bus: Riding With the Campaign Press Corps* (New York: Ballantine Books, 1976).

29. Michael Parenti, *Inventing Reality* (New York: St. Martin's Press, 1986), p. 4.

30. Quoted in David Bollier, "The Strange Politics of 'Fairness'," *Channels* (January/February 1986), p. 48.

31. Friendly, chaps. 2-3.

32. Halberstam, p. 744.

33. Halberstam, p. 663.

34. Halberstam, p. 560.

35. Halberstam, pp. 707, 709.

36. Peter J. Boyer, "CBS News In Search of Itself," *New York Times Magazine*, Dec. 28, 1986, pp. 17-18.

37. See Rather's letter to the *Times*, Aug. 7, 1986, p. C13, and his op-ed article, "From Murrow to Mediocrity?" Mar. 10, 1987, p. A27.

38. See Stephen Hess, in Hiebert and Reuss, p. 272.

39. S. Robert Lichter and Stanley Rothman, "Media and Business Elites," *Public Opinion* (October/November 1981), pp. 42-60; S. Robert Lichter, Stanley Rothman, and Linda S. Lichter, *The Media Elite* (Bethesda, MD: Adler & Adler, 1986).

40. Lichter and Rothman, 1981, p. 44.

41. Herbert Gans, "Are U.S. Journalists Dangerously Liberal?" in the *Columbia Journalism Review* (November/December 1986), pp. 29-33.

42. Gans, p. 32.

43. Gay Talese, *The Kingdom and the Power* (New York and Cleveland: World Publishing Co., 1969), pp. 293-97.

44. Halberstam, p. 716.

45. Boylan, p. 34.

46. John Chancellor, Donald G. Herzberg Memorial Lecture, Columbia School of Journalism, Dec. 3, 1984, transcript p. 11.

47. Maura Clancy and Michael Robinson, "General Election Coverage: Part I," *Public Opinion* (December/January 1985), p. 50.

48. Clancy and Robinson, p. 50.

49. Michael Robinson and Margaret Sheehan, *Over the Wire and On TV: CBS and UPI in Campaign '80* (New York: Russell Sage Foundation, 1983).

50. Martin Moyer, "Television," *Harper's* (December 1971), pp. 40-42.

51. Don Kowet, *A Matter of Honor: General William C. Westmoreland Versus CBS* (New York: Macmillan Publishing Co., 1984), p. 63.

52. Bob Brewin and Sydney Shaw, *Vietnam on Trial: Westmoreland v. CBS* (New York: Atheneum, 1987), p. 33. After the interview, Crile wrote to Wallace: "The interview was a classic. . . . It was wonderful having you as our champion." Brewin and Shaw, p. 34.

53. Kowet, p. 77.

54. Burton Benjamin, *Fair Play: CBS, General Westmoreland, and How a Television Documentary Went Wrong* (New York: Harper & Row, 1988), p. 167.

55. Renata Adler, "Annals of Law: Two Trials—II," *New Yorker*, June 23, 1986, p. 34.

56. Brewin and Shaw suggest two other reasons: (1) Westmoreland was running out of money and knew that CBS would appeal if it lost; (2) the judge's instructions to the jury made it very difficult for Westmoreland to win. The instructions required "clear and convincing evidence," not just a preponderance of evidence, that the CBS broadcast was false. Brewin and Shaw, pp. 352-53.

57. *Facts on File Yearbook, 1983* (New York: Facts on File, Inc., 1984), p. 944.

58. "A Question of Access," *The Military and the News Media*, transcript of the Media and Society Seminars, Columbia University School of Journalism, 1985, p. 22.

59. *The Military and the News Media*, pp. 16-18, 24-25.

60. "National Security and Freedom of the Press," *The Constitution: That Delicate Balance*, transcript of the Media and Society Seminars, Columbia University School of Journalism, 1985, pp. 28-29.

61. "National Security and Freedom of the Press," *The Constitution: That Delicate Balance*, pp. 20, 23, 25, 51.

62. See, for example, the debate between Ernest Lefever and William Small, in McKenna, pp. 75-83.

63. Robert MacNeil, "The Mass Media and Public Trust," Remarks at dedication of the Gannet Center for Media Studies, Columbia University, Mar. 13, 1985. (Occasional Paper No. 1). MacNeil added: "I get that feeling sometimes reading *The Columbia Journalism Review.*"

64. James Madison (Publius), *The Federalist* No. 10.

65. Robert D. Hershey Jr., "F.C.C. Votes Down Fairness Doctrine in 4-0 Decision," *New York Times*, Aug. 5, 1987, p. 1.

66. Jerome Barron, *Freedom of the Press for Whom?* (Bloomington, IN: Indiana University Press, 1973).

67. Peter M. Sandman, David M. Rubin, and David Sachsman, *Media: An Introductory Analysis of American Communications*, 2d ed. (Englewood Cliffs, NJ: Prentice-Hall, Inc., 1976), pp. 217-18.

15

Interest Groups

The Death and Life of the B-1 Bomber

The B-1 is a gray, needle-nosed aircraft that looks more like a fighter than a bomber. Yet it is a craft designed for carrying nuclear bombs into the heart of the Soviet Union. It was to be a replacement for the aging B-52 (a plane first deployed in the early 1950s), and it was to be capable of screaming along the treetops at speeds just below sound, dumping its deadly payload on enemy targets and, with any luck, returning home. It was to be a very fast plane (much faster than the lumbering B-52), designed to get off the runway on five minutes' notice. In case the enemy's missiles start arriving as it takes off, the B-1 has curtains that can be drawn to protect its crew from the blinding flashes of nuclear explosions. Presumably, it is hard to spot on enemy radar: Its radar cross section is only 1 percent as visible on the screen as that of the B-52, and it contains a variety of electronic devices that can make the plane appear to be where it is not. *

To its supporters, past and present, the B-1 is vital to American security. To its critics, it is a ridiculous gold-plated boondoggle, a scan-

392

The B-1 bomber was the object of a ten-year lobbying war that involved a broad range of interest groups fighting for and against its funding from Congress.

dalous waste of taxpayers' money. For a time in the 1970s, the critics' view prevailed, and President Carter cut off funds for the B-1. But in the end, its supporters got their way. It took a 10-year lobbying war, but they won.

That war began in earnest in 1970, two years after the Johnson administration awarded the contract to produce the plane to Rockwell International, a multibillion-dollar aerospace corporation that had been working on plans for the B-1 since 1961. Almost immediately, opponents, some of whom were members of Congress, began to organize. A year earlier, a group of Congressmen had issued a 40-page document on proposed military expenditures that had featured a scathing review of the B-1: It would cost too much (the estimated price was $100 million per plane; today it costs more than double that figure), and its military capabilities were not that much greater than the B-52's. Despite these arguments, the anti-B-1 members of Congress were hopelessly outnumbered. The Nixon administration's request for funding sailed through with little debate.

But outside of Congress, pressure against the B-1 was building. It grew out of a general antiwar mood that was sweeping the nation, a reaction to the seemingly endless war in Vietnam. College campuses around the nation exploded in student riots and sit-ins, giant antiwar demonstrations were held in Washington, and each day the mass media brought more reports of the misery caused by American bombers.

Soon there was a broad coalition of pressure groups opposed to the B-1. In 1973 the Quaker-founded American Friends Service Committee (AFSC) organized a meeting of opposition groups. Out of that meeting

*This account is drawn from the following sources: Nick Kotz, *Wild Blue Yonder: Money, Politics, and the B-1 Bomber* (New York: Pantheon Books, 1988); Norman J. Ornstein and Shirley Elder, *Interest Groups, Lobbying and Policymaking* (Washington: Congressional Quarterly, Inc., 1978), pp. 187-220; Stratford P. Sherman, "How Rockwell Kept the B-1 Alive," *Fortune*, November 2, 1981, pp. 106 + ; Orr Kelly, "The B-1: When Pentagon, Politicians Joined Hands," *U.S. News and World Report*, July 11, 1983, pp. 34-35; *Department of State Bulletin* (December, 1981), pp. 67-68; *Newsweek*, October 12, 1981, p. 41; and *New York Times*, June 30, 1985, p. 20.

came The National Campaign to Stop the B-1 Bomber. They scraped up the money to hire a full-time staff director, Robert P. Brammer, a 1971 graduate of Earlham College. Although Brammer was a novice to Washington politics, he caught on fast. More and more groups joined his campaign against the B-1: Common Cause, a liberal-oriented citizens' lobby; the National Taxpayers Union, a more conservative group opposed to government waste; the Federation of American Scientists, a pacifist-oriented group of scientists formed in 1946; and two other well-known peace groups, Women's International League for Peace and Freedom, and SANE (Citizens Committee for Sane Nuclear Policy). In terms of funds, it was a shoestring operation, but by sharing resources, from experts to duplicating machines, The National Campaign to Stop the B-1 Bomber was able to bring enormous pressure to bear on Congress.

By the mid-1970s, Brammer's people were almost winning some close votes in Congress. But their greatest single achievement came during the 1976 presidential campaign. Jimmy Carter, seeking the Democratic nomination, appeared before the platform committee at the start of the Democratic convention. With little knowledge of the B-1 but much respect for the coalition that opposed it, Carter decided to take a stand. Deploring "exotic weapons which serve no real function," Carter cited the B-1 as a weapon "which should not be funded and would be wasteful of taxpayers' dollars."[1] After that, it was just a matter of reminding President Carter of what candidate Carter had said. "We really drummed on that statement," Robert Brammer later recalled.[2] At a news conference on June 30, 1977, Carter officially announced his decision to cut off further funding of the B-1. Opponents were jubilant. "If people get organized," Brammer said, "they can even fight the Pentagon." But the optimism was premature. The B-1 opponents had won a battle—but now the second, and decisive, phase of the war was beginning.

Shortly after Carter's press conference, Robert Anderson, chairman and chief executive of Rockwell International, sat in the Concordia Club in Pittsburgh, not far from his office, trying to dispel his gloom with a dry Tanqueray martini. "It was like a death in the family," he recalled later.[3] But grieving was not enough; Rockwell could not afford to lose a contract that size, and Anderson had no intention of giving up.

Anderson had some powerful allies, like the United States Air Force, which had its own connections to sympathetic legislators. And on this issue it was not hard to generate sympathy. Construction of the B-1 would employ about 140,000 people throughout the country. Although its main frame was to be assembled in California, many parts would be produced by subcontractors—5,200 in all, located in every state of the union except Hawaii and Alaska. Even some outspoken doves like Senator Alan Cranston of California—the state where the main work was to be done—became strong advocates of the B-1.

Robert Anderson finished his drink and went to work on his immediate task—to keep the B-1 alive. In this he was helped by some ambiguities in Carter's speech. First, while rejecting the B-1, Carter believed that bombers should still play a major role in American defense. He thought the old B-52s would still do, provided they were equipped with cruise missiles, tiny unmanned jet planes with warheads that could be launched from B-52s. Carter did say, however, that he was willing to appropriate money for continued testing of B-1 prototypes in "the unlikely event" that cruise missiles did not work. Anderson used some of that "testing" money to (1) warehouse the expensive tools for building B-1

FIGURE **15-1**

Pieces of the Action

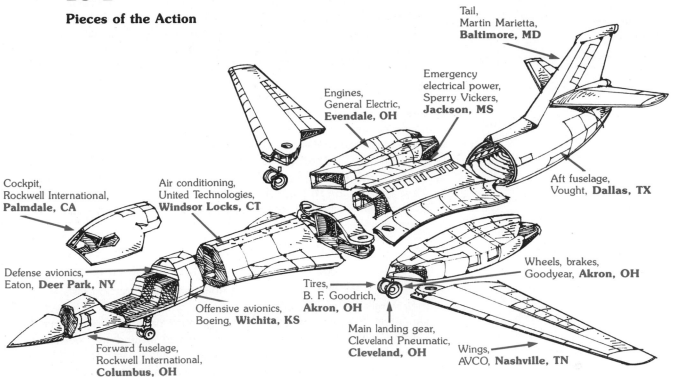

Tail,
Martin Marietta,
Baltimore, MD

Engines,
General Electric,
Evendale, OH

Emergency
electrical power,
Sperry Vickers,
Jackson, MS

Cockpit,
Rockwell International,
Palmdale, CA

Air conditioning,
United Technologies,
Windsor Locks, CT

Aft fuselage,
Vought, **Dallas, TX**

Defense avionics,
Eaton, **Deer Park, NY**

Tires,
B. F. Goodrich,
Akron, OH

Wheels, brakes,
Goodyear, **Akron, OH**

Offensive avionics,
Boeing, **Wichita, KS**

Main landing gear,
Cleveland Pneumatic,
Cleveland, OH

Wings,
AVCO, **Nashville, TN**

Forward fuselage,
Rockwell International,
Columbus, OH

Source: U.S. News & World Report, July 11, 1983, p. 35. Reprinted with permission.

The controversial B-1 bomber received support in part because its components were made in every state except Alaska and Hawaii. Support was also generated by fears that Soviet advances in missiles and bombers had left the U.S. vulnerable and that our aging fleet of B-52s was nearly obsolete.

planes, (2) keep as many B-1 employees on the payroll as possible, and (3) redesign the plane to make it even more state-of-the-art. He gave rides on the B-1 to 28 key Washington decision makers, including two senators and six congressmen. And he continued to pass out reports to Congress showing how many constituents depended on the plane for their livelihood.

In September 1980 Anderson got his first big break. Congress directed the Defense Department to select a plane capable of carrying both bombs and cruise missiles and to turn it into a squadron by 1987. On the drawing boards was a new Stealth bomber, capable of evading radar detection, but it was still almost a decade away from completion. The best *available* plane for meeting the 1987 deadline was Rockwell's B-1. All that was needed was the go-ahead for production.

The presidential election turned out to be Anderson's second big break. Ronald Reagan, long an advocate of a strong national defense, claimed that Carter's defense budgets had opened a "window of vulnerability." In October 1981 he announced his plans for closing the window. Included in them was the decision to build a fleet of 100 improved B-1 bombers. As their prime contractor, Rockwell International stood to gain $10 billion in sales and $400 million in earnings by 1987. All of a sudden, its stock shot up from $24 to more than $32 a share.

But by this time the bomber, which had been originally designed in the 1960s, was no match for improved Soviet surface-to-air missiles. The

B-1 was redesigned, as the B-1B bomber, and an additional 24 tons of defensive gimmicks were installed just to guarantee the plane's own safety. By the time the last of the 100 planes rolled off the assembly line in 1987, the B-1 was under new attack by critics who charged that the plane was technologically obsolete before it was even deployed. The B-1's defenders, while admitting that the plane was not perfect, insisted that it would serve as a good stopgap until the stealth bomber was perfected.

At this point the critics' attack was somewhat academic, for the fight was over. Robert Anderson of Rockwell told a writer from *Fortune* magazine how pleased he was that things had turned out as they had. It was not just the profits, it was the satisfaction of winning a long, intense lobbying war. "That's the way I enjoy life, I guess—that and winning at tennis."[4] Nick Kotz, a former *Washington Post* reporter, took a harsher view. For him, the B-1 war showed that "the defense network, pursuing its goal with relentless determination, can wear down and outlast any opposition."[5]

*   *   *   *   *

The B-1 controversy gives us a small glimpse of how lobbyists swing their weight around. A lobbyist is someone whose task it is to influence legislation or policymaking. Lobbyists got their name in the early nineteenth century from their practice of hanging around the lobbies of legislatures, waiting to buttonhole lawmakers who were entering and leaving the legislative chambers. Lobbyists work for interest groups, also called "pressure groups" or "special interests"—organized groups whose members share certain views and seek to translate those views into policy. Sometimes that means winning approval for a certain policy; in the case of Rockwell International, it meant struggling to get the go-ahead and the funds to build a fleet of B-1s. In other cases, lobbyists try to block approval of some proposal they do not like, as did the opponents of the B-1.

Interest groups have a long history and a bad reputation. In *Federalist* No. 10, written in 1788, James Madison called them "factions." A faction, wrote Madison, is a group motivated by a common interest or "passion" that is opposed to "the rights of other citizens, or to the permanent and aggregate interests of the community." Later in the chapter we will look at Madison's proposed cure for factions, but for now it is enough to see that he considered them to be evil by definition. This view is widely shared today. Mention interest-group politics, and people think of sleaze and corruption. We all know those cartoons of potbellied lobbyists manipulating legislators on behalf of "special interests." The victim is usually a little guy who has been turned upside down and is being shaken by his ankles; coins are falling from his pockets. His name is John Q. Public or The Taxpayer.

But this predator-victim view of politics does not help us understand how interest-group politics works; it may even get in the way of our understanding. Take the B-1 controversy. Who are the villains? Many people—Ronald Reagan, for example—sincerely believed that the B-1 was essential to our defense. Others believed just as sincerely that it was a waste of money. At the time there were respectable arguments on both sides. One side, of course, stood to profit financially from the outcome, but what is so evil about that? People make profits whenever the government builds anything, from bombers to day-care centers and libraries. The point is that we do not need the hypothesis of bad motives in order to understand the B-1 controversy, and in science the rule is this: If you don't need an *extra* hypothesis to explain something—don't use it!

These observations are not meant to banish all concern about interest groups. Valid questions remain: Are not some interest groups simply out to make money? Doesn't money distort public debate? Shouldn't we give more weight to the arguments of general interest groups, like Common Cause, that do not stand to make a nickel? Do we really need *any* interest groups? What good do they do?

These issues form the agenda of this chapter. Let us begin by considering the interest groups we have in America and the roles they play in our politics.

Interest Groups in America

"In no country of the world," wrote Alexis de Tocqueville, a French visitor to the United States in the 1830s, "has the principle of association been more successfully used, or more unsparingly applied to a multitude of different objects, than in America."[6] De Tocqueville was impressed by the tendency of Americans to form voluntary associations for a wide variety of purposes. This is still true today; there are more than 100,000 associations in America. And now the stakes are much higher than they were in the 1830s. Because government plays a much greater role in our lives, groups of all kinds try to influence it to lean one way or another. We can classify these groups by their primary focus: economics, issues, ideology, civil rights, religion, "public interest," and state and local interests.

ECONOMIC INTEREST GROUPS

Most interest groups are those associated with economic and occupational interests: business, labor, farm, and professional groups. These groups fight mainly over bread-and-butter issues—issues that involve the question of who gets what, when, and how.

TABLE **15-1**

The Power to Persuade

Lobby Registration, February 1989	
Type	Number
Businesses and corporations	81
Trade associations	43
Labor	3
State and local governments	13
Citizens' groups (misc.)	10
Foreign governments	4

Data source: Congressional Quarterly Weekly Report, June 3, 1989, pp. 1354-59.

As of 1989 there were 154 different registered lobby groups vying for congressional support of local and global issues. Here is acknowledgment of the power of association and its attempt to influence lawmakers.

Business.   The National Association of Manufacturers (NAM) and the Chamber of Commerce of the United States are two business groups. The Chamber has surpassed the once-powerful NAM as the most respected business lobby in Washington. Four of its lobbyists in Congress watch the progress of each bill that worries the business community, then send out an alert to local affiliates when a key vote is pending. The members of these local groups are then able to besiege Congress with letters, telegrams, and telephone calls. The Chamber of Commerce helped Rockwell International during the B-1 fight by distributing a Rockwell-made film on the bomber to its local branches.

Labor.   The AFL-CIO, the largest labor federation in the country (its 16 million members include 105 separate unions), dominates the labor groups. The unions come from the widest variety of industries. Among the affiliates, for example, are the Retail Clerks International Union; the United International Union of Automobile, Aerospace and Agricultural Implement Workers of America; the United Auto Workers (UAW); the Postal Workers' Union; and the American Federation of Musicians. In addition, there are a number of independent unions, such as the Teamsters and the United Mineworkers. Historically, unions first arose to give workers some leverage against the businesses that employed them. Today, although there is still much competition between labor and business groups, the two sometimes find themselves on the same side. In the B-1 controversy, for example, the UAW, many of whose members make their living by building airplanes, teamed up with Rockwell International to get the B-1 approved. When it comes to environmental issues, labor and business have on occasion stuck together to get something built that environmental lobbies have opposed.

Farm.   The many varieties of farm groups roughly correspond to the income and philosophy of their members. The largest group is the American Farm Bureau Federation. Formed back in 1920 and with strong ties to the Department of Agriculture, it favors programs to subsidize farmers but opposes government regula-

In 1979 the National Farmers' Organization staged a tractor parade in Washington, D.C., in an effort to obtain higher prices for their crops. Other farm groups have other interests, and one organization does not necessarily speak for all farmers.

tion. A smaller farmers' organization, the Farmers' Union, claims to represent the interests of less affluent farmers. It favors programs to regulate the production and marketing of farm commodities. A still newer group, the National Farmers' Organization, calls for aggressive tactics in meeting the needs of farmers. It wants farmers to withhold produce from the market in order to raise prices; in the 1970s it organized an attention-getting (and traffic-snarling) "tractor parade" in Washington, D.C.

Professional. Included here are organizations of teachers, doctors, lawyers, nurses, and various other specialists. The American Political Science Association is a professional organization. Most of these groups are not as politically oriented as business, labor, and farm groups. But there are some notable exceptions. One is the American Medical Association (AMA), which for more than 40 years has successfully lobbied against government health insurance despite poll results showing a majority of Americans in favor of it. Another politically oriented professional group is the National Education Association, which includes many elementary and secondary school teachers. Its former president, Mary Futrell, once remarked that "instruction and professional development have been on the back burner to us, compared with political action."[7] Over the past decade the NEA has become a powerful and controversial lobby, with some highly activist members and a large Washington staff. One of its trophies is the Department of Education. Education used to be only one part of a larger cabinet department—Health, Education, and Welfare—but in 1976 the NEA got presidential candidate Jimmy Carter to pledge to make it a separate department, a promise he kept. Even more remarkable, NEA helped keep the department alive despite Ronald Reagan's 1980 pledge to abolish it. In the 1984 election campaign the NEA spent more than $2.4 million, eight times the amount it had spent in 1980, to support the Mondale–Ferraro ticket and the other candidates it backed.

SINGLE-ISSUE INTEREST GROUPS

These are interest groups that form around one issue, or perhaps several related issues. The National Campaign to Stop the B-1 Bomber, the broad umbrella group that fought the B-1, would seem to fit in this category. In most cases, such groups are not directly concerned with bread and butter. They often involve moral questions, or what are called "social issues." During the Vietnam War, for example, antiwar groups that worked toward American withdrawal saw the war as immoral. Today other moral issues spawn interest-group activity: the environment, abortion, school prayer, gun control, nuclear disarmament. The National Right to Life Committee has been trying to work toward a legal ban on abortion, while the National Abortion Rights Action League wants to make sure that abortion stays legal. On limiting the sale of guns, there is the National Rifle Association on one side and a number of other groups, including the National Coalition to Ban Handguns, on the other. There are some social issues in which the divisions are not so clear-cut. The Sierra Club, for example, is anti-pollution, but its opponents are not pro-pollution groups. Instead, the Sierra Club often finds itself fighting business and labor groups when they oppose environmental laws on the grounds that the laws unnecessarily harm productivity and employment opportunities.

Single-issue groups have a long history in America. In the nineteenth and early twentieth centuries there were groups favoring the abolition of slavery, the limitation of foreign immigration, the banning of liquor, the abandonment of the gold standard, and women's suffrage. Some of their causes have been vindicated by history, others have ended up on the scrap heap. All were urged with crusading zeal, and their proponents were not always particular about methods. Abolitionist John Brown broke into a federal arsenal and killed five people. Prohibitionist Carrie Nation smashed up saloons with a hatchet. Suffragettes chained themselves to fences and fought off the police officers who tried to unchain them. Some single-issue activists today also use tactics that seem extreme. At the fringes of the anti-abortion movement are people who have bombed abortion clinics to get their message across. Leaders of the movement have denounced the bombings but some of them support nonviolent acts of civil disobedience, like blocking entrances to abortion clinics. Other groups, such as those protesting nuclear weapons, have used similar aggressive methods. The wisdom of doing so is a topic much debated within the movements. Some proponents worry about being labeled "extremist," a deadly label in the American political arena, while others agree with the civil rights lyric of the 1960s:

> It isn't nice to block the doorway,
> It isn't nice to go to jail . . . ,
> There are nicer ways to do it,
> But the nice ways always fail.[8]

IDEOLOGICAL INTEREST GROUPS

In chapter 13 we defined *ideology* as a series of beliefs connected in a coherent pattern. The two major ideologies in America are liberalism and conservativism. Liberal and conservative groups also get beyond bread-and-butter issues and take sides on moral questions. But unlike single-issue groups, liberal and conservative groups are devoted to a broad array of issues. For example, Americans for Democratic Action (ADA), a liberal group, takes positions on issues ranging from minimum-wage laws (they favor an increase) to abortion (the liberal position is pro-choice). ADA tracks the voting records of legislators and gives them scores based upon how closely their votes agree with ADA positions. The ADA's conservative counterpart, the American Conservative Union (ACU), does the same thing, and its scores are mirror images of the ADA's. (Legislators who receive 100 percent ADA scores are likely to get ACU scores in the range of 0–10 percent.)

People for the American Way is a liberal group founded by Norman Lear, producer of the television sitcom "All in the Family." It played a central role in the campaign against Robert Bork, whom President Reagan tried to put on the Supreme Court in 1987. The National Conservative Political Action Committee (NCPAC) is another active player in Washington politics. NCPAC is a PAC, or political action committee. (PACs will be discussed later in the chapter.)

CIVIL RIGHTS INTEREST GROUPS

These groups consider themselves the victims of some practice or condition in America and seek government assistance to protect individual rights. Included here are the National Association for the Advancement of Colored People (NAACP), the oldest black organization, founded in 1910. The Congress of Racial Equality (CORE) is a newer black organization, as is the National Urban League. Other groups in this category include the National Organization for Women (NOW), founded by feminist writer Betty Friedan in 1966, and the Mexican-American Legal Defense Fund. Traditionally, these groups have taken positions similar to those of liberal groups. NOW, for example, has sometimes opposed female candidates in favor of males whose views it considers more progressive. However, the liberal orientation of some of these groups may be changing. In recent years, CORE has taken tough positions on criminal justice that liberals have opposed, and a new women's group, Women Exploited By Abortion (WEBA), lobbies for pro-life legislation, which is opposed by NOW and other liberal groups.

RELIGIOUS INTEREST GROUPS

Catholic, Protestant, Jewish, and other religious groups sometimes try to influence policymaking in Washington. American Catholic bishops have supported poverty programs, a nuclear freeze, and a ban on abortion. The National Council of Churches, a Protestant organization, lobbies for many causes connected with the Third World, such as majority rule in South Africa. Jewish organizations, like the American Jewish Committee and the B'nai B'rith, work for a variety of causes, from civil rights and religious tolerance to support for the state of Israel.

PUBLIC INTEREST GROUPS

There are groups that claim to rise above specific interests, whether liberal, conservative, bread-and-butter, religious, or moral. These groups, who call themselves "citizen" or "consumer" groups, claim to speak for all of us. One such group is Common Cause, founded in 1970 by John Gardner, former secretary of Health, Education and Welfare in the Johnson administration. A self-styled citizens' action group, Common Cause has worked successfully, usually in league with other groups, in getting action from Congress on a number of items, including the regulation of campaign spending, the passage of the eighteen-year-old age voting amendment, the withdrawal of funds from the Vietnam War, and the modification of the seniority system in Congress. Common Cause was also one of the groups fighting the B-1 bomber.

Ralph Nader became a prominent figure in the 1960s by attacking the auto industry in his book *Unsafe at Any Speed*. Since then, he and his research and advocacy groups (often referred to as Nader's Raiders) have focused attention on issues that affect consumers, including health care costs, tax reform, and unsafe products.

Another public interest group is actually a series of 23 separate groups with close ties to Ralph Nader, who claims to speak for consumers and citizens alike. Nader became prominent in the 1960s when his book *Unsafe at Any Speed* convinced Congress to bring automobile design under federal control. He was harassed for a time by General Motors agents. He then sued and won a large ($400,000) financial settlement. That money, plus book royalties and lecture fees, has enabled Nader to create a conglomerate of groups that fight for a number of causes, from tax reform to openness in government. Nader's empire spans the country. It has public interest research groups (PIRGs) in almost every state, and many colleges use student activity money to assist PIRGs in providing services to students.

Critics of these groups say that it is presumptuous for any group to claim to represent "the citizen" or "the consumer." Virtually all Americans are citizens and consumers, yet many do not agree with the goals of these groups. For example, many Americans wanted the B-1 in spite of Common Cause's opposition to it. They included not only the employees of Rockwell International and the other companies that built the B-1, but other Americans who honestly believed that the B-1 was essential to the defense of the country.

STATE AND LOCAL INTEREST GROUPS

All the activities of interest groups in the national arena are reproduced in the states and local areas across the country. If anything, they may be even more intense in these areas because of cutbacks in federal expenditures and the increased vitality of state and local governments in recent years.[9] In the capital city of each state, hundreds of organizations with axes to grind have their headquarters. Still others

TABLE **15-2**

Types of Interest Groups

Who Supports What

Economic
  Chamber of Commerce
  AFL-CIO
  American Farm Bureau Federation
  American Medical Association

Single-Issue
  National Campaign to Stop the B-1 Bomber
  National Right to Life Committee
  National Abortion Rights Action League
  National Rifle Association
  National Coalition to Ban Handguns

Ideological
  Americans for Democratic Action (ADA)
  American Conservative Union (ACU)
  People for the American Way

Civil Rights
  National Association for the Advancement of Colored People (NAACP)
  Congress of Racial Equality (CORE)
  National Organization for Women (NOW)

Religious
  National Council of Churches
  B'nai B'rith
  Council of Catholic Bishops

Public Interest
  Common Cause
  Public interest research groups (PIRGs)

State and Local
  American Automobile Association
  Liquor interests

Strength in numbers is clearly evidenced by the number of lobbies and by the variety of their causes. The diversity of their interests—from ideological to economic—suggests that these factions, as Madison would have called them, interact to check and balance each other to promote the *nation's* best interest. Listed above are a few examples of the different types of interest groups.

send representatives when some issue affecting their vital interests comes before the legislature. Alphabetically, the associations may range from the American Automobile Association to the YWCA, and the policies in which they have an interest may range from AIDS to zoning. Teacher organizations, trade associations, labor groups, insurance, mining, real estate, and banking are among the most visible lobbying groups in many states—although, of course, the lineup varies from state to state. In some states a few interests dominate statehouse politics, but in most there is open competition among interest groups, with no single group or coalition leading the way.[10]

Lobbyists openly work the state capitols, buttonholing legislators and attempting to get their vote. Often, they are preaching to the already-converted, and their purpose is to make sure of the vote and of continued support. Sometimes they can actually change minds, or at least get a legislator to question a view.[11] Some lobbyists

(Continued on page 403)

GLOBAL PERSPECTIVES:

Interest Groups in Israel

A number of interest groups influence policymaking in Israel. The largest and most influential is the Histadrut, General Federation of Labor in Israel. Its importance goes beyond its influence on policy, for it is also the largest single entrepreneur and employer and a major influence on cultural and educational life. Other Israeli interests wielding great power include the military, the press, agricultural organizations, religious groups, and *diaspora* Jewry. The latter term refers to Jews living outside Israel, especially those in the United States, who play a crucial role in supporting Israel. There are also interest groups representing various ethnic divisions, including the so-called Oriental Jews, who come from such Middle Eastern countries as Yemen. Some interest groups are bitterly opposed to one another. Peace Now, a group seeking accommodation with the Palestinians, frequently clashes with Gush Emunim (Bloc of the Faithful), a militantly nationalist group.

Israeli interest groups operate much differently from ours. Instead of directly lobbying legislators or administrators, they work almost entirely within the political party system. Nearly every significant interest group is represented through one or more of the parties, which, like those in Europe, are strong and disciplined. Legislators and administrators are deeply indebted to the party leaders. The way to influence policy, therefore, is to get the ear of those leaders.

This need for a party connection has important implications. One is that public lobbying is much less important in Israel than in the United States. Since the chief task of the successful Israeli lobbyist is to get through to a handful of leaders, there is no need to reach the public through computerized mailings or advertising. Nor do street demonstrations have much effect on policy. When they happen, it is usually because regular party channels have become clogged or overloaded. Sooner or later the protesting group is brought back into a party, and its leaders become insiders again.

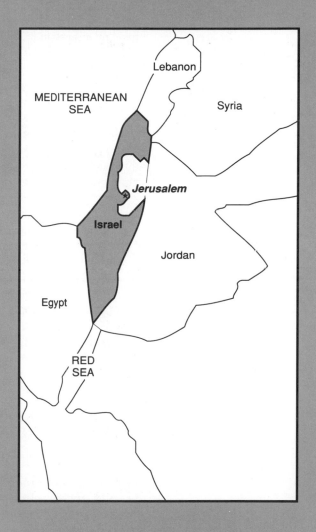

(Continued from page 402)

get results through bribery and other corrupt methods, although it is obviously difficult to say how much of this goes on. Because state governments have enacted a number of laws aimed at curbing corruption in recent years, it seems likely that these methods are not used as often as in the past.

At the local level too, there is almost always some kind of lobbying by interests concerned about zoning, school board policies, or the proposed location of roads, housing projects, factories, and shopping malls. These groups often use professional lobbyists skilled in the art of dealing with local councils, but they also bring out ordinary people, people who have never made a speech before local city or town meetings. Overflow crowds of such people have been known to have profound effects on the votes of local politicians. Most of the time, however, local government in America is carried on in nearly empty council chambers. There is massive apathy at the local level of American politics.

IS THERE A PUBLIC INTEREST?

Is there such a thing as "the general interest," an interest that transcends all particular interests? Take clean air, for example. All of us—black and white, rich and poor—have an interest in it. All of us have to breathe. Therefore, on this issue environmental interest groups like the Sierra Club represent the interests of us all. But, you may reply, although it is true that everyone needs clean air, the *degree* of cleanness required is open to discussion. If you are an unemployed worker and a factory is coming into your town, you may decide to tolerate a higher level of pollution than your environmentalist neighbor, who happens to be a tenured college professor. If he or she tells you that everyone has an interest in clean air, you can reply that everyone also has an interest in eating. This is true of many of the seemingly universal causes that public interest groups champion. There are usually people on the other side who are going to be injured if the public interest group gets what it wants. In that case, can it really be said that the group represents the public? It almost seems presumptuous.

Still, we need the distinction between special interests and the general interest. One way of making this distinction was suggested by political scientist E. E. Schattschneider. "Is it possible," he asked, "to distinguish between the interests of the National Association of Manufacturers and members of the American League to Abolish Capital Punishment?" Yes, he answered. The "*members of the A.L.A.C.P. obviously do not expect to be hanged.*" The distinction, then, turns upon whether the group benefits personally in any special way from the outcome they seek. To ignore that distinction, Schattschneider said, forces us into arguing that some people "have special interests in the common good." Maybe that argument can be made, "but it seems a long way around to avoid a useful distinction."[12]

JUSTIFYING INTEREST GROUP POLITICS: PLURALIST THEORY

Most interest groups are frankly self-serving—although none would accept the label "selfish." Interest group leaders speak of their "constituents," their "people." Some social scientists welcome this vast array of self-serving groups. They see them as a practical means by which all reasonable positions can find some sort of representation in government. It is natural and understandable, they say, for people to form groups. Indeed, the whole of American government can be understood in terms of the interaction of groups.

Pluralism has deep roots in America. If any American can be called its founder, it was James Madison. In *Federalist* No. 10, Madison seemed to have interest groups in mind when he discussed factions. He did not like factions. Yet, Madison reflected, the tendency to form factions is "sown in the nature of man." The best way to deal with factions is to let them proliferate—indeed, to encourage them to proliferate. The more factions the better because they will all check and balance each other. "Extend the sphere [of the nation] and you take in a greater variety of parties and interests; you make it less probable that a majority of the whole will have a common motive to invade the rights of other citizens." More factions equal more diversity; more diversity equals more liberty.

Slightly more than a century and a half after *The Federalist* papers appeared, pluralism became very popular with political science professors. The central premise of pluralism was that our political system is one "in which all the active and legitimate groups in the population can make themselves heard at some crucial stage in the process of decision."[13] In the 1950s it seemed like an accurate description of the American political process. Washington politics at that time worked in fairly predictable fashion. Each group—farm, labor, business, and so on—bargained to get its slice of the pie. Farmers wanted subsidies, labor unions wanted to raise the minimum wage, businesses wanted tariffs, and so on. Political scientists defined politics as the process by which "who gets what, when, and how." Everyone, or at least every organized group, could hope to get something, but each group had to settle for less than it bargained for. Pluralism put a premium on compromise and gradualism.

When the 1960s came along, the pluralist framework became shaky. The civil rights movement and the Vietnam War raised broad moral questions that could not be compromised or put off to some future date. "Freedom now" was the slogan of the civil rights revolution. Other movements arose, all equating the word *compromise* with *sellout*. Today, however, these movements seem to have less vitality. Some have been taken over by fanatics and hustlers, and the public has grown weary of their sermons and nonnegotiable demands. The time may be ripe for the theory of pluralism to make a comeback. Pluralism tolerates wide differences of opinion, encourages compromise, and dampens extremism. Yet pluralism has also been criticized on a number of grounds. Three in particular stand out.

First, pluralism seems to leave no room for interests that are not organized. You can win your slice of the pie only if you have an organization to lobby for you. But what about migrant farm laborers, employees in nonunion sweatshops, and many white-collar workers, who have no organization to fight for them? Are they to be left out of the system? Second, the assumption behind pluralism seems to be that every organized interest can play the game on roughly equal terms. This is a questionable assumption. A generation ago, political scientist E. E. Schattschneider argued that our system of pressure groups is skewed in favor of powerful corporate interests. The pressure system, he wrote, "has an upper-class bias."[14] The same point was made more recently by political scientists Kay L. Schlozman and John T. Tierney.

> Taken as a whole, the pressure community is heavily weighted in favor of business organizations: 70 percent of all organizations having a Washington presence and 52 percent of those having their own offices represent business.[15]

The dominance of business may be more apparent than real, since the various business lobbies often lack coordination in fighting against common adversaries.[16] Still, it is hard to imagine the Washington pressure system as a completely level playing field.

A third criticism of pluralism is that, by viewing America as a patchwork of groups, each with its own particular interest, pluralism seems to ignore the *national* interest. The United States is more than the sum of its groups. The Constitution does not say "We the Peoples." It says "We the *People*." Surely there are interests that bind us all, give us the unity by which we can call ourselves a "people." Pluralism, as a framework for discussion, seems to leave little room for such considerations.

Some critics have gone further and denied that American politics is really pluralistic. They argue that, behind all the seeming diversity and competition of groups, there is a small group that makes all the big decisions for America. The late sociologist C. Wright Mills argued this thesis in a book entitled *The Power Elite*.[17] It is still being argued today by a number of critics. (The Taking Sides section of chapter 1 presents a debate on the power elite thesis.)

Speak now

or forever hold your breath.

We all know about air pollution. Urban smog and airborne toxics threaten the health of 150 million Americans. Acid rain kills our lakes, forests, and wildlife. We need to end them now.

To find out how to make your voice heard, contact Sierra Club. Isn't it about time we cleared the air?

Write to: **Sierra Club**
730 Polk Street
San Francisco, CA 94109

Or call: **415-776-2211**

SIERRA CLUB

The Sierra Club is an environmental interest group that attempts to educate and inform the public about issues such as air pollution. Paid advertisements, such as this one, are used regularly to increase the group's membership and to generate public support.

How to Succeed in Lobbying

Those who argue that America is run by a power elite often point to the great wealth that is in the hands of the few. Wealth, however, does not always translate into power. Other factors play a role in the success of an interest group in translating its interests into a favorable outcome. What are these factors?

In the world of Washington politics, at least seven can contribute to the success of lobbying: respectability, information, coordination, media support, staying power, White House support, and wealth.

RESPECTABILITY

How respectable is a group? Is it considered a moderate organization, or is it widely regarded as a fringe group? Washington policymakers are sensitive to the charge that they may be on the side of extremists, so any serious interest group seeks to cultivate a moderate image. In the B-1 controversy, the foes of the bomber were helped by having the National Taxpayers Union (NTU), a rather conservative organization, in their coalition. "They really helped us in our lobbying effort on Capitol Hill," said Robert Brammer. "NTU is well respected there."[18] The anti-B-1 lobby was also helped by the support of the Federation of Scientists, which includes 35 Nobel Prize winners on its board of directors.

Respectability can increase or decrease with swings in public mood. The anti-B-1 forces thrived during the early 1970s, when Jane Fonda could call American airmen "hired killers" without causing a furor. But by 1980, the huge increase in Soviet defense spending, the Soviet advances in Africa, and the Soviet invasion of Afghanistan made the American public more receptive to building a new bomber. This made the going somewhat tougher for the B-1's foes and correspondingly easier for its promoters.

TABLE **15-3**

407

How to Succeed
in Lobbying

What Lobbyists Do

Techniques Used to Exercise Influence	Percentage of Organizations Using
Testifying at hearings	99%
Contacting government officials directly to present your point of view	98
Engaging in informal contacts with officials—at conventions, over lunch, and so on	95
Presenting research results or technical information	92
Sending letters to members of your organization to inform them about your activities	92
Entering into coalitions with other organizations	90
Attempting to shape the implementation of policies	89
Talking with people from the press and the media	86
Consulting with government officials to plan legislative strategy	85
Helping to draft legislation	85
Inspiring letter writing or telegram campaigns	84
Shaping the government's agenda by raising new issues and calling attention to previously ignored problems	84
Mounting grass-roots lobbying efforts	80
Having influential constituents contact their congressional representative's office	80
Helping draft regulations, rules, or guidelines	78
Serving on advisory commissions and boards	76
Alerting congressional representatives to the effects of a bill on their districts	75
Filing suit or otherwise engaging in litigation	72
Making financial contributions to electoral campaigns	58
Doing favors for officials who need assistance	56
Attempting to influence appointments to public office	53
Publicizing candidates' voting records	44
Engaging in direct-mail fund-raising for your organization	44
Running advertisements in the media about your position on issues	31
Contributing work or personnel to electoral campaigns	24
Making public endorsements of candidates for office	22
Engaging in protests or demonstrations	20

Source: Kay Lehman Schlozman and John T. Tierney, *Organized Interests and American Democracy* (New York: Harper & Row, 1986), p. 150. Reprinted with permission.

The folklore of the potbellied lobbyist who "buys" legislators is largely mythical. The majority of lobbyists spend their time testifying at hearings and trying to persuade lawmakers to their points of view. On the whole, in spite of lurid tales of bribery and corruption to the contrary, they lead prosaic lives.

INFORMATION, COORDINATION, AND MEDIA APPEAL

A successful lobby keeps careful tabs on the people it is lobbying, noting their views, seeing if these views are beginning to change, finding out when key votes are coming up. This requires solid information and good coordination. "Communication was the key to our success," said Robert Brammer after his initial defeat of the B-1. "Eventually, we were able to tell you at any hour where every congressman was— who was in town, who wasn't."

Good relations with the press are helpful, particularly if the issue has become public. The pro-B-1 forces tried to cultivate good press relations by sending representatives to editorial offices with arguments in favor of the plane. The anti-B-1 forces were probably helped by the David and Goliath image of themselves that they had cultivated: the little citizens' group fighting the huge corporation, powerful labor unions, and the Pentagon. The underdog theme has much appeal in pressrooms.

If you cannot woo reporters, you might still be able to buy your way into their newspapers. In the 1980s some business lobbyists who felt their organizations were being badly treated in the media started purchasing "advocacy" advertisements. As pointed out in chapter 14, groups like Mobil Oil put pieces in newspapers charging unfair coverage and purporting to set the record straight. Other groups—such as Planned Parenthood, the American Federation of Teachers, and the Sierra Club— now regularly use paid advertisements to help get their messages across. How successful these methods are is open to question. They probably enhance the image of these groups and help generate mail to lawmakers, but they also may raise the ire of their opponents and stimulate counter-lobbying. In any event, they cost a lot of money and are thus not available to groups with small purses.

Whatever route you take—whether through paid ads or other forms of publicity—it is better not to come on too strong. A successful lobbyist is courteous and low-keyed, never obnoxious. It is usually unwise to insult decision makers or "muscle" them too obviously. At one point in the B-1 controversy, the Senate was considering an amendment by then-Iowa Senator John Culver that would have delayed production of the plane. A Rockwell lobbyist distributed a fact sheet pointing out the added costs and lost jobs that the amendment would cause. That was all right. But the sheet also charged that the Culver amendment "furthers USSR objectives." That item angered not only Culver but also many senators who had been planning to vote against his amendment. As a result, they changed their minds and voted *for* it.

STAYING POWER

One of the keys to Rockwell's eventual success was its ability to hold the B-1 project together while waiting for a better political climate. Robert Anderson was able to keep together a team of 5,000 people who worked on the original B-1 and to warehouse the expensive tools used in its construction. Rockwell could do this because it was an established corporate institution with plenty of other projects to keep it going. The anti-B-1 coalition, on the other hand, was a temporary alliance of different groups, a coalition that unraveled after Jimmy Carter left office. Staying power helps to explain the success of many other lobbies. The National Rifle Association, for example, has its own large office building in Washington, while the various anti-gun lobbies tend to be more unstable and impermanent.

WHITE HOUSE SUPPORT

As we saw from the B-1 controversy, White House support can sometimes be critical. Jimmy Carter's decision not to produce the B-1 sent the project into hibernation. Ronald Reagan's decision to go ahead with B-1 production revived it. The president's power is considerable. Not only can he veto bills, but he has a variety of means by which to influence votes in Congress. When Carter was president, he dangled public works projects in front of legislators (sewer construction projects for their districts) in return for promises to vote against the B-1.[19] On many other issues, too, from school prayer to tax cuts, the person in the White House can help shape outcomes.

The march of the homeless on Washington in 1989 demonstrated that even the poor can mobilize and hopefully influence legislation. In the past, the plight of the homeless was primarily the concern of local governments in urban areas, but as the problem worsened in the 1980s, city, state, and federal governments became involved in finding solutions.

WEALTH

There is no denying the power of money in the lobbying process. It buys many things: a large professional staff, impressive offices, advertisements in the media, dinners and drinks for legislators, contributions to their campaigns, and so on. Yet its influence should not be overstressed. The coalition of anti-B-1 groups operated on a shoestring budget, yet—for a time, at least—they brought the B-1 to a standstill. Other modestly funded groups have enjoyed more lasting victories. In 1970 a rag-tag assortment of environmental groups was able to prevent the government from funding a supersonic transport plane (SST) that, the groups claimed, was a waste of taxpayers' money and an environmental hazard. It did this with a very small budget and in the teeth of opposition from the Boeing Corporation, several unions, key senators, and the president of the United States. The anti-SST groups succeeded because they were well-coordinated, because they used smart lobbying tactics, because the public mood was pro-environment, and because the groups were able to dramatize their cause in the media. These factors also enabled Ralph Nader to succeed in his early days as a penniless consumer advocate.

In spite of all the lurid tales of payoffs—some of which have turned out to be true—the world of interest-group politics is far less gaudy than it looks in the popular media. The main influence of wealth is not in bribery, but in campaign contributions. Even then, money does not necessarily buy a senator or a representative. The total contributions from any single source are far less than the total cost of any campaign. Seasoned political observers think of campaign contributions primarily as "door openers." In the words of one: "They give entrée—that's the key."[20]

Discussion of campaign contributions leads us to a closer examination of a special type of committee used by interest groups to help—or sometimes hurt—legislators in their campaigns. It is called the "political action committee," or "PAC" for short.

PACs—Interest Groups in Campaigns. Political action committees (PACs) serve a particular need of interest groups: getting involved in political campaigns usually by giving money or sponsoring advertisements. PACs first appeared in the 1940s because federal law banned direct contributions to political campaigns by corporations and labor unions. The way around it was to make indirect contributions. In 1948 the AFL-CIO founded the first PAC, the Committee on Political Education (COPE), which funneled union money to labor-backed candidates. It played a critical role in helping the Democrats in the 1948 elections and was denounced by Republicans as an insidious threat to democracy. Later, business started setting up its own PACs, beginning in 1963 with the creation of the Business-Industry Political Action Committee (BIPAC).

The real growth in PACs, particularly business PACs, began in the 1970s. This was partly the result of legislation passed by Congress in 1974 that explicitly legitimized PACs and partly the result of a later Supreme Court decision, *Buckley v. Valeo* (1976), which struck down part of the 1974 legislation that had attempted to limit congressional campaign spending. Soon PACs began popping up everywhere, spending large sums of money on behalf of candidates. In 1974 there were 600 PACs; by 1982 there were 3,400—an increase of almost 600 percent. Growth in the number of PACs leveled off in the 1980s; by 1987 there were about 4,100 PACs, and the number has not changed much since then.

PACs contributed almost $150 million to all congressional campaigns for the 101st Congress (1987-88). Most of the money went to Democrats. In the Senate, Democratic candidates received $24.9 million from PACs, while Republicans got $21.5 million. The difference was much greater in the House of Representatives, which has a larger percentage of Democrats. Democratic legislators got more than $66.9 million in PAC money, while Republicans received about half that amount, $34.9 million. News of this caused both Republicans and Democrats to gloat. "All of the Democrats' expressions of concerns about the Republicans being the party of moneyed interests are shown by these figures to be absolutely false," said John Buckley, a spokesman for the National Republican Congressional Committee. But for Anita Dunn, a spokeswoman for the Democratic Senatorial Campaign Committee, the figures showed that her party ran stronger candidates, who in turn were able to attract more contributions.[21] Figures compiled in 1987 showed that more than half the U.S. Senate—51 senators—had received more than a million dollars apiece from PACs during their congressional careers.[22] For the 1988 elections, the three biggest PAC contributors were the National Association of Realtors, the International Brotherhood of Teamsters, and the American Medical Association, which together contributed more than $8 million to Senate and House campaigns. As Table 15.4 shows, PACs and other contributors did much to help reelect well-known members of Congress like Lloyd Bentsen (D-Texas), Robert Dornan (R-California), and Joseph P. Kennedy (D-Massachusetts).

PACs come in many varieties. There are PACs supporting businesses, from independent grocers to funeral directors. There are labor PACs, civil rights PACs, pro-Israeli PACs, Arab-American PACs, PACs on both sides of the abortion issue. There is even a PAC called "Citizens for a Funnier Future." (Its purpose, says its founder, is "to make quality humor more accessible to the average American.")[23] Some PACs are explicitly liberal or conservative, but most are not concerned with ideology. Business PACs, for example, are just as likely to contribute to liberals like Edward Kennedy of Massachusetts as they are to legislators who go out of their way to sing the praises of "our free enterprise system."[24] What business PACs really like to do is to back winners, regardless of party or ideology, and that usually means backing incumbents. One conservative Republican, Representative Robert Dornan of California, put it rather bluntly: "Corporate managers . . . don't care who's in office, what party or what they stand for. They're just out to buy you."[25]

PACs that donate funds directly to the campaigns of candidates are bound by

(Continued on page 412)

TABLE 15-4

Politicians and PACs

Top Political Action Committee Contributors to Federal
Candidates in 1988 Elections

Rank	Organization	Dollars
1	National Association of Realtors	$ 3.0 million
2	International Brotherhood of Teamsters	2.9 million
3	American Medical Association	2.3 million
4	National Education Association	2.1 million
5	National Association of Retired Federal Employees	2.0 million
6	United Auto Workers	1.9 million
7	Association of Trial Lawyers of America	1.9 million
8	National Association of Letter Carriers	1.7 million
9	American Federation of State, County & Municipal Employees	1.6 million
10	International Association of Machinists and Aerospace Workers	1.5 million

Members of Congress Receiving Most Money for 1988
Election Campaigns from PACs and Other Sources

Rank	Member of Congress	Dollars
	Senate	
1	Pete Wilson, R-California	$11.4 million
2	Lloyd Bentsen, D-Texas	8.3 million
3	George V. Voinovich, R-Ohio*	7.8 million
4	Pete Dawkins, R-New Jersey*	7.8 million
5	Herb Kohl, D-Wisconsin	7.6 million
6	Howard Metzenbaum, D-Ohio	7.3 million
7	Frank Lautenberg, D-New Jersey	7.1 million
8	Leo McCarthy, D-California*	7.0 million
9	John Heinz, R-Pennsylvania	5.3 million
10	Connie Mack, R-Florida	5.2 million
	House of Representatives	
1	Jane Eskind, D-Tennessee*	$ 2.6 million
2	Philip Bredesen, D-Tennessee*	1.9 million
3	Robert Dornan, R-California	1.7 million
4	Joseph J. Dioguardi, R-New York*	1.6 million
5	Gary K. Hart, D-California*	1.5 million
6	Thomas Campbell, R-California	1.4 million
7	Joseph P. Kennedy II, D-Massachusetts	1.4 million
8	Nita M. Lowey, D-New York	1.3 million
9	John Miller, R-Washington	1.3 million
10	Jim Moody, D-Wisconsin	1.3 million

*Lost election

Source: Federal Election Commission. Reprinted from the *New York Times* with permission.

Political action committees (PACs) gave almost $150 million to reelect federal candidates in 1988 elections. The ten senators receiving the most money from PACs and other sources grossed more than $74 million; the top ten representatives grossed $16 million. These millions of dollars in campaign funds, however, did not guarantee the reelection of incumbents; in fact, the two senators ranked third and fourth in monies received lost their elections, as did the two top-ranked representatives.

PROFILE IN POWER: THE REALTORS' PAC

In 1988 the National Association of Realtors decided that Democrat Greg Laughlin did not have a chance to win the contest for a congressional seat in southeastern Texas held by Representative Mac Sweeney, a Republican. The Realtors' Political Action Committee (RPAC) gave Sweeney the maximum allowed by law, $10,000, to run his campaign. But Laughlin turned out to be one of the very tiny minority of challengers in 1988 who defeated incumbent members of Congress. A few days after Laughlin assumed his seat in Congress, a representative of RPAC walked into his office offering him help for his reelection in 1990: $10,000 in checks.

The realtors learned a lesson the hard way from their experience in 1986. In that year they spent sizable sums to help elect Republicans to the House and Senate. Most of the Republicans lost, and many of their victorious Democratic opponents were angered at RPAC. So the realtors adopted a new, "friendly incumbent" rule: It would support any incumbent, of either party, who looked like a winner and whose positions on real estate issues were considered reasonably friendly to the industry, even if the incumbent's opponent was more to the liking of realtors. The policy seemed to work. In the 1988 race, the candidates supported by RPAC won in 98 percent of the House races and more than four-fifths of the Senate campaigns.

Most of the big PACs in Washington operate this way, although RPAC stands out because of its financial resources and its extensive grass-roots ties. For the 1988 elections, it raised $6.2 million (making it the third-ranked fund-raiser among all PACs) and spent $5.9 million. It has more than 800,000 members around the country; in the 1988 election, it made contributions in every Senate race and in 432 of the 435 House districts. RPAC's decision making starts at the grass roots. Local member associations recommend which congressional candidates to support, and their recommendations are forwarded to RPAC's 23 trustees, who represent 13 regions of the nation.

At least one of RPAC's goals coincides with the interests of American homeowners: in 1986 it successfully fought off attempts in Congress to eliminate the tax deductibility of mortgage interest rates. Other RPAC interests may not coincide so directly with those of middle-class Americans. In 1989 it embarked on a campaign to persuade Congress to help stave off bankruptcy among America's savings and loan associations (Adapted from the *New York Times*, June 29, 1989, pp. 1, B6).

(Continued from page 410) limits set by Congress in 1974. The law states that PACs may contribute no more than $5,000 to any one candidate's campaign in any one election.[26] (This would permit a maximum of $10,000 if the candidate ran both a primary and a general election campaign.) *But*—and it is a big "but"—if a PAC is independent, not tied to the organization of a particular party or candidate, it can spend as much as it can raise. Take a hypothetical example. Suppose we organize a PAC called "Committee to Protect American Jobs," which favors high tariffs against Japanese products. If our PAC contributes to the campaign of Congressman Smith, who favors tariffs, it can give no more than $5,000. But suppose the PAC stays clear of the Smith organization and spends its money instead on commercials to defeat Smith's opponent, Jones, who opposes tariffs. It is then an independent PAC and can spend as much as it wants. This was the ruling of the Supreme Court, which has equated the right to spend money on campaigns with the right of free speech.[27] The PAC that really pioneered this approach was the National Conservative Political Action Committee (NCPAC). In 1980 NCPAC paid for a large number of "negative advertisements" on television, advertisements attacking several liberal senators. Four of the five senators NCPAC targeted were defeated in that election. (In more recent elections it has not been as successful; some of its negative advertisements may even have backfired.)

Former CBS News commentator Bill Moyers has expressed his concern about the power of independent PACs: "I am troubled by the ability of organized money . . . to caricature people in the political process, and I think many of their commercials did indeed caricature the politicians they were trying to beat."[28] "Caricatures," however, tend to be in the eye of the beholder. One person's caricature is another's fair criticism. Anyway, suppose there is caricature—so what? Painting one's opponent in lurid colors has been going on since the early days of the republic. It is a kind of American folk art. Liberals do it, conservatives do it, even moderates do it. Perhaps it is a regrettable practice, but caricature seems to be an integral part of American politics. Indeed, Moyers's own remark about "organized money" sounds a little like the caricature of the potbellied lobbyist we talked about earlier in the chapter. If, instead, "organized money" just means "money collected by an organization"— what's wrong with that? The "organization" could be a group of students, professors, or other decent folk.

A more serious case against PACs has been made by Washington reporter Elizabeth Drew. She charges that PACs have made money the dominant factor in Washington politics. By funneling huge amounts of money into campaigns, they have made it virtually impossible for challengers to compete on equal terms with incumbents in elections. However, this charge is disputed by others who think that the influence of money has been exaggerated and that, in any case, the many different competing PACs check and balance each other. The arguments are presented in this chapter's Taking Sides section on the following page.

Most PAC money goes to incumbents, and in the 1988 congressional elections, nearly 99 percent of House incumbents (and 85 percent of the senators who ran) got reelected.[29] It is hard to pin down the causal connection between getting PAC money and winning. Do incumbents win because of PAC donations, or are PACs attracted to incumbents because they are likely to win? Or is it some combination of the two? Whatever the connections, the fact that the turnover rate in Congress is lower than that of the Supreme Soviet of the USSR is embarrassing to many Americans. Public-interest lobbies like Common Cause have been fighting for a long time to control PACs with rather mixed support from the politicians. In the past, liberal Democrats tended to back laws aimed at placing limits on campaign spending and contributions, which would affect PAC spending. (Some of these laws are examined in chapter 17.) Republican leaders were less enthusiastic, partly for philosophical reasons—Republicans tend to oppose government regulation of the economic sphere—and partly because they hoped that Republican-oriented PACs would help their side.[30] But during the 1980s, Democrats in the House of Representatives perfected the technique of extracting money from groups ordinarily inclined to support Republicans. Then-majority whip Tony Coelho (D-California) would approach the groups, refresh their memories as to which party controlled the House, and suggest that they might want to think about their best business interests.[31]

Coelho's "offer you can't refuse" approach steered so much PAC money into Democratic campaign coffers that many House incumbents had money left over after

"Senator, according to this report, you've been marked for defeat by the A.D.A., the National Rifle Association, the A.F.L.-C.I.O., the N.A.M., the Sierra Club, Planned Parenthood, the World Student Christian Federation, the Clamshell Alliance . . ." *Drawing by Dana Fradon; © 1980 The New Yorker Magazine, Inc.*

(Continued on page 415)

Points to Remember

1. Successful lobbying requires both skill and good fortune.

2. The following factors contribute to success in pressuring the government: respectability; information, coordination, and media support; staying power; a friend in the White House; and lots of money.

3. Some successful groups may be weak in one or two of these crucial factors but make up for it in strength in others. For example, some lobbies (like environmental groups) that operate with little money are often successful because of favorable media coverage.

4. PACs are the means by which lobbies funnel money into political campaigns and otherwise get involved in the electoral process. They have become controversial because of their spectacular growth since the early 1970s, the large sums of money they spend, and their use of negative advertising.

SIDES

Do PACs Corrupt the Political Process?

YES Elizabeth Drew

Based upon Elizabeth Drew, *Politics and Money: The New Road to Corruption* (New York: Macmillan Publishing Company, 1983).

Drew notes that PACs have grown tremendously since they were officially legalized in 1974—from 600 in 1974 to 3,400 in 1982. (Today there are more than 4,000 PACs.) It is clear, she says, "that the politicians' anxiety about having access to enough money corrodes, and even corrupts, the political system." Politicians turn to PACs to fund their increasingly expensive campaigns and in return listen carefully to PAC demands. She quotes Richard Wirthlin, a Republican pollster: "Money not only can make the difference but can make a huge difference." At best, she says, politicians worry about how their votes will affect their ability to raise money. "At worst, votes are actually traded for money." She claims that the average House winner receives more than a third of his or her campaign money from PACs, much of it from PACs representing powerful business interests. The poor, meantime, get very little representation by PACs. Drew proposes a number of measures to eliminate the need for PAC money, including free television advertisements for all candidates, public funding of congressional elections, and spending limits placed on so-called independent PACs.

NO Robert J. Samuelson

Based upon Robert J. Samuelson, "The Campaign Reform Failure," *The New Republic*, September 5, 1983.

Samuelson cautions that "Drew's reporting is precisely the kind that young reporters ought to be warned away from vigorously." Her evidence of PAC corruption, he says, is misleading. Individual fund-raising, not PAC contributions, still accounts for the lion's share of congressional funds. In any case, it is wrong to assume that only PAC interests get represented on Capitol Hill. There were no Food Stamp PACs, or Nutrition PACs, or Medicare PACs—yet we have all these programs because members of Congress saw merit in them and knew there were constituencies for them. Anyway, even where there are powerful moneyed interests on Capitol Hill, it does not mean that money is all-powerful. "PACs tend to check each other. When one interest organizes a PAC, competing interests do likewise." Besides, there are other checks on the power of PACs, including "the spotlight of public attention focused by the press, groups like Common Cause, and other politicians." His conclusion: Our system "is still working to accommodate conflicting interests and ideals."

Postscript

PACs present us with a delicate problem. On the one hand, democracy demands free expression and participation, including the right to expend effort and money on behalf of issues and candidates. On the other hand, there is the risk that large sums of money will give some points of view much more power than others. Democracy is based upon the assumption that points of view will prevail on their merits, not on the depths of the purses that fund them.

Edward Roeder has edited a useful directory of PACs, supplying information about their sources, their funds, and whom they support. See his *PACs Americana: A Directory of Political Action Committees and Their Interests*, 2d Edition (Washington, DC: Sunshine Service, 1986). Larry Sabato's *PAC Power: Inside the World of Political Action Committees* (New York: Norton, 1984) is a comprehensive overview of PACs: what they are, how they operate, and what their impact is. Frank J. Sorauf's *What Price PACs?* (Dallas: Priority Press, 1985) studies PAC financing and its implications today. For an excellent general study of interest groups, including PACs, see Graham K. Wilson, *Interest Groups in the United States* (Oxford University Press, 1981).

FIGURE **15-2**

415

Uses and Abuses
of Lobbies

**Monies Received by Candidates
House and Senate Races, 1977-1988**

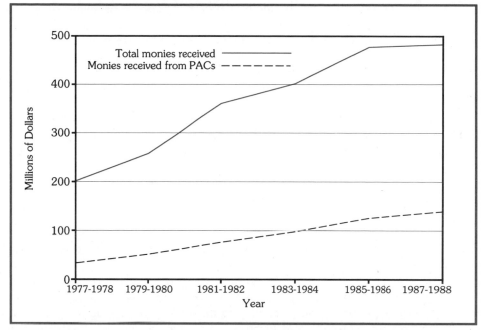

Source: Congressional Quarterly Weekly Report, March 4, 1989, p. 478. Reprinted with permission.

In 1977 federally elected officials received $200 million for their election campaigns. Of that money, $40 million came from PACs. In 1988 the total amount received was $480 million, with $140 million coming from PACs. In 11 years the total monies received by candidates more than doubled, while the amount from PACs more than tripled.

(Continued from page 413)

their 1988 victories. Now it was time for Republicans to demand congressional campaign reforms. In June 1989 President Bush proposed a package of them, including a proposal for the elimination of all PACs supported by corporations, unions, or trade associations, which together account for 90 percent of all PAC contributions. Bush and other Republicans viewed this proposal as a means of ending what they called "the permanent Congress." Democrats were less than enthusiastic. "The President's proposal is wholly inadequate," said Senate majority leader George Mitchell (D-Maine). "It is obviously crafted with one objective: to help Republicans."[32] Both sides of the controversy may have overreacted to the publicity about PACs in campaigns. As Figure 15.2 shows, although the proportion of campaign money donated by PACs has been growing since the 1970s, it still constitutes only a third of the total funds received by congressional candidates. The rest of the money comes largely from political parties and individuals.

Uses and Abuses of Lobbies

Lobbies are often aggressive and loud. They spend a lot of money and time to influence lawmakers. Some of their goals are selfish, others are no doubt foolish. Yet they render valuable services to the democratic process.

First, they *help to promote an interest in public affairs*. They publicize issues and seek supporters everywhere. In so doing, they help to promote citizen involvement in the political process, which is vital to democracy. Second, they *provide information and support to lawmakers*. One team of researchers working in the 1960s found that members of Congress usually welcomed communications from lobbyists. "To many congressmen," the researchers concluded, "the interest organization is a source of information about the attitudes of significant groups in his public, a source of research data and speech material, and an unofficial propaganda ally to help him put his case forward."[33]

Third, they *serve as watchdogs*. They can sound the alarm when some new government policy threatens the interests of their members; in the process they may point out critical weaknesses and dangers in the proposed policy. In that respect lobbies serve to implement the philosophy of checks and balances, which the Framers rightly cherished.

Fourth, lobbies *help represent citizens in government*. Our legislative districts and states represent us by geography. But we Americans are more than New Yorkers, Californians, and so on. We are also workers, businesspeople, Jews, Catholics, blacks, and others who belong to interests that cut across geographic lines, and it is lobbies that help to represent us in these ways. Political scientists Allan J. Cigler and Burdett A. Loomis have been impressed by the expanded reach of interest groups over the past generation. "Population groupings such as blacks, hispanics, and women have been mobilized since the 1950s and 1960s; even animals and the unborn are represented in the interest group arena, as is the broader 'public interest,' however defined."[34]

Yet the operation of lobbies in America has also been criticized. Some of the criticisms are similar to the criticisms of pluralist theory, reviewed earlier in the chapter (see page 404): Lobbies give voice only to those who are organized; they do not represent people equally. Some lobbying groups are much more powerful than others, and they pay little attention to what James Madison called "the permanent and aggregate interests of the community." But besides these criticisms, some additional ones should be noted.

Lobbyists attempt to influence politicians and legislative decisions at all levels of government. Lobbyists are so named because they often hang around the lobbies of legislative chambers, waiting for lawmakers.

First, many lobbies that claim to speak for a segment of the population really do not; at best, they speak for a segment of the segment. A farmers' organization like the American Farm Bureau Federation speaks for big agribusiness groups, not the small family farmers of America. Veterans' groups like the American Legion would be better entitled "right-wing veterans' groups." This is also true of some women's groups. They really speak only for those women who agree with the agenda of the feminist movement.[35] The leaders of groups that claim to speak for blacks, workers, and others may also be promoting views not shared by "their" people.

Second, the pressure on policymakers exerted by lobbies can sometimes get so intense that responsible policymaking becomes difficult. Regarding the work of PACs, one congressman said the reason Congress has not passed a number of bills is that "you get PACs fighting PACs, so it is just easier to do nothing."[36]

Third, the action of interest groups can heat up public debate so much that reasonable discussion gets lost. That has sometimes happened in current fights over abortion, school prayer, civil rights, and nuclear arms. Interest groups alone cannot be entirely blamed, for the issues are emotional. Nor is emotion always bad—there are some things we should feel strongly about. But when emotion destroys reason, and when groups on either side start to stoke the fires of unreason, the real losers are the American people.

REGULATING INTEREST GROUPS

Because of these and other criticisms, at various times the government has attempted to regulate interest-group lobbying. Congress has not attempted to prohibit lobbying, only to require lobbyists to tell us who they are, whom they represent, and how much they are spending. Such disclosure requirements lie at the heart of the Regulation of Lobbying Act of 1946. The act requires paid congressional lobbyists to file quarterly reports and to register with the House of Representatives and the Senate. These reports must list all contributions, expenditures, and the name and address of anyone who contributed over $500 or received payments. The act was challenged on First Amendment grounds and upheld by the Supreme Court in the case of *U.S. v. Harriss* (1954). However, in upholding the act, the Supreme Court construed it to require registration only if the primary purpose of a lobbying group was to influence legislation and only if the lobbyist directly contacted a member of Congress. As a result, many large organizations, such as the National Association of Manufacturers, do not register as lobbyists because they contend that lobbying is not the principal purpose for which they collect and receive funds. Other lobbyists contend that their contacts with Congress are designed to inform, not influence, and thus do not constitute lobbying.

The Lobbying Act has other loopholes as well. It does not apply to lobbying aimed at the executive branch, only to legislative lobbying, and it does not cover testifying before congressional committees. What is more, it has penalties for violation but no enforcement provisions. Despite the Lobbying Act, then, there is no way to tell how much money is being spent to influence key decisions made in Washington. "All that can be said with certainty," one student of the subject concluded, "is that the amount reported to Congress and the public is a very, very small fragment of the total."[37]

Other limitations on lobbying have been aimed at curbing conflicts of interest. A conflict of interest occurs when a public official has some outside ties that tempt him or her to subordinate the public interest to personal profit. During the Reagan administration, Michael Deaver, a former White House aide, was criticized for allegedly attempting to use his old White House connections to help clients, including the governments of Canada, South Korea, and Singapore, to the possible detriment of the United States. In 1988 Deaver was convicted of lying to Congress about the

Former White House aide Michael Deaver was the subject of an FBI inquiry and was convicted of lying to Congress about the extent of his private lobbying activities. He was accused of using his old White House connections to help his clients to the possible detriment of the United States. Such conflicts of interest are not rare in government, and Congress has passed a number of rules aimed at preventing some of these conflicts.

extent of his lobbying activities. The following year, President George Bush's nominee for secretary of defense, former Texas senator John G. Tower, was rejected by the Senate—in part because of charges of excessive drinking and womanizing, but also because of his ties to defense contractors. Tower had served as a U.S. representative at the START negotiations with the Soviets during the mid-1980s and, shortly afterward, as a consultant to the contractors. Tower's defenders saw irony in the anti-Tower vote not only because it was well known that some of the senators who voted and spoke against his confirmation were themselves drinkers and/or womanizers, but because conflicts of interest are not rare in Congress. Every senator or House member who takes money from a PAC or who accepts a generous speaking fee from a special interest is at least potentially in such a situation. As Representative Barney Frank (D-Massachusetts) put it: "Elected officials are the only—only human beings I know of who are supposed to accept large amounts of money from relative strangers for important purposes that have no influence whatsoever on their behavior."[38]

Congress has passed a number of rules aimed at curbing conflicts of interest, and in 1978 these were codified in the Ethics in Government Act of 1978. Among its chief provisions:

- All members of Congress, their principal assistants, high-level executive branch employees, and federal judges must file a financial disclosure form every year, listing the sources and amounts of all outside income, including the income of their spouses.
- For one year after leaving government service, former executive-branch employees may not represent clients before any agency or body in the government for which they had previously worked.
- An Office of Government Ethics is authorized to develop rules and regulations pertaining to conflicts of interest in the executive branch.
- The attorney general must investigate all allegations of serious wrongdoing by the president or other high-level federal officers and apply to a special court unit to appoint a special prosecutor if he or she concludes that the allegations appear to be substantiated.

Suggestions have been made for new laws aimed at curbing conflicts of interest. One proposal would make it mandatory for pressure groups to disclose a list of contributors. This would make clearer just who is behind those groups with ties to policymakers. The proposal, however, raises serious questions about civil liberty and fairness. It would probably scare away a lot of contributors who, for perhaps good reasons, wish to remain anonymous. (Imagine, for example, an employee of a tobacco company who wants to contribute to an antismoking lobby.) Detailed disclosure requirements would also increase the paperwork and costs to groups attempting to petition the government, which is particularly burdensome for small groups with modest budgets.

Points to Remember

1. Lobbies promote interest in public affairs, provide useful information, serve as watchdogs over government and each other, and help represent the interests of citizens.

2. Lobbies have been criticized for ignoring the wider interests of the community, not representing all those they claim to represent, producing confusion and deadlock in Congress, and generating so much emotion that they make reasoned discussion difficult.

3. The government has attempted to regulate lobbies by requiring them to register with federal agencies and disclose lists of their contributors and the amounts contributed. However, the law has many loopholes, such as the fact that those who do not directly contact members of Congress need not register.

For better or for worse, interest groups—factions, James Madison called them—are here to stay. Governments can, of course, jail people for belonging to factions, and in totalitarian systems that commonly happens. But it is hard to disagree with Madison's conclusion that repression is "a remedy worse than the disease." Our First Amendment protects free speech and press; it also explicitly protects the right of people to assemble peaceably and "petition the Government for a redress of grievances."

Madison accepted interest groups as a necessary evil, but perhaps a more positive case can be made for them. As we noted in this chapter, interest groups serve a variety of purposes, from providing information to stirring up interest in politics. Yet we persist in using such terms as *special interests* to describe them. Well, to describe *some* of them—the ones we do not like. The ones *we* favor we call "citizens' groups" or "public interest groups" or some more pleasant name.

Are there genuine public interests, interests that reach beyond the narrow concerns of a single group? Yes—at least in theory. Civil rights issues concern not just blacks, but all Americans. Pollution control should interest anyone with lungs. Automobile safety and consumer protection safeguard us all. In practice, however, these universal interests sometimes conceal special interests. Some whites complain that, in practice, affirmative action programs set up to benefit blacks and women actually penalize white males. Environmental laws, which in theory help us all, in practice may result in plant closings that hurt working-class people. Auto safety devices, designed to protect everyone, add to the cost of cars, making it still more difficult for the poor to buy them. In short, there is sometimes a hidden class bias behind the public interest.

Still, it would seem unwise to abandon the distinction between public interest groups and special interests. As E. E. Schattschneider noted, the members of the American League to Abolish Capital Punishment do not expect to be hanged. They have nothing to gain personally from the abolition of capital punishment. That makes them different from members of the AFL-CIO or the American Petroleum Institute, who lobby for self-serving ends. Not that there is anything wrong with self-interest. In helping themselves, interest groups may also help others. And even when they do not, the sheer variety and multiplicity of interest groups help to ensure a healthy competition. Out of that competition, something like the national interest may emerge. It may leave out some interests that are not organized, but perhaps that will have to do until we finally realize the ideal invoked by President John Kennedy in his inaugural address: "Ask not," he said, "what your country can do for you; ask what you can do for your country."

Notes

1. Norman J. Ornstein and Shirley Elder, *Interest Groups, Lobbying and Policymaking* (Washington: Congressional Quarterly, Inc., 1978), p. 214.

2. Ornstein and Elder, p. 214.

3. Stratford P. Sherman, "How Rockwell Kept the B-1 Alive," *Fortune*, Nov. 3, 1981, p. 106.

4. Sherman, p. 107.

5. Nick Kotz, *Wild Blue Yonder: Money, Politics, and the B-1 Bomber* (New York: Pantheon Books, 1988), p. 249.

6. Alexis de Tocqueville, *Democracy in America* (New York: Vintage Books, 1945), I, p. 198.

7. See Allan Brownfield's review of Samuel L. Blumenfeld's *NEA: Trojan Horse in American Education*, in *Washington Times*, Jan. 14, 1985, p. 4B.

8. Lyrics from the song "It Isn't Nice" by Malvina Reynolds, copyright 1964 by Schroder Music Co. (ASCAP) used with permission; all rights reserved. Recorded by Judy Collins in Town Hall, New York, Mar. 21, 1964, in *Judy Collins, Fifth Album*.

9. Charles G. Bell, "Legislatures, Interest Groups and Lobbyists: The Link Beyond the District," *Journal of State Government* (Spring 1986), p. 14.

10. L. Harmon Ziegler and Hendrik van Dalen, "Interest Groups in State Politics," in Herbert Jacob and Kenneth Vines, eds., *Politics in the American States*, 3d ed. (Boston: Little, Brown, Inc., 1976), pp. 98-101.

11. L. Harmon Ziegler, "The Effects of Lobbying: A Comparative Assessment," *Western Political Quarterly* (March 1969), pp. 122-40.

12. E. E. Schattschneider, *The Semi-Sovereign People* (New York: Holt, Rinehart and Winston, Inc., 1960), pp. 224, 226.

13. Robert A. Dahl, *Preface to Democratic Theory* (Chicago: University of Chicago Press, 1956), p. 137.

14. Schattschneider, p. 32.

15. Kay L. Schlozman and John T. Tierney, *Organized Interests and American Democracy* (New York: Harper & Row, 1986), p. 68.

16. David Vogel, *Fluctuating Fortunes: The Political Power of Business in America* (New York: Basic Books, Inc., 1989), chap. 9.

17. C. Wright Mills, *The Power Elite* (New York: Oxford University Press, 1956).

18. Quoted in Ornstein and Elder, p. 201.

19. Sherman, p. 108.

20. Quoted by Orr Kelly, "The B-1: When Pentagon, Politicians Joined Hands," *U.S. News and World Report*, July 11, 1983, p. 35.

21. "Democrats Spent More on Election," *New York Times*, Feb. 26, 1989, p. 27.

22. *New York Times*, Aug. 10, 1987, p. A17.

23. *New York Times*, Oct. 27, 1986, p. A20.

24. Graham K. Wilson, *Interest Groups in the United States* (Oxford: Clarendon Press, 1981), p. 74.

25. Quoted in Wilson, p. 74.

26. Campaign finance laws are studied in more detail in chapter 17.

27. *Federal Election Commission v. National Conservative Political Action Committee* (1985).

28. Bill Moyers, "Campaign Spending: Money and Media," *The Constitution: That Delicate Balance*, transcript of 13-part television series on PBS (Fall 1984), p. 12.

29. "How PAC Money Flows to Party Leaders," *New York Times*, June 17, 1989, p. B7.

30. See Elizabeth Drew's interviews with Republican leaders William Brock and Lee Atwater in *Politics and Money: The New Road to Corruption* (New York: Macmillan Publishing Company, 1983), pp. 20-21, 24-25.

31. Charles R. Babcock, "Money Has Big Role in Coelho's Career," *Washington Post*, May 28, 1989, p. A25. See further, Brooks Jackson, *Honest Graft* (New York: Alfred A. Knopf, Inc., 1988).

32. Maureen Dowd, "Bush Urges Campaign Fund Curbs and Limits on Fees for Congress," *New York Times*, June 30, 1989, p. A12.

33. Raymond A. Bauer, Ithiel de Sola Pool, and Lewis A. Dexter, *American Business and Public Policy, The Politics of Foreign Trade* (New York: Atherton Press, 1963), pp. 440-41.

34. Allan J. Cigler and Burdett A. Loomis, eds., *Interest Group Politics* (Washington: Congressional Quarterly, 1983), p. 27.

35. For the failure of feminist groups to represent a large portion of America's women, see Jane M. Mansbridge, *Why We Lost the ERA* (Chicago: University of Chicago Press, 1987). One of the most remarkable demonstrations of the gap between these groups and the majority of American women came in 1984, when feminists strenuously opposed the reelection of President Reagan. When the election was over, it was discovered that 57 percent of American women had voted for Reagan, and only 42 percent for Mondale. Feminist groups kept a lower profile during the 1988 election, but they backed Dukakis. Bush beat Dukakis by one percentage point among women voters (50 percent to 49 percent).

36. Quoted in Elizabeth Drew, *Politics and Money: The New Road to Corruption* (New York: Macmillan Publishing Company, 1983), p. 90.

37. James Deakin, *The Lobbyists* (Washington: Public Affairs Press, 1966), p. 23.

38. Quoted in "Campaign Spending: Money and Media," *The Constitution: That Delicate Balance*, p. 4.

16

Political Parties

I seen my opportunities
and I took 'em.

George Washington Plunkitt,
Tammany Hall Boss

Anyone acquainted with native Chicagoans in the 1960s **The Siege of Chicago**
knew them as a serious, industrious people: rather old-
fashioned in their mores, firmly attached to their routines. To some out-of-
towners, they seemed excessively restrained and distant. Journalist
Theodore H. White (a native Bostonian) called them "uptight to
strangers."[*][1]

In the last week of August 1968, Chicago was invaded by strangers.
About 10,000 people, many from outside the city, converged on "the

[*]This account is drawn from the following sources: *Rights in Conflict: Chicago's 7 Brutal
Days* (The Official "Walker Report" to the National Commission on the Causes and
Prevention of Violence; New York: Grosset & Dunlap, 1968); Lewis Chester, Godfrey
Hodgson, and Bruce Page, *An American Melodrama: The Presidential Campaign of 1968*
(New York: Dell Publishing Co., 1969); Norman Mailer, *Miami and the Siege of Chicago*
(New York: The New American Library, Signet Books, 1968); Theodore H. White, *The
Making of the President 1968* (New York: Atheneum Publishers, 1969); David Lewis
Stein, *Living the Revolution: The Yippies in Chicago* (Indianapolis, IN: Bobbs-Merrill
Company, 1969).

421

Loop," Chicago's downtown area. Some of the strangers were very strange indeed. They hung out in Grant Park, where they smoked dope, danced naked, made love on the lawn, climbed on top of the statues and spray-painted them with peace symbols in fierce Day-Glo colors.

The strangers had descended upon Chicago because the Democratic presidential convention was being held there. They had come to protest the Vietnam War—"Johnson's War," they called it, referring to the administration of Democratic President Lyndon B. Johnson. Most of the protesters were peaceful. They were content to stage illegal marches and go limp when arrested. But some were not so peaceful. They threw rocks, tiles, bricks, and bags of feces at the police, screamed at them, and called them "pigs." They bought live pigs at the stockyards and released them into the streets. They trampled American flags and waved Communist flags in the air. Some of the demonstrators were self-declared Marxists; some more nearly resembled liberals. Still others had no philosophy at all, only a slogan: "Revolution for the hell of it." One thing all the demonstrators seemed to agree upon was this: The Democratic party convention of 1968 was rigged; it was a fraud.

The man the convention was to designate as its nominee for president of the United States, Hubert H. Humphrey, had not entered a single primary election in 1968. Other contenders for the nomination had. Minnesota senator Eugene J. McCarthy had started off by entering the New Hampshire primary in March to challenge President Johnson for the Democratic nomination. Although Johnson, a write-in candidate in New Hampshire, won the primary, McCarthy got a surprising 42.3 percent of the vote. Then Robert Kennedy, brother of the late president and senator from New York, entered the Democratic primaries. In the meantime, Lyndon Johnson decided he had had enough and announced that he had no intention of running again for president. His choice for a successor was Vice President Hubert Humphrey, who was widely perceived as "Johnson's man" and therefore pro-war. Fairly or not, the anti-Vietnam movement saw Humphrey as a tool of the administration.

Robert Kennedy's quest for the presidency ended on June 5, 1968, when he was assassinated. That left McCarthy, South Dakota senator George McGovern, and a few minor candidates. And, of course, Hubert Humphrey. Humphrey's failure to enter the primaries did not matter. Almost all the major party leaders—party wheelhorses, bigwigs, and bosses—supported Humphrey. In particular, his nomination was supported by Chicago's mayor, Richard Daley, the most powerful boss of all. A round, red-faced man with three chins, Daley, who had been mayor of Chicago for 13 years, controlled the votes of the huge Illinois delegation. As host of the 1968 convention, he could pull strings everywhere. "The boss of bosses," they called him. Mayor Daley was firmly committed to Hubert Humphrey. That meant that Humphrey was going to be nominated, even though he had not entered a single primary.

It was not just anger over the power of men like Daley—a power that could cancel primary victories—that brought the demonstrators to Chicago. The "boss" method about to be used to nominate Humphrey did not differ greatly from the methods that had been employed in the past to nominate Franklin Roosevelt, Adlai Stevenson, and John Kennedy. There had been no mass protests then. The underlying issue behind the Chicago demonstrations in 1968 was not "boss rule"; it was the war. At that point, half a million American soldiers were in Vietnam. American bombs and shells were falling all over the tiny country, both in the Communist north and in the anti-Communist south. Villages had been destroyed, thousands of Americans had died, hundreds of thousands of Vietnamese were dead or maimed or homeless.

Although public opinion polls revealed that a majority of Americans supported the war, an activist minority was outraged by it. This minority drew heavily from the campuses of the nation's most prestigious universities: Harvard, Yale, Columbia, the University of Michigan, Berkeley, the University of Chicago, and so on. Some of its members were professors, some were teaching assistants, some were students, some were dropouts who still congregated on the various campuses. There were also young professionals who had recently graduated from law schools and medical schools.

Eugene McCarthy drew his support from these antiwar activists. McCarthy's workers were young, well-educated, and headed toward careers in the professions and the media. Morally and esthetically, McCarthy's supporters were repelled by the sleazy characters who hung around local Democratic clubhouses, but they had not yet given up on the party system. They wanted to make it work—for them and for their cause. A year before, many of "McCarthy's kids," as they were known, were walking around in tie-dyed T-shirts, cutoffs, and "Che" Guevara beards. Now it was time for sportcoats and blazers, penny loafers, and Black Watch miniskirts. They were going to be "clean for Gene." Few had any illusions that their candidate would get the nomination, but they all hoped to get a peace plank into the Democratic platform that would call for a unilateral halt in the bombing of North Vietnam. If they could not get the nomination for McCarthy, maybe they could force Humphrey to stand on McCarthy's platform.

It was all wishful thinking. Some party leaders, including Daley, had private misgivings about the war but no intention of insulting President Johnson with a peace plank. Nor was the vice president about to repudiate his chief. The peace plank was voted down. To the McCarthy delegates, it meant the end of their dreams. As they saw it, an insane system had triumphed over reason. Standing at the back of the convention hall, they shouted their frustration and despair. Many wept. Someone distributed black armbands for McCarthy's people to put on. They sang "We Shall Overcome" and "The Battle Hymn of the Republic" but were drowned out by the convention band playing "We Got a Lot of Livin' to Do."

That night, the streets outside the Hilton Hotel, where most of the conventioneers were staying, exploded in violence. Demonstrators gathered on Michigan Avenue and Balbo Drive; they taunted the police and pelted them with various objects (149 police officers were hurt that night). From the open windows of Hilton rooms high above the streets, more debris rained down on the police, presumably from "McCarthy's kids." Then the police, who had been working 12- and 15-hour shifts for three days and had been provoked beyond endurance, went berserk. Theodore H. White described the scene as viewed from the Hilton's twenty-fifth floor:

Slam! Like a fist jolting, like a piston exploding from its chamber, comes a hurtling column of police from off Balbo into the intersection, and all things happen too fast: first the charge as the police wedge cleaves through the mob; then screams, whistles, confusion, people running off into Grant Park, across the bridge, into hotel lobbies. And as the scene clears, there are little knots in the open clearing—police clubbing youngsters, police rushing them by the elbows, their heels dragging, to patrol wagons, prodding recalcitrants who refuse to enter quietly.[2]

Chicago police clash with demonstrators in August 1968. The clash occurred during the 1968 Democratic National Convention. The Vietnam War was raging at the time, and Democratic reformers tried to nominate an antiwar Democrat, Senator Eugene McCarthy, for president and tried to get a peace plank into the Democratic platform. They failed to accomplish either objective and charged that the convention was rigged. Demonstrators gathered in the streets and pelted police with various objects; the exhausted and overworked police went berserk and responded with violence.

It looked like a massacre. The police were beating people who had already surrendered, beating news reporters, beating everyone who looked young or radical or sympathetic to the demonstrators. Blood was spurting from head wounds, people were staggering, falling, getting beaten on the ground. Much later, when the night was nearly over, the police went inside the Hilton, burst into the rooms of McCarthy's staffers, and beat everyone they could find.

So Hubert Humphrey won the Democratic nomination in 1968. But he won it amid wild scenes of violence and recrimination. The "regular" Democrats and the "reform" Democrats hated each other, screamed at each other, and blamed each other for the bloodshed. Even before the last confrontation on Michigan Avenue, Theodore H. White scribbled in his notebook: "The Democrats are finished."[3]

* * * * *

In one sense, White was right: The *old* Democratic party was finished. But out of its ashes arose a new Democratic party. The Democrats, regulars and reformers alike, were determined that the events of 1968 must never happen again. The way to prevent them from happening, they concluded, was to change the rules for selecting convention delegates. Over the next four years, the Democratic party rewrote its delegate selection rules. The power of the bosses was to be curbed. Party democracy was to prevail.

Later in the chapter, we will discuss the rules changes. For now it is enough to say that the changes turned the party upside down. Those who were on the bottom in 1968 were on the top by 1972, and vice versa. The McCarthy and McGovern forces, the outsiders in 1968, controlled the 1972 convention. The regulars, the forces of Mayor Daley and the other leaders, had faded into the background. The revolution can be seen in a single vignette: Ann Wexler, a McCarthy delegate to the Chicago convention, had burst into tears as the peace plank went down in 1968. Burying her head in the chest of a sympathetic reporter, she had sobbed, "They got us into a corner and did this to us."[4] In 1972 Wexler was a major party leader; she helped to write the new rules. And where was Mayor Daley, kingmaker, the man who had doomed the peace plank? Daley was barred from a seat as a delegate to the 1972 convention.

The Democratic party was no longer controlled by urban machines, labor unions, blue-collar northerners, and rural white southerners. Some of the old groups, particularly the labor unions, still had some say in Democratic politics. But the party's basic makeup had changed. It was now, increasingly, a party of professors and professionals, feminists and peace marchers. The new leaders were the leisured, professional people who had the time and money to spend on political activism. The "amateur Democrats," as one political scientist called them, had triumphed. Would their victory bring a new infusion of reason and democracy into the American electoral process, or, as their critics charged, would it make the whole process even more confused, more elitist, more irrational? This issue, first raised in 1972, is still with us and still unresolved.

This controversy is part of a larger series of issues concerning the American party system. What *is* a political party? How did parties develop in America? What purposes do they serve? How do they differ from one another? How have they changed? What is their future—or do they have one?

Nature and Purpose of American Political Parties

In some respects, political parties resemble interest groups, which were discussed in the previous chapter. Similar to an interest group, a political party is an association of people who agree on certain ideas or goals, which they try to get translated into law. But there are two important differences between a party and an interest group. First, a party is usually broader than an interest group. At some point, it begins to spell out its views not just on one or two issues, but on a range of issues; in other words, it develops a program or platform. The reason for this is that a party usually holds together—and sometimes juggles uneasily—different groups in the population. Because each group usually has its own agenda, party leaders must be skillful in building platforms that do not alienate any of the groups. The second difference between a party and an interest group is that a party does not want merely to influence government. It wants to run the government. An interest group stands on the outside; it lobbies policymakers. A party wants to *be* the policymaker. Putting these points together, we may define a political party as a political association that seeks to acquire and maintain control of the government.

FIGURE **16-1**

Organization of American Political Parties

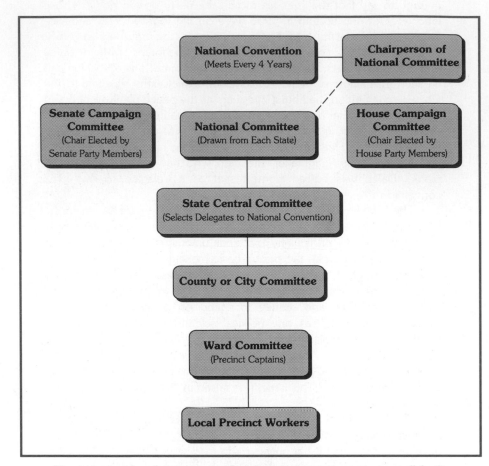

The organization of American political parties to some extent parallels the governing structures of the United States. It contains local, state, and national components. At the bottom of the structure are local precinct (neighborhood) workers who help drum up support and get people to vote for candidates. Then there are ward, county, state, and national units of the party. In recent years, national leadership has assumed greater importance.

Political parties are found throughout the world, but they are not all the same. All parties do have smaller groups within them, for example, but in some cases the range of groups is quite narrow. The British Labour party is meant to appeal to British workers and certain intellectuals who believe in socialism. It does not attempt to appeal to business, for example, or to farmers. This is even more true of political parties on the European continent, which are usually committed to specific programs. In order to govern, these European parties must sometimes form working coalitions in the national legislature, for no one party has a majority of seats. Continental parties are invariably <u>multiparty systems</u>. The systems in Great Britain and the United States are two-party systems.

THE LOOSENESS OF AMERICAN PARTIES

American political parties are looser than most European, Asian, and African parties. Ours is called an <u>indistinct party system</u>, meaning that Democrats and Republicans tend to agree on many issues. Both parties, for example, pay homage to patriotism, to the family, to capitalism (free enterprise), to Social Security, to environmental protection, and to civil rights; both parties agree that the Soviet Union has been an adversary of the United States; both agree that we must negotiate with the Soviets. The area of general agreement is extensive. But there are also real differences, as we shall see later in this chapter.

Aside from the fact that the two major parties agree on many basic issues, there is another sense in which American parties are "looser" than parties in Europe, Asia, Africa, and elsewhere. In most countries, parties play a greater role, both in the nominating process and in the lives of citizens. Virtually the only way for a person to become a candidate for elective office in most countries is to be nominated by party leaders. Campaigns are run by the party, using party funds and workers, not by the candidate. Once in office, the candidate is expected to vote strictly along party lines. Party membership is taken seriously, even by ordinary citizens. People join a party and, in some nations, pay dues and attend public meetings. Parties sponsor political and cultural events: They run youth groups, labor groups, even chess clubs. In America, this kind of attachment does not exist—indeed, it would probably be regarded with suspicion. Americans pride themselves on their independence, their refusal to follow a party line. Being a member of a political party is usually limited to declaring oneself a member of one party or another on a voter registration form. Even there, greater and greater numbers of Americans are registering as independents.

In contrast to the system in other countries, then, our party system is two-party and indistinct. What else can be said about it? One distinguishing characteristic is so obvious that we hardly notice it: Ours is a competitive party system—another way of saying that it is not a one-party system. Democrats and Republicans tolerate one another and compete with one another; neither is assured of dominance on the national scene, and even many local "one-party" areas have become competitive in recent years. In countries like China, Cuba, and the Soviet Union, only one party is permitted. Other one-party systems, such as those in Indonesia and Egypt, do not reach so deeply into people's private lives but are no less intolerant of opposition. Still others—for example, Yugoslavia's—permit only one party but allow open factionalism within the party. Finally, there are *de facto* one-party systems that permit opposition parties to exist but govern principally through the dominant party.

THE EMERGENCE OF AMERICAN PARTIES

Political parties are not mentioned in the Constitution; the Founders did not like them. Thomas Jefferson declared: "If I could not go to heaven but with a party, I would rather not go there at all." The Founders tended to think of parties as conspiracies. George Washington, in his Farewell Address, condemned "all combinations and associations, under whatever plausible connection, with the real design to direct, control, counteract or awe the regular deliberation of the constituted authorities."[5]

FEDERALISTS VERSUS REPUBLICANS

This dislike did not, however, prevent the Founders from belonging to parties. Washington himself became the mainstay of the Federalists, our first political party, and Jefferson entered the White House on the back of a new party called the Jeffersonian Republican party, which later became the Democratic-Republican party.

It was not hypocrisy for Washington, who condemned parties, to lead the

Federalists. The Federalists did not think of themselves as a party. They got their name from the fact that they were champions of the new Constitution, the document that replaced the Articles of Confederation. By the 1790s, the Constitution was no longer controversial. It had been ratified by nearly all the states and was on its way to becoming a sacred document.

Not surprisingly, it was Washington, the hero of the Revolution and the man who presided at the Constitutional Convention, who was unanimously elected president. A figure of awesome dignity, George Washington seemed to be "above politics." But the drift of the Washington administration toward East Coast, trading, and banking interests at the expense of rural, western, and southern interests prepared the ground for the emergence of a rival party, the Jeffersonian Republicans (not to be confused with today's Republican party). Led by Jefferson and James Madison, the Republicans were also committed to the Constitution, but their policies were different. They championed majority rule.

The Jeffersonian Republicans became the party of what we would today call "the little people": small farmers and frontier settlers. They denounced the rich and the privileged, the eastern money interests. Internationally, the Republicans saw the French Revolution as a movement toward democracy. In 1800 the Jeffersonian Republicans won their first major battle against the Federalists. Their candidate, Thomas Jefferson, unseated Federalist president John Adams. From then on, the Federalist party's fortunes declined, and after 1816 it ceased to exist.

In retrospect, the withering away of the Federalists seemed almost inevitable. Preoccupied with the interests of the East Coast and afraid of the mass of the people, they had the misfortune to live in a nation that was rapidly expanding westward and increasing in numbers. But perhaps a more critical factor was their inability to compromise, to build coalitions. Jefferson cherished his own interests (he once described farmers as God's "chosen people"), but he knew how to forge alliances with others of different interests and temperaments. In 1791 Jefferson and fellow Virginian James Madison journeyed into New York State, ostensibly on a botanical field trip, and helped to build an alliance with New York Republicans that paid off in 1800 when the Republicans carried the state.

IMPROBABLE ALLIANCES

The early success of the Jeffersonian Republicans in cementing alliances between different interests was repeated again and again in the history of American parties. In the 1830s and 1840s the flood of impoverished Irish immigrants found a home in the new Democratic party (formerly the Democratic-Republican party), which managed to link them together in a victorious coalition with western pioneers and southern farmers. As the Civil War approached, the slavery issue split the Democrats but helped to create a new party, the Republicans. The modern Republican party was the product of a rather strange alliance. It included eastern manufacturers, bankers, and traders; middle western farmers; abolitionists; "nativist" groups (groups opposed to immigration); and a wide variety of "reformers": saints, cynics, bigots, dreamers, and hustlers. Yet they all agreed that slavery must not be extended into the new territories, and that was enough to hold the new party together. In 1860 it elected its first president, Abraham Lincoln, and from that year until 1912 the party virtually dominated national politics. In 1912 Woodrow Wilson, a Democrat, was elected president. By 1920 it was the Republicans' turn again, and they remained the dominant party until the Depression ruined the party's reputation as "the party of the full dinner pail."

The Depression and Franklin Roosevelt restored the fortunes of the Democrats,

(Continued on page 429)

FIGURE **16-2**

Major American Political Parties

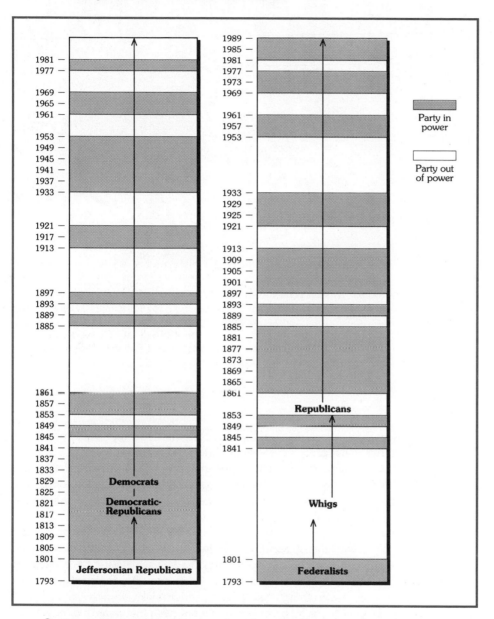

Our two major national parties have long histories. The Democratic party traces
its roots to Thomas Jefferson and the 1800 election, when the party was called
the "Republican" or "Jeffersonian Republican" party. The present-day Republican party was assembled in the 1850s out of pieces of older parties, particularly
the Whigs, and several minor parties.

but some years before Roosevelt's 1932 victory, the Democrats were starting to make
a comeback. As early as 1928 they began assembling a coalition of groups: Irish city
bosses and their followers; the newer Catholic immigrants from southern and eastern
Europe; Jews from Russia, Poland, and Germany; rural Protestants from the South;
even some northern blacks. It was another improbable alliance. Many of these groups
hated each other—but because they hated poverty more, they learned to stick
together. At the start of his administration in 1933, Franklin Roosevelt promised

Political cartoonist Thomas Nast was the first to portray the Republican party as an elephant. In this cartoon, from the November 7, 1874, issue of *Harper's Weekly*, the rampaging elephant, apparently frightened by an ass (the *New York Herald* newspaper) dressed in a lion's skin, is about to fall into chaos. At the bottom of the picture is the Democratic party, portrayed as an extremely wary little fox.

Americans a New Deal, a reshuffling of the old economic deck, that would permit the lower classes to rise. That promise was enough to weld these groups into a winning electoral coalition pledged to an activist government, a government that would experiment with programs to end the Depression. The New Deal alliance held together for almost 20 years until it was undermined by postwar affluence and the rise of new and divisive issues like communism.

In surveying the sweep of party history, one quality of our parties seems to stand out: their almost breathtaking opportunism. In the 1830s Irish immigrants barely off the boat were greeted by American-born party leaders who must have despised everything about the newcomers—their looks, their poverty, their religion, their accents and manners—everything, that is, except their ability to cast ballots. Years later, the descendants of these Irish immigrants would (with the greatest of reluctance and against their better judgment) share some of *their* power with the newer immigrants and with other people they did not much like.

SOME FUNCTIONS OF PARTIES

It may seem strange to say this, but the opportunism of America's parties has done democracy a service. It has helped bring together peoples from all over the world and has taught them the art of democratic government. American democracy was and is very far from being an ideal democracy. But because of parties, America became a democracy that, however imperfectly, began to serve the needs of quite ordinary people. Although they have been weakened in recent years (for reasons we shall soon explore), parties continue to serve valuable functions. *(Continued on page 432)*

GLOBAL PERSPECTIVES:

Political Parties in Brazil

Traditionally, power in Brazil has been in the hands of strong executives—monarchs, generals, and dictators. Not until the mid-1950s did Brazil finally establish a constitutional republic with sufficient pluralism to permit meaningful party competition. From then until 1964 a succession of shaky civilian governments tried vainly to cope with the nation's economic troubles—unemployment, foreign debt, and skyrocketing inflation. In 1964, alarmed at the leftist tendencies of the government, the military took over and ruled for 21 years.

The generals did not permit civilian government to return until 1985, but they eased the way in 1979 by enacting the Party Reform Bill. Under its provisions, new political parties could be established. They would be granted the freedom to formulate platforms as long as the platforms were not ideological and did not favor any one economic class.

A number of new parties soon appeared. The largest is the PMDB (Brazilian Democratic Movement party), an ostensibly left-of-center party, although it has a conservative wing. In January 1985, the PMDB's candidate for president, Tancredo Neves, easily won the presidency in an indirect election through an electoral college. But the ailing, 75-year-old Neves died before his inauguration, and the military directed the electoral college to pick a successor. It chose Neves's vice-presidential running mate, José Sarney, who was not from the PMDB but from the Liberal Front party (PFL), which had teamed up with the PMDB for the 1985 election. Sarney's party was more conservative than the PMDB, and many of its members had connections with the military.

Sarney was constitutionally barred from succeeding himself, and the next presidential election, held in November 1989, featured candidates from 22 different parties. Neither of the two highest vote-getters, Luis Inacio da Silva and Fernando Collor de Mello, won a majority, so a runoff election was held in December. Collor, a 39-year-old conservative, was virtually unknown the previous year but his youth and good looks, combined with frequent television appearances, turned him into the front-runner. His party, the National Reconstruction Party, was founded less than a year before the election. Collor's rival, da Silva, was a candidate of the leftist Workers' Party and after the November election he was endorsed by the Communists and the new Green Party. These two presidential candidates represented parties that jointly controlled less than 5 percent of the seats in the Brazilian Congress.

All of this points out the weakness of Brazil's new party system, which in actuality continues long-standing practices in the country. The widespread scattering of parties fractionalizes the voters and makes rational choice difficult. The influence of television on a poorly educated electorate (only 31 percent of the population has finished primary school) may make personality more important than party platforms, which generally remain vague. Meanwhile, party organization conforms to traditional alliances and the "rules" of patronage. One observer concluded: "Democratic *forms* are in place in Brazil; the substance remains to be realized."

(Continued from page 430) **Bringing in the "Outs."**   American parties exert a powerful force for bringing in the "outs." What was accomplished through violent revolution in Europe has been done loudly, rudely, sometimes crookedly, but more or less peacefully by political parties in America. The Democratic party leaders who greeted the Irish immigrants getting off boats in the 1830s soon found themselves outnumbered. It did not take long for these immigrants to seize control of the machines. In the process, an angry and disorderly proletariat was absorbed into a peaceful political system. They in turn passed power on to still newer groups that came to America in the early years of the twentieth century.

But the immigrants were not the only "outs"; some older groups who felt threatened by the immigrants soon formed their own party, the American or Know-Nothing party (so called because its members, who felt the need for secrecy, invariably answered "I know nothing" when asked about their party). The Know-Nothings were absorbed into the new Republican party in 1856. There were many other parties for people who felt left out of the system, the most prominent being the People's party, better known as the Populists, of the 1880s and 1890s. The Populists claimed that both parties were controlled by wealthy eastern interests. By the end of the nineteenth century, they had been absorbed by the Democrats.

There seems to be a recurring pattern in our party system: A group or interest that feels itself ignored by the regular parties forms its own party or in some other way demonstrates its political clout. If it is a serious movement with a real following, one of the major parties suddenly finds great merit in it, which makes it ripe for the picking. One of the major parties then begins to appropriate some of its positions and/or recruit its leaders. Soon the protest movement or party has been swallowed up by a major party. It happens all the time. In the 1970s the Republicans picked up at least one plank of George Wallace's American Independent party of 1968—its opposition to busing for the sake of racial balance—and promptly pulled into their party many of Wallace's followers. At the same time, the Democrats pulled in the followers of Martin Luther King, Jr., and other blacks who had been alienated from the old Democratic party. The success of black politicians like the Reverend Jesse Jackson and the late Chicago mayor Harold Washington is in part attributable to a new and reshaped Democratic party.

The motive for all this wooing of the "outs" is anything but idealistic. Parties do it because they like to win elections. They are opportunists. But the effect of the opportunism is good: The party reaches out and brings into the system those who have been left out. The Democrats have appealed to groups, such as feminists and environmentalists, that at first were not taken seriously by politicians. The Republicans, for their part, have turned to pro-lifers and "born-again" Christians who felt shut out of the political system. Whatever you think of any of these groups, surely you agree that in a democracy they deserve to be heard. Thanks to our political parties' relentless chasing after votes, these groups have been given that opportunity. This is much better than an abstract "right" to participate; it is a practical, concrete *means* of participating.

Expanding Political Participation.   Related to bringing in the "outs" is a second function of political parties—whipping up enthusiasm for politics and getting ordinary people more deeply involved in the political process. Here is how John Adams, writing in the 1760s, depicted a political meeting in his neighborhood:

> This day learned that the Caucus club meets at certain times in the garret of Tom Dawes, the Adjutant of the Boston regiment. He has a large house, and he has a movable partition in his garret which he takes down, and the whole club meets in one room. There they smoke tobacco till you cannot see from one end of the garret to the other. There they drink flip, I suppose, and they choose a moderator who puts questions to the vote regularly; and selectmen, assessors, collectors, firewards, and representatives are regularly chosen before they are chosen in the town.[6]

PARTIES: BAD OR GOOD?

George Washington, Farewell Address (1796):

"Let me warn you in the most solemn manner against the baneful effects of the spirit of party generally. This spirit . . . exists under different shapes in all government . . . but in those of the popular form it is seen in its greatest rankness and is truly their worst enemy."

Clinton Rossiter, political scientist and historian, *Parties and Politics in America* (1960):

"Political parties and democracy are inseparable phenomena. The surge toward democracy first gave life to parties as we know them, and parties in their turn were major spurs to the onward course of democracy."

What Adams was describing so indignantly was a party <u>caucus</u>. A caucus is a group of party members who meet together informally and select candidates to support for office. After taking their votes in Tom Dawes's garret, these Bostonians pledged themselves to vote for their chosen candidates. Here, quite literally, was a "smoke-filled room" in action.

It may have been the tobacco and the flip (a spicy alcoholic punch) that really bothered Adams's Puritan conscience. For when it came to caucuses, Adams was soon skilled in their operation. He was picked by the Federalist caucuses to be that party's standard-bearer. In fact, it is hard to see what was so wrong about caucuses, at least for that time; if anything, they brought more people into the political process. Prior to the development of the caucus, the business of nominating candidates for office was largely done by landowning and mercantile elites plus those lucky enough to form connections with them. The development of the party caucus permitted politicians to bring the names of others before the voters. That, in turn, helped to dissolve the quasi-aristocratic system of elite politics that colonial America had inherited from the British.

Caucuses, then, helped to broaden and extend democracy in the new nation. But soon some caucuses were criticized as being undemocratic. Presidential candidates were nominated by congressional caucus: All the members of Congress from the same party would get together and decide on the party's presidential nominee. This system seemed too cozy, too elitist to the rising young party leaders who were not members of Congress, and by the 1820s there was pressure to broaden participation in the nominating process. In 1832 the Democratic followers of Andrew Jackson hit upon a new way of nominating the party's presidential candidate: the <u>convention system</u>—a great gathering of local party leaders from throughout the nation. Once again, thanks to the centrifugal forces generated by parties, political participation was broadened.

Participation was broadened in other ways as well. Politics became pageantry, with torchlight parades and stump speaking. Political campaigns became popular festivals. To some people, the transformation represented a cheapening and coarsening of political life. Perhaps that is true. But in the process, politics was made understandable—and fun—to ordinary people. The prestige of parties swelled, and so did participation. In 1824 only 26.9 percent of eligible voters went to the polls, but in 1828 the turnout was over 57 percent, and in 1840 it was 80.2 percent. Democracy exists as a potential when the mass of people have the right to vote; it begins to take on real meaning when people exercise that right. American parties helped to turn the promise of participation into a noisy and boisterous reality.

"The man who has filled the measure of his Country's Glory." JEFFERSON.

Jackson,

DEMOCRACY, And our Country.

"*The Union must be Preserved.*"

Although detested as an ignorant vulgarian by the enlightened classes of the time, Andrew Jackson, elected president in 1828, was an extremely popular figure who helped strengthen the foundations of the Democratic party by uniting western frontiersmen and urban workers into a coalition claiming the support of "the common people."

Standing for (and Against) Something. Imagine going to the polls and choosing from a great array of candidates—from presidential candidates on down to those at the local level—without the benefit of party labels. It would be hard to vote unless you looked up the proposals and biographies of each and every candidate. To be sure, doing so would be a good exercise, but most Americans do not have the time or inclination for exhaustive research. Parties make it easier to choose between candidates. Candidates run on party labels; a party embraces a candidate because the candidate's philosophy is more or less compatible with the party's philosophy. All the voter has to do, then, is to know what the party stands for and then to vote for the party's slate, that is, the list of candidates nominated by the party. This greatly simplifies choosing without making the choice utterly irrational.

A word of caution: we have already pointed out that American parties are "loose" or indistinct. Some Republican candidates do not act very much like Republicans, and the same is true of some Democrats. None of the candidates is bound to the platform of his or her party, and there are few ways of punishing elected politicians who stray from their party's program.

Nevertheless, our party platforms are not meaningless. One analysis of about fourteen hundred promises made between 1944 and 1964 in the platforms of the two major parties showed that 72 percent of them were in fact carried out.[7] Nor is it fair to say, as George Wallace used to, that "there ain't a dime's worth of difference" between the two parties. Each party has linked a wide variety of interests, but these interests have had certain goals in common—goals that have been quite different from those shared by members of the opposition party. In Andrew Jackson's day in the 1830s, the Democrats combined small businessmen, farmers, and laborers into a coalition against the big merchants and manufacturers of the East. These interests produced identifiable party platforms: against national banks and other enterprises that granted exclusive benefits to "the favored few" and against artificial barriers to advancement; for "equality of opportunity," for "the common man," the small entrepreneur, and the blue-collar worker. The Republicans, like the Democrats, also were an improbable alliance of diverse interests, but from the outset, they supported tariffs to protect business, opposed labor unions, worried about excessive immigration, and wanted slavery limited or abolished. Through the years, Democrats and Republicans have continued to show considerable differences in what they endorse and what they reject. During the New Deal period of the 1930s, for example, the Democrats supported an activist role for government in helping the poor and regulating business, while Republicans generally opposed the idea of an activist state.

DEMOCRATS AND REPUBLICANS: IDEOLOGICAL DIFFERENCES

There have been times in our history when it has been hard to see much difference between the parties. One such period was during the 1880s, when Democratic leaders like President Grover Cleveland were scarcely distinguishable from Republicans. Another such period was during the 1950s. In the "Happy Days" decade, both parties endorsed a kind of mild welfarism (Republicans called it "modern Republicanism"), both parties paid homage to private enterprise, neither party said much about civil rights, and the two parties outdid each other in anti-Communist rhetoric. As late as 1960 anyone who watched the famous presidential debates between Republican Richard Nixon and Democrat John Kennedy would find it hard to remember what they disagreed on. But by the end of the 1960s the two parties had begun to develop rather clear ideological differences, and those differences widened during the 1970s and 1980s. Today it is not hard to see their differences on a number of issues:

(Continued on page 435)

DEMOCRATIC AND REPUBLICAN PLATFORMS, 1988

Issue	Democrats	Republicans
Defense	Endorse "stable" defense spending; oppose "dubious new weapons."	Modernize nuclear forces: B-1, B-2, Trident, MX; 600-ship navy; update chemical weapons.
Policy Toward Soviets	Test Soviets' sincerity on arms control, human rights, etc. If they are sincere, we will reciprocate.	Avoid "naive inexperience or overly enthusiastic endorsement of current Soviet rhetoric."
Central America	Support regional peace plan advanced by Costa Rican president Arias; no mention of Contras.	Support Contras.
Trade	Use all means to "export more goods and fewer jobs."	Support free trade.
Economics	Provide advance notice of plant closings; opposed to "unproductive mergers."	Support for "enterprise zones" and deregulation.
Taxes	The "wealthy and the Pentagon should pay their fair share."	"We oppose any attempts to raise taxes."
Housing	Progress toward providing "a decent place to live for every American."	"The best housing policy is sound economic policy."
Environment	Support aggressive enforcement of toxic cleanup, anti-dumping laws, etc.	Provide first a cost-benefit analysis of cleanups; build future nuclear plants according to uniform designs.
Women	Support ERA, comparable worth, right to abortion regardless of ability to pay.	Oppose ERA; support rights of fetus; oppose abortion funding.
Minorities	Support affirmative action, minority set-asides.	Support equal opportunity, oppose quotas.
Crime	Ban "cop-killer" bullets; seek to end greed in economy.	Death penalty for capital crimes; no prison furloughs for murderers.

Source: Adapted from *Congressional Quarterly Weekly Report*, October 22, 1988, pp. 3042-43.

- The Democrats would reduce budget deficits by cutting defense spending and increasing taxes; the Republicans would do it by cutting welfare spending.
- The Democrats endorse race-conscious affirmative action programs as a means of achieving racial equality; the Republicans oppose such programs.
- The Democrats want the Equal Rights Amendment revived; the Republicans say nothing about it in their platform. If asked about it, Republican politicians are generally cool to it.
- Beginning in 1976 the Democrats have endorsed the pro-choice position on abortion in their presidential platforms; Republican platforms endorse the pro-life position.
- The Democrats oppose an amendment allowing prayer in public schools; the Republicans support such an amendment.
- In 1984 Ann Lewis, then director of the Democratic National Committee,

said, "Gay rights is no longer a debatable issue within the Democratic party."
The Republicans have never even considered such a plank.

- The Democrats have opposed the B-1 bomber, the MX missile, and the "Star Wars" antimissile defense; the Republicans have endorsed all of them.
- Democrats have officially endorsed a nuclear freeze; the Republicans have never taken an official position on it, but during the 1980s leading Republicans like President Reagan opposed it.
- Throughout the 1980s most Republicans in Congress supported military aid to the Contras fighting the Marxist-Leninist government of Nicaragua; most Democrats opposed Contra aid.

These positions roughly correspond to the list of liberal and conservative positions discussed in chapter 13. Clearly, the Democrats opt for liberal positions, and the Republicans for conservative ones. Of course, there are a number of mavericks in both parties. Republicans like Kansas senator Nancy Kassebaum argue for the pro-choice position on abortion; Democrats like Oklahoma senator David Boren supported the Contras in the 1980s. But it is probably safe to say most Democrats are more liberal than most Republicans.

Behind the disagreements on specific issues is a general philosophical difference between the two parties. Democrats tend to favor an activist government that seeks solutions to social problems through governmental agencies. Republicans tend to view governmental solutions with suspicion, arguing that problem solving should come through voluntary action. (This is what George Bush meant during the 1988 presidential campaign when he talked about "a thousand points of light.") The fallback Republican position is that if government must get involved, let it be local rather than federal government. Clearly, then, the parties lean in opposite directions on many issues, and that gives the voters a choice when they go to the polls.

THIRD PARTIES

We have been talking entirely about Democrats and Republicans, but there are many lesser political parties in the United States. In the 1988 presidential election there were 17 others, each with its own candidate. But so-called third parties do not do very well in American politics. In 1988 the closest competitor to Republican George Bush and Democrat Michael Dukakis was Ron Paul of the Libertarian party, who won 431,499 votes, or 0.47 percent of the total. The other 16 minor parties fared much worse. The Consumer party, for example, headed by former senator Eugene McCarthy (the candidate of the young dissidents at the stormy 1968 Democratic convention) received 0.03 percent of the total ballots cast (see Table 16.1).

In other presidential elections, minor parties and candidates have played a somewhat greater role, although never as great as people thought they were going to play. Take John Anderson, for example. In 1980 Anderson, then a Republican congressman from Illinois, entered the race for the Republican presidential nomination. When Reagan got the nomination, Anderson bolted from the party and made himself the candidate of his own National Unity party. Anderson was an attractive candidate. With snow-white hair and a resonant voice, he looked "presidential," and he had an enthusiastic corps of volunteers. Nor could he complain of a news blackout. He was on television just about every night, and he kept winning endorsements from movie stars. Some people hoped, and others feared, that he might just pull it off. The result? Less than 7 percent of the popular vote.

When President Harry S. Truman ran in 1948 against Republican governor Thomas E. Dewey, Truman had to worry about parties on his right and left that could siphon off Democratic votes. On the Right were the Dixiecrats, composed of former

TABLE 16-1

437

Party Votes in the 1988 Presidential Election

Candidate and Party	Popular Vote	Percent
George Bush, Republican	48,881,011	53.37
Michael S. Dukakis, Democrat	41,828,350	45.67
Ron Paul, Libertarian	431,499	0.47
Lenora Fulani, New Alliance	218,159	0.24
David Duke, Populist	48,267	0.05
Eugene McCarthy, Consumer	30,510	0.03
James Griffin, American Independent	27,818	0.03
Lyndon LaRouche, National Economic Recovery	25,082	0.03
William Mara, Right to Life	20,497	0.02
Ed Winn, Workers League	18,579	0.02
James Warren, Socialist Workers	13,338	0.01
Herbert Lewin, Peace and Freedom	10,312	0.01
Earl Dodge, Prohibition	7,984	0.01
Larry Holmes, Workers World	7,719	0.01
Willa Kenoyer, Socialist	3,800	0.00
Delmar Dennis, American	3,456	0.00
Jack Herer, Grassroots	1,949	0.00
Louie Youngkite, Independent	372	0.00
John Martin, Third World Assembly	236	0.00
None of these candidates	6,934	0.01

Data source: Associated Press; *New York Times*, Dec. 29, 1988, p. B6. Reprinted with permission.

Third parties get very sparse support in the United States, as is shown by the results of the 1988 presidential election. Of the 17 minor parties running presidential candidates, the Libertarians did the best—with less than half of 1 percent of the vote!

southern Democrats upset by the Democrats' civil rights plank. On the Left were the Progressives, composed of liberal Democrats and others much further to the Left. Neither minor party received enough votes to make a dent in Truman's victory.

Other third parties have included the American Independent party, a creation of then-Alabama governor George Wallace, who was its 1968 presidential candidate; the Populist (or People's) party, which flourished during the 1890s; and the Socialists, who reached their high point in 1912 with the presidential candidacy of Eugene V. Debs.[8] Although each of these parties has had its season in the sun, none has lasted very long. There are at least four reasons for this.

First, the states have made it hard for third parties to get on the ballot. In most states, a candidate must file a petition signed by a certain proportion of registered voters (which election officials squint very hard at, trying to invalidate signatures whenever they can). Many states also require early filing deadlines and high fees for filing. The Supreme Court has struck down some of these practices as discriminatory, but others have been left standing.[9]

Second, our winner-take-all electoral system discriminates against third parties. Congressional races are by district. One—and only one—candidate can win the contest to represent the district in Congress. In these races, the third party candidate is almost always the odd man out. When this happens in 435 districts, it produces zero seats for third parties in the House of Representatives. The same happens in the 50 states when Senate elections are held. At the presidential level, the electoral college system awards *all* of the state's electoral votes to the candidate who wins a majority of popular votes in the state. Again, the third parties get crowded out.

Third, our two major parties steal planks from third party platforms once they discover that the planks are popular. Starting in 1896 the Democrats stole (more accurately, cloned) planks from the Populists, and the Republicans after 1968 did the same to some of the planks of George Wallace's American Independent party. By doing this, the Democrats and Republicans can say to voters: "Why vote for the third party? We offer some of their best planks, and, unlike them, *we* can win!" It is an offer that is hard to refuse.

Fourth, the minor parties are perceived by many American voters as narrow, extremist, or both. Socialist parties have never done well here, in part because Americans are wary of any movement aimed at abolishing private property and the Socialists have never been able to adapt themselves to that fact.[10] Single-issue parties, such as the Right-to-Life party, also do poorly, either because they seem too narrow or extremist or because one of the major parties adopts a similar plank.[11]

Party Reform

As we have seen, political parties have helped expand democratic participation. Yet parties have also been criticized for being elitist, boss-run organizations. This has been a constant theme of reformers over the years: getting rid of the "smoke-filled rooms," "back-room dealings," and pot-bellied "bosses" with big cigars. The caricatures had some truth in them. The business of nominating candidates for public office *was* largely in the hands of the professional politicians who ran the parties. But things changed dramatically in the 1970s. The Democrats spearheaded the revolution, but the Republicans also felt it. The revolution came in the form of rule changes.

This chapter opened with an account of the riots at the 1968 Democratic convention in Chicago. The focus of the protest was Vietnam, but what kept things stirred up was the widespread sense that the Democratic party was running a rigged convention. The peace candidates and peace planks were being methodically crushed by the bosses, who were able to use the rules to their own advantage. The deck was stacked. Nothing was left, then, but to get a new deck.

(Continued on page 440)

Points to Remember

1. A political party is an association that seeks to acquire and maintain control of the government. The American political party system is an indistinct and competitive two-party system.

2. The Founders did not like political parties, but their dislike did not prevent them from joining such parties. The first party under the Constitution was the Federalist party. It was soon challenged by the Jeffersonian Republicans.

3. The Federalist party died out because it was too narrowly based. Since then, the major American parties have been broad coalitions of diverse groups. The major parties are opportunists. To win elections, they often steal planks from minor parties or popular movements—one reason third parties do not last long in America.

4. Parties have served American democracy in at least three ways: They have brought in the "outs"; they have expanded participation; and they have simplified choice.

5. Although ours is an indistinct two-party system, there are recognizable differences between the two major parties. The Democrats tend to be more liberal than the Republicans on specific issues like abortion, public school prayer, and gay rights. More generally, Democrats tend to favor greater federal involvement in solving of social problems.

6. Third parties have done poorly in America for these four reasons: First, the states have made it hard for them to get on the ballot; second, our winner-take-all system works against them; third, the major parties steal their best planks; fourth, many voters perceive them as extremist.

The Socialist party reached its highest level of public support in the early years of the twentieth century. One of the party's most charismatic leaders was Eugene V. Debs, who ran for president in every election from 1900 through 1912 and again in 1920. In the latter election he won almost one million votes, even though he was in prison for violating the 1917 Espionage Act by publicly denouncing America's participation in World War I.

VARIOUS THIRD PARTIES IN AMERICAN HISTORY

Election	Party	Platform	Percentage of Votes
1832	Anti-Masonic Party	Opposed to Masons and Andrew Jackson.	7.8
1860	Constitutional Union	Conservative southerners and northerners opposed to secession.	12.6
1892	Populist	Endorsed anti-monopoly, regulation of railroads, free silver, progressive income tax.	8.5
1912	Progressive ("Bull Moose")	Aimed at regulating "big business."	27.4
1924	Progressive	Supported public ownership of natural resources and railroads, popular election of judges, outlawing war, reducing armaments.	16.6
1948	Progressive	Endorsed peace with Soviets; opposed alliance with "fascist" regimes and Marshall Plan.	2.4
1948	States' Rights ("Dixiecrat")	Opposed racial desegregation.	2.4
1968	American Independent	Headed by Alabama governor George Wallace, opposed busing, civil rights laws, tax increases; endorsed tougher laws on street crime.	13.5
1980	Independent (National Unity party)	Supported women's rights, defense cuts, tougher environmental laws, tax reform.	6.6

TABLE **16-2**

Votes Cast for Minor Parties Since 1920*

Year	Candidate	Party	Votes
1920	Eugene Debs	Socialist	919,799
	P. P. Christensen	Farmer-Labor	265,411
1924	Robert LaFollette	Progressive	4,831,269
1928	Norman Thomas	Socialist	267,835
1932	Norman Thomas	Socialist	881,951
	William Z. Foster	Communist	102,785
1936	William Lemke	Unionist	882,479
	Norman Thomas	Socialist	187,720
1948	Strom Thurmond	States' Rights	1,176,125
	Henry Wallace	Progressive	1,157,326
1952	Vincent Hallinan	Progressive	140,023
1956	T. Coleman Andrews	States' Rights	111,123
1968	George Wallace	American Independent	9,906,473
1972	John Schmitz	American Independent	1,009,482
1976	Eugene McCarthy	Independent	756,691
	Roger McBride	Libertarian	173,011
1980	John Anderson	Independent	5,720,060
	Ed Clark	Libertarian	921,299
1984	David Bergland	Libertarian	228,314
1988	Ron Paul	Libertarian	431,499
	Lenora Fulani	New Alliance	218,159

*Only candidates with more than 100,000 votes are included.

Data source: Statistical Abstract, 1987, p. 228; Associated Press; *New York Times.*

THE DEMOCRATS: CHANGING THE RULES

To understand the post-1968 rules changes in the Democratic party, we must first understand how the party—in fact both parties—nominated presidential candidates prior to the Chicago convention. In the past, the nomination was done by the votes of delegates at a national party convention. Sometimes it took many ballots before one candidate emerged with a clear majority. (In 1924 it took 103 ballots before the Democrats nominated John W. Davis.) The delegates got to the convention through a variety of means, depending on the laws and party practices in the various states. Mayors, governors, members of Congress and most other elected officials from the party were virtually assured of delegate status. Other delegates arrived at the convention as a result of caucus meetings. For Democratic and Republican conventions, the caucus structure was pyramid-shaped: Many little caucuses from local areas, or <u>precincts</u>, would meet and pick delegates to fewer but larger delegate-selection bodies; these, in turn, would pick the state's delegates to the national convention. On paper this method looked very democratic because the delegates were the result of a long series of votes. But what usually happened was that established party leaders guided the whole operation. Politicians from the local party clubhouses went to the precinct caucuses and voted as they were told to vote.

Sometimes there were surprises. In 1963-64 Senator Barry Goldwater's enthusiastic supporters "crashed" local Republican precinct caucuses and voted for Goldwater delegates to the 1964 national convention. The convention was then packed with Goldwaterites. (Senator Henry Cabot Lodge, a Republican regular, looked around at the convention and asked, "Who are these people?") But such takeovers were rare—and rarer still in the Democratic party, where leaders had firm control. When, in the months before the 1968 convention, Eugene McCarthy's volunteers tried to do what Goldwater's people had done four years earlier, they found themselves frustrated at every turn. They would show up at a precinct caucus, only to find out that the meeting place had been changed at the last minute. By the time they found the new place, Humphrey delegates had already been selected and the voting was over. Or they would find out that all the delegates had been picked much earlier. Or they would show up to vote and find themselves barred by a variety of rules hastily enacted before the meeting.

One way to avoid such tricks is to select convention delegates by means of primary elections instead of precinct caucuses. A primary election is a formal, secret-ballot election, usually limited to party members, that decides who is to be the party's candidate. Primaries were first introduced in 1903, but until the 1970s they played a minor role in the nomination of presidential candidates. In 1952, for example, Senator Estes Kefauver of Tennessee won most of the Democratic primaries he entered but was beaten for the nomination by Illinois governor Adlai E. Stevenson II. Very few states had presidential primaries. As late as 1968, only 17 states did, and in some the primaries were just "beauty contests," designed to test the popularity of candidates; the actual delegates were picked by caucuses. (This is still true in some states.) Only a little more than one-third of the delegates to the 1968 Democratic convention got there through primaries. The rest were largely composed of mayors, governors, other office-holders, and those picked through boss-controlled precinct caucuses.

THE NEW RULES AND THEIR RESULTS

Even though the 1968 Democratic convention was dominated by the regulars, the convention majority made one concession to the reformers. It voted to set up a special Commission on Party Structure and Delegate Selection to propose rule changes for future conventions. The commission was co-chaired by South Dakota senator George McGovern and Representative Donald W. Fraser. In 1970 the McGovern-Fraser Commission issued a report whose major recommendations included these:

1. *Fair-play rules.* Party caucuses must be open to all members, announced in advance, held in public places, and governed by written rules.
2. *Affirmative action.* Call it a system of "numerical goals," or call it a "quota system." Whatever the name, the commission thus spelled out the meaning: Women, minorities, and young people 18 or more years old must be represented at all future conventions "in reasonable relationship to their presence in the population." If 12 percent of the state is black, at least 12 percent of the delegates must be black.
3. *Democratic selection procedures.* Three-quarters of the delegates must be selected either by fair-play caucuses or by primary elections.
4. *No unit rule.* An end to the practice, used by some state delegations (California, for example), of casting all of the state's votes for the candidate who received a majority of votes among the state's delegates.

Even though the regulars still controlled the party in 1970, they agreed to the commission's proposals; they thought they were throwing a bone to the reformers to

(Continued on page 442)

TABLE **16-3**

1988 Convention Delegates and the Public on the Issues

	Democratic Delegates	— The Public —			Republican Delegates
		Dem. voters	Total adults	Rep. voters	
Political philosophy					
Describe own political views as conservative	5%	22%	30%	43%	60%
Describe own political views as liberal	39	25	20	12	1
Size of government					
Prefer smaller government providing fewer services	16	33	43	59	87
Prefer bigger government providing more services	58	56	44	30	3
Domestic policy					
Favor increased federal spending on education programs	90	76	71	67	41
Favor increased federal spending on day care and after-school care for children	87	56	52	44	36
Say abortion should be legal, as it is now	72	43	40	39	29
Say Government is paying too little attention to the needs of blacks	68	45	34	19	14
Foreign and military issues					
Favor keeping spending on military and defense programs at least at current level	32	59	66	73	84
Are more worried about Communist takeover in Central America than about U.S. involvement in a war there	12	25	37	55	80
Support use of military to stop inflow of drugs	54	61	61	63	67

Source: Reprinted from the *New York Times* with permission.

Delegates' views were based on telephone interviews with 739 delegates to the Republican National Convention, conducted July 22–August 4, 1988, and with 1,059 delegates to the Democratic National Convention, conducted June 20–July 12, 1988. Views of "total adults" and each party's registered voters were based on telephone interviews conducted as part of *New York Times*/CBS News polls in March, May, July, or August 1988.

(Continued from page 441) prevent any more party splits like the one in Chicago two years earlier. They did not realize that by agreeing to these changes, they were signing their own political death warrants. For, as a major study by political analyst Byron E. Shafer has shown, the effect of the rule changes was to constrict—squeeze out—the old leadership and replace it with a new class of leaders.[12] The fair-play rules now permitted amateur activists to join the party caucuses and elect their own delegates. The quota system meant that feminist and black activists were now assured of a much larger member-

(Continued on page 443)

TABLE **16-4**　443

1988 Convention Delegates and How They Compare

	Rep.	Dem.		Rep.	Dem.
Sex			**Age**		
Men	63%	48%	18-29 years	4%	4%
Women	37	52	30-39	13	22
Race			40-49	28	33
White	96	70	50-59	30	25
Black	3	21	60 and older	25	16
Hispanic	3	8	**Religion**		
Education			Protestant total	70	51
High school education or less	10	9	White Protestant	67	31
Some college	21	18	Catholic	24	30
College graduate	26	21	Jewish	2	6
Beyond college	42	52	**Occupation**		
Political philosophy			Lawyer	14	14
Very liberal	*	15	Executive	21	11
Somewhat liberal	1	24	Other profession	12	17
Moderate	36	50	Union official	0	6
Somewhat conservative	41	3	Public official	16	16
Very conservative	19	1	Government employee	2	9
Party activity			White collar	10	12
Work year-in, year-out	82	74	Blue collar	2	3
Work if candidates, issues matter	16	22	Homemaker or volunteer	7	3
Delegate to previous convention?			Retired	8	5
Yes	41	38	**Family income**		
No	59	62	Under $25,000	2	6
Position holders			$25,000-49,999	21	33
Hold party position now	60	43	$50,000-99,999	39	40
Hold elected public office now	28	26	$100,000 or more	27	16
			Marital status		
			Married	83	70
			Widowed	4	4
			Divorced, separated	6	13
			Never married	6	12

*Less than one half of 1 percent

Source: Reprinted from the *New York Times* with permission.

(Continued from page 442)

ship at the convention. In general, the new selection procedures forced the regulars either to let the new people into their caucuses or give up on caucuses altogether and move toward primary elections. Either way, they would find themselves elbowed out of power. The effect, writes Shafer, was to shuffle the traditional class constituencies served by the parties:

> Before reform, there was an American party system in which one party, the Republicans, was primarily responsible to white-collar constituencies and in which another, the Democrats, was primarily responsible to blue-collar constituencies. After reform, there were two parties each responsive to quite different white-collar coalitions, while the old blue-collar majority within the Democratic party was forced to try to squeeze back into the party once identified predominantly with its needs.[13]

By 1972 the changes were evident in the makeup of the presidential convention. The traditional coalition of big city officials and union leaders had been evicted. Only 10 percent of the delegates were union officials, less than a third had ever held any party or governmental office, and only 11 percent had attended the 1968 convention. The representation of women, on the other hand, went from 13 percent in 1968 to 38 percent in 1972; blacks increased from 5.5 percent to nearly 15 percent. And 27 percent of the delegates were under thirty. This convention nominated George McGovern for president.

The general election of 1972 gave critics of the new rule changes an opportunity to say "I told you so!" McGovern was roundly defeated by President Richard Nixon, who won 60.7 percent of the popular vote to McGovern's 37.5 percent. (McGovern won the electoral votes of only one state, Massachusetts, plus the District of Columbia's three electoral votes.) Blue-collar workers deserted him in droves. So did Catholics and white southerners. Critics charged that the reason for these defections was that McGovern was perceived as an extreme liberal. He promised a guaranteed annual income for all Americans, amounting to an annual $1,000 for every man, woman, and child. He also said that he would "crawl to Hanoi on my knees" if necessary to achieve peace in Vietnam. Such talk did not endear him to the majority of American voters.

Was there some sort of link between the new rules and the nomination of candidates like McGovern? Yes, said the critics. For the rule changes made the party responsive to wealthy liberals, black radicals, feminists, college professors, and other elites cut off from "middle America." These elites wrote new platforms that included planks supporting gay rights, abortion, tax increases, racial quotas, and other positions rejected by many traditional Democrats. The new rules led to new rulers and new platforms that were out of touch with the American mainstream; therefore, the Democrats would continue to lose elections.

Today the critics think their prophecy has come to pass. Although the Democrats narrowly won the White House in 1976, they lost in 1980, 1984, and 1988. The reason seems to be that, at least when it comes to presidential races, they have lost the support of critical constituencies—groups like Catholics, white ethnics, and white southerners—who were once the backbone of the Democratic party. The Solid

"My God! I went to sleep a Democrat and I've awakened a Republican."
Drawing by Dana Fradon; © 1984 The New Yorker Magazine, Inc.

FIGURE **16-3**

445

Party Reform

Young Voters Move to the G.O.P.

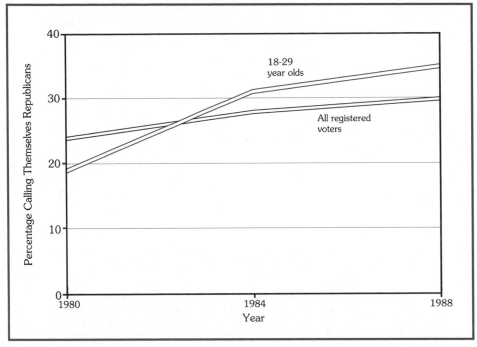

Source: New York Times/CBS News Poll, October 31, 1988, p. B4. Reprinted with permission.

Since the beginning of the 1980s, the Republican party has been enjoying support from younger voters (those 18-29 years of age). Whether or not it will continue to do so remains to be seen, but the general tendency of Americans has been to stick with the party that attracted them when they reached voting age. If that trend continues, many of the young Republicans of the 1980s will probably stay Republican as they get older.

South once meant "solidly Democratic," and Catholics were so Democratic that one joke had Mrs. Murphy, after hearing that Tommy Breen had gone Republican, exclaim, "That couldn't be—I just saw him at Mass last Sunday!" If Tommy Breen goes to Mass today, there is a better than even chance he voted for George Bush in 1988.

More ominously, perhaps, from the Democrats' standpoint, there is evidence that young voters, those from 18 to 29, have been moving toward the GOP—Grand Old Party, a term applied to the Republican party. In 1980 only 19 percent of young voters called themselves Republicans, while 42 percent identified themselves as Democrats. By 1988 the Republicans were almost even with the Democrats among voters under 30. There is a double irony here: First it was the Democrats who went out of their way to appeal to young people by starting an affirmative action plan to guarantee their "reasonable" representation at conventions; second, it was during the tenure of Ronald Reagan, our oldest president, that young people started their move toward the Republicans. If this movement continues, or even if the Democrats are unable to win back those who have joined the Republicans, it could make it difficult for Democrats to stage a comeback.

Still, the prophecies of Democratic doom must be taken with several grains of salt. Remember, the Democrats managed to win the White House in 1976 despite— or perhaps because of—the rule changes. Jimmy Carter took advantage of the new rules, coming out of nowhere to get the nomination through a string of victories in primaries and new-style caucuses. He then went on to beat a seasoned Republican

TABLE **16-5**

Party Balance in Congress

Congress	Years	President	Senate (100 Members)			House (435 Members)		
			Dem.	Rep.	Other	Dem.	Rep.	Other
89th	1965-67	Johnson (D)	68	32		295	140	
90th	1967-69	Johnson (D)	64	36		248	187	
91st	1969-71	Nixon (R)	58	42		243	192	
92nd	1971-73	Nixon (R)	54	44	2	255	180	
94th	1973-75	Nixon/Ford (R)	56	42	2	242	192	1
94th	1975-77	Ford (R)	61	37	2	291	144	
95th	1977-79	Carter (D)	61	38	1	292	143	
96th	1979-81	Carter (D)	58	41	1	277	158	
97th	1981-83	Reagan (R)	46	53	1	242	190	
98th	1983-85	Reagan (R)	46	54		269	166	
99th	1985-87	Reagan (R)	47	53		253	182	
100th	1987-89	Reagan (R)	54	46		258	177	
101st	1989-91	Bush (R)	55	45		262	173	

Source: Clerk of the House of Representatives and Secretary of the Senate.

Listed above are the party affiliations of members of the House and Senate for the 89th to the 101st Congress. The figures represent membership at the beginning of each term, except for the 101st Congress, which lists figures as of the 1988 congressional elections. The 97th Congress had three vacancies in the House of Representatives.

Massachusetts Republican Enrique Matos displays a sign expressing his feelings toward Democratic presidential candidate Michael Dukakis at the Republican National Convention in 1988. Most Hispanic voters are Democrats, but some, particularly Cubans, tend to favor Republicans. In the future, both parties will be vigorously competing for the Hispanic vote.

politician, Gerald Ford. True, Carter lost the White House in 1980, but it is very hard to isolate the reasons for that loss. Our elections are decided by many factors, including personality, media coverage, the state of the economy, incumbency, campaign spending, good or bad campaign advice, and luck.

Carter got bad media coverage, had bad luck (the Iran hostage crisis, the Soviet invasion of Afghanistan), got hit with soaring oil prices that fueled high inflation, and ran against "The Great Communicator" (Ronald Reagan). It seems far-fetched to blame his defeat on the rule changes in his party. As for Democratic losses in the 1984 and 1988 races, should they be attributed to McGovernite domination of the Democratic nominating process or to the dull, untelegenic personalities of Walter Mondale and Michael Dukakis? Anyway, if we leave aside the last three presidential races, the Democrats have not done badly in electoral contests since 1972. They continue to control both houses of Congress (in 1986 they won the Senate back from the Republicans) and most of the state governments. Many of their planks and goals, such as trimming the defense budget, nonintervention in Nicaragua, and increasing funds for drug control, remain popular with the American majority.

SUPERDELEGATES, BROKERED CONVENTIONS

The changes in the Democratic party between 1968 and 1972 have been modified in various ways. Subsequent party reform commissions made new recommendations, many of which were adopted. The most important of these came in 1984 when the party provided for superdelegates. Numbering more than 600 and drawn almost entirely from the ranks of Democratic office-holders—especially governors, senators, and House members—superdelegates are party members who are guaranteed seats at the convention. They do not have to compete in caucuses or primaries, and they are not tied to any particular candidate. The idea behind superdelegates is to give more input to political professionals in selecting presidential candidates; their political experience and expertise are meant to balance the zeal of the "committed" delegates.

In a way, this represents a retreat from the spirit of the original 1972 reforms. The complaint then was that professional politicians had *too much* control over the nomination process; the idea behind the reforms was to reach out to the rank and file who participate in primaries and caucuses. The reformers wanted no more brokered conventions, conventions in which the candidate was selected through a series of quiet deals made between party professionals who controlled blocs of delegates.

In 1984 and 1988 the Democrats incurred no risk of a brokered convention because their leading candidates (Walter Mondale in 1984 and Michael Dukakis in 1988) each had won a majority of delegates by convention time. But it could happen in 1992 or at any future convention if none of the leading candidates secures a majority. In 1988 it looked for a while as if neither Michael Dukakis nor his nearest rival, Jesse Jackson, would get a majority. There was talk then of the 600-plus superdelegates going to the "inevitable winner," the candidate with the largest plurality. Nobody knows whether or not that really would have happened. Suppose, for example, that Jesse Jackson came in second in a race that produced no absolute majority. Would black superdelegates pass over Jackson to support a white candidate with only a plurality?

The prospect of a splintered Democratic convention may haunt the Democrats in 1992 because of new rule changes. In response to demands from the Jackson forces at the 1988 convention, the party mandated (1) fewer superdelegates for the next convention, (2) a reduction in bonuses (extra delegates) for states carried by the Democrats in the last election, and (3) the elimination of winner-take-all district primary elections.

THE REPUBLICAN RESPONSE

The Republicans have never gone as far as the Democrats in changing the rules. They have no affirmative action guidelines for selecting delegates, nor have they set up as many rules for challenging the credentials of state delegations. According to political scientists William J. Crotty and Gary C. Jacobson:

> [Republican change] has not followed the participant-oriented, structural-change path taken within the Democratic party. Rather, the Republican party has emphasized increased nationalization and institutionalization of the party by, in effect, making the national party more relevant in politically traditional ways: providing new services and support. [14]

The Republicans have streamlined their convention procedures and enhanced communication among the delegates. They have also prohibited racial discrimination and urged—but, unlike the Democrats, not required—their state delegations to encourage broad-based participation. The philosophy underlying the Republican changes is that the national party organization should be a coordinating and service agency for the state parties. [15]

Still, the Republicans have been carried along by legal and social changes initiated by the Democrats. During the 1970s Democratically-controlled state legislatures began mandating presidential primaries, so that by 1988 about 65 percent of the delegates in both national conventions were selected by that means. Most of the rest were selected by caucuses, and even here the changes put in place by the Democrats have affected the Republicans. The caucuses are now more visible than they were in

(Continued on page 448)

Before 1968

Party-Dominated

The nomination decision is largely in the hands of party leaders. Candidates win by enlisting support of state and local party machines.

Few Primaries

Most delegates are selected by state party establishments, with little or no public participation. Some primaries are held, but their results do not necessarily determine the nominee.

Short Campaigns

Candidates generally do not begin their campaign until early in the election year.

Easy Money

Candidates frequently are able to raise large amounts of money quickly by tapping a handful of wealthy contributors. There are no federal limits on spending by candidates.

Limited Media Coverage

Campaigns are followed by print journalists and, in later years, by television. But press coverage of campaigns is not intensive and generally does not play a major role in influencing the process.

Late Decisions

Events early in the campaign year, such as the New Hampshire primary, are important but not decisive. States that pick delegates late in the year, such as California, frequently play an important role in selecting nominee.

Open Conventions

National party conventions frequently begin with nomination still undecided. Outcome determined by maneuvering and negotiations among party factions, often stretching over multiple ballots.

Source: Congressional Quarterly, Inc., *Elections*, 1988. Reprinted with permission.

Since 1968

Candidate-Dominated

Candidates' campaigns are independent of party establishments. Endorsements by party leaders have little effect on nomination choice.

Many Primaries

Most delegates are selected by popular primaries. Nominations are determined largely by primary results.

Long Campaigns

Candidates begin laying groundwork for campaigns three or four years before the election. Candidates who are not well organized at least 18 months before the election may have little chance of winning.

Difficult Fund-Raising

Campaign contributions are limited to $1,000 per person, so candidates must work endlessly to raise money from thousands of small contributors. Campaign spending is limited by law at the national and state level.

Media-Focused

Campaigns are covered intensively by the media, particularly television. Media treatment of candidates plays crucial role in determining nominee.

"Front-Loaded"

Early events, such as the Iowa caucuses and New Hampshire primary, play an increasingly important role in nomination. The nomination may be decided even before many major states vote.

Closed Conventions

Nominee is determined before convention, which does little more than ratify decision made in primaries and caucuses. Convention activities are focused on creating favorable media image of candidate for general-election campaign.

(Continued from page 447) the past; the news media pay much more attention to them. The effect of all this is to sweep Republicans as well as Democrats into the drama of participatory politics. It has also made it easier for Republican outsiders to get nominated with support from grass-roots enthusiasts, in much the same manner as Jimmy Carter was able to secure the Democratic nomination in 1976. Ronald Reagan, for example, was not the favorite of Republican "insiders," the party professionals and office-holders, in 1980. If the nomination had been left to them, they might have named a centrist like Robert Dole or Gerald Ford or George Bush. Reagan, they feared, would get tagged as an

(Continued on page 450)

Has Party Reform Succeeded?

YES William J. Crotty

Based upon William J. Crotty, *Decision for the Democrats: Reforming the Party Structure* (Johns Hopkins University Press, 1978).

Crotty, a political science professor who served as a consultant to the McGovern–Fraser Commission, says that the rule changes "introduced a remarkable era to American politics"—one in which grass-roots participation was at last possible in the Democratic party. "The party was opened and, in the process, made more responsive to the representatives of its rank and file." The work of the McGovern–Fraser Commission "was responsible for turning a relatively closed nominating process, controlled primarily by party regulars, into one directly reflective of the concerns of those party members who chose to participate in delegate selection." Summing up the position of the "reformers," Crotty says that they "would argue that the grass-roots party members should be represented in all party bodies and should . . . control their deliberations." The reformers "believe in a participant-oriented party, accessible to those who cared to identify with it and take part in its activities, and open to influence from below." The new rule changes have also established "a code of fair and decent behavior" in the nominating process, bringing rationality, openness, and equity to a complex system.

NO Everett Carll Ladd

Based upon Everett Carll Ladd, Jr., *Where Have All the Voters Gone?* (W. W. Norton & Company, Inc., 1978).

Ladd, also a political science professor, says that the supporters of the rule changes "could not be more wrong" in their "notion that it is 'rank-and-file citizens' who benefit from party 'reform' and the elite who suffer; just the opposite is the case." For a century and a half, says Ladd, parties served to extend democracy by giving lower-class voters candidates who served their interests. "In fact, it has been upper-middle-class groups, not the broad mass of Americans, who have confronted the party organizations . . . who have attacked the legitimacy of 'bosses,' who have urged 'democratization.' And it is these highly educated, well-informed, relatively prosperous groups who have primarily benefited from party 'reform,' for they tend to participate in more open nomination processes at a rate that far exceeds that of 'rank-and-file-citizens.' " Ladd cites figures showing the extremely low turnout of eligible voters for presidential primaries and suggesting that these political elites also tend to be economic and educational elites; these voters, he says, not the less affluent, are the chief beneficiaries of party "reform."

Postscript

Behind Crotty's and Ladd's conflicting views on party reform is a fundamental disagreement on the meaning of *democracy*. For Crotty, the reforms were democratic because they expanded the *opportunity* for grass-roots participation; Ladd suggests that the *effect* of the reforms was antidemocratic because in fact, so he contends, the reforms *increased* the influence of amateur-activist elites within the parties.

A provocative and still-relevant book on party reform is Austin Ranney's *Curbing the Mischiefs of Faction* (Berkeley, CA: University of California Press, 1975). For an study of how political "machines" have worked, see Martin and Susan Tolchin, *To the Victor . . . Political Patronage from the Clubhouse to the White House* (New York: Vintage, 1972). Byron E. Shafer, *Quiet Revolution: The Struggle for the Democratic Party and the Shaping of Post-Reform Politics* (New York: Russell Sage Foundation, 1983) is a comprehensive "inside story" of the changes wrought in the Democratic party between 1968 and 1972.

(Continued from page 448) extremist, another Barry Goldwater. It was the primary system and the new attention to grass-roots party members that allowed Reagan to be nominated—and, in a more subtle way, that may have helped move Republican centrists closer to Reagan's positions on issues.

Only a minority of eligible voters, usually between 20 and 30 percent, vote in primary elections, and an even smaller minority bothers to come out to caucuses. Primaries and reformed caucuses tend to attract the activist, who generally feels very strongly about issues. Among the Republicans, primaries tend to bring out the more conservative members of the party; Democratic primaries bring out the more liberal voters. It appears, then, that the party reforms first put into place in 1972 have helped to make the Democrats more liberal and the Republicans more conservative than they were in the 1950s and 1960s. Whether or not the reforms have made the parties more democratic remains debatable. In this chapter's Taking Sides section (on the previous page), two political scientists, William J. Crotty and Everett Carll Ladd, Jr., disagree on whether the rule changes really democratized the parties.

The Future of Parties

Where are our political parties headed? Are they in decline? Many observers think so. They note the great increase in those who call themselves "independents," voters belonging to no party. In 1952, 22 percent of Americans so described themselves; today about a third of American voters classify themselves as independent. There has also been a great increase in ticket-splitting, voting for one party's candidate for Congress and another party's candidate for president. In 1948 about a third of the voters interviewed by pollsters said they had split their tickets; by 1968 nearly one-half had; in 1988 over 60 percent had. People just do not have the kind of party loyalties they used to have. Certain groups, such as blacks and Jews, still seem to be wedded to one party, but most voters have been indulging in promiscuous relationships with both parties.

Moreover, the party organizations lack the power they once had. They have lost control over the nominating process. They do not have reliable workers. What factors lie behind this apparent weakening of political parties? Over the past half-century or so, four developments have had an adverse effect on parties.

FIGURE **16-4**

451

The Future of
Parties

**Congressional District Winners:
1988 Presidential-House Voting**

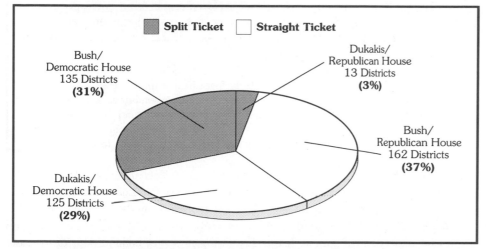

Source: Congressional Quarterly Weekly Report, July 8, 1989, p. 1710. Reprinted with permission.

In the past, Americans tended to vote straight party tickets, that is, to vote for the same party for president as for Congress. Today, many split their tickets, as evidenced by the 1988 national elections, in which over a third did so. Democrats split tickets more often than Republicans; in 1988 large numbers of registered Democrats voted for a Democratic Congress and a Republican president.

WHY PARTIES ARE NOT WHAT THEY USED TO BE

The Spread of Primaries. More and more primaries have become the principal method of nominating candidates. This takes away from the power of party leaders and weakens party organizations. It permits outsiders with no ties to the party organization to get the nomination by piling up a string of primary victories.

The weakened condition of the party organization is shown in the diminished importance of the national party convention. At one time, these conventions were grand deliberative assemblies, infused with drama and excitement. After all, the convention decided who was going to be the party's nominee for the highest office in the land. All sorts of wheeling and dealing, bargaining, and compromising went on before the delegates finally lined up behind a winning candidate. Most of that is gone today. Although the Democrats have tried to give some power back to the political professionals by reserving seats for superdelegates, it has not really restored the old convention. In theory the superdelegates can play a pivotal role at the convention, but in fact they apparently will do no more than back the candidate who has already won the greatest number of delegates in the months *before* the convention. Prior to 1972 the main function of the party convention was to nominate the party's candidate for president of the United States. After 1972 that function was turned into the much more passive one of merely registering the votes of the various candidates and announcing the winner. Of course, there are other things to do, like writing platforms and whipping up party spirit for the coming campaign. But platforms do not bind the candidates, and the old "give 'em hell" oratory often sounds pompous and tedious these days. The television networks, in fact, have decided to give up live convention coverage.

"Boss Tube." Long before the networks decided to abandon live convention coverage, television had already damaged the prestige of parties. To begin with, it took over much of the communications role that party organizations once performed. There was a time in American life when ward heelers—party workers who went door-to-door to make sure that people voted for the organization's candidate—were a major source of information about politics. Now the television correspondent and anchorperson tell us what is going on in politics, make judgments about which politicians are up-and-coming, and retail all the political gossip. *New York Times* correspondent Hedrick Smith writes:

> In effect, Boss Tube has succeeded Boss Tweed of Tammany Hall, Boss Crump of Memphis, and the Daley machine in Chicago. . . . Television brings politicians right into the living room and lets voters form their own impressions, rather than voters having to depend on what local party bosses, union leaders, church spokesmen, or business chiefs say. . . . For many candidates it has replaced going door to door.[16]

Smith may be a bit naive to think that television "lets voters form their own impressions." Television correspondents are seldom shy about giving us their impressions. But his larger point is correct: They have taken away the job that used to be performed by party leaders and their lieutenants.

The politicians, of course, know this very well. Every waking hour of the day, they are trying to figure out how to get on television and how to look good while they are there. "Today, you don't use your brain or your gut," one prominent senator grumbled in 1986, "all you use is your pollster and your filmmaker. They've replaced the party boss."[17] The television news reporters are contemptuous of this lust for coverage. This bring us to another, more subtle, way that television has hurt parties.

Parties, of course, are run by politicians, and television has a way of making all politicians look like crooks, or fools, or at least crass opportunists. Television, being a visual medium, accentuates the lurid aspects of politics. And television reporters seem to have an especially cynical view of politicians. Political analyst Edward Jay Epstein, who spent over a year interviewing television journalists and watching them at work, noted how they regarded politicians:

> The working hypothesis almost universally shared among correspondents is that politicians are suspect; their public images probably false, their public statements disingenuous, their moral pronouncements hypocritical, their motives self-serving, and their promises ephemeral.[18]

This attitude, as Epstein shows in his book, works its way into television accounts of political events. The content of what goes on is often downplayed in favor of "colorful" pieces on the misdeeds of politicians. With this kind of coverage, it is difficult for Americans to have much respect for those who run our political parties.

Reduction of Patronage. Parties once derived a reliable and loyal body of workers from patronage—that is, rewarding good campaigners with jobs once the party got in power. But beginning in 1883 with the passage of the Pendleton Act, party patronage began to be threatened by civil service reform. The Pendleton Act set up a procedure for granting federal jobs on the basis of competitive examinations. During the next half-century, the civil service concept worked its way throughout the federal bureaucracy and into state and local government as well. Although there are still large numbers of patronage jobs at the state and local level, most of the jobs in the federal bureaucracy are filled by competitive exams, and even at the state and local level, the federal government's standards have made inroads. For example, many federal grant-in-aid programs require that the jobs be filled by the candidates who score highest on competitive examinations.

New York City's Tammany Hall is decked out in gala attire for the Democratic Convention in 1924. This famous clubhouse dominated politics in New York City for well over a century, since it controlled nominations and patronage in a heavily Democratic city. Its power was broken at the end of the 1950s, and its last leader, Carmine DeSapio, went to prison for corruption.

The reduction of patronage means that one of the chief rewards for loyal party workers has been severely cut back. For many people, party zeal is a sufficient motivator, but people are usually zealous about causes more than about parties. Their loyalty to the party lasts only as long as the parties do what they want. That is not the kind of loyalty that sustains party organizations through good times and bad.

Decline of Parties as Charitable Organizations. Historically, our national parties derived their strength from local party organizations, which in turn built their power not only through patronage—even in the gaudiest days of patronage, there were not enough jobs for everyone—but by helping people in need. At the turn of the century, George Washington Plunkitt, a leader of New York City's Tammany Hall, revealed how he recruited new Democratic voters. Every time he heard a fire engine, he chased after it to see who had gotten burned out of their home. Plunkitt explained what would happen then:

If a family is burned out . . . I don't refer them to the Charity Organization Society, which would investigate their case in a month or two and decide they were worthy of help about the time they are dead of starvation. I just get quarters for them, buy clothes for them if their clothes were burned up, and fix them up till they get things runnin' again. It's philanthropy, but it's politics, too—mighty good politics. Who can tell how many votes one of these fires brings me? The poor are the most grateful people in the world, and let me tell you, they have more friends in their neighborhoods than the rich have in theirs.[19]

Such philanthropy was once a common feature of local political parties. The widow got free coal delivery and food baskets through her local party leaders. She and her relatives repaid this favor with a kind of gut loyalty that always puzzled and annoyed middle-class reformers. But today the chances are that the single parent, and the people who are burned out of their homes, have other resources. There are professional social workers and agencies, welfare money, food stamps, Social Security, and other forms of assistance that do not depend upon the charity of political leaders. This "professionalization of welfare" has taken away an important function that parties once served and thus weakened their support among the population at large.

WHAT THE CHANGES MEAN

All these factors together have sapped some of the organizational strength of political parties. This loss of vigor has been deplored by many writers and perhaps with good reason. Parties still serve a number of good purposes. Yet the weakening of parties, at least from what they once were, is probably an irreversible process. We can no more abolish primaries than we can abolish television or Social Security pensions. (Nor, presumably, would many of us want to do so.) We cannot turn back the clock to the time when parties were quite different from what they are today.

It is also possible that too much has been made of the decline of parties. Although Americans will still split their tickets and switch loyalties from time to time, and although a substantial portion of them will call themselves independents, most will probably continue to identify with one party or another, vote along party lines, and run for office on party labels. The parties will still incline toward differing philosophies and programs and thus give Americans a choice when they go to the polls.

Points to Remember

1. Political parties have been weakened by the spread of primary elections, the influence of the mass media, the reduction of patronage, and the decline of parties as charitable institutions.

2. Primaries have turned over the nomination process to rank-and-file party members, undermining the power of party leaders to designate the nominees.

3. Mass media, especially television, have replaced party organizations as sources of political information and gossip, and television news reporters tend to denigrate all politicians.

4. Civil service reform has gradually eaten into the power that parties once had to hand out massive numbers of jobs.

5. Parties once functioned as charitable institutions—there was the proverbial free coal delivery for the widow—but since the 1930s charity has become professionalized and has been taken over by the government, thus removing another function of parties.

6. Despite the weakening of party ties, our two-party system seems here to stay. You cannot win national office without the backing of one of them, for most Americans still identify themselves as Democrats or Republicans. Parties continue to offer Americans different philosophies and programs.

Nor should we forget one of the other important functions that parties have served and still do serve. They have brought together people of very different backgrounds—blacks and whites, Jews and Christians, agnostics and fundamentalists, old-line Americans and recent immigrants—and taught them the art of compromise. That lesson lies at the heart of democracy, and our parties teach it to each new generation of Americans that comes along.

Reflections

It does not take much imagination to figure out what the party recruiters must have thought of the Irish they saw coming down the gangplank in the late 1840s. They must have despised everything about them: their accents, their religion, their attitudes. But they greeted them warmly: "Hello. Welcome to America. We're from the Democratic party. . . ."

The Protestant party leaders were going to use the Irish. The Irish would pass out campaign literature and buttons and ribbons. They would get their people out to torchlight parades. Above all, they would swell the voters' rolls. Yes, the Irish would make good foot soldiers. But soon the Irish were not content to be foot soldiers, they wanted to be generals. They wanted to run the Democratic machines—and within a few decades, they did.

Fifty years later, Irish ward heelers were greeting the latest immigrants: Jews, Poles, Italians, and other white ethnics. They probably had no more liking for these new arrivals than the earlier groups had had for them, but they needed the votes. Then, after a while, the new immigrants began to rise through the ranks. Over the next half-century, the Irish were forced to share power with them. In Chicago, Poles became a force to be reckoned with. In New York City, an Italian took over Tammany Hall, the famous Democratic clubhouse. Jews were becoming increasingly powerful in party circles.

The votes of women, blacks, and Hispanics had been largely taken for granted over the years. Sometimes planks have been put into platforms to attract their votes. Surely that will be enough, the party leaders reasoned. But it is not enough. It never is. The newest "arrivals" (some of them have been here for centuries) are bulldozing their way into the clubhouse. The old party politicians are dismayed. What do these newcomers want? The answer is simple: They want to run things.

As the Democrats have found a place for foreigners, blacks, and women in their political circle, so have the Republicans invited many different groups into their party. Since its formation in the 1850s, the Republican party has been full of strange bedfellows: abolitionists, eastern bankers, midwestern farmers, utopians, capitalists. More recently, it has taken the leavings of the new, post-1972 Democratic party. By the end of the 1970s, it was apparent that many evangelical Protestants, traditional Catholics, right-to-lifers, southern whites, anti-Communist activists, and other former Democrats no longer felt at home in the party. They were ignored, sometimes even scorned as "Archie Bunkers" by the new leaders. In 1980 the Republican party actively courted these discontented Democrats, and they switched. The Republican regulars, who had very little in common with them socially and did not even much agree with them philosophically, thought they could appease them with a few planks in the platform and some speeches by "The Great Communicator." That ought to keep them happy. But by the end of the decade, the new Republicans were starting to move into the circles of power once confined to the country club set.

Now it should be clear what has been going on in this republic since its early days. Political parties have been bringing the "outs" into the system, giving them the sense—and the reality—of participation in democratic government. The aliens, the outsiders, the people looked down upon by those who consider themselves respectable society, have gotten power through political parties. Party leaders have not willingly shared power; what they have really wanted to do was to keep riding the tiger. Instead they end up inside—but in the process, the tiger gets tamed. In the nineteenth century, the Irish were transformed from an unruly proletariat into a powerful and disciplined voting bloc. In the twentieth century, Jews and Italians were steered away from the attractions of foreign ideologies and movements; they were given a secure home in an American political party. In the 1960s blacks and Hispanics were burning down our cities; today, more and more, they are running them.

Seen from this standpoint, the violence at the 1968 Democratic convention begins to assume a familiar meaning. The raining-down of debris on the Chicago police, the sudden solidarity between McCarthy's young workers and the crazy street demonstrators—was it anything other than a collective howl of frustration at being locked out of their political party? That was the way the party regulars finally understood it; the lesson was driven home by Hubert Humphrey's narrow defeat in the November election, in part attributable to the bitter fight in Chicago.

Did the Democrats go too far in accommodating "McCarthy's kids" (most of them now in their forties)? Has the party become too closely identified with feminists, academics, and black nationalists? If so, chances are you will hear voices calling for new approaches to straying traditional Democrats. Is that opportunism? Of course it is. Our political parties like to win elections. Opportunism has served American democracy well: It has forced the parties to cast a very wide net in fishing for support. Without our parties, some groups might remain outside our political system, waiting for the chance to demolish it. One or the other of our parties has always asked them in and given them a place. Our loose, indistinct party system will never satisfy those who insist upon absolute purity of principle. But it has helped to give us a stable and democratic government. That is also a principle worth preserving.

Notes

1. Theodore H. White, *The Making of the President 1968* (New York: Atheneum Publishers, 1969), p. 258.

2. White, p. 298.

3. White, p. 298.

4. Lewis Chester, Godfrey Hodgson, and Bruce Page, *An American Melodrama: The Presidential Campaign of 1968* (New York: Dell Publishing Co., 1969), p. 648.

5. Jefferson, "Letter to Francis Hopkinson, March 13, 1789," in Edward Dumbauld, ed., *The Political Writings of Thomas Jefferson: Representative Selections* (Indianapolis, IN: Bobbs-Merrill Company, 1955), p. 46; Washington, quoted in J. D. Richardson, ed., *Messages and Papers of the Presidents*, vol. 1 (Washington, DC: U.S. Congress, 1987), p. 217.

6. Quoted in William Nisbet Chambers, *Political Parties in a New Nation* (New York: Oxford University Press, 1963), pp. 4-5.

7. Gerald M. Pomper, *Elections in America* (New York: Dodd, Mead, 1971), p. 178.

8. George McKenna, ed., *American Populism* (New York: G. B. Putnam's Sons, 1974); Irving Howe, *Socialism and America* (New York: Harcourt Brace Jovanovich, 1985).

9. *Williams v. Rhodes*, 393 U.S. 23 (1968); *Anderson v. Celebrezze*, 460 U.S. 780 (1983).

10. See the discussion in Irving Howe, *Socialism and America*, pp. 73-86.

11. For a more comprehensive discussion of why third parties have failed in America, see Clinton Rossiter, *Parties and Politics in America* (Ithaca, NY: Cornell University Press, 1960), pp. 3-11.

12. Byron E. Shafer, *Quiet Revolution: The Struggle for the Democratic Party and the Shaping of Post-Reform Politics* (New York: Russell Sage Foundation, 1983).

13. Shafer, p. 530.

14. William J. Crotty and Gary C. Jacobson, *American Parties in Decline* (Boston: Little, Brown, 1980), pp. 159-60.

15. Alan R. Gitelson, M. Margaret Conway, Frank B. Feigert, *American Political Parties: Stability and Change* (Boston: Houghton Mifflin, 1984), p. 93.

16. Hedrick Smith, *The Power Game: How Washington Works* (New York: Random House, 1988), p. 36.

17. Senator Thomas Eagleton, quoted in Smith, p. 138.

18. Edward J. Epstein, *News From Nowhere* (New York: Vintage Books, 1974), p. 215.

19. William L. Riordan, *Plunkitt of Tammany Hall* (New York: E. P. Dutton & Co., Inc., 1963), p. 28.

V. O. Key, *The Responsible Electorate*

17

Campaigns, Elections, and Voting

In 1952 the Republicans nominated Dwight D. Eisenhower **The Checkers Speech**
for president. "Ike," commander of the Allied forces in
Europe during World War II, was not only a national hero but a beloved
figure. "I Like Ike," bumper stickers said. The vice-presidential candidate
was a thirty-nine-year-old senator from California named Richard M.
Nixon. He was young—two years younger than another vice-presidential
candidate, Dan Quayle, would be 36 years later—and he was ambitious;
he knew it was a great honor to be on the ticket with Eisenhower.*

*This account is drawn from the following sources: Garry Wills, *Nixon Agonistes*
(Boston: Houghton Mifflin Company, 1969), chap. 5; Richard M. Nixon, *Six Crises*
(Garden City, NY: Doubleday & Company, 1962), section 2; Sherman Adams,
Firsthand Report (New York: Harper & Brothers, 1961), pp. 38-42; Kathleen Hall
Jamieson, *Packaging the Presidency* (New York: Oxford University Press, 1984), pp.
69-74; Congressional Quarterly Service, *Congress & the Nation, 1945-1964* (Washing-
ton: Congressional Quarterly Service, 1965), p. 18; Stephen E. Ambrose, *Nixon: The
Education of a Politician, 1913-1962* (New York: Simon and Schuster, 1987), chap. 14.
The text of the Checkers speech was reprinted in the *New York Times*, September 24,
1952, p. 22.

But Nixon was no Eisenhower: He seemed never to be able to disguise his ambition, never to look relaxed. He had acquired a reputation of being a young man who played a very rough game of politics. Indeed, the term *ruthless* often came up when Washington politicians talked about Dick Nixon. He had made a lot of enemies.

It was probably one or more of those enemies who leaked the story to the press that Nixon had been the beneficiary of an $18,000 campaign fund put up by a group of California industrialists. The story was true but misleading; there was such a fund, but it was perfectly legal. (Later it was discovered that Adlai E. Stevenson II, the Democratic presidential candidate, had a similar fund.) Still, it did not look good, especially in the newspapers. The headline in the *New York Post* screamed, "SECRET NIXON FUND: SECRET RICH MEN'S TRUST FUND KEEPS NIXON IN STYLE FAR BEYOND HIS SALARY." Nixon tried to ignore the story, but it kept building. At every stop on the campaign trail he was met by hecklers and picket signs. "Tell us about the $18,000," they demanded. The fund issue was starting to become the *only* issue of the campaign. Soon there was talk of dumping Nixon from the ticket. Most of that talk was coming from the eastern establishment wing of the party—the big businessmen from the northeastern industrial states and the writers and publicists who shared their point of view. This last group included the publishers of most of the major media in the East.

A wide chasm separated Nixon from the party's establishment. Its leading members were wealthy, had been born so; Nixon had been born poor. They had gone to elite prep schools and Ivy League colleges; he had attended public schools and Whittier College. The establishment stood for big business; Nixon, for small business and farmers. The establishment was eastern-based; Nixon grew up in California. The leaders were relatively liberal; Nixon was tied in with the party's conservatives. Their attitude toward Nixon was a mixture of cynicism and contempt: They thought he might be useful for pulling in the yokel vote.

They did like Eisenhower, however. They saw him as a winner. (The Democrats themselves had once courted him.) Ike's brand of "modern Republicanism" seemed just right for the times. Finally, after 20 years, the Republican party was going to capture the White House—unless Nixon fouled up everything. The first sign that Nixon was in deep trouble with his own party came when the New York *Herald Tribune*, the most powerful Republican newspaper in the East, called for his withdrawal. Since the *Tribune* was practically a house organ of the eastern establishment, Nixon drew the appropriate conclusion. "That sounded like the official word from Eisenhower himself," he later recalled.[1]

Eisenhower hardly knew Nixon. But what he knew he did not like. Nixon seemed too political to him. (Eisenhower liked to cultivate an image of being above politics.) Ike would have been glad to see Nixon disappear, but he could not openly ask for his withdrawal. Instead, he remained officially silent while meeting privately with the press. At one of those meetings Eisenhower admitted that Nixon was probably innocent but added that was not enough. Nixon should prove himself innocent in some kind of public forum—or else get off the ticket.

After much painful soul-searching, Nixon decided to ask the Republican National Committee for the money to purchase a half-hour of television time. He would explain the "Nixon fund" to the American people, tell them how the $18,000 was used and why it was necessary. And he would do more. He would reveal everything about himself, from his humble beginnings to his present-day earnings and debts. The

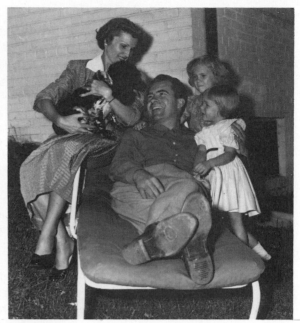

Richard Nixon's 1952 Checkers speech was a dramatic demonstration of the political potential of television. Diverting attention away from a controversial "gift" of $18,000 to his campaign fund, Nixon tugged at heartstrings around the nation as he talked about the gift of a cocker spaniel puppy. The emotional speech secured Nixon's position as vice-presidential running mate on the Republican ticket. At right, the Nixons pose with their famous pet.

Republican National Committee came up with $75,000, and at 5:50 P.M. on September 23, 1952, Richard Nixon entered the El Capitan Theater in Hollywood, California. As Nixon had insisted, the 750-seat theater was empty except for the camera crew and the electricians onstage. Nixon was exhausted; he had hardly slept for the last three days, and his nerves were frazzled. One of Eisenhower's men had telephoned him from the East Coast just before he had left his hotel and had said the consensus was that Nixon should offer his withdrawal at the end of the speech. The caller wanted to know Nixon's answer so that he could inform the others. "Just tell them I haven't the slightest idea as to what I am going to do," Nixon shouted and banged down the receiver.[2]

Now Nixon sat behind a desk waiting for his cue. He watched the second hand go around on the clock. Then the director pointed at him. "My fellow Americans," Nixon began, and all the nervousness went out of him. "My integrity has been questioned because I have taken $18,000 from a group of supporters. There is nothing illegal about getting the money, but that isn't enough. The question is, was it morally wrong?" Yes, he answered, "I say that it *was* morally wrong . . ." [dramatic pause] "*if* any of that $18,000 went to Senator Nixon, for my personal use," and *if* "it was secretly given and secretly handled," and *if* "any of the contributors got special favors for the contributions that they made." Nixon then demonstrated that none of these "ifs" applied to him. But, Nixon said, that still was not enough. Maybe some folks thought he was hiding something. "And so now what I am going to do—and, incidentally, this is unprecedented in the history of American politics—I am going at this time to give to this television and radio audience a complete financial history, every-

459

thing I have earned, everything I have spent, everything I own." He proceeded to list all of his assets, from "a 1950 Oldsmobile car" to his $4,000 in life insurance, and all of his debts: the mortgages on his California and Washington houses, a bank loan, the money he owed on his life insurance, and the money he had borrowed from his parents. There was one more item on his list:

We did get something, a gift, after the nomination. A man down in Texas heard Pat on the radio mention the fact that our two youngsters would like to have a dog and, believe it or not, the day before we left on this campaign trip we got a message from Union Station in Baltimore, saying they had a package for us. . . . You know what it was? It was a little cocker spaniel dog, in a crate that he had sent all the way from Texas—black and white, spotted, and our little girl Tricia . . . named it Checkers. And you know, the kids . . . loved the dog, and I just want to say this right now, that regardless of what they say about it, we are going to keep it.[3]

Having revealed everything, Nixon dared the Democrats to do the same. Let the Democrats stand up and talk about *their* finances. This led Nixon to raise an issue: Should higher office in the United States be the exclusive province of the wealthy? The chairman of the Democratic National Committee had "made the statement that if a man couldn't afford to be in the United States Senate, he shouldn't run for the Senate." Nixon disagreed. He thought that people of modest means should also have a chance at higher office, "because, you know—remember Abraham Lincoln, remember what he said—'God must have loved the common people, he made so many of them.' "[4]

There was much more to the speech. So much, in fact, that Nixon ran out of time. At the very end he was suggesting that those who thought he should stay on the ticket might want to write in, when the red light blinked off. He was off the air, and he had not told his supporters where to write! All the weeks of pent-up tension burst out: Nixon threw his notes on the floor and stalked out of the building. Afterward, as his car pulled away, a playful Irish setter ran alongside, barking. Looking gloomily out the window, Nixon said, "At least I won the dog vote tonight."[5]

In fact, Nixon had won a lot more. Reams of telegrams piled up at Republican headquarters around the country; switchboards were jammed. People had figured out whom to write and call. Eisenhower, who had been eager to dump Nixon the day before, now summoned him to his side. Nixon flew to West Virginia, where Ike was campaigning. As he started to get off the plane, Eisenhower rushed up the stairs and embraced him. Embarrassed, Nixon said: "General, you didn't need to come out to the airport." Ike beamed at him. "Why not?," he said, "You're my boy!"

*　　　*　　　*　　　*　　　*

The Checkers speech was a milestone in American politics because it offered the first real glimpse of the political potential of television. Literally overnight a candidate who was about to be kicked off the ticket became a national hero. Nixon himself never forgot one lesson of Checkers. A football fan, he called it a "long bomb," one of those dramatic forward passes that suddenly turns the tide of the game.

This story raises some interesting and troubling questions. Do American political campaigns turn too much on long bombs—dramatic moves designed to win elections by stirring up emotions? When Nixon talked about the gift of a cocker spaniel puppy, he diverted people's attention from the more controversial "gift" of $18,000 to his campaign fund. "Regardless of what they say about [the dog], we are going to keep it," Nixon said. Well, of course. What kind of monster would take a beloved puppy away from two little girls? Somehow, the $18,000 was forgotten. Is there too much play on the emotions in our campaigns? Can American elections be won by image making and manipulation?

The Checkers incident raises still more questions. One was brought up by Nixon himself in his speech: How *should* a candidate who is not a millionaire get the money to run for office? Nixon was surely right to insist that political campaigns must be open to all, not just to the wealthy. How, then, do people who are not affluent obtain the money to run for office? Nixon turned to wealthy friends. Is there anything wrong with that? Should there be more limits on campaign spending and contributions? Should the federal government help pay for the costs of campaigning?

A final issue relates to the background of the Checkers speech. As we saw, Nixon was pressured into making the speech by key members of his own party. Most of the eastern establishment wing of the Republican party in 1952 could be considered moderate or liberal in ideology. But that wing hardly exists anymore; even George Bush, who was born into it, has been transformed into a "westerner" and a conservative. And it is not only the Republican party that has changed. Change within the Republican party has a parallel in what has happened in the Democratic party. What has happened? Some observers think that our parties have been realigning. Without trying to spell out the full meaning of *realignment*—we will return to it later in the chapter—it appears that some groups of Americans who used to vote Democratic are now voting Republican, whereas others who once sided with the Republicans have now become Democrats. What has caused these shifts? Are they permanent?

Let us begin with the basics—voting in America—and consider voter turnout and voter preferences.

Voting in America

The right to vote is basic to a democracy. Not all issues can or should be referred directly to the people for a decision (see chapter 1), but the people must be able to decide who will represent them—which brings up the importance of voting, or suffrage, as it is often called.

WHO VOTES?

Some of the Founders worried about suffrage. They were afraid that if the propertyless masses were allowed to vote, they would flock to the polls and use their ballots to overthrow the elites. John Dickenson of Delaware favored suffrage restrictions as "a necessary defense against the dangerous influence of those multitudes without property and without principle, with which our country, like all others, will in time abound."[6]

FIGURE **17-1**

**How Many Vote in the United States:
Presidential Election Turnouts, 1932-1988***

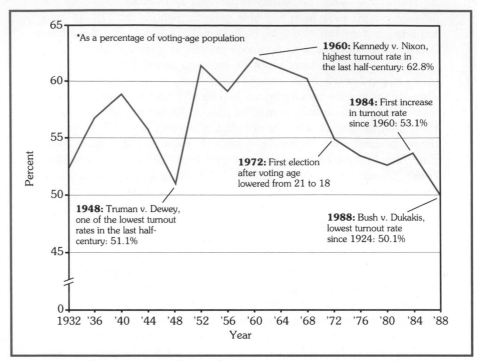

Source: Congressional Quarterly Weekly Report, October 1, 1988, p. 2702. Adapted with permission.

Voting turnout in the United States varies with the times, although it is hard to say precisely what it is that affects turnout. The high turnout of 1960 may have been a result of the excitement generated by the first presidential television debates or the glamour of John F. Kennedy or the optimism of the times or some combination of the three. The low turnouts in 1948 and 1988 may have been a reflection of voter dissatisfaction with the candidates of both major parties.

Dickenson need not have worried. The fact is that the poor and the less educated are the least likely Americans to vote. In a book entitled *The Real Majority*, Richard Scammon and Ben Wattenberg wrote that American voters tend to be "unpoor, unblack, and unyoung."[7] The summary is succinct, if somewhat oversimplified. Black citizens are less likely to vote than whites. Young people—caught up with grades, careers, romances, and the like—are less likely to vote than the middle aged. As people reach their mid-sixties, voter participation drops off again, probably because of the difficulty of getting to the polls. Some poor people and black people— often one and the same—may ignore politics because they cherish little hope that it will bring improvement. The strongest variable, though, is not race but education. (Black voters with little education are actually more likely to vote than their white counterparts.) It may simply be that people who lack knowledge also lack interest.

What concerns many observers of American elections is that so many of our eligible voters seem to be screening themselves out of the electoral process. In 1988 only 50.1 percent of eligible voters in this country participated in the presidential election, the lowest turnout since 1924. (It usually gets much lower in off-year congressional elections, when nobody is running for president, and in state and local races.) We can see a sharp contrast when we compare our turnouts with those of most other industrial democracies such as Sweden, Great Britain, and West Ger-

TABLE **17-1**

463

Voting in America

Voter Turnout Worldwide: Industrial Democracies

Country	Year	Turnout
United States	1988	50.1%
United States	1984	53.1
Australia*	1984	94.2
Austria	1983	92.6
Belgium*	1985	93.6
Canada	1984	75.7
Denmark	1984	88.4
Finland	1983	75.7
France	1981	85.8
Great Britain	1983	72.8
Greece	1983	80.2
Israel	1985	78.8
Italy*	1984	89.0
Japan	1983	71.4
Netherlands	1986	85.7
New Zealand	1986	88.5
Norway	1981	81.2
Portugal	1985	78.2
Spain	1986	70.7
Sweden	1986	89.8
Switzerland	1985	48.9
West Germany	1983	89.1

*Voting is compulsory

Source: Congressional Research Service

The voter turnout rate in the United States—50.1 percent in the 1988 presidential election—lags behind the turnout rates of most other industrial democracies. Note the high voter turnout rates in Australia, Belgium, and Italy, where voting is compulsory.

many. In recent years Great Britain has had a turnout of 72.8 percent. The closest we came to that in this century was in 1960 (the Kennedy-Nixon election), when the turnout fell 10 points below that figure. As for the voting rates in West Germany, Austria, and Sweden, which fall into the range of 89 to 93 percent, we have never come anywhere near them.

Our low turnout is a source of embarrassment to the United States and its elected officials. How can our presidents claim a mandate of the people if half the electorate has not even bothered to vote? The reason for this low turnout is not easy to determine; from a comparative perspective, the figures may be somewhat deceptive. In this country we calculate turnout by comparing actual voters with *eligible* voters, that is, those citizens 18 years old and older who are not otherwise disqualified. In Europe they compare actual voters to *registered* voters. That, of course, will produce higher numbers, since the people who have taken the trouble to register are more likely to vote. This brings us to one possible reason for the low turnouts in the United States: Registration requirements, which vary from state to state, may discourage some voters. In many states one must register at least 30 days before voting. Political scientists Raymond E. Wolfinger and Steven J. Rosenstone have estimated that abolishing this requirement—allowing registration at the time of voting—would increase turnout 3 to 9 percent nationally.[8] Still, registration requirements do not explain the ups and downs of voter turnout in America. Why was it comparatively high in 1960 and so low in 1988? We do not know for sure. Is it

Voting is an important form of political participation. But low voter turnout is a source of embarrassment to the United States and its elected officials. It may suggest widespread distrust or apathy. It could also be interpreted as evidence of widespread satisfaction with the performance of those in office, but the theory of democracy assumes that even satisfied people will turn out to vote.

FIGURE **17-2**

Why Some People Do Not Vote

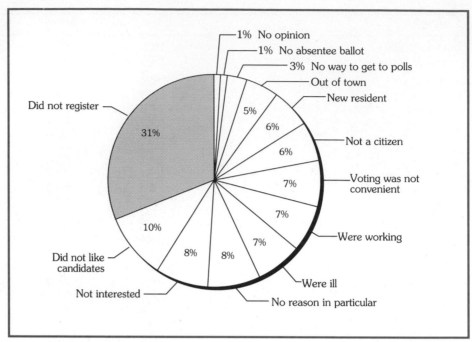

1% No opinion
1% No absentee ballot
3% No way to get to polls
Out of town
New resident
Not a citizen
Voting was not convenient
Were working
Were ill
No reason in particular
Not interested
Did not like candidates
Did not register

31%
5%
6%
6%
7%
7%
7%
8%
8%
10%

Source: A November 1984 Gallup poll.

There are many different reasons why some people in the United States do not vote. The most common reason is that they have not registered to vote. In many states people must register at least one month before an election. In recent years some have suggested that this period be shortened; some have even suggested that registration be allowed on the same day as voting. Advance registration was originally required to prevent such fraud as voting in two or more places. Critics worry that same-day registration may encourage other fraudulent voting practices.

because in recent years many Americans have become "turned off" by politics and politicians? Or are they now so content with the way their system works that they do not feel the need to get involved? Maybe it is some combination of the two: People are soured by politics *and* relatively content with the results. Some such mixture may account for the low turnout of 1988.

WHO VOTES FOR WHAT PARTY?

A voter's demographic characteristics—whether that person is Catholic, Protestant, black, white, male, female, southern, northern, and so on—often correlate with the way he or she will vote. Over the years we can find some rather consistent correlations between demographic characteristics and party preference, which makes it possible in some cases to predict how the majority of certain groups are likely to vote. Take a look at the Table 17.2, on pages 466 and 467: The most reliable predictor of voting preference is race. The percentage of nonwhites (the category includes blacks, Asians, and American Indians) voting Democratic in presidential elections has not dipped below 82 percent since 1960. An almost equally predictable category is religion. Except for the 1964 and 1968 presidential elections, the majority of Protestants has voted for the Republican candidate *every* four years. This statement, however, requires some qualification. In the past, *southern* white Protestants tended to be Democrats. That has changed in recent years, particularly since 1980, when the Republicans deliberately courted born-again Christian voters. Since then, evangelical Christians, particularly in the South, have been strongly Republican.[9]

Now look at the education category. Most people with college degrees vote Republican (1964 was an exception), whereas those with less than a high-school degree tend to vote Democratic (although narrow majorities went Republican in 1972). White-collar workers usually vote Republican (except in 1964); blue-collar workers usually vote Democratic (except in 1972 and 1984). Perhaps more surprisingly, the majority of female voters has chosen Republicans in *every* presidential election year except 1964 and 1968. After the 1980 election there was much discussion in the media about a gender gap. Ronald Reagan's margin of victory in the 1980 election was smaller among women (5 percent) than it was among men (15 percent). That gave feminists in the Democratic party some hope that they could mobilize the women's vote to defeat Reagan. The gender gap reappeared in 1984 and 1988, but it did not give the Democrats much comfort. Reagan won an even larger majority of women's votes than he had in 1980 (57 percent, compared to 47 percent), and his support among male voters was still larger—61 percent, in contrast to Walter Mondale's 37 percent of the male vote. In 1988 George Bush won 50 percent of women's votes, compared to Michael Dukakis's 49 percent. But Bush did better among men (57 percent) than he did among women, and Dukakis much worse (41 percent). At least at the presidential level, the gender gap seems to benefit the Republicans.

Other groups seem to have lost their constancy. In the 1930s and the 1940s, Catholics were as loyal to the Democrats as nonwhite voters are today. But those days are over. In 1972, 1980, and 1984 the majority of Catholics voted for the Republican presidential candidate. Southerners, another category of people who were once solidly Democratic, have seesawed back and forth since 1956. Much of this fluctuation may have to do with the black-white composition of the southern vote. Blacks, whether northern or southern, are reliable Democrats. But the Democrats have failed to win a majority of *white* southern voters since 1964. The switch of these voters from the Democrats to the Republicans in presidential elections has been dramatic. White southerners, one of the most reliably Democratic groups since the end of the Civil War, began turning against their party in presidential races in the 1960s, in part because of the national Democratic support for civil rights. Even Jimmy Carter, a Georgian, was unable to win a majority of the white South in 1976. Between 1984 and 1988 their identification with the Republican party sharply increased. The reasons for this are not entirely clear, but they may be connected with high personal regard for Ronald Reagan and support for Republican conservatism on social issues like abortion and crime. At any rate, by 1988 George Bush had reaped the benefits of it. According to a *Los Angeles Times* exit poll, 74 percent of southern white Protestants voted for George Bush, as compared with 25 percent for Michael Dukakis.[10]

CRITICAL OR REALIGNING ELECTIONS

Although these shifts of groups in and out of our two major parties do not happen very often, they have long intrigued political scientists.[11] In the past most groups have supported their parties from election to election. But every so often a critical, or realigning, election takes place—one in which key voting groups enter one party (usually because they have left the other party) and form a victorious coalition that lasts for many years. *(Continued on bottom of page 466)*

TABLE 17-2

Vote by Groups in Presidential Elections Since 1952

National	1952		1956		1960		1964		1968		
	Stevenson	Eisenhower	Stevenson	Eisenhower	Kennedy	Nixon	Johnson	Goldwater	Humphrey	Nixon	Wallace
National	**44.6%**	**55.4%**	**42.2%**	**57.8%**	**50.1%**	**49.9%**	**61.3%**	**38.7%**	**43.0%**	**43.4%**	**13.6%**
Sex											
Men	47	53	45	55	52	48	60	40	41	43	16
Women	42	58	39	61	49	51	62	38	45	43	12
Race											
White	43	57	41	59	49	51	59	41	38	47	15
Nonwhite	79	21	61	39	68	32	94	6	85	12	3
Education											
College	34	66	31	69	39	61	52	48	37	54	9
High school	45	55	42	58	52	48	62	38	42	43	15
Grade school	52	48	50	50	55	45	66	34	52	33	15
Occupation											
Prof. & business	36	64	32	68	42	58	54	46	34	56	10
White collar	40	60	37	63	48	52	57	43	41	47	12
Manual	55	45	50	50	60	40	71	29	50	35	15
Age											
Under 30 years	51	49	43	57	54	45	64	36	47	38	15
30-49 years	47	53	45	55	54	46	63	37	44	41	15
50 years & older	39	61	39	61	46	54	59	41	41	47	12
Religion											
Protestants	37	63	37	63	38	62	55	45	35	49	16
Catholics	56	44	51	49	78	22	76	24	59	33	8
Politics											
Republicans	8	92	4	96	5	95	20	80	9	86	5
Democrats	77	23	85	15	84	16	87	13	74	12	14
Independents	35	65	30	70	43	57	56	44	31	44	25
Region											
East	45	55	40	60	53	47	68	32	50	43	7
Midwest	42	58	41	59	48	52	61	39	44	47	9
South	51	49	49	51	51	49	52	48	31	36	33
West	42	58	43	57	49	51	60	40	44	49	7
Labor Union											
Union Families	61	39	57	43	65	35	73	27	56	29	15

*Less than one percent
Note: From 1976 onwards, results do not include vote for minor party candidates.

Source: The Gallup report, Report No. 278, November 1988. Reprinted with permission.

(Continued from page 465) The best example of a critical election is the 1932 presidential election. Blacks, who had formerly voted Republican (the antislavery party), started voting Democratic because the Democrats and their candidate, Franklin Delano Roosevelt, promised to end the Depression. Many immigrants, who had either not voted at all or had voted Republican previously, became Democrats for the same reason. Then there were Republican reformers who had grown impatient with their party's inability (or unwillingness) to do something about the Depression—they too switched to the Democrats. These groups became the New Deal coalition: workers, southerners, blacks, intellectuals, and those in big-city "machines." They added up to a majority of voters. The coalition held together long enough to make the Democrats winners in 1932, 1936, 1940, 1944, and 1948.

Other critical elections took place before the turn of the century. For example,

1972		1976			1980			1984		1988	
McGovern	Nixon	Carter	Ford	McCarthy	Carter	Reagan	Anderson	Mondale	Reagan	Dukakis	Bush
38%	62%	50%	48%	1%	41%	51%	7%	41%	59%	46%	54%
37	63	53	45		38	53	7	36	64	44	56
38	62	48	51	*	44	49	6	45	55	48	52
32	68	46	52	1	36	56	7	34	66	41	59
87	13	85	15	*	86	10	2	87	13	82	18
37	63	42	55	2	35	53	10	39	61	42	58
34	66	54	46	*	43	51	5	43	57	46	54
49	51	58	41	1	54	42	3	51	49	55	45
31	69	42	56	1	33	55	10	34	66	NA	NA
36	64	50	48	2	40	51	9	47	53		
43	57	58	41	1	48	48	5	46	54		
48	52	53	45	1	47	41	11	40	60	37	63
33	67	48	49	2	38	52	8	40	60	45	55
36	64	52	48	*	41	54	4	41	59	49	51
30	70	46	53	*	39	54	6	39	61	42	58
48	52	57	41	1	46	47	6	39	61	51	49
5	95	9	91	*	8	86	5	4	96	7	93
67	33	82	18	*	69	26	4	79	21	85	15
31	69	38	57	4	29	55	14	33	67	43	57
42	58	51	47	1	43	47	9	46	54	51	49
40	60	48	50	1	41	51	7	42	58	47	53
29	71	54	45	*	44	52	3	37	63	40	60
41	59	46	51	1	35	54	9	40	60	46	54
46	54	63	36	1	50	43	5	52	48	63	37

political scientists agree that the 1896 election resulted in party realignment. From 1876 to 1896 the Democrats and Republicans were almost evenly matched. Although the Democrats managed to win only two presidential elections, the popular margins were very close. In 1896 the Democrats fused with the Populist party, and both parties endorsed the same presidential candidate, William Jennings Bryan. The Populist, or People's, party was one of those short-lived third parties that agitates the waters for a time and then disappears.

During its heyday, from 1890 to 1900, the People's party denounced Wall Street financiers, the railroads, and eastern bankers and businessmen. It stood for what it called "the plain people," ordinary Americans who did not have a lot of money, education, or fancy manners. In fact, the Populist idea of ordinary people usually turned out to be farmers or small-town Americans from the South or West. In the

FIGURE **17-3**

Three Presidential Elections: Shifting Choices

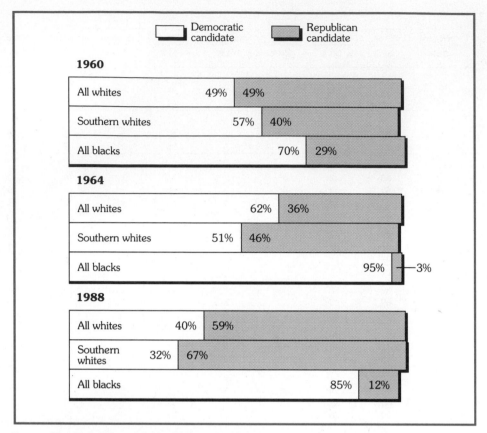

Source: New York Times, July 2, 1989, p. 16. Reprinted with permission.

The 1964 presidential election marked a turning-point in American politics. Black voters, who had been showing some interest in the Republican party, turned to the Democrats in overwhelming numbers, while southern whites began their move away from their traditional party. Although a majority of southern whites still voted Democratic in the 1964 presidential election, it was the last time it was to happen. By 1988, most whites, but especially southern whites, were voting Republican in presidential contests, while the vast majority of blacks had moved into the Democratic camp.

East the Populists were viewed with suspicion, and not just by the wealthy. The party was suspected of being anti-immigrant, anti-city, anti-Catholic, and anti-Jewish. Bryan, the Democratic-Populist presidential candidate, was a dramatic orator whose style was like that of a fundamentalist preacher. He did not really appeal to working-class voters of the East and upper Midwest, and he terrified middle-class voters from those key areas.

The result was a disaster for the Democrats. Except for Woodrow Wilson's two terms (1913–1921), the Republicans controlled the White House from 1896 to 1932. The Republicans had put together a winning coalition of workers and business based upon the promise of mutual prosperity. They promised business protection against foreign competition and they promised workers "a full dinner pail." The link lasted until the Depression of the 1930s.

The 1860 election also qualifies as critical. That year marks the emergence of the

FIGURE **17-4**

469

Voting in America

A Critical Election: 1932

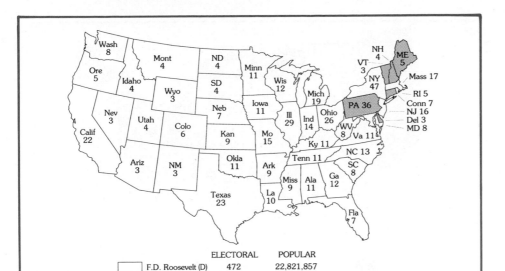

	ELECTORAL	POPULAR
F.D. Roosevelt (D)	472	22,821,857
Hoover (R)	59	15,761,841

In the election of 1932, the Democrats put together a coalition of southerners, Catholics, Jews, and ethnic minorities from the northern cities. This broad support proved enduring: It kept the White House under Democratic control for 20 years and produced Democratic majorities in Congress.

Republican party as a victorious coalition. The Republicans had been born four years earlier, when they ran John C. Frémont for president in the 1856 election. Frémont lost to James Buchanan, a Democrat. By 1860 the Democrats were divided into northern and southern branches, with southern Democrats defending slavery and northern Democrats waffling on the issue. Then there was the old Whig party (renamed the Constitutional Union party); it simply remained silent on slavery, hoping the issue would go away. Its failure to take a stand alienated supporters who opposed slavery. The Republican party built its victory—and its core support—from the antislavery Whigs, together with some northern Democrats and voters from a sprinkling of minor parties.

A NEW CRITICAL ELECTION?

Have we had a critical election lately? Some observers think that a critical shift occurred in the 1980s. At the 1985 convention of the American Political Science Association (APSA), Thomas E. Mann, the executive director, declared that it was time for political scientists to stop "quibbling over details." According to Mann, the shift had indeed occurred, and "it is crazy to keep denying the existence of the political events of the 1980s."[12] The events of the 1984 election that impressed Mann were discussed earlier in the chapter: the shift to the Republicans of groups once considered the backbone of the Democratic party—Catholics, white southerners, and blue-collar workers. Others at the APSA convention, however, urged caution. Do not be too quick, said political scientist Herbert F. Weisman, to talk about 1984 as a critical election. In the past, he said, realignment has meant at least three consecutive presidential victories for a party. "The realignment test," he concluded, is whether the Republicans can keep the White House in the 1988 election."[13]

FIGURE **17-5**

A Critical Election: 1896

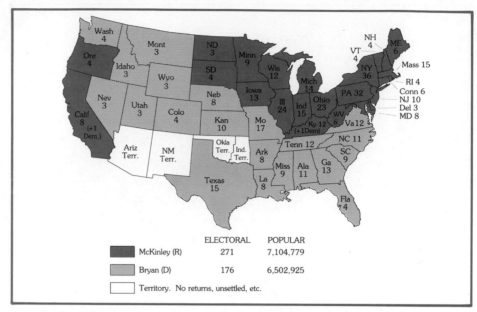

	ELECTORAL	POPULAR
McKinley (R)	271	7,104,779
Bryan (D)	176	6,502,925
Territory. No returns, unsettled, etc.		

In the 1896 election the Democrats nominated William Jennings Bryan, who was also endorsed by the Populist party, a party that denounced Wall Street and demanded reform of "big business." Bryan's evangelistic style frightened away many voters—the Republicans won in 1896 and remained the dominant national party for a generation—yet the Populist theme of economic reform was worked into future Democratic platforms.

This campaign poster for William Jennings Bryan dates from the critical 1896 presidential election. Bryan, who was backed by the Democrats and Populists, lost to Republican William McKinley. Except for the two terms of Woodrow Wilson (1913-1921), the Republicans continued to occupy the White House for the next 36 years.

They did, of course, and while George Bush's margin of victory was not as dramatic as Ronald Reagan's in 1984, it was large enough (53 to 45 percent) to be unambiguous. Moreover, Bush kept the loyalty of many "Reagan Democrats." Decisive majorities of Catholics, southerners, and families with moderate incomes ($25,000 to $35,000 annually) voted Republican for the presidential slot. Finally, what had embarrassed the Democrats most in 1984 happened again: Young people, those in the 18-29 age bracket, preferred Bush to Dukakis by a margin of 52 to 47 percent. For the Democrats, who aspire to be the party of youth and the future, this was particularly painful.

However, the Democrats retained majorities in Congress, state legislatures, and governorships in 1988, which left grounds for interpreting the result as an ambiguous Republican victory. (Under the headline "G.O.P. Hope of Dominance Is Delayed," a *New York Times* correspondent called it a "muddled verdict.")[14] Still, the results offered limited consolation to the Democrats. Congressional and state races usually turn on local questions and personalities rather than on major party differences, and, for a variety of reasons unrelated to the issues of the campaign, voters tend to favor incumbents, who are usually Democrats.

DEALIGNMENT

Whatever happened to the parties in 1984 and 1988, we *can* say that it was not the kind of clear-cut realignment that occurred in 1932 and in earlier elections. The bond between most voters and their parties of choice does not seem to be as strong as in

FIGURE **17-6**

471

Voting in America

A Critical Election: 1860

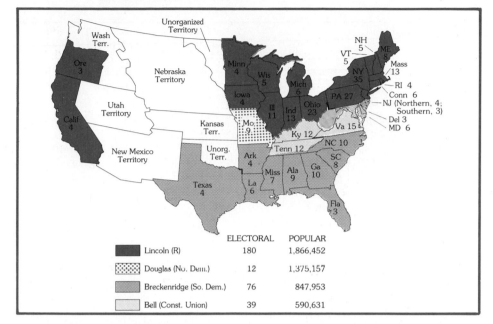

	ELECTORAL	POPULAR
Lincoln (R)	180	1,866,452
Douglas (No. Dem.)	12	1,375,157
Breckenridge (So. Dem.)	76	847,953
Bell (Const. Union)	39	590,631

In 1860 the Republican Party, founded six years earlier, captured the White House for the first time with the election of Abraham Lincoln. The Republicans were assembled from fragments of the Democratic and Whig parties and several minor parties, such as the Free Soil, Liberty, and Know-Nothing parties. They were united in their opposition to the extension of slavery into the territories of the West.

the past. In the 1980s more than a third of all voters called themselves "independents," compared to less than a fifth in the 1950s. Voters frequently switch their party affiliation from one election to the next, making it almost impossible to determine their allegiances. They also split their tickets now, something that was seldom done in the past; typically, Americans in recent years have been voting Republican at the presidential level and Democratic at the state and congressional levels. Although some groups, notably blacks and Jews, tend to vote a straight Democratic ticket, most voting groups seem reluctant to put all their eggs in either party's basket. This trend has led some political scientists to use the term <u>dealignment</u>, meaning a general weakening of ties between the voters and *both* parties.[15]

It could be, then, that the long-awaited realignment is never going to occur because voters today do not exhibit long-term party loyalty. As political scientists David G. Lawrence and Richard Fleisher put it: "It may be that we are seeing a series of short-term candidate-based coalitions, rather than the long-term party attachments that exist in a stable party system."[16] Political scientist Everett Carll Ladd thinks that the whole debate about contemporary realignment has been a waste of time. "Let's bury the concept," he says.[17] Still, if the concept does nothing else, it reminds us that some very important things have been happening in our political system over the past generation. We should be careful lest we "bury" a concept that provides a framework for serious thought about them. Nevertheless, do all these happenings add up to a fundamental shift in the strength and composition of our two parties? Or is realignment still elusive? There is another possibility. Maybe—at least at the presidential level—we had our party realignment some years ago. From this perspective, two elections, one in 1964 and one in 1972, seemed to change radically the lineup of groups comprising the two parties. The 1964 election realigned the Republicans and

TABLE **17-3**

The Last Presidential Campaign: Public Attitudes

	Bush Supporters	Dukakis Supporters	Total Voters
Describe the 1988 campaign as dull	52%	54%	53%
Say they wish there were choices other than Bush and Dukakis	55	72	64
Say this year's campaign has been more negative than past campaigns	49	48	48
Say there has been less discussion of the issues this year than in past campaigns	43	55	48
Say neither candidate is talking enough about the particular issue the voter says should be the most important	51	59	54
Say Bush is spending more time attacking Dukakis than explaining what he would do as president	30	77	51
Say Dukakis is spending more time attacking Bush than explaining what he would do as president	59	31	47
Say one or both campaigns have made unfair charges:			
Just the Bush campaign has	4	24	12
Just the Dukakis campaign has	18	3	11
Both campaigns have	48	47	49
Of those who have seen each candidate's ads in the past week:			
Say at least some of Bush's television commercials are false	33	76	52
Say at least some of Dukakis's television commercials are false	58	41	50

Source: New York Times, October 26, 1988, p. A22. Reprinted with permission.

> Many voters were unhappy with the so-called negative aspects of the 1988 presidential campaign. But compared to some earlier campaigns, the 1988 tactics were a model of civility. The data here were based upon interviews with 1,287 registered voters nationwide, conducted by telephone Oct. 21-24, and weighted to reflect a "probable electorate."

the 1972 election realigned the Democrats.[18] Each of these elections needs a closer examination.

As we discussed earlier, in 1952 the two wings of the Republican party were the liberal eastern establishment wing and the more conservative wing, which backed Nixon. The powerful liberal wing included Eisenhower's chief boosters and such notables as former New York governor Thomas E. Dewey and (governor-to-be) Nelson A. Rockefeller. Eight years later, when Nixon was seeking the Republican nomination for president, he had to make his peace with the liberals; otherwise, Rockefeller would have challenged him for the nomination. Meeting privately with Rockefeller, Nixon agreed to put some key liberal planks into the platform (for example, medical care for the elderly and civil rights).

The conservatives, crying that they had been sold out, vowed to nominate a real conservative in 1964. They did and in the process changed the base of the Republican party. Their nominee, Arizona senator Barry Goldwater, was badly

In 1964 the Republicans nominated the conservative Barry Goldwater for president. He is seen here surrounded by followers, some of whom are carrying Y.A.F. (Young Americans for Freedom) signs. Goldwater was badly beaten in the election by Democrat Lyndon B. Johnson.

beaten in the election, but he managed to win his home state of Arizona plus five Deep South states: Alabama, Georgia, Louisiana, Mississippi, and South Carolina. He also did fairly well (slightly more than 40 percent or higher) in Florida, Idaho, Indiana, Kansas, Nebraska, North Carolina, Oklahoma, South Dakota, Tennessee, Utah, Virginia, and Wyoming.[19] The Republicans, who had once had their base in the Northeast, became the party of the South and West. In the process, the eastern establishment wing lost its leverage.

That election brought no real change to the Democratic party, which nominated Lyndon B. Johnson, a traditional Democrat who favored welfare and a strong national defense. The critical year for the Democrats was 1972, when they lost much of the working class. As we saw in the last chapter, the rule changes adopted by the Democrats between 1968 and 1972 brought a "new class" of Democrats into power. They nominated Senator George McGovern, who, like Barry Goldwater in 1964, was badly beaten in the election, even in areas that the Democrats had traditionally carried. McGovern did manage to carry Massachusetts and the District of Columbia, and he won 42 percent or more of the votes in the following states: California, Michigan, Minnesota, Rhode Island, Oregon, South Dakota, and Wisconsin. Leaving aside South Dakota (McGovern's home state), it may be possible to designate these states as areas of potential Democratic strength, since even during a Republican landslide, they gave some comfort. All states that McGovern won in 1972, or where he carried at least 42 percent of the vote, continued to hold up fairly well during the Democrats' second major defeat in 1984. That year Walter Mondale lost every state in the union except Minnesota, but he won at least 42 percent of the vote in all of the McGovern states (except Michigan, where he won 41 percent). In 1988 Michael Dukakis did better, beating George Bush in all of these states except Michigan and California.

A pattern begins to emerge. Taking into account the record of the two parties during disastrous elections, we can mark out areas of Democratic and Republican strength. Look at Figure 17.7 on page 474. There is something fascinating about this map, especially when you compare it with Figure 17.5 on page 470, the critical

FIGURE **17-7**

Democratic and Republican Strongholds

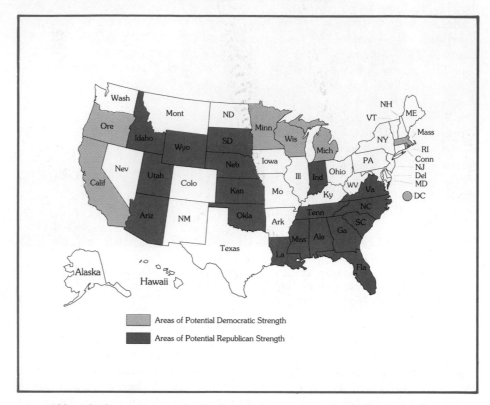

Although the outcomes of presidential elections in individual states may be determined by a number of factors, in recent years there has emerged a rough pattern of Democratic strength in New England and the upper Midwest and Republican strength in the South and the West. This is almost the reverse pattern of Democratic and Republican strength during the New Deal era.

election of 1896. What has happened, as you can see, is that over the past century the Democratic and Republican parties have come close to switching places. Republican strength is now in the South and West (except for California and Oregon), the very states where William Jennings Bryan, the Democratic-Populist candidate, did well in 1896. The Democrats, meanwhile, have their bastions in New England, the upper Midwest, California, and Oregon—areas that were once Republican strongholds.[20]

THE ELECTORAL COLLEGE

The question of sectional realignment is very important in American politics because presidential candidates win by *states*. Who can win the South? Who will do well in the Northeast, in the Great Lakes states, or in the West? These are the typical anxieties of American politicians before a presidential election. For better or for worse, elections for the highest office in the land are decided not by popular votes, but by *electoral votes*, in which states play a major role. For this we can praise or blame our Founders, who gave us the electoral college.

The electoral college has no campus, and it never meets as a whole. It is composed of 50 state delegations (plus 1 from the District of Columbia) that meet separately in their state capitals a month after the November presidential election.

There they vote to tell us what we already know: who the next president and vice president will be. Today the electoral college's role is entirely ceremonial, but that is not what the Founders originally intended.

The Constitution set up the electoral college system as follows: Each state receives an allotment of electoral votes equal to its total number of U.S. representatives plus its two senators. So, for example, if a state has 20 representatives in the House, it has 22 electoral votes. These votes are to be cast by electors, who the Founders assumed would be wise and upright men chosen by their fellow citizens in statewide elections. The electors from each state would then use their own discretion in voting for president and vice president.

The Founders thus gave us an indirect system of electing the president. The people would choose the electors, but the electors would select the president. It was an aristocratic idea—election by the wise—but by 1800, aristocracy had given way to democracy. Political parties had taken over the electoral system, offering voters the choice between *slates* of electors who were pledged to vote for their parties' candidates for president and vice president.

FAITHLESS ELECTORS AND WINNER-TAKES-ALL

Today, as in 1800, voters go to the polls in a presidential election and choose between rival slates of electors pledged to party candidates. For example, in the 1988 election a voter in New York State who cast a ballot for Michael Dukakis was actually voting for a slate of 36 Democratic electors (equal to New York's 34 representatives plus its 2 senators) pledged to vote for Dukakis. In all except a few states, the electors are not bound by law to vote for the candidates to whom they are pledged, and there have been a few cases of faithless electors—electors who have turned against their own party's candidate and voted for somebody else. Even so, with a total of 538 electoral votes, an occasional faithless elector will not make much difference.[21]

A somewhat more believable nightmare has to do with the winner-takes-all nature of the electoral college. When a presidential candidate wins a majority of popular votes in a state, *all* of that state's electoral votes go to that candidate. Even if the loser is defeated by a paper-thin margin, he or she gains no portion of that state's electoral votes. In 1988, for example, Michael Dukakis received 3,227,518 votes in New York, and George Bush received 2,974,190 votes. Dukakis won *all* of New York's 36 electoral votes; Bush received none. Overall, adding together all the states' electoral votes, the effect is to "amplify" (some would say "distort") the winner's margin of victory.

Some degree of amplification may be acceptable. It may even be desirable in order to give the victor an unambiguous mandate to govern.[22] But what happens if a candidate wins the popular vote and loses in the electoral college? Mathematically, that can happen, and in fact, it has. In 1888 President Grover Cleveland won a majority of popular votes yet failed to win reelection because he lost in the electoral college. There were two earlier elections, in 1824 and 1876, in which an apparent popular-vote winner lost the presidency (although the cases were not as clear-cut as in the 1888 election). Would Americans today accept as their president someone who had actually lost the popular vote to an opponent, or would they consider it a "stolen" election?

SHOULD WE ABOLISH THE ELECTORAL COLLEGE?

Because of the possibility of a "stolen" election as well as other reasons, some observers argue that the electoral college should be abolished. There is much to be said for and against this proposal. If we abolished the electoral college and relied on a *(Continued on page 477)*

FIGURE **17-8**

Winner-Takes-All: The 1988 Presidential Campaign

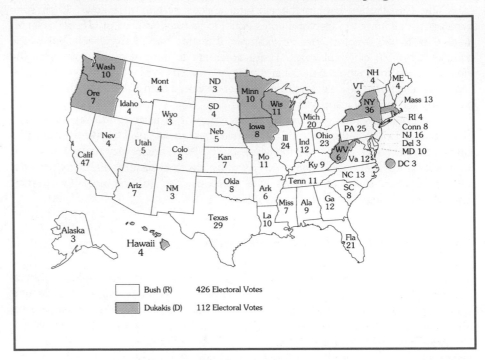

	Bush (R)	426 Electoral Votes
	Dukakis (D)	112 Electoral Votes

	Electoral Vote		Percentage Popular Vote			Electoral Vote		Percentage Popular Vote	
	Dukakis	*Bush*	*Dukakis*	*Bush*		*Dukakis*	*Bush*	*Dukakis*	*Bush*
Total	**112**	**426**	**46**	**54**					
Alabama	—	9	40	60	Missouri	—	11	48	52
Alaska	—	3	38	62	Montana	—	4	47	53
Arizona	—	7	39	61	Nebraska	—	5	40	60
Arkansas	—	6	43	57	Nevada	—	4	38	60
California	—	47	48	52	New Hamp-shire	—	4	37	63
Colorado	—	8	46	54	New Jersey	—	16	43	57
Connecticut	—	8	47	53	New Mexico	—	5	48	52
Delaware	—	3	43	57	New York	36	—	52	48
District of Columbia	3	—	86	14	North Carolina	—	13	42	58
Florida	—	21	39	61	North Dakota	—	3	43	57
Georgia	—	12	40	60	Ohio	—	23	45	55
Hawaii	4	—	55	45	Oklahoma	—	8	42	58
Idaho	—	4	37	63	Oregon	7	—	53	47
Illinois	—	24	49	51	Pennsylvania	—	25	49	51
Indiana	—	12	40	60	Rhode Island	4	—	56	44
Iowa	8	—	55	45	South Carolina	—	8	38	62
Kansas	—	7	43	57	South Dakota	—	3	47	53
Kentucky	—	9	44	56	Tennessee	—	11	42	58
Louisiana	—	10	45	55	Texas	—	29	44	56
Maine	—	4	44	56	Utah	—	5	33	67
Maryland	—	10	49	51	Vermont	—	3	49	51
Massachusetts	13	—	54	46	Virginia	—	12	40	60
Michigan	—	20	46	54	Washington	10	—	51	49
Minnesota	10	—	54	46	West Virginia	6	—	52	48
Mississippi	—	7	40	60	Wisconsin	11	—	52	48
					Wyoming	—	3	39	61

Source: New York Times, November 10, 1988, p. B5. Reprinted with permission.

The electoral college greatly exaggerates the victor's winning margin because *all* of a state's electoral votes go to the candidate who wins a majority of the state's popular votes. In Pennsylvania, for example, George Bush won 51% of the state's popular votes in 1988, compared to 49% for Dukakis, yet Bush won all of Pennsylvania's 25 electoral votes.

Points to Remember

1. Those Americans most likely to vote are affluent, educated, middle-aged whites. The most reliable predictor of whether or not a person will vote is years of education.

2. The Democrats' strongest supporters are blacks, Jews, and union members. The majority of white southerners vote Republican. Other groups are less predictable.

3. When major voting blocs shift their party preference, it sometimes results in a critical, or realigning, election. At present, we may have entered an era of dealignment.

4. The electoral college is a winner-takes-all system. It amplifies the extent of the winner's victory. On at least one occasion, in 1888, it led to the defeat of a candidate who had won the majority of popular votes.

5. Abolition of the electoral college would eliminate the dangers of "another 1888," but it might lead to worse dangers: a splintering of the majority, the proliferation of minor parties, and the possibility of electing a candidate who would not represent the will of the majority.

(Continued from page 475)

popular nationwide election, what would happen? One result would probably be a great proliferation of minor parties. As we discussed in chapter 16, the present system is very hard on minor parties because it denies them electoral votes. (The last notable minor party candidate, John Anderson in 1980, got about 7 percent of the popular vote but no electoral votes.) Abolishing the electoral college would encourage every party to run candidates because *now they could get something for their efforts.* Without the electoral college, Americans might also be more inclined to vote for a minor party candidate instead of settling on one of the two major party candidates. We could then have an election that would result in something like this: The Democratic presidential candidate gets 39 percent of the vote; the Republican gets 38 percent; the candidate of Minor Party A gets 10 percent; the candidate of Minor Party B, 7 percent; the candidate of Minor Party C, 6 percent. Who wins? Some would say the Democrat. But the Democrat received only 39 percent of the vote—not a clear majority. Suppose, then, there was a runoff election between the top two candidates. That would mean a new election, another round of campaigning, and another delay before the new president is named. More ominously, it would mean that all the little splinter parties could throw their weight around, promising to support one of the major parties in return for concessions. The "swing vote" of a tiny, unrepresentative party could thus determine the election—a very undemocratic outcome.

Packaging Candidates

Before people can vote, they have to decide for whom to vote. How voters decide, how the candidates help them decide, and what kinds of means (fair or foul) the candidates use as political salesmanship are examined in this section.

During the Checkers speech, Nixon held forth for half an hour, alternately sitting and standing in front of a live camera. Without any music or voiceovers or dissolving images, Nixon managed to talk his way into the hearts of his audience. Nowadays a candidate would hire a political consultant, who will "package" the candidate. This means that the consultant will generate as much publicity as possible for the candidate and at the same time make him or her look like the most wonderful—yet humble—person ever to run for public office.

The art of packaging candidates has a long history. In 1840 the supporters of William Henry Harrison knew all about packaging. To attract attention, they rolled a large paper ball from Kentucky to Baltimore, Maryland, where the National Convention of Whig Young Men was held. (This is the origin of the phrase "keep the ball

In the 1888 presidential election, supporters of Benjamin Harrison rolled a large
paper ball across the country. The packaging stunt, first used by William Henry
Harrison in 1840, gave rise to the expression "keep the ball rolling."

rolling.") They also invented the myth, later justly appropriated by Lincoln's campaign,
that their candidate had grown up in a log cabin. In fact, Harrison was raised in a
house in Ohio that had 22 rooms and was covered with clapboards. Like today, the
nineteenth and the early twentieth centuries were full of this kind of campaign
ballyhoo, with exaggeration and slogans often substituting for rational argument.

The importance of packaging candidates has increased over the past 50 years.
Now that there is television, every serious candidate for high office needs a media
expert. Second, and perhaps most important, the decline of state and local party
organizations and the proliferation of primary elections have meant that the candidate is now thrown back on his or her own resources for winning office. The
candidate must personally woo voters as never before. And one very, very important
tool for wooing voters is television, as discussed in chapter 14.

Television can also be used against opponents. In recent years "negative"
advertising has become increasingly common. In the 1988 presidential election
George Bush's campaign aired a series of television advertisements that depicted
Bush's opponent, Michael Dukakis, as being soft on crime and criminals. The most
controversial of these commercials showed prisoners going through a revolving door
while a voiceover reminded viewers that, as governor of Massachusetts, Dukakis had
authorized weekend furloughs for convicts, including murderers. The highly effective
advertisement angered Dukakis's supporters, who regarded it as an appeal to raw
emotions.

All of this raises troubling questions. Has television made it possible for
candidates to be elected solely on the basis of their "images," without any reference to
their positions on issues? Can voters be manipulated by political advertisements?

CAN CANDIDATES BE SOLD?

In 1969 a young reporter named Joe McGinnis published a book suggesting that people can indeed be manipulated by television advertisements. The book, *The Selling of the President 1968*, outlined the techniques used by Richard Nixon's campaign staff during the 1968 presidential election.[23] Drawn mostly from the world of advertising, his campaign staff was well equipped to change Nixon's image. They put together a series of clever television advertisements that portrayed a "new Nixon"—one who was relaxed, serene, and able to respond coolly to the toughest questions. In one of the television spots, Nixon was shown standing alone, without notes, in front of an audience that included blacks, students, and senior citizens. Individuals would ask him how he stood on controversial questions, and Nixon, looking very confident, would shoot back articulate answers. In fact, the audience was hand-picked and the questions were rehearsed. These and other slick television spots were used with increasing frequency as Election Day approached.

"I'm still undecided—I like Dukakis' make-up and camera angles, but I'm impressed with Bush's backdrops and twenty-second sound bites!" *Drawing by Doug Marlette for the* Atlanta Constitution.

In the sixteenth century an exiled Florentine statesman named Niccolò Machiavelli wrote that "the mass of mankind is always swayed by appearances"; to be a successful prince, therefore, you must understand the art of deception, the art of "seeming."[24] Machiavelli had a certain grandness of vision that helped to qualify his cynicism. In McGinnis's book, Nixon's advisers came across as Machiavellians minus the grandeur. They just wanted to sell their candidate, and they operated on the assumption that American voters can be sold anything because they are mentally feeble. As one of them put it: "Voters are basically lazy, basically uninterested in making an *effort* to understand. . . . Reason pushes the viewer back, it assaults him, it demands that he agree or disagree; impression can envelop him, invite him in, without making an intellectual demand."[25]

This is cynicism, but it is also naiveté. The assumption seems to be that voters can be manipulated—that their belief systems can be moved this way and that—by clever commercials. There is very little empirical evidence to support that assumption and much to belie it. In 1968 Nixon won, but his opponent, Hubert Humphrey, kept gaining on him *even as the Nixon ad campaign intensified*. Later studies of political advertisements by political scientists Thomas Patterson and Robert McClure suggested that *certain* kinds of advertisements can have an effect on undecided voters but that "image" advertisements, the ones with the pretty music and the pictures of candidates being wonderful people, do not change many people's minds. Those voters who liked the candidate to begin with will like his or her advertisement, and those opposed to the candidate will say, "Look at that phony!".[26]

But if image advertising does not brainwash viewers, it is not for lack of trying. Its whole intent is to short-circuit reasoning, appealing instead to primitive fantasies and fears. The 1988 presidential election featured some of these appeals, such as the revolving-door television advertisement on prison furloughs mentioned earlier, but it certainly was not the first time that such tactics were used. In 1828 Andrew Jackson's supporters put out the word that Jackson's opponent, John Quincy Adams, was a part-time pimp![27] In 1884 the Republicans kept reminding voters about Democrat Grover Cleveland's illegitimate child by repeating this refrain: "Ma, Ma, where's my pa?" (After Cleveland's victory, the Democrats countered with, "He's in the White House, ha-ha-ha.") Then there was the famous daisy commercial of 1964. During that election year President Johnson's media people put together a television advertisement aimed at his opponent, Arizona senator Barry Goldwater, who was often accused of being too hawkish. The commercial showed a little girl in a white dress pulling the petals off a daisy. She was counting, "One, two, three, four. . . ." When she got to "nine," a man's voice took over: "ten, nine, eight, seven, six. . . ." At "zero," the scene dissolved into a nuclear explosion, and then President Johnson's voice came on: "These are the stakes. To make a world in which all of God's children can live, or go into the dark. . . ." Goldwater's staff cried, "Foul," and Johnson pulled the commercial, but the uproar attracted the attention of the network television news shows. They ran the commercial in its entirety—to the delight of Johnson's staff.[28]

ADVERTISEMENTS AGAINST JUDICIAL CANDIDATES: ANTI-BORK

Even though negative advertisements go back a long way in American history, in 1987 something unprecedented occurred: For the first time they were used to influence opinion against a *judicial* nominee. In July 1987 President Reagan nominated Federal Appeals Court judge Robert H. Bork to fill a vacancy on the U.S. Supreme Court. Judge Bork's judicial philosophy, described by him as exemplifying "judicial restraint," put him at odds with a number of liberal, civil rights, feminist, and pro-choice interest groups, and they in turn sponsored many anti-Bork advertisements. One television advertisement, paid for by People for the American Way (PAW), a liberal interest group, used actor Gregory Peck to say "we found out that there is something *strange* about Judge Bork." Then, with haunted-house music playing in the background, Peck went on: "He defended poll taxes and literacy tests, which kept many Americans from voting. He opposed the civil rights law that ended 'whites only' signs at lunch counters. He doesn't believe the Constitution protects your right to privacy." PAW also sponsored a newspaper advertisement charging that Bork stood for "sterilizing workers, no privacy," and an intent to "turn back the clock on civil rights." Another newspaper advertisement, this one from the National Abortion Rights Action League (NARAL), asserted that Bork would "wipe out every advance women have made in the 20th century" (see illustration opposite). NARAL sent out a mass mailing of a letter signed by actress Joanne Woodward stating that "NARAL is mobilizing its largest and most critical campaign ever—to stop the nomination of Judge Bork. $500,000 is needed immediately to cover costs of full-page newspaper ads, to launch demonstrations nationwide, to pay for a massive media campaign. . . . All Americans must be reminded of the desperate days of back-alley abortions and the maiming and death of women driven to extreme measures."[29] Bork's nomination was defeated in the Senate, although it is not clear whether or not these advertisements played a major role in his defeat.

Bork's supporters charged that his record and his positions were being wildly distorted, and even the liberal *Washington Post* worried about elements of "intellectual vulgarization and personal savagery" in the anti-Bork campaign.[30] But the campaign against Bork raises a concern that is even more troubling. Some worry our judicial confirmation process may be turning into an election contest, complete with advertisements, celebrities, and fund-raising. In our system of government the federal judiciary is not supposed to be an elected branch. Yet the Bork controversy assumed many of the aspects of a political campaign. "We're getting perilously close to electing a Supreme Court Justice," said Lloyd N. Cutler, a Washington lawyer and prominent Democrat.[31]

SHOULD POLITICAL ADVERTISEMENTS BE BANNED?

Disgust at the manipulative intent of television advertisements and the fear that the cost of those advertisements will discourage would-be candidates of modest means have led some critics to advocate their abolition. One such critic is journalist Elizabeth Drew. In place of television advertisements, she suggests that "free" air time be donated to candidates for public office.[32] Her proposal is not without precedent (this practice is common in Europe), but it raises several questions. First, would banning

(Continued on page 482)

What women have to fear from Robert Bork.

You wouldn't vote for a politician who threatened to wipe out every advance women have made in the 20th Century. Yet your Senators are poised to cast a vote that could do just that. Senate confirmation of Robert Bork to the Supreme Court might cost you the right to make your most personal and private decisions. His rulings might leave you no choice—in relationships, in childbearing, in your career. He must be stopped. Tell your Senators. Our lives depend on it.

If Robert Bork is confirmed to the Supreme Court, he'll be the deciding vote on questions that affect every aspect of our lives.

The fair-minded, deliberate, balanced Supreme Court we're all familiar with will be a thing of the past. A right-wing 5-4 majority will prevail for decades.

Robert Bork's writings and his record demonstrate a hostility to rights most women would consider fundamental, from personal privacy to the equality of women and men before the law. And he's threatened to overturn any Supreme Court precedent that stands in his way.

According to Bork, women can be forced to choose between being sterilized and losing their jobs...

A state can declare the use of birth control illegal and invade your privacy to enforce the law...

You wouldn't even be protected against sexual harassment at work (Robert Bork doesn't believe such coercion is "discriminatory").

The fact is, Robert Bork's nomination threatens almost every major gain women have made since we won the right to vote. He would deny women the freedom, fairness and independence we've come to expect as first-class citizens.

Stripped of our most basic Constitutional guarantees of personal privacy and equal protection, women would have no defense against the "moral majority" extremists.

First to go? Your right to make a private decision about abortion. With Bork on the Court, your basic freedom to decide when, whether and under what circumstances to bear children could be taken away forever.

A state could ban both birth control and abortion—throwing women back to the age when pregnancy was, in effect, compulsory and women risked their lives to terminate a pregnancy.

Far-fetched? Far from it.

Attempts have already been made to officially permit discrimination against women who've chosen abortion—even though abortion is entirely legal. Women who made this profoundly private decision, protected by our Constitution, could be singled out and denied education and employment opportunities.

The Supreme Court nominee doesn't think vital Constitutional guarantees apply to women.

And a Supreme Court dominated by the right would do nothing to stop it.

Whatever your personal feeling about abortion, the decision must be up to you—not imposed by some political appointee.

But then, that's precisely why Robert Bork was nominated to the Supreme Court. His expedient reading of the Constitution allows "moral majority" extremists to hope they can force their dogma on the rest of us under penalty of law.

Beginning with abortion. But extending from there into every aspect of women's lives, personal and professional, as if the U.S. Constitution simply didn't apply to women.

The choice is stark.

Your Senators can confirm Robert Bork—inviting right-wing extremists to challenge every right we possess.

Or they can reject Robert Bork—and uphold the Constitutional standards of freedom and fairness.

This is your chance to determine the course of our country and the status of women in a free society. Act now.

Or a man you've never met will decide your future for you.

We're one vote away from losing our most fundamental rights... one Justice away from injustice. Your Senators must hear from you. Many are undecided on Bork... and wonder if you know how much is at stake. Mail the coupons immediately. Robert Bork must be stopped. And it's your turn to make history.

This full-page advertisement in the *New York Times* was one of the many directed against Judge Robert Bork in 1987 after he was nominated to the Supreme Court. There were also radio and television spots and mass mailings against Bork, whose nomination was later rejected by the Senate. The anti-Bork campaign marked the first time in American history that political advertisements in major media were used for the purpose of defeating a Supreme Court nominee. Some worried that the precedent could turn future judicial nominations into electoral contests.

(Continued from page 480) advertisements limit free speech? The First Amendment prohibits government from interfering with our right of self-expression. Second, who will pay for the "free" air time? If the networks are forced to donate the time, they will raise the price for other advertisements, and advertisers will then pass the increased cost along to consumers. The voters will pay for it. If the advertisements are paid for by the government, the money will come from the taxpayers—the voters again. Third, who will be given all this "free" air time? Only candidates from the major parties, or those from the minor parties as well? If the latter, then expect to see advertisements from a lot of parties on television. And if all the candidates in primary elections also get "free" air time, the public may get terminally weary of politics.

Money in Political Campaigns

Although the money spent trying to sell the candidate on television usually takes the biggest slice out of every campaign budget pie, funds are needed for many other things as well: for the salaries of aides; for hotels, meals, travel, and telephone bills; for private polls; for postage; for bumper stickers, posters, and balloons. The cost of running a campaign is growing astronomically. In 1988 the presidential election was financed by more than $92 million in taxpayers' money. Nevertheless, the parties also managed to raise another $137 million in private contributions, plus several million dollars more earmarked for "operating expenses."[33] The cost of campaigning for Congress is also rising dramatically. Campaign spending on House and Senate races totaled $457 million in 1988, more than double the amount spent a decade earlier.[34] One prominent California politician said, "[Money is] the mother's milk of politics."[35] How do politicians get that "milk"?

CAMPAIGN FINANCING

In the nineteenth and early twentieth centuries much of the money for campaigning came from political parties. The parties bankrolled the candidates, and, in turn, party members were rewarded with patronage jobs by their successful candidates. Gradually, the civil service laws enacted in the late nineteenth century, which awarded jobs

Points to Remember

1. Political packaging has a long history in America, going back at least as far as William Henry Harrison's Log Cabin campaign of 1840.

2. In the past 40 or 50 years, the importance of packaging has increased due to the arrival of television, the increase in the number of primaries, and the weakening of party organizations—all of which have forced the candidates to sell themselves to a mass public.

3. People cannot be manipulated by "image" advertisements on television, although the ones discussing issues can affect the decisions of undecided voters.

4. Many voters were unhappy with the "negative" tone of the 1988 presidential campaign, but negative campaigns are not uncommon in the United States.

5. In 1987, for the first time in our history, television advertisements were used for the purpose of defeating a nominee for a Supreme Court position, Robert H. Bork.

6. Some have proposed a ban on paid political television advertisements, and their replacement by the donation of "free" air time. This proposal raises a variety of questions, such as whether or not such a ban would violate the First Amendment, would be fair to all parties, and would lead to an excessive amount of political speechmaking on television.

on the basis of competitive exams, began to dry up patronage. The professionalization of "welfare," the spread of primary elections, and the increasing sophistication of former immigrant voting blocs have also hurt party "machines" in this century. By mid-century, party organizations had already stopped being the principal source of funding, which is one reason why Nixon turned to his industrialist friends for help in 1952.

Today parties play an even more marginal role. (In House races, for example, the average candidate received only 6 percent of his or her funds from party coffers in the mid-1980s.)[36] Not being wealthy himself, Nixon's own system was to find affluent friends. In the 1972 presidential campaign his top 10 contributors gave him more than $4 million. One of them, W. Clement Stone of Chicago, donated $2 million in 1972 alone out of a total of $4.7 million between 1968 and 1972. According to Stone, Nixon told him on at least two occasions: "Clem, you and I know that I wouldn't be here if it weren't for you."[37] Nixon's campaign staff also solicited funds from well-to-do interest groups. Dairy interests contributed more than half a million dollars to Nixon's

GLOBAL PERSPECTIVES:

Campaigning in Great Britain

In *The Governance of Great Britain*, published in 1976, former British prime minister Harold Wilson recounted how he came to be nominated as Labour party leader in 1963. Wilson was in the United States when he received the news that then-Labour leader Hugh Gaitskill had fallen gravely ill. An American friend, upon hearing that Wilson's party colleagues had called him back to England, realized that Wilson was now a serious candidate for the Labour nomination. He offered Wilson $10,000 to help with the "campaign." "I replied," said Wilson, "that I could not take a penny from him, or any other American friend; moreover, the campaign, as he would put it, would not cost $10,000 in all. He was amazed, and when he asked me how much I estimated, I said, 'Two bob, at most'; i.e., two old shillings, ten new pence—at the then-current exchange rate, twenty-eight cents."

Wilson's American friend did not believe him even after Wilson explained that getting the nomination in Great Britain meant winning the approval of other Labourites in Parliament who have known him for years. "Canvassing," as it is called there, going around the country to campaign for the nomination, is actually counterproductive. After getting the nomination, Wilson sought to quell his friend's disbelief by sending him a complete audit of his nomination expenses. "It amounted to eight

(old) pence, a little over nine cents, and was accounted for by telephone calls to two over-enthusiastic supporters of mine who were defying my ban on canvassing."

reelection campaign in 1972. International Telephone and Telegraph (ITT) picked up a bill of $400,000 to help pay for the Republican Convention in 1972. A deluge of illegal cash contributions was made to the Nixon reelection fund by a variety of major corporations. What did these special interests get in return? The full story may never come to light, but we know that Nixon's Department of Agriculture raised price supports for milk shortly after the Republicans began receiving payments from the milk lobby; we also know that Nixon officials pressured the Justice Department to drop a lawsuit against ITT once its contribution arrived. These and many other questionable activities were revealed during the Watergate investigation.

Watergate was discussed more fully in chapter 10. For our purposes here, we need to remember this: By 1974, the year Nixon resigned, Watergate had become more than a news story; it had become a symbol. Watergate had come to stand for everything underhanded in American politics. In the area of campaign finance, it stood for laundered money—for all the big contributions that came into Nixon headquarters and were routed through a Mexican bank account and back up to Miami in order to remove the names of the original contributors. It stood for shakedowns of corporations—implied promises to help them if they contributed and threats to hurt them if they did not. It stood for the suitcases full of untraceable cash that were flown into Washington, D.C.—cash that was later used to hire the Watergate burglars and then bribe them to keep quiet after they were caught. By this point, the mix of money and politics was really overripe. Congress knew it had to act, and in 1974 it did.

FEDERAL ELECTION CAMPAIGN AMENDMENTS, 1974

The same Congress that forced the resignation of President Richard Nixon in the summer of 1974 also passed a series of amendments to the Federal Election Campaign Act of 1971. Together, the original law and the new amendments contained the following provisions:

1. *Spending Limits.* All candidates for federal elections (for the Senate, the House, and the office of President) were limited in the amount of money they could spend. Different formulas were used to set the spending limits for each type of race. As we shall see shortly, this provision was later struck down by the Supreme Court. It is not operative today, although the rest of the act is.
2. *Contribution Limits.* Individuals could contribute no more than $1,000 to each candidate in each election. (That would mean a $2,000 limit per candidate if the candidate ran in both the primary and the general election.) There were also limits on how much a person could give to political parties and Political Action Committees (PACs).
3. *Disclosure.* Candidates were required to file periodic reports disclosing the names and addresses of everyone who donated more than $100 and listing all expenditures of more than $1,000.
4. *Public Financing of Presidential Campaigns.* Presidential candidates had the option of accepting money to help pay for both primaries and the general election. The money was provided from a special fund fed by federal income tax checkoffs.
5. *Federal Election Commission (FEC).* A special Federal Election Commission was set up—the majority of its members to be appointed by Congress—to oversee the whole process, disburse the funds, and release the lists of contributors to the public.

The federal income tax checkoff for public financing works like this: Your annual federal income tax form has a box to check if you want $1 of the taxes you owe ($2 on joint returns) diverted into a special fund to help subsidize presidential elections. The fund subsidizes both primary and general elections. Primary candidates must first "qualify" to receive funds by collecting $100,000 on their own. To ensure that the candidates do not receive all their qualifying money from one or two wealthy people, the law limits individual contributions to no more than $5,000 each and requires that they be sent in from at least 20 states. Candidates are then given a matching check for $100,000 from the government. Once a candidate receives the nomination, he or she is entitled to more public money to run in the general election.

Public financing is limited to presidential elections. In 1974 a provision extending it to congressional races passed the Senate but was defeated in the House. Since then, several attempts to reintroduce it have also been defeated. Supporters of public financing claim that it has worked well at the presidential level, moderating the influence of "special interest money." They see the real problem now in congressional races, where the power of PACs and other special interests is formidable. Opponents, however, say that public financing would be tantamount to an "incumbent protection act" because contributors are especially eager to bankroll those already in power.

Almost immediately after their passage in 1974, the amendments to the Federal Election Campaign Act of 1971 were challenged in court. The main complaint was that the spending and contribution limits violated free speech. In 1976, in *Buckley v. Valeo*, the U.S. Supreme Court partly agreed.

BUCKLEY v. VALEO (1976): SPENDING LIMITS VIOLATE THE FIRST AMENDMENT

In the 1976 case of *Buckley v. Valeo*, the Court ruled that the spending limitations in the 1974 amendments violated the First Amendment's protection of free speech. Restricting the amount of money one person or group can spend on communication during a campaign, the Court said, "reduces the quantity of expression by restricting

Should *Buckley v. Valeo* Be Overturned?

YES Jonathan Bingham

Based upon Jonathan Bingham, "Democracy or Plutocracy? The Case for a Constitutional Amendment to Overturn *Buckley v. Valeo*," *Annals of the American Academy of Political and Social Science* (July 1986), pp. 103–114.

Bingham, a former New York congressman, calls money a "curse" in politics, not only because it enables the wealthy to exert undue influence but for two other reasons as well: It erodes public confidence in democracy and discourages good people from running for or staying in office. "There is no doubt that *every two years* valuable members of Congress decide to retire because they are fed up with having constantly to beg." The spending limits enacted by Congress in 1974 would have moderated these evil effects of money in politics, but the *Buckley* decision wiped them out. Bingham considers the Court's decision "doctrinaire" because it proceeds from an extreme view of free speech and misunderstands the real spirit of the First Amendment: the protection of give-and-take argument, not slick promotion. According to Bingham, a constitutional amendment, carefully worded to ensure free speech, should be enacted to reverse *Buckley*.

NO David Broder

Based upon David Broder, transcript of "Campaign Spending: Money and Media," p. 17, from the PBS series *The Constitution: That Delicate Balance*. This segment was broadcast on October 30, 1984.

Appearing on the television series *The Constitution: That Delicate Balance* on the Public Broadcasting System on October 30, 1984, to discuss the role of money in politics, *Washington Post* columnist David Broder argued that the Supreme Court was right to strike down spending limits. He also thought that the Court's distinction between spending and contribution limits made sense. According to Broder, a contribution is an effort by someone to *give* voice to a candidate or a cause, whereas expenditures "*are* voice" [emphasis added]. Since Broder identifies expenditures with voice, he concludes that limiting expenditures limits speech. "I am disturbed," Broder said, "that there are so many liberals in this room who cannot see as a constitutional principle that you are treading on very dangerous ground when you say to an individual in this country, 'You may not spend your own money legitimately in the cause of seeking office in this country.'"

Postscript

As Broder observes, many liberal writers and politicians support spending limits. Yet liberals are usually strong supporters of free speech. The obvious question is whether or not this is, as Broder believes, a contradiction. "Money talks," the old saying goes, which raises less obvious but more perplexing questions having to do with the distribution of money and the rights of the wealthy in our society.

Elizabeth Drew's *Politics and Money: The New Road to Corruption* (New York: Macmillan, 1983) agrees with Bingham about the "curse" of money in campaigns and suggests means of limiting spending. But Gary Jacobson's *Money in Congressional Elections* (New Haven, CT: Yale University Press, 1980) argues that spending limits usually benefit incumbents. For a longer look at the history of money in campaigns since George Washington's time, see George Thayer, *Who Shakes the Money Tree?* (New York: Simon & Schuster, 1973).

the number of issues discussed, the depth of their exploration, and the size of the audience reached." Why is that? The Court noted that because our society is dominated by the mass media, candidates who cannot buy media time are as good as silenced. To limit the amount of money they can spend, therefore, is to limit their right to speak.

The Court, however, refused to strike down the law's limit on *contributions* because, it said, such limits did not impair free speech. Even though, according to the law, contributors can give only $1,000 to each of their favorite candidates, they can voice their views through a variety of other means, such as buying air time to speak on behalf of the candidates. Meanwhile, candidates can go elsewhere for money as soon as one contributor's limit has been reached. The Court made an analogy between the right to speak and the right to drive: If you say, "You may spend no more than two dollars on gas," then you have effectively limited someone's right to drive. But if you say, "You may get no more than two dollars' worth of gas from *any one gas station*," then you have not limited the right to drive; you have merely forced the driver to go to several sources.[38]

Despite this explanation, many critics think that the Court's distinction between spending limits and contribution limits is questionable; some even say the decision was wrong and should be reversed. One of these critics is former Democratic congressman Jonathan Bingham, who favors a constitutional amendment reversing it. On the other side of the argument is *Washington Post* columnist David Broder. Their contrasting views are presented in this chapter's Taking Sides section.

THE *NCPAC* CASE (1985): NO LIMIT ON INDEPENDENT PAC SPENDING

In *Buckley* the Court struck down the spending limitations in the 1974 amendments. However, the Court said that a candidate who elects to receive public money for the general election must be subject to spending limits. Now, suppose the candidate takes the public money and accepts the spending limits. Suppose also that an *independent* Political Action Committee (PAC) decides to spend money in support of the candidate by taking out advertisements on his or her behalf. Does the independent PAC have to accept spending limits? By a vote of 7–2 in *Federal Election Committee v. NCPAC* (1985), the Court answered no.

NCPAC (pronounced "nickpack") stands for National Conservative Political Action Committee, a conservative PAC that supported Ronald Reagan in the 1980 and 1984 presidential campaigns. The Federal Election Committee tried to impose a $1,000 spending limit on NCPAC in 1984, on the grounds that it was supporting a candidate—Reagan—who had taken public money and was thus bound by spending limits. NCPAC argued that it was an independent entity, not controlled by the Reagan reelection committee and that therefore no limits could be placed on its spending. The Court agreed. The opinion, written by Justice William Rehnquist, said that forbidding the expenditure of more than $1,000 to present political views "is much like allowing a speaker in a public hall to express his views while denying him the use of the amplifying system." Once again, as in *Buckley*, the Court was saying that it is not possible to separate the freedom to speak from the freedom to spend.[39]

Points to Remember

1. Money has always been necessary to run political campaigns in the United States. But today, because of high media costs, huge sums are required.

2. In the past, campaign money was supplied largely by political parties. Today, with party organizations in a decline, the candidates must go elsewhere for money.

3. The Watergate affair demonstrated the danger of accepting large sums of money from wealthy individuals and special interests. The scandal motivated Congress in 1974 to pass a series of amendments to the Federal Election Campaign Act of 1971. The 1974 amendments included (1) spending limits, (2) contribution limits, (3) disclosure requirements, (4) public financing of presidential elections, and (5) the establishment of a Federal Elections Commission to monitor the whole process.

4. The 1974 amendments' spending limits were struck down by the Supreme Court in *Buckley v. Valeo* (1976). However, the Court upheld the contribution limits.

5. In the *NCPAC* case of 1985 the Court said that independent PACs could spend as much as they wanted and that any attempt to limit their spending would violate the First Amendment.

Reflections

Much has changed in the area of campaign spending since Nixon's Checkers speech, although much of what was to come was prefigured in that speech. The powerful eastern establishment wing of the Republican party was chastened by his speech; today it is a ghost of its former self. A few Republican liberals remain, but most have died, grown more conservative, or become Democrats. For their part, Democratic conservatives have also become an endangered species. The South, their traditional home, has been growing more Republican since the 1960s, and many of their old supporters, such as Catholics, are no longer very loyal Democrats.

At first glance the two parties seem to have been trading off blocs of constituents. It is not yet clear which party will be the long-term beneficiary. Perhaps neither party will be: Perhaps voters are actually swinging back and forth between the two parties, no longer wedded to either of them. It could be that the parties are not realigning, but dealigning. Only time will tell.

Time has already told us much about another aspect of the Checkers speech—the use of television. In those days television programming came to us on small, blurry black-and-white screens. "Checkers" was a half-hour production—by today's standards, an amateurish "talking head" show. By the 1960s everything had changed: television was fast-moving, it was in color, and it gave us sophisticated visuals, voiceovers, and dissolving images—all in a 30-second commercial. This is the type of political advertising we see today, and it worries many observers. Can pure "image" commercials manipulate viewers into voting for a candidate just because he or she looks good on camera? Can candidates be marketed like a detergent? In fact, the evidence seems to point in a different direction. Voters get whatever message they want to get out of image commercials, including messages contrary to the intent of those who make them.

Although their effectiveness varies, television advertisements are now a staple of American political campaigns. As with all other campaign costs, their costs have been skyrocketing. How should candidates get the money they need just to survive in a campaign? In the past, local parties had provided it. But by 1952 local parties were already losing power; Nixon, as we know, went to his business friends.

Maybe there is a better way. With the 1974 amendments to the Federal Election Campaign Act of 1971, Congress provided for public financing of presidential campaigns, and there is a movement to extend it to congressional campaigns. Is it right for taxpayers to pay the cost of politicians' campaigns (even when they do so voluntarily, as in the tax checkoff system)? Would public financing of congressional campaigns amount to an "incumbent protection act"? There may or may not be good answers to these questions, but public financing is worth thinking about. One way of formulating the problem with American political campaigns is to say that they are overspent. Another way is to say that they are underfinanced. These two formulations point toward different solutions: spending limitations on the one hand, and government help on the other. The experts cannot agree. What do *you* think?

Notes

1. Richard M. Nixon, *Six Crises* (Garden City, NY: Doubleday & Company, 1962), p. 86.
2. Nixon, pp. 110-11.
3. *New York Times*, Sept. 24, 1952, p. 22.
4. *New York Times*, p. 22.
5. Garry Wills, *Nixon Agonistes* (Boston: Houghton Mifflin Company, 1969), p. 110.
6. Max Farrand, ed., *Records of the Federal Convention* (New Haven, CT: Yale University Press, 1927), vol. II, p. 201.
7. Richard Scammon and Ben J. Wattenberg, *The Real Majority* (New York: Coward, McMann, Inc. 1970), p. 55.
8. Raymond E. Wolfinger and Steven J. Rosenstone, *Who Votes?* (New Haven, CT: Yale University Press, 1980), p. 130.
9. A. James Reichley, "Religion and Political Realignment," *The Brookings Review* (Fall 1984), pp. 29-35.
10. Cited in Everett Carll Ladd, "The 1988 Elections: Continuation of the Post-New Deal System," *Political Science Quarterly* (Spring 1989), p. 15.
11. See, for example, V. O. Key, Jr., "A Theory of Critical Elections," *The Journal of Politics* (February 1955), pp. 3-18; Walter Dean Burnham, *Critical Elections and the Mainsprings of American Politics* (New York: W. W. Norton, 1970).
12. *New York Times*, Sept. 1, 1985, p. 26.
13. *New York Times*, p. 26.
14. *New York Times*, Nov. 10, 1988, p. B6.
15. See, for example, James L. Sundquist, *Dynamics of the Party System: Alignment and Realignment of Political Parties in the United States*, 2d ed. (Washington, DC: Brookings Institute, 1983); Everett Carll Ladd, Jr., with Charles D. Hadley, *Transformations of the American Party System: Political Coalitions from the New Deal to the 1970s* (New York: W. W. Norton, 1975).
16. David G. Lawrence and Richard Fleisher, "Puzzles and Confusions: Political Realignment in the 1980s," *Political Science Quarterly* (Spring 1987), p. 90. The authors, however, point to one serious weakness in the "dealignment" thesis: its failure to explain why election outcomes seem to tilt toward the Republicans at the presidential level.
17. Everett Carll Ladd, p. 18.
18. This is an adaptation of a thesis developed by political scientist James Q. Wilson. See Wilson, "Realignment at the Top, Dealignment at the Bottom," in Austin Ranney, *The American Elections of 1984* (Washington, DC: American Enterprise Institute, 1985), pp. 297-310. Wilson, however, claims that the realignment has taken place only among party "elites." This seems questionable, unless we define *elites* so broadly as to take in all who vote for a party because they agree with what the party stands for, in contrast to those who vote out of sheer inertia or habit. If *elites* means what it usually means, namely those *few* who go to the conventions, write the platforms, and otherwise play prominent roles in party affairs, then the revolution in the two parties has spread far beyond elite circles. A 35-year-old New York City advertising executive whose father was a liberal Republican and who now votes Democratic because of the Democrats' support of the pro-choice stand on abortion is not necessarily a party elite, nor is a 25-year-old Alabama truck driver whose father was a New Deal Democrat and who votes Republican because of the Democrats' support of gay rights.
19. For present purposes, the somewhat arbitrary figure of 42 percent was used. Decrease it and more states will become "potential" Republican strongholds; increase it and there will be fewer. In both cases the *regional pattern* will look the same: The "Republican" states will tend to cluster in the South and West.
20. Kevin Philips, *The Emerging Republican Majority* (New Rochelle, NY: Arlington House, 1969).
21. But see Joseph A. Mulusky, "An Electoral College Fable: How the Carter-Ford Election Might Have Made Ronald Reagan President in 1976," *Presidential Studies Quarterly* (Summer 1981), pp. 384-386.
22. See Martin Diamond, *The Electoral College and the American Idea of Democracy* (Washington, DC: American Enterprise Institute, 1977).
23. Joe McGinnis, *The Selling of the President 1968* (The Trident Press, 1969).

24. Niccolò Machiavelli, *The Prince* (Arlington Heights, IL: AHM Publishing Corporation, 1947), p. 52. Originally published in 1513.

25. Machiavelli, p. 224.

26. Thomas E. Patterson and Robert D. McClure, *The Unseeing Eye: The Myth of Television Power in National Elections* (New York: G. P. Putnam's Sons, 1976); Thomas Patterson, *The Mass Media Election* (New York: Praeger Publishers, 1980). According to Patterson and McClure, the most effective advertisements are the ones dealing with issues, and such advertisements are not without content, although, of course, they address the issues in a biased way. Voters actually learn from them; in fact, they may even learn more about the issues from such advertisements than they do from television news programs!

27. See letter of Fred I. Lewis, *New York Times*, Nov. 20, 1988, p. 22.

28. Kathleen Hall Jamieson, *Packaging the Presidency* (New York: Oxford University Press, 1984), p. 200.

29. Fund-raising letter for NARAL, signed by Joanne Woodward.

30. Editorial in *Washington Post*, Oct. 5, 1987, p. A14.

31. Quoted in Stuart Taylor, "Politics in the Bork Battle," *New York Times*, Sept. 28, 1987, p. 1.

32. Elizabeth Drew, *Politics and Money: The New Road to Corruption* (New York: Macmillan, 1983), p. 150.

33. Richard L. Berke, "Some True Tales of Campaign Cash," *New York Times*, Dec. 11, 1988, p. 43.

34. "Democrats Spent Most on Election," *New York Times*, Jan. 26, 1989, p. 27.

35. Jesse Unruh, quoted in Fred W. Friendly and Martha J. H. Elliott, *The Constitution: That Delicate Balance* (New York: Random House, 1984), p. 91.

36. Gregg Easterbrook, "What's Wrong With Congress?" *The Atlantic Monthly* (December 1984), p. 64.

37. *New York Times*, Aug. 4, 1973, p. 13; Aug. 4, 1973, V, p. 2.

38. *Buckley v. Valeo*, 424 U.S. 1, (1976).

39. *Federal Election Commission v. National Conservative Political Action Committee, et al.*, 470 U.S. 480 (1985).

PART V

Domestic and Foreign Policies

To understand American government we need to study not only its institutions and processes, but also its major policies. This section examines the evolution, present positions, and future directions of our domestic and foreign policies. Chapter 18, which discusses our domestic economy, considers a number of issues: the causes of poverty and conceivable remedies, the uses and limitations of welfare, the balancing of our domestic budget, and the changes in our tax system. Chapter 19 studies American foreign policy in historical perspective, putting into context the exciting changes that have occurred in the past few years. Chapter 20, on national defense policies, strikes a more somber note as it examines the defense organizations and the defense theories and policies of the United States, its allies, and its adversaries.

18

Poverty, Welfare, and Taxes

The universal regard for money is the one hopeful fact in our civilization, the one sound spot in our social conscience.

George Bernard Shaw, preface to *Major Barbara*

At 68th Street and Park Avenue in New York City, the **The Other Park Avenue**
rhododendrons are blooming in front of Hunter College.
Crossing the avenue at 69th Street is a uniformed maid pushing a baby in
an English pram. Numbers 700 and 710 Park Avenue are imposing 14-story
penthouses with roof gardens. Across the avenue are some particularly
handsome brownstones, with brass carriage lamps in their doorways to
light the night. Walking past are a man of perhaps 60, sporting a bow tie,
and two boys about 10, one of them carrying a baseball bat that appears
not to have been used. On the corner of 75th and Park stands a shop:
"Flowers By Cort." A Cadillac limousine, with its windows shut, idles its
engine while the chauffeur runs inside.*

At 86th Street a hint of change appears. On this busy thoroughfare
people seem more hurried, less sure of themselves. Some black faces
(aside from servants) can be seen among the pedestrians.

*This account is drawn from the author's observations.

492

A man crouches amid squalor and graffiti in New York City. At one end of Park Avenue in New York City are gorgeous penthouses; at the other end are depressing slums. Why is there such a division of rich and poor in America? What causes poverty? The answers to these questions seem to vary according to ideology.

At 96th Street everything comes apart. The avenue's green center mall disappears and is replaced by a rusty iron fence. Twenty feet below lie railroad tracks. The penthouses have vanished, their places taken by rundown tenements, each half a block long with backs linked by clotheslines. The walls are spray-painted with graffiti—the baroque designs of aerosol artists. A bent old woman with a shopping bag in each hand peers into the garbage cans in front of the "Spanish-American Grocery."

At 100th and Park the railroad tracks slope upward and Park Avenue slopes downward. It is now divided by a stone wall several feet high that forces traffic into a narrow lane with the wall on one side and tenements on the other. The smell of dampness mixes with the smell of urine and uncollected garbage. At 103d Street a young man, staring aimlessly, sits on a box in front of New York Marble Works.

At 115th Street the stone wall is replaced by giant rusty stilts holding up the railroad tracks. Below are abandoned cars stripped of tires, their windshields smashed, the crushed glass scattered around the ground. Loud noises blare nearby. They blare from a suitcase-size radio. On this weekday afternoon men and boys are loitering around the radio, looking idle, bored, full of despair and defeat.

The trip between the two Park Avenues of New York City takes slightly more than five minutes by car. It can be duplicated in almost any other larger American city—in Chicago by driving from the Near North Side to South State Street; in Boston by driving from Beacon Hill to South Boston; in San Francisco by driving from the Marina to the Fillmore area; in Los Angeles by driving from Westwood to Watts; and so on.

494

This is *urban* poverty. Rural poverty, the poverty of the American countryside, is in some ways worse, although it is harder for the casual observer to see. Many rural areas are picturesque. Americans may pass through them on their vacations, little realizing—maybe not wanting to realize—that right behind the Holiday Inn there are shacks housing very poor people. In some rural areas there are hardly any visitors. Parts of Appalachia, a 13-state region running from New York to Mississippi, provide views of strip-mined hillsides, polluted streams, junked cars at the side of the road. Appalachia has an unemployment rate that approaches 20 percent, three times the national average.[1]

There has always been poverty. You can read about it in the Bible, in Shakespeare, in Dickens and Dostoyevsky. But that was *then*—in ancient times, in Elizabethan times, in nineteenth-century Europe. This is *today*, this is modern America. We are living in "the affluent society," as economist John Kenneth Galbraith called it in the 1950s. Poverty was hardly noticed until the 1960s, and when it was it was described in terms of "pockets of poverty." These "pockets" were going to be eliminated in one final campaign—a war on poverty. Since then, America has spent billions on job training programs, preschool learning programs, community action programs, urban renewal programs, school lunch programs, cultural uplift programs, food stamp programs, and outright cash grants.

Yet the slums remain, the urban ghettos remain, the poverty in the cities and the countryside—all remain. Some observers think it has gotten worse. More and more people seem to be dependent on welfare; families are falling apart; illegitimacy is increasing; the slums are full of crack addicts and drug dealers; AIDS is taking its grim toll; many young people are failing to learn essential skills—even reading and writing are beyond the reach of an increasing number. What is happening?

* * * * *

This chapter will discuss a number of questions concerning the American economy. But the issue that really haunts this chapter is the question *why*. Why does poverty persist? Where does the fault lie? What can be done about it?

Often, answers to these questions are shaped by ideology. Those on the ideological Left are inclined to talk about "rich and poor" in America.[2] Some of the arguments of the Left are subtle and sophisticated, but in cruder form the claim is that people are poor on the uptown end of Park Avenue because people living on downtown Park Avenue are rich. The rich have gotten that way at the expense of the poor. Their solution is redistribution. Find some means of taking money away from the rich and giving it to the poor.

Those on the ideological Right warn that schemes for redistributing wealth will end up by making everyone poor. Conservatives emphasize economic incentives: People should be encouraged to be productive. Reduce taxes for the rich and they will put their money to work; cut welfare to the poor and they will have to work.

On one point, all critics of our welfare system seem to agree: Poverty and welfare cannot be studied apart from the rest of the economy. Conservatives warn that schemes for redistributing wealth may kill the goose that laid the golden egg by hurting the nation's ability to generate wealth. Liberals insist that we have to look at poverty in relation to our economic system, which, they say, is what is keeping the poor poor. Both sides press for a larger focus than poverty itself. The point is well taken, and this chapter will attempt to meet that challenge. Starting with a discussion of the nature and extent of poverty in America, we will examine some of the successes and failures of government poverty programs. We will then turn to some of the broader issues of government taxing and spending policies.

Poverty in Modern America

According to a 1987 government report, 13.5 percent of Americans could be classified as poor, a much lower percentage than the nearly 20 percent who were living in poverty a generation ago. Still, it meant that 32.5 million Americans were living below the poverty line.[3] But what does it mean when we talk about the poverty line? How can we draw such a line?

HOW MANY POOR ARE THERE?

The Census Bureau defines the poverty line by calculating the annual cost of a basic, nutritionally adequate diet for a family of four, then multiplying it by three because the cost of food constitutes about a third of a family's annual expenditures. In 1987, a family of four was classified as poor if it had a cash income of less than $11,611.[4] This definition has often been criticized. Some critics say that it sets the poverty line too low. There is some evidence that poor people now spend less than one-third of their income on food, so to be more accurate the basic food budget may have to be multiplied by more than three.[5] Others think the definition puts the poverty line too high, for in calculating annual incomes it leaves out the noncash payments received by the poor, such as subsidized medical care, housing, and food stamps. Of course, if we compare the official poverty line in 1987 of $11,611 for a family of four with the median family income of Americans of $24,897 in that year, $11,611 is a very minimal standard indeed.

However, if we were to define poverty as "below median income," we would wind up with a *relative* definition of poverty. That would make poverty a totally insoluble problem, for (unless we equalize incomes) some people are always going to be making less than others. The opposite extreme is an *absolute* definition, which is based upon a fixed "bundle of goods" and makes that the dividing line between poverty and nonpoverty. By that calculus, hardly anyone is poor today. In 1900 only 15 percent of all living quarters had flush toilets; now almost 99 percent do. In 1900 only 3 percent of all dwellings had electricity; today 99 percent do. And who had television sets in 1945? Today just about every poor family has one. You can continue with this analysis, but what does it prove? That there are no poor people in America? Take a walk up Park Avenue in New York City. Or walk into the slums of any other city. Or go into the rural hollows of Appalachia.

Admittedly, poverty is more than the condition of material deprivation; it also includes the feeling that one is trapped in this condition. "Poverty in its truest sense," writes one authority on the subject, "is more than want; it is want mixed with a lack of hope."[6] To be poor today means not only to lack the basic amenities Americans have come to associate with a decent life; it also means to be left out, left back, and stuck at the low end of the economic scale while others move upward.

Who are these poor? As Table 18.1 (on page 496) indicates, the poor belong to a number of categories. Two-thirds are white and one-third black, although the percentage of blacks living in poverty is almost three times that of whites. Regionally,

Carmen Motta, a single mother, is photographed in one of the two small rooms she shares with her four children in a New York City welfare hotel. In 1986 she was receiving $422 in welfare payments and $61 in food stamps every month. Many single mothers and their children live in chronic poverty. Sadly, chronic poverty and dependence on welfare is often passed on to the next generation.

TABLE 18-1

Who Is Below the Poverty Level

	Number Below Poverty Level (in thousands)				Percent Below Poverty Level			
	All races	White	Black	Hispanic	All races	White	Black	Hispanic
National	32,546	21,409	9,683	5,470	13.5	10.5	33.1	28.2
Age								
Under 16 years old	11,859	7,289	4,007	2,493	21.2	16.2	46.7	40.6
16-21 years old	3,455	2,148	1,144	565	15.9	12.1	36.0	27.5
22-44 years old	9,596	6,470	2,647	1,628	10.7	8.5	25.1	21.2
45-64	4,145	2,905	1,007	536	9.1	7.4	23.5	20.4
65 years old and over	3,491	2,597	808	247	12.2	10.1	33.9	27.4
Region								
Northeast	5,476	3,860	1,391	1,232	11.0	8.9	28.8	36.6
Midwest	7,499	5,185	2,041	366	12.7	9.9	36.6	27.5
South	13,287	7,426	5,648	1,910	16.1	11.5	34.5	31.0
West	6,285	4,939	603	1,962	12.6	11.5	24.3	23.0

Data source: Statistical Abstract, 1989, No. 736, p. 454, which is based upon the U.S. Bureau of the Census, Current Population Reports, series P-60, No. 161.

This survey shows the number of people by race, age, and region who were below the poverty level as of March 1988. The figures for *all races* include other races that are not shown separately. Hispanic totals include Hispanics of any race.

the South is the hardest hit: 16.1 percent of its people are poor compared, for example, to 11 percent in the Northeast. The poor live in the central cities and in the countryside. (Not surprisingly, only a small percentage live in suburbs.) Taking all races and locations into account, the largest single group of poor people in this country are children under the age of 16. Over 21 percent of these children, numbering almost 12 million, live in poverty.

The Feminization of Poverty. Particularly worrisome is the fact that large and growing numbers of poor children live in households headed by women. Between 1970 and 1987 the percentage of American children living in households headed by single mothers increased from less than 11 percent to 21.3 percent (see Table 18.2). More than half of these children are poor—eight times the percentage of poor children in two-parent families. The so-called feminization of poverty is of great concern because someone who has to raise and train children *and* enter a tough job market to earn money to sustain the family is not in a good position to do any of these things very well. The number of single-mother families below poverty level doubled between 1970 and 1986.[7]

Points to Remember

1. The poverty level in America is calculated by multiplying by three the annual cost of a nutritionally adequate diet for a family of four. It does not include food stamps or other in-kind benefits that the family receives.

2. It is difficult to define poverty in strictly material terms. It is, as one authority put it, "want mixed with a lack of hope."

3. One of the most worrisome elements of today's poverty is its feminization, the growth of poor families headed by mothers only. Their number is growing rapidly.

TABLE **18-2**

497

Children under 18 Years Old Living with Both Parents/Mother Only

		Percent Living with	
Race and Year	Number (in thousands)	Both Parents	Mother Only
All Races			
1970	69,162	85.2	10.8
1980	63,427	76.7	18.0
1985	62,475	73.9	21.0
1986	62,763	73.9	20.9
1987	62,932	73.1	21.3
White			
1970	58,790	89.5	7.8
1980	52,242	82.7	13.6
1985	50,836	80.0	15.6
1986	50,931	79.9	15.8
1987	51,112	79.1	17.2
Black			
1970	9,422	58.5	29.5
1980	9,375	42.4	43.9
1985	9,479	39.5	51.0
1986	9,532	40.6	50.6
1987	9,612	40.1	50.5
Hispanic			
1970	4,006	77.7	(NA)
1980	5,459	75.4	19.6
1985	6,057	67.9	26.6
1986	6,430	66.5	27.7
1987	6,647	65.5	27.7

Data Source: *Statistical Abstract 1989*, No. 71, p. 52, which is based on upon the U.S. Bureau of the Census, *Current Population Reports*, series P-20, No. 423 and earlier reports.

For this data the *all races* category includes other races not shown separately and the Hispanic totals include Hispanics of any race. The *mother only* totals include women who are divorced or widowed, have never married, or are married but spouse is absent.

A number of reasons for this have been suggested: the loss of manual jobs, which left many unskilled male workers unemployed and caused them to lose self-respect; the difficulty of adjusting to modern urban life; the culture of the slums; the decline of church influence; the new sexual mores; and a hedonistic life-style promoted by television.[8] It has also been argued that the increases in social welfare payments since the 1960s have helped to perpetuate poverty. This argument has been vigorously disputed, but before we can even understand it, we need to know more about the growth and structure of welfare spending in the United States.

The Structure of American Welfare

Welfare programs are designed to relieve the effects of poverty by providing cash, food, or other benefits to needy people or by providing special educational or training programs to help people escape from poverty. But if you ask the average American what welfare is, you will get a much shorter definition: giveaway programs. Americans do not like the word *welfare*. Polls show that 69 to 78 percent of Americans oppose increases in welfare spending. However, if you change the language and call it "aid to the needy" or "helping the poor," as many as 67 percent support increases.[9] It seems as if Americans are against welfare increases but for more government spending to help the poor. Is this a contradiction?

Not to Americans. In 1981 President Reagan showed that he understood these nuances when he proposed cuts in welfare spending, for he promised that the "truly needy" would not be hurt by them; a "safety net" would be provided. Reagan realized that Americans do not want to turn their backs on people they perceive as truly needy, such as those physically unable to work. But what about the able-bodied? If they are able-bodied and out of work temporarily, Americans will support them—but *temporarily* is the key word. Americans believe that ours is a land of opportunity and that if you try hard enough you will eventually succeed.[10]

Europeans do not share our negative attitudes toward state support, which is probably one reason why the welfare state arrived much earlier in Europe. Germany became one as early as 1889, England in 1908, and Sweden in 1913. In the United States it took the worst depression in our history to nudge the federal government in the direction of a welfare state.

Welfare I: The Legacy of the 1930s

When the stock market crashed in October 1929, it set off a series of economic disasters. Banks collapsed, houses and farms were repossessed, and whole industries were crippled and paralyzed. By the time of Franklin Roosevelt's election in 1932, one-quarter of the work force was unemployed; in some places the unemployment rate reached more than 60 percent. Breadlines and soup lines became common in the cities, and in the countryside starving people wandered from region to region in search of work.

"I pledge you, I pledge myself," Roosevelt said as he accepted the Democratic nomination for president, "to a new deal for the American people." The term New Deal has come to stand for the various programs launched by the Roosevelt administration to pull the country out of the Depression: a temporary bank holiday, closer supervision of business practices, the use of government spending to stimulate the economy, stock market reforms, and so on. *New Deal* has also come to stand for the effort of the administration and its congressional allies to relieve some of the human misery resulting from the Depression. It tried to put the unemployed to work, to aid people who could not find work, and to set up a support system for those too old to work or otherwise unable to do so.

The Civilian Conservation Corps (CCC) and Works Progress Administration (WPA) put the unemployed to work on a wide variety of government-financed projects, ranging from planting trees in the countryside to painting murals in post offices. Its Public Works Administration (PWA) financed public projects, including low-cost housing. Its Home Owners Loan Corporation helped impoverished homeowners pay their mortgages and lent them money at low interest rates to pay for repairs and renovations. The administration also set up programs and subsidies for farmers. Many of these projects were dissolved when prosperity returned with World War II, but they set important precedents for federal involvement in the fight against poverty. *(Continued on page 500)*

GLOBAL PERSPECTIVES:

The Welfare State in Sweden

The foundations of the Swedish welfare state were laid early in this century, but its most durable features were put in place in the 1930s: Unemployment insurance, expanded old-age pensions, health insurance, housing, and a much more extensive system of public works projects than the United States had ever tried before date from that period. They survived World War II and were greatly expanded during the 1950s and 1960s by the ruling Social Democrats.

Today Sweden has a general family allowance for children under 16 years of age, who receive more than $400 per year tax-free; each child receives free medical and dental care and free vitamins. Child-rearing consultations are provided by the Advice Bureau for Child and Youth Mental Care, and all children now enjoy access to day-care centers, provided on a limited basis.

Education is free at comprehensive schools, high schools, and county colleges. Advanced tuition and graduate studies at universities are also free. Meals, books, and school supplies are free in comprehensive and high schools. After the age of 16, a student is eligible for a monthly allowance.

Sweden has a comprehensive system of health insurance. The Regional Social Insurance Office pays the costs of hospitalization at virtually every type of hospital facility. Vital medicines such as insulin are provided free, and all other medicines are available at half price. Patients suffering from venereal disease and alcoholism are given free treatment, the latter in government hospitals, where they live under special supervision. Marriage and maternity benefits range from home furnishing loans to free advice on contraception and abortion by state-appointed medical officers. A cash maternity allowance is paid regardless of income. Services of a trained midwife are available before, during, and after childbirth. "Social home help" is provided to all disabled people.

All these services carry a price tag. Sweden is the most heavily taxed country in the West. A family earning the equivalent of $13,500 per year—the poverty line in Sweden—must pay 40 percent of its income in taxes! The effect of this is to make families with one wage earner virtually obsolete. Husband and wife must both work to pay their taxes and make ends meet. Some 80 percent of working-age women in Sweden have jobs, compared to 61 percent in the United States.

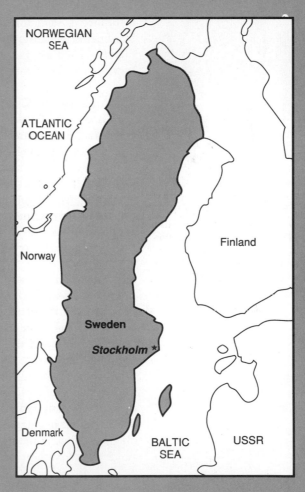

When the stock market on New York City's Wall Street collapsed in 1929, it set off a panic that triggered the Great Depression of the 1930s. The misery of the Depression became the occasion for the New Deal programs of the Roosevelt administration, programs aimed at regulating business, relieving poverty, and setting up a national pension system for retired Americans.

THE SOCIAL SECURITY ACT OF 1935

The most ambitious antipoverty legislation of the New Deal years was the Social Security Act of 1935: Its programs form the backbone of our present national welfare system. In its original form the Social Security Act contained three basic provisions that have since been amended.

Old Age and Survivor's Insurance.   Later amended to Old Age, Survivors, and Disability Insurance (OASDI), this provision (which is usually what people mean when they speak of Social Security) provides pensions for workers when they retire or become disabled. The pensions are paid out of a trust fund fed by a special payroll tax levied on workers and their employers. If *welfare* means aid to the needy, it may be arguable that OASDI is *not* welfare. Its payments are not means-tested; that is, tied to the amount of income recipients possess; instead, payments are based upon the length of time the recipients have worked. Some of the richest people in America receive Social Security checks. This may seem to be an absurd waste of money, but one must keep in mind the theory behind OASDI. It is supposed to be a pension and insurance system for workers. They pay out money, and they get it back with increments when they retire or become disabled. In this way they can preserve their dignity: They are not receiving welfare payments because they have *earned* this money. However, that is not quite what happens in practice, as we shall see later.

Unemployment Compensation.   The purpose of Unemployment Compensation is to provide workers with payments to tide them over during periods of temporary joblessness. Like OASDI, Unemployment Compensation is paid for out of a payroll tax, but the funding is different in two respects: First, only the employers pay it; and second, the state governments play a key role. (They play no role at all in OASDI.) Individual state governments collect these taxes, the amount of which is shaped by federal guidelines, and place them in a special national trust fund to which the federal government also contributes. However, separate accounts are kept for each state, and the states disburse the monies. If they overdraw on their accounts, they can borrow from the federal government.

Aid to Families with Dependent Children (AFDC).   This is the amended name for a feature of the original Social Security program that was combined with programs for the blind. Of the three provisions of the act, this is the one that most clearly fits the definition of means-tested *welfare*. AFDC payments are geared to family income and the number of children in the family. The money comes from regular federal taxes; state governments also share in the cost. Since control of AFDC is largely in the hands of the states, payment amounts vary widely from state to state. The inclusion of AFDC in the original Social Security Act was hardly noticed at the time; it was assumed that its chief beneficiaries would be widows with small children. Today the major category of AFDC recipients consists of unmarried women and their children. Their numbers are growing rapidly, and so is the controversy over AFDC.

THE FUTURE AND PRESENT OF SOCIAL SECURITY

There was great optimism about its future when President Franklin Roosevelt signed the Social Security Act on August 14, 1935. "Today," Roosevelt said, "a hope of many years' standing is in large part fulfilled." He saw it as a means by which the nation could at last provide "some measure of protection to the average citizen and to his family against the loss of a job and against poverty-ridden old age." Has it worked out that way?

In 1940 this Portuguese farming family living near Falmouth, Massachusetts, posed for a photograph. The father of this family had been able to supplement the income from his seven-acre plot by working as a day laborer at a nearby army camp, and the family had just purchased its first cow. On the wall, near the calendars and the painting of the Last Supper, is a photo of President Franklin D. Roosevelt.

To a great extent, yes. Social Security's OASDI program, which has paid benefits to over 115 million people since it began, has turned out to be a powerful weapon in the fight against poverty. About two-thirds of the elderly now get at least half their income from it, an important reason why the poverty rate among old people has fallen from 35 percent a quarter of a century ago to less than 14 percent today. Indeed, Social Security seems to be the single most powerful program for redistributing income in the United States. In December 1988 the Census Bureau released the results of a major study showing the effects of tax and benefit programs upon the real incomes of Americans.[11] By real incomes the bureau meant the amount of cash and in-kind benefits available to people after their taxes are taken out and government benefits are provided. The report showed that while Americans as a whole paid out more than they got back from the government, the elderly came out ahead: Their median household income was nearly $3,000 more after the government got through taxing and subsidizing them (see Figure 18.1 on page 502). Small wonder that Social Security is so popular. Ronald Reagan learned this the hard way in the 1980s. His proposed cuts in the program in 1981 caused such a furor that by his 1984 campaign he swore that the program would be deemed inviolate during his second term. In 1985, on the fiftieth anniversary of Social Security, he pronounced it "one of the most successful and popular programs ever established by the Federal Government."[12] Yet it may have serious flaws. The most intensively debated issue is whether or not the system is headed for bankruptcy.

In theory Social Security is an insurance or pension-type program: Workers pay into it and get back from it. In fact, the government has been increasing benefit levels so steeply over the years that the contribution of any generation of workers bears little relationship to what it gets back. In addition, OASDI payments are now indexed, (adjusted to keep up with inflation). The demographic shifts in America over the past

FIGURE **18-1**

Income v. Real Income

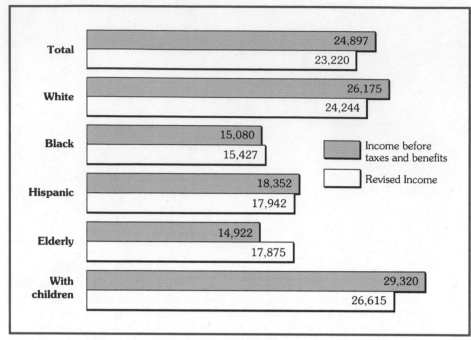

Source: *New York Times*, December 28, 1988, p. A1. Reprinted with permission.

According to a comprehensive study by the Census Bureau, Social Security and other in-kind benefits have provided an effective weapon against poverty, significantly reducing income inequality in the United States.

half-century have also changed the picture. When the system began in the 1930s, only 6.8 percent of the population was more than 65 years old; today it is 12 percent and climbing; shortly after the end of this century it will be about 23 percent. Payments for all these people come from the Social Security trust fund, which is fed by the taxes paid by present-day workers and employers. Of course, *they* are going to expect even higher benefits when they retire, and those benefits will come from the paychecks of people in the labor force at that time. And so on. Even some admirers admit that the system has the appearance of a giant pyramid scheme, with each generation getting higher benefits paid for by the next generation.[13] Is the whole structure going to crash?

No, say the program's defenders, not as long as the trust fund is there. But by the middle of the 1970s the trust fund was being depleted: Payments were outstripping revenues. In 1977 the Carter administration and Congress increased the tax, promising that this would make the system sound through the year 2030. By 1983 it was going broke again. By then Ronald Reagan was in the White House, and he had learned from experience to approach Social Security very carefully. He appointed a bipartisan National Commission on Social Security Reform. The commission recommended a variety of measures, including a higher payroll tax, a gradual increase in the retirement age, taxing Social Security benefits paid to people with incomes above certain levels ($25,000 a year for an individual, $32,000 for a couple), and a requirement that new federal employees join Social Security. In an unusual bipartisan spirit, Congress enacted the recommendations with almost no debate. President Reagan signed the measure in April 1983 with House Speaker ("Tip") O'Neill smiling beside him.[14]

FIGURE **18-2**

503

Welfare I: The
Legacy of the
1930s

How Americans View Social Security

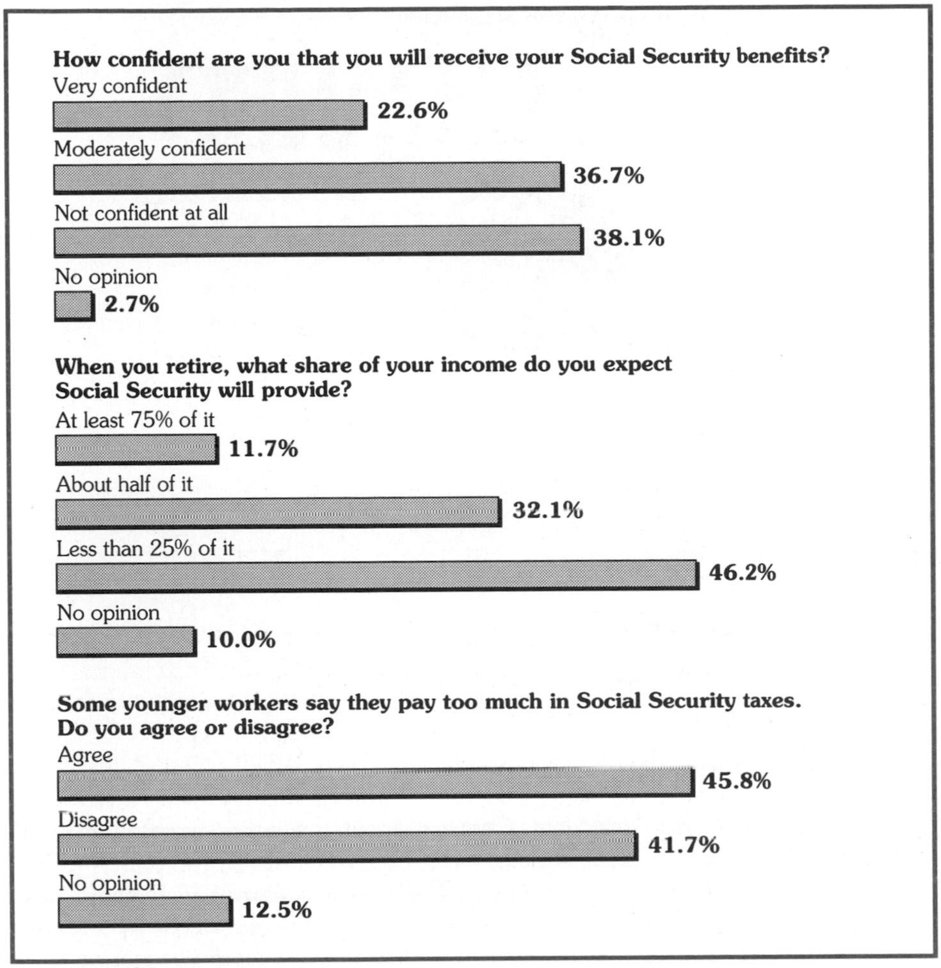

How confident are you that you will receive your Social Security benefits?

Very confident

22.6%

Moderately confident

36.7%

Not confident at all

38.1%

No opinion

2.7%

**When you retire, what share of your income do you expect
Social Security will provide?**

At least 75% of it

11.7%

About half of it

32.1%

Less than 25% of it

46.2%

No opinion

10.0%

**Some younger workers say they pay too much in Social Security taxes.
Do you agree or disagree?**

Agree

45.8%

Disagree

41.7%

No opinion

12.5%

Source: *U.S. News & World Report*, August 12, 1985, p. 41.

Results of a poll of 1,500 people indicate that many Americans believe that their Social Security benefits will provide 50 percent or less of their retirement income, and over one-third of those polled do not believe they will receive any benefits at all. The aging of the U.S. population has raised concerns that younger workers are paying to support a system that will not be able to support them when they retire.

But some critics charge that the system is putting an unfair burden on the young. In 1985, through Social Security payments alone, the government transferred $200 billion in wealth from the young to the old. Many of the young people paying for this transfer were workers struggling to make ends meet, while the recipients include some of the wealthiest people in America. Of course, the young workers of today will someday get their benefits, but, according to *Washington Post* writer Paul Taylor, they will never get back as much as present recipients are getting.

Today's Social Security beneficiary receives, on average, three dollars back for every one dollar that he and his employer contributed to the system plus real interest. A typical young worker entering the labor force today, even under assumptions widely regarded as optimistic, won't get back even $1 for every $1 he and his employer put in plus real interest.[15]

At some point this may become a big campaign issue. But for now the politicians do not want to touch it. As one senator put it, "No one wants to be accused of granny bashing."[16]

Drawing by Mike Luckovich; Copley News Service.

Welfare II: The Legacy of the 1960s

World War II ended the Depression: For five years much of the American labor force was in the armed services or working in defense industries. Unemployment, which had been 25 percent, shrank to 3 percent. With the end of the war unemployment went up slightly, but it never again approached Depression levels.

Poverty, however, had not vanished, and it was rediscovered in the 1960s. Campaigning in West Virginia in 1960, John Kennedy was horrified when he saw half-starved Appalachian residents. Concern about the poor increased after the publication in 1962 of a book by socialist writer Michael Harrington. Called *The Other America*, it vividly described the situation of Americans who had seemed invisible during the 1950s.[17] It was widely read in Washington, reportedly by President Kennedy himself, and helped nudge his administration toward sponsoring major antipoverty legislation. But the real campaign against poverty did not begin until after Kennedy's death in November 1963.

Despite the national mourning over the death of Kennedy, hope for the future was bright when Lyndon Johnson became president. Johnson talked of achieving a Great Society, a flowering of democracy and dignity in America. Every person would be able to reach his or her potential; people would be provided with all the education, training, and essential services they deserved. A generation earlier, in the 1930s, Lyndon Johnson had been a young Texas congressman who greatly admired Franklin Roosevelt. As president he resolved to pick up where Roosevelt left off. "This administration," he declared in his first State of the Union message, "today here and now declares unconditional war on poverty in America."[18]

THE ECONOMIC OPPORTUNITY ACT OF 1964

If Johnson's version of the New Deal was his Great Society, his counterpart to the New Deal's Social Security Act was the Economic Opportunity Act of 1964. Like Social Security, it was to be the centerpiece of his administration's antipoverty effort. But there the parallels begin to disappear. Social Security is basically a cash-disbursal program. The Economic Opportunity Act used a very different strategy. It concentrated on training and services to the poor; its underlying philosophy was to teach the poor to help *themselves*. The motto was "A hand, not a handout." To lend this hand—to teach the poor the skills for getting out of poverty—a number of agencies were set up:

- A Job Corps to train low-skilled young people for entering the work force.
- A Neighborhood Youth Corps to provide part-time jobs to youngsters and give them money and incentive to stay in school.
- A Comprehensive Employment Program to find jobs and develop marketable skills for poor people.
- Upward Bound, a program designed to help bright underachieving children from poor families get into college.
- Project Head Start, which was to enroll preschool children from poverty areas and improve their basic learning skills.
- A Community Action Program (CAP), which funded local Community Action Agencies (CAAs) in poverty areas around the country to get the poor to participate in their own poverty programs. In a phrase that was later the subject of controversy and derision, the statute said that the agencies were to get the "maximum feasible participation" from local residents.

These programs were to be coordinated by a major new executive agency, the Office of Economic Opportunity (OEO). The weight and importance accorded to the OEO was evident from its location in the Executive Office of the President.

Today the OEO no longer exists. Some programs, such as the preschool programs in Project Head Start, have been preserved under the control of cabinet-level agencies, but in general the "services" approach adopted during the Johnson years has never lived up to its promise.

Some supporters of the OEO charged that the problem was a lack of adequate funding. One year after launching it, President Johnson began escalating the Vietnam War. Soon the war was costing $20 billion a year; funding for OEO's programs never reached above $2 billion annually. But there were also problems with the programs themselves. The Office of Economic Opportunity created a giant welfare bureaucracy that often got bogged down in red tape. It gave administrative jobs to many middle-class blacks and whites, but it did not help the poor very much.

Another problem was the power struggle between the new Community Action Agencies and entrenched local governments. OEO's mandate to solicit maximum feasible participation from the poor was interpreted by some OEO workers as a mandate to organize the poor for confrontations with city hall. Mayors and other local officials found their offices disrupted by picketing, sit-ins, and angry shouting that often ended up on the evening news. They complained to their legislators that OEO was "funding revolution." Congress responded by cutting the agencies' funds and bringing them under the control of local bureaucracies.[19]

The training programs administered under various OEO grants produced very uneven results. Poor people signed up for the job training programs, but many had such serious learning problems that they could not absorb the lessons. Some dropped out. Others stayed on but could not find jobs to match their new skills.

FOOD STAMPS

The Economic Opportunity Act may have been President Johnson's most ambitious welfare program, but there were others begun during his administration that have had a longer life and have run up much higher bills. One was a program that began very modestly in 1964; it was called Food Stamps.

A program of food coupons, or food stamps, as they are more commonly called, was begun at the end of the 1960s and expanded greatly during the 1970s. Food stamps were designed to ensure that poor people received an adequate diet, and by the close of the 1970s investigators concluded that malnutrition in the U.S. had significantly declined. During the 1980s, critics of the Reagan administration charged that "hunger" had made a comeback, but their methodology was criticized by some observers.

Under this program, a poor family received stamps (actually coupons) that could be exchanged for selected food items. When Congress first established the program in 1964, its scope was limited. Only the poorest families were eligible, and they had to purchase the stamps. By the end of the 1960s a series of well-publicized studies of hunger in the U.S., including a CBS documentary, increased the pressure for expansion of the program. Eligibility was broadened, and in 1977 Congress eliminated the requirement that the stamps be purchased. As a result, the Food Stamp program grew from a marginal experiment to one of the largest welfare programs of the federal government.

MEDICARE AND MEDICAID

Although every Democratic president since Harry Truman declared himself in favor of a national health care program for the aged, it took the Johnson landslide of 1964 to tip the balance in Congress. The influx of liberal Democrats created a sympathetic majority on the House Ways and Means Committee, which handles taxes and Social Security. The result was the Medicare Act of 1965, which set up two separate programs central to our welfare system today.

Medicare, the original goal of reformers, is a program of medical care for the aged. Grafted onto the Social Security retirement system, it covers hospitalization and at least part of doctors' bills. Medicare is not means-tested, which is to say that it is available for all regardless of their income or financial need. All Social Security retirees are eligible for it. It is financed entirely by the federal government through the Social Security Administration.

Medicaid provides health care to the poor through payments to health care providers such as hospitals, doctors, clinics, and nursing homes. Unlike Medicare, it is

FIGURE **18-3**

507

Welfare II: The
Legacy of the
1960s

Federal Food Stamp Programs, 1970-1987

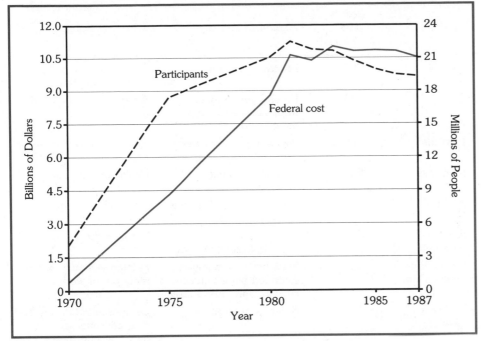

Source: 1989 Statistical Abstract, p. 364.

In one decade, between 1970 and 1980, the number of people receiving federal food stamps increased from 4.3 million to over 21 million, and the federal cost of the program increased from $550 million to almost $9 billion. During the Reagan years, federal food stamp expenditures stayed in the range of $10-11 billion, although the number of people receiving food stamps eventually decreased by about 2 million.

means-tested and is aimed specifically at the poor (those receiving other public assistance) and at all age groups. The other key difference from Medicare is that Medicaid is partly financed by the states (the federal government helps through matching grants) and is largely run by them. Although the federal government sets standards, the states are the basic providers; they can set ceilings on benefits and guidelines for the choice of physicians.

WHERE ARE WE NOW?

The 1930s and the 1960s gave us the main components of our present welfare system. The New Deal of the 1930s produced Social Security (OASDI), Unemployment Compensation, and Aid to Families with Dependent Children (AFDC); the Great Society initiatives of the 1960s gave us Medicaid, Medicare, food stamps, and a variety of helping agencies. To be sure, not every major welfare program is a product of those decades. Veterans' programs, which now cost about $27 billion per year, were begun in the 1940s. In 1972 Congress added Supplemental Security Income (SSI) by amendment to the Social Security Act. Administered by the Social Security Administration, SSI gives out roughly $15 billion a year to the low-income elderly. Table 18.3 on page 508 provides an overall view of our federal welfare system.

TABLE **18-3**

Major Federal Welfare Programs

Program	Cost in 1987 (in billions)	Method of Funding	Purpose
OASDI	$201.7	Federal trust fund	Pension system for elderly and disabled
SSI	$14.8*	Federal government; most states also supplement	Assistance to aged and poor
Medicare	$80.0	Payroll tax plus member contributions	Health insurance for aged
Medicaid	$50.0*	Federal matching grants to states	Health care for poor
AFDC	$18.4*	State funded with federal reimbursements	Financial aid to poor mothers for child care
Food Stamps	$12.5*	Federal funding; states pay administrative costs	Nutrition for the needy
Unemployment Compensation	$14.4*	State tax on employers; extended benefits funded by state and federal taxes	Helping workers temporarily out of work
Veterans Benefits	$26.8	Federal government	Compensation for disabilities, education benefits, death benefits, home loan guarantees, medical care

*Federal and state expenditures

Source: 1989 Statistical Abstract.

The federal government now supports a variety of welfare and social insurance programs. Begun during the New Deal period of the 1930s and greatly expanded during the Great Society period of the 1960s, these programs now constitute the largest segment of the federal government's overall budget expenditures.

If we include Social Security payments, social welfare expenditures in 1986 constituted almost 50 percent of total federal government outlays, compared to 28.1 percent in 1960 (see Table 18.4). One reason for the growth in welfare programs since the early 1960s is connected with the proliferation of <u>entitlement programs</u>. These are programs in which the government is obligated to pay benefits to all applicants who meet criteria set by law. Entitlement spending grows automatically according to the size of the population that falls into its categories. Social Security, Medicare, Food Stamps, and AFDC are among the major entitlement programs. Unless the basic eligibility criteria for receiving assistance under these programs are altered, the programs are virtually inviolate.

THE REAGAN YEARS: SAFETY NETS AND CUTBACKS

The long-term growth of welfare spending since the early 1960s has troubled many observers. Even liberals now worry about the danger of welfare dependency. But conservatives have been the most outspoken critics. They complain that welfare wastes taxpayers' money, rewards idleness, and bloats the size of government. In

TABLE **18-4**

509

Welfare II: The
Legacy of the
1960s

How Much is Spent on Welfare

Welfare Expenditures as Percentage of Total Federal
Government Outlays, 1960–1986

Year	Percentage	Year	Percentage
1960	28.1	1974	52.5
1961	28.4	1975	53.8
1962	29.8	1976	57.0
1963	29.8	1977	56.3
1964	30.0	1978	55.3
1965	32.7	1979	54.9
1966	35.0	1980	54.3
1967	35.0	1981	54.0
1968	35.1	1982	52.4
1969	35.1	1983	51.9
1970	40.1	1984	50.2
1971	44.9	1985	47.8
1972	47.4	1986	47.6
1973	50.5		

Source: U.S. Census Bureau, *Statistical Abstract 1964, 1969, 1976, 1985, 1987*, and *1989*.

The percentage of our annual budget devoted to social welfare payments peaked in 1976 at 57.0 percent of total outlays but then slowly began to decline in the 1980s, owing to Reagan's military buildup, which increased the percentage devoted to the military.

1981 President Reagan came into office on a conservative platform that included the promise to "get government off our backs." He and his staff immediately set to work trying to trim welfare expenditures.

To what extent did Reagan succeed in cutting welfare and preserving the safety net? In *By the Few for the Few*, researchers Tom Joe and Cheryl Rogers trace the effects of several policy changes in AFDC rules that the Reagan administration persuaded Congress to enact in 1981. Congress tightened eligibility rules and reduced the amount of income that could be earned before AFDC payments stopped. Summarizing studies from the General Accounting Office (GAO) and other public and private agencies, the authors claim that the changes led to increasing hardship— "more hunger, larger debts, worsening medical care. The General Accounting Office found that families had to borrow money more often and turned more often to food pantries and soup kitchens." Another researcher, Dorothy Wickenden, in a *New Republic* article published in 1985, claimed that deep cuts in housing assistance, AFDC, child nutrition, food stamps, low-income energy assistance, and low-income housing had made the lives of the poor desperate. The poor, she said, "have suffered at the hands of the Reagan administration."[20] Yet economist John Weicher studied the data and concluded that "both the budget and program changes turn out to be smaller than much of the public discussion would suggest."[21] What Reagan succeeded in doing, he said, was to cut the *rate of increase* in welfare spending but not actually to cut it back. Table 18.5 on page 511 provides a glimpse of some of the changes in welfare payments during the 1980s.

The problem, of course, is that the cost of living keeps going up in the United States, and both state and federal payments are not keeping up with that increase. A March 1989 study by the staff of the House Ways and Means Committee revealed that on average, purchasing power of AFDC payments has declined one-third since

FIGURE **18-4**

Growing Commitments

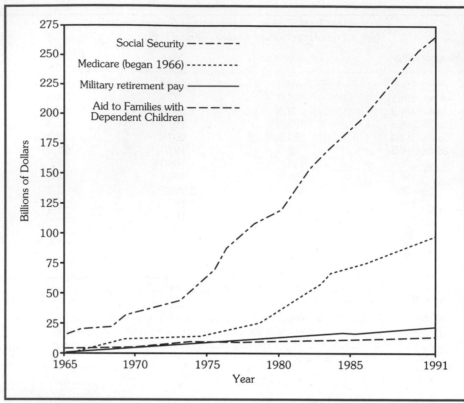

Source: *New York Times*, February 9, 1986, IV, p. 4. Reprinted with permission.

Federal entitlement programs cannot be cut unless the criteria for the grants are themselves altered. Some entitlement payments, especially Social Security, have increased sharply since the 1960s, while others, such as Aid to Families with Dependent Children, have not even kept up with inflation. Note that figures after 1985 are estimates.

1970. In eight states, the study found, AFDC benefits and food stamps combined still left a family of three with less than 60 percent of the poverty-level threshold (see Figure 18.5 on page 512).

CONTINUING PROBLEMS: HUNGER AND HOMELESSNESS

In 1988 Robert Fersh, executive director of the Food Research and Action Center, a hunger activist group, told a special House Select Committee on Hunger that there are "unconscionable levels of hunger in our country today." Professor J. Larry Brown, head of the Harvard-based Physicians' Task Force on Hunger, claimed that his group had "uncovered overwhelming evidence" that hunger was "created and spread by government policies."[22] Reagan officials discounted much of this testimony as politically motivated.

Largely neglected in the fracas was the question of how to define *hunger*. As a useful analytical concept, the term is maddeningly elusive. The real question is whether or not people are chronically hungry because they cannot afford to buy enough food. Even then, the only *measurable* phenomenon is not the subjective

TABLE **18-5**

511

Welfare II: The
Legacy of the
1960s

Federal Benefits in the 1980s

Programs	Federal Spending on Benefits for Persons with Limited Income Major Programs: 1980 and 1986 (in millions of dollars)	
	Dollars Spent	
	1980	1986
Aid to Families with Dependent Children (AFDC)	6,964	9,536
Supplemental Security Income (SSI)	6,365	10,307
Food Stamps	9,195	12,528
Housing Benefits	9,606	13,250
Medicaid	14,550	24,995

Source: *Statistical Abstract 1988*, No. 557.

Advocates and critics cite various data to argue the effects of program changes
initiated by Reagan's administration. Determining the causes of the continuing
problems of hunger and homelessness, however, is as difficult as finding the
solutions.

feeling of hunger but the nutritional data: the amount and kinds of foods people are
eating and the effects of the food (or its lack) on people's health.

If people do not eat properly, they will eventually suffer malnutrition. How
widespread is malnutrition in America? In 1967 the Field Foundation sent a team of
researchers into a number of areas in the country and concluded that 20 million
Americans were suffering from malnutrition.[23] But in 1978 the Field Foundation sent
out a new team, including many of the same physicians who were on the first team,
and reported to Congress in 1979 that malnutrition had practically disappeared. Food
stamps, it concluded, had made the difference.

Did widespread malnutrition make a comeback during the 1980s? In 1985 the
Physicians' Task Force concluded that in 150 counties around the United States
"hunger today is approaching the magnitude of the 1960s." The report's methodology, however, was sharply criticized. Its conclusion that there are 20 million hungry
was reached by comparing census reports on the number of people living below the
poverty line with the number receiving food stamps (on the assumption that those not
regularly receiving food stamps were going without food). This assumption did not
take into account the rural poor who grew their own food, seasonal workers who
might have needed food stamps for only part of the year, people who were able to get
help from relatives, and possibly many others. Joseph J. O'Hara, director of the
Missouri Division of Social Services, said: "Trying to do an analysis of food stamps
and income leads you to gibberish."[24]

Other studies that also suggest people were not getting enough to eat came
under fire as well. One report by the U.S. Conference of Mayors showed an 18
percent rise in emergency food demand in 1987. "Unfortunately," wrote Peter Rossi,
a University of Massachusetts demographer, "the data presented are of unknown and
suspect quality," and "the prudent assessor must simply set aside the report as a
credible document."[25] Earlier, an advocacy group for the poor produced statistics on
Massachusetts children with stunted growth, but it turned out that the statistical
sample used by the group included disproportionate numbers of Asian children, who
were stunted only in comparison to the tallest (non-Asian) children in the sample.[26]

In short, it is hard to prove that malnourishment resulting from economic
deprivation is widespread in today's America. Some studies even show poor women
consuming more calories per capita than females of all incomes.[27] This does not

FIGURE **18-5**

AFDC Benefit Levels: Losing Value

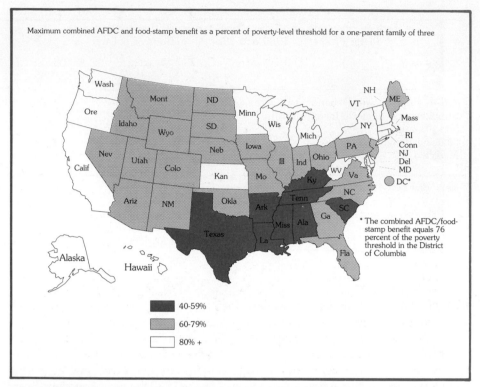

Source: *Congressional Quarterly Weekly Report*, May 20, 1989, p. 1192.

According to a March 1989 study by the staff of the House Ways and Means Committee, the average purchasing power of the AFDC benefit has declined by one-third since 1970. Data showed that in eight states the value of these benefits and food stamps *combined* leaves a family of three with less than 60 percent of the federal poverty-level threshold, which was $10,060 in 1989.

mean that there is not widespread malnourishment, only that existing research methods have failed to detect credible, systematic evidence of it. Nor does it mean that there is no real poverty in the U.S. There is plenty of that, and some of it is painfully visible.

Sleeping in cars or alleyways, begging in the streets, prowling bus and train stations, America's homeless have become a national scandal. Nobody knows for sure how many there are. The estimates range from a low of about a quarter of a million, cited by the Department of Housing and Urban Development (HUD) in a 1984 study, to a high of 2 to 3 million, cited by most advocacy groups.[28] As with hunger, the methods of estimating numbers are part of the controversy. A congressional hearing exposed methodological flaws in the HUD study and suggested its figures were too low. Yet the figure of 2 to 3 million cited by advocates of the homeless was reached by a rather impressionistic method.[29] The higher figure was finally reached by adding another million or so to cover "the hidden homeless," those who might not have been counted.[30] Whatever the faults, however, all serious commentators now agree that the 1984 HUD figure of 250,000 is much too low. Early in 1988 Reagan's own secretary of Housing and Urban Development, Samuel Pierce, estimated the number to be 500,000 or 600,000.[31] By now there might be more than a million homeless.

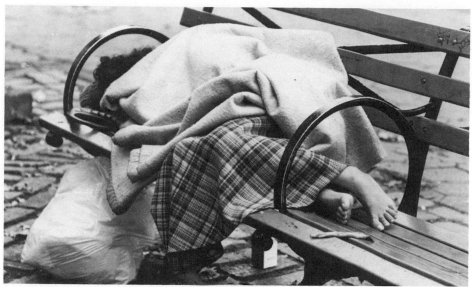

One of America's homeless tries to sleep on a Houston Street park bench in New York City. Estimates of the numbers of homeless in the United States range from 250,000 to 3 million. The methods used to make these estimates were not very rigorous, so the actual numbers are not known. Homelessness has been blamed on everything from lack of sufficient low-income housing projects to the policy of discharging the mentally ill from hospitals.

DEFINING THE GROUP THAT MAKES UP THE HOMELESS

Who are these people? Another disputed question. In a farewell interview with ABC correspondent David Brinkley, President Reagan implied that the homeless were largely made up of people who belong in mental institutions. Advocates for the homeless characterize this as "blaming the victim." They say that people are homeless not because they are crazy but because they cannot afford housing, and they picture the homeless as families with small children. There is some truth in both images. Beginning in the early 1980s a growing proportion of the homeless consisted of young families headed by women. Yet there is also evidence that many in the homeless population are mentally disturbed or are drug addicts.[32]

We should thus be wary of easy so-called solutions to the homeless problem. One part of the solution is probably more affordable housing. During the Reagan years Congress, at the urging of the president, diminished the money spent to build low-income housing, although Reagan increased the funds available for rent vouchers. Affordable housing is sometimes also constricted at the local level by tangles of bureaucratic regulations, often enforced by incompetent and corrupt officials. Local rent-control laws may also have the unintended effect of causing the deterioration of buildings and thus reducing the supply of affordable housing.[33] Obviously, we need a sweeping reexamination of our laws and financial commitments. But this cannot be the only strategy. Some of the homeless need hospital care, but since the wave of deinstitutionalization in the 1960s, it has become almost impossible to confine people against their will unless they pose an *immediate* danger to themselves or others. Moreover, an adequate number of facilities and trained personnel simply do not exist. A comprehensive approach to homelessness, then, will require changes in many quarters. Civil libertarians may have to modify their opposition to enforced confinement, taxpayers may have to pay for an expansion of housing and treatment programs, and local residents may have to put up with such facilities in their neighborhoods. Without mutual sacrifice and cooperation, it is hard to see how the problem of homelessness can be resolved.

Welfare Reform

Has welfare spending been a failure? Many Americans think so. As its defenders remind us, however, it has accomplished a great deal. Carnegie Foundation president Alan Pifer is emphatic about its success:

> Looking backward over the past two decades, we can see that it is myth, not fact, that Federal social programs have failed. On the contrary, they greatly reduced poverty, hunger, malnutrition, infectious disease, and infant mortality—the last of these by 50%. They increased equality of opportunity for minorities and women. They made health care much more widely available. They gave dignity and opportunity to many of our fellow citizens.[34]

Yet disturbing questions remain. Do government welfare programs create problems of their own? Do they rob people of initiative? Do they hurt the family structure? A long series of experiments with income maintenance programs has underscored these concerns.

THE SIME/DIME EXPERIMENTS: MAKING THINGS WORSE?

Income maintenance experiments were conducted in a number of states, including New Jersey and Indiana, but the largest and best-evaluated ones were conducted in Seattle and Denver between 1971 and 1978. This has earned the entire program the musical-sounding title of SIME/DIME (Seattle Income Maintenance Experiment/Denver Income Maintenance Experiment). In the SIME/DIME experiments, groups of poor families were made beneficiaries of a negative income tax. They were given cash grants on a sliding scale according to family income level: The less the family members earned at their jobs, the more money they were given. These groups were then compared with control groups who received no such benefits.

The results of the experiments suggested that the negative income tax caused husbands to work 9 percent less and wives to work 20 percent less than they would have without it.[35] What is more, when recipients of these cash grants lost their jobs, they took much longer in finding new ones. It took husbands 9 weeks longer and wives 50 weeks longer to find new jobs than did their counterparts in the control group. If these experiments are valid and can be generalized, it would appear that welfare, at least when it takes the form of a negative income tax, reduces work effort.

Citing the results of SIME/DIME and a number of other studies, conservative researcher Charles Murray argued in 1984 that poverty in America actually got worse as a result of the initiatives of the 1960s.[36] Murray contended that the gains the poor might have made in obtaining money and in-kind benefits were more than offset by the destruction of the incentive to work and to hold families together. The most damning fact about welfare, Murray said, is its effect on latent poverty. *Latent poverty* is a term he used to measure not only those whose incomes fall below the poverty line but also those whose incomes *would* fall below it if they did not get welfare. According to Murray's calculations, latent poverty fell steadily during the 1950s and early 1960s; in 1968 it started going up, and it continued to climb in the 1970s.[37] In Murray's view the problem with making welfare easily available is that it destroys poor people's incentive to get *themselves* out of poverty. It also contributes to illegitimacy and family breakups, which mire young people in cycles of poverty. In a CBS television documentary on the black family, a welfare mother told commentator Bill Moyers: "I don't like welfare because it makes me lazy."[38] That, in a nutshell, was Murray's point.

The point was contested by a number of critics.[39] Among the best known was sociologist Christopher Jencks, who challenged Murray's claim that "latent poverty" has increased since the 1960s. Jencks also denied any causal link between welfare and illegitimacy. Citing a 1984 study by David Ellwood and Mary Jo Bane that compared illegitimacy rates in states with high and low AFDC payments, he noted that the authors found *less* illegitimacy in states with high payments.[40]

THE UNDERCLASS

Another critic of Murray, sociologist William Julius Wilson, suggested an alternative explanation for the rise of dependency and families headed by women since the 1960s. The culprit, said Wilson, is not welfare but "the extraordinary rise of black male joblessness."[41] He attributed this rise to the increasing scarcity of low-skill manufacturing jobs in the central cities where blacks are concentrated. White-collar jobs have increased in many cities, but many black men lack the education and skills for them. Why? In Wilson's view the fault lies with inner city public schools, which he thinks are too authoritarian.[42]

Wilson's suggestion that inner-city public schools are too authoritarian is open to challenge. Some think that the problem is too little authority and structure.[43] Nevertheless, Wilson's focus on the shortcomings of the educational system seems justifiable. William B. Johnston and Arnold H. Packer, authors of a major study by the Hudson institute, a social research organization, found that average young adults, 21 to 25 years old, are reading at a level significantly lower than the level necessary to perform the average jobs available in 1984 and even further below what will be needed for the jobs expected to be created between 1984 and the end of this century.[44] Replying to criticism that his administration had not done enough to fight poverty, President Reagan often referred to the many pages of "help wanted" ads he saw in the morning paper. But it is questionable whether or not many of those jobs could be performed by America's poor. Corporate experience suggests that poor minority groups are among those least well served by public schools; the result may turn out to be a colossal, tragic mismatch between surplus jobs and young people who cannot perform them. In the fall of 1989, for example, the MCI Communications Corporation in Boston was having a hard time filling positions for telephone salespersons, positions that paid $7.10 per hour plus incentives. "Now, we have 52 job slots," the sales manager said, "but only 38 employees." Her difficulty was in finding qualified candidates to fill the positions.[45]

"A rising tide lifts all boats." During the early 1960s officials in the Kennedy administration used this metaphor to justify tax cuts, which they claimed fostered business prosperity, thus helping to get the unemployed back to work. The old adage was revived during the Reagan administration in the 1980s to justify Reagan-supported tax cuts, and by the end of his term Reagan boasted that 19 million new jobs had been created during the decade. The trouble is that those who live near or at the bottom of American society—such as ex-convicts, teenage delinquents, drug addicts, welfare mothers—suffer from limitations that make it very difficult for them to enter the job market. Collectively, these individuals are sometimes referred to as the underclass.

Most observers now agree that it is going to take more than a prosperous economy to help the underclass. A rising tide may lift all boats, but it will not raise shipwrecks from the bottom of the sea. The approach favored by many reformers and public officials is some combination of incentives, training, and special job opportunities. There is evidence suggesting that the right mix of these can get *some* of the hard-core unemployed into the work force.

Some fascinating experiments in helping the underclass have been conducted by the Manpower Demonstration Research Corporation (MDRC), a private research agency based in New York City. MDRC studies in several states have shown modest success in "supported work" programs, in which training and counseling are given to special categories of the underclass who are then given jobs with salaries paid for by MDRC. After a period of this supported work, MDRC tries to place them in the regular job market. In his book *The Underclass*, *New York Daily News* columnist Ken Auletta reported that of the four categories of the underclass enrolled in MDRC programs (welfare mothers, ex-addicts, ex-convicts, and teenage delinquents), two clearly profited from the experience. Welfare mothers benefited the most; about 40 percent of them finished the program and went on to regular employment. Second-best were former drug addicts, whose public assistance payments went down and whose employment went up. The program had no significant effect on their addiction (it did not help them to stop), but at least it let them earn money to support their habits so they did not have to commit crime. Juvenile offenders and ex-convicts were hardly helped at all: The juveniles were too immature and the ex-offenders too angry.[46]

MAKING WELFARE WORK: REFORM PROPOSALS

These experiments pushed lawmakers to try fresh approaches to solving the underclass problem. The innovations began at the state level in the 1980s as federal support for traditional welfare programs waned. Over half the states revised their systems to permit or require workfare, welfare assistance in return for work or job training. Massachusetts started an Employment and Training program for welfare mothers, inevitably dubbed "E.T." It provides career counseling, job placement, training, and support services such as child care. About 86 percent of those who complete it are able to stay off welfare.[47] New Jersey tried a slightly different approach that was based upon a contract. The welfare recipient promises to get a job, to train for one, or to go to school. The state promises to provide day care for children, health benefits, and transportation to work.[48]

The concepts embodied in these and other state plans eventually found their way into federal law. In 1987 Senator Daniel P. Moynihan (D-New York) sponsored a welfare reform package based upon a plan adopted by the National Governors Association. When the Family Welfare Reform Act became law in the fall of 1988, Moynihan said: "This is the moment we've been waiting for for half a century."[49] The act contains the following major provisions:

- Provides $3.34 billion in federal contributions to welfare over a five-year period.
- Requires participating states to initiate measures to withhold wages from absentee fathers and provide child-care support to enable welfare mothers to join the work force.
- Requires the states to establish education and training programs as a condition for receiving federal money for welfare.
- Requires one adult in each two-parent welfare household to participate in a job search and if no job is found, to put in 16 hours a week of community service. (This provision will not take effect until 1994.)

The most controversial part of the program is that requiring states to put welfare recipients to work. Some Democrats in Congress called it "slavefare." But in the end it was so watered down that it may turn out to be largely symbolic. Even when it takes effect in 1994, it will apply at first only to 40 percent of two-parent families; only 5 percent of welfare families *have* two parents. The sobering fact that only a small percentage of welfare families have two parents at home brings us back to a point touched upon earlier in the chapter: the breakdown of the family structure in the United States.

Strong intact families that have both male and female role models present may be the most efficient vehicles for transmitting to children the skills and attitudes necessary for them to succeed. The problem, as noted earlier, is that households headed by women that have no male present have been growing alarmingly. Many black leaders and educators have contended that this problem is particularly acute in the black community. Writing in 1985, Georgetown University law professor Eleanor Holmes Norton noted that in 1965 "two-and-a-half times as many black families as white ones were headed by women. Today it is almost three-and-a-half times as many—43 percent of black families compared with 13 percent of white families."[50] Roger Wilkins, a former member of the *New York Times* editorial board who is now a history professor at George Mason University, contends that the black family needs special attention because of the damage wrought by emigration from country to city a generation ago, at the very time when opportunities for unskilled work were shrinking. Some families, he says, survived this transition, while others became "disoriented and redundant."

It is the children and grandchildren of these leftover Americans that Dr. Samuel D. Proctor, the retired pastor of the Abyssinian Baptist Church, mentioned when I asked him what the biggest lesson of his years in Harlem had been. He said, "Children without parents," referring to babies born to mothers who are still children. "Being born without parents is like being born without skin."[51]

There is now a broad consensus that the family needs support, in some cases restoration. The question is how to do it. Are there suitable public remedies? The issue has to be approached carefully. The family, after all, is essentially a *private* institution, and too much reliance on government might do more harm than good. Yet there may be ways in which the public sphere, private sphere, and families themselves can work together to strengthen ties. Roger Wilkins recommends multi-purpose family service centers connected with elementary schools that can bring parents and children together with trained counselors and therapists.[52] Eleanor Holmes Norton favors public assistance programs tied to work opportunities and training, "consciousness-raising," and voluntary service (such as counselors and surrogate parents and grandparents) by the black middle classes.[53] A 1989 Ford Foundation report suggests that experiments with informal support networks and role models, combined with comprehensive medical and social services for teen mothers, have in some cases helped to break the cycle of dependency.[54] These solutions sound a bit vague, and perhaps they are—but at least they try to come to grips with the tragedy of family deterioration, which has contributed not only to poverty and dependency but to crime and delinquency.

Deficits and Taxes

It is unlikely that we will soon be hearing of any new total or unconditional war on poverty, for one lesson we have learned is that massive expenditures do not guarantee success. And even if they could, there is a second post-1960s lesson: We just do not have money to spend frivolously. At least the politicians do not think we do. "Twenty years ago," says writer James Fallows, "politicians were arguing about which programs to expand; now everyone argues about where to cut."[55]

If we want government programs, we need money. Where do we get it? We can shift the money from one sector to another. We can raise taxes. Or we can hope that tax revenues will grow without raising taxes, through economic growth. Or we can spend more taxes than we take in and finance the difference through borrowing. Each alternative has virtues and dangers.

DEFICITS: CAUSES AND CURES

Borrowing has the virtue of being the least painful alternative—at least over the short run. If we borrow the money, we do not have to take it from other programs or raise taxes. Instead, the Treasury Department gets the money by selling bonds and notes to the public; when the bonds and notes mature, the Treasury pays them back with interest. This creates debt, of course, and we all know what happens to individuals when they cannot pay their debts: They go bankrupt. Can the federal government go bankrupt? No one knows for sure; it has never happened.

18-6

The Budget Deficit[1]

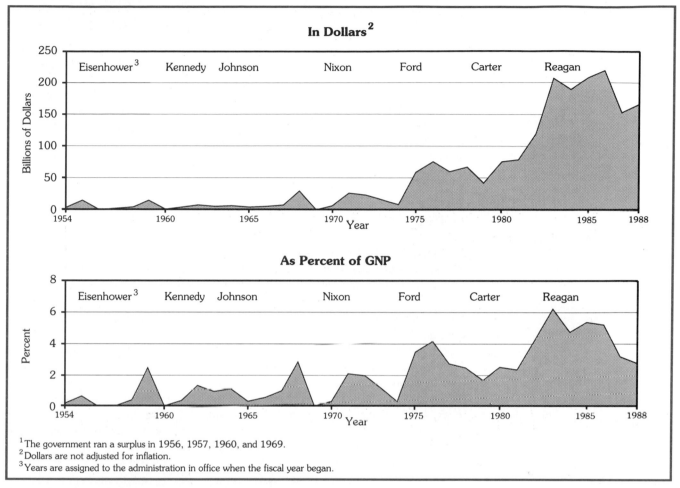

In Dollars[2]

Eisenhower[3]   Kennedy   Johnson   Nixon   Ford   Carter   Reagan

(Billions of Dollars; Year: 1954, 1960, 1965, 1970, 1975, 1980, 1985, 1988)

As Percent of GNP

Eisenhower[3]   Kennedy   Johnson   Nixon   Ford   Carter   Reagan

(Percent; Year: 1954, 1960, 1965, 1970, 1975, 1980, 1985, 1988)

[1] The government ran a surplus in 1956, 1957, 1960, and 1969.
[2] Dollars are not adjusted for inflation.
[3] Years are assigned to the administration in office when the fiscal year began.

Source: Congressional Quarterly Weekly Report, November 26, 1988, p. 3379.

In terms of dollars, the present budget deficit rests near the peak of a gigantic mountain created during the Reagan years. Measured against our gross national product, however, the deficit has declined rather steeply in the last few years and is lower today than it was during the last year of the Ford administration and the early years of Carter's. Economists are divided over whether the deficit is a serious danger to the economic health of the U.S.

Since the 1930s some economists have argued that federal debt can actually help the economy. When Franklin Roosevelt came into office he criticized the extravagance of his predecessor, Herbert Hoover, and promised to balance the budget. Within a few years, however, New Deal spending had gotten the budget even further in the red. By that time many thinkers in the administration had taken over the ideas of British economist John Maynard Keynes (1883-1946), who was convinced that idle savings were responsible for business stagnation. In his view, the government should borrow the money and use it to put people to work, thus stimulating demand. Deficits, then, are not necessarily a problem; indeed, in Keynesian theory, they are part of the solution when the economy is not producing at full capacity.

This attitude toward deficit financing became part of the credo of liberal Democrats from the New Deal through the 1970s. It horrified conservative Republicans, who tried for years to make a campaign issue out of deficits. Then, in the 1980s something curious happened: The two sides just about reversed their positions. Liberal Democrats now insisted that soaring deficits would ruin the nation, and conservative Republicans seemed to want to change the subject. Why the switch in positions? Part of the reason is political.

Like Franklin Roosevelt, Ronald Reagan came into office complaining about excessive government spending. And, again like Roosevelt, Reagan soon presided over a gigantic mountain of deficits. Within the first four years of Reagan's presidency, deficits had reached their highest rate in our history: over $200 billion, 6.4 percent of our gross national product (GNP). Since this happened during Reagan's presidency, you can see why the Democrats tried to make a campaign issue out of deficits in 1984 and 1988. Why did our deficits grow so large? Was it Reagan's fault? Opinions differ. Reagan and his supporters put the blame on big-spending Democrats in Congress. Reagan's critics blamed them on what they called "voodoo economics."

SUPPLY-SIDE ECONOMICS

The term *voodoo economics* was coined by George Bush when he ran against Reagan in the 1980 Republican primaries. It was used to sum up the "all this and heaven too" philosophy of Ronald Reagan. Reagan wanted an increase in defense spending, a tax *decrease*, and a "safety net" in welfare spending so that the truly needy would be taken care of. Reagan promised all this *plus* a gradual decrease in deficits!

The key was to be a combination of tax reduction and domestic spending cuts. The tax reduction would leave more money in people's pockets, and business would use the money to expand plant capacity. This would have several effects: It would reduce inflation by putting more goods on the market; it would put more people to work, thus reducing welfare costs; and it would increase government revenues by increasing taxable profits and salaries. This economic theory has been called supply-side economics. Advocated by a number of New Right spokesmen, such as economist Arthur Laffer and then-New York congressman Jack Kemp (the present secretary of Housing and Urban Development), supply-side economics is a kind of inverted Keynesianism. Keynes advocated putting money in the hands of consumers, thus stimulating demand. Supply-side economics aims at stimulating business in order to increase productivity, or the supply of goods. Reagan's strategy was to combine supply-side economics with cuts in domestic spending eventually to make the deficit go down. Instead, the deficit shot up. Why?

Liberal Democrats said it was the combination of a tax cut and the increase in military spending. In 1981, Reagan persuaded Congress to pass a 25 percent three-stage cut in income tax that benefited high-income taxpayers. He also convinced Congress to increase military spending from $157 billion in 1981 to nearly $221 billion in 1984, an increase of over 40 percent. Put the two together, said the liberals, and you explain the huge increase in the deficit.

Conservative Republicans pointed out that the Reagan tax cuts were cuts in the tax *rate*, not cuts in revenue collected by the government, and that tax revenues grew substantially between 1980 and 1984 (except for 1983, when a recession trimmed tax receipts). For conservatives, the basic cause of the deficit was not the tax cut, but a very large increase in overall government spending—from roughly $591 billion in 1981 to nearly $852 billion in 1984. What caused the increase? Even conservatives admitted that part of it was the increase in military spending between 1981 and 1984. But, they added, Reagan's defense increases did no more than restore military spending to the place it had occupied in the mid-1970s. What really caused the deficit to skyrocket, say conservatives, is that spending on social programs kept going up in

FIGURE **18-7**

521

Deficits and Taxes

The Federal Government Dollar

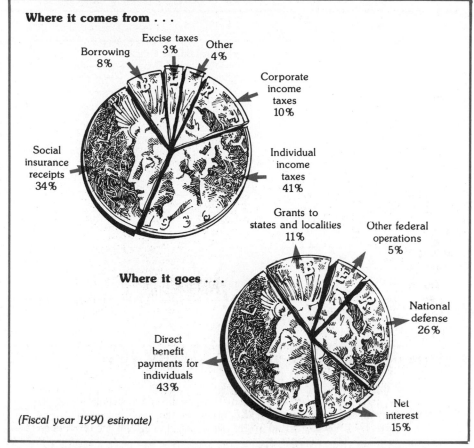

Where it comes from . . .

Borrowing
8%

Excise taxes
3%

Other
4%

Corporate
income
taxes
10%

Social
insurance
receipts
34%

Individual
income
taxes
41%

Grants to
states and localities
11%

Other federal
operations
5%

Where it goes . . .

National
defense
26%

Direct
benefit
payments for
individuals
43%

Net
interest
15%

(Fiscal year 1990 estimate)

Source: Congressional Quarterly Weekly Report, January 14, 1989, p. 65.

The key issue in current proposals to balance the federal budget is where to find sources of revenue and where to make spending cuts without jeopardizing major social services or placing too great a burden on the American taxpayer.

the 1980s, despite Reagan's efforts to cut it back. Welfare spending went up at a slower *rate* than in the 1970s, but it still went up; added to Reagan's "catch-up" military spending, it produced the big deficits.

But whatever its causes and whoever was responsible for it, it was hard to be nonchalant about a $200 billion deficit. By the middle of the 1980s, debt service alone on the $200 billion deficit was consuming nearly $4 out of every $10 that the government was collecting. A consensus developed in Congress that something drastic had to be done. So something was done, and it was drastic. Former senator Howard Baker called it "a riverboat gamble." New York senator Daniel P. Moynihan called it a "suicide pact."

GRAMM-RUDMAN: A REMEDY FOR DEFICITS?

Its official name is the Balanced Budget and Emergency Deficit Control Act of 1985, but it is better known as Gramm-Rudman-Hollings, or just Gramm-Rudman. Its chief sponsors were Senators William Gramm (R-Texas), Warren Rudman (R-New

FIGURE **18-8**

Deficit Projections

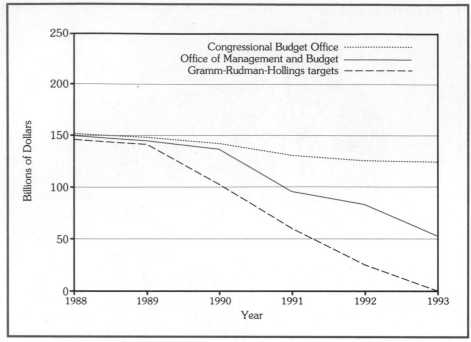

Source: *Congressional Quarterly Weekly Report*, November 26, 1988, p. 3380.

Beyond the debate over where to make cutbacks and where to increase revenues lies the fundamental question: What really is an *acceptable* deficit? Answers differ depending upon who is asked, as the three projections show here. Targets for 1993 range from a $121 billion deficit to a complete elimination of the budget deficit.

Hampshire), and Ernest Hollings (D-South Carolina). Its purpose was to bring the federal budget into balance; its method was to force Congress and the administration to raise taxes, or agree on selected spending cuts, or both—or else. The "or else" is the prospect of *unselected*, across-the-board spending cuts. These indiscriminate cuts would be so horrendous that the thought of them would make the politicians think twice before doing any more overspending. As one congressman explained: "The theme in what we did was to make this thing so irrational, so ugly, that it works as a club."[56]

Gramm-Rudman's club is a meat-ax, and it is wielded by the Office of Management and Budget (OMB) in the executive branch.[57] If Congress and the president fail to agree on spending cuts or a tax increase, the OMB cuts all government spending—except for certain exempted programs—by a certain amount. This is called <u>sequestering</u>. The amount to be sequestered will vary by the year. The great danger of such automatic cuts is that they must be indiscriminate and across the board. They would thus kill good programs along with less valuable ones. Of course, as defenders of Gramm-Rudman kept pointing out, Congress and the president can prevent indiscriminate cuts by making their own selected cuts or by raising taxes.

Still, many people are worried about Gramm-Rudman. Critics charge that it has fostered a spirit of short-sightedness, budgetary gimmickry, and outright deceptiveness. They cite, for example, Congress's decision in 1989 to move a military payday from October 1, which marked the beginning of fiscal year 1990, to September 29, which was still in the 1989 fiscal year; Congress did so in order to claim that it had "cut" $2.9 billion from its 1990 fiscal budget. This was one of the examples cited by Senator Hollings in his criticism of the law that he helped to sponsor. Calling the Gramm-Rudman-Hollings act a "shotgun marriage" that had now gone "on the rocks," in the fall of 1989 he announced his intention of filing for "divorce." But defenders of the law, including Gramm and Rudman, claim that it has fulfilled its main purpose, that of holding down federal spending and cutting back on the deficit. Whatever its flaws, it has made progress toward its goals. Gramm and Rudman conclude: "Just as we don't judge the success of a religion by the number of saints but by whether or not the world is better off, so should we judge Gramm-Rudman-Hollings."[58]

In the 1988 presidential race, George Bush promised no tax increases. As he began his new term, the Democrats in Congress waited to see if he was going to renege on that promise. If not, the only alternative was massive spending cuts—but where? Liberal Democrats would fight very hard against curbs on social spending, and conservative Republicans would be no less hostile to cuts in military spending. If neither side won and both sides refused to compromise, the Gramm-Rudman cuts would automatically be made.

Even as Americans awaited the resolution of these policy dilemmas, experts were debating the question of whether or not deficits really hurt the economy. In this chapter's Taking Sides section, on the following page, economists C. Fred Bergsten and Robert E. Hall present opposing views on the issue.

TAXES AND LOOPHOLES

Americans hate taxes. No people on earth really like them, but Americans have a special aversion to them. The American Revolution was fought over taxes, and part of our heritage is the belief that government should leave private property alone as much as possible. Our salaries are a form of private property, and Americans tend to begrudge government any portion of their paychecks. Every year at tax time we hear accounts of how many months of work it takes to pay the taxes due to Uncle Sam each year.

And yet—however grudgingly—Americans acknowledge that taxes are necessary if government is to carry out its essential functions. The Constitution gives Congress the power to tax and spend for the general welfare. The issue is not taxes but the extent and fairness of our taxes. Brought on in part by the Gramm-Rudman law, the new mood among lawmakers may well hold down the extent of taxing. The remaining question concerns the fairness of our tax code, particularly the income tax, which produces more than half the government's revenue.

The income tax is a relatively new development in American history. In the nineteenth century the federal government obtained its revenues mainly from tariffs (taxes on goods coming into the country), excise taxes (taxes on domestic goods), and the sale of public lands. The income tax levied in 1863, during the Civil War, was repealed at the end of the war in 1865. In 1894 Congress enacted the first peacetime income tax, a 2 percent tax on all incomes exceeding $4,000. Even this modest beginning was aborted by the Supreme Court, which declared it unconstitutional.[59] The Court's decision was reversed 18 years later by the Sixteenth Amendment, ratified in 1913. In that year Congress enacted the law that set up our present system. Even so, most of our working population paid hardly any federal income tax until the 1940s when the government started the practice of withholding income taxes from paychecks.

In theory the income tax is a progressive tax, meaning that a person's tax rate goes up according to his or her yearly earnings. By 1986 there were 14 different tax *(Continued on page 525)*

Do Deficits Harm the United States?

YES   C. Fred Bergsten

Based upon C. Fred Bergsten, "Yes, They Invite A Dollar Crisis—If Not Worse," *New York Times*, December 21, 1988, p. A35.

Unless something is done about deficits, says Bergsten, we risk inflation, recession, and major financial disruptions. "These risks stem mainly from the stubborn trade deficit and its financial implications." Our trade deficit, which exceeds $100 billion, cannot be brought down by present policies. Since the early 1980s foreign investors "have financed our deficit, pouring in $700 billion. They may now be nearing their saturation levels." Once their capital inflow stops, Bergsten believes, the dollar will fall precipitously in value, which in turn will send import prices up sharply, causing domestic prices to do the same. The inflationary pressures may cause the Federal Reserve to raise interest rates, triggering a recession. The only way to avoid these events is to adhere strictly to the Gramm-Rudman timetable and balance our budget by 1992. "History clearly demonstrates that imbalances as large as our trade and budget deficits are unsustainable." The remaining question, says Bergsten, is whether or not the correction will come through deliberate rational action on our part or by deep cuts "that create enormous pain."

NO   Robert E. Hall

Based upon Robert E. Hall, "No, In Fact Overall Debt Is Now Falling," *New York Times*, December 21, 1988, p. A35.

"Wall Street's and Washington's hysteria over the Federal budget deficit is unwarranted." Hall bases this conclusion on the fact that the debt constitutes a very small percentage of our national income (3 percent at the end of 1988) and may be getting even smaller. "Simply put, the national debt is rising more slowly than the economy is growing." He concedes that a smaller deficit would be better, but "the economy is still humming along in a very satisfactory way." Hall says that the danger of the hysteria about deficits is that it might cause Congress to overreact by raising taxes or suddenly slashing spending, throwing the economy into a tailspin. Yet the hysteria may have one good effect: making Congress more prudent and judicious about spending. For example, Congress has cut down on energy subsidies to business. Members of Congress who could not understand the silliness of taxing one part of the economy to subsidize another do understand that government cannot go on spending money it does not have. Thus, as Hall states, it turns out that "a slightly unhealthy deficit, from an economic point of view, has favorable political effects."

Postscript

Bergsten and Hall disagree on the dangers of the deficit but apparently agree that Congress is right to trim spending. Bergsten sees it as a means of averting disaster, and Hall seems to favor it on principle. Both, then, seem favorably disposed to Gramm-Rudman.

In *Day of Reckoning: The Consequences of American Economic Policy Under Reagan and After* (New York: Random House, 1988), Benjamin Friedman argues that the accumulation of a nearly $3 trillion national debt during the Reagan years represents a decisive break with the past and will saddle our children with a frightful burden. This general thesis is challenged by Robert Heilbroner and Peter Bernstein in *The Debt and the Deficit: False Alarms/Real Possibilities* (New York: W. W. Norton, 1989). They claim that the national debt as a percentage of our gross national product remains about where it was in 1962 and has actually shrunk since 1945; they do not regard it as a serious burden on the future, for, they argue, the same generation that will pay it off will also receive its proceeds.

(Continued from page 523)

brackets ranging from 11 to 50 percent. In practice very few paid half their income in taxes. The rich hired attorneys and accountants who found convenient loopholes in the law. Loopholes are tax code exceptions that allow people to pay much less in taxes. Most of the loopholes take the form of tax exemptions, which allow a person to subtract a certain amount from his or her taxable income. (Another, less common form of exception is a tax credit, which is a subtraction from the final tax bill.) There have been all sorts of loopholes: exemptions for capital gains, for municipal bonds, for pension earnings, and for dividends and interest; business exemptions for meals and drinks, for seminars on cruise ships, and for skyboxes at sporting events.

TAX REFORM ACT OF 1986

There have been periodic attempts to reform the system, to eliminate loopholes and simplify tax forms. In the 1970s the movement toward tax reform was spearheaded by liberal citizen lobbies like Common Cause. Such efforts were always balanced by special interest lobbyists who persuaded Congress to add new loopholes that just made the code more complicated. By the early 1980s, the reformers had all but given up.

Then something strange happened. In 1985 a conservative Republican president with lots of wealthy friends went on television to announce that he was going to push for comprehensive tax reform. President Reagan said he wanted taxes simplified, special interest loopholes eliminated, and tax breaks for the working poor. Reagan added that these reforms would constitute the number one domestic priority of his second term. Although the public at large did not seem to know or care much about Reagan's plan, it evoked a variety of reactions from political insiders. Many Democrats, including some of his old enemies, lavished praise on the plan; but conservative Republicans tended to be wary of it (to some it sounded like another "soak the rich" scheme), and many economic interests were appalled.[60]

The fight began in earnest when Reagan submitted his plan to Congress. Flocks of Lear jets descended on Washington as corporate interests girded themselves for battle. City and state governments also opposed one of Reagan's proposed changes, his proposal to drop federal tax deductions for the payment of state and local taxes. They feared that its effect would be to put pressure on states to reduce taxes. (Reagan finally neutralized their opposition by allowing this change to be eliminated.) But there was also strong support from influential senators and representatives on both sides of the aisle who were determined not to let reform get nibbled to death. In the end—after a year and a half of passionate debates, all-night meetings, deadlocks, near-derailments, and at one point public tears—the Tax Reform Act of 1986 became law. Here are some of its key provisions:

* The existing 14 tax brackets were reduced to 3: a rate of 15 percent for a married couple (filing jointly) making less than $30,000, 28 percent for a similar couple making roughly $30,000 to $72,000, and a 33 percent rate for a couple making $72,000 to approximately $150,000. (Those earning above that amount could be taxed at either the 28 percent rate or the 33 percent rate, depending on circumstances and not permitting personal exemptions.)
* Corporate taxes were reduced from 46 percent to 34 percent.
* The personal exemption was increased from $1,080 to $2,000, removing about 6 million working poor from the tax rolls.
* It closed or narrowed several loopholes, including deductions for business lunches (they are now only 80 percent deductible), investment tax credit, and capital gains tax exclusion (both entirely eliminated).

"I'm an American taxpayer! I've *already* been ripped off!" *Drawing by George Booth. Reproduced by special permission of Playboy Magazine © 1973 by Playboy.*

How successful has the law been in achieving its objectives? That is hard to say right now. It takes a number of years for the effects of any tax changes to be felt, and some of the provisions of the new code were phased in over a three-year period. Both liberal and conservative analysts seem to agree that the new code has helped the working poor as Reagan promised (although to a lesser degree than was expected) and that it has increased taxes on at least some categories of the wealthy.[61] It has also succeeded in cutting out some historic deductions. One thing it has conspicuously failed to do is to simplify our taxes. Within two years, the new law had spawned 2,704 changes in the Internal Revenue Code, 42 regulations, 65 announcements, 32 revenue rulings, and 48 new tax forms. The business magazine *Forbes* reported that the law made taxes a growth industry, giving rise to countless new lobbyists, accountants, and tax lawyers. One tax expert said: "When young people ask if it's still worth studying tax, I tell them their grandchildren will go to college on the fees they earn from the 1986 tax simplification."[62]

In 1989 Congress and the White House returned to the topic of taxes, this time to consider President Bush's plan for reducing taxes on capital gains (the sale of stocks, bonds, real estate, and other investments). This time there was no bipartisan accord between the president and the opposition leaders; both sides were ready to draw a line in the dust. Bush insisted that capital gains tax breaks would stimulate the economy and actually generate more tax revenues, helping all Americans. Democratic leaders called the Bush plan a "giveaway program to the rich," which in the long run would cost the Treasury billions each year. In September 1989, Democratic House leaders were stunned when it passed the House by a sizable majority made possible by the defection of 64 Democratic representatives. In the Senate, too, momentum seemed to be building toward passage of some form of capital gains tax reduction. "We're getting rolled," said New York senator Daniel P. Moynihan, a leading Democratic opponent of the measure.[63] But a threatened filibuster from Senator Howard Metzenbaum (D-Ohio) and other Senate liberals kept the measure from reaching the Senate floor for a vote, so the tax cut was defeated—for the time being.

Reflections

Between 1960 and 1980 the United States was transformed from a warfare state into a welfare state. In 1960 America spent 52.2 percent of its total federal budget on defense and 28.1 percent on welfare; in 1980 it spent 23.2 percent on defense and

54.3 percent on welfare. It was permanently committed—through Democratic and Republican administrations—to a complex series of social programs.

The roots of the commitment go back to the Social Security Act and other programs passed during the 1930s. But these beginnings were extremely modest in comparison with our present-day commitments. Even through the Great Depression, federal welfare spending in the 1930s was seen as a marginal and temporary expedient. It was for the widow and her small children, for the man who was temporarily out of work; it was to help people through the rough times in their lives. It certainly was not regarded as a solution to poverty or a substitute for work; the cure for poverty, Americans assumed, could only come through business recovery. The American assumption has always been that the normal way of getting money is to work for it.

It was during the 1960s that the government became involved in a major, long-term commitment to welfare. President Lyndon Johnson declared total war on poverty and launched a series of poverty programs. But even these were justified in traditional terms of helping people to help *themselves*. The slogan was "A hand, not a handout," and the intent was to help people to become self-sufficient. In 1967 it was discovered that the training programs were not working very well. Soon programs that simply handed out cash and benefits began to dwarf them. By 1980, in constant dollars, per capita expenditures on public aid were seven times what they had been in 1960.

Then Ronald Reagan came into the White House. He was determined, as he put it, to "restore the military balance" that had been lost during the 1970s. He persuaded Congress to increase the military budget and to cut taxes on the grounds that such a cut would stimulate the economy. Soon the national deficit had climbed to more than $200 billion a year. In desperation, Congress passed the Gramm-Rudman-Hollings law. "Stop me before I kill again," Congress seemed to be saying. Gramm-Rudman provides that if Congress and the president cannot agree on selected spending cuts or tax increases, the budget will automatically be cut—and cut across the board. Neither Congress nor the president, neither liberals nor conservatives, could derive any joy from such cuts. The theory is that the prospect will force compromise.

Gramm-Rudman forces us all to think about national priorities. How much should we spend on guns and how much on butter? Should we take more from one area and give it to another? One lesson we have learned since the 1960s is that we cannot do everything. We have to choose, and that requires careful thought. It also brings us to the question of results. If we are going to make a major commitment to a war on poverty, we have to ask whether or not a strategy is going to work. The poverty war begun in the 1960s worked in one sense: It dramatically reduced desperation and malnutrition. Poor people are better off physically today than they were a generation ago. What the new poverty programs failed to do was to decrease dependency, the condition that makes poor people constantly require assistance from the government. The real challenge of the future is what to do about the increase in the homeless, welfare mothers, and absentee fathers.

We began this chapter with a journey up Park Avenue, starting with the wealthy section at 68th Street and ending up on Harlem's East Side. In five minutes we went from penthouses to abandoned tenements, from English prams to smashed cars and broken glass. The two Park Avenues seem to be in two different worlds. Why have our poverty programs failed to change the poor end of Park Avenue?

We have raised these questions and provided some material for thinking about them, but we have not suggested any definitive answers. Modern poverty is extremely complex, involving everything from the breakdown of traditional values to the scarcity of unskilled blue-collar jobs. This does not mean that we should abandon the search for solutions. On the contrary, the time may now be ripe for a fresh start. There is a new spirit of realism and accommodation in the air. We have examined a few pieces of legislation, such as the Tax Reform Act of 1986 and the Welfare Reform

Act of 1988, which give tax relief to the working poor and encourage the nonworking poor to find jobs. These are probably no more than palliatives. What is encouraging about them is that they were both products of a broad bipartisan consensus. If that consensus can be sustained—if Democrats and Republicans can put aside old grudges and at least work around old ideologies—then maybe we can make progress toward fulfilling the great promise of American life: giving all our people the chance to do honest work, to take pride in it, and to get a decent reward for doing it.

Notes

1. See Ben A. Franklin, "Despite 20 Years of Federal Aid, Poverty Still Reigns in Appalachia," *New York Times*, Aug. 11, 1985, pp. 1, 26.

2. In the ensuing discussion, "Left," "Right," "liberal," and "conservative" are used. These terms were defined and discussed in chapter 13.

3. *Statistical Abstract 1989*, No. 734, p. 452.

4. *Statistical Abstract 1989*, p. 420.

5. Robert Pear, "Is Poverty a Condition Or Is It a Definition?" *New York Times*, Sept. 1, 1985, IV, p. 4.

6. Herman P. Miller, *Rich Man, Poor Man* (New York: Thomas Crowell Company, 1971), p. 111.

7. *Statistical Abstract 1989*, No. 741, p. 456.

8. William Julius Wilson, *The Truly Disadvantaged: The Inner City, the Underclass, and Public Policy* (Chicago: University of Chicago Press, 1987); Marie Winn, *The Plug-in Drug* (New York: Penguin Books, 1985); Eleanor Holmes Norton, "Restoring the Traditional Black Family," *The New York Times Magazine*, June 2, 1985, pp. 43-98.

9. A 1972 survey by Louis Harris and associates put the figure at 69 percent; a 1976 poll by Yankelovich, Skelly, and White found that only 18 percent favored an increase; 47 percent wanted less spent on welfare, and 31 percent thought it should remain at the same level. However, the Harris and Yankelovich polls showed 62 percent and 51 percent respectively favoring increases in funds for helping the poor. See further, Survey by ABC News/*Washington Post*, July 28-Aug. 1, 1983.

10. ABC News/*Washington Post* poll, Nov. 3-7, 1983. By a margin of 2-1 those polled agreed that "if you work hard, eventually you will get ahead."

11. Robert Pear, "Social Security Marking Golden Anniversary," *New York Times*, Aug. 14, 1985, p. B6. Robert Pear, "Social Security Said to Bridge the Gap in Income," *New York Times*, Dec. 28, 1988, p. A1.

12. Quoted in Pear, 1985.

13. See, for example, economist Paul Samuelson, quoted by AP writer Christopher Connell, "Generations Clash Over Social Security," *Journal-News* (Rockland County, NY), Aug. 25, 1985, p. AA4.

14. *New York Times*, Apr. 21, 1983, p. A17. Reagan predicted that the new changes "will allow Social Security to age as gracefully as all of us hope to do ourselves, without becoming an overwhelming burden on generations still to come." Whether or not this prophecy is sound will depend on a number of factors, including the state of the economy. One of those who worries about the future of Social Security is a former assistant to President Reagan for policy development. See Doug Bandow, "Sun City for Social Security," in *The American Spectator* (October 1985), pp. 17-20. For a sample of the almost incredibly complex debate surrounding the future of Social Security, see Peter G. Peterson's two-part article in the *New York Review of Books*, Dec. 2 and Dec. 16, 1982, followed by readers' replies and Peterson's rejoinder in the Mar. 17, 1983 issue (pp. 41-57).

15. Paul Taylor, "The Old Get Richer, the Young Get Poorer," *The Record* (Bergen County, NJ), Jan. 10, 1986, p. 0-4.

16. Senator David Durenbeger (R-Minnesota), quoted by Taylor.

17. Michael Harrington, *The Other America* (New York: Macmillan, 1962).

18. *1964 Congressional Quarterly Almanac*, p. 862.

19. Daniel P. Moynihan, *Maximum Feasible Misunderstanding* (New York: Free Press, 1969); James L. Sundquist, *Politics and Policy* (Washington, DC: The Brookings Institution, 1968). For an interesting case study of confrontation between local government and a Community Action Agency, see Huey Perry, *"They'll Cut Off Your Project": A Mingo County Chronicle* (New York: Frederick A. Praeger, Inc., 1972).

20. Tom Joe and Cheryl Rogers, *By the Few for the Few* (Lexington, MA: Lexington Books, 1985), p. 99. Dorothy Wickenden, "Abandoned Americans," *New Republic*, Mar. 18, 1985, p. 21.

21. John C. Weicher, "The Safety Net after Three Years," in *Maintaining the Safety Net* (Washington, DC: American Enterprise Institute, 1984), p. 17.

22. Quoted in Carolyn Lochhead, "How Hungry? How Many?" *Insight*, June 27, 1988, p. 8.

23. See U.S. Congress, "Senate Select Committee on Nutrition and Human Needs," *Hearings, Nutrition and Human Needs*, 90th Congress, 2d Session, 1968, part 4.

24. Quoted in Matthew L. Wald, "Study Suggests Hunger Common in Rural U.S.," *New York Times*, Jan. 15, 1986, p. A16. Compare with Robert Pear, "Counting the Hungry—a Contentious Census," *New York Times*, Nov. 15, 1987, IV, p. 5.

25. Quoted in Lochhead, p. 9.

26. See George G. Graham, "Searching for Hunger in America," *The Public Interest* (Winter 1985), pp. 4-17.

27. Nick Eberstadt, "Economic and Material Poverty in the U.S.," *The Public Interest* (Winter 1988), p. 63.

28. U.S. Department of Housing and Urban Development, *A Report to the Secretary on the Homeless and Emergency Shelters* (Washington: Office of Policy Development and Research, 1984).

29. Estimates were obtained from shelter operators in 21 selected American cities in 1986; later, estimates from some other cities were added. Then an effort was made to imagine how many homeless people were in the suburbs, and that number was added on to the total. Even then, the figure only came to 1.5 million, not 2 to 3 million.

30. Jonathan Kozol, *Rachel and Her Children: Homeless Families in America* (New York, Crown Publishers, Inc., 1988), pp. 10-11.

31. Robert Pear, "Data Are Elusive on the Homeless," *New York Times*, Mar. 1, 1988, p. B6.

32. A 1987 survey by the New York State Psychiatric Institute estimated that nearly two-thirds of those using homeless shelters throughout the state had some mental disorder. In the same year New York City's Deputy Human Resources Administrator for adult services estimated that roughly one-third of the city's shelter population suffered from mental illness and another third had drug, alcohol, or behavior problems. In Chicago a team of demographers from the University of Massachusetts studied the homeless population in 1987 and found that 23 percent reported having been in mental hospitals, 16 percent had attempted suicide, 41 percent had been jailed for two or more days, and 33 percent had been in drug or alcohol detoxification programs. Josh Barbanel, "New York's Shelters: Who Uses Them and Why," *New York Times*, Jan. 26, 1988, p. B2. Peter H. Rossi et al., "The Urban Homeless: Estimating Composition and Size," *Science*, Mar. 13, 1987, pp. 1138-39.

33. Suzanne Daley, "The Ruin of a Building Owned by New York," *New York Times*, Feb. 9, 1988, p. B1. William Tucker, "The Economics of Public Hearing," *The American Spectator* (November 1989), pp. 26-29.

34. Alan Pifer, "The Social Role of Government in a Free-Enterprise System," in Kurt Finsterbusch and George McKenna, eds., *Taking Sides: Clashing Views on Controversial Social Issues*, 3d ed. (Guilford, CT: The Dushkin Publishing Group, 1984), pp. 191-92.

35. The entire Fall 1980 issue of the *Journal of Human Resources* is devoted to analyzing the results of SIME/DIME. Compare with Robert A. Moffit, "The Negative Income Tax: Would It Discourage Work?" *Monthly Labor Review* (April 1981), pp. 23-27.

36. Charles Murray, *Losing Ground: American Social Policy, 1950-1980* (New York: Basic Books, 1984).

37. Murray, pp. 64-65.

38. "CBS Reports: The Black Family," broadcast Jan. 25, 1986. For another anecdotal account that reveals some of the "disincentives" of the welfare system, see Susan Sheehan, *Welfare Mother* (Boston: Houghton Mifflin Co., 1976), pp. 30-35, 42-43.

39. See, for example, Michael Harrington, "The Future of Poverty," *Commonweal*, Nov. 2-16, 1984, pp. 625-32; Robert Greenstein, "Losing Faith in 'Losing Ground,' " *New Republic*, Mar. 25, 1985, pp. 12-17; Murray has replied to many of the criticisms. See his exchange with Greenstein in *New Republic*, Apr. 8, 1985, pp. 21-23 and his "Have the Poor Been 'Losing Ground'?" in *Political Science Quarterly* (Fall 1985), pp. 427-45.

40. Christopher Jencks, "How Poor Are the Poor?" *New York Review of Books*, May 9, 1985, p. 45.

41. Wilson, p. 104.

42. Wilson, p. 103.

43. See, for example, Frank E. Armbruster, *Our Children's Crippled Future: How American Education Has Failed* (New York: Quadrangle/New York Times Book Co., 1977); Gerald Grant, "Schools That Make an Imprint: Creating a Strong Positive Ethos," in John H. Bunzel, ed., *Challenge to American Schools: The Case for Standards and Values* (New York: Oxford University Press, 1985), pp. 127-43; Joseph Adelson, "What Happened to the School?" *Commentary* (March 1981), pp. 36-41; Andrew Oldenquist, " 'Social Triage' Against Black Children," in Beatrice and Ronald Gross, eds., *The Great School Debate: Which Way for American Education?* (New York: Simon & Schuster, Inc., 1985), pp. 254-63.

44. Edward B. Fiske, "Impending U.S. Jobs 'Disaster': Work Force Unqualified to Work," *New York Times*, Sept. 25, 1989, p. B6.

45. Fiske, p. B6.

46. Ken Auletta, *The Underclass* (New York: Random House, 1982), pp. 222-30.

47. *Boston Globe*, Feb. 3, 1986, p. 1.

48. William K. Stevens, "The Welfare Consensus," *New York Times*, June 22, 1988, pp. A1, 21.

49. Martin Tolchin, "Conferees Approve Welfare Revisions; Moynihan Lauded," *New York Times*, Sept. 28, 1988, p. A1.

50. Norton, p. 79.

51. Roger Wilkins, "The Black Poor Are Different," *New York Times*, Aug. 22, 1989, p. A23.

52. Wilkins, p. A23.

53. Norton, p. 98.

54. *The Common Good: Social Welfare and the American Future*, Policy Recommendations of the Executive Panel (New York: The Ford Foundation, 1989), p. 43.

55. James Fallows, "The Three Fiscal Crises," *The Atlantic* (September 1985), p. 24.

56. Congressman Leon Panetta (D-California), quoted by *Washington Post* columnist David Broder, "Gramm-Rudman: Fraud and Failure," in *The Record* (Bergen County, NJ), Dec. 11, 1985, p. A31.

57. As amended by Congress in 1987. In the original 1985 legislation, the power was given to the comptroller general, head of Congress's General Accounting Office. This was declared unconstitutional by the Supreme Court in 1986 on the grounds that such power is by nature executive and thus belongs in the executive branch of government rather than in the legislative branch.

58. The respective views of Hollings and Gramm-Rudman are in the *New York Times*, Oct. 25, 1989, A31.

59. *Pollock v. Farmer's Loan and Trust Co.*, 1895.

60. A *Washington Post*/ABC News poll in 1985 revealed that only 22 percent of those polled expressed firm support for Reagan's plan, another 22 percent opposed it, and 56 percent said they knew too little about it to take a stand. See *The Record* (Bergen County, NJ), Sept. 29, 1985, p. A8. For the reactions of insiders, see the report of *Congressional Quarterly* writer Robert Rothman, "Tax Reform Finds Strange Partisans," in *Washington Times*, July 16, 1985, p. 6A.

61. Robert S. McIntyre, "The Populist Tax Act of 1989," *The Nation*, Apr. 2, 1988, pp. 462-63; Edwin Rubenstein, "Truth in Taxation," *National Review*, Feb. 19, 1988, p. 18. Compare with *Consumer Reports* (March 1988), pp. 142-48, which did its own study based upon subscribers' self-reporting. "Upper-middle class subscribers with household incomes of $50,000 to $74,999 are most likely to feel the pinch of a tax increase" (p. 142).

62. "The Tax Nightmare," *Newsweek*, Feb. 29, 1988, p. 40; Laura Saunders and Jonathan Clements, "One Man's Problem is Another's Opportunity," *Forbes*, Mar. 7, 1988, pp. 105-06.

63. David E. Rosenbaum, "Senate Democrats Working to Devise Their Own Tax Cut," *New York Times*, Sept. 30, 1989, p. 1.

19

American Foreign Policy

Sunday morning, September 2, 1945. In Tokyo Bay, Japan, a vast flotilla of American warships was assembled in the harbor, their guns trained on the Japanese coast. But there was no shooting this day. In a few minutes, World War II would be officially over in the Pacific—this terrible war that had lasted six years, killed 40 million people, and left eight nations in rubble.[*]

The Japanese Surrender

A formal ceremony was about to take place aboard the battleship USS *Missouri*, which less than a month earlier had been pounding the Japanese coast with her 16-inch guns. General Douglas MacArthur, the Supreme Allied Commander of the Pacific, was there, along with his chief admirals and staff and representatives of other countries that had fought Japan. Everything was prepared. The deck was swept clean; the flag that

[*]This account is drawn from the following sources: Theodore H. White, "The Danger from Japan," *New York Times Magazine* (July 28, 1985), pp. 19ff; Samuel Eliot Morison, *The Two-Ocean War* (Boston: Little, Brown and Company, 1963), pp. 570–77; Spencer Davis, "Unconditional Surrender," Associated Press Report, September 2, 1945 (reprinted in Rockland County, NY, *Journal-News*, September 1, 1985, p. AA3).

531

September 1945: A Japanese general signs the official articles of surrender aboard the USS *Missouri*, marking the end of World War II. U.S. General of the Army Douglas MacArthur, who is seen here looking on (far left), voiced the hope that this peace would be permanent, yet within a few years the cold war had begun.

had flown over Pearl Harbor in December 1941 was flying above the mainmast. In the center of the deck was a table, draped in blue, bare except for the articles of surrender laid upon it.

Soon an American naval launch arrived, carrying Japanese foreign minister Mamoru Shigemitsu, formally attired in top hat, morning coat, and striped pants, and army chief of staff General Toshijiro Umezu. The atmosphere was frigid as they came aboard and they were escorted to the front of the table. They waited in silence under a gray sky.

After three or four minutes General MacArthur appeared with two of his admirals. He took his place in front of the microphones and made a short speech. It concluded on this note:

It is my earnest hope—indeed the hope of all mankind—that from this solemn occasion a better world shall emerge out of the blood and carnage of the past, a world founded upon faith and understanding, a world dedicated to the dignity of man and the fulfillment of his most cherished wish for freedom, tolerance and justice.[1]

Someone brought Foreign Minister Shigemitsu a chair; he had been crippled years before in an assassination attempt. Removing his top hat and hunching forward, he signed the articles of surrender. Umezu, the military commander, stood stiffly in front of the table, then abruptly bent at the waist to sign. MacArthur signed, his hand shaking a little at first. He steadied himself and finished. Then he called on the representatives of the other Allied governments to sign.

As the last signature was scrawled on the documents, a crack appeared in the clouds; the whole scene was suddenly flooded in morning light. Then came another event almost as miraculous in timing. Journalist Theodore H. White, a spectator, later remembered it this way:

> As MacArthur intoned "These proceedings are closed," we heard a drone and looked up. It is difficult to recall now, after years of floundering and blunder, how very good we were in those days, with what precision we ordered things. Four hundred B-29s had taken off from Guam and Saipan hours before to arrive over the *Missouri* at this precise moment of climax. They stretched across the rim of the horizon, and their heavy droning almost instantly harmonized with a softer buzzing as 1,500 fleet aircraft from our flattops joined them.[2]

*   *   *   *   *

In 1945 the United States was at the zenith of its power. Great Britain was crippled, and continental Europe was devastated. The Soviet Union had lost 20 million people. China was near collapse. The major industrial cities of Japan had been incinerated. There was no Third World: India, Africa, and Southeast Asia were colonies, and Latin America lay securely within the U.S. sphere of influence.

The United States was not only untouched, it had been helped by the war. The war had forced its industry to modernize, leading to a dramatic increase in output and a proliferation of new products. By 1945 the United States had become the industrial giant of the world. But more important than industrial leadership was our moral leadership. The United States had rescued Europe from tyranny, closed down the Nazi death camps, liberated Asia from the Japanese, and given even Japan itself a democratic government. Every country in the world—including the Soviet Union, whose wartime alliance with the United States was already falling apart—looked up to the United States. Whether the U.S. liked it or not, it had become a global leader. And it was seen as a good leader, a force for democracy, liberty, and compassion.

What person living in those times could have imagined that in less than 25 years serious writers would be comparing the United States with Nazi Germany and holding "war crimes tribunals" to condemn its leaders? Who could have predicted the transformation of the United States' reputation from leader of the free world to Yankee imperialist? Who could have foreseen its humiliation or could have pictured the stunned, blindfolded American hostages being led around by Iranian militants?

By the 1970s an American president openly talked of his country becoming "a pitiful, helpless giant." More than a decade after that, in spite of presidential assurances that the United States could stand tall again, there were fresh humiliations. There were still American hostages in the Middle East. In an effort to get them back, American arms were sent to a nation that called us "the great Satan" and trampled on our flag. France would not let our planes fly over it to bomb Colonel Muammar al-Qadaffi's Libya. In West Germany, a public opinion poll showed that a majority of respondents had more admiration for the president of the Soviet Union than they did for our president. In Nicaragua a Marxist-Leninist government took over in 1979 and was still firmly in control a decade later; in neighboring El Salvador a war between the government and leftist rebels had cost 70,000 lives and was tearing the society apart. Other governments in the region seemed at least as worried about the dangers of American intervention as they were about Communist subversion.

Throughout much of the world, from Korea to West Germany, from Lebanon to Great Britain, American military forces were threatened by terrorists and picketed by protestors. Even American civilians no longer felt safe as they boarded airplanes; they wondered whether or not some terrorist group might take over the plane—or blow it up. What has happened to the United States' reputation and strength? Is the decline of the United States as a world power in some way related to our foreign policy? What is our foreign policy, and what changes, if any, should be made in it? These are the questions we probe in this chapter.

Who Makes Foreign Policy?

Let us start with the basics. Before we can understand the evolution of American foreign policy and some of the lessons that observers have tried to derive from it, we must first examine the processes and institutions of policymaking. Who makes foreign policy? The question is not easily answered, for it is a complex process involving the participation of the president and his administration, Congress, pressure groups, public opinion, and international agencies.

THE PRESIDENT: SOLE ORGAN

The president's power derives from a unique status as the nation's chief foreign policy spokesperson. In a famous 1936 case, *United States v. Curtiss-Wright*, the Supreme Court characterized the president as being the sole organ of foreign relations. Only the president is allowed to negotiate for this country; only the president is allowed to decide when, where, and *if* to negotiate. The president represents this country in its relations abroad. The president receives, or refuses to receive, ambassadors and foreign ministers of other countries. A presidential visit to another country is a signal that the United States considers the country's regime one with which it can deal on a friendly basis. President Nixon's visit to China in 1972 suddenly eased relations between the two countries, relations that had been severely strained since the Communists won the 1949 civil war in China. When President Reagan visited the Soviet Union in 1988 and put his arm around Soviet general secretary Gorbachev, the gesture probably did more to melt the ice of the cold war than a score of international conferences.

In shaping foreign policy the president works within a framework of executive agencies. Some of them are cabinet departments that have been around since the early days of the Republic. Others are of more recent creation.

THE STATE DEPARTMENT

The State Department, established by the First Congress in 1789, is one of the oldest cabinet agencies. State Department employees perform a variety of tasks, from hand-carrying diplomatic documents between Washington and its 143 embassies abroad to advising the president on virtually every facet of foreign policy. Among its more important bureaus are the Arms Control and Disarmament Agency (ACDA), which does research in methods of arms control and negotiates these issues with other

FIGURE **19-1**

The U.S. Department of State

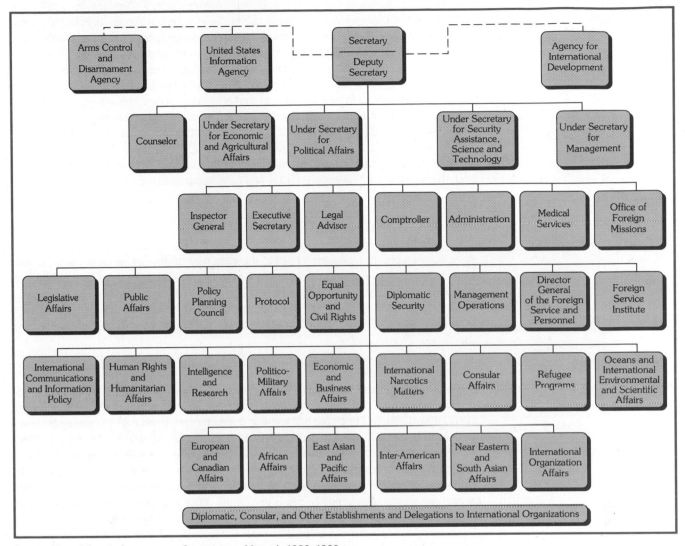

Source: United States Government Organization Manual, 1988–1989.

The U.S. Department of State is one of the oldest agencies of the executive branch of the government. Among its many tasks in shaping foreign policy are information, research, public relations, and foreign-aid program administration.

countries; the United States Information Agency (USIA), a public relations agency for the United States in other countries (it operates libraries and information centers as well as Voice of America radio broadcasts); and the Agency for International Development (AID), which administers foreign aid programs.

The State Department is headed by a secretary of state. The secretary of state is the chief cabinet officer in charge of foreign policy, but in fact, the secretary's power depends upon a number of factors, including the individual's personality and how much use the president decides to make of him or her. Some secretaries, such as Dean Acheson (who served under Truman) and John Foster Dulles (Eisenhower's secretary of state) have been forceful in shaping policy; some, such as William P. Rogers (Nixon's first secretary of state), have played a more passive role.

THE DEPARTMENT OF DEFENSE

The Defense Department is discussed at greater length in the next chapter. Still, it is important to mention its connection with foreign policy. Set up in 1789, the Department of Defense was originally called the War Department. In 1949 the name was changed to *Defense*, mainly for public relations purposes but also to employ a term more inclusive of its area of expertise—war *and* diplomacy. There is a relationship between the two: One need not go as far as the famous Prussian general Von Clausewitz, who said that "war is politics by other means"; it is sufficient to say that U.S. presidents consider it essential that all foreign policy options are investigated before employing any risky military initiatives. The president often seeks the advice of the secretary of defense and the Joint Chiefs of Staff (JCS)—the chief officers of our armed services (the chiefs of staff of the Army, Navy, and Air Force and the commandant of the Marine Corps)—who, with a staff of 400, advise the president and the secretary of defense on U.S. military needs and options.

THE NATIONAL SECURITY COUNCIL

A newer organization designed to help the president make foreign policy was created by The National Security Act, passed in 1947: The National Security Council (NSC). Its formal membership consists of the president, vice president, secretary of state, and secretary of defense. In fact, participation in NSC meetings is much broader; it includes members of the Joint Chiefs of Staff, the Central Intelligence Agency, and the White House staff.

According to law its job is "to advise the president with respect to the integration of domestic, foreign, and military policies relating to the national security" and to perform "such other functions as the president may direct." The "other functions" clause leaves room for the president to make whatever use he or she sees fit for the NSC. It is not limited to giving advice; the president can involve it in actual operations. In the early 1960s President Kennedy got impatient with the delays, red tape, and lack of response in the State Department, so he bypassed it, preferring to make policy informally through the NSC and his personal staff. That marked the ascension of the president's national security adviser to a key role in carrying out foreign policy. It may also have planted the seeds of the Iran-Contra affair that germinated 25 years later.

The use of the NSC to circumvent the State Department was expanded under President Nixon's administration. His national security adviser, Henry Kissinger, was adept at bureaucratic infighting, and he quickly overshadowed Secretary of State William P. Rogers. (Nixon later appointed Kissinger secretary of state.) In Jimmy Carter's administration there was a kind of standoff between his national security adviser, Zbigniew Brzezinski, and Secretary of State Cyrus Vance. Brzezinski was a hawk; Vance was more dovish. Vance finally resigned after losing a closed-door argument about whether or not to send a military expedition into Iran to rescue the American hostages (a mission that ended in disaster). The ideological tensions between anti-Communist hardliners in the NSC and doves in the State Department intensified during the Reagan administration.[3] In these contests the NSC usually lost. Indeed, the post of adviser became a revolving door. Six NSC advisers came and went during Reagan's two terms. The best-known of these, Navy rear admiral John Poindexter, acquired national recognition because of the Iran-Contra scandal. He and his assistant, Marine lieutenant colonel Oliver North, took funds from arms sales to Iran and diverted them to the Contras, the antigovernment guerrillas in Nicaragua. During the height of the scandal, some critics thought the roots of "Irangate" went deeper than the misdeeds of two men. They saw them as inevitable products of an agency shrouded in secrecy and largely uncontrolled by Congress. They wanted to strip the NSC of any further operational role, forcing the president to rely more heavily upon the State Department. But one reason that the NSC accumulated so much power in the first place was that presidents no longer trusted State Department bureaucrats to carry out their policies with speed and reliability. By the end of the Reagan administration, it appeared that a tacit understanding had been reached: The NSC would not be crippled by Congress, but in the future only seasoned foreign-policy professionals should head the agency. When George Bush entered the White House in 1989, he appointed retired Air Force general Brent Scowcroft national security adviser. Scowcroft had occupied the same post during the Ford administration in the 1970s and enjoyed a good reputation in Congress.

The National Security Act states that the Central Intelligence Agency (CIA) is to advise the National Security Council, to acquire and analyze information concerning other countries, and to perform such other functions and duties as the National Security Council directs. A succession of presidents and CIA directors have interpreted these other functions as a license to conduct covert operations. In the 1950s the CIA helped to overthrow unfriendly governments in Guatemala and Iran; in 1961 the CIA planned and directed the ill-fated Bay of Pigs invasion of Cuba; it later plotted the assassination of several foreign leaders, including Cuban dictator Fidel Castro, and supported a secret anti-Communist army in Laos.

In the early 1970s newspaper revelations about improper behavior by the CIA led to investigations into its activities. Senator Frank Church of Idaho, whose committee conducted a sweeping investigation of CIA activities, said that the agency had become a "rogue elephant." Congress passed new legislation forcing the CIA to notify no less than eight different congressional committees before embarking on any covert actions. Since members of Congress and their staffs are not very good at keeping secrets, the effect of this was to turn covert action into overt action, and that usually meant no action. As former president Gerald Ford later put it, "If you start out with the assumption that, for one reason or another, it's going to be out there in every newspaper, forget it."[4] Responding to complaints that the CIA had been paralyzed by all this scrutiny, Congress later cut back on the number of congressional committees with access to CIA files. But it still required the president to submit official findings to select congressional panels before undertaking any covert action through the CIA. This action gave every member of Congress an effective veto over covert actions; if the legislator opposed a particular action, he or she could stop it simply by leaking it to the press.

The CIA has become the most controversial of American intelligence services, but it is not the only one. In fact, it employs only 10 percent of personnel involved in intelligence activities. Most intelligence analysts work in the Department of Defense, which houses such important agencies as Air Force Intelligence and The National Security Agency. Air Force Intelligence operates the spy satellites that give us vital information about Soviet missile sites and other installations that the agency deems threatening to our security. The National Security Agency is largely concerned with cryptology—breaking the secret codes of other countries and protecting our own codes.

THE ROLE OF CONGRESS

The president's power of initiative in foreign policy does not mean that Congress has no role to play. Article II, Section 2, of the Constitution specifically empowers one of its houses by making presidential treaties dependent upon the "advice and consent of the Senate." Since George Washington's time the "advice" part has been left up to the discretion of the president. At one point Washington went to the Senate with the draft of an Indian treaty. The treaty had seven headings, and he wanted the senators' yea or nay on each. The senators told the president they wanted more involvement than that—whereupon, according to one of those present, Washington "started up with a

FIGURE **19-2**

Congressional Control of Foreign Policy: Federal Funding

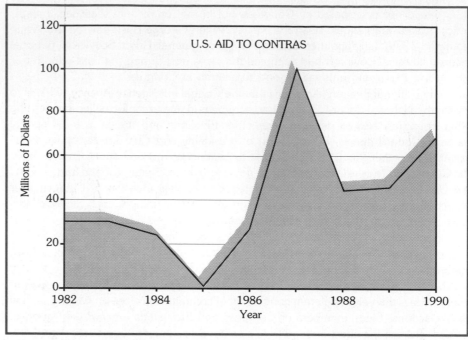

Source: Congressional Quarterly Weekly Report, April 15, 1989, p. 834. Reprinted with permission.

The important role that the U.S. Senate plays in refining presidential directives on foreign policy stems from its power to withhold consent, to initiate investigations, and most especially, to control the purse. The 1988 withdrawal of financial support for President Reagan's Contra-aid policy prompted some in his administration to finance the Contras with the money from arms sales to Iran; the resulting scandal further weakened the Reagan administration.

violent fret."[5] Never again did he journey to the Senate for advice on treaties, nor have any of his successors, although some have conferred informally with key senators during the treaty-making process.

Treaty Ratification. It is wise for a president to take soundings of Senate opinion while shaping treaties because the Senate's consent is by no means assured. Woodrow Wilson suffered a catastrophic defeat in 1919 when the Senate refused to ratify the treaty he negotiated at the end of World War I. In more recent history, in 1980 Jimmy Carter withdrew from Senate consideration an arms limitation treaty (SALT II) that he had worked out with the Soviets because he knew that he lacked the votes for ratification.

Power of the Purse. Another influence that Congress has over foreign policy is control of the purse. In the early 1970s Congress forced President Nixon to stop bombing Cambodia by cutting off funds for the bombing, and in 1975 Congress cut off all assistance to the South Vietnamese army. In the 1980s Congress's cutoffs and limitations of aid to the Nicaraguan Contras (see Figure 19.2) put a crimp in President Reagan's Central American policy and led to the search for alternative sources of funding that culminated in the Iran-Contra scandal.

Hearings. The Iran-Contra investigation should remind us of another congressional device for shaping American foreign policy: investigations. In the early 1950s investigations by Senator Joseph McCarthy and others into alleged Communist subversion in the State Department pushed policymakers into adopting a harder line on any dispute involving Communist forces in the world.[6] In the late 1960s congressional liberals took their turn to reexamine those hard-line policies. Hearings on the Vietnam War conducted by Senator William Fulbright (D-Arkansas) and others contributed to the erosion of public support for the war and pressured the administration to seek ways of getting out. Congressional hearings can thus set the framework for policymaking. Under the glare of klieg lights and the frowns of members of Congress, executive officials often lose their appetite for policies that are clearly unacceptable on the Hill.

Lawmaking. Congress can influence foreign policy in a more direct way by passing laws. In chapter 9 we discussed the War Powers Resolution of 1973, which sought to impose limits on presidential warmaking. There have been other attempts to influence foreign policy through legislation. The Neutrality Acts of 1935, 1936, and 1937 attempted to keep the United States out of the war developing in Europe by prohibiting American arms shipments and loans to nations at war. With a similar intent the Clark Amendment, passed by Congress in 1975, prohibited the United States from giving aid to either side in the civil war then raging in Angola. The various Boland Amendments passed by Congress in the 1980s limited the amount and kind of assistance that could be given to the Contras in Nicaragua.

President Reagan and his supporters were often exasperated by congressional limitations on the president's foreign policies. They considered this "micromanagement" and complained that congressional statutes lack the flexibility to deal with the day-to-day changes that occur in the international arena. In reply, congressional supporters insisted that legislation was necessary to prevent the kind of runaway foreign policy that had gotten the United States involved in Vietnam. The Bush administration seems more inclined to work with Congress instead of accusing it of meddling. Still, in various forms, the micromanagement charge sometimes resurfaces. After the unsuccessful attempt by Panamanian military officers to overthrow General Manuel Noriega in October 1989, some in Congress criticized Bush for not doing enough to get rid of the dictator. In reply, Bush aides complained that past congressional actions had tied the hands of the present administration. They cited specifically congressional pressure in the 1970s that had forced then-President Ford to ban assassinations by the CIA, thus limiting any assistance the United States could give to the anti-Noriega military officers involved in the attempted overthrow (assassination of Noriega may have been one of their options to ensure the success of their revolt). National Security Adviser Brent Scowcroft complained that "Congress, by its actions and demeanor, certainly leaned us against the kinds of things they're now saying we should have done." This was angrily disputed by Senator David Boren (D-Oklahoma), head of the Senate Intelligence Committee, who insisted that his panel had given the administration full authority to take decisive action against Noriega.[7] There were angry feelings on both sides, although President Bush and key Democrats in Congress did not seem too far apart in their basic premises; both sides tacitly agreed that in this case the United States had the right to intervene militarily in another country. This consensus would have been unlikely during the Reagan years.

PRESSURE GROUPS AND PUBLIC OPINION

The arguments on foreign policy issues should remind us of another source of influence: pressure groups. They lobby, sometimes very emotionally, for and against certain policies. Often they divide along philosophical lines: There are liberal and conservative groups, hawkish and dovish groups. The Committee on the Present

FIGURE **19-3**

Our Opinion of Reagan's Foreign Policy, 1981-1987

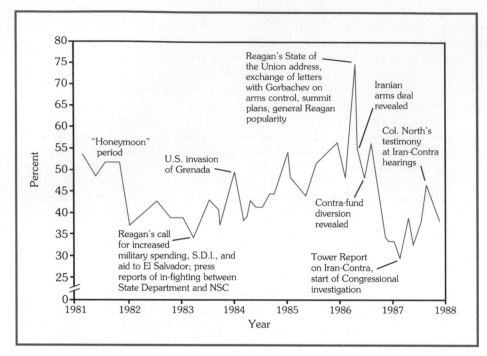

Source: New York Times/CBS news poll, 1981-1987, in Harold W. Stanley and Richard G. Niemi, *Vital Statistics on American Politics.* Adapted with permission.

The percentage of Americans approving of Ronald Reagan's foreign policy rose and fell throughout Reagan's time in office. Public approval reached a high of 75 percent in early 1986, following Reagan's discussions with Gorbachev on arms control; public approval fell below 30 percent in early 1987 at the start of the Congressional investigation of the Iran-Contra fund diversion. The question asked in this poll was: Do you approve or disapprove of the way Ronald Reagan is handling foreign policy? The percentage shown is of those approving.

Danger is a hawkish group. Founded in 1976 by a group of prominent public figures (its membership includes former UN ambassador Jeane Kirkpatrick and *Commentary* editor Norman Podhoretz), the committee believes that American policymakers need to take more seriously security threats to the United States. On the other side are a variety of dovish groups, including the National Committee for a Sane Nuclear Policy and the Union of Concerned Scientists, which worry about warlike confrontations in a nuclear age.

Some pressure groups are more interested in bread-and-butter issues than in ideology. Business and labor unions often lobby for protective tariffs against foreign competition. There are pressure groups centering on religion, race, and ethnicity. These groups usually claim to represent not just their own interests but "what is best for America." They know the importance of public support; without it, a controversial policy initiative runs the risk of derailment. President Reagan's policy of arming the Contras was never really popular in Congress, in part because legislators knew that such aid was not supported by the majority of Americans. On the other hand, the majority of Americans polled did approve of the presence of American troops in Grenada in 1983, and when that became clear to congressional critics of Reagan's invasion, most of them decided to say no more.[8] The ups and downs of public sentiment on Reagan's foreign policy—and some possible reasons for some of the shifts—are indicated in Figure 19.3.

THE UNITED STATES AND THE UNITED NATIONS

Unlike all the institutions and groups mentioned above, the United Nations plays a distinctly marginal role in American foreign policy. Today the United States and other member nations use the UN as a forum for presenting their views and, more informally, for meeting representatives of other countries.

Of course, the UN is not a world government and was never intended to be one. Each member nation retains complete sovereignty and independence. As stated in the 1945 charter, its purposes are more limited: to keep the peace, to develop friendly relations between states, and to work out cooperative solutions to the common problems facing mankind. It has many organs, but the principal ones are the General Assembly, consisting of all its members; a Security Council, consisting of 15 members; a Secretariat; an Economic and Social Council; and an International Court of Justice. In theory each of these organs aims at keeping world peace in its own way. The General Assembly and the Economic and Social Council are authorized to pass resolutions addressing the underlying causes of world tension, such as poverty and injustice. The Security Council can go further: Its 15 members (the United States, the USSR, the United Kingdom, France, and China, plus 10 other rotating members) can pass resolutions regarding the use of force to suppress acts of aggression. (This seems to be an exception to the general powerlessness of the UN; however, it has been used very rarely, since each council member has a veto that can overturn the decisions of the majority.) The International Court can adjudicate certain controversies concerning international law and hand down decisions, although it has no power to enforce them.

The United Nations has undergone many changes since its founding in 1945, but perhaps none has been as striking as the change in its membership. In 1945 the UN had 51 members, most of them from Europe and the western hemisphere. Today it has 159 members, with a large representation from states in Asia and Africa. Most of these are former European colonies, many are tiny in size (32 have under a million in population), and the total monetary contribution of half of them amounts to 2 percent of the UN budget.[9] Yet their power in the General Assembly is considerable. In this "town meeting of the world," as it was once called, the United States often finds itself outmaneuvered and outvoted because the smaller states have learned to band together and vote in blocs. There is, for example, the 20-member Arab bloc, the 42-member Islamic Conference, and a more loosely structured nonaligned bloc, which often opposes the United States on major votes.

How well has the UN performed? Its accomplishments include the 1968 treaty banning the proliferation of nuclear weapons, the successful negotiation of border disputes between India and Pakistan, the resettlement of refugees, and the work of some specialized agencies in fighting disease and famine. More recently there has been a string of successes. In 1988 the UN set the stage for a ceasefire in the Iran-Iraq war, Soviet withdrawal from Afghanistan, Cuban withdrawal from Angola, independence from South Africa for Namibia, and negotiations between Greece and Turkey for the unification of Cyprus. Supporters also often point to the General Assembly as a place where nations can talk out grievances—"blow off steam"—instead of fighting.

Critics focus on the UN's apparent double standard of political morality. The UN has condemned the white regime in South Africa, in fact expelled it from membership, while remaining silent on atrocities committed by black regimes in Africa. It has condemned right-wing oppression in Chile, but it has said little about Communist oppression in Cuba and Nicaragua. It has frequently criticized the United States and its allies but has never criticized the Soviet Union by name even when the Soviets invaded Afghanistan; it has equated *Zionism* (a code word for Israel) with *racism* and extended official recognition to the Palestine Liberation Organization (PLO) but has shown little sensitivity to Israel's own worries about Arab militance. As for the assumed therapeutic value of "blowing off steam," critics charge that the General

"What is most depressing is that these platitudes are being simultaneously translated into five languages." *Drawing by Mahood;* © 1971 *The New Yorker Magazine, Inc.*

(Continued on page 543)   541

FIGURE **19-4**

The United Nations

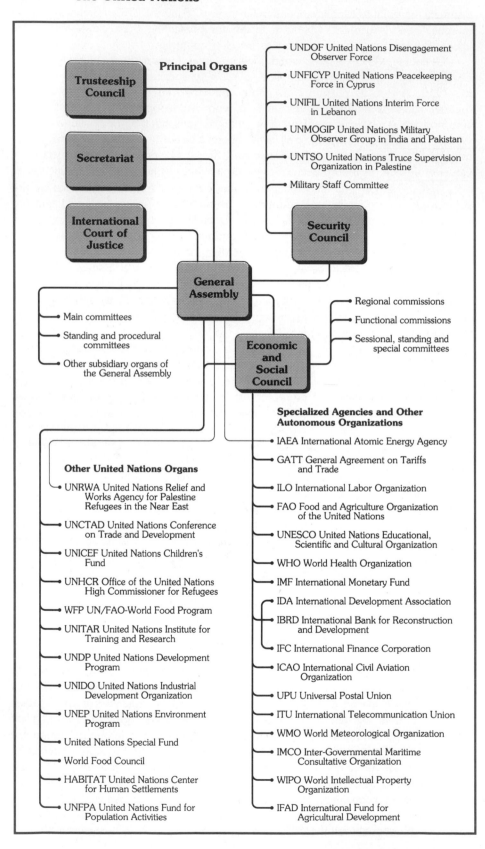

Principal Organs

Trusteeship Council

Secretariat

International Court of Justice

General Assembly

Security Council

Economic and Social Council

- UNDOF United Nations Disengagement Observer Force
- UNFICYP United Nations Peacekeeping Force in Cyprus
- UNIFIL United Nations Interim Force in Lebanon
- UNMOGIP United Nations Military Observer Group in India and Pakistan
- UNTSO United Nations Truce Supervision Organization in Palestine
- Military Staff Committee

- Main committees
- Standing and procedural committees
- Other subsidiary organs of the General Assembly

- Regional commissions
- Functional commissions
- Sessional, standing and special committees

Other United Nations Organs

- UNRWA United Nations Relief and Works Agency for Palestine Refugees in the Near East
- UNCTAD United Nations Conference on Trade and Development
- UNICEF United Nations Children's Fund
- UNHCR Office of the United Nations High Commissioner for Refugees
- WFP UN/FAO-World Food Program
- UNITAR United Nations Institute for Training and Research
- UNDP United Nations Development Program
- UNIDO United Nations Industrial Development Organization
- UNEP United Nations Environment Program
- United Nations Special Fund
- World Food Council
- HABITAT United Nations Center for Human Settlements
- UNFPA United Nations Fund for Population Activities

Specialized Agencies and Other Autonomous Organizations

- IAEA International Atomic Energy Agency
- GATT General Agreement on Tariffs and Trade
- ILO International Labor Organization
- FAO Food and Agriculture Organization of the United Nations
- UNESCO United Nations Educational, Scientific and Cultural Organization
- WHO World Health Organization
- IMF International Monetary Fund
- IDA International Development Association
- IBRD International Bank for Reconstruction and Development
- IFC International Finance Corporation
- ICAO International Civil Aviation Organization
- UPU Universal Postal Union
- ITU International Telecommunication Union
- WMO World Meteorological Organization
- IMCO Inter-Governmental Maritime Consultative Organization
- WIPO World Intellectual Property Organization
- IFAD International Fund for Agricultural Development

Source: Encyclopedia Americana, International Edition (Danbury, CT: Grolier, Inc., 1989), vol. 27, p. 443. Reprinted with permission.

Although the United Nations has grown into a complex array of bureaus and provides a world forum for hearing the voices of member governments, it presently plays no significant role in determining U.S. foreign policy.

TABLE 19-1   543

The Evolution of
American Foreign
Policy

Evaluation of the UN: Passing Grades

	Public Opinion of the United Nations				
	West Germany	Great Britain	France	Japan	United States
How is the UN doing in solving the problems it has had to face?					
Very good job	2%	7%	2%	1%	5%
Good job	46	39	45	11	46
Poor job	21	28	22	43	27
Very poor job	6	9	3	5	13
Don't know	26	17	28	41	10
Does the Third World have too much influence in the UN?					
Yes	13	31	25	12	42
No	45	48	37	17	42
Depends/Don't know	42	21	38	71	16
Would the world be better off without the UN?					
Yes	5	11	11	1	13
No	56	69	45	56	78
Makes no difference	16	7	21	8	-
Don't know	23	13	23	35	9

Based on 950 interviews conducted in West Germany from May 17 through 29; 888 in Great Britain from May 8 through 13; 980 in France from May 15 through 22; 1,446 in Japan from May 9 through 13; and 1,509 in the United States from May 29 through June 2.

Source: New York Times, June 26, 1985, p. A8

Public opinion polls conducted in five industrial democracies reveal mixed feelings toward the United Nations. Although only small minorities in each country think that the UN does a very good job, most do not believe that the world would be better off without the UN.

(Continued from page 541)
Assembly has become a place where hot rhetorical vapors inflame world tensions instead of easing them.[10]

But whatever the perceived flaws of the UN, a poll of respondents in major countries suggests that most people are generally satisfied with its performance (see Table 19.1). Although few are ready to say it does a very good job, most apparently think the world would be worse without it.

The Evolution of American Foreign Policy

We have been discussing the groups and processes that produce American foreign policy. That does not tell us *how* foreign policy is made, any more than listing the ingredients of a cake tells us how the cake is made. The questions really turn upon how the ingredients are combined and for what purpose. What are the aims of American foreign policy? What role should the various agencies play in fulfilling those aims? What can be accomplished by diplomacy? When must we resort to force?

There are no definite answers to any of these questions. All we can do is explore some of the approaches to foreign policy that have been tried over the years. We began this chapter aboard the USS *Missouri* in September 1945. General MacArthur stood at the microphones and made his brief speech. He spoke of his hope for a better world that would somehow emerge "from the blood and carnage." The vanquished signed the articles of surrender. The sun broke through the clouds, and the planes flew over. It was like a movie ending from one of the popular black-and-white films of the period, time for the music to swell and *The End* to appear on the screen. And in a way, that is what it was. It ended a period in American foreign policy that had begun 25 years earlier. Lessons were learned from it: One lesson, so it appeared at the time, was the danger of isolationism. To understand that lesson, we need to go back much further in time.

WASHINGTON AND HAMILTON: NATIONAL SELF-INTEREST

The term isolationism stands for a policy of avoiding "entangling alliances" with other countries, alliances that—so it is argued by isolationists—may drag our nation into wars in which it has no stake. At the other end of the scale from isolationism are internationalism, the willingness to enter into closer relations with other countries, and interventionism, the willingness to use American military force in other countries.

The term *entangling alliances* paraphrases an expression used by President George Washington. In September 1796 he said: "Observe the good faith and justice of all nations. Cultivate peace and harmony toward all. An attachment for one nation or another produces a variety of evils. It is our true policy to steer clear of all foreign entanglements." Washington's remarks were influenced by the thinking of his treasury secretary, Alexander Hamilton (who may in fact have written them). Hamilton's views are best seen in his "Pacificus" articles. In 1793 the Washington administration proclaimed American neutrality in the war between France and Great Britain, setting off a furious debate. In the eyes of some American statesmen, the proclamation violated a treaty we had made with France 15 years earlier. Besides, were not the French our friends, who had helped us in our revolution? Therefore, shouldn't we help them now? No, said Hamilton, writing under the pen name "Pacificus." There is nothing in this war for us. To enter it out of gratitude to France would be folly. Selfless gratitude is fine between individuals, but leaders of nations have others to think of besides themselves. "Existing millions, and for the most part future generations, are concerned in the present measure of a government."[11] *(Continued on page 546)*

GLOBAL PERSPECTIVES:

The Foreign Policy of India

India is a major world power. Its population of 700 million is greater than the populations of Latin America and Africa combined. It ranks as the tenth-largest industrial nation of the world and fourth in the size of its armed forces. The reality of its actual power, and still more its potential power, is a fact with which nations in Southwest Asia and the world must reckon. But India husbands its power carefully and tries to avoid imprudent commitments.

Since achieving independence in 1947, India has claimed to pursue a policy of neutrality in the struggle between the Communist world and the West. At times this policy has been the occasion for controversy with the United States. John Foster Dulles, President Eisenhower's secretary of state, declared neutralism "an immoral and shortsighted conception" and hinted that India had to choose between the United States and the USSR. In reply, Indian statesmen reminded the United States of its own early years, when it, too, avoided "entangling alliances."

A more common U.S. complaint against India is not that it is neutral, but that it is *not* neutral. In 1956 India criticized Great Britain, France, and Israel for invading Egypt but refused to condemn the Soviets for their bloodier—and permanent—invasion of Hungary. This, U.S. critics charge, has been a pattern of Indian foreign policy. It criticized the U.S. presence in Vietnam in the 1970s but defended the Soviet occupation of Afghanistan in the 1980s; it refused to enter into any treaty arrangements with the United States, but in 1971 it signed a treaty of "peace, friendship, and cooperation" with the Soviet Union. It refused to condemn Libyan terrorism but wasted no time in denouncing the U.S. bombing of Libya.

To the American charge that it "tilts" toward the USSR, Indian spokesmen reply that it has been the United States' own "tilting" that has forced their country into greater dependence on the Soviet Union. Since the 1950s the United States has given large amounts of money and arms to Pakistan, India's neighbor and adversary. India and Pakistan have been at war three times in the past 40 years. During one of these fights, in 1971, it was reported in the American press that Secretary of State Henry Kissinger actually used the word "tilt" in advising President Nixon to support Pakistan.

Statesmen in both the United States and India were hopeful that relations between the two countries might improve after the assassination of Prime Minister Indira Gandhi in 1984. Her son, Rajiv, who assumed her position, was young and politically inexperienced (he was a former airline pilot), but these were seen by many as genuine virtues. He seemed free of old ideologies and habits of mind, and he brought into government many like him: practical-minded young people ready to take a fresh approach to foreign policy. By the close of the 1980s, however, most of the enthusiasm for Rajiv Gandhi had cooled. U.S. officials watched warily as scandals clouded the future of his regime. Indian peacekeeping troops in Sri Lanka were accused of murdering civilians, and news stories about bribery and kickbacks in the purchase of military hardware fed popular suspicions of high-level corruption. In the November 1989 elections, Gandhi's Congress party lost its parliamentary majority, and a new prime minister, V. P. Singh, was put in charge of India's foreign policy.

NINETEENTH-CENTURY ISOLATIONISM

Hamilton's view became the guiding principle of American foreign policy for the next century. With a few exceptions, such as the War of 1812, we steered clear of foreign involvements. Nineteenth-century American isolationism was always qualified by self-interest. We stayed out of the affairs of Europe because it was not necessary to get involved. After Napoleon's downfall in 1815, a long peace followed in Europe that England and its navy were strong enough to police. But in Asia the American navy forced China and Japan to open their borders to American trade; we were not very isolationist there. And even the most isolationist-minded politicians always made an exception in the case of Latin America; we were determined that there would be no foreign powers on our doorstep. In 1823 President James Monroe enunciated the so-called Monroe Doctrine by declaring that "the American continents" would no longer "be considered as subjects for future colonization by any European power."

Not until the twentieth century did the United States get seriously involved in the affairs of Europe. In 1914 the delicate, century-long balance of power that England had maintained was suddenly upset as German armies swept into France. World War I began, and three years later the United States was in it. President Woodrow Wilson led the nation in a war to "make the world safe for democracy." Wilson's moralism has often been criticized, but the real flaw in his approach was his assumption that moral ideals could be achieved without the use of power. Wilson went to Europe to put an end to power politics. His wartime allies, particularly Great Britain and France, had other ideas. During the negotiations at Versailles they pushed through peace accords that settled a number of old scores with their enemies and set the stage for financial collapse in Germany. Wilson gave in to their demands for a punitive peace. The remaining pillar in his "partnership of right" crumbled when the U.S. Senate refused to ratify American entry in the new League of Nations, a forerunner of the United Nations. America slipped back into isolationism.

TWENTIETH-CENTURY ISOLATIONISM

American isolationism of the 1920s and 1930s was very different from that of the nineteenth century. People thought that all we had to do was ignore the squabbles of the European nations. This naive policy was simply the mirror image of Wilson's internationalism. In both cases, the assumption was that the United States should not get its hands dirty.

A typical product of this kind of thinking was the Kellogg-Briand Pact of 1929. Two years earlier, Aristide Briand, the French foreign minister, proposed that the major world powers sign an agreement renouncing "war as an instrument of national policy."[12] The State Department, headed by Frank B. Kellogg, was cool to the idea, but under prodding from Columbia University president Murray Butler, the *New York Times*, and other sources, the United States signed the treaty and the Senate ratified it. Sixty-one other nations signed the Kellogg-Briand pact in 1929, including Japan, Italy, and Germany. Two years later the Japanese invaded Manchuria; six years later the Italians invaded Ethiopia; seven years later the Germans invaded the Rhineland; nine years later the Germans invaded Austria; ten years later the Germans invaded Czechoslovakia and Poland; twelve years later the Japanese bombed Pearl Harbor.

WORLD WAR II AND ITS AFTERMATH

Six years of blood and carnage ended after the United States dropped atomic bombs on the Japanese cities of Hiroshima and Nagasaki. Then came the dramatic surrender aboard the *Missouri*. "These proceedings are closed," MacArthur said.

Alexander Hamilton (1755-1804), shown here in a famous painting by John Trumbull, believed that the United States should stay away from foreign wars and binding ties to other countries unless it could be shown that they advance U.S. interests in the world.

From left to right, British prime minister Winston Churchill, U.S. president Franklin D. Roosevelt, and Soviet dictator Josef Stalin pose for a photograph during the Yalta conference of 1945. The conference concerned the postwar relationships that were to prevail in Eastern Europe, and critics of the conference charged that Roosevelt, who was mortally ill at the time, made concessions to Stalin that led to Soviet domination of the region.

New proceedings had already begun. In 1944, the Dumbarton Oaks Conference, with the United States, the USSR, and Great Britain attending, proposed establishment of the United Nations. In a solemn ceremony in San Francisco on June 16, 1945, the charter of the United Nations was signed. It says, "We, the people of the United Nations, determined to save succeeding generations from the scourge of war, which twice in our lifetime has brought untold sorrow to mankind . . . do hereby establish an international organization to be known as the United Nations."

The guiding principles behind the United Nations had been worked out a year earlier. The Big Four—the United States, Great Britain, China, and the USSR—agreed to set up a new international organization whose membership would be open to all "peace-loving" states and whose purpose would be to keep the peace, develop friendly relations between states, and work out cooperative solutions to the problems facing all peoples.

Still unresolved were a number of questions, including whether or not vetoes should be allowed on the Security Council and what the criteria should be for membership. These questions were settled in February 1945 during the Yalta Agreements, named after the place in the Russian Crimea where President Roosevelt, Soviet dictator Joseph Stalin, and British prime minister Winston Churchill met near the end of the war in Europe. The purpose of the meeting was to work out arrangements for a postwar world. One of the big questions was the future of the Eastern European countries that had been occupied by Germany. In a "Declaration of Liberated Europe" the parties solemnly agreed that each of the countries in Eastern Europe would be able to set up its own government through democratic elections.

THE COLD WAR

The founding of the United Nations in 1945 marked the high point in Western-Soviet cooperation. By 1946 relations had begun to deteriorate. The Soviets took over Poland, Rumania, Yugoslavia, Albania, Bulgaria, Hungary, and half of Germany, giving each a Soviet-controlled Communist government. When the Western powers objected, Stalin accused the West of stirring up trouble. British prime minister Winston Churchill coined a new term in a historic speech delivered at Westminster College in Fulton, Missouri, in 1946. "From Stettin in the Baltic to Trieste in the Adriatic," he told his startled audience, "an iron curtain has descended across the Continent." Since then, the term iron curtain has been used to denote the barrier dividing Soviet-bloc countries from the rest of the world.

Thus began the cold war, a war of nerves, feints, threats, propaganda, subversion, spying, trickery, and accusations; a war of rival alliances and in some cases actual shooting. But the shooting has been between proxy states, like North and South Korea, or between established regimes and guerrilla fighters.

The big chill came in 1948. In that year the Soviets engineered a coup d'etat in the one remaining democracy of Eastern Europe, Czechoslovakia, which then became another Soviet satellite. (In the same year, however, they lost Yugoslavia, which stayed Communist but took an independent line.) Was the iron curtain moving west? Fears were reinforced by another Soviet move in 1948: the military blockade of Berlin. Berlin, the former capital of Germany, was located deep within Soviet-controlled East Germany. The city had been divided into sectors, with the Western powers guaranteed access to their zones. In 1948 the Soviets blockaded all land routes to Berlin. In response the Western powers started the Berlin airlift to bring in necessary supplies. The Soviets finally lifted their blockade after 15 months.

"Operation Vittles," the American pilots called it. The Berlin Airlift seemed an impossible venture. To function normally, the city needed 8,000 tons of food a day, which meant a takeoff or landing every minute and 48 seconds. But young American, British, and French pilots rose to the challenge, risking their lives to keep West Berlin alive. They succeeded. After 15 months the Soviets gave up the blockade.

THE DOCTRINE OF CONTAINMENT

The Berlin airlift was a particular defense against a particular Soviet initiative, but an overall policy for dealing with the Soviet Union was needed. It was formulated in a 1947 article in the magazine *Foreign Affairs* by a man identified only as "X." Anonymity was necessary because the author was then serving as counselor of the U.S. embassy in Moscow. He was George F. Kennan.

Kennan was pessimistic about Soviet intentions. The Soviets' overall ideology had "taught them that the outside world was hostile and that it was their duty eventually to overthrow the political forces beyond their borders." Kennan also worried about what he considered the gullibility of many Americans. Every time the Soviets have wanted something from us, he cited, they start sounding conciliatory, at which point "there will always be Americans who will leap forward with gleeful announcements that 'the Russians have changed.' . . ." But, he cautioned, let no one be deceived: "There can never be on Moscow's side any sincere assumption of a community of aims between the Soviet Union and powers which are regarded as capitalist."[13] Kennan advocated "a policy of firm containment, designed to confront the Russians with unalterable counterforce at every point where they show signs of encroaching upon the interests of a peaceful and stable world."[14]

By the early 1960s the policy of containment enjoyed broad political support in the United States. There were no hawks and doves in those days. All the major opinion leaders were hawks. "We shall pay any price, bear any burden," President Kennedy had said in his inaugural address, "to assure the survival and the success of liberty." He was backed by major American opinion leaders when he began sending American military "advisers" to South Vietnam. Indeed, two years later when a more cautious Kennedy remarked that the Vietnam War was "their war," meaning a war for the South Vietnamese to fight, not the Americans, the *New York Times* took him to task. It was not just "their war," the *Times* said, but also "our war—a war from which we cannot retreat and which we dare not lose."[15]

VIETNAM: A TURNING POINT

But as casualties mounted with no apparent end in sight and as horror stories of American bombings and atrocities began drifting back, American opinion leaders had second thoughts about Vietnam. They wanted to get out by any means. By the 1970s that idea had become the political consensus. In 1971 Congress declared it "the policy of the United States to terminate at the earliest practicable date all military operations of the United States in Indochina."[16] In 1972 Nixon's national security adviser, Henry Kissinger, announced "peace is at hand." He had worked out an agreement with the Communist-backed North Vietnamese that provided for a ceasefire and the withdrawal of all American forces from Vietnam. The South Vietnamese premier, fearing a sellout, objected furiously. In January 1973 he reluctantly signed the agreement, along with representatives of the United States and the Communist forces. "We have finally achieved peace with honor," Nixon declared.

But the accords proved meaningless; the fighting went on, this time without American troop support. The Communists gained ground. American bombing of Communist positions was no longer possible because in June 1973 Congress cut off funds for that purpose. Then Congress began cutting military aid to South Vietnam itself. Nixon protested, but by now he was too caught up in the Watergate scandal to have much influence. Congress continued to cut funds for the South Vietnamese

The Vietnam War ended on an apocalyptic note in the spring of 1975. As North Vietnamese troops rode into Saigon, the capital city, the last of the Americans were fleeing in helicopters and planes. Terrified South Vietnamese, many of them former employees of the Americans, also rushed to board the aircraft. Some, as in this picture, had to be punched back to prevent the evacuation planes from being overloaded.

army, and delays blocked most of the rest from reaching it.[17] By the spring of 1975 South Vietnamese troops were running away from the Communist forces, throwing down their weapons and stripping off their uniforms.

The final scenes were apocalyptic. The remaining Americans and some of their South Vietnamese friends—the lucky ones—were evacuated from Saigon by fleets of helicopters. Thousands of other hysterical Vietnamese rushed toward the takeoff spots. Some clung to the skids of the ascending helicopters, held on until their strength gave out, and then fell to their deaths. At 11 A.M. on the morning of April 30, 1975, a squadron of Soviet-built tanks rumbled down Thong Nhut Boulevard in Saigon and crashed through the gates of the presidential palace. The war that "we dare not lose," as the *New York Times* had called it, was over now, and we had lost it.

FROM CONTAINMENT TO DÉTENTE

The United States had lost more than a war. It had lost its nerve. Many American opinion leaders began to wonder about whether or not their country had any legitimate role to play in world politics. American foreign aid commitments, which as a percentage of our gross national product had been dwindling for a generation, fell off further between 1972 and 1976 (see Figure 19.5). Conservatives in Congress tended to favor cutoffs in economic aid, while congressional liberals preferred to cut military aid. (As already noted, the 1975 Clark Amendment prohibited military aid to either side in the Angolan civil war.) Neither liberals nor conservatives showed much enthusiasm anymore for President Kennedy's ringing promise to "pay any price, bear any burden" to protect freedom in the world. Containment had proven to be a very heavy burden.

Ironically, one of the most outspoken critics of containment was George Kennan, who had promoted it in the famous "Mr. X" article of 1947 but thought that it was outdated in an age of nuclear missiles.[18] Many American opinion leaders now agreed with his revised view, and they helped set the stage for détente, a French word that means "relaxation of tension." The roots of détente go back to the Nixon administration. Nixon and Kissinger first promoted this new attitude in a series of bilateral meetings with Soviet leaders. For them, "relaxation of tension" had a subtle meaning. We would still compete with the Soviets; but we would try to avoid nuclear one-upmanship with them, and we would give them incentives (for example, the prospect of better trade relations) to moderate their aggressiveness. Détente was a strategy, not an end in itself.

But in selling détente to the American people and the world, Nixon oversold it. He told the UN General Assembly that it would displace "the old patterns of power politics," and he told the American people that it meant a "new era [of] durable peace."[19] War-weary Americans could scarcely be blamed for thinking that détente now meant the end of the cold war. After 30 years of glacier-like relations with the Soviets, it appeared that spring had finally come. Elected in 1976, President Jimmy Carter gave voice to this sentiment in a speech at Notre Dame University in 1977 when he announced that Americans were "now free" of what had been their "inordinate fear of communism."[20] For many Americans, détente meant a new era of goodwill and mutual understanding.

There was, perhaps, something prophetic about that interpretation of détente, for in little more than a decade the Soviet Union under General Secretary Mikhail Gorbachev did seem to be moving in that direction. But this was the 1970s, and the Soviet Union was controlled by hard-liners like General Secretary Leonid Brezhnev. During the Brezhnev era the USSR looked at détente as evidence of American weakness. Soviet writers stressed that the Marxist–Leninist concept of peace "is not of an abstract-pacifist, but rather of a class character." It "distinguishes between just wars, wars of liberation, and unjust wars."[21] The spirit of Soviet détente was not conciliatory

FIGURE **19-5**

Declining Commitment to Foreign Aid

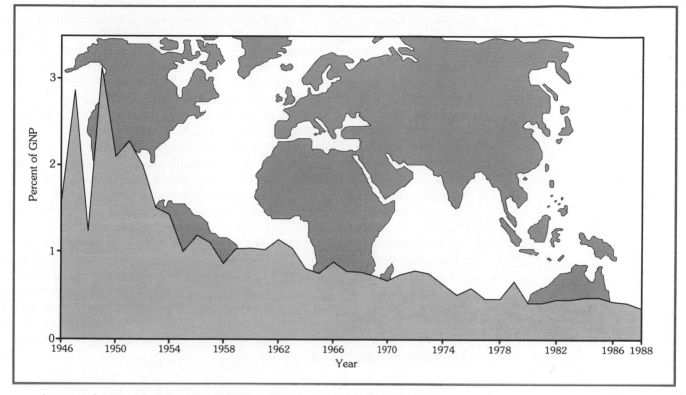

American foreign aid as a percent of GNP reached high levels right after World War II and at the end of the 1940s, when such programs as the Marshall Plan and aid to Greece and Turkey were given high priority by American policymakers. Our aid commitments fell off sharply through the 1950s, then steadily dwindled in the 1960s and 1970s. Our level of commitment hardly changed in the 1980s, despite President Reagan's desire for a greater American role in world affairs.

but triumphant. An official Soviet theoretician asserted that the struggle between "imperialism"—by which he meant the western, non-Communist world—and communism will continue "right up to the complete and final victory of communism on a world scale."[22]

During his last two years in office, President Carter became increasingly alarmed by Soviet foreign and military policies. What finally really angered Carter was the Soviet invasion of Afghanistan in December 1979. In a television interview just hours after hearing the news, Carter burst out: "This action of the Soviets has made a more dramatic change in my own opinion of what the Soviets' ultimate goals are than anything they've done in the previous time I've been in office."[23]

By then Americans had formed a view of Carter as a weak and irresolute president. They yearned for strong leadership and a return of old-fashioned patriotism. Ronald Reagan appealed to those yearnings.

THE REAGAN DOCTRINE: GLOBAL CONTAINMENT?

Ironically, some of the themes trumpeted by Ronald Reagan during the presidential campaign had been sounded 20 years earlier by one of the Democratic party's most revered presidents. John F. Kennedy's inaugural address was full of crusading zeal. "In the long history of the world," Kennedy said, "only a few generations have been granted the role of defending freedom in its hour of maximum danger." It emphasized the need for military strength ("we dare not tempt them with weakness") and announced a willingness to use American power anywhere necessary in the world ("we shall pay any price, bear any burden").[24] In similar fashion, President Reagan came into office promising "peace through strength," proclaiming that the United States now faced a major "test of moral will and faith," and warning against the danger of weakness. Ronald Reagan shared Kennedy's belief that the United States was in its "hour of maximum danger."[25] He regarded the USSR as a huge empire ruled by an elite that holds all power and all privilege, which now extended into Africa, Asia, and South America.[26] His plan was not only to stop the advance of the Soviet empire, but to nibble at its edges, reversing wherever possible its most recent gains by aiding anti-Communist insurgencies and promoting American-style democracies in the Third World. *New Republic* editor Charles Krauthammer called it the Reagan Doctrine, which he characterized as "American support for anti-Communist revolution as the centerpiece of a revised policy of containment." An opponent called it "global containment."[27]

The Reagan Doctrine met strenuous opposition from the Democratic leadership in Congress, the mass media, and the academic community. Prominent writers and policy analysts accused Reagan of "bear-baiting" the Soviets and deliberately seeking worse relations with them, of being unable to "handle the complexities involved in the pursuit of détente," of pursuing policies that were "at best obsolete and at worst primitive," of having a "preference for hectoring the Soviet Union instead of negotiating with it," and of viewing the world "through the distorting prism of anti-Communist ideology."[28]

THE EVOLUTION OF REAGAN'S FOREIGN POLICY

For his part, Reagan sought to revive the interventionist spirit of Roosevelt, Truman, Eisenhower, and Kennedy. The very language of his speeches sometimes sounded like a mix of Kennedy and Eisenhower. "Let us now begin," he told the British Parliament in 1982, "a major effort to secure the best—a crusade for freedom that will engage the faith and fortitude of the next generation."[29]

Whatever the merits of Reagan's policies, they were consistent in certain respects. Based upon the cold war premise of an expanding Soviet empire, they sought to counter the advance by the vigorous application of American power. But during his second term, Reagan put some nuances into his global anti-Communism in two areas: human rights and East-West negotiations.

Human Rights.   During Reagan's first term in office, his human rights policy was influenced by the views of Jeane Kirkpatrick, his UN ambassador from 1981 to 1985. As Kirkpatrick saw it, Carter's attempt at even-handedness in human rights policy was based upon a failure to appreciate the difference between authoritarianism and totalitarianism. Most right-wing dictatorships are authoritarian, Kirkpatrick asserted. Authoritarianism limits freedom but does not destroy it; furthermore, authoritarian regimes are susceptible to eventual liberalization. But totalitarian regimes—the Soviets and their client states—are more thorough in destroying liberty and more impervious to internal change. The conclusion: Do not be too ready to denounce human rights violations by right-wing authoritarian regimes; you may destabilize them, cause revolutions, and end up with Communist regimes.[30] Kirkpatrick's philosophy was dominant during the early Reagan years, but beginning in 1986 there were signs that the administration was modifying this doctrine. It was now prepared to criticize openly and even take action against friendly authoritarian regimes. In a message to Congress in March of that year, President Reagan said: "The American people believe in human rights and oppose tyranny in whatever form, whether of the left or the right."

Negotiating with the Soviets. During his first four years in office, Reagan seemed reluctant to negotiate with the Soviets. Convinced that the 1970s had undermined the United States' military strength, he preferred to wait until the United States was in a better negotiating position. Moreover, he sometimes wondered aloud whether or not the Soviets were capable of good faith negotiations. "I know of no leader of the Soviet Union," he said, "that has not more than once repeated . . . their determination that their goal must be the promotion of world communism and a one-world socialist or communist state."[31]

By 1985 Reagan had begun to shift emphasis. Whether it was because he now felt confident that the United States could negotiate from strength or because he felt pressure from the peace movement, Reagan stressed the need for serious negotiations with the Soviets. The Soviets seemed to be of like mind. In January 1985 they resumed arms-control talks with the United States, which they had unilaterally suspended a year earlier. The Soviets had their own reason for confidence. After the death—within three years—of two aged leaders, a new and vigorous one came to power: Mikhail Gorbachev. The time was ripe for a face-to-face meeting of U.S. and Soviet heads of state.

In October 1985 Reagan and Gorbachev met for 15 hours in Geneva, Switzerland. No substantive breakthroughs came out of the talks, although the two agreed to initiate new cultural exchanges, set up new consulates, and improve communications.

Two presidents, one American and one Soviet, listen to their respective national anthems at a welcoming ceremony in front of the White House in 1987. By then, even skeptics seemed to agree that the ice of the cold war was melting with astonishing speed.

At a second summit held in Reykjavik, Iceland, in October 1986, the two leaders considered proposals for sweeping cuts in nuclear arsenals. The talks broke down after Gorbachev demanded a 10-year moratorium on U.S. field tests of components of the Star Wars antiballistic missile, which he claimed violated the 1972 SALT I treaty with the Soviets (see chapter 20, pages 583-84). Reagan refused to discuss such a moratorium, and the Reykjavik summit ended in stalemate.

The next summit meeting was more productive. Held in Washington in December 1987 it got the two leaders together to sign the INF Treaty, a treaty scrapping all intermediate-range nuclear force (INF) missiles (see chapter 20, page 584). The two also agreed to meet again the following year, which set the stage for Reagan and Gorbachev's fourth summit meeting, held in Moscow from May 29 to June 2, 1988. The meeting was short on specifics but long on symbolism. Standing beneath a bust of Lenin, Reagan lectured students of Moscow University on the blessings of freedom. Later, as he and Gorbachev strolled around Red Square together, a reporter asked Reagan if he still considered the Soviet Union an "evil empire." Reagan replied, "I was talking about another time, another era."

Pictured here are President George Bush and President Mikhail Gorbachev as they met aboard the Soviet cruise ship *Maxim Gorky* off Malta for the first meeting of the 1989 summit.

THE BUSH POLICY: BEYOND CONTAINMENT

In May 1989 President George Bush spelled out what he said was to be the chief foreign policy theme of his administration. In a speech at Boston University, Bush stated his intention to move "beyond containment" of the Soviet Union. He would move "to integrate the Soviets into the community of nations, to help them share the rewards of international cooperation." In a later press conference he called the concept "a bold one." Bush officials said that it was to be accomplished by an incremental, "step-by-step" process, and at each stage the Soviets would be expected

(Continued on page 556)

Points to Remember

1. During the nineteenth century, the United States followed a policy of isolationism based upon the idea that there was no need to become involved in the affairs of Europe. After intervening in World War I, the United States tried unsuccessfully to return to isolationism.

2. Shortly before the Japanese surrender in 1945, the United States and the other Great Powers (Great Britain, China, and the USSR) drew up the charter for the United Nations. At Yalta Great Britain, the USSR, and the United States also agreed that the future of eastern Europe would be decided by free elections.

3. The cold war began in 1946 when the Soviet Communist party line returned to the theme of class warfare and the West accused the

Soviets of violating the Yalta Agreements by setting up puppet governments in eastern Europe.

4. The doctrine of containment governed American policymaking in the late 1940s and the 1950s. As spelled out by George Kennan, containment meant the application of counterforce at any place on the globe where the Soviets used force. After the Vietnam disaster, American policymakers welcomed détente, which they defined as a relaxation of tensions with the Soviets. The Soviets understood détente very differently. In their view it marked the triumph of Soviet arms. The "imperialists," the Soviets said, were now on the defensive. The Soviets would aid "national liberation struggles," which in turn would move the world toward a final Communist victory.

5. The Reagan Doctrine—a revised version of containment that included American support for anti-Communist revolutions—did not enjoy the bipartisan support that containment enjoyed in the 1950s and early 1960s. It was unpopular in academia, the media, and in liberal Democratic circles.

6. Reagan later seemed to modify his foreign policy. Administration spokespersons sometimes criticized right-wing violations of human rights. In U.S.-Soviet relations, Reagan participated in four summit meetings and signed a major arms-control treaty with the Soviets.

7. Early in his administration, President George Bush expressed his desire to move beyond containment.

The Cold War: Is the End in Sight?

YES John Lewis Gaddis

Based upon "How the Cold War Might End," *The Atlantic* (November 1987).

Historian John Lewis Gaddis believes that it is no longer utopian imagining to foresee an end to the cold war. "The geopolitical ice is shifting beneath our feet these days in unexpected ways." For the first time since the end of World War II, the two superpowers have begun the elimination of an entire category of nuclear weapons, intermediate-range nuclear missiles. Moscow has allowed on-site inspections, which it never did before. All this happened during the presidency of a man who once called the Soviet Union the "focus of evil" in the world. Gaddis believes we may live to see "the emergence of a new international system capable of moving beyond the condition of perpetual confrontation that has overshadowed our lives for the past four decades."

Throughout the cold war we have pretended that the relations between the superpowers have been "zero-sum," meaning that one side's gain is the other side's loss. But, says Gaddis, it does not have to be that way. It is possible for *both* sides to develop a mutual interest in each other's survival. For example, if Soviet control of eastern Europe disintegrates, that may bring back all the national and ethnic fights that plagued the region between the two world wars. Gaddis admits that we also need to think about human rights in Soviet-occupied areas, but peace must precede justice "as the compromise with power that has to take place before one can begin to address—as one ultimately still has to—questions of right and wrong."

NO Richard M. Nixon

Based upon Richard Nixon, "Dealing with Gorbachev," *New York Times Magazine*, March 13, 1988, p. 21t.

Former president Nixon warns Americans against the dangers of peace at any price. We should respect the Soviet Union "as a strong and worthy adversary" but never delude ourselves that it will become our friend. Whether or not Gorbachev survives as leader, he, like his predecessors and successors, "seeks to expand the influence and power of the Soviet Union." Indeed, Nixon argues, "he has preserved the long-term objective of pushing for global dominance." Nixon favors negotiations with the Soviets, for we and they have a common interest in avoiding nuclear war. This makes peace possible "despite the political differences that make continued conflict inevitable."

Negotiate, then, but do it shrewdly, writes Nixon. We should give Gorbachev what he wants—a relaxation of tension and expanded economic ties—only in return for what *we* want: "the elimination of Soviet superiority in first-strike land-based nuclear missiles; a reduction in Soviet repression at home as called for by the Helsinki Accords; and a halt to Soviet aggression abroad." Nixon thinks that Americans are naive about the Soviets because they tend to believe that conflict is just a result of misunderstanding. "But what moves the world for good or ill is power. . . . This is an immutable aspect of national character."

Postscript

Both Nixon and Gaddis steer clear of extreme positions. Gaddis is not saying that the cold war will end in a burst of love, only that it has become a nuisance to both sides. For his part, Nixon is advocating not war but hardnosed bargaining with the Soviets. Yet there are marked differences: Gaddis thinks that a new era is dawning, while Nixon insists that power politics never changes.

In *The Nuclear Delusions: Soviet-American Relations in the Atomic Age* (New York: Pantheon, 1982), the "new" George Kennan explains why he modified his views on containment. A useful study of détente in the era before Gorbachev is Raymond L. Garthoff, *Détente and Confrontation: American-Soviet Relations from Nixon to Reagan* (Washington, DC: Brookings, 1985).

(Continued from page 554)

to reciprocate U.S. initiatives. The aim, said a high-level Bush aide, was to make the Soviet Union "a full partner in the international system and to enjoy the benefits of a system that has supported political freedom and economic prosperity around the world."[32] The Soviets seemed cool to the initiative or at least to the phrasing of it, which they considered somewhat condescending. "To put it mildly," said *Pravda*, the Soviet party newspaper, "we are bewildered at the attempts of the president to pose conditions under which the U.S. will work to include the USSR in the world community."[33] Still, U.S.-Soviet relations seemed to proceed constructively. A series of informal meetings were held between Secretary of State James A. Baker and his Soviet counterpart, Foreign Minister Eduard Shevardnadze at Baker's vacation home in Montana. These meetings helped smooth the way for new understandings and a Bush-Gorbachev summit meeting at Malta in December 1989.

The Future of American Foreign Policy

As the 1990s get underway the United States faces a dangerous and uncertain world. From the Middle East, with its jumble of warring factions, terrorists, and fanatics, to Central America, which seems to be sliding into chaos and economic catastrophe, the United States has all it can do to cope with day-to-day crises, let alone formulate any guiding policy. The one bright spot is our new relationship with the Soviet Union, which appears to be more cordial than at any time in recent history. Some have referred to it as Détente II, but it is really better than détente because it is more clearly reciprocal, at least in words. Largely missing from Soviet statements is the rhetoric of the Brezhnev era. Now the official line is mutual cooperation between Communist and capitalist countries in securing "the universal values of humankind," such as ensuring peace and cleaning up the environment.[34] In July 1988 Soviet foreign minister Eduard Shevardnadze came close to repudiating the whole concept of inevitable struggle between communism and capitalism. He told a conference of foreign policy specialists that "the struggle between two opposing systems is no longer a determining tendency of the present era."[35] It is not clear how long this mood will last—or, indeed, how long Gorbachev will last. But for the time being, it appears that the cold war is melting with astonishing speed. Is it, then, over? Have we reached the end of the cold war? In this chapter's Taking Sides section, former president Richard M. Nixon and historian John L. Gaddis present very different views on the issue.

The debate on whether or not the cold war is ending is one facet of a larger debate on what sort of assumptions or expectations should underlie American foreign policy. In his book *Public Opinion*, the famous journalist and political commentator Walter Lippmann introduced the word *stereotype* into the language of social science. "Stereotypes," wrote Lippmann, are the "pictures in our heads," the simple models or "fictions" we use to represent the complex world in which we live. Lippmann is often misunderstood as condemning stereotypes. Actually, he insisted that we cannot do without them. "For the real environment is altogether too big, too complex, and too fleeting for direct acquaintance. We are not equipped to deal with so much subtlety, so much variety, so many permutations and combinations." We use these models just as we use road maps; like maps, they are schematic representations of reality. Stereotypes are bad only when they become complete fictions, when they do not fit the facts, when they mislead us rather than guide us.[36]

What kinds of fictions, models, "pictures in the head" have guided American policymakers? During the height of the cold war in the 1950s, policymakers pictured a bipolar world: communism versus the "free" world. This model fit the facts very imperfectly. Many of the nations counted in the "free" world, such as South Korea and South Vietnam, were dictatorships. Another problem with the model was that it failed to take nonaligned states into account. By the early 1960s the bipolar picture was blurred further by the split between the USSR and China, the two Communist superpowers. To account for these discrepancies, the model was modified somewhat; policymakers now talked about a "loose" bipolar world. But by the end of the 1960s even that did not seem to fit very well. It appeared that there were now many different varieties of communism, plus a large number of Third World countries heading in every direction, from Islamic fundamentalism to atheistic Marxism.

American policy analysts now talked about multipolarity and even pluralism. The heyday of this model was the late 1970s when for the first time since the start of the cold war, an American president warned of the "inordinate fear of Communism." But the pluralist model was seriously damaged after the Soviet invasion of Afghanistan, and in the early 1980s bipolarity made something of a comeback, at least within the Reagan administration. Reagan's speech referring to the "evil empire" seemed to be based upon that model of the world.

These various models were not created out of pure imagination; behind them were some major historical events of the twentieth century, events that policymakers soon began to regard as object lessons. Two analogies in particular have been extremely powerful—and competing. Their proponents engage in vigorous debate about which one of them best fits the facts. We can sum up the two with the words *Munich* and *Vietnam*.

THE MUNICH ANALOGY: AVOID APPEASEMENT

In the 1930s Adolf Hitler started conquering Europe by stages. He took over one piece of territory after another. Each time he could have been stopped if nations had had the courage and the will to do it. If the French had met him with military force when he marched into the Rhineland in 1936, he would have retreated. If the French and British had threatened war when he took over Austria in 1938, he might have been deterred. Instead, they let him go on. He demanded a portion of Czechoslovakia (the part inhabited by many ethnic Germans) and at the 1938 Munich Conference, named after the German city where it was held, Great Britain and France gave it to him. Hitler had assured them that this was his last demand; he was appeased. British prime minister Neville Chamberlain came back from Munich assuring his nation that he had brought "peace with honor." "I believe," he said, "it is peace for our time." A year later, Hitler invaded Poland. This was too much even for the British and the French, and World War II began.

The Munich analogy long outlived Adolf Hitler. Was Stalin's takeover of eastern Europe much different from that of Hitler? American policymakers did not think so. The whole doctrine of containment was built on an implied Munich model. If the Soviets try any more pushing, we will push them back. In the 1960s it was applied to Vietnam. North Vietnam, a Soviet surrogate, was trying to take over South Vietnam by force. It was relying largely on guerrillas rather than regular forces, but what difference did that make? It was aggression, and aggressors must never be appeased.

THE VIETNAM ANALOGY: AVOID QUAGMIRES

Vietnam looked like an easy fight. A confident Secretary of Defense Robert MacNamara said that this war could not go on very long. He had maps and he had a pointer, and he pointed at little circles on the maps that were marked "pacified

Robert MacNamara, secretary of defense in the Kennedy and Johnson administrations during the 1960s, uses a pointer in 1964 to indicate the progress made in defeating the enemy in Vietnam. MacNamara frequently resorted to pointers and maps to reassure Americans that the war was being won, but by the end of the 1960s many Americans had come to regard Vietnam as a quagmire, a swamp, that swallowed up all our efforts.

villages." Those were the villages that were free of Communist control. The encouraging news was that in the last six months the number of pacified villages had increased by such-and-such percent. At this rate—well, he did not want to get too optimistic, but it was clear that there was already light at the end of the tunnel. Later, there would be some bad news. The North Vietnamese Communists had stepped up their infiltration into the South. There were some sneak attacks on American installations, and there were some ambushes of our allies, the Army of South Vietnam. It would be necessary to increase the American presence by another 25,000 men. That would not only reverse the Communist gains, but bring us much closer to victory.

The American presence escalated from 16,000 American military advisers at the time of Kennedy's death to over 500,000 American troops five years later. With every new round of escalation, the story was the same: We are doing fine, we are winning, but we just need a little more to finish the job. The war dragged on, we became more and more committed, and we never seemed to be able to win. Some 55,000 men were killed; many more returned blind or crippled. We never seemed to reach the light at the end of the tunnel. In the end, when we withdrew unilaterally, the bitter joke among the remaining soldiers was: "Last one out, turn off the light at the end of the tunnel."

Vietnam has become a cautionary tale. Journalist David Halberstam called it a "quagmire," a swamp. We kept marching into it, deeper and deeper, and it swallowed us up. In 1965 Halberstam's viewpoint was heresy; within five years it had become orthodox, at least among the intellectuals and writers who shape American opinion. The shift from the Munich to the quagmire analogy was almost like a religious conversion experience: The old religion was suddenly overturned in favor of the new one. It framed foreign policy debates throughout the 1970s. All sides had to keep in mind the danger of getting bogged down in "another Vietnam."

During the 1980s the Vietnam analogy was challenged. Proponents of the Reagan Doctrine insisted that the real danger was another Munich. Whether the immediate issue was aid to the antigovernment rebels in Angola, confronting Libyan dictator Muammar al-Qadaffi, supporting the Contras in Nicaragua, or sending military advisers to El Salvador, the ultimate issue was whether the United States was going to stand up to aggression or encourage it by appeasement.

Reagan was often accused of being simplistic, but that misses the point. Of course the Munich analogy is simplistic; so is the Vietnam analogy. All models are simple. They are supposed to be in order to make sense of the booming, buzzing confusion of facts that surround us. The question is not whether or not a model is simple but whether or not it takes the facts into consideration without requiring too many modifications.

VIETNAM OR MUNICH: WHICH FITS?

Which analogy better fits the facts today? We look around the world, and we see some very ugly facts. Terrorists are kidnapping and murdering people and blowing planes out of the sky. Revolutions begun in the name of freedom have put anti-American dictators into power. In many supposedly "uncommitted" countries, the United States' name is a curse, and sometimes even our allies are reluctant to support us when we need them. *How do we account for all these facts?*

The Vietnam analogy does not directly answer this question, but it has a bearing on it. Those who invoke it suggest that its real lesson has to do with the limitations of American military power. The United States has gotten itself in trouble because it has tried to use military force to make over the world in its own image. The lesson of Vietnam is that we must learn to respect other ways of life. When we see anti-Americanism in the world, we must realize its root causes are usually poverty, social injustice, and memories of American imperialism. We cannot deal with the causes by sending in the marines; we need to show goodwill through diplomacy, economic aid, and cooperation with regional and international bodies.

The Munich analogy explains the facts much differently. It suggests that the United States lost much of its prestige and power during the 1970s because it made itself contemptible. The problems go back to the early 1970s when leading Americans started abusing their country in public. Soon every thug in the world joined in, and after our Vietnam defeat they realized they could go beyond words; they could injure the United States without cost to themselves. President Carter wanted to make the United States loved in the world and apparently never entertained the thought that "it is much safer to be feared than loved."[37] Now we reap the harvest of spinelessness and appeasement.

Which of these two explanations better explains the facts? The answer can be worked out only by patient analysis of particular issues. Take, for example, terrorism and Central America. Here is the way the two are usually argued.

Terrorism. Over the past decade thousands of innocent people have died in terrorist attacks. Most of these attacks have been of incredibly mindless brutality, like the 1985 murder of the crippled Leon Klinghoffer aboard the hijacked cruise ship *Achille Lauro* or the 1988 bombing of the Pan Am airliner over Scotland. Often these attacks are sponsored by terrorist organizations or by states such as Syria, Iran, and Libya. Most observers agree on these facts. The question is, which response is appropriate? If we operate from the Vietnam paradigm, we will be wary of military responses. We would argue as follows: "Military retaliation just sets off more terrorism. Then what? A still *larger* show of force? That is the way we got drawn into Vietnam. In the meantime, we make only heroes and martyrs of the terrorists." "You do not understand," says the advocate of the Munich paradigm. "The terrorists do not get to be heroes because they get hurt—They get to be heroes because they *do not* get hurt. They show that they can get away with it. If you up the ante, if you make terrorists pay a big price for their acts, they will begin to think twice. Anyway, we have got to take action. We cannot just do nothing. You have no real policy for dealing with terrorism."

"But we do have a policy," replies the critic. "Consult with our allies. Work through the United Nations. Isolate the offending nation politically. Press for economic sanctions. Let us seek international and diplomatic paths." "Those things do not work," says the advocate of the Munich model. "Our allies are too scared to do much of anything. It is the 1930s all over again. We must teach them not to be bullied, and the way to do that is not to be bullied ourselves." The rejoinder: "That is exactly the kind of talk that led us into Vietnam."

The validity of each argument turns in part on how well each takes account of the facts. When did the terrorism begin? To what extent was it provoked by American military acts? How willing are the United States' allies to put pressure on terrorist groups and terrorist states? How effective has nonmilitary action been? What evidence is there that American military responses have deterred terrorism?

Central America. The Sandinista's promise of democracy and civil liberties for Nicaragua has never been fully realized. Opposition groups have been intimidated; antigovernment demonstrations have sometimes been permitted but sometimes broken up with rifle butts. For years the only independent newspaper, *La Prensa*, was heavily censored. The censorship was lifted in 1988, but the editors still complain of harassment and interference by the government. Advisers, economic aid, and war matériel pour into the country from the Soviet Union, East Germany, North Korea, Vietnam, and Cuba. At the end of the 1980s, opposition parties were mobilizing in an attempt to oust the Sandinistas in the national elections scheduled for 1990 but feared that the Sandinistas would either cancel the elections, rig them, or intimidate opponents through the use of *turbas*, Sandinista mobs.

In neighboring El Salvador, closely allied to the United States, a decade-long civil war has claimed more than 70,000 lives. The United States has sunk more than $4 billion into El Salvador without much result. In March 1989 the right-wing ARENA party, which has been linked to death squads, defeated the more moderate Christian Democrats in a presidential election. In November 1989 six Jesuit priests, their housekeeper, and her daughter were brutally murdered by a death squad. "For all our aid, for all the genuine commitment to democracy," said Senator Mark Hatfield (R-Oregon), "things in El Salvador are getting worse."[38] In Panama, General Manuel Noriega, already under indictment in American courts for drug-trading, ignored the results of an election that defeated his hand-picked candidate; Noriega remained in power by military might. A nearly-successful coup by disgruntled elements of the military in October 1989 failed; he was finally ousted by American troops in December 1989.

What should the United States do? For some, American attempts to "do" too much in Central America are what got us into trouble in the first place. They put the argument this way: "American meddling—helping the antigovernment Contras in Nicaragua, sending military advisers to El Salvador, trying to oust other governments we do not like—only gets us deeper into quicksand. The people of Central America have long memories of Yankee intervention. More meddling by us will probably make things worse."

Other observers, with the Munich analogy in mind, look at the situation much differently. "Look at what has happened. First Cuba became Communist, then Nicaragua, and now El Salvador is in big trouble. It is not just a matter of communism. American weakness encourages all kinds of Central American dictators to think they can get away with subverting the region."

Both analyses have serious limitations. There are problems in Central America—hunger, economic chaos, exploitation—that are not caused by Communists or drug kingpins. There are also armed demagogues and drug-running tyrants in the region with ties to Cuba and Nicaragua. The situation is extremely complex, involving considerations of economic justice, political liberty, and American security. While neither the Vietnam nor the Munich paradigm quite fits the facts, both may provide partial visions of the whole.

Reflections

Everything about the scene aboard the USS *Missouri* in 1945—the dignity of the proceedings, the sudden sunlight, the flyover of the American planes—suggested the position in which the United States found itself in 1945, a position of unrivaled power and prestige.

How different it all was 30 years later! In April 1975 American helicopters were evacuating the last of the Americans from Saigon. Vietnamese friends and employees were frantically trying to go with them. Some lucky ones did manage to squeeze into the helicopters. Others had to be kicked and punched in the face so that the helicopters could take off. This scene, too, has taken on symbolic significance. It sums up our humiliation in the wake of the Vietnam disaster.

What caused the humiliation? Was it that we had attempted too much, tried to be the world's policeman? Or was it caused by a failure of nerve and determination? Everyone agrees that we must have "no more Vietnams." The disagreement comes over what we should learn from the Vietnam experience.

We began as an isolationist country; our splendid isolation continued until World War I. After those few years of war, the United States tried to retreat again into isolationism. But it was too late. Events in Europe and the Pacific forced us into a second international war. Then came the cold war: the spying, the intrigues, the confrontations, the polemics—then the Korean War (bringing more confusion to an already uneasy United States). A decade later Vietnam began, and by the time it ended in 1975, the United States had entered a period of soul-searching. Maybe we had been too obsessed with communism. Maybe it was time for a thaw, time for détente.

The cold war returned with the Soviet invasion of Afghanistan. Soviet troops have gone home now, and the cold war also seems to be in retreat. Perhaps it will disappear for good. Or is it another false spring? Nobody really knows. All we can do is search for some kind of analogy to try to make sense of things and to warn us what to avoid in the future.

It may be that neither Munich nor Vietnam really explains today's predicament. The present state of the world may be unique, and no analogy from the past will do. If so, a new model should be crafted to put the facts into context. We should be ready to change our models when the facts no longer fit.

But the present danger seems to be not fixation on a model, but the lack of *any* model. We seem to be overwhelmed by events. We turn on the television news and see crowds and demonstrations, pickets and banners; we see bloody figures sprawled on the ground; angry faces and raised fists; we hear shouts of rage, indignant speeches, weeping. Depending on what we see and hear, we may be angry or frightened, pugnacious or conciliatory, ready for a fight or sorry we ever got into one. We are pulled this way and that.

The worst policy the United States could ever pursue would be one that simply responded to day-to-day events and moods. Americans need a long-range approach, one with a clear vision of where we want to go and how we are to get there. If we are to move beyond containment, what is there in that "beyond" that we seek? We may need new sketches, new models, new road maps. We have entered a challenging and exciting era of American foreign policy.

Notes

1. Quoted in Spenser Davis, "Unconditional Surrender," Associated Press report, Sept. 2, 1945; reprinted in *Journal News* (Rockland County, NY), Sept. 1, 1985, p. AA3.

2. Theodore H. White, "The Danger from Japan," *New York Times Magazine*, July 28, 1985, p. 21.

3. Constantine C. Menges, *Inside the National Security Council* (New York: Simon & Schuster, 1988); Frank McNeill, *War and Peace in Central America* (New York: Charles Scribner's Sons, 1988).

4. President Ford's remarks at Media and Society Seminar, "War Powers: The President and Congress," *The Constitution: That Delicate Balance*, PBS broadcast, Sept. 25, 1984, transcript p. 4.

5. Senator William Maclay of Pennsylvania, quoted in Edward S. Corwin, *The President: Office and Powers, 1787-1957*, 4th rev. ed. (New York: New York University Press, 1957), p. 209.

6. David Halberstam, *The Best and the Brightest* (New York: Random House, 1972), chaps. 1-5.

7. Stephen Engelberg, "Bush Aide and Senator Clash over Failed Coup in Panama," *New York Times*, Oct. 9, 1989, pp. A1, A7.

8. David Shribman, "Poll Shows Support for Presence of U.S. Troops in Lebanon and Grenada," *New York Times*, Apr. 6, 1983, II, p. 8.

9. Flora Lewis, "The U.N. at 40," *New York Times*, Oct. 25, 1985, p. A27.

10. Elaine Sciolino, "Worldwide, UN Tackles Problems Large and Small," *New York Times*, Sept. 22, 1985, p. 16.

11. Alexander Hamilton, "Pacificus," quoted in Robert A. Goldwin, ed., *Readings in American Foreign Policy*, 2d ed., revised by Harry M. Clor (New York: Oxford University Press, 1971), p. 633.

12. In fact, Briand's message was written by a Columbia University professor named James Shotwell. A disappointed proponent of American entry into the League of Nations, Shotwell was convinced that civilization and modern war were incompatible. See Julius W. Pratt, *A History of United States Foreign Policy*, 2d ed. (Englewood Cliffs, NJ: Prentice Hall, Inc., 1965), pp. 316-17.

13. "X" (George F. Kennan), "The Sources of Soviet Conduct," *Foreign Affairs* (July 1947), pp. 569, 572.

14. Pratt, p. 581.

15. Editorial, *New York Times*, Sept. 6, 1963, p. 28.

16. Arthur Schlesinger, Jr., *The Imperial Presidency* (Boston: Houghton Mifflin Company, 1973), p. 194.

17. Stanley Karnow, *Vietnam: A History* (New York: The Viking Press, 1983), p. 661. See further, Gareth Porter, *A Peace Denied: The United States, Vietnam, and the Paris Agreement* (Bloomington and London: Indiana University Press, 1975), pp. 272-73.

18. See Kennan's reflections in *The Nuclear Delusion: Soviet-American Relations in the Atomic Age* (New York: Pantheon Books, 1982).

19. Raymond L. Garthoff, *Détente and Confrontation: American-Soviet Relations from Nixon to Reagan* (Washington: The Brookings Institution, 1985), p. 29.

20. Quoted in Garthoff, p. 568.

21. Andrei Melvil, "The Leninist Concept of Foreign Policy in Our Time," *Reprints From the Soviet Press*, Sept. 30, 1981, p. 34.

22. F. Ryzhenko, quoted in Garthoff, p. 42.

23. Quoted in Garthoff, p. 950.

24. See Kennedy's 1961 inaugural address, in Theodore C. Sorensen, *Kennedy* (New York: Harper & Row, 1965), pp. 245-48.

25. Sorensen, p. 248.

26. "Reagan Address on East-West Relations," *1982 Congressional Quarterly Almanac* (Washington: Congressional Quarterly, Inc., 1983), p. 22E.

27. Charles Krauthammer, "The Poverty of Realism," *The New Republic*, Feb. 17, 1986, p. 15. The opponent, Christopher Lane, was quoted by Krauthammer on p. 16.

28. Strobe Talbott, *The Russians and Reagan* (New York: Vintage Books, 1984), pp. 70-71; Richard W. Stevenson, *The Rise and Fall of Détente* (Urbana and Chicago: University of Illinois Press, 1985), p. 208; Alexander Dallin and Gail Lapidus, "Reagan and the Russians: The United States Policy toward the Soviet Union and Eastern Europe," in Kenneth A. Oye et al., *Eagle Defiant: United States Foreign Policy in the 1980s* (Boston: Little, Brown and Company, 1983), p. 223; Richard Barnet, "Dancing in the Dark," in John Stack, ed., *Policy Choices: Critical Issues in American Foreign Policy* (Guilford, CT: Dushkin Publishing Group, 1983), p. 27; Charles W. Kegley and Eugene R. Wittkopf, "The Reagan Administration's World View," in Stack, p. 37.

29. Ronald Reagan, "Address to Members of Parliament, June 8, 1982," reprinted in Talbott, p. 118.

30. Jeane Kirkpatrick, "Dictatorships and Double Standards," *Commentary* (November 1979), pp. 34-45. See chapter 1 for a discussion of use and misuse of the terms *authoritarianism* and *totalitarianism*.

31. Quoted in Dallin and Lapidus, p. 205.

32. Don Oberdorfer, "Bush Finds Theme of Foreign Policy: 'Beyond Containment,'" *Washington Post*, May 28, 1989, p. A30.

33. Oberdorfer, p. A30.

34. "Present-Day Concept of Socialism," speech by Politburo member Vadim, in *Reprints From the Soviet Press*, Nov. 15, 1988, p. 15.

35. Bill Keller, "Gorbachev Deputy Criticizes Policy," *New York Times*, Aug. 7. 1988, p. 11.

36. Walter Lippmann, *Public Opinion* (New York: The Free Press, 1965), pp. 10-11.

37. Niccolò Machiavelli, *The Prince* (Arlington Heights, IL: AHM Publishing Corporation, 1947, originally published in 1513), p. 48.

38. Robert Pear, "Cristiani's Victory Complicates U.S. Decisions," Mar. 21, 1989, p. A8.

20

National Defense

At the approach of danger there are always two voices that speak with equal power in the human soul: one very reasonably tells a man to consider the nature of the danger and the means of escaping it; the other, still more reasonably, says that it is too depressing and painful to think of the danger, since it is not in man's power to foresee everything and avert the general course of events, and it is therefore better to disregard what is painful till it comes, and to think about what is pleasant.

Leo Tolstoy, *War and Peace*

Not long after the atomic bomb was dropped on **Hiroshima**
Hiroshima in 1945, author John Hersey visited the Japanese city and interviewed some of the survivors. Among them was Mrs. Hatsuyo Nakamura, a poor widow with three children who worked as a seamstress. When the bomb exploded, Hersey notes, Mrs. Nakamura was looking out the window of her house. Her first instinct was to run back toward her children.

She had taken a single step . . . when something picked her up and she seemed to fly into the next room over the raised sleeping platform, pursued by parts of her house. Timbers fell around her as she landed, and a shower of tiles pommelled her; everything became dark, for she was buried. The debris did not cover her deeply. She rose up and freed herself. She heard a child cry, "Mother, help me!" and saw her youngest—Myeko, the five-year-old—buried up to her breast and unable to move. As Mrs. Nakamura started frantically to claw her way toward the baby, she could see or hear nothing of her other children.[1]   *(See footnote on bottom of page 564)*

Mrs. Nakamura managed to free Myeko and the two other children, who were bruised and dirty but alive. They staggered into the street and saw their block in ruins, saw flames break out from the rubble that had been people's houses. A neighbor from across the street, Mrs. Nakamoto, came over, told Mrs. Nakamura that her baby had been badly cut, and asked if she had any bandages.

Mrs. Nakamura did not, but she crawled into the remains of her house again and pulled out some white cloth that she had been using in her work as a seamstress, ripped it into shreds, and gave it to Mrs. Nakamoto. While fetching the cloth, she noticed her sewing machine; she went back for it and dragged it out. Obviously, she could not carry it with her, so she unthinkingly plunged the symbol of her livelihood into the receptacle which for weeks had been her symbol of safety—the cement tank of water in front of her house, of the type every household had been ordered to construct against a possible fire raid.[2]

Little remained of Hiroshima. Two-thirds of the city's buildings had been destroyed and another 6,000 damaged beyond repair. Mrs. Nakamura and her family later suffered prolonged nausea from radiation, but compared to others, they had been very lucky. More than 100,000 people were dead, about 25 percent from direct burns, the rest from radiation and other causes. Many died immediately, but others took weeks and months to die. Hersey describes the condition of some of the victims:

The eyebrows of some were burned off and skin hung from their faces and hands. Others, because of pain, held their arms up as if carrying something in both hands. Some were vomiting as they walked. Many were naked or in shreds of clothing. On some undressed bodies, the burns had made patterns—of undershirt straps and suspenders and, on the skin of some women (since white repelled the heat from the bomb and dark clothes absorbed it and conducted it to the skin), the shapes of the flowers they had had on their kimonos.[3]

In his account of the Nakamura family, Hersey writes that they set off for the park, along with other survivors, hoping to find some refuge there. On the way, they were met by a German Jesuit Priest, Father Wilhelm Kleinsorge, who invited them to a Jesuit novitiate. There they were given food and a place to sleep. A week later, though still suffering radiation sickness, they managed to move to the nearby town of Kabe, where they stayed with Mrs. Nakamura's sister-in-law. The next day, Hersey writes, Mrs. Nakamura returned to Hiroshima to find out what had happened to her mother, brother, and sister.

She discovered that her family were all dead. She went back to Kabe so amazed and depressed by what she had seen and learned in the city that she could not speak that evening.[4]

The survivors of Hiroshima tried to figure out what had happened to their city. Some, says Hersey, thought that flash-powder had been dropped on it and ignited. Others, smelling the electric odor that followed the nuclear blast, thought it might be gas. Ordinary people could not understand what kind of bomb could have tossed freight cars through the

*This account is drawn from the following source: John Hersey, *Hiroshima* (New York: Alfred A. Knopf, Inc., 1966). Copyright, 1946, 1985, by John Hersey. Excerpts from book reprinted with permission.

The aftermath of Hiroshima. Two dazed survivors walk through the devastation caused by the first atomic bomb dropped on a city. It destroyed two-thirds of the city's buildings and killed more than 100,000 people, yet by today's standards it was a mere tactical weapon. A one-megaton missile warhead today would produce a blast 80 times as great as the Hiroshima explosion.

air like matchboxes and exposed X-ray films that had been locked in hospital vaults. But Japanese physicists, entering the city with electroscopes and electrometers, knew what had happened.

After a time the scientists determined that the radiation levels in Hiroshima had diminished enough to permit a return to the city. By that time, Hersey relates, Mrs. Nakamura had remembered that "on the morning of the explosion she had literally sunk her means of livelihood,"[5] her sewing machine, into the water tank in front of her house. She sent her brother-in-law to look for it. "It was still submerged in the water tank, and when he brought it home, she saw, to her dismay, that it was all rusted and useless."[6]

*　　*　　*　　*　　*

The nuclear bomb dropped on Hiroshima was small compared to the bombs in today's arsenals. It was measured in kilotons, or thousands of tons of TNT. Today we usually discuss strategic weapons—the long-range kind carried on bombers and intercontinental missiles—in terms of *megatons*, or millions of tons of TNT. One-megaton warheads seem to be the most common. A one-megaton warhead would produce a blast 80 times larger than that of the Hiroshima bomb. But even that is tiny compared to some of the weapons now targeted on the United States. *New Yorker* writer Jonathan Schell says that the Soviets now have a sizable arsenal of 20-megaton bombs meant to be carried on intercontinental bombers.[7] One such bomb would produce a blast 1,600 times larger than the Hiroshima explosion.

For at least a generation now, political leaders with quite different ideological outlooks have agreed that a nuclear war would be hellish. In

1963 Soviet premier Nikita Khrushchev said that after a full-scale nuclear exchange, "The survivors would envy the dead." In 1985 President Ronald Reagan said, "A nuclear war cannot be won and must never be fought." But despite these official expressions of horror, the nuclear arsenals of the world are well stocked. Why?

Nations value peace, but they value other goals as well, including their territorial integrity, and for this they are usually ready to go to war. Peace is one goal, but it is not the only one. Moreover, it is a *goal*, not a *policy*. A policy is a means of reaching a goal. What sort of policies will best preserve peace? The answer may depend on circumstances. One lesson of the 1930s is that appeasement does not always bring peace; sometimes it leads to war. On the other hand, the constant preparation for war, especially for nuclear war, may turn into a kind of self-fulfilling scenario, which leads to the very war it is meant to deter. In the case of nuclear war, this could spell the end of life on this planet.

The issues, then, are full of moral dilemmas and mortal dangers. How has our nation sought to defend itself against its chief adversaries? What basic strategies has it relied upon? How have they worked out in practice? Do they need revision? This chapter will examine these questions as it studies the organization and operation of American defense in the modern age.

Defense Organization and Defense Spending

The modern defense establishment in the United States owes its origins to Pearl Harbor. World War II began in 1939, but for two years the United States did not enter the war. President Franklin Roosevelt tried to aid Great Britain but he had an uphill fight against the isolationists in Congress. "Why die for Danzig?" they kept asking. (Danzig was in the section of Poland invaded by Germany in 1939; it was that invasion that touched off the war.) The isolationists enjoyed much public support.

PEARL HARBOR: THE DANGER OF UNPREPAREDNESS

Pearl Harbor changed everything. On December 7, 1941, the Japanese, who were allied with Germany, launched a surprise attack on the American naval base at Pearl Harbor, in the Hawaiian Islands. Their aircraft destroyed five of the eight battleships stationed there, plus a number of warships and 140 airplanes. Over 2,000 servicemen lost their lives during this day "which will live in infamy," as President Roosevelt called it. Suddenly—literally overnight—isolationist sentiment evaporated. The day after Pearl Harbor Congress declared war on Japan with only one dissenting vote; three days later Congress unanimously voted for war against Germany and Italy. The lesson was seared into the American consciousness: Never again must we be caught unprepared.

Determined to crush its enemies, the United States created a giant war machine of 11 million men and women in uniform, a huge civilian bureaucracy, and a whole network of defense industries that produced the tanks, airplanes, bombs, and the other apparatus of modern war. It was during World War II that the Pentagon was built, a massive, five-sided building in Arlington, Virginia, just across the Potomac River from Washington. With 17½ miles of corridors and 83 acres of rooms, the Pentagon became the largest office building in the world. The finished structure was three times the size of the Empire State Building and twice the size of the

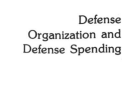

An American battleship destroyed by the Japanese surprise attack on Pearl Harbor, Hawaii, in December 1941. It was, said President Roosevelt, a day "which will live in infamy," and American leaders vowed that this country would never again be caught unprepared for war.

Merchandise Mart in Chicago. The Capitol building could fit into one wing of the Pentagon.[8]

At the end of the war, the defense machinery was stripped down and partially demobilized. But the cold war that began in the late 1940s clinched the national commitment to constant defense. By 1948 the Soviet takeover of Eastern Europe and the increasingly shrill tone of Soviet rhetoric had convinced the Western powers that military unity was necessary to ensure the security of Western Europe. Great Britain and other northern European countries began planning a defense pact, and soon the United States joined as an active participant. In 1949 these discussions culminated in the signing of the North Atlantic Treaty by ten European nations as well as the United States and Canada. The treaty stipulated that each nation would come to the assistance of any other that might be attacked; it set up a permanent body, the North Atlantic Treaty Organization (NATO), to coordinate its political and military agreements. In response, the Soviet Union drew its own eastern European satellites— Poland, Hungary, Rumania, Bulgaria, Czechoslovakia, and East Germany—closer together. In 1955 it created the Warsaw Pact, a network of military alliances, with these satellite states and kept Soviet troops stationed in these countries to supervise military operations.

It was during the cold war that our National Security Act was passed. As we saw in the previous chapter, this act established the National Security Council (NSC) and the CIA, locating them within the central circles of power in the executive branch. It also unified the Army, Navy, Marines, and Air Force under joint control. Finally, it was a 1949 amendment to the National Security Act that changed the name of the old War Department to the Department of Defense (DOD).

The DOD is headed by a secretary of defense, who by law must be a civilian.

A view of the Pentagon, the giant building that houses the U.S. Department of
Defense in Arlington, Virginia, just across the Potomac River from Washington.
With its 17½ miles of corridors and 83 acres of rooms, it is the world's largest
office building. The Capitol Building could fit into one wing.

According to the National Security Act of 1947, the secretary is to be "the principal
assistant to the president in all matters relating to the national security." His or her
duties are to "establish general policies and programs . . . exercise general direction,
authority and control" over the department and "take appropriate steps to eliminate
unnecessary duplication or overlapping in the fields of procurement, supply, transportation, storage, health, and research."

Since 1949 the secretary's task of eliminating wasteful duplication has been
taken with various degrees of seriousness. During the Kennedy and Johnson
administrations in the 1960s, Secretary of Defense Robert McNamara tried hard to
eliminate inefficiencies by bringing in a staff of young management experts to
supervise procedures used by the military services. Called "McNamara's whiz kids,"
the young efficiency experts were not much appreciated by the generals and the
admirals, but they underscored McNamara's determination to bring businesslike
procedures into the Defense Department. More recently Congress has championed
the cause of efficiency and rational decision making. After the Grace Commission
reported Pentagon expenditures that included $91 screws and $600 toilet seats,
President Reagan appointed a special blue-ribbon commission to recommend reforms in the Pentagon. Commonly known as the Packard Commission (it was headed
by industrialist David Packard), the commission recommended tighter coordination of
the individual services. In May 1986 the Senate unanimously passed a bill that
incorporated some of the commission's key recommendations. It was a sweeping
measure that would greatly enlarge the advisory role of the chairman of the Joint
Chiefs of Staff and reduce the autonomy of the individual services.[9] Such changes
may or may not bring about real reform. Both Congressional supporters and critics of
the military welcome reform, but some critics worry that new legislation may end up
creating more red tape and bureaucracy.[10] *(Continued on page 570)*

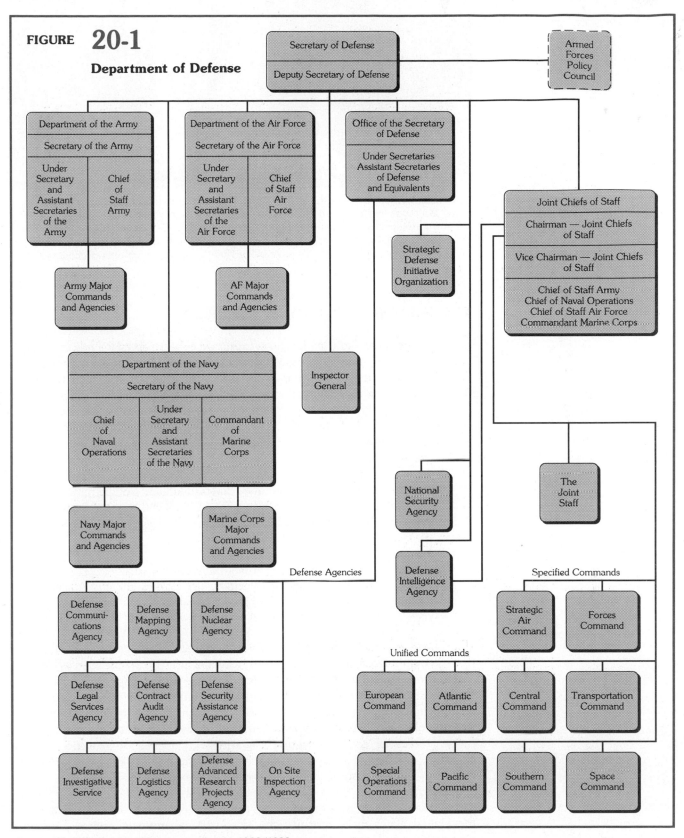

FIGURE 20-1

Department of Defense

Source: The United States Government Manual, 1988/1989.

The Department of Defense, headed by Defense Secretary Dick Cheney, includes the major armed services (Army, Navy, Marines, and Air Force), 12 defense agencies, the Joint Chiefs of Staff, and 10 specified commands for various areas (from specific regions in the country and the world to outer space).

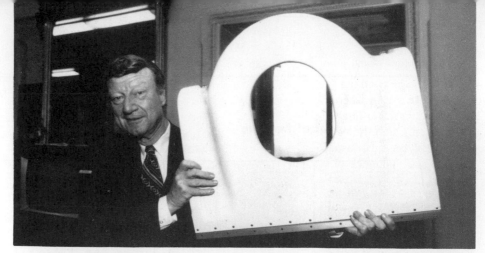

Senator William V. Roth, Jr. (R-Delaware) displays a toilet seat purchased by the Pentagon for $600. In the 1980s the Pentagon came under fire for paying inflated prices for some of the goods it ordered. The Grace Commission, which investigated government waste, concluded that the Pentagon and many other government agencies could save billions by tightening purchasing procedures.

THE MILITARY-INDUSTRIAL COMPLEX

Some writers and political leaders have expressed concern about the role of the DOD and defense contractors in shaping policies. The large number of employees directly dependent upon the DOD for their livelihood (such as the men and women in uniform) is itself a source of influence. But an even larger number of people are employed indirectly by working in industries that make the guns, airplanes, tanks, bombs, and other apparatus of war. These industries employ millions of people who, like their employers, have a vested interest in defense spending. As we saw in the case of the B-1 bomber (chapter 15), defense industries can exert great pressure on legislators who make the decisions on military procurement and policy.

One of those who worried about the combined influence of the military and the defense industries was himself a general and a president of the United States, Dwight D. Eisenhower. When Eisenhower left the presidency in 1961, he warned against the power of what he called the "military-industrial complex":

> In the councils of Government we must guard against the acquisition of unwarranted influence, whether sought or unsought, by the military-industrial complex. The potential for the disastrous rise of misplaced power exists and will persist. We must never let the weight of this combination endanger our liberties or democratic processes.

The warning was timely in 1961. The United States was spending more than half its budget on defense, and the Democrats, who had just won the presidential election, were claiming that the United States suffered from a "missile gap" as compared with the Soviets—a claim that turned out to be false. Since Eisenhower's time the term *military-industrial complex* has been used so often that its original meaning has become obscured. Eisenhower was warning that we ought to be on guard *lest* the military-industrial complex acquire unwarranted influence. Within a few years, however, defense critics were implying that the complex had already acquired such influence—indeed, had become an all-powerful conspiracy.[11]

Used in this way the meaning is less clear. If it means that some corporations make money from defense spending, it is true—but not very startling. Corporations in the United States make money from all sorts of government activity. Computer companies make money processing welfare claims; construction companies make money building state and federal highways; medical laboratories make money from government health services; and so on. The real question is not whether or not corporations make money from the state, but whether or not they make money by foisting products on the American taxpayer that are useless, superfluous, or counter-productive. Writings about the military-industrial complex are usually based upon the premise that this is indeed the case, that military contractors are in effect swindling the taxpayers. Often, however, there is little attempt to prove the premise; it is simply assumed.[12] Another aspect of the argument has to do not with the products, but with the political influence of the military-industrial complex. The contention, stated or implied, is that defense industries are driving the nation toward ever-increasing militarization. If so, it is reasonable to expect that the defense budget has been climbing relentlessly over the years, gobbling ever-larger portions of the federal budget. This expectation is not borne out by the facts.

THE UPS AND DOWNS OF DEFENSE SPENDING

Since the 1960s we have had an up-and-down pattern in our defense budgets, but overall it has been down. Defense spending as a percentage of total federal outlays has shrunk from 52.2 percent in 1960 to slightly more than 25 percent today. Spending on social programs has gone in the other direction: from 28.1 percent of total federal outlays in 1960 to more than 50 percent today. The biggest spender among federal government departments today is no longer the Department of Defense; it is Health and Human Services (HHS). In 1986, when the Defense Department spent $286 billion, HHS spent $334 billion.[13]

In actual dollars, defense spending has gone from about $48 billion in 1960 to its present level of roughly $300 billion. But if we control for inflation by measuring the increase in constant 1982 dollars, the growth looks more modest: from $192.1 billion in 1960 to $243.5 billion in 1988. Even more revealing is the pattern of growth and decline in defense spending since 1960. Most of the initial growth occurred during the Vietnam War buildup in the late 1960s. During the 1970s American defense spending shrank dramatically. Measured in 1982 dollars, the United States was spending

TABLE **20-1**

The Ups and Downs of Defense Spending

	Amount spent in current dollars[a]	Amount spent in constant 1982 dollars[a]	Percent of GNP
Kennedy/Johnson (yearly average, 1961-1968)	$ 59.0	$207.8	8.9%
Nixon/Ford (yearly average, 1969-1976)	81.8	189.3	6.8
Carter (yearly average, 1977-1980)	113.0	158.1	4.9
Reagan (yearly average, 1981-1988)	234.2[b]	216.9[b]	6.1

[a]Billions of dollars
[b]Includes 1988 estimates

Source: New York Times, November 27, 1988, IV, p. 1.

A spending decline in the 1970s followed a spending increase to fuel the Vietnam War in the late 1960s. The most recent increase, during the Reagan administration, will likely be followed by a spending decrease in the 1990s.

FIGURE **20-2**

**Defense Spending, World Events, Domestic Politics:
U.S. Military Expenditures, 1967-1987***

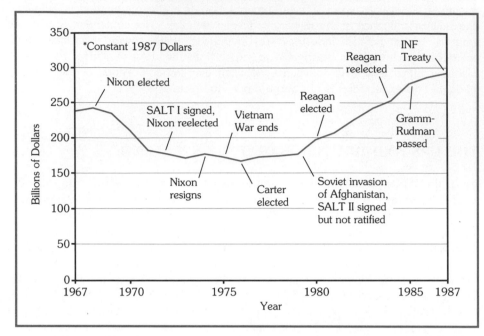

Source: U.S. Arms Control and Disarmament Agency, *World Military Expenditures and Arms Transfers, 1988.*

> U.S. defense spending declined during the 1970s as the United States retreated from Vietnam and sought détente with the Soviets. Defense spending began to increase in 1979, but the Soviet invasion of Afghanistan in December of that year and the election of Ronald Reagan in 1980 marked the beginning of a more rapid increase in defense spending. It seems likely that in the 1990s U.S. defense spending will decline again.

almost $17 billion *less* on defense in 1973 than it was in 1960.[14] The gap got even wider as the decade went on, so that by 1978 the nation was spending 14 percent less on defense in constant dollars than it was in 1960.

In more recent years the rate of defense spending has gone up sharply, but it is starting to go down again. The increases began even before Jimmy Carter left office, but they shot up during the first four years of the Reagan administration. By 1982 spending was slightly higher than it was in 1960, and by 1985 it topped the 1960 level by 23 percent. But in 1986 and 1987 defense growth stalled. In 1985 President Reagan reluctantly went along with a zero-growth military budget for 1986.

Then came the 1985 Gramm-Rudman-Hollings Resolution (see chapter 18). It requires Congress to reduce federal deficits by stages until the budget is fully balanced in 1991. The effect of Gramm-Rudman was to force tough decisions on lawmakers: raise taxes, cut spending, or do both. Since the president vowed to veto any tax increase, only spending cuts remained. But where to cut? Reagan suggested cuts in domestic spending, risky during an election year. Polls show that most Americans would rather cut defense.[15] In 1986 Congress decided to do just that. Even the Republican Senate reduced the president's military spending proposal of $320 billion by $19 billion; the House version cut the president's request by $35 billion. The much-vaunted military-industrial complex was profoundly demoralized. Military contractors around the country began girding for austerity, bitter competition, and increasing demands for efficiency and cost cutting. A headline in the business section of the *New*

FIGURE **20-3** 573

Defense
Organization and
Defense Spending

U.S.-Soviet Defense Spending, 1967-1987: A Comparison*

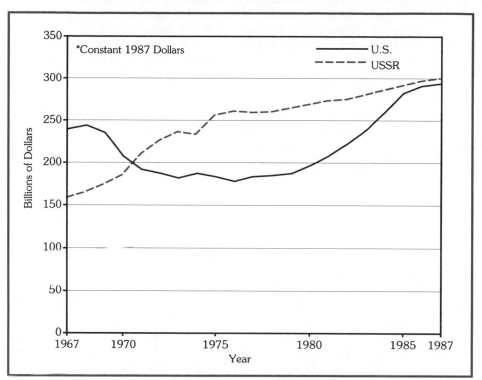

Source: U.S. Arms Control and Disarmament Agency, *World Military Expenditures and Arms Transfers, 1988.* Data prepared by Doru Tagana; Graduate Center, City University of New York.

> At the very time American military expenditures were falling, during the early part of the 1970s, Soviet military expenditures were rapidly rising. During the last years of the Carter administration and for most of the Reagan years, the level of American military expenditures started catching up with those of the Soviets.

York Times summed it up: "Stern Times for Arms Makers."[16] Under Bush the economic situation of the arms makers got even grimmer, as tight budget constraints and the new, warmer relationship with the Soviets combined to produce major defense cuts. "We're in a business that has fallen out of favor," said John O'Brien, chairman of the Grumman Corporation, a military aircraft manufacturer in Long Island, New York.[17] The military budget now stood at $300 billion, which in constant dollars was about the same as it was in 1953. As a percentage of the gross national product (GNP), however, it was much lower than in 1953, when it stood at 14.5 percent; by 1989 it was down to 5.8 percent of the GNP and even further shrinkage is expected in the 1990s.[18]

SOVIET MILITARY POWER

How much *should* we spend on defense? During the cold war, any reasonable response had to take account of what the Soviets were spending. Figure 20.3 compares American and Soviet defense spending over the years. As the United States reduced its level of defense spending during the 1970s, the Soviets increased theirs.

There are technical difficulties in estimating Soviet cash expenditures.[19] Still, it is safe to assume that it is quite a large burden. Starting in the 1970s and continuing until today, the Soviets have been engaged in a major program of weapons modernization. Despite President Reagan's efforts to reverse what he called "the decade of neglect," the Soviets have increased their lead over the United States in almost every category of arms. Some examples: In 1983 we had 16 percent more helicopter gunships than we had in 1980, but the Soviets had 64 percent more than they had in 1980. The size of our Navy's surface fleet increased by 1 percent during that period; the Soviets increased theirs by 5 percent. Their antisubmarine aircraft increased by 14 percent, while ours actually decreased by 6 percent.[20] In nuclear weapons the Soviet advances are also impressive. In 1976, when U.S. observers first began to worry about the Soviet buildup, the Soviets had a force of roughly 2,500 nuclear warheads on their land-based missiles. Then they began adding about 500 warheads a year, and they now have more than 6,000. The United States still leads the Soviets in the overall number of warheads (almost 13,000), but that is because of our lead in sea- and bomber-based warheads. The Soviets lead in the more dangerous land-based strategic warheads.[21]

Still, there is reason for caution in assessing Soviet military strength. Counting troops and weapons is one thing; assessing their reliability is another. To what extent can the Soviets still rely upon troops from countries like Poland or Hungary? How accurate are Soviet missiles? How well do Soviet tanks work? In *The Myth of Soviet Military Supremacy*, reporter Tom Gervasi argues that despite the Soviet buildup in the 1970s, American military superiority was never seriously challenged.[22]

Is it possible that military buildups on both sides are contributing to national weakness instead of national strength? That is a point suggested by historian Paul Kennedy in his book *The Rise and Fall of the Great Powers*. Kennedy's argument has many critics, and this chapter's Taking Sides section on page 576 pits Kennedy against one leading critic, political economist W. W. Rostow.

American Defense

American nuclear defense is based upon the theory of <u>deterrence</u>, the threat of nuclear retaliation against any country that launches a nuclear attack on the United States. To make good this threat the United States relies on three kinds of nuclear delivery systems: land-based intercontinental ballistic missiles (ICBMs), missile-

TABLE **20-2**

575

American Defense
Theories

Who Has More: Vital U.S.-Soviet Statistics

A comparison of key national security and economic statistics

	United States	Soviet Union
Population	245 million	280 million
Active duty military personnel	2.1 million	5.1 million
Budget deficit as a percent of GNP	3.4%	4%
Gross national product, per capita	$18,556	$8,360
Defense outlays as a percent of GNP	5.7%	15-17%
Oil reserves in billions of barrels	32	50-80
Attack submarines	76	200
Main battle tanks	14,016	53,300
Strategic offensive nuclear warheads (estimated total)	13,000	11,000

Source: *Wall Street Journal Reports*, January 20, 1981, p. 27R.

The Soviet Union is far ahead of the United States in its numbers of tanks and submarines. Our country has a greater number of nuclear warheads, but that is because of our lead in the less dangerous sea- and bomber-based warheads. The Soviets spend a much larger percentage of their gross national product (GNP) on defense than we do; whether or not this commitment to military spending will continue in the new, warmer climate of U.S.-Soviet relations remains to be seen.

carrying submarines, and long-range bombers. Together these are called our strategic defense triad.

Each component ("leg") of the defense triad has its own advantages and disadvantages. Bombers are the time-tested vehicles. They are accurate and dependable, but they are also slow and vulnerable to anti-aircraft fire. ICBMs are faster and harder to shoot down but still remain largely untested in actual war, and they can be destroyed before they get off the ground. Submarines, since they are constantly moving under water, are much less vulnerable than land-based missiles, but the accuracy of their missiles is poor: They can wipe out entire cities but not smaller military targets such as missile sites. Whatever the individual weaknesses of these three legs of our triad, their combined strength is considered sufficient to form the base of U.S. strategic defense.

THE MAD THEORY

Let us now take a closer look at one leg of the structure, the land-based missiles. At one time they seemed to provide great reassurance that we would never be caught in a nuclear Pearl Harbor. The development of Minuteman solid-fuel rockets in the early 1960s enabled us to put our missiles deep underground in silos and harden (insulate) them with layers of reinforced concrete. The purpose of hardening was to give the United States what is called a second-strike capacity, which means that if an enemy were to hit us with nuclear missiles, our missiles could absorb the blow and hit back. Our cities might be in ruins, but our missile force would be ready for retaliation. In the end, both countries would be destroyed. Just the thought of that should be enough to deter an enemy from launching a first strike. This is the basic premise of the doctrine of mutually assured destruction (MAD). Put crudely, it says: "If you blow us up, we'll blow you up." MAD has some interesting and rather disquieting implications.

(Continued on page 577)

Is Defense Spending Weakening the United States?

YES Paul Kennedy

Based upon *The Rise and Fall of the Great Powers* (New York: Random House, 1987).

Kennedy contends that the great powers in history (such as Rome, Spain, and England) declined because of "imperial overreach": They took over too many lands and peoples. In trying to maintain their holdings by military force, they exhausted their wealth. Since the end of World War II and particularly since the end of the 1960s, that has been happening to the United States. We have more than half a million troops scattered around the world, which has tripled our defense budget since the 1970s. Our overreach is draining away precious resources. The United States "continues to invest a massive amount of its R&D [research and development] activities into military-related production while the Japanese and West German concentration is upon commercial R&D." More than half of our scientists and engineers are working on military-related projects instead of designing better consumer products. Kennedy argues that this heavy investment in arms, "while bringing greater security in the short term, may so erode the commercial competitiveness of the American economy that the nation will be *less* secure in the long term." The Soviets are doing the same thing, and *both* powers may soon be eclipsed by expanding states like China and Japan.

NO W. W. Rostow

Based upon "Beware of Historians Bearing False Analogies," *Foreign Affairs* (Spring 1988), pp. 863-68.

Rostow begins with a reminder that military spending as a percentage of our gross national product has not been increasing but decreasing since the 1950s. It was 13 percent during the Korean War, almost 9 percent during Vietnam, and 6.5 percent at the end of 1987. "The image that emerges from Kennedy's rhetoric and analysis—of the United States in the grip of a linear expansion in its military outlays until it self-destructs—is justified neither by past trends nor by reasonable expectations for the future." Other states that spend proportionately more than we do on the military (for example, Taiwan and South Korea) are enjoying much larger growth rates than we are. "The capacity to reconcile a high rate of growth with a nation's security requirements is a much more complex affair than Kennedy allows." What we need right now, Rostow concludes, is steadiness of purpose in strengthening our alliances while holding out to the Soviets the possibility of a "soft landing" from the cold war. This is possible; it can be done. But Rostow says a blind and precipitous retraction of our security commitments, "which Paul Kennedy's false analogies tend to encourage, could destroy that possibility."

Postscript

Kennedy's analogies to Spain and England suggest that the United States too has become an overgrown imperial power and will suffer the consequences. Is that a fair comparison? Do the United States' post–World War II alliances add up to an imperial system? Some observers agree without hesitation; others take Rostow's view that the label is false and dangerous.

Although written years earlier, *The Permanent War Economy* (New York: Simon & Schuster, 1974) by economist Seymour Melman argues a thesis similar to Kennedy's: Excessive military spending weakens a country. H. L. Nieburg's *In the Name of Science* (Chicago: University of Chicago, 1966) argues that the American military establishment has gotten into an alliance with industry that is unhealthy for both of them. For a much different perspective on security and defense, see Norman Podhoretz, *The Present Danger* (New York: Simon & Schuster, 1980). He agrees that the United States has declined but blames it on a loss of will and nerve, not on excessive military spending.

FIGURE **20-4**

577

American Defense
Theories

American Missiles: A Strategy for Delivery

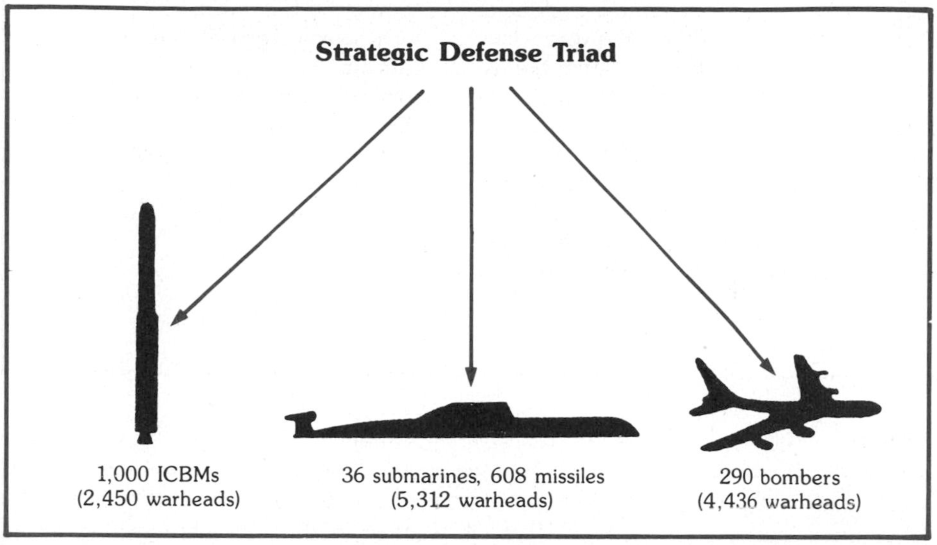

Strategic Defense Triad

| 1,000 ICBMs | 36 submarines, 608 missiles | 290 bombers |
| (2,450 warheads) | (5,312 warheads) | (4,436 warheads) |

Data Source: Defense Intelligence Agency, Center for Defense Information, *U.S. News and World Report*, June 12, 1989, pp. 32-33.

Although each leg of this nuclear triad contains its individual strengths and weaknesses, the Pentagon theory is that their collective power will deter any would-be aggressors.

(Continued from page 575)

First, it means that the enemy too should be encouraged to build up its second-strike force. "If you blow us up, we'll blow you up" has a corollary: "If we blow you up, you get to blow us up." Thus, the United States sought to understand the Soviets when they started building up their missile force in the late 1960s. After all, the reasoning went, the Soviets also need to be ready for a second strike—against *us*.

Second, the logic of MAD works against any kind of civil defense or antimissile program. These are seen as destabilizing. If you start building fallout shelters or Star Wars antimissile systems (see Strategic Defense Initiative on page 586), it must mean that you think you can protect your civilian population against retaliation for a first strike, and that must mean that you are contemplating a first strike. For MAD to work best, each side should offer its civilians as hostages. "If we strike you first, here are our city dwellers: See, we're not even trying to protect them."

Third, MAD leads to a countervalue instead of a counterforce strategy. The term *countervalue* means targeting enemy cities, while *counterforce* means concentrating on enemy military targets, particularly those capable of hitting your country with bombs or missiles. Why would a country use a counterforce strategy? Because it plans to wipe out its enemy's retaliatory capacity. And why would any country want to do that? Because it is contemplating a first strike. On the other hand, if a country is targeting its enemy's cities, that must mean that it has no first-strike intentions, since it has left its enemy with the means of retaliation. Thus, to be bloodthirsty is to be humane: If you plan to kill your enemy's women and children, that means your intentions are peaceful. The logic sounds like it was borrowed from George Orwell's *1984*, but MAD proponents insist that it has kept the United States and the USSR out of war.[23]

MAD is a purely American theory; there is no evidence that the Soviets have ever believed in it. The evidence, in fact, points in the opposite direction. Since the beginning of the nuclear age, the Soviets have had an extensive program of civil defense. Soviet schoolchildren regularly participate in air-raid drills, and Soviet authorities have worked out plans for evacuating cities. Whether these plans would work (especially in light of what we know of the bungled evacuation after the Chernobyl nuclear accident in 1986) is another matter. We are talking about intentions, and it is clear that the Soviets do not intend to offer their civilians as hostages.

Another destabilizing element actively pursued by the Soviets is antimissile defense. If that is what Star Wars means, the Soviets have been working on their own Star Wars system since the mid-1960s. The Soviets possess the world's only operational antiballistic missile (ABM) system, located around Moscow. In 1980 they began to upgrade and expand that system to the limit allowed by the 1972 ABM treaty—and, many thought, beyond it.

Nuclear Arms Control Negotiations

Because of the terrifying weapons we now have—and the terrifying logic that can lead sane people to think of using them—the Soviet Union and the United States have both come to the conclusion that something has to be done to reduce the stockpiles of such weapons. The history of nuclear arms control negotiations with the Soviet Union goes back to the early years of the cold war at the end of the 1940s, but the negotiations have usually foundered on the Soviet refusal to permit on-site verification of agreements. Not until 1963 did the two countries reach agreement on one small segment of the nuclear arms controversy: They agreed to stop atmospheric testing of nuclear weapons. This treaty presented no compliance problems, since neither side could hope to hide such tests. The box on page 580 lists the major arms agreements between the United States and the USSR since 1963. A few of them need a somewhat longer discussion.

SALT I (1972)

SALT I was the first Soviet-American treaty that concerned the production and deployment of strategic weapons. SALT stands for "strategic arms limitation talks." These talks had been going on formally since 1969, after President Nixon and Henry Kissinger approved the SALT concept. Finally, after two and a half years of hard bargaining, the two sides forged the first SALT agreement in 1972. It came in two parts: *(Continued on page 580)*

GLOBAL PERSPECTIVES:

Canada's Defense Forces

Since the beginning of the nuclear age in 1945, defense systems of Canada and the United States have been viewed as interdependent. The degree of that interdependence, however, has varied with the times and the regimes in power.

Canada has been a member of NATO since its establishment in 1949, and during the 1950s it entered into more specific defense arrangements with the United States. The two countries developed a series of early warning systems to alert defense forces of approaching Soviet bombers. In 1958 they established the North American Air Defense Command (NORAD), an integrated defense command. American nuclear-armed bombers regularly flew missions over Canada. (The Soviets warned that Canada was seriously jeopardizing its own security by permitting such flights.)

But by the end of the 1960s feelings began to change. Canadians felt less threatened by the Soviets and more troubled by the American involvement in Vietnam. In 1968 Prime Minister Pierre Trudeau came to power promising a reassessment of Canadian defense commitments. He soon began

a series of drastic cuts in military spending, from 20 percent in 1966 to 10.7 percent in 1975. In 1974 just 2.1 percent of Canada's gross national product went to the military. Among NATO countries only Luxembourg spent less.

Canada's defenses improved after Trudeau left office, and it has undertaken a major weapons modernization program. The strident anti-Americanism that underlay much of Trudeau's policies (in 1971 the Canadian defense minister described NORAD as protecting "not just against a Soviet incursion, but also against potential American incursion") has given way to a more cooperative posture. Still, it is likely that Canada will continue to steer an independent course even as it recognizes the need for working with the United States in matters of mutual concern. Canadians have always been sensitive to the danger of becoming a U.S. satellite. In 1938 a Canadian author voiced a sentiment that is still widely shared among Canadians: "Whatever our fate, it is to be hoped that our own government shall decide it."

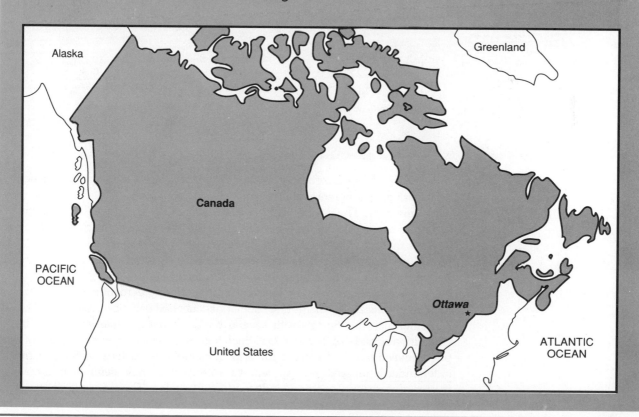

1963

"Hot Line" Agreement

Established a direct teleprinter link between the two governments.

Partial Test Ban

Prohibited nuclear testing above ground or in the atmosphere, where it would spread radiation to other countries.

1967

Outer Space Treaty

Prohibited sending nuclear weapons into earth orbit.

1968

Nonproliferation Treaty

Prohibited the transfer of nuclear weapons or know-how to other countries.

1971

Seabed Treaty

Prohibited placing nuclear weapons on the ocean floor beyond a nation's 12-mile limit.

Nuclear Accidents Agreement

Provided for immediate notification in case of accidental detonation of a nuclear weapon.

1972

Antiballistic Missile Treaty

Limited the number of sites, launchers, and anti-ballistic missiles that each country may employ.

SALT I

Called for a five-year freeze on the testing and deployment of ICBMs and submarine-launched missiles.

1973

Agreement on the Prevention of Nuclear War

Provided that the United States and the Soviet Union would refrain from threatening each other or their allies with nuclear war.

1974

Threshold Test-Ban Treaty

Limited the power of weapons to be tested underground (never ratified by the United States).

Vladivostok Accords

Limited the number of delivery vehicles available to each country, including missiles and bombers.

1976

Peaceful Nuclear Explosions Treaty

Prohibited underground tests for peaceful purposes of devices yielding more than 150 kilotons.

1979

SALT II

Limited the number of ground-based strategic missile launchers, submarine-based missiles, heavy bombers, and air-to-surface missiles. The treaty was never ratified by the U.S. Senate.

1987

INF Treaty

Provided for the elimination of all intermediate-range nuclear missiles.

(Continued from page 578)

1. *ABM Treaty.* Based upon the logic of MAD, which views antimissile defense as destabilizing, this agreement limited each side to one antiballistic missile (ABM) deployment site. The development of ABM technology was also severely limited. For example, apart from the one permissible ABM site, the construction of any radar facilities that could be used for detecting and shooting down incoming missiles was prohibited. Early warning radar systems could be therefore constructed only at the periphery of the two countries, not deep in their interiors.

2. *Interim Agreement on Offensive Arms.* This agreement imposed a five-year quantitative freeze on ICBMs and submarine-launched ballistic missiles (SLBMs). The agreement left the Soviets with several hundred more missile launchers than the United States had—2,347 to 1,710. Such figures, however, took no account of a new phenomenon that had entered the arms race in the late 1960s: MIRVs, or multiple independently targeted reentry vehicles. Missiles were now being built to contain a cluster of warheads, each one independently targeted. The missile itself serves as a kind of bus, carrying the warheads over the enemy's territory. Then the warheads are released and go off to their separate targets. MIRVed missiles made it even more

difficult to negotiate nuclear arms limits; the clusters of warheads multiplied by an unknown factor the number of explosions that could be visited upon each country.

The MIRV problem and other issues were discussed by President Ford and Soviet general secretary Brezhnev at Vladivostok, in the USSR, in 1974. An agreed framework for a new treaty was signed that set a limit on the number of MIRVed missile launchers. It also set overall force limits for each side while leaving each side free to shape defense strategy as it saw fit. But it left major problems unresolved. By this time, the Soviets had produced a new bomber (called Backfire by the Americans) that was a supersonic craft capable of reaching the United States. Brezhnev claimed that it was intended primarily as a medium-range bomber and should therefore be left out of the count of long-range weapons. The United States was not satisfied with Brezhnev's explanation. The Soviets in turn expressed concern about U.S. cruise missiles. A cruise missile is a jet-powered vehicle that can be launched from a bomber and is capable of carrying a nuclear warhead. Should it be counted among strategic delivery vehicles? The Soviets said yes; we said no, since the missile itself was incapable of intercontinental flight.

SALT II: AN UNRATIFIED TREATY

The problems occasioned by the Backfire bomber and the cruise missile were among those tackled during the extensive negotiations leading to SALT II, signed in June 1979 by President Carter and General Secretary Brezhnev.

SALT II is a bewildering document, more than a hundred pages long and crammed with technical jargon. At its heart is an attempt to tie up the loose ends from SALT I and Vladivostok. What do we do about the new bombers and cruise missiles? What do we do about MIRVed missiles? The SALT II method was to set numerical limits and sublimits. For example:

- Within a year the total number of launching vehicles (land-based launchers, bombers, and submarines) was to be limited to 2,250.
- The number of long-range cruise missiles was to be limited to an average of 28 per bomber.
- Total MIRVed missiles could not exceed 1,200.
- Limits were set on the number of warheads allowed in each missile (10 for each ICBM, 14 for each submarine-launched missile).

One provision of SALT II that later became important was the prohibition of any more than one new ICBM. The United States was to accuse the Soviets of violating this provision.

SALT II has never had the force of law, for it was never ratified. The president negotiates treaties, but the Senate must approve them. President Carter submitted SALT II to the Senate but, knowing that it would be defeated, he withdrew it in 1980. The treaty displeased key senators, among them the late Henry Jackson (D-Washington). Jackson and others opposed it because it left the Soviet Backfire bomber largely undisturbed and also because it left open a number of questions about Soviet compliance. Still, as of December 1979 the treaty had a 50-50 chance of ratification.

Then came the Soviet invasion of Afghanistan. Shocked and angered at the Soviets, President Carter knew that their invasion spelled doom for the treaty. He asked the Senate to delay consideration of it, and the Senate complied.

SALT II was legally stillborn, but the Soviets announced that they would honor its terms provided that the United States did the same. This put pressure on Carter to do what the Senate was apparently unwilling to do: bind our nation to the terms of a highly controversial document. When Ronald Reagan entered the White House in 1981, the stage was set for a new national security debate. At issue was whether or

President Jimmy Carter and Soviet leader Leonid Brezhnev sign the SALT II treaty in 1979. The treaty was never ratified by the U.S. Senate: Carter withdrew it from consideration after he realized that he did not have the votes for ratification. Senate critics charged that the treaty harmed U.S. interests, and their opposition won increasing support in the Senate after the Soviets invaded Afghanistan in December 1979.

not the United States should continue to honor the unratified SALT II treaty even after its scheduled expiration date and even in the face of evidence that the Soviets were violating it.

Another issue, debated not so much in the United States as in Western Europe, was whether or not the United States should continue deploying intermediate-range missiles (those with ranges of 600 to 3,400 miles) based in Europe. The United States and other NATO countries had resolved to deploy them in 1980 in response to the Soviet deployment of similar missiles targeted on European NATO countries. The deployment set off massive protest demonstrations throughout Western Europe, and the Soviets called the deployment provocative. The next round of peace talks thus began on a sour note. These talks were called the START talks.

THE START TALKS

Reagan came into office determined to reverse the military cutbacks of the 1970s. During his first term, defense budgets soared; tanks, cruise missiles, B-1 bombers, and other new military hardware went into production. Although the United States and the Soviets engaged in discussions on intermediate-range missiles as early as 1981, it was not until mid-1982 that discussions on strategic weapons got under way. Reagan, who shared the misgivings of Senator Jackson and others regarding SALT, gave the new talks a different name: START (Strategic Arms Reduction Talks). The name reflected Reagan's philosophy that the ultimate goal of both sides should not simply be a slowdown in the arms race, but a reversal—a *reduction* in nuclear arms.

Reagan wanted to negotiate cuts in existing nuclear arsenals. The Soviets objected that his proposals would require them to make deeper cuts than the Americans in certain categories of weapons. Still, everything was negotiable until the Soviets walked out at the end of 1983. Their price for returning was U.S. removal of the intermediate-range missiles it had deployed in Europe. The Reagan administration refused. This put Reagan in a delicate position, especially during the 1984

Then-vice president George Bush and a Soviet missile inspector watch the destruction of U.S. intermediate-range missiles in September 1988. The systematic destruction of INF missiles by both the U.S. and the Soviet Union was the result of the INF treaty the two nations signed in December 1987. The treaty was considered an important first step in nuclear arms reduction.

election campaign. The Democrats pressed the peace issue, noting the administration's failure to reach any arms agreements with the Soviets. Reagan kept insisting that he wanted nothing more than to reach such an agreement—if only the Soviets would come back to the bargaining table.

THE INF TREATY (1987)

A little more than a year later the Soviets did come back and were soon negotiating in earnest for a ban on intermediate-range missiles, known officially as "Intermediate-range Nuclear Force" (INF). Early in his first term Reagan had proposed a "zero-zero" arrangement on INF missiles: If the Soviets would destroy all of their missiles, we would destroy all of ours. For the first time, the Soviets accepted the offer. They also agreed to allow on-site inspection to ensure treaty compliance. The Reagan administration was almost bound to accept the offer—otherwise it would be accused of "refusing to take 'yes' for an answer."

While these negotiations were going on, President Reagan and General Secretary Gorbachev were meeting together to discuss a number of East-West issues, including arms control. They met in Geneva, Switzerland, at the end of 1985 and in Reykjavik, Iceland, in October 1986. They were to meet two more times before Reagan left office, but the 1986 Reykjavik meeting was perhaps the most interesting. Although it produced no agreement, it was the first meeting in which leaders on both sides discussed the possibility of banning *all* ballistic missiles. At that meeting, which the Americans thought was going to be informal, Gorbachev surprised the American side by introducing a package of arms reduction proposals linked to a proposal to limit research on the Star Wars missile defense system. Reagan countered with his own proposal to ban all offensive missiles, but the Soviets refused to consider this unless the Americans also agreed to limit Star Wars. The meeting ended inconclusively and on a rather tense note.

Some of Reagan's advisers abhorred the thought of abandoning missiles. For them, that would be the equivalent of sawing off two legs of the deterrent triad, for it would eliminate ICBMs as well as submarine-launched missiles. We would be left only with bombers to respond to, perhaps, a massive Soviet conventional attack on Western Europe. Yet it may be that Reykjavik helped loosen the ice of the cold war and prepare the way for the INF Treaty.

Signed in December of 1987 in Washington, the INF Treaty was hailed as a major step forward in lessening the danger of nuclear war and putting the United States and the Soviets on a more civil footing. Some, however, expressed deep concern. General Bernard Rogers, then commander of NATO, said that it would make Europe "safe for conventional war" by removing any European-based nuclear deterrent to a Soviet attack on Western Europe with conventional forces (where the Soviets possess at least a numerical advantage).[24] Columnist George F. Will said it would leave the United States with no "graduated response" to a Soviet invasion of Western Europe. If we were confronted with an overwhelming Soviet advantage in conventional forces, Will believed that the U.S. choice would be to surrender Europe or launch strategic weapons from U.S. soil; if we decided on the latter, we would be inviting Soviet retaliation against American cities. "Europeans," it was argued, "would reasonably doubt America's readiness to sacrifice Chicago to protect, or avenge, Hamburg."[25] In reply, defenders of the treaty noted that it left undisturbed hundreds of short-range (600 miles or less) missiles on both sides, which would permit a degree of graduated response.

But even short-range missiles were put in jeopardy in April 1989 after West German chancellor Helmut Kohl, responding to internal pressures, demanded superpower talks aimed at removing short-range missiles from German soil. West Germans had become increasingly fearful of these missiles, since in a nuclear exchange they would be exploding all over their country. Kohl's demand put the United States in a bind. Short-range missiles are the last credible deterrent to a Soviet conventional attack on Western Europe, but to refuse Kohl flatly could ruin our relations with a key NATO ally. Soviet president Gorbachev skillfully exploited the situation by announcing that he was unilaterally withdrawing 500 of the USSR's short-range missiles. President George Bush, however, soon turned the situation around. At the NATO summit held in Brussels, Belgium, in May 1989, Bush proposed dramatic mutual reductions in *conventional* forces, to be followed by talks on short-range missiles.

Conventional American and Soviet troop ceilings would be 275,000, which meant that Soviet troop withdrawals would be 325,000 compared to 30,000 for the United States. Bush placated German fears by proposing a short timetable for

---

Points to Remember

1. The 1972 SALT I treaty consisted of two parts: a provision banning nationwide ABM systems and an interim freeze on ICBMs and submarine-launched missiles.

2. SALT II was a more ambitious attempt to slow the growth of offensive nuclear weapons. It set limits and sublimits on warheads and launching vehicles. The treaty was never ratified by the U.S. Senate.

3. The START talks, so named by President Reagan, were aimed not just at putting limits on the growth of nuclear weapons, but on effecting cuts in existing arsenals.

4. Ronald Reagan, who had called the Soviet Union an "evil empire," left office with a seemingly changed view of the Soviets. He had met Soviet president Gorbachev on four separate occasions and in 1987 signed the INF Treaty, a major U.S.-Soviet agreement banning intermediate-range nuclear weapons.

5. Critics of the INF Treaty contended that it would make Europe safe for "conventional war." The reply was that we still had short-range missiles. But the West Germans wanted these missiles out as well, and George Bush promised negotiations aimed at cutting their numbers once the Soviets and Americans implemented cuts in conventional forces.

conventional troop reductions; he estimated that a deal could be worked out with the Soviets and implemented by 1992 or 1993. Then we could start talking about a partial cutback of short-range missiles. (Bush opposed their complete elimination.) The proposal was received with enthusiasm by our NATO allies, especially the Germans, and was incorporated into a formal document signed by the NATO states. Bush had regained the diplomatic initiative, and the Soviets seemed uncertain about how to react. At first, their foreign minister characterized the Bush plan as "a serious and important step in the right direction," but the next day he said he was "disappointed" with the plan because it put conventional troop reductions ahead of missile cuts.[26]

Alternatives to MAD

The doctrine of mutually assured destruction (MAD) rests on the assumption that the hardened missile silos of both superpowers guarantee to each a second-strike capability. That assumption is now very dubious. The combination of the ABM system, civil defense, super-accurate missiles, and MIRVing may now permit a nation to launch a first strike without paying an unacceptable price. The inner logic of MAD is thus challenged. Moreover, even if retaliation is still an option, the morality of threatening to kill millions of people because their leaders threaten to kill millions of your people is, at the very least, questionable. What other options are there? Let us consider four.

DISARM UNILATERALLY

This is sometimes implied or hinted at, but it has few outright proponents—and those few tend to come not from politics, but from the field of arts and entertainment. Composer and conductor Leonard Bernstein advocated it in a 1980 commencement address at Johns Hopkins University. "Suppose—just suppose," Bernstein said, that we disarmed unilaterally. What would the Soviets do? Take us over? He answered with a series of rhetorical questions.

> But would they really? What would they do with us? Why would they want to assume the responsibility for, and administration of, so huge, complex and problematical a society as ours? And in English yet![27]

We need not linger long over this proposal. The idea of ending the arms race by throwing away our weapons—and hoping that the Soviets will find us too burdensome to rule—has little popular appeal in the United States.

POSSESS BUT NEVER USE NUCLEAR WEAPONS

This appears to be the official position of the American Catholic bishops, who accept the need for deterrence and thus do not rule out the possession of nuclear weapons. Using such weapons, however, seems to be impossible under the constraints adopted by the bishops. They rule out any first use of nuclear weapons, even to deter a massive conventional assault on Western Europe. What about second use—using them in retaliation for a nuclear first strike? That too seems to be ruled out in practice. The bishops oppose the use of nuclear weapons against civilian population centers.[28] The alternative is counterforce strategy (targeting military installations). But so many military installations are near or within cities that striking them would still kill millions of civilians. It would be "morally disproportionate, even though not intentionally

"Oooooooooooooooo!"

Beyond the Far Side *cartoon by Gary Larson is reprinted with permission of Chronicle Features, San Francisco, CA.*

indiscriminate."[29] Suppose, then, that we target only missile sites in the isolated wastes of Siberia? That too is undesirable because "a purely counterforce strategy may seem to threaten the viability of other nations' retaliatory forces, making deterrence unstable in a crisis and war more likely." (The bishops accept the logic of MAD: If we blow you up, you get to blow us up. That means we have to leave your missiles alone.) It is hard to see, then, what legitimate target remains for our missiles. In essence, the bishops would let us possess nuclear weapons and even threaten to use them in retaliation for a first strike, but never *actually* use them. The bishops would allow us only to make empty threats.

DETER WITHOUT NUCLEAR WEAPONS

In 1982 *New Yorker* writer Jonathan Schell published a book called *Fate of the Earth*. It was a frightening account of what would happen to the earth and its inhabitants in a full-scale nuclear war. But the book failed to offer any solution to the problem of nuclear weapons. All Schell could come up with was the utopian solution of abolishing independent nation-states.[30] In 1984 Schell published a new book that sought a more realistic solution to the nuclear menace. His main suggestion was to get all the nations of the world to agree to dismantle their nuclear weapons.

On its face, that seems as utopian as abolishing the nation-state. Even if all nations dismantled their nuclear bombs, they could not destroy the knowledge of how to make them. But Schell thinks it is precisely that fact that makes his proposal practical after all. Since a nation can make a new bomb in less than a month, we can have deterrence without actually having nuclear weapons. Let us all agree to dismantle the weapons. If it is discovered later that a nation is cheating (by hiding bombs or secretly making more), its adversary can start making them too, and in a short while deterrence would be back to where it is today. But at least more steps would have been added to the ladder of escalation. At present the only step we have is the final, apocalyptic one of actually pushing the button. Schell calls his idea "weaponless deterrence" and claims that it would stretch the time between the first threats and the final holocaust from seven minutes to four weeks. The problem is that it would tempt one side—or perhaps both—to cheat by hiding some weapons.[31]

SEEK A RELIABLE DEFENSE

MAD assumes that there is no defense against missiles. The Soviets, however, have never accepted that assumption and have been working on antimissile weapons since the 1960s. They have the only operational ABM system in the world, built up over the last 17 years. They have developed mobile ABM radars and missiles, located at ICBM sites all around the Soviet Union, and, for several years were building a radar station in Siberia that was apparently intended to be a component of a larger missile defense system.[32] In October 1989 the Soviets admitted that this radar station did indeed violate the 1972 ABM treaty, and they promised to dismantle it.

In an address to the nation in March 1983, President Reagan unveiled his plan for the United States to start its own research on antimissile defense; he called his research program the Strategic Defense Initiative, or SDI. His critics had another name for it. Massachusetts senator Edward Kennedy contemptuously referred to it as "Star Wars." The name stuck.

The basic idea behind Star Wars is quite simple: Shoot down incoming Soviet missiles and warheads before they land on our country. To do this, we would use three layers of defense: a *launch defense*, a *terminal defense*, and a *point defense*. The critical layer is *launch defense*, also called the *boost phase*. If we could destroy

FIGURE **20-5**

How Star Wars Would Work

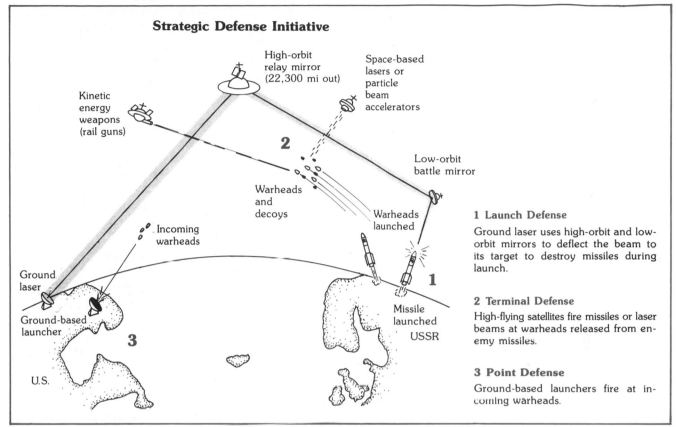

Strategic Defense Initiative

High-orbit relay mirror (22,300 mi out)

Space-based lasers or particle beam accelerators

Kinetic energy weapons (rail guns)

Low-orbit battle mirror

2

Warheads and decoys

Warheads launched

Incoming warheads

Warheads launched

Missile launched USSR

Ground laser

Ground-based launcher

1

3

U.S.

1 Launch Defense

Ground laser uses high-orbit and low-orbit mirrors to deflect the beam to its target to destroy missiles during launch.

2 Terminal Defense

High-flying satellites fire missiles or laser beams at warheads released from enemy missiles.

3 Point Defense

Ground-based launchers fire at incoming warheads.

Data Source: New Haven Register, November 10, 1985, p. A46; UPI release.

Soviet missiles before they leave their launch pads or at least before they get very far in the air, we could then knock out a whole cluster of MIRVed warheads at a single blow. *Terminal defense* would take place once the rocket "bus" had released its warheads in space and they began descending toward the American continent. This defense would be difficult because each single rocket will have spawned several warheads. Finally, there is *point defense*—ground-based artillery for shooting down each descending warhead as it heads toward its individual target. This type of technology has been around since the 1960s; as mentioned earlier, the Soviets already have it in place around Moscow. However, it is questionable as to how effective it would be against a pack of multiple warheads: It could probably knock out some, but how many? Still, SDI proponents claim that, *taken together*, the three layers could eventually filter out 97 percent or more of the incoming rounds, making the United States not completely safe, but much safer than at present. (No serious proponent of SDI has ever contended that it would place an impenetrable "stadium dome" over the country and make it perfectly safe from attack.)

Reagan's proposal set off a vigorous debate about the feasibility and desirability of such a system. Critics doubted that it would work and feared that it would escalate the arms race. Defenders pointed to a series of successful preliminary tests and insisted that it was purely defensive, not aggressive. Whatever the merits of these arguments, by the end of the 1980s they had become largely academic. The Gramm–Rudman budget cuts forced large cutbacks in SDI research, and the new Bush administration was not very enthusiastic about the program. Dick Cheney, President Bush's defense secretary, said that the system had "great potential" but had been "oversold" by the Reagan administration and needed to be balanced against other goals.[33]

Another factor to be taken into account is nuclear proliferation—the spread of nuclear weapons to other countries. In 1968 the United States and the USSR signed a nonproliferation treaty prohibiting the transfer of nuclear weapons or knowledge of how to build them to nonnuclear countries. But it is impossible to hold back such knowledge and technique. China has had nuclear weapons since the 1960s, and now many other nations are about to enter the nuclear club. According to CIA director William H. Webster, Egypt, Argentina, and Iraq have joined forces on a nuclear missile project. Other developing countries working on such projects include North Korea, Syria, Israel, Iran, Libya, Brazil, India, and Pakistan. "Although missiles being developed by these countries are somewhat crude and inaccurate," Webster says, "many of them have capabilities well beyond the battlefield, and can strike in a matter of minutes."[34] This development is a kind of wild card. It may make missile defense more difficult yet also strengthen the case for it, since these other countries are not used to playing by the delicate, implicit rules of deterrence worked out by the two superpowers.

Reflections

The word *apocalypse* comes from a Greek word meaning "uncovering" or "revelation." Early Christian writers gave that name to a strange vision recounted by John, one of the apostles of Jesus.

The Apocalypse, also called the Book of Revelation in the Bible, is a prophecy of the end of the world. In John's vision, four ghostly horsemen ride into the world, representing war, strife, famine, and sickness. The earth begins shaking. The sun turns black, the moon blood-red, and all the stars seem to be falling. "And the kings of the earth, and the princes, and the tribunes, and the rich, and the strong, and everyone, bond and free, hid themselves in the caves and in the rocks of the mountains." Then a large "pool of fire" descends from the sky, a punishment for those who have transgressed against God's law.

To anyone in Hiroshima on August 6, 1945, who had read and remembered the Apocalypse—like the Jesuit fathers who helped the Nakamura family—it must have seemed as if a vision much like John's was being played out. In the history of warfare there had never been anything like this: a city wiped out in one blinding flash and people instantly cremated, with only their shadows left on sidewalks and on the broken walls of buildings. Then came the nightmare of the survivors wandering in the ruins under a dark noonday sky.

By today's standards, the Hiroshima bomb would be called a tactical weapon—a local battlefield bomb, not serious enough for intercontinental warfare. The typical warhead today is about 80 times as powerful, although there are some warheads more than 1,000 times so. The Soviets and the Americans have a combined total of about 20,000 nuclear bombs and warheads; in the event of a general, total war between them, there is no reason to think that all 20,000 would not be shot off. Thus, even if the other nuclear powers stayed out of the fight, the superpowers might themselves be able to bring all life on earth to an apocalyptic end.

Both hawks and doves seem to agree on this much: Arms limitation, the philosophy underlying the two SALTs, is not enough. Slowing down the production of bombs and missiles when we already have thousands and thousands of them will neither prevent a first strike nor make the world appreciably safer. We already have too many bombs. How do we deal with this predicament?

An infallible defense system is impossible. But proponents of Star Wars research contend that it is possible to build one that is 97 percent effective by the end of the century. At the present level of nuclear stockpiles, that would still allow more than 250 warheads to fall on the United States. It would be an unparalleled disaster—but it would allow the United States to retaliate. Maybe that is the best argument for SDI: It could serve to enhance our deterrent by allowing us to reply effectively to a first strike. But the SDI debate may soon become moot. Funding cuts and general lack of enthusiasm by the Bush administration have already slowed research on the system. The whole issue is presently being outpaced by political events. Could it be that the cold war is finally ending? The Soviet Union of Mikhail Gorbachev is undergoing dramatic internal change. Unless that change is reversed, some variant of democracy may even emerge. That may not end U.S.-Soviet rivalry, but it will put it on a different plane because ordinary people, who are not ideologues, do not want global power as much as they want decent housing, food, and consumer goods. There are few of these things in the Soviet Union. Imperial ambitions will have to be subordinated, and this could set the stage for real understanding.

Other world developments are less reassuring. Nuclear weapons and the know-how to build them are becoming available to many countries, including some of the most fanatical and unstable. In the future we may have to orient our defense differently. We will need to pay closer attention to the various loose cannons throughout the world and—perhaps in cooperation with the Soviets—make sure that one or more of them do not set off an apocalypse.

Notes

1. John Hersey, *Hiroshima* (New York: Alfred A. Knopf, Inc., 1966), pp. 12-13.
2. Hersey, p. 28.
3. Hersey, pp. 39-40.
4. Hersey, p. 83.
5. Hersey, p. 94.
6. Hersey, p. 97.
7. Jonathan Schell, *The Fate of the Earth* (New York: Alfred A. Knopf, 1982), p. 52.
8. Congressional Quarterly, *The Power of the Pentagon* (Washington, DC: Congressional Quarterly, 1972), p. 104.
9. "Senate Approves Military Changes," *New York Times*, May 8, 1986, p. 1. The role of the Joint Chiefs of Staff was discussed in the previous chapter.
10. See, for example, Jim Courter and Gregory A. Fossedal, "The Military-Congressional Complex," *American Spectator* (June 1986), pp. 17-18.

11. See, for example, Marc Pilisuk and Thomas Hayden, "Is There a Military-Industrial Complex?" *Journal of Social Issues* (July 1965), pp. 67-117. The authors conclude that our entire nation is a giant military-industrial complex. For a more recent statement of this thesis, see Ira Katznelson and Mark Kesselman, *The Politics of Power* (New York: Harcourt Brace Jovanovich, 1975), p. 194: "The arms race probably represents in good part a subsidy to powerful interests within the United States."

12. See, for example, E. P. Thompson, "Look Who's Really Behind Star Wars," *The Nation*, Mar. 1, 1986, p. 234. The author attacks the proposed program of research on antimissile systems (Star Wars) by asserting that major defense contractors will profit from the research. He makes no attempt to prove that the research will be fruitless; it is enough for him that "eighty-seven percent of the [antimissile] contracts in fiscal 1983 and 1984 were received by ten companies."

13. *1988 Statistical Abstract*, no. 476, p. 297.

14. *1989 Statistical Abstract*, no. 526, p. 326.

15. In a poll for *Time* magazine by Yankelovich, Skelly & White, Inc., 64 percent of those who said that the best way to reduce budget deficits is to cut the budget indicated that they would put the military budget at the top of their "hit list." See *Time*, May 20, 1985, p. 15.

16. *New York Times*, July 3, 1986, p. D1.

17. Quoted in Eric Schmitt, "The Area's Economy Feels the Austerity of the Pentagon," *New York Times*, Apr. 16, 1989, IV, p. 26. See further, William J. Broad, "Military Research Facing the Pinch of Tight Budgets," *New York Times*, July 3, 1989, p. 1.

18. *New York Times*, June 8, 1989, p. A18.

19. The figures are based upon estimates of what Soviet spending amounts to in cash figures. The CIA does this, and its method is to analyze each component of the Soviet military—each weapon, each soldier, each item constructed—and then to estimate what it would cost in the United States. The method is full of pitfalls, since costs in the controlled Soviet economy have little to do with supply and demand. Moreover, the cost of a Soviet soldier, who is drafted and paid next to nothing, is difficult to compare with the wages of a volunteer soldier in the United States. Andrew Cockburn has remarked, "It may be that the Soviet authorities themselves do not know the precise economic burden of their defense industry on the overall economy." See Andrew Cockburn, *The Threat: Inside the Soviet Military Machine* (New York: Random House, 1983), p. 80.

20. Figures supplied by John Collins of the Congressional Research Service, cited by James Fallows, "The Spend-Up," *The Atlantic* (July 1986), p. 28.

21. *U.S. News & World Report*, June 12, 1989, pp. 32-33.

22. Tom Gervasi, *The Myth of Soviet Military Supremacy* (New York: Harper & Row, 1986). See further, John Pardos, *The Soviet Estimate* (New York: Dial Press, 1982).

23. Paul M. Kattenburg, "MAD Is the Moral Position," in Charles W. Kegley, Jr., and Eugene R. Wittkopf, eds., *The Nuclear Reader: Strategy, Weapons, War* (New York: St. Martin's Press, 1985), pp. 77-84.

24. "What's Wrong with 'Zero': NATO's Boss Speaks Out," *Newsweek*, Apr. 27, 1987, p. 27.

25. George F. Will, "The Opiate of Arms Control," *Newsweek*, April 27, 1987, p. 86.

26. "Soviets Welcome Bush Arms Plan," *New York Times*, May 31, 1989, p. A14; James M. Markham, "NATO Proposal 'Disappoints' Shevardnadze," *New York Times*, June 1, 1989, p. A12.

27. Leonard Bernstein, "Just Suppose We Disarmed," *New York Times*, June 10, 1980, p. 19.

28. National Conference of Catholic Bishops, "Nuclear Strategy and the Challenge of Peace: Ethical Principles and Policy Prescriptions," in Kegley and Wittkopf, p. 46.

29. Kegley and Wittkopf, p. 55.

30. Schell, pp. 217-31.

31. Schell tries to answer this objection by saying that if one side hid weapons and then used them on its disarmed opponent, the victim could get revenge by rebuilding the missiles and using them on the cheater. See Schell, *The Abolition* (New York: Alfred A. Knopf, 1984), p. 134. But could a nation that had just survived a nuclear attack start rebuilding its arsenal? Schell seems to have forgotten about the horrible chaos (that he himself depicted in his *Fate of the Earth*) caused by a nuclear attack.

32. "U.S. Experts Condemn Soviet Radar," *Science*, Mar. 22, 1985, p. 1442; McGeorge Bundy, George F. Kennan, Robert S. McNamara, and Gerald Smith, "The President's Choice: Star Wars or Arms Control," *Foreign Affairs* (Winter 1984-85), p. 275; compare with Strobe Talbott, "Questions about Soviet Cheating," *Time*, Dec. 3, 1984, pp. 19-21.

33. Andrew Rosenthal, "Missile Shield Must Be Balanced Against Other Goals, Cheney Says," *New York Times*, Mar. 29, 1989, p. B6.

34. Stephen Engelberg, "C.I.A.'s Chief Campaigns Against Missile-Making by Third World," *New York Times*, Mar. 31, 1989, p. A6.

The Declaration of Independence

IN CONGRESS, JULY 4, 1776

(The unanimous Declaration of the Thirteen United States of America)

PREAMBLE

When, in the course of human events, it becomes necessary for one people to dissolve the political bands which have connected them with another, and to assume, among the powers of the earth, the separate and equal station to which the laws of nature and of nature's God entitle them, a decent respect to the opinions of mankind requires that they should declare the causes which impel them to the separation.

New Principles of Government

We hold these truths to be self-evident; that all men are created equal, that they are endowed by their Creator with certain unalienable rights, that among these are life, liberty, and the pursuit of happiness.

That, to secure these rights, governments are instituted among men, deriving their just powers from the consent of the governed;

That whenever any form of government becomes destructive of these ends, it is the right of the people to alter or to abolish it, and to institute new government, laying its foundation on such principles, and organizing its powers in such form, as to them shall seem most likely to effect their safety and happiness. Prudence, indeed, will dictate that governments long established should not be changed for light and transient causes; and accordingly all experience hath shown that mankind are more disposed to suffer while evils are sufferable, than to right themselves by abolishing the forms to which they are accustomed. But when a long train of abuses and usurpations, pursuing invariably the same object, evinces a design to reduce them under absolute despotism, it is their right, it is their duty, to throw off such government, and to provide new guards for their future security.

Reasons for Separation

Such has been the patient sufferance of these colonies; and such is now the necessity which constrains them to alter their former systems of government. The history of the present king of Great Britain is a history of repeated injuries and usurpations, all having in direct object the establishment of an absolute tyranny over these states. To prove this, let facts be submitted to a candid world.

He has refused his assent to laws the most wholesome and necessary for the public good.

He has forbidden his governors to pass laws of immediate and pressing importance unless suspended in their operation till his assent should be obtained; and when so suspended, he has utterly neglected to attend to them.

He has refused to pass other laws for the accommodation of large districts of people, unless those people would relinquish the right of representation in the legislature, a right inestimable to them, and formidable to tyrants only.

He has called together legislative bodies at places unusual, uncomfortable, and distant from the depository of their public records, for the sole purpose of fatiguing them into compliance with his measures.

He has dissolved representative houses repeatedly, for opposing, with manly firmness, his invasions on the rights of people.

He has refused, for a long time after such dissolutions, to cause others to be elected; whereby the legislative powers, incapable of annihilation, have returned to the people at large for their exercise; the state remaining, in the mean time, exposed to all the dangers of invasion from without and convulsions within.

He has endeavored to prevent the population of these states; for that purpose obstructing the laws of naturalization of foreigners, refusing to pass others to encourage their migration hither, and raising the conditions of new appropriations of lands.

He has obstructed the administration of justice, by refusing his assent to laws for establishing judiciary powers.

He has made judges dependent on his will alone for the tenure of their offices, and the amount and payment of their salaries.

He has erected a multitude of new offices, and sent hither swarms of officers to harass our people and eat out their substance.

He has kept among us, in times of peace, standing armies, without the consent of our legislature.

He has affected to render the military independent of, and superior to, the civil power.

He has combined with others to subject us to a jurisdiction foreign to our constitution and unacknowledged by our laws, giving his assent to their acts of pretended legislation:

For quartering large bodies of armed troops among us;

For protecting them, by a mock trial, from punishment for any murders which they should commit on the inhabitants of these states;

For cutting off our trade with all parts of the world;

For imposing taxes on us without our consent;

For depriving us, in many cases, of the benefits of trial by jury;

For transporting us beyond seas, to be tried for pretended offenses;

For abolishing the free system of English laws in a neighboring province, establishing therein an arbitrary government, and enlarging its boundaries, so as to render it at once an example and fit instrument for introducing the same absolute rule into these colonies;

For taking away our charters, abolishing our most valuable laws, and altering, fundamentally, the forms of our governments;

For suspending our own legislatures, and declaring themselves invested with power to legislate for us in all cases whatsoever.

He has abdicated government here, by declaring us out of his protection and waging war against us.

He has plundered our seas, ravaged our coasts, burned our towns, and destroyed the lives of our people.

He is at this time transporting large armies of foreign mercenaries to complete the works of death, desolation, and tyranny already begun with circumstances of cruelty and perfidy scarcely paralleled in the most barbarous ages and totally unworthy the head of a civilized nation.

He has constrained our fellow citizens, taken captive on the high seas, to bear arms against their country, to become the executioners of their friends and brethren, or to fall themselves by their hands.

He has excited domestic insurrections among us, and has endeavored to bring on the inhabitants of our frontiers the merciless Indian savages, whose known rule of warfare is an undistinguished destruction of all ages, sexes, and conditions.

In every stage of these oppressions we have petitioned for redress in the most humble terms; our repeated petitions have been answered only by repeated injury. A prince whose character is thus marked by every act which may define a tyrant is unfit to be the ruler of a free people.

Nor have we been wanting in attention to our British brethren. We have warned them, from time to time, of attempts by their legislature to extend an unwarrantable jurisdiction over us. We have reminded them of the circumstances of our emigration and settlement here. We have appealed to their native justice and magnanimity; and we have conjured them, by the ties of our common kindred, to disavow these usurpations, which would inevitably interrupt our connections and correspondence. They, too, have been deaf to the voice of justice and of consanguinity. We must, therefore, acquiesce in the necessity which denounces our separation, and hold them, as we hold the rest of mankind, enemies in war, in peace, friends.

We, therefore, the representatives of the United States of America, in General Congress assembled, appealing to the Supreme Judge of the world for the rectitude of our intentions, do, in the name and by authority of the good people of these colonies, solemnly publish and declare, that these united colonies are, and of right ought to be, free and independent states; that they are absolved from all allegiance to the British crown, and that all political connection between them and the state of Great Britain is, and ought to be, totally dissolved; and that, as free and independent states, they have full power to levy war, conclude peace, contract alliances, establish commerce, and do all other acts and things which independent states may of a right do. And, for the support of this declaration, with a firm reliance on the protection of Divine Providence, we mutually pledge to each other our lives, our fortunes, and our sacred honor.

SIGNERS OF THE
DECLARATION OF INDEPENDENCE
According to the Authenticated List Printed by
Order of Congress of January 18, 1777

John Hancock.

New Hampshire	Josiah Bartlett, Wm Whipple, Matthew Thornton.
Massachusetts Bay	Saml Adams, John Adams, Robt Treat Paine, Elbridge Gerry.
Rhode Island and Providence, &c	Step. Hopkins, William Ellery.
Connecticut	Roger Sherman, Saml Huntington, Wm Williams, Oliver Wolcott.
New York	Wm Floyd, Phil. Livingston, Fran^s Lewis, Lewis Morris.
New Jersey	Richd Stockton, Jno. Witherspoon, Fra^s Hopkinson, John Hart, Abra. Clark.
Pennsylvania	Robt Morris, Benjamin Rush, Benja. Franklin, John Morton, Geo. Clymer, Ja^s Smith, Geo. Taylor, James Wilson, Geo. Ross.
Delaware	Caesar Rodney, Geo. Read.
Maryland	Samuel Chase, Wm Paca, Thos Stone, Charles Carroll, of Carrollton.
Virginia	George Wythe, Richard Henry Lee, Th^s Jefferson, Benj^a Harrison, Thos Nelson, J^r, Francis Lighfoot Lee, Carter Braxton.
North Carolina	Wm Hooper, Joseph Hewes, John Penn.
South Carolina	Edward Rutledge, Thos Heyward, jun^r, Thomas Lynch, jun^r, Arthur Middleton.
Georgia	Button Gwinnett, Lyman Hall, Geo. Walton.

The Constitution of the United States

PREAMBLE

We the People of the United States, in Order to form a more perfect Union, establish Justice, insure domestic Tranquility, provide for the common defence, promote the general Welfare, and secure the Blessings of Liberty to ourselves and our Posterity, do ordain and establish this Constitution for the United States of America.

ARTICLE I
Congress

Section I. All legislative Powers herein granted shall be vested in a Congress of the United States, which shall consist of a Senate and House of Representatives.

House of Representatives

Section 2. The House of Representatives shall be composed of Members chosen every second Year by the People of the several States, and the Electors in each State shall have the Qualifications requisite for Electors of the most numerous Branch of the State Legislature.

No person shall be a Representative who shall not have attained to the Age of twenty five Years, and been seven Years a Citizen of the United States, and who shall not, when elected, be an Inhabitant of that State in which he shall be chosen.

Representatives and direct Taxes shall be apportioned among the several States which may be included within this Union, according to their respective Numbers, which shall be determined by adding to the whole Number of free Persons, including those bound to Service for a Term of Years, and excluding Indians not taxed, three fifths of all other Persons. The actual Enumeration shall be made within three Years after the first Meeting of the Congress of the United States, and within every subsequent Term of ten Years, in such Manner as they shall by Law direct. The Number of Representatives shall not exceed one for every thirty Thousand, but each State shall have at Least one Representative; and until such enumeration shall be made, the State of New Hampshire shall be entitled to chuse three, Massachusetts eight, Rhode-Island and Providence Plantations one, Connecticut five, New-York six, New Jersey four, Pennsylvania eight, Delaware one, Maryland six, Virginia ten, North Carolina five, South Carolina five, and Georgia three.

When vacancies happen in the Representation from any State, the Executive Authority thereof shall issue Writs of Election to fill such Vacancies.

The House of Representatives shall chuse their Speaker and other Officers; and shall have the sole Power of Impeachment.

Senate

Section 3. The Senate of the United States shall be composed of two Senators from each State, chosen by the Legislature thereof, for six Years; and each Senator shall have one Vote.

Immediately after they shall be assembled in Consequence of the first Election, they shall be divided as equally as may be into three Classes. The Seats of the Senators of the first Class shall be vacated at the Expiration of the second Year, of the second Class at the Expiration of the fourth Year, and of the third Class at the Expiration of the sixth Year, so that one third may be chosen every second Year; and if Vacancies happen by Resignation, or otherwise, during the Recess of the Legislature of any State, the Executive thereof may make temporary Appointments until the next Meeting of the Legislature, which shall then fill such Vacancies.

No Person shall be a Senator who shall not have attained to the Age of thirty Years, and been nine Years a Citizen of the United States, and who shall not, when elected, be an Inhabitant of that State for which he shall be chosen.

The Vice President of the United States shall be

President of the Senate, but shall have no Vote, unless they be equally divided.

The Senate shall chuse their other Officers, and also a President pro tempore, in the Absence of the Vice President, or when he shall exercise the Office of President of the United States.

The Senate shall have the sole Power to try all Impeachments. When sitting for that Purpose, they shall be on Oath of Affirmation. When the President of the United States is tried, the Chief Justice shall preside: And no Person shall be convicted without the Concurrence of two thirds of the Members present.

Judgment in Cases of Impeachment shall not extend further than to removal from Office, and disqualification to hold and enjoy any Office of honor, Trust or Profit under the United States: but the Party convicted shall nevertheless be liable and subject to Indictment, Trial, Judgment and Punishment, according to Law.

Congressional elections, prerogatives, and procedures

Section 4. The Times, Places and Manner of holding Elections for Senators and Representatives, shall be prescribed in each State by the Legislature thereof; but the Congress may at any time by Law make or alter such Regulations, except as to the Places of chusing Senators.

The Congress shall assemble at least once in every Year, and such Meeting shall be on the first Monday in December, unless they shall by Law appoint a different Day.

Section 5. Each House shall be the Judge of the Elections, Returns and Qualifications of its own Members, and a Majority of each shall constitute a Quorum to do Business; but a smaller Number may adjourn from day to day, and may be authorized to compel the Attendance of absent Members, in such Manner, and under such Penalties as each House may provide.

Each House may determine the Rules of its Proceedings, punish its Members for disorderly Behaviour, and, with the Concurrence of two thirds, expel a Member.

Each House shall keep a Journal of its Proceedings, and from time to time publish the same, excepting such Parts as may in their Judgment require Secrecy; and the Yeas and Nays of the Members of either House on any question shall, at the Desire of one fifth of those Present, be entered on the Journal.

Neither House, during the Session of Congress, shall, without the Consent of the other, adjourn for more than three days, nor to any other Place than that in which the two Houses shall be sitting.

Section 6. The Senators and Representatives shall receive a Compensation for their Services, to be ascertained by Law, and paid out of the Treasury of the United States. They shall in all Cases, except Treason, Felony and Breach of the Peace, be privileged from Arrest during their Attendance at the Session of their respective Houses, and in going to and returning from the same; and for any Speech or Debate in either House, they shall not be questioned in any other Place.

No Senator or Representative shall, during the Time for which he was elected, be appointed to any civil Office under the Authority of the United States, which shall have been created, or the Emoluments whereof shall have been encreased during such time; and no Person holding any Office under the United States, shall be a Member of either House during his Continuance in Office.

Section 7. All Bills for raising Revenue shall originate in the House of Representatives; but the Senate may propose or concur with Amendments as on other Bills.

Every Bill which shall have passed the House of Representatives and the Senate, shall, before it become a Law, be presented to the President of the United States; If he approve he shall sign it, but if not he shall return it, with his Objections to that House in which it shall have originated, who shall enter the Objections at large on their Journal, and proceed to reconsider it. If after such Reconsideration two thirds of that House shall agree to pass the Bill, it shall be sent, together with the Objections, to the other House, by which it shall likewise be reconsidered, and if approved by two thirds of that House, it shall become a Law. But in all such Cases the Votes of both Houses shall be determined by yeas and Nays, and the Names of the Persons voting for and against the Bill shall be entered on the Journal of each House respectively. If any Bill shall not be returned by the President within ten Days (Sundays excepted) after it shall have been presented to him, the Same shall be a Law, in like Manner as if he had signed it, unless the Congress by their Adjournment prevent its Return, in which Case it shall not be a Law.

Every Order, Resolution, or Vote to which the Concurrence of the Senate and House of Representatives may be necessary (except on a question of Adjournment) shall be presented to the President of the United States; and before the Same shall take Effect, shall be approved by him, or being disapproved by him, shall be repassed by two thirds of the Senate and House of Representatives, according to the Rules and Limitations prescribed in the Case of a Bill.

Congressional powers

Section 8. The Congress shall have Power To lay and collect Taxes, Duties, Imposts and Excises, to pay the Debts and provide for the common Defence and general Welfare of the United States; but all Duties, Imposts and Excises shall be uniform throughout the United States;

To borrow Money on the credit of the United States;

To regulate Commerce with foreign Nations, and among the several States, and with the Indian Tribes;

To establish an uniform Rule of Naturalization, and uniform Laws on the subject of Bankruptcies throughout the United States;

To coin Money, regulate the Value thereof, and of foreign Coin, and fix the Standard of Weights and Measures;

To provide for the Punishment of counterfeiting the Securities and current Coin of the United States;

To establish Post Offices and post Roads;

To promote the Progress of Science and useful Arts, by securing for limited Times to Authors and Inventors the exclusive Right to their respective Writings and Discoveries;

To constitute Tribunals inferior to the supreme Court;

To define and punish Piracies and Felonies committed on the high Seas, and Offences against the Law of Nations;

To declare War, grant Letters of Marque and Reprisal, and make Rules concerning Captures on Land and Water;

To raise and support Armies, but no Appropriation of Money to that Use shall be for a longer Term than two Years;

To provide and maintain a Navy;

To make Rules for the Government and Regulation of the land and naval Forces;

To provide for calling forth the Militia to execute the Laws of the Union, suppress Insurrections and repel Invasions;

To provide for organizing, arming, and disciplining, the Militia, and for governing such Part of them as may be employed in the Service of the United States, reserving to the States respectively, the Appointment of the Officers, and the Authority of training the Militia according to the discipline prescribed by Congress;

To exercise exclusive Legislation in all Cases whatsoever, over such District (not exceeding ten Miles square) as may, by Cession of particular States, and the Acceptance of Congress, become the Seat of the Government of the United States, and to exercise like Authority over all Places purchased by the Consent of the Legislature of the State in which the Same shall be, for the Erection of Forts, Magazines, Arsenals, dockYards, and other needful Buildings;—And

To make all Laws which shall be necessary and proper for carrying into Execution the foregoing Powers, and all other Powers vested by this Constitution in the Government of the United States, or in any Department or Officer thereof.

Limitations on congressional power

Section 9. The Migration or Importation of such Persons as any of the States now existing shall think proper to admit, shall not be prohibited by the Congress prior to the year one thousand eight hundred and eight, but a Tax or duty may be imposed on such Importation, not exceeding ten dollars for each Person.

The Privilege of the Writ of Habeas Corpus shall not be suspended, unless when in Cases of Rebellion or Invasion the public Safety may require it.

No Bill of Attainder or ex post facto Law shall be passed.

No Capitation, or other direct, Tax shall be laid, unless in Proportion to the Census or Enumeration herein before directed to be taken.

No Tax or Duty shall be laid on Articles exported from any State.

No Preference shall be given by any Regulation of Commerce or Revenue to the Ports of one State over those of another; nor shall Vessels bound to, or from, one State, be obliged to enter, clear, or pay Duties in another.

No Money shall be drawn from the Treasury, but in Consequence of Appropriations made by Law; and a regular Statement and Account of the Receipts and Expenditures of all public Money shall be published from time to time.

No Title of Nobility shall be granted by the United States: And no Person holding any Office of Profit or Turst under them, shall, without the Consent of the Congress, accept of any present, Emolument, Office, or Title, of any kind whatever, from any King, Prince, or foreign State.

Limitations on powers of state

Section 10. No State shall enter into any Treaty, Alliance, or Confederation; grant Letters of Marque and Reprisal; coin Money; emit Bills of Credit; make any Thing but gold and silver Coin a Tender in Payment of Debts; pass any Bill of Attainder, ex post facto Law, or Law impairing the Obligation of Contracts, or grant any Title of Nobility.

No State shall, without the Consent of the Congress, lay any Imposts or Duties on Imports or Exports, except what may be absolutely necessary for executing its inspection Laws: and the net Produce of all Duties and Imposts, laid by any State on Imports or Exports, shall be fore the Use of the Treasury of the United States; and all such Laws shall be subject to the Revision and Controul of the Congress.

No State shall, without the Consent of Congress, lay any Duty of Tonnage, keep Troops, or Ships of War in time of Peace, enter into any Agreement or Compact with another State, or with a foreign Power, or engage in War, unless actually invaded, or in such imminent Danger as will not admit of delay.

ARTICLE II
The President

Electing the president

Section 1. The executive Power shall be vested in a President of the United States of America. He shall hold his Office during the Term of four Years, and, together with the Vice President, chosen for the same Term, be elected, as follows:

Each State shall appoint, in such Manner as the Legislature thereof may direct, a Number of Electors, equal to the whole Number of Senators and Representatives to which the State may be entitled in the Congress: but no Senator or Representative, or Person holding an Office of Trust or Profit under the United States, shall be appointed an Elector.

The Electors shall meet in their respective States, and vote by Ballot for two Persons, of whom one at least shall not be an Inhabitant of the same State with themselves. And they shall make a List of all the Persons voted for, and of the Number of Votes for each; which List they shall sign and certify, and transmit sealed to the Seat of the Government of the United States, directed to the President of the Senate. The President of the Senate shall, in the Presence of the Senate and House of Representatives, open all the Certificates, and the Votes shall then be counted. The Person having the greatest Number of Votes shall be the President, if such Number be a Majority of the whole Number of Electors appointed; and if there be more than one who have such Majority, and have an equal Number of Votes, then the House of Representatives shall immediately chuse by Ballot one of them for President; and if no Person have a Majority, then from the five highest on the List the said House shall in like Manner chuse the President. But in chusing the President, the Votes shall be taken by States, the Representation from each State having one Vote; A Quorum for this Purpose shall consist of a Member or Members from two thirds of the States, and a Majority of all the States shall be necessary to a Choice. In every Case, after the Choice of the President, the person having the greatest Number of Votes of the Electors shall be the Vice President. But if there should remain two or more who have equal Votes, the Senate shall chuse from them by Ballot the Vice President.

The Congress may determine the Time of chusing the Electors, and the Day on which they shall give their Votes; which Day shall be the same throughout the United States.

No Person except a natural born Citizen, or a Citizen of the United States, at the time of the Adoption of this Constitution, shall be eligible to the Office of President; neither shall any Person be eligible to that Office who shall not have attained to the Age of thirty five Years, and been fourteen Years a Resident within the United States.

In Case of the Removal of the President from Office, or of his Death, Resignation, or Inability to Discharge the Powers and Duties of the said Office, the Same shall devolve on the Vice President, and the Congress may by Law provide for the Case of Removal, Death, Resignation or Inability, both of the President and Vice President, declaring what Officer shall then act as president, and such Officer shall act accordingly, until the Disability be removed, or a President shall be elected.

The President shall, at stated Times, receive for his Services, a Compensation, which shall neither be encreased nor diminished during the Period for which he shall have been elected, and he shall not receive within that Period any other Emolument from the United States, or any of them.

Before he enter on the Execution of his Office, he shall take the following Oath or Affirmation:—"I do solemnly swear (or affirm) that I will faithfully execute the Office of President of the United States, and will to the best of my Ability, preserve, protect and defend the Constitution of the United States."

Powers and duties of the president

Section 2.   The President shall be Commander in Chief of the Army and Navy of the United States, and of the Militia of the several States, when called into the actual Service of the United States; he may require the Opinion, in writing, of the principal Officer in each of the executive Departments, upon any Subject relating to the Duties of their respective Offices, and he shall have Power to grant Reprieves and Pardons for Offences against the United States, except in Cases of Impeachment.

He shall have Power, by and with the Advice and Consent of the Senate, to make Treaties, provided two thirds of the Senators present concur; and he shall nominate, and by and with the Advice and Consent of the Senate, shall appoint Ambassadors, other public Ministers and Consuls, Judges of the supreme Court, and all other Officers of the United States, whose Appointments are not herein otherwise provided for, and which shall be established by Law: but the Congress may by Law vest the Appointment of such inferior Officers, as they think proper, in the President alone, in the Courts of Law, or in the Heads of Departments.

The President shall have Power to fill up all Vacancies that may happen during the Recess of the Senate, by granting Commissions which shall expire at the End of their next Session.

Section 3.   He shall from time to time give to the Congress Information of the State of the Union, and recommend to their Consideration such Measures as he shall judge necessary and expedient; he may, on extraordinary Occasions, convene both House, or either of them, and in Case of Disagreement between them, with Respect to the Time of Adjournment, he may adjourn them to such Time as he shall think proper; he shall receive Ambassadors and other public Ministers; he shall take Care that the Laws be faithfully executed, and shall Commission all of the Officers of the United States.

Section 4.   The President, Vice President and all civil Officers of the United States, shall be removed from Office on Impeachment for, and Conviction of, Treason, Bribery, or other high Crimes and Misdemeanors.

ARTICLE III
Federal Judiciary

Section 1.   The judicial Power of the United States, shall be vested in one supreme Court, and in such inferior Courts as the Congress may from time to time ordain and establish. The Judges, both of the supreme and inferior Courts, shall hold their Offices during good Behaviour, and shall, at stated Times, receive for their Services, a Compensation, which shall not be diminished during their Continuance in Office.

Section 2.   The judicial Power shall extend to all Cases, in Law and Equity, arising under this Constitution, the Laws of the United States, and Treaties made, or which shall be made, under their Authority;—to all Cases affecting Ambassadors, other public Ministers and Consuls;—to all Cases of admiralty and maritime Jurisdiction;—to Controversies to which the United States shall be a Party;—to Controversies between two or more States;—between a State and Citizens of another State;—between Citizens of different States,—between Citizens of the same State claiming Lands under Grants of different States, and between a State, or the Citizens thereof, and foreign States, Citizens or Subjects.

In all Cases affecting Ambassadors, other public Ministers and Consuls, and those in which a State shall be Party, the supreme Court shall have original Jurisdiction. In all the other Cases before mentioned, the supreme Court shall have appellate Jurisdiction, both as to Law and Fact, with such Exceptions, and under such Regulations as the Congress shall make.

The Trial of all Crimes, except in Cases of Impeachment, shall be by Jury; and such Trial shall be held in the State where the said Crimes shall have been committed; but when not committed within any

State, the Trial shall be at such Place or Places as the Congress may by Law have directed.

Section 3. Treason against the United States, shall consist only in levying War against them, or in adhering to their enemies, giving them Aid and Comfort. No Person shall be convicted of Treason unless on the Testimony of two Witnesses to the same overt Act, or on Confession in open Court.

The Congress shall have Power to declare the Punishment of Treason, but no Attainder of Treason shall work Corruption of Blood, or Forfeiture except during the Life of the Person attainted.

ARTICLE IV
Relations among the States

Section 1. Full Faith and Credit shall be given in each State to the public Acts, Records, and judicial Proceedings of every other State. And the Congress may by general Laws prescribe the Manner in which such Acts, Records, and Proceedings shall be proved, and the Effect thereof.

Section 2 The Citizens of each State shall be entitled to all Privileges and Immunities of Citizens in the several States.

A Person charged in any State with Treason, Felony, or other Crime, who shall flee from Justice, and be found in another State, shall on Demand of the executive Authority of the State from which he fled, be delivered up, to be removed to the State having Jurisdiction of the Crime.

No Person held to Service or Labour in one State, under the Laws thereof, escaping into another, shall, in Consequence of any Law or Regulation therein, be discharged from such Service or Labour, but shall be delivered up on Claim of the Party to whom such Service or Labour may be due.

Section 3. New States may be admitted by the Congress into this Union; but no new State shall be formed or erected within the Jurisdiction of any other State; nor any State be formed by the Junction of two or more States; or Parts of States, without the Consent of the Legislatures of the States concerned as well as of the Congress.

The Congress shall have Power to dispose of and make all needful Rules and Regulations respecting the Territory or other Property belonging to the United States; and nothing in this Constitution shall be so construed as to Prejudice any Claims of the United States, or of any particular State.

Section 4. The United States shall guarantee to every State in this Union a Republican Form of Government, and shall protect each of them against Invasion; and on Application of the Legislature, or of the Executive (when the Legislature cannot be convened) against domestic Violence.

ARTICLE V
Amending Procedures

The Congress, whenever two thirds of both Houses shall deem it necessary, shall propose Amendments to this Constitution, or, on the Application of the Legislatures of two thirds of the several States, shall call a Convention for proposing Amendments, which, in either Case, shall be valid to all Intents and Purposes, as part of this Constitution, when ratified by the Legislatures of three fourths of the several States, or by Conventions in three fourths thereof, as the one or the other Mode of Ratification may be proposed by the Congress; Provided that no Amendment which may be made prior to the Year One thousand eight hundred and eight shall in any Manner affect the first and fourth Clauses in the Ninth Section of the first Article; and that no State, without its Consent, shall be deprived of its equal Suffrage in the Senate.

ARTICLE VI
Supremacy Clause

All Debts contracted and Engagements entered into, before the Adoption of this Constitution, shall be as valid against the United States under this Constitution, as under the Confederation.

The Constitution, and the Laws of the United States which shall be made in Pursuance thereof; and all Treaties made, or which shall be made, under the Authority of the United States, shall be the supreme Law of the land; and the Judges in every State shall be bound thereby, any Thing in the Constitution or Laws of any State to the Contrary notwithstanding.

The Senators and Representatives before mentioned, and the Members of the several State Legislatures, and all executive and judicial Officers, both of the United States and of the several States, shall be bound by Oath or Affirmation, to support this Constitution; but no religious Test shall ever be required as a Qualification to any Office or public Trust under the United States.

ARTICLE VII
Ratifying the Constitution

The Ratification of the Conventions of nine States, shall be sufficient for the Establishment of this Constitution between the States so ratifying the Same.

Done in Convention by the Unanimous Consent of the States present the Seventeenth Day of September in the Year of our Lord one thousand seven hundred and Eighty seven and of the Independence of the United States of America the Twelfth IN WITNESS whereof We have hereunto subscribed our Names,

G°· Washington   Presid^t. and deputy from Virginia.

New Hampshire   John Langdon, Nicholas Gilman.
Massachusetts   Nathaniel Gorham, Rufus King.
Connecticut   Wm. Saml. Johnson, Roger Sherman.

New York	Alexander Hamilton.
New Jersey	Wil: Livingston, David Brearley, Wm. Paterson, Jona: Dayton.
Pennsylvania	B Franklin, Thomas Mifflin, Robᵗ Morris, Geo. Clymer, Thos. FitzSimons, Jared Ingersoll, James Wilson, Gouv Morris.
Delaware	Geo: Read, Gunning Bedford jun, John Dickinson, Richard Bassett, Jaco: Broom.
Maryland	James McHenry, Dan of Sᵗ Thos. Jenifer, Danˡ Carroll.
Virginia	John Blair—, James Madison Jr.
North Carolina	Wm. Blount, Rich'd Dobbs Spaight, Hu Williamson.
South Carolina	J. Rutledge, Charles Cotesworth Pinckney, Charles Pinckney, Pierce Butler.
Georgia	William Few, Abr Baldwin.

Attest: William Jackson, Secretary.

AMENDMENTS

[The first 10 Amendments, known as the Bill of Rights, were ratified on December 15, 1791.]

AMENDMENT I
No Religious Establishment; Freedom of Religion, Speech, Press, and Assembly

Congress shall make no law respecting an establishment of religion, or prohibiting the free exercise thereof; or abridging the freedom of speech, or of the press; or the right of the people peaceably to assemble, and to petition the Government for a redress of grievances.

AMENDMENT II
Right to Bear Arms

A well regulated Militia, being necessary to the security of a free State, the right of the people to keep and bear Arms, shall not be infringed.

AMENDMENT III
Quartering of Soldiers

No Soldier shall, in time of peace, be quartered in any house, without the consent of the Owner, nor in time of war, but in a manner to be prescribed by law.

AMENDMENT IV
Searches and Seizures

The right of the people to be secure in their persons, houses, papers, and effects, against unreasonable searches and seizures, shall not be violated, and no Warrants shall issue, but upon probable cause, supported by Oath or affirmation, and particularly describing the place to be searched and the persons or things to be seized.

AMENDMENT V
Grand Jury Indictments, Double Jeopardy, Self-Incrimination, Due Process, and Just Compensation

No person shall be held to answer for a capital, or otherwise infamous crime, unless on a presentiment or indictment of a Grand Jury, except in cases arising in the land or naval forces, or in the Militia, when in actual service in time of War or public danger, nor shall any person be subject for the same offence to be twice put in jeopardy of life or limb; nor shall be compelled in any criminal case to be a witness against himself, nor be deprived of life, liberty, or property, without due process of law; nor shall private property be taken for public use, without just compensation.

AMENDMENT VI
Fair Trials

In all criminal prosecutions, the accused shall enjoy the right to a speedy and public trial, by an impartial jury of the State and district wherein the crime shall have been committed, which district shall have been previously ascertained by law, and to be informed of the nature and cause of the accusation; to be confronted with the witnesses against him; to have compusory process for obtaining witnesses in his favor, and to have the Assistance of Counsel for his defence.

AMENDMENT VII
Jury Trials

In Suits at common law, where the value in controversy shall exceed twenty dollars, the right of trial by jury shall be preserved, and no fact tried by a jury, shall be otherwise reexamined in any Court of the United States, than according to the rules of the common law.

AMENDMENT VIII
No Excessive Bail or Cruel and Unusual Punishment

Excessive bail shall not be required, nor excessive fines imposed, nor cruel and unusual punishments inflicted.

AMENDMENT IX
Not an Exhaustive List of Rights

The enumeration in the Constitution, of certain rights, shall not be construed to deny or disparage others retained by the people.

AMENDMENT X
Reserved Powers

The powers not delegated to the United States by the Constitution, nor prohibited by it to the States, are reserved to the States respectively, or to the people.

AMENDMENT XI
Suits against States

[Ratified February 7, 1795]

The Judicial power of the United States shall not be construed to extend to any suit in law or equity, commenced or prosecuted against one of the United States by Citizens of another State, or by Citizens or Subjects of any Foreign State.

AMENDMENT XII
Separate Ballots for President and Vice President

[Ratified June 15, 1804]

The Electors shall meet in their respective states and vote by ballot for President and Vice-President, one of whom, at least, shall not be an inhabitant of the same state with themselves; they shall name in their ballots the person voted for as President, and in distinct ballots the person voted for as Vice-President, and they shall make distinct lists of all persons voted for as President, and of all persons voted for as Vice-president, and of the number of votes for each, which lists they shall sign and certify, and transmit sealed to the seat of the government of the United States, directed to the President of the Senate;- The President of the Senate shall, in the presence of the Senate and House of Representatives, open all the certificates and the votes shall then be counted;- The person having the greatest number of votes for President, shall be the President, if such number be a majority of the whole number of Electors appointed; and if no person have such majority, then from the persons having the highest numbers not exceeding three on the list of those voted for as President, the House of Representatives shall choose immediately, by ballot, the President. But in choosing the President, the votes shall be taken by states, the representation from each state having one vote; a quorum for this purpose shall consist of a member of members from two-thirds of the states, and a majority of all the states shall be necessary to a choice. And if the House of Represen-

tatives shall not choose a President whenever the right of the choice shall devolve upon them, before the fourth day of March next following, then the Vice-President shall act as President, as in the case of the death or other constitutional disability of the President. The person having the greatest number of votes as Vice-President, shall be the Vice-President, if such number be a majority of the whole number of Electors appointed, and if no person have a majority, then from the two highest numbers on the list, the Senate shall choose the Vice-President; a quorum for the purpose shall consist of two-thirds of the whole number of Senators, and a majority of the whole number shall be necessary to a choice. But no person constitutionally ineligible to the office of President shall be eligible to that of Vice-President of the United States.

AMENDMENT XIII
Abolition of Slavery

[Ratified December 6, 1865]

Section 1. Neither slavery nor involuntary servitude, except as a punishment for crime whereof the party shall have been duly convicted, shall exist within the United States, or any place subject to their jurisdiction. *Section 2.* Congress shall have power to enforce this article by appropriate legislation.

AMENDMENT XIV
Citizenship, Due Process, and Equal Protection

[Ratified July 9, 1868]

Section 1. All persons born or naturalized in the United States, and subject to the jurisdiction thereof, are citizens of the United States and of the State wherein they reside. No State shall make or enforce any law which shall abridge the privileges or immunities of citizens of the United States; nor shall any State deprive any person of life, liberty, or property, without due process of law; nor deny to any person within its jurisdiction the equal protection of the laws. *Section 2.* Representatives shall be apportioned among the several States according to their respective numbers, counting the whole number of persons in each State, excluding Indians not taxed. But when the right to vote at any election for the choice of electors for President and Vice president of the United States, Representatives in Congress, the Executive and Judicial Officers of a State, or the members of the Legislature thereof, is denied to any of the male inhabitants of such state, being twenty-one years of age, and citizens of the United States, or in any way abridged, except for participation in rebellion, or other crime, the basis of representation therein shall be reduced in the proportion which the number of such male citizens shall bear to the whole number of male citizens twenty-one years of age in such State. *Section 3.* No person shall be a Senator or Representative in Congress, or elector of President and Vice President, or hold any office, civil or military, under the United States, or under any State, who having previously taken an oath, as member of Congress, or as an officer of the United States, or as a member of any State legislature, or as an executive or judicial officer of any State, to support the Constitution of the United States, shall have engaged in insurrection or rebellion against the same, or given aid or comfort to the enemies thereof. But Congress may by a vote of two-thirds of each House, remove such disability.

Section 4. The validity of the public debt of the United States, authorized by law, including debts incurred for payment of pensions and bounties for services in suppressing insurrection or rebellion, shall not be questioned. But neither the United States nor any State shall assume or pay any debt obligation incurred in aid of insurrection or rebellion against the United States, or any claim for the loss or emancipation of any slave; but all such debts, obligations and claims shall be held illegal and void.

Section 5. The Congress shall have power to enforce, by appropriate legislation, the provisions of this article.

AMENDMENT XV
Voting Rights

[Ratified February 3, 1870]

Section 1. The right of citizens of the United States to vote shall not be denied or abridged by the United States or by any State on account of race, color, or previous condition of servitude.

Section 2. The Congress shall have power to enforce this article by appropriate legislation.

AMENDMENT XVI
Income Tax

[Ratified February 3, 1913]

The Congress shall have power to lay and collect taxes on incomes, from whatever source derived, without apportionment among the several States, and without regard to any census or enumeration.

AMENDMENT XVII
Direct Election of Senators

[Ratified April 8, 1913]

The Senate of the United States shall be composed of two Senators from each State, elected by the people thereof for six years; and each Senator shall have one vote. The electors in each State shall have the qualifications requisite for electors of the most numerous branch of the State legislatures.

When vacancies happen in the representation of any State in the Senate, the executive authority of such State shall issue writs of election to fill such vacancies: *Provided,* That the legislature of any State may empower the executive thereof to make temporary appointments until the people fill the vacancies by election as the legislature may direct.

This amendment shall not be so construed as to affect the election of term of any Senator chosen before it becomes valid as part of the Constitution.

AMENDMENT XVIII
Prohibition

[Ratified January 16, 1919]

Section 1. After one year from the ratification of this article the manufacture, sale, or transportation of intoxicating liquors within, the importation thereof into, or the exportation thereof from the United States and all territory subject to the jurisdiction thereof for beverage purposes is hereby prohibited.

Section 2. The Congress and the several States shall have concurrent power to enforce this article by appropriate legislation.

Section 3. This article shall be inoperative unless it shall have been ratified as an amendment to the Constitution by the legislatures of the several States, as provided in the Constitution, within seven years from the date of the submission hereof to the States by the Congress.

AMENDMENT XIX
Women's Suffrage

[Ratified August 18, 1920]

The right of citizens of the United States to vote shall not be denied or abridged by the United States or by any State on account of sex. Congress shall have power to enforce this article by appropriate legislation.

AMENDMENT XX
Lame Duck Amendment

[Ratified January 23, 1933]

Section 1. The terms of the President and Vice President shall end at noon on the 20th day of January, and the terms of Senators and Representatives at noon on the 3d of January, of the years in which such terms would have ended if this article had not been ratified; and the terms of their successors shall then begin.

Section 2. The Congress shall assemble at least once in every year, and such meeting shall begin at noon on the 3d day of January, unless they shall be law appoint a different day.

Section 3. If, at the time fixed for the beginning of the term of the President, the President elect shall have died, the Vice President elect shall become President. If a President shall not have been chosen before the time fixed for the beginning of his term, or if the President elect shall have failed to qualify, the Vice President elect shall act as President until a President shall have qualified; and the Congress may by law provide for the case wherein neither a President elect nor a Vice President elect shall have qualified, declaring who shall then act as President, or the manner in which one who is to act shall be selected, and such person shall act accordingly until a President or Vice President shall have qualified.

Section 4. The Congress may by law provide for the case of death of any of the persons from whom the House of Representatives may choose a President whenever the right of choice shall have devolved upon them, and for the case of the death of any of the persons from whom the Senate may choose a Vice President whenever the right of choice shall have devolved upon them.

Section 5. Sections 1 and 2 shall take effect on the 15th day of October following the ratification of this article.

Section 6. This article shall be inoperative unless it shall have been ratified as an amendment to the Constitution by the legislatures of three-fourths of the several States within seven years from the date of its submission.

AMENDMENT XXI
Repeal of Prohibition

[Ratified December 5, 1933]

Section 1. The eighteenth article of amendment to the Constitution of the United States is hereby repealed.

Section 2. The transportation or importation into any State, Territory, or possession of the United States for delivery or use therein of intoxicating liquors, in violation of the laws thereof, is hereby prohibited.

Section 3. This article shall be inoperative unless it shall have been ratified as an amendment to the Constitution by conventions in the several States, as provided in the Constitution, within seven years from the date of the submission hereof to the States by the Congress.

AMENDMENT XXII
Two-Term Limit on President

[Ratified February 27, 1951]

Section 1. No person shall be elected to the office of the President more than twice, and no person who has held the office of President, or acted as President for more than two years of a term to which some other person was elected President shall be elected to the office of the President more than once. But this Article shall not apply to any person holding the office of President when this Article was proposed by the Congress, and shall not prevent any person who may be holding the office of President, or acting as President, during the term within which this Article becomes operative from holding the office of President, or acting as President, during the remainder of such term.

Section 2. This article shall be inoperative unless it shall have been ratified as an amendment to the Constitution by the legislatures of three-fourths of the several States within seven years from the date of its submission to the States by the Congress.

AMENDMENT XXIII
Electors for the District of Columbia

[Ratified March 29, 1961]

Section 1. The District constituting the seat of Gov-

ernment of the United States shall appoint in such manner as the Congress may direct:

A number of electors of President and Vice President equal to the whole number of Senators and Representatives in Congress to which the District would be entitled if it were a State, but in no event more than the least populous State; they shall be in addition to those appointed by the States, but they shall be considered, for the purposes of the election of President and Vice President, to be electors appointed by a State; and they shall meet in the District and perform such duties as provided by the twelfth article of amendment.

Section 2. The Congress shall have power to enforce this article by appropriate legislation.

AMENDMENT XXIV
Anti-Poll Tax Amendment

[Ratified January 23, 1964]

Section 1. The right of citizens of the United States to vote in any primary or other election for President or Vice President, for electors for President or Vice President, or for Senator or Representative in Congress, shall not be denied or abridged by the United States or any State by reason of failure to pay any poll tax or other tax.

Section 2. The Congress shall have power to enforce this article by appropriate legislation.

AMENDMENT XXV
Presidential Disability

[Ratified February 10, 1967]

Section 1. In case of the removal of the President from office or of his death or resignation, the Vice President shall become President.

Section 2. Whenever there is a vacancy in the office of the Vice President, the President shall nominate a Vice President, who shall take office upon confirmation by a majority vote of both Houses of Congress.

Section 3. Whenever the President transmits to the President pro tempore of the Senate and the Speaker of the House of Representatives his written declaration that he is unable to discharge the powers and duties of his office, and until he transmits to them a written declaration to the contrary, such powers and duties shall be discharged by the Vice President as Acting President.

Section 4. Whenever the Vice President and a majority of either the principal officers of the executive departments or of such other body as Congress may by law provide, transmit to the president pro tempore of the Senate and the Speaker of the House of Representatives their written declaration that the President is unable to discharge the powers and duties of his office, the Vice president shall immediately assume the powers and duties of the office as Acting President.

Thereafter, when the President transmits to the President pro tempore of the Senate and the Speaker of the House of Representatives his written declaration that no inability exists, he shall resume the powers and duties of his office unless the Vice President and a majority of either the principal officers of the executive department or of such other body as Congress may by law provide, transmit within four days to the President pro tempore of the Senate and the Speaker of the House of Representatives their written declaration that the President is unable to discharge the powers and duties of his office. Thereupon Congress shall decide the issue, assembling within forty-eight hours for that purpose if not in session. If the Congress, within twenty-one days after receipt of the latter written declaration, or, if Congress is required to assemble, determines by two-thirds vote of both Houses that the President is unable to discharge the powers and duties of his office, the Vice President shall continue to discharge the same as Acting President; otherwise, the President shall resume the powers and duties of his office.

AMENDMENT XXVI
Eighteen-Year-Old Vote

[Ratified June 30, 1971]

Section 1.   The right of citizens of the United States, who are eighteen years of age or older, to vote shall not be denied or abridged by the United States or by any State on account of age.

Section 2.   The Congress shall have the power to enforce this article by appropriate legislation.

The Federalist No. 10
James Madison, 1787

TO THE PEOPLE OF THE STATE OF NEW YORK

Among the numerous advantages promised by a well-constructed union, none deserves to be more accurately developed than its tendency to break and control the violence of faction. The friend of popular governments, never finds himself so much alarmed for their character and fate, as when he contemplates their propensity to this dangerous vice. He will not fail, therefore, to set a due value on any plan which, without violating the principles to which he is attached, provides a proper cure for it. The instability, injustice, and confusion introduced into the public councils, have, in truth, been the mortal diseases under which popular governments have everywhere perished; as they continue to be the favourite and fruitful topics from which the adversaries to liberty derive their most specious declamations. The valuable improvements made by the American constitutions on the popular models, both ancient and modern, cannot certainly be too much admired; but it would be an unwarrantable partiality, to contend that they have as effectually obviated the danger on this side, as was wished and expected. Complaints are everywhere heard from our most considerate and virtuous citizens, equally the friends of public and private faith, and of public and personal liberty, that our governments are too unstable; that the public good is disregarded in the conflicts of rival parties; and that measures are too often decided, not according to the rules of justice, and the rights of the minor party, but by the superior force of an interested and overbearing majority. However anxiously we may wish that these complaints had no foundation, the evidence of known facts will not permit us to deny that they are in some degree true. It will be found, indeed, on a candid review of our situation, that some of the distresses under which we labour have been erroneously charged on the operation of our governments; but it will be found, at the same time, that other causes will not alone account for many of our heaviest misfortunes; and, particularly, for that prevailing and increasing distrust of public engagements, and alarm for private rights, which are echoed from one end of the continent to the other. These must be chiefly, if not wholly, effects of the unsteadiness and injustice, with which a factious spirit has tainted our public administrations.

By a faction, I understand a number of citizens, whether amounting to a majority or minority of the whole, who are united and actuated by some common impulse of passion, or of interest, adverse to the rights of other citizens, or to the permanent and aggregate interests of the community.

There are two methods of curing the mischiefs of faction: The one, by removing its causes; the other, by controlling its effects.

There are again two methods of removing the causes of faction: The one, by destroying the liberty which is essential to its existence; the other, by giving to every citizen the same opinions, the same passions, and the same interests.

It could never be more truly said, than of the first remedy, that it was worse than the disease. Liberty is to faction what air is to fire, an aliment without which it instantly expires. But it could not be a less folly to abolish liberty, which is essential to political life, because it nourishes faction, than it would be to wish the annihilation of air, which is essential to animal life, because it imparts to fire its destructive agency.

The second expedient is as impracticable, as the first would be unwise. As long as the reason of man continues fallible, and he is at liberty to exercise it, different opinions will be formed. As long as the connection subsists between his reason and his self-love, his opinions and his passions will have a reciprocal influence on each other; and the former will be objects to which the latter will attach themselves. The diversity in the faculties of men, from which the rights of property originate, is not less an insuperable obstacle to an uniformity of interests. The protection of these faculties is the first object of government. From the protection of different and unequal faculties of acquiring property, the possession of different degrees of kinds of property immediately results; and from the influence of these on the sentiments and views of the respective proprietors, ensues a division of the society into different interests and parties.

The latent causes of action are thus sown in the nature of man; and we see them everywhere brought into different degrees of activity, according to the different circumstances of civil society. A zeal for different opinions concerning religion, concerning government, and many other points, as well of speculation as of practice; an attachment to different leaders ambitiously contending for preeminence and power; or to persons of other descriptions whose fortunes have been interesting to the human passions, have, in turn, divided mankind into parties, inflamed them with mutual animosity, and rendered them much more disposed to vex and oppress each other, than to cooperate for their common good. So strong is this propensity of mankind, to fall into mutual animosities, that where no substantial occasion presents itself, the most frivolous and fanciful distinctions have been sufficient to kindle their unfriendly passions and excite their most violent conflicts. But the most common and durable source of factions, has been the various and unequal distribution of property. Those who hold, and those who are without property, have ever formed distinct interests in society. Those who are creditors, and those who are debtors, fall under a like discrimination. A landed interest, a manufacturing interest, a mercantile interest, a moneyed interest, with many lesser interests, grow up of necessity in civilized nations, and divide them into different classes, actuated by different sentiments and views. The regulation of these various and interfering interests form the principal task of modern legislation, and involves the spirit of the party and faction in the necessary and ordinary operations of the government.

No man is allowed to be a judge in his own cause; because his interest will certainly bias his judgment, and, not improbably, corrupt his integrity. With equal, nay, with greater reason, a body of men are unfit to be both judges and parties at the same time; yet what are many of the most important acts of legislation, but so many judicial determinations, not indeed concerning the right of single persons, but concerning the rights of large bodies of citizens? And what are the different classes of legislators, but advocates and parties to the causes which they determine? Is a law proposed concerning private debts? It is a question to which the creditors are parties on one side, and the debtors on the other. Justice ought to hold the balance between them. Yet the parties are, and must be, themselves the judges; and the most numerous party, or, in other words, the most powerful faction, must be expected to prevail. Shall domestic manufactures be encouraged, and in what degree, by restrictions on foreign manufactures? are questions which would be differently decided by the landed and the manufacturing classes; and probably by neither with a sole regard to justice and the public good. The apportionment of taxes, on the various descriptions of property, is an act which seems to require the most exact impartiality; yet there is, perhaps, no legislative act, in which greater opportunity and temptation are given to a predominant party to trample on the rules of justice. Every shilling, with which they overburden the inferior number, is a shilling saved to their own pockets.

It is in vain to say, that enlightened statesmen will be able to adjust these clashing interests, and render them all subservient to the public good. Enlightened statesmen will not always be at the helm: nor, in many cases, can such an adjustment be made at all, without taking into view indirect and remote considerations, which will rarely prevail over the immediate interest which one party may find in disregarding the rights of another, or the good of the whole.

The inference to which we are brought is, that the *causes* of faction cannot be removed; and that relief is only to be sought in the means of controlling its *effects*.

If a faction consists of less than a majority, relief is supplied by the republican principle, which enables the majority to defeat its sinister views, by regular vote. It may clog the administration, it may convulse the society; but it will be unable to execute and mask its violence under the forms of the constitution. When a majority is included in a faction, the form of popular government, on the other hand, enables it to sacrifice to its ruling passion or interest, both the public good and the rights of other citizens. To secure the public good, and private rights, against the danger of such a faction, and at the same time to preserve the spirit and the form of popular government, is then the great object to which our inquiries are directed.

Let me add, that it is the great desideratum, by which alone this form of government can be rescued from the opprobrium under which it has so long laboured, and be recommended to the esteem and adoption of mankind.

By what means is this object attainable? Evidently by one of two only. Either the existence of the same passion or interest in a majority, at the same time, must be prevented; or the majority, having such coexistent passion or interest, must be rendered, by their number and local situation, unable to concert and carry into effect schemes of oppression. If the impulse and the opportunity be suffered to coincide, we well know that neither moral nor religious motives can be relied on as an adequate control. They are not found to be such on the injustice and violence of individuals, and lose their efficacy in proportion to the number combined together; that is, in proportion as their efficacy becomes needful.

From this view of the subject, it may be concluded, that a pure democracy, by which I mean a society consisting of a small number of citizens, who assemble and administer the government in person, can admit of no cure for the mischiefs of faction. A common passion or interest will, in almost every case, be felt by a majority of the whole; a communication and concert, results from the form of government itself; and there is nothing to check the inducements to sacrifice the weaker party, or an obnoxious individual. Hence, it is, that such democracies have ever been spectacles of turbulence and contention; have ever been found incompatible with personal security, or the rights of property; and have in general been as short in their lives, as they have been violent in their deaths. Theoretic politicians, who have patronized this species of government, have erroneously supposed, that by reducing mankind to a perfect equality in their political rights, they would, at the same time, be perfectly equalized and assimilated in their possessions, their opinions, and their passions.

A republic, by which I mean a government in which the scheme of representation takes place, opens a different prospect, and promises the cure for which we are seeking. Let us examine the points in which it varies from pure democracy, and we shall comprehend both the nature of the cure and the efficacy which it must derive from the union.

The two great points of difference, between a democracy and a republic, are, first, the delegation of the government, in the latter, to a small number of citizens, elected by the rest; secondly, the greater number of citizens, and greater sphere of country, over which the latter may be extended.

The effect of the first difference is, on the one hand, to refine and enlarge the public views, by passing them through the medium of a chosen body of citizens, whose wisdom may best discern the true interest of their country, and whose patriotism and love of justice, will be least likely to sacrifice it to temporary or partial considerations. Under such a regulation, it may well happen, that the public voice, pronounced by the representatives of the people, will be more consonant to the public good, than if pronounced by the people themselves, convened for the purpose. On the other hand the effect may be inverted. Men of factious tempers, of local prejudices, or of sinister designs, may by intrigue, by corruption, or by other means, first obtain the suffrages, and then betray the interest of the people. The question resulting is, whether small or extensive republics are most favourable to the election of proper guardians of the public weal; and it is clearly decided in favour of the latter by two obvious considerations.

In the first place, it is to be remarked that, however small the republic may be, the representatives must be raised to a certain number, in order to guard against the cabals of a few; and that however large it may be, they must be limited to a certain number, in order to guard against the confusion of a multitude. Hence, the number of representatives in the two cases not being in proportion to that of the constituents, and being proportionally greatest in the small republic, it follows, that if the proportion of fit characters be not less in the large than in the small republic, the former will present a greater option, and consequently a greater probability of a fit choice.

In the next place, as each representative will be chosen by a greater number of citizens in the large than in the small republic, it will be more difficult for unworthy candidates to practise with success the vicious arts, by which elections are too often carried; and the suffrages of the people being more free, will be more likely to centre in men who possess the most attractive merit, and the most diffusive and established characters.

It must be confessed, that in this, as in most other cases, there is a mean, on both sides of which inconveniences will be found to lie. By enlarging too much the number of electors, you render the representatives too little acquainted with all their local circumstances and lesser interests; as by reducing it too much, you render him unduly attached to these, and too little fit to comprehend and pursue great and national objects. The federal constitution forms a happy combination in this respect; the great and aggregate interests being referred to the national, the local and particular to the state legislatures.

The other point of difference is, the greater number of citizens, and extent of territory, which may be brought within the compass of republican, than of democratic government; and it is this circumstance principally which renders factious

608

The Federalist
No. 10

combinations less to be dreaded in the former, than in the latter. The smaller the society, the fewer probably will be the distinct parties and interests composing it; the fewer the distinct parties and interests, the more frequently will a majority be found of the same party; and the smaller the number of individuals composing a majority, and the smaller the compass within which they are placed, the more easily will they concert and execute their plans of oppression. Extend the sphere, and you take in a greater variety of parties and interests; you make it less probable that a majority of the whole will have a common motive to invade the rights of other citizens; or if such a common motive exists, it will be more difficult for all who feel it to discover their own strength, and to act in unison with each other. Besides other impediments, it may be remarked, that where there is a consciousness of unjust or dishonourable purposes, communication is always checked by distrust, in proportion to the number whose concurrence is necessary.

Hence, it clearly appears, that the same advantage, which a republic has over a democracy, in controlling the effects of faction, is enjoyed by a large over a small republic,—is enjoyed by the union over the states composing it. Does this advantage consist in the substitution of representatives, whose enlightened views and virtuous sentiments render them superior to local prejudices, and to schemes of injustice? It will not be denied that the representation of the union will be most likely to possess these requisite endowments. Does it consist in the greater security

afforded by a greater variety of parties, against the event of any one party being able to outnumber and oppress the rest? In an equal degree does the increased variety of parties, comprised within the union, increase the security? Does it, in fine, consist in the greater obstacles opposed to the concert and accomplishment of the secret wishes of an unjust and interested majority? Here, again, the extent of the union gives it the most palpable advantage.

The influence of factious leaders may kindle a flame within their particular states, but will be unable to spread a general conflagration through the other states; a religious sect may degenerate into a political faction in a part of the confederacy; but the variety of sects dispersed over the entire face of it, must secure the national councils against any danger from that source: a rage for paper money, for an abolition of debts, for an equal division of property, or for any other improper or wicked project, will be less apt to pervade the whole body of the union than a particular member of it; in the same proportion as such a malady is more likely to taint a particular county or district, than an entire state.

In the extent and proper structure of the union, therefore, we behold a republican remedy for the diseases most incident to republican government. And according to the degree of pleasure and pride we feel in being republicans, ought to be our zeal in cherishing the spirit, and supporting the character of federalists.

PUBLIUS

The Federalist No. 51
James Madison, 1788

To what expedient then shall we finally resort for maintaining in practice the necessary partition of power among the several departments, as laid down in the constitution? The only answer that can be given is, that as all these exterior provisions are found to be inadequate, the defect must be supplied, by so contriving the interior structure of the government, as that its several constituent parts may, by their mutual relations, be the means of keeping each other in their proper places. Without presuming to undertake a full development of this important idea, I will hazard a few general observations, which may perhaps place it in a clearer light, and enable us to form a more correct judgment of the principles and structure of the government planned by the convention.

In order to lay a due foundation for that separate and distinct exercise of the different powers of government, which to a certain extent, is admitted on all hands to be essential to the preservation of liberty, it is evident that each department should have a will of its own; and consequently should be so constituted, that the members of each should have as little agency as possible in the appointment of the members of the others. Were this principle rigorously adhered to, it would require that all the appointments for the supreme executive, legislative, and judiciary magistracies, should be drawn from the same fountain of authority, the people, through channels, having no communication whatever with one another. Perhaps such a plan of constructing the several departments would be less difficult in practice than it may in contemplation appear. Some difficulties however, and some additional expense, would attend the execution of it. Some deviations therefore from the principle must be admitted. In the constitution of the judiciary department in particular, it might be inexpedient to insist rigorously on the principle; first, because peculiar qualifications being essential in the members, the primary consideration ought to be to select that mode of choice, which best secures these qualifications; secondly, because the permanent tenure by which the appointments are held in that department, must soon destroy all sense of dependence on the authority conferring them.

It is equally evident that the members of each department should be as little dependent as possible on those of the others, for the emoluments annexed to their offices. Were the executive magistrate, or the judges, not independent of the legislature in this particular, their independence in every other would be merely nominal.

But the great security against a gradual concentration of the several powers in the same department, consists in giving to those who administer each department, the necessary constitutional means, and personal motives, to resist encroachments of the others. The provision for defense must in this, as in all other cases, be made commensurate to the danger of attack. Ambition must be made to counteract ambition. The interest of the man must be connected with the constitutional rights of the place. It may be a reflection on human nature, that such devices should be necessary to control the abuses of government. But what is government itself but the greatest of all reflections on human nature? If men were angels, no government would be necessary. If angels were to govern men, neither external nor internal controls on government would be necessary. In framing a government which is to be administered by men over men, the great difficulty lies in this: You must first enable the government to control the governed; and in the next place, oblige it to control itself. A dependence on the people is no doubt the primary control on the government; but experience has taught mankind the necessity of auxiliary precautions.

This policy of supplying by opposite and rival interests, the defect of better motives, might be traced through the whole system of human affairs, private as well as public. We see it particularly displayed in all the subordinate distributions of power; where the constant aim is to divide and arrange the several offices in such a manner as that each may be a check on the other; that the private interest of every individual, may be a sentinel over the public rights. These inventions of prudence cannot be less requisite in the distribution of the supreme powers of the state.

But it is not possible to give to each department an equal power of self defense. In republican government the legislative authority, necessarily, predominates. The remedy for this inconveniency is, to divide the legislature into different branches; and to render them by different modes of election, and different principles of action, as little connected with each other, as the nature of their common functions, and their common dependence on the society, will admit. It may even be necessary to guard against dangerous encroachments by still further precautions. As the weight of the legislative authority requires that it should be thus divided, the weakness of the executive may require, on the other hand, that it should be fortified. An absolute negative, on the legislature, appears at first view to be the natural defense with which the executive magistrate should be armed. But perhaps it would be neither altogether safe, nor alone sufficient. On ordinary occasions, it might not be exerted with the requisite firmness; and on extraordinary occasions, it might be perfidiously abused. May not this defect of an absolute negative be supplied, by some qualified connection between this weaker department, and the weaker branch of the stronger department, by which the latter may be led to support the constitutional rights of the former, without being too much detached from the rights of its own department?

If the principles on which these observations are founded be just, as I persuade myself they are, and they be applied as a criterion, to the several state constitutions, and to the federal constitution, it will be found, that if the latter does not perfectly correspond with them, the former are infinitely less able to bear such a test.

There are moreover two considerations particularly applicable to the federal system of America, which place that system in a very interesting point of view.

First. In a single republic, all the power surrendered by the people, is submitted to the administration of a single government; and usurpations are guarded against by a division of the government into distinct and separate departments. In the compound republic of America, the power surrendered by the people, is first divided between two distinct governments, and then the portion allotted to each, subdivided among distinct and separate departments. Hence a double security arises to the rights of the people. The different governments will control each other; at the same time that each will be controlled by itself.

Second. It is of great importance in a republic, not only to guard the society against the oppression of its rulers; but to guard one part of the society against the injustice of the other part. Different interests necessarily exist in different classes of citizens. If a majority be united by a common interest, the rights of the minority will be insecure. There are but two methods of providing against this evil: The one by creating a will in the community independent of the majority, that is, of the society itself, the other by comprehending in the society so many separate descriptions of citizens, as will render an unjust combination of a majority of the whole, very improbable, if not impracticable. The first method prevails in all governments possessing an hereditary or self appointed authority. This at best is but a precarious security; because of power independent of the society may as well espouse the unjust views of the major, as the rightful interests, of the minor party, and may possibly be turned against both parties. The second method will be exemplified in the federal republic of the United States. While all authority in it will be derived from and dependent on the society, the society itself will be broken into so many parts, interests and classes of citizens, that the rights of individuals or of the minority, will be in little danger from interested combinations of the majority. In a free government, the security for civil rights must be the same as for religious rights. It consists in the one case in the multiplicity of interests, and in the other, in the multiplicity of sects. The degree of security in both cases will depend on the number of interests and sects; and this may be presumed to depend on the extent of country and number of people comprehended under the same government. This view of the subject must particularly recommend a proper federal system to all the sincere and considerate friends of republican government: Since it shows that in exact proportion as the territory of the union may be formed into more circumscribed confederacies or states, oppressive combinations of a majority will be facilitated, the best security under the republican form, for the rights of every class of citizens, will be diminished; and consequently, the stability and independence of some member of the government, the only other security, must be proportionally increased. Justice is the end of government. It is the end of civil society. It ever has been, and ever will be pursued, until it be obtained, or until liberty be lost in the pursuit. In a society under the forms of which the stronger faction can readily unite and oppress the weaker, anarchy may as truly be said to reign, as in a state of nature where the weaker individual is not secured against the violence of the stronger: And as in the latter state even the stronger individuals are prompted by the uncertainty of their condition, to submit to a government which may protect the weak as well as themselves: So in the former state, will the more powerful factions or parties be gradually induced by a like motive, to wish for a government which will protect all parties, the weaker as well as the more powerful. It can be little doubted, that if the state of Rhode Island was separated from the confederacy, and left to itself, the insecurity of rights under the popular form of government within such narrow limits, would be displayed by such reiterated oppressions of factious majorities, that some power altogether independent of the people would soon be called for by the voice of the very factions whose misrule had proved the necessity of it. In the extended republic of the United States, and among the great variety of interests, parties and sects which it embraces, a coalition of a majority of the whole society could seldom take place on any other principles than those of justice and the general good; and there being thus less danger to a minor from the will of the major party, there must be less pretext also, to provide for the security of the former, by introducing into the government a will not dependent on the latter; or in other words, a will independent of the society itself. It is no less certain than it is important, notwithstanding the contrary opinions which have been entertained, that the larger the society, provided it lie within a practicable sphere, the more duly capable it will be of self government. And happily for the *republican cause,* the practicable sphere may be carried to a very great extent, by a judicious modification and mixture of the *federal principle.*

PUBLIUS

Presidents of the United States

Year	President	Party	Vote	Electoral Vote	Percentage of Popular Vote
1789	George Washington	no designation		69	
1792	George Washington	no designation		132	
1796	John Adams	Federalist		71	
1800	Thomas Jefferson	Democratic-Republican		73	
1804	Thomas Jefferson	Democratic-Republican		162	
1808	James Madison	Democratic-Republican		122	
1812	James Madison	Democratic-Republican		128	
1816	James Monroe	Democratic-Republican		183	
1820	James Monroe	Democratic-Republican		231	
1824	John Quincy Adams	Democratic-Republican	108,740	84	30.5
1828	Andrew Jackson	Democratic	647,286	178	56.0
1832	Andrew Jackson	Democratic	687,502	219	55.0
1836	Martin Van Buren	Democratic	765,483	170	50.9
1840	William H. Harrison	Whig	1,274,624	234	53.1
1841	John Tyler*	Whig			
1844	James K. Polk	Democratic	1,338,464	170	49.6
1848	Zachary Taylor	Whig	1,360,967	163	47.4
1850	Millard Fillmore*	Whig			
1852	Franklin Pierce	Democratic	1,601,117	254	50.9
1856	James Buchanan	Democratic	1,832,955	174	45.3
1860	Abraham Lincoln	Republican	1,865,593	180	39.8
1864	Abraham Lincoln	Republican	2,206,938	212	55.0
1865	Andrew Johnson*	Democratic			
1868	Ulysses S. Grant	Republican	3,013,421	214	52.7
1872	Ulysses S. Grant	Republican	3,596,745	286	55.6
1876	Rutherford B. Hayes	Republican	4,036,572	185	48.0
1880	James A. Garfield	Republican	4,453,295	214	48.5
1881	Chester A. Arthur*	Republican			
1884	Grover Cleveland	Democratic	4,879,507	219	48.5
1888	Benjamin Harrison	Republican	5,447,129	233	47.9
1892	Grover Cleveland	Democratic	5,555,426	277	46.1
1896	William McKinley	Republican	7,102,246	271	51.1
1900	William McKinley	Republican	7,218,491	292	51.7
1901	Theodore Roosevelt*	Republican			
1904	Theodore Roosevelt	Republican	7,628,461	336	57.4
1908	William H. Taft	Republican	7,675,320	321	51.6
1912	Woodrow Wilson	Democratic	6,296,547	435	41.9
1916	Woodrow Wilson	Democratic	9,127,695	277	49.4
1920	Warren G. Harding	Republican	16,143,407	404	60.4
1923	Calvin Coolidge*	Republican			
1924	Calvin Coolidge	Republican	15,718,211	382	54.0
1928	Herbert C. Hoover	Republican	21,391,993	444	58.2
1932	Franklin D. Roosevelt	Democratic	22,809,638	472	57.4
1936	Franklin D. Roosevelt	Democratic	27,752,869	523	60.8
1940	Franklin D. Roosevelt	Democratic	27,307,819	449	54.8
1944	Franklin D. Roosevelt	Democratic	25,606,585	432	53.5
1945	Harry S. Truman*	Democratic			
1948	Harry S. Truman	Democratic	24,105,812	303	49.5
1952	Dwight D. Eisenhower	Republican	33,936,234	442	55.1
1956	Dwight D. Eisenhower	Republican	35,590,472	457	57.6
1960	John F. Kennedy	Democratic	34,227,096	303	49.9
1963	Lyndon B. Johnson*	Democratic			
1964	Lyndon B. Johnson	Democratic	43,126,506	486	61.1
1968	Richard M. Nixon	Republican	31,785,480	301	43.4
1972	Richard M. Nixon	Republican	47,169,905	520	60.7
1974	Gerald R. Ford†	Republican			
1976	Jimmy Carter	Democratic	40,827,394	297	50.0
1980	Ronald Reagan	Republican	43,899,248	489	50.0
1984	Ronald Reagan	Republican	54,450,603	525	58.8
1988	George Bush	Republican	47,946,422	426	53.9

*Succeeded to presidency upon death of the incumbent.
†Succeeded to presidency upon resignation of the incumbent.

Glossary

Absorption The view that the Fourteenth Amendment "absorbs" or assimilates those provisions in the Bill of Rights that are "of the essence of a scheme of ordered liberty." Also called **selective incorporation**. **140**

Actual malice The burden that any public figure must assume in suing someone for libel or slander; it means that he or she must prove that the speech in question was not only false and defamatory but made with the knowledge that it was false or in "reckless disregard" of its accuracy. **93**

Affirmative action Discriminating in favor of women or minorities in hiring or in admitting to training or education programs in order to make up for past discrimination against them. **103**

Air Force Intelligence Agency that operates the spy satellites that give us vital information about Soviet missile sites and other installations. **537**

Amendments Additions to the U.S. Constitution; there are 26 in all. **40**

Amici curiae "Friends of the court," individuals not officially parties to a lawsuit but who are concerned about the outcome of the case and submit arguments for one side or the other. **307**

Anarchy The absence of government. **6**

Aristocracy Literally, "rule by the best"; historically it has meant rule by a hereditary elite. **15**

Articles of Confederation The United States' first national charter; replaced by the Constitution in 1789. **25**

Attitude A general outlook or perspective on social policies. **335**

Authoritarianism A system of government that severely limits freedom but does not extinguish it. **15, 552**

Bandwagon effect The supposed effect of polls in influencing people to vote for perceived winners and to desert losers. **354**

Berlin airlift An airlift of food and other necessities to West Berlin in 1948 to counter a Soviet blockade of the city. **548**

Bicameralism A legislative system that requires the approval of two houses or chambers. **166**

Bill of Rights First 10 amendments to the Constitution, which restrain government and protect rights. **43**

Bipartisanship Cooperation and friendship across party lines in Congress. **194**

Black Codes Laws that severely limited the rights of the newly freed slaves: preventing them in most states from testifying in court against whites, limiting their opportunities to find work, and relegating them to the status of second- or third-class citizens. **106**

Block grants Federal grants to states or localities for services in broad program areas. **66**

Bread-and-butter issues Issues that involve the question of who gets what, when, and how. **397**

Briefs A summary of the written arguments in a judicial case. **306**

Brokered conventions Conventions in which the presidential candidate is selected by negotiation between party leaders controlling blocs of delegates. **447**

Bureaucrat An unelected administrator or public servant charged with implementing the laws. **269**

Bureaus Working agencies of the government. **271**

Cabinet Group of 14 secretaries, answerable to the president, who head major departments of the federal government. **270**

Categorical grants Federal grants to states or localities for a specifically described category of services. **66**

Caucus A conference of party members in Congress. A small meeting of party leaders, usually officeholders. **200, 433**

Central Intelligence Agency (CIA) An organization established in 1947 to gather and analyze information about other countries and to perform such "other functions and duties" as the National Security Council directs. **537**

Chair The head of a congressional committee or subcommittee; the chair is always selected from the majority party. **170**

Checks and balances A system designed to protect liberty by giving the three branches of government—executive, legislative, and judicial—partial control over the others. **39**

Civil rights Positive acts of government designed to protect people against arbitrary or discriminatory treatment by government or individuals. **106**

Civil Rights Act of 1964 First major civil rights statute passed in the 1960s; it desegregated public accommodations and banned employment discrimination. **109**

Civil Rights Act of 1968 A statute that outlaws racial discrimination in housing. **109**

Civil War Amendments Thirteenth, Fourteenth, and Fifteenth Amendments to the U.S. Constitution; enacted during or shortly after the Civil War; guarantee basic rights to blacks. **47**

Classical liberals In the nineteenth century, those who favored as little government intervention as possible. **345**

Clear and present danger Formula used by Justice Oliver Wendell Holmes, Jr., in *Schenck v. United States* (1919) that allows the government to punish speech which incites unlawful acts. **80**

Closed rule Decision by the House Rules Committee that a bill may not be amended on the House floor. (See **open rule**) **172**

Cloture A procedure for ending a filibuster and bringing a bill to a floor vote in the Senate; if three-fifths of the Senate votes to end debate, speakers are then allowed only one hour on the floor. **175**

Coercion The use of force. **6**

Cold war Term used to denote a state of hostility, short of direct military conflict, between Communist countries and the West. **548**

Commerce clause Clause in Article I, Section 8, of the Constitution that authorizes Congress to "regulate Commerce with foreign Nations, and among the several States, and with the Indian Tribes." **64**

Committee of the Whole An agreement by the House of Representatives to consider itself a committee for purposes of discussing a bill or some other matter; this permits the House to relax its parliamentary rules a bit and thus to expedite the discussion. **173**

Committee on the Present Danger A pressure group founded in 1976 that argues that American policymakers need to take more seriously security threats to the United States. **539**

Common Cause A self-styled citizens' action lobby, which claims to represent the public interest. **401**

Comparable worth A strategy for mandating equal pay for "comparable" jobs; measured in terms of effort, skill, degree of responsibility, and other qualities. **123**

Competitive party system A political system in which no single party dominates elections or can be assured of victory in all of them. **427**

Concurrent powers Powers shared by both federal and state governments, such as road building and the punishment of lawbreakers. **55**

Concurring opinions Occurs when a member or members of the Supreme Court agree with the Court's ruling but disagree with the reasons for it. **307**

Confederation A loose association or "compact" of states over which the central government has no coercive powers. **54**

Conference committee A joint House-Senate committee that meets to iron out differences between House and Senate versions of a bill. **164, 175**

Conflicts of interest Situations in which the personal interests of lawmakers may influence their decisions and tempt them to subordinate the public interest to personal profit. **417**

Congressional oversight Congress's responsibility to see how well the executive branch is carrying out the laws passed by Congress. **183**

Connecticut Compromise A compromise worked out at the Constitutional Convention of 1787 in which one house of Congress was to represent states in proportion to their population and the other house would provide two senators for each state regardless of population. **26**

Consensus A viewpoint or assumption that is very widely shared. **20**

Constituency service The practice, common in the House and Senate, of helping out people in home districts or states in various ways; for example, investigating complaints against some agency of the federal government, cutting bureaucratic red tape, helping to get sons or daughters of constituents into West Point or the Naval Academy. **180**

Constitutional democracy Majority rule, but with limitations on the power of the majority and protections for the rights of minorities. **16**

Contracting out The practice, common in the federal government, of turning over work to private agencies and paying them to do it. **277**

Convention system A method of nominating presidential candidates by gathering together party officials from throughout the nation. **433**

Core values Basic commitments to moral positions. **335**

Counterforce A strategy targeting nuclear missiles on the adversary's missile sites. **577**

Countervalue A strategy targeting nuclear missiles on the adversary's cities. **577**

Court of Claims A federal court that hears suits for damages brought against the federal government by private individuals and companies. **305**

Court of Customs and Patent Appeals A federal court which hears appeals from the Court of International Trade, the U.S. Patent Office, and the U.S. Tariff Commission. **305**

Court of International Trade A federal court that decides cases involving tariffs. **305**

Court of Military Appeals A special legislative court set up by Congress to hear appeals from military tribunals. **305**

Critical election An election in which key voting groups enter or leave a party and form a victorious coalition that lasts for many years. Also called **realigning election**. **465**

Cruise missiles Tiny pilotless jet-powered vehicles with warheads that are launched from bombers. **581**

***De facto* segregation** Segregation "in fact," resulting from the decisions of people, not from any legal requirement. **107**

***De jure* segregation** Segregation required by law. **107**

Dealignment General voter dissatisfaction with both political parties. **471**

Deist One who believes that God wound up the universe like a clock, then let it run by its own mechanical laws; the belief was fashionable among intellectuals in the 18th century. **96**

Delegated powers Powers explicitly given to the federal government by the Constitution. **55**

Democratic-Republican party See **Jeffersonian Republican**. **427**

Demographic characteristics Social characteristics such as age, race, income, occupation, and gender. **464**

Departments Each is headed by a secretary (except the Justice Department, which is headed by the Attorney General); the 14 make up the cabinet. **270**

Desegregation The abolition of state-imposed separation of the races. **115**

Détente Literally, "relaxation of tensions": a search for a less hostile relationship with the Soviets; begun under President Nixon in the 1970s. **550**

Deterrence Defense theory based on the premise that other countries will not attack the United States if they are certain that we will respond militarily. **574**

Direct democracy Rule by the majority in which the people themselves, not elected representatives, make laws. **10**

Direction Describes the position of an opinion along a political ideology scale of "Left" to "Right." **334**

Discharge petition A device for getting a bill dislodged from a committee; if a majority of the House sign such a petition and if the majority then votes to consider the bill, it is taken from the committee and brought up for a vote in the House. **171**

Disclosure requirements The legal requirement that lobbyists must reveal their interests, the names of their clients, and their expenditures. **417**

District courts One of the first levels of the federal judiciary, where federal cases are usually tried in the first instance. **304**

Economic and Social Council An organ of the United Nations that is authorized to pass resolutions addressing the presumed causes of world tension, including poverty and social injustice. **541**

Economic individualism The belief that individual effort is what gives people the right to wealth. **338**

Elastic clause Last clause of Article I, Section 8, of the Constitution, which authorizes Congress to "make all Laws which shall be necessary and proper for carrying into Execution" the powers of the federal government. Also called **implied powers clause**. **61**

Electoral college The collectivity of electoral votes from the various states and the District of Columbia; a majority of electoral votes determines who the next president and vice president will be. **474**

Entitlement programs Programs in which the federal government is obligated to pay benefits to applicants who meet criteria set by law. **508**

Equal Pay Act of 1963 Statute banning pay discrimination based upon gender. **123**

Equal Rights Amendment (ERA) A proposed constitutional amendment stating that equality of rights may not be abridged because of sex; proposed by Congress in 1972, it failed to win the necessary ratification by three-fourths of the state legislatures. **121**

Equality of condition The notion that people are entitled to an equal share, regardless of effort or output. **338**

Equality of opportunity The equal right of each individual to better his or her lot in life. **338**

Ethics in Government Act of 1978 A law that requires all federal policymakers and judges to disclose their outside incomes and forbids (for a period of one year) all former federal executives from representing clients before the federal agency for which they had worked. **418**

Exclusionary rule Judge-made rule that evidence seized through illegal searches and seizures or coerced confessions may not be used against a defendant in a courtroom. **141**

Executive agreements Bilateral understandings between the president and foreign governments that, unlike treaties, do not require ratification by the Senate. **218**

Executive orders Directives signed by the president requiring executive agencies or individuals to take specific actions. **221**

Executive privilege A claim of confidentiality occasionally invoked by the president when investigators have demanded materials or summoned administration officials to testify. **251**

Factions A term used by James Madison in *Federalist* No. 10 to define any group motivated by a common interest that is opposed to "the rights of other citizens, or to the permanent and aggregate interests of the community." **396**

Fairness doctrine A doctrine proclaimed by the Federal Communications Commission (FCC) that required broadcasters to air controversies and to allow time for replies to controversial viewpoints; the FCC abolished the doctrine in 1987. **386**

Faithless electors Electors who desert the presidential candidate to whom they are pledged. **475**

Family Welfare Reform Act Federal statute enacted in 1988 that provides welfare payments tied to education and training programs, job searches, and community service. **517**

Federal Communications Commission (FCC) A federal regulatory commission that makes rules governing broadcasting and may punish violators. **386**

Federal system An arrangement in which authority is subdivided between central and regional or local governments. **54**

Federalists The first successful national party in the United States; the party of George Washington. **427**

Feminization of poverty The increasing incidence of poverty among female-headed families. **496**

Fighting words One of the exceptions to First Amendment protection of speech activities; it allows the government to punish direct incitements to violence. **82**

Filibuster "Talking a bill to death" or attempting to do so: taking the floor of the Senate for marathon speech-making, thus preventing a vote on a bill; allowed in the Senate but not the House. 167, **175**

Floor leader See **Senate majority leader**. **201**

Folkways Unwritten rules promoting cohesion and cooperation in the House and Senate; rules that have fallen into disarray over the past generation. **194**

Gender gap Differences in voting preferences between males and females. **465**

General Assembly A United Nations forum that includes all member nations, giving each a single vote. **541**

Good-faith exception In certain circumstances, police may be exempted from the strict letter of the law on suspects' rights, provided that they have done their best to comply with it. **144**

Government At its most general level, the body of people who exercise control over society. **6**

Government corporations Government-run agencies that, like private corporations, are expected to make a profit. **274**

Government foundations and institutes Government agencies whose purpose it is to promote science, the spread of knowledge, and scholarship. **274**

Grace Commission A presidential commission (1982–83) headed by industrialist J. Peter Grace that exposed waste in government and recommended reforms. **286**

Grandfather clauses Clauses inserted in statutes in former slave states during the late nineteenth and twentieth centuries that limited rights of suffrage to those who had voted before 1867 or were children or grandchildren of those who had; such clauses effectively disenfranchised blacks. **106**

Grants-in-aid Money given to states or localities by the federal government to use for various public purposes. **66**

Great Society The name used by the administration of President Lyndon Johnson in the 1960s for its new social welfare programs. **504**

Hatch Act A law passed in 1939 that prohibits federal civil service employees from taking an active part in elections. **281**

Hearings Discussions, testimony, and questioning of witnesses conducted by a Senate or House committee or subcommittee. **172**

Honeymoon period The period at the beginning of a president's term when public trust and goodwill are at the highest point. **333**

Honoraria Fees members of Congress receive from speaking engagements. **206**

House majority leader Assistant to the Speaker of the House. **200**

House majority whip One who serves as a communications link between the leadership and the rank and file in the House of Representatives. **200**

House minority leader Leader of the minority party in the House of Representatives. **200**

House minority whip Assistant to the House minority leader; serves as liaison between the leader and rank-and-file members. **200**

Ideology A set of political beliefs or values that are systematically and predictably linked. **343**

Impeach To bring a formal accusation or indictment against the president; this can be done only by the House of Representatives. **246**

Implied powers clause Clause in Article I, Section 8, of the Constitution that gives Congress the right to make "all Laws which shall be necessary and proper for carrying into Execution the foregoing Powers." Also called **elastic clause**. 32, **62**

Independent agencies Various offices in the executive branch of the federal government that are independent of the cabinet departments. **272**

Independent regulatory commission A type of independent agency in the federal government that has the authority to create and interpret its own rules and to make decisions based upon these rules; these agencies are free of direct control by the president or Congress. **272**

Indistinct party system A system in which the parties are not radically divided on major issues. **426**

INF Treaty A 1987 treaty banning intermediate-range nuclear missiles. **554**

Initiative A procedure that permits voters to place policy options on the ballot by gathering signatures on petitions. **11**

Intensity The depth of feeling people have about an issue. **333**

Interest groups Organized groups whose members share certain views and seek to translate those views into policymaking; also called "pressure groups" or "special interests." **396**

International Court of Justice A United Nations organ that adjudicates controversies between nations on points of international law; it can hand down decisions but has no power to enforce them. **541**

Internationalism A doctrine that advocates American involvement in world affairs. **544**

Interposition The doctrine that a state government may "interpose" itself between the federal government and its own people, blocking the enforcement of a federal law within the state. **53**

Interventionism A doctrine advocating use of American military force in other countries. **544**

Iron curtain A metaphor, first used by British prime minister Winston Churchill in 1946, to denote the barrier dividing Soviet-dominated countries from the rest of the world. **548**

Iron triangle A three-way, mutually beneficial relationship between an interest group, a government bureau, and a congressional committee or subcommittee. **287**

Isolationism A doctrine that opposes "entangling alliances" and commitments to other countries in the world. **544**

Issue networks Clusters of interest groups, some of which may be opposed to one another, that establish relationships with particular bureaus and congressional committees. **288**

Jeffersonian Republican Party headed by Thomas Jefferson, which defeated the Federalist party in the election of 1800; later known as the **Democratic-Republican Party**. **427**

Jim Crow The name given to laws in the South that discriminated against blacks. **108**

Joint Chiefs of Staff (JCS) Chief military officers of the United States armed forces, who advise the president and the secretary of defense on military needs and options. **536**

Judicial activists Supreme Court justices who believe that the Court should closely scrutinize any statue limiting the freedoms spelled out in the Bill of Rights and should not hesitate to strike down any statute that seems to limit these preferred freedoms. (See **preferred freedoms**) **310**

Judicial review The authority of the judicial branch to declare unconstitutional an act of the legislative or executive branches of the government. **302**

Judicial self-restraint A judicial philosophy based upon the premise that courts should assume that whatever the legislative branch does is constitutional unless there is clear and convincing evidence of unconstitutionality. **310**

Kellogg-Briand Pact A 1929 treaty renouncing "war as an instrument of national policy." **546**

Keynesian theory An economic theory that promotes government spending as a means of stimulating the economy. **519**

Keystone clause See **supremacy clause**. **32**

Lame duck A political official who has been defeated in an election or whose term is about to expire, but who is still in office. **301**

Latent poverty A term used by author Charles Murray to measure not only those whose incomes fall below the poverty line but also those whose incomes *would* fall below it if they did not receive welfare payments. **515**

Legislative courts Courts set up by Congress for certain specialized purposes. **305**

Legislative veto A provision in a statute giving Congress the right to reverse a decision delegated by the statute to the president. **221**

Legitimacy The widely shared assumption that those who govern society have gotten their power by right, not simply by force. **5**

Libel A written statement that is false and defamatory (injurious to a person's reputation or career). **93**

Line-item veto The executive authority to veto a single item in a bill instead of having to veto all of it; power possessed by 43 governors but not the president. **228**

Lobbyists People whose task it is to influence legislation or policymaking. **396**

Locke, John British philosopher (1632-1704) who expounded a doctrine of natural rights ("life, liberty, and property") that influenced the founders of the United States. **20, 30**

Mace A three-foot club with an eagle on top that rests on a pedestal on the House Speaker's desk; removal of the mace from its pedestal signals the transformation of the House into a Committee of the Whole. (See **Committee of the Whole**) **174**

McCarthyism A term that has come to stand for a number of practices attributed to the late Senator Joseph R. McCarthy (R-Wisconsin), including the bullying of witnesses and defaming of people by making false charges against them. **183**

McGovern-Fraser Commission A reform commission set up by the Democrats to suggest rule changes for candidate selection for their 1972 convention. **441**

Means-tested Programs that pay people according to economic need. **500**

Media elites Those who hold key positions of power and influence in the major news media of the United States. **368**

Medicaid A program of medical care for poor people. **506**

Medicare A program of medical care for the aged that is part of the Social Security program. **506**

Merit system A system of federal employment based upon the use of civil service examinations. **281**

Miranda warnings Four facts that police must give a suspect at the time of arrest: you have a right to remain silent, a right to consult with a lawyer, a right to have a court-appointed lawyer if you cannot afford one, and anything you say may be used against you. **143**

MIRVs Multiple independently targeted reentry vehicles: clusters of warheads launched from a single missile. **580**

Monarchy Hereditary rule by one person. **15**

Multiparty systems Political systems with three or more major parties. **426**

Multiple independently targeted reentry vehicles See MIRVs. **580**

Multiple referral Sending different parts of a bill to different House or Senate committees for consideration. **170**

Munich conference A 1938 conference at which British prime minister Neville Chamberlain agreed to let Nazi Germany take over part of Czechoslovakia. **557**

Mutually assured destruction (MAD) A defense theory based upon the ability to destroy another country after it has destroyed your country; if both are destroyable, neither would wish to initiate a nuclear exchange. **577**

National Committee for a Sane Nuclear Policy A pressure group that is concerned about warlike confrontations in a nuclear age. **540**

National News Council An organization set up by major news media with the task of investigating charges of press bias and unfairness; founded in 1973; expired in 1985. **385**

National security adviser The person who presides over the National Security Council (NSC), an organization established in 1947 to advise the president on national security matters and to "perform such other functions as the President may direct." **536**

617

Glossary

The National Security Agency Agency that is concerned with cryptology, breaking the secret codes of other countries and protecting our own codes. **537**

National Security Council (NSC) Agency in the Executive Office of the President that oversees the operation of the CIA and deals with other sensitive foreign policy operations. **224**

Natural rights Rights held to be inherent in human beings and not dependent upon government. **19**

Negative checks The various methods that can be used to block the passage of hasty and ill-considered legislation. **178**

Negative income tax Welfare payments tied to income; the less one earns, the larger the payments. **514**

New Deal Term used for the various programs launched by the administration of President Franklin Roosevelt in the 1930s; the programs were designed to pull the country out of the Depression. **498**

New Federalism A term with two meanings: President Nixon used it to denote the shared use of tax revenue by federal and state authorities; President Reagan used it for the title of his proposed "swap" of welfare programs (full federal financing of Medicaid in return for full state support of AFDC, Food Stamps, and other programs). **69**

New Jersey Plan Proposal at Constitutional Convention of 1787 that would modify the Articles of Confederation without radically changing them and would provide equal representation for the states regardless of population; favored by the small states. **26**

News spin The way a news correspondent interprets or embellishes the facts when reporting a story. **376**

Newsroom revolution The new power and prestige acquired by news correspondents during the 1960s. **370**

Nonrecorded teller votes See **voice votes**. **203**

North Atlantic Treaty Organization (NATO) An organization established in 1949 by the United States, Canada, and several nations in Europe to counter a perceived Soviet threat. **567**

Nuclear proliferation The spread of nuclear weapons systems to many countries in the world. **588**

Office of Management and Budget (OMB) The agency in the Executive Office of the President that has the responsibility of drawing up the president's budget for submission to Congress. **224**

Ombudsman Government official appointed to investigate citizen complaints against government agencies; exists in Scandinavian countries and in some states of the United States, but not in the federal government. **290**

Open rule Decision by the House Rules Committee that a bill may be amended on the House floor. (See **closed rule**) **172**

Opinions Judgments about current events. **334**

Override A vote to pass a bill despite a presidential veto; it requires a two-thirds vote of both the House of Representatives and the Senate. **176**

Packard Commission Special commission appointed by President Reagan that recommended tighter coordination of the major branches of the armed services. **568**

Patronage A system by which those in government provide jobs to friends, relatives, and supporters. A system of rewarding loyal party workers with jobs once the party gets in power. (See **spoils system**) **278, 452**

Pendleton Act (the Civil Service Act) A law passed in 1883 setting up the federal civil service system; designed to provide government employment on the basis of a merit system. (See **merit system**) **281**

Pentagon Five-sided building in Arlington, Virginia, that houses the United States' defense bureaucracy. **566**

Platform A list of goals or policies agreed upon by party members. **425**

Plebiscitary presidency A concept of the presidency that would limit internal checks upon the presidency; in this view, the president is responsible to the people every four years but is otherwise free to operate with little or no restraint. **263**

Pluralism A doctrine, popular among political science professors in the 1950s, based upon the premise that our political system fairly represents all active and legitimate groups in the population. **405**

Pocket veto A rare opportunity for a president to kill a bill by doing nothing; if he "pockets" a bill (holds on to it without signing it) and if Congress adjourns within 10 days, the bill dies. **178**

Police powers Powers, ordinarily reserved to state authorities by the Tenth Amendment, to protect the health, morals, and safety of individuals residing within the state. **139**

Political party A political association that seeks to acquire and maintain control of the government. **425**

Political questions A self-limiting doctrine of the Supreme Court in which the Court consigns certain questions to the "political" process, saying in effect that courts have no business trying to resolve such questions. **320**

Political socialization The process by which people acquire their political views and values. **348**

Poll taxes Taxes that had to be paid in many states before citizens were permitted to vote; such taxes helped to disenfranchise blacks and others who could not afford to pay. **106**

Populist party An agrarian-based party of the late 1880s and the 1890s that called for regulation of railroads, antitrust policies, the progressive income tax, and other social reforms. **119**

Pork-barrel legislation Appropriations for projects aimed primarily at providing jobs and other benefits to people who live in the home district or state of a legislator. **166**

Precincts Local areas of political parties. **440**

Preferred freedoms A term used by judicial activists to designate those freedoms spelled out in the Bill of Rights. (See **judicial activists**) **310**

Presidential Succession Act of 1947 Law that determines the order of succession if the president is removed from power; power transfers to the vice president, then the House speaker, then the president pro tempore of the Senate. **236**

Presumptive privilege The assumption, which must be honored by the judiciary, that the records of all White House conversations belong to the president; any litigant seeking an exception to this assumption must prove that the exception is warranted. **252**

Primary elections Elections to decide who the party's nominees will be. **441**

Prior restraint Censorship or any other act by the government to prevent a speech activity from taking place. **89**

Private bills Bills introduced in Congress that are designed to help out specific individuals or deal with specific matters rather than general affairs. **182**

Professionalism The ethos of "objective" reporting: restraining of one's own biases while covering a story. **374**

Progressive movement A reform movement of the early 1900s that called for women's suffrage, antitrust legislation, the elimination of urban political corruption, and other political and social reforms. **119**

Progressive tax A tax that increases in percentage along with income. **523**

Random sampling Selecting interviewees for a public opinion poll in such a manner that each person within the area to be covered has an equal chance of being interviewed. **352**

Ratification Approval by three-quarters of the state legislatures or by special conventions held in three-quarters of the states; amendments to the Constitution can be ratified by either means. **40**

Realigning election See **critical election**. **465**

Recidivism Continuing to commit crimes after release from prison. **148**

Reconstruction The period beginning at the end of the Civil War and lasting until 1877 (when federal troops were withdrawn from the South) during which former Confederate states were placed under federal supervision and forced to grant civil rights to blacks. **106**

Referendum An election in which the electorate is permitted to vote "yes" or "no" on policy questions that are placed on the ballot. **11**

Regulation of Lobbying Act of 1946 Law requiring paid lobbyists to file quarterly reports and to register with the House of Representatives and the Senate. **417**

Representative democracy A system of majority rule in which the people vote for representatives, who in turn make the laws. **10**

Reserved powers Powers not delegated to the federal government that, therefore, normally belong to states and localities (for example, education, traffic regulations, drinking laws). **55**

Revenue sharing A form of federal grants-in-aid in which federal funds were made available to states and localities to be used largely at their discretion; Congress terminated this program in 1986. **66**

Reverse discrimination Discriminating against white males in job and educational opportunities in favor of women and minorities. **104**

Revolution Overturning one government and replacing it with another. **6**

Rider An amendment to a bill that has nothing directly to do with that bill. **163**

Right of privacy A right not explicitly mentioned in the Constitution but derived from it by the Supreme Court in the case of *Griswold v. Connecticut* (1965); it became the basis for the Supreme Court's 1973 decision legalizing abortion. **124**

Roll call vote A vote in which each member's vote is recorded and associated with his or her name. **174**

SALT I The first Soviet–American treaty concerning the production and deployment of strategic weapons; signed in 1972, it included a limit on antimissile defenses and a freeze on intercontinental missiles. **578**

Sampling error The percentage range by which the figures cited in a poll could be in error; the size of this range is inversely proportional to the size of the sample. **353**

SDI See **Strategic Defense Initiative**. **586**

Second-strike capacity The ability to absorb a nuclear strike from another country and hit back with one's own missiles. **575**

Secretariat The chief administrative organ of the United Nations, headed by a secretary general, who exerts both administrative and political leadership over the world body. **541**

Section VII of the 1964 Civil Rights Act Section banning employment discrimination based upon gender. **123**

Security Council A United Nations body of 15 members: the United States, the USSR, Great Britain, France, and China, plus 10 rotating members. **541**

Selective incorporation The view that the Fourteenth Amendment makes some of the provisions in the Bill of Rights applicable to the states: those provisions that are "of the very essence of a scheme of ordered liberty." Also called **absorption**. **140**

Senate majority leader The one responsible for marshalling the majority party's forces in the Senate. Also called **floor leader**. **201**

Seniority system Unwritten understanding in Congress that the person from the majority party with the longest number of years of continuous service on a committee was to be its chair. **203**

Sequestering Indiscriminate cuts in government spending by a certain percentage; required under the Gramm-Rudmann-Hollings Act of 1985 in the event that the president and Congress cannot agree on how to progress toward a balanced budget. **522**

Shays's Rebellion Farmers' uprising in western Massachusetts, 1786-87, in protest against farm foreclosures; led by Daniel Shays, a former captain in the Revolutionary War. **25**

Sit-ins Peaceful demonstrations by blacks in which they seated themselves at whites-only lunch counters and other public facilities, asking for service and refusing to leave when requested by the management. **109**

Slander An oral statement that is false and defamatory (injurious to a person's reputation or career). **93**

Slate A list of candidates for various offices nominated by a political party. **434**

Socialism The doctrine that calls for state (or community) ownership of basic industries. **338**

Spoils system Derived from the expression "to the victors go the spoils"; a patronage system. (See **patronage**) **279**

Stability The extent to which an opinion stays the same over time. **333**

Standing committees Committees that remain operating from one session of Congress to the next. **170**

START (Strategic Arms Reduction Talks) A series of U.S.-Soviet talks aimed at reducing the size of the two countries' nuclear arsenals; begun during the Reagan administration. **582**

State A government, together with the people it governs and the territory it occupies. **6**

State of nature An imagined time and place before there was government. **8**

Statutory interpretation An authoritative judicial statement on the meaning of a law passed by the legislature. **303**

Strategic Defense Initiative SDI or Star Wars: an antimissile defense system proposed by President Reagan. **586**

Strategic defense triad Name for the United States' three kinds of nuclear delivery systems: bombers, missile-carrying submarines, and land-based intercontinental missiles. **575**

Subcommittee bill of rights A congressional reform of the 1970s that gave subcommittees and their chairs greater autonomy and freedom from control by the parent committee. **203**

Suffrage Voting. **461**

Sunset clauses Sections of laws that automatically expire after a given number of years unless renewed by Congress. **206**

Sunset law A law that creates an agency with a limited life span; these laws are designed to expire after a given period unless Congress renews them. **292**

Sunshine laws Rules requiring committee meetings to be open to the public. **204**

Superdelegates Democratic party members, mainly officeholders, who are guaranteed seats at Democratic presidential conventions. **446**

Supply-side economics An approach to economics that encourages tax cuts as a means of stimulating business activity and thus increasing tax revenues through prosperity. **520**

Supremacy clause Clause in Article VI of the Constitution stating that the Constitution and laws of the United States "shall be the supreme Law of the Land;" binding on all state judges regardless of what their state constitutions say. Also called **keystone clause**. **32**

Symbolic speech Actions intended primarily to make a statement, such as burning a flag or draft card. **82**

Tax credit A subtraction of a certain amount from one's total tax bill. **525**

Tax exemptions Subtraction of a certain amount from one's taxable income. **525**

Tax Reform Act of 1986 A federal statute passed in 1986 that collapsed the existing 14 tax brackets into three and eliminated a number of tax loopholes. **525**

Ticket-splitting Voting for one party's nominee for one office and another party's nominee for another office. **450**

Total incorporation The view that the Fourteenth Amendment makes the entire Bill of Rights applicable to the states. **140**

Totalitarianism A system of government that comes closest to the total destruction of freedom: its decrees are shifting and unpredictable, it intrudes deeply into the private realm, and it punishes people not just for what they say or do but for who they are. **15, 552**

The underclass Those who live near or at the bottom of American society. **516**

Unicameral A single-house legislature. **167**

Unintended effects Effects of reforms that nobody wanted or foresaw. **202**

Union of Concerned Scientists A pressure group, composed of scientists and social thinkers, that argues for disarmament. **540**

Unitary government A system in which all authority is in the hands of the central government. **54**

U.S. Courts of Appeals Courts that hear cases appealed from lower levels of the federal judiciary. **304**

Virginia Plan Proposal at Constitutional Convention of 1787 for strong central government with representation based upon population; favored by the large states. **25**

Voice votes Votes in Congress that leave no record of how members voted. Also called **non-recorded teller votes**. **203**

Volatile An unstable, changing public opinion. **333**

Voting Rights Act of 1965 Statute that prevents attempts to bar blacks from voting; the statute calls for sending federal registrars into areas that have discriminated against blacks at the polls. **109**

Wall of separation A metaphor used by Thomas Jefferson in a letter to a group of Baptists in Danbury, Connecticut, to illustrate his view that church and state should be radically separate in the U.S. **96**

War Powers Resolution Law passed by Congress in 1973, over President Nixon's veto, that requires the president to notify Congress when American troops are sent into war zones and requires that the troops be withdrawn in 60-90 days unless Congress declares war or extends the time period. **217, 252**

Warsaw Pact A network of military alliances, established in 1955, between the Soviet Union and its Eastern European satellites. **567**

Weber, Max German sociologist who viewed bureaucracy as an assemblage of offices, not personalities; his ideal bureaucracy has three distinguishing characteristics: hierarchy, specialization, and the rule of law. **275**

Welfare capitalism Individualism qualified by the belief that poor people should be given an opportunity to help themselves—"a hand, not a handout." **338**

Whistle-blowers Those bureaucrats who expose wrongdoing in the bureaucracy by informing Congress or the media. **290**

White flight The movement of whites out of the cities to the suburbs in the United States. **116**

White-only primary elections Primaries that banned blacks from voting; outlawed by the Supreme Court in 1944. **106**

Winner-takes-all Our system of awarding all of a state's electoral votes to the presidential candidate who wins a majority of the popular votes in the state. **475**

Workfare Welfare payments that encourage or require recipients to work in gainful employment, or at least to seek such employment. **516**

Writ of certiorari A statement by the Supreme Court that it is prepared to hear the arguments in a case. **306**

Writ of mandamus A judicial order requiring a public official to act in a prescribed manner. **302**

Yalta Agreements A series of 1945 agreements between President Franklin Roosevelt, British prime minister Winston Churchill, and Soviet dictator Joseph Stalin concerning the future of Eastern Europe. **547**

Index

Page numbers in **boldface** refer to glossary terms. Page numbers in *italics* refer to tables, figures, boxes, and captions.

common people, 460; and
Congress, 220; and Douglas
debate, 31; packaging of,
478; political career of, 230;
on public sentiment, 363;
and Republican party, 428,
471; and South's rebellion,
217
Line-item veto 227, **228**
Lippmann, Walter, 366, 556
Little Rock, school desegregation
in, 110
Lobbyists: 205, **396**; citizen
involvement and, 415-416;
as citizen representation,
416; and Congress, 396,
416; coordination of, 407;
criticisms of, 416-417;
government and, *416*; House
of Representatives and, 417;
information for, 407; on
local level, 403-404; mass
media and, 408; political
process and, 415-416;
power of, 408; registration
of, *397*; respectability of,
406; Senate and, 417; on
state level, 402-403; success
factors, 406-415; techniques
of, *407*; as watchdogs, 416;
and wealth, 409-415; White
House support for, 408
Local government: federal aid to,
69; and federal government,
66; regulations of, 57
Locke, John, 8, **20**, **30**, 34, *34*,
338
Lockeanism, 19, 388
Lodge, Henry Cabot, 441
Loomis, Burdett A., 416
Lott, Trent, 193
Loury, Glenn C., *114*
Lowi, Theodore, *262*
Lucas, William, 255
Luther v. Borden, 320

MacArthur, Douglas, 531, 532,
543
Mace, **174**
Machiavelli, Niccolò, 479
MacNamara, Donal E. J., *157*
MacNamara, Robert, 557, 568
MacNeil, Robert, 384
Madison, James, 8, 9, 24, *25*,
27, 33, 34, 45, 96, 98; on
bias judgment, 385; checks
and balances, theory of, 14,
39; on community interests,
426; on democracy, 10; on
expressed powers, 61; on
factions, 396, 404, 419; and
The Federalist papers, 37;
on federation, 39; on
government branches, 39;

and Jeffersonian-Republican
party, 428; as secretary of
state, 301; and the Virginia
Plan, 32;
Magazines, 41, 59, 90, 92, 118,
352, 375
*The Making of the President,
1960* (White), 215
Malcolm X, 106
Manchester, William, 214
Manes, Susan, 485
Mann, Thomas E., 469
Mapp v. Ohio, 141, 142, 144,
146
Mapplethorpe, Robert, 92
Marbury, William, 302
Marbury v. Madison, 255, 302,
303, 304, 307, 308, 316
Marcuse, Herbert, 343
Marshall, John, 255, 256, 301;
and Bill of Rights, 65; and
commerce clause, 64; on
implied powers, 62, 63; on
judicial review, 300, *302*,
302-303
Marshall, Thurgood, 156, 313,
314, 324; dissent from
Constitution celebration, *36*;
and Fourteenth Amendment,
37;
Marxism-Leninism, 5, 145, 422,
550
Mason, George, 34, 37
Mass media: advertisements, 412,
478, 480; bias of, 372-381,
378; and business, 365,
367, 370, 387; cable pro-
grammers, *369*; conglom-
erates, 365, 367-369, 389;
economic and social
pressure on, 386-387; and
elite attitudes, *373*; and
ethics, 374; and Grenada
invasion, 382, 384;
influence on public opinions,
350, 363; libel suits against,
93, 94, 380-381; liberalism
and, 374, *378*, 387;
lobbying, 407, 408; military
and, 379-381, 382;
monopoly of, 364-371; and
national security, 382-384;
negative advertising and,
412; networks in, 365-369;
and Nixon fund, 458;
opinions on *368*; owners
and sponsors of, 369-370,
371; and political campaigns,
374, *376*, 376, 377, *378*,
487; and nominating
processing, 448; Supreme
Court on, 385-386; on
Vietnam War, 393. *See also*
Newspapers; Press;
Television
Matching grants, 66

Mattingly, Mack, *227*
McCarthy, Eugene J., 422, 423,
424, 425, 436, 441
McCarthy, Joseph: investigating
committee of, 183, 251, 267
McCarthyism, **183**, 186
McCloskey, Frank, 191-192
McClure, Robert, 479
McCord, James W., Jr., 243
McCormack, Robert, 370
McCorvey, Norma, *125; See also
Roe v. Wade*
McCulloch, James, 62
McCulloch v. Maryland, 62, 64
McCurdy, Howard E., 181
McEwen, Bob, 190
McGinnis, Joe, 479
McGovern, George, 341, 374,
422, 425, 441, 444, 473
McGovern-Fraser Commission,
441, 449
McIntyre, Richard, 191-192
McKinley, William, 470
Means-tested, **500**
Media elites, **368**, 371, 373,
374; liberalism of, 374; on
national security and foreign
policy, 374; and social
issues, *373*
Medicaid, 69, **506**, 506-507,
508
Medicare, **506**, 506-507, 508
Meese, Edwin, 187, 250, 259,
317
Mellon, Andrew, 296
Mencken, H. L., 13
Menem, Carlos Saul, 342
Menninger, Karl A., 147
Merit system, **281**; federal
government employees and
percentage under, *281*
Merit Systems Protection Board
(MSPB), 289
Metzenbaum, Howard, 175
Mexican-American Legal Defense
Fund, 400
Mexico, bureaucracy in, *279*
Military: confidence in, *340*;
convention delegates on,
442; and Department of
Defense, 536; desegregation
in, 221; expenditures of,
568, *572*; force, 558; in
Grenada, 382, 384; and
media, 382; in Panama,
539; reform, 568; spending,
520, 582; strength in 1970s,
553; and terrorism, 534,
559; and World War II, 566
Military-industrial complex,
570-571
Miller, Clem, 193
Miller, Mark Crispin, *378*
Miller v. California, 58, 91, 92
Mills, C. Wright, 405
Minor parties, *440*

1 Costa Rica   12
2 Soviet Union   38
3 Nigeria   56
4 Zaire   88
5 Republic of South Africa   113
6 China   145
7 Great Britain   173
8 Great Britain   199
9 France   218
10 Federal Republic of Germany   249
11 Mexico   279
12 Japan   315
13 Argentina   342
14 German Democratic Republic   372
15 Israel   403
16 Brazil   431
17 Great Britain   483
18 Sweden   499
19 India   545
20 Canada   579

Numbers on the map refer to chapters in which the countries are discussed in Global Perspective boxes. Page references are listed above.

Credits

Chapter 1. 3 Library of Congress; 5 Baldev—Sygma; 8 Library of Congress; 9 UPI/Bettmann Newsphotos; 11 George Bellerose—Stock, Boston; 19 Library of Congress.

Chapter 2. 25 Library of Congress; 27 Paul Hosefros—New York Times Pictures; 28 Library of Congress; 29 Library of Congress; 33 Library of Congress; 34 The Bettmann Archive, Inc.; 36 UPI/Bettmann Newsphotos.

Chapter 3. 53 Birmingham News Post Co.; 57 UPI/Bettmann Newsphotos; 61 UPI/Bettmann Newsphotos; 62 Library of Congress; 63 Library of Congress; 65 Library of Congress; 67 © John Bryson—Photo Researchers, Inc.

Chapter 4. 77 T. Simon—Gamma Liaison; 80 Pach/Bettmann; 85 UPI/Bettmann Newsphotos; 91 UPI/Bettmann Newsphotos; 97 Courtesy Krause Publications; 98 Reuters/Bettmann Newsphotos.

Chapter 5. 104 AP/Wide World; 107 Library of Congress; 108 UPI/Bettmann Newsphotos; 109 UPI/Bettmann Newsphotos; AP/Wide World; 118 Library of Congress; 120 Library of Congress; 127 UPI/Bettmann Newsphotos.

Chapter 6. 135 UPI/Bettmann Newsphotos; 142 © Eugene Gordon 1985—Photo Researchers, Inc.; 147 UPI/Bettmann Newsphotos; 151 The Bettmann Archive, Inc.; Stock, Boston.

Chapter 7. 163 United Nations photo by Peter Magubane; 167 New York Public Library; 174 K. Jewell—U.S. House of Representatives; 175 UPI/Bettmann Newsphotos; 184-185 Pamela Carley Petersen.

Chapter 8. 191 Library of Congress; 193 George Tames—New York Times Pictures; 196 UPI/Bettmann Newsphotos; 198 UPI/Bettmann Newsphotos; 201 UPI/Bettmann Newsphotos; Architect of the Capitol; 202 UPI/Bettmann Newsphotos.

Chapter 9. 214 UPI/Bettmann Newsphotos; 219 UPI/Bettmann Newsphotos; 223 UPI/Bettmann Newsphotos; 231 AP/Wide World; 237 Historical Pictures Service.

Chapter 10. 243 UPI/Bettmann Newsphotos; 245 UPI/Bettmann Newsphotos; 246 Library of Congress; 247 Library of Congress; 251 UPI/Bettmann Newsphotos; 253 UPI/Bettmann Newsphotos; 256 UPI/Bettmann Newsphotos; 257 UPI/Bettmann Newsphotos; 258 Chicago Historical Society.

Chapter 11. 267 UPI/Bettmann Newsphotos; 274 TVA Washington Office & Tom Sweeten, TVA News Desk, Knoxville, TN; 276 AP/Wide World; 280 New York Public Library Picture Collection; 283 UPI/Bettmann Newsphotos; 290 UPI/Bettmann Archive; 296 UPI/Bettmann Newsphotos.

Chapter 12. 302 The Bettmann Archive, Inc.; 307 Yoichi R. Okamoto—Photo Researchers, Inc.; 309 The Granger Collection; The Bettmann Archive, Inc.; 310 UPI/Bettmann Newsphotos; 312 UPI/Bettmann Newsphotos; 314 UPI/Bettmann Newsphotos; 318 UPI/Bettmann Newsphotos.

Chapter 13. 329 UPI/Bettmann Newsphotos; 338 © Christopher Morrow—Stock, Boston; 345 UPI/Bettmann Newsphotos; 352 UPI/Bettmann Newsphotos.

Chapter 14. 361 UPI/Bettmann Newsphotos; 366 A. Tannenbaum—Sygma; 370 UPI/Bettmann Newsphotos; 381 UPI/Bettmann Newsphotos; 387 Courtesy CBS News.

Chapter 15. 393 U.S. Air Force; 398 Teresa Zabala—New York Times Pictures; 401 UPI/Bettmann Newsphotos; 409 UPI/Bettmann Newsphotos; 416 UPI/Bettmann Newsphotos; 417 UPI/Bettmann Newsphotos.

Chapter 16. 424 UPI/Bettmann Newsphotos; 430 Library of Congress; 433 Tennessee Historical Society; 439 Library of Congress; 446 UPI/Bettmann Newsphotos; 453 UPI/Bettmann Newsphotos.

Chapter 17. 459 UPI/Bettmann Newsphotos; 462 Smithsonian Institution; 470 Library of Congress; 473 UPI/Bettmann Newsphotos; 478 Library of Congress; 481 Courtesy NARAL.

Chapter 18. 493 United Nations photo by P. S. Sudhakaran; 495 Jim Wilson—New York Times Pictures; 500 UPI/Bettmann Newspapers; 501 Library of Congress; 506 Pamela Carley Petersen; 513 United Nations photo by P. Sudhakaran.

Chapter 19. 532 UPI/Bettmann Newsphotos; 546 The Bettmann Archive, Inc.; 547 National Archives; 548 Walter Sanders—Life Magazine, © 1948 Time, Inc.; 549 UPI/Bettmann Newsphotos; 553 UPI/Bettmann Newsphotos; 554 UPI/Bettmann Newsphotos; 558 UPI/Bettmann Newsphotos.

Chapter 20. 565 UPI/Bettmann Newsphotos; 567 National Archives; 568 UPI/Bettmann Newsphotos; 570 Dennis Brack—Black Star; 582 UPI/Bettmann Newsphotos; 583 AP/Wide World.

Staff

Editor Jeannine Ciliotta
Copy Editor Joanne Wlodarczyk
Production Manager Brenda S. Filley
Designers Harry Rinehart and Charles Vitelli
Art Editor Pamela Carley Petersen
Photo Researcher Mary L. Strieff
Typesetting Supervisor Libra Ann Cusack
Typesetter Juliana Arbo
Graphics Assistant Shawn Callahan
Systems Coordinator Richard Tietjen
Proofreader Diane Barker

Charts/Graphs/Maps by Rex Doane.
Cover design by Harry Rinehart.
    Photo, Philadelphia Electric Company.